2002

THINGS TO DO WITH YOUR KIDS

CARYL WALLER KRUEGER

GALAHAD BOOKS
NEW YORK

CONTENTS

Book 1

1001
Things
to Do
with Your
Kids

TO

Chris, Carrie, and Cameron,
who enjoyed many of these ideas,
and to Cliff,
who still enjoys life with our now grown-up kids

Contents

The author speaks to you . . .

his book is geared to the needs of a busy family, possibly one with two career parents. It includes ideas for toddlers up through the teen-age years, with some chapters for children who like to do puzzles or play in the yard and other chapters for kids who want to earn extra money or give great parties. In keeping with your busy schedule, you'll be able to enjoy many of these ideas "in the cracks"—a term that means doing something without taking additional time.

Before you start, let me share with you how to get the most out of this book. First, scan the book, getting a feel for the many categories of family life covered. Then read the sections that have greatest interest for you and your children. You may want to share a few ideas at suppertime each day.

Check off the ideas you've tried; make a note of those you want to repeat. But most important: Don't feel you have to do all 1001! This book isn't a test. Its purpose is to help you enjoy parenting!

Note that in some sections ideas are suggested for younger children, for older children, and for all children. Since children mature at different paces, the division between "younger" and "older" comes when a child has learned to read fairly well and is permitted to go about the neighborhood on his own. In using this book, let your child enjoy the freedom of new ideas, in keeping with normal safety precautions.

Because I lecture regularly on child development and have written articles and books about many areas of family life, I wanted this book to fill a special need. So, this book is *not* about toilet training, picking up toys, handling divorce, or major discipline problems. Instead, it's about intelligent things that you can do with your children in the course of ordinary family events. These ideas will make those ordinary events more enjoyable and educational.

The operative word in the title of this book is *with*. These are things to do *with* your child, not things *to* do to your child or *for* your child or things to get a child out of your hair. Family life is an adventure when parent and child work together, learn together, and have fun together. That's what builds memories. Expensive toys, world trips, and designer jeans may have their place, but the things that are memorable to children are the times you walked in the rain, lived by candlelight during a power outage, or took them into your confidence and asked their opinion on some important topics.

So don't let precious time slip by. Start a new way of life *with* your child today.

Caryl Waller Krueger

Acknowledgments

o one writes 1001 ideas all alone. My parents, husband, and children made this book possible by wanting to live adventurously. When it came to putting ideas into the computer and getting them into book form, others were of invaluable help.

My special thanks to the "Marvelous Moms" team members who contributed ideas from their own current experiences as moms and grandmoms. The team included working mothers, moms in bi-racial families, at-home moms, single mothers, stepmothers, teachers, librarians, mothers and grandmothers of twins, and some marvelous dads, too!

Moms and dads who helped include: Marie Addario, Linda Bowman, Mary Ann Brady, Sally Buttner, Barbara and Larry Hauser, Connie King, Danielle and Lance McCune, Jan and Mike McCurties, Marsha and Chris Moersch, Elieth Robertshaw, Debbie and Jim Waller, JoAnn Worthington, and Margaret Worthington.

Special thanks to: Nancy Sager, who helped with ideas on fitness and nutrition; my librarian friends Merna Bennett, Jean Mosteller, and Jean Stewart, who helped in compiling the book lists; Cameron Krueger, who introduced me to computer writing and devised many of the systems and macros that made writing and editing such a joy; my secretary, Sheila Kinder, for watchdogging spelling and punctuation while also contributing ideas.

ONE

HOMEMADE FUN

Home should be the center of family life, so the home should be a happy place for tots and teens. Try these ideas for in-home activities—simple, inexpensive, challenging fun for weekdays, rainy days, busy days, and weekends. For additional ideas read: *How to Play with Your Children* (Brian Sutton-Smith, Dutton, 1974).

★

★

SECTION 1: GAMES AND PUZZLES

FOR YOUNGER CHILDREN

☐ **1. MAGIC CARPET.**   All you need is a small, soft rug, a child, and two parents with imagination to share. The child sits or stretches out on the rug and holds the edges. Where does he want to go? The ocean? (Hold the corners of the rug and lift it just off the floor, as you take the magic carpet to the bathroom.) Are there whales here? Fish? Sand? Touch the water; is it cold? Where next? The grocery store? (Carry him off to the kitchen.) What shall we shop for? Milk? A cracker? Sorry, we have no money! Let's go somewhere else. To the library! (Transport the magic carpet to a bookshelf.) Other trips are to the theater (in front of the TV), to the repair shop (the garage or workshop), to the clothing store (his closet), and to the Land of Nod (his bed). Let your imagination be your guide.

☐ **2. THE LONE RANGER.**   Using a string, hang a rigid bracelet (any hoop about three inches across will do) from a ceiling light fixture or a nail in a doorway. Depending on the age of the children, make the string longer or shorter. Next, make the Lone Ranger's silver bullets. Using foil, roll silver bullets about 1 ¼ inches long. Then let the players make simple Lone Ranger masks. Start kids close to the ring for practice in throwing the bullets through the hoop. Then start the game, dividing the silver bullets among the players and giving a point for each one thrown through the hoop. After each round, move back one more foot. The winner is the one who scores twenty-five.

☐ **3. BALLOONS.**   Keep a supply on hand for moments when diversion is needed. Eye-hand coordination is taught when you play to keep the balloon up in the air in these ways: using only one hand or foot to hit it; using two hands; using your head; alternating between two children; hitting it with a spoon, a sheet of newspaper, or a flyswatter.

☐ **4. CARD GAMES.**   With a deck of cards, deal five cards to each player. Each player puts his own hand of cards in front of him, face up. Put the remaining cards in the center of the table, face down. This is the stack. Players take turns turning over a card from the stack. If a player can match the card value with a card in his own hand (for example, a four of spades with a four of diamonds, or a jack of hearts with a jack of clubs), he turns his matching card face down. He keeps turning a card from the stack as long as he can make a match. When he doesn't match, the next player turns a card from the stack, and so forth. When the stack is gone, turn it over and go through again. The first player to get all his cards turned over (or the player with the most turned over) wins. As children begin to understand this simple game, make it harder by matching the number and the color (red or black).

☐ **5. PATIENT PUZZLES.**   Start a young child's puzzle on a low table, kitchen counter, or some place in her room where it won't be disturbed. Don't put it together all at one time. Tell her to add a piece each time she goes past. You add a piece now and then, too. Some families put a simple wood puzzle on the bathroom counter and let each family member add a piece at a time. Who says bathrooms can't be fun!

FOR OLDER CHILDREN

☐ **6. MIRROR PICTURES.**   Give each player paper and pencil. Take turns sitting down facing a large mirror and drawing an object while looking only in the mirror. Start with simple things, such as a pig or a house and work up to more difficult drawings, such as a bicycle rider or letters of the alphabet. Try it yourself; it's harder than it sounds.

☐ **7. WALKING CHESS.**   Put a chess game on a table, in the hall or just inside the living room or family room. Two family members start playing, moving one of their pieces each time they feel like it, whenever they happen to pass by. Provide a poker chip or other marker (a fifty-cent piece is perfect) for the player to put under the piece he last moved. Occasionally both players may meet at the same time at the table, but you can also play the entire game without encountering your partner or taking a special time to play. The winner takes on another family member.

☐ **8. REBUS.**   This word game (enjoyed by Benjamin Franklin) uses numbers, letters, and words to indicate other words or parts of words. Start with these simple ones, then make up some for your children. Next, make up harder ones for each other.

(1) Draw an eye, the letters C and A, and a dog : I see a dog. (2) Draw the letter U, the words "stepped on," the letter M followed by an eye and a shoe : You stepped on my shoe. (3) Draw the letter M followed by an eye, then a cat, a heart, and a fish: My cat loves fish.

You can make them harder by the placement of the words, for example:

$$\frac{stand}{I} = \text{I understand.}$$

/R/E/A/D/I/N/G/ = Reading between the lines.

```
R
R O A D
A
D      = Crossroad
```

You and your child can write a short story in rebus form and let the family decipher it.

□ 9. THEME CHARADES.
Introduce kids to this all-ages game. In charades you may not speak but instead must act out the words. Start by selecting a theme: Disney characters, TV shows, songs, children's books. Take turns acting out the charade. Let younger children have a parent or older child to consult with for ideas. Show children the charade hand signs for how many words (use fingers), little word (use thumb and index finger close together), rhymes with (place hands parallel), and so on.

□ 10. EQUATIONS.
This word game can be played one-a-day at breakfast or as an after-supper or party game. The object is to tell what the letters stand for. Example: 16 = O. in a P. Answer: Ounces in a Pound. For younger children, you may have to fill in more of the missing words. So, in #1, you'd use the word "Days" instead of the letter D. Once children get the knack of this game you'll be surprised how quickly they can solve each equation. (The answers are at the end of this section.)

1. 7 = D. in the W.
2. 10 = F. on two H.
3. 52 = W. in the Y.
4. 60 = M. in an H.

5. 2.2 = C. in an I.
6. 26 = L. of the A.
7. 7 = W. of the A. W.
8. 57 = H. V.
9. 1001 = A. N.
10. 88 = P. K.
11. 8 = S. on a S. S.
12. 54 = C. in a D. (including 2 J.)
13. 9 = P. in the S. S.
14. 13 = S. on the A. F.
15. 18 = H. on a G. C.
16. 32 = D. F. at which W. F.
17. 90 = D. in a R. A.
18. 3 = B. M. (S. H. T. R.)
19. 4 = Q. in a G.
20. 24 = H. in a D.
21. 1 = W. on a U.
22. 11 = P. on a F. T.
23. 1000 = W. that a P. is W.
24. 64 = S. on a C. B.
25. 29 = D. in F. in a L. Y.

☐ **11. PALINDROMES.** These are words or sentences spelled the same from right to left as from left to right. "Palindromos" is a Greek word meaning "running back again." Look together for simple palindrome words such as noon, peep, radar, pup, mom, dad, bib, did, gag, hah, pop, sis, tot, and wow. Then look for names such as Otto, Hannah, Ada, and Eve. Napoleon supposedly came up with this palindrome sentence: "Able was I ere I saw Elba." Humorists say that Adam spoke this palindrome to Eve: "Madam, I'm Adam."

FOR ALL CHILDREN

☐ **12. HIDE-AND-SEEK PAIRS.** This takes four or more to play. Pair parents or older children with young children. "Hide-and-Seek" in the dark isn't scary when you have a buddy to hide or seek with. When playing with three or more pairs, change the game this way: One pair hides, other pairs seek. When a pair finds a hiding pair, they hide with them. No giggling! The game can be played in the day, of course, but the dark makes it more fun.

☐ 13. THE NEW "SIMON SAYS." Children love this game in English, and they'll find it as much fun in Spanish—or any language you choose. The rules are the same: One player is Simon, who stands before the others and issues orders to do various things. The others follow his order if he begins it with "Simon says," but they ignore the order if he does not say "Simon says." One who makes a mistake sits down and is out for that game. The last one still up becomes the next Simon. To play in Spanish, you need these words:

> *Simon dice* (see-mon dee-say): Simon says
> *toque su* (toe-kah soo): touch your
> *nariz* (nah-ris): nose
> *ojo* (o-ho): eye
> *oreja* (oh-ray-hah): ear
> *boca* (bow-kah): mouth
> *mejilla* (may-hee-yah): cheek
> *mano* (mah-no): hand
> *estomago* (es-toe-mah-go): stomach
> *rodilla* (row-dee-yah): knee
> *codo* (co-dough): elbow
> *dedo* (day-dough): finger
> *zapato* (sa-pa-toe): shoe
> *amigo* (ah-mee-go): friend

Simon can give some orders in English and others in Spanish until the new words are known. As the game progresses, Simon should give the orders faster and faster.

☐ 14. HOT AND COLD. Use this for teens as well as toddlers. It's also great on gift-days when you want to have a child find a big gift that can't be easily wrapped, such as a wagon or stereo. But for a family game, take turns hiding a small object anywhere in the house. (Start by hiding it in the room where you are, while others close their eyes; the next time hide it far away from where you'll start.) The first time, parents should hide the object and give the hints. Depending on how close the child is getting to the hidden object, the hint words are: burning hot (very close), hot, warm, cool, cold, and freezing (not at all close). The one searching always leads in walking and looking; others stand back and give the hints. When the object is found, the finder is the next to hide it and give the hot-cold clues. You can make it more difficult by limiting the number of hints to ten and giving a hint only when the seeker requests one.

ANSWERS TO EQUATIONS: (1) Days in the Week, (2) Fingers on Two Hands, (3) Weeks in the Year, (4) Minutes in an Hour, (5) Centimeters in an Inch, (6) Letters of the Alphabet, (7) Wonders of the Ancient World, (8) Heinz Varieties, (9) Arabian Nights, (10) Piano Keys, (11) Sides on a Stop Sign, (12) Cards in a Deck (including Two Jokers), (13) Planets in the Solar System, (14) Stripes on the American Flag, (15) Holes on a Golf Course, (16) Degrees Fahrenheit at which Water Freezes, (17) Degrees in a Right Angle, (18) Three Blind Mice (See How They Run), (19) Quarts in a Gallon, (20) Hours in a Day, (21) Wheel on a Unicycle, (22) Players on a Football Team, (23) Words that a Picture is Worth, (24) Squares on a Chess Board, (25) Days in February in a Leap Year.

★

SECTION 2: LET'S PRETEND

☐ **15. THE TRUNK.**   Use a toy trunk, a large old suitcase, or a sturdy carton to gather things that make fantasy: masks, clothes, hats, shoes, gloves, old jewelry, scraps of fabric, safe makeup, some gadgets, handbags, and wallets. Ask grandparents to contribute old-style clothing, old but still usable phonograph records, old tools and kitchen equipment that can be used for imaginative play. If you're using a carton, decorate it like a trunk, with marking pen trim and lock.

☐ **16. CREATE A FAMILY.**   Plan a week of doll corner play by helping a child give "character" to many dolls: mom, dad, children, cousins, a neighbor, store owner, repair person. Then create a situation to start off each day's play, for example, "It is the day before Dad's birthday and Billy and Betsy have no money to buy a gift" or "Mom works at the real estate office, but today the repair person is coming to fix the sink and Cousin Melissa and Uncle Charlie are coming for dinner." These situations give a boost to a child's imaginative play.

☐ **17. WHAT IS IT, REALLY?**   Go to a garage sale with the family. You'll find many interesting items: clothes for the dress-up trunk, objects for the doll corner, unusual tools. Give each child fifty cents to spend on the most interesting item she can find. When home, let everyone suggest the new uses for these outdated items. Keep the ones that are the most fun and put the duds in a box for your own garage sale.

☐ **18. DRESS-UP DRAWER.**   When parents are going out for the evening, let children pretend they're going, too. It makes the parents' being away easier. Have a low drawer in the parents' bedroom for clothing items the parents no longer enjoy wearing: dresses, shirts, slacks, hats, scarves, shoes. Let both girls and boys dress at the same time parents dress, doing many of the same things (makeup, after-shave, jewelry, tying a tie, etc.). Let them pretend they're going to your event. What will they say? What will they do? Who will they meet? What will they eat? The next day talk about what you really did.

☐ **19. BE A CHARACTER.**   Let children act out a simple story they know. Join in the play, especially at the beginning. Volunteer to be the giant or the queen and dress up for your role. If you plan to read the newspaper, make a salad, or work in the garden, let the play follow you. If the play starts in the afternoon, let it continue through supper, including other family members in the play.

☐ **20. TEDDY'S CLOTHES.**   Show a child how to make clothes for stuffed animal or doll friends. Start with a simple jacket for Teddy. Use fabric glue to begin with; sewing can come later. Let the newly clothed friends have a place of honor at the supper table so they can show off.

☐ **21. DOLLS IN CHARGE.**   Talk with a child about his dolls and stuffed animals. Help him choose one that will be "in charge" of the playtime. Say a doll named Mark is chosen. Then, all the others have to be obedient to Mark. Show a child how Mark "speaks." Mark says, "It's naptime for everyone" (all dolls and children must pretend); Mark says, "Now we'll all do a trick" (all dolls and children get in strange poses); and so on. Another day, a different doll or animal can be in charge. It is interesting to see how this doll with a different personality makes for different play.

☐ **22. LIVING TV.**   Take a clue from TV and come up with a fantastic set of characters. Help your child assign parts of TV characters to siblings, dolls, animals—even you! These can be from any show the family knows. Big Bird, Minnie Mouse,

Superwoman—any character she knows can be included. Make up a simple situation such as "Rainbow Brite has walked into the forest and can't find her way home." Then let the TV show develop from imagination. Help older children start a soap opera with just one character's life, then add another character for interaction. Add more and see how the story develops. There may be time warps and other stretches of the imagination as each new character is added to the play, but that makes for fun.

★

SECTION 3: TRANSPORTATION, BLOCKS, AND CITIES

☐ **23. A POEM TO LEARN.**   The joy of creative play at home is well expressed in these lines from Robert Louis Stevenson's poem "Block City." Help your child memorize this poem and play with it in mind.

> What are you able to build with your blocks?
> Castles and palaces, temples and docks.
> Rain may keep raining, and others go roam,
> But I can be happy and building at home.
> Let the sofa be mountains, the carpet be sea,
> There I'll establish a city for me.

☐ **24. CHRISTMAS IN JULY.**   Bring out the electric train in midsummer and set it up as you would at Christmas. Let everyone work together to assemble it. Use the train to deliver small objects put in boxcars or flatcars. Play after supper with only the train lights for illumination. If a child's friend also has a train, let them make a setup with both trains, being sure to remember one another's possessions.

☐ **25. BLOCK ROOM.**   Using building blocks, show a child how to recreate in miniature the room she's in (kitchen, bedroom, family room). Is the room square or rectangular? The building block room should have the same shape. Then, with other blocks, create in simple form the major furniture items. Next, take a few more blocks and, using washable marking pens, make them into people and pets.

☐ **26. BIG CITY.** Provide a place that won't need to be vacuumed for about two weeks. Start youngsters setting up the Big City. Use the train, blocks for city buildings, motocross roadways, landscaping, toy figures and animals, and other related toys. Don't worry if the scale isn't perfect. See how fabulous a setup can be made. Let everyone's imagination create a situation (the governor is coming to speak, a foot of snow just fell, a bear escaped from the zoo) and play with all the toys using that theme.

☐ **27. LITTLE CITY.** Using scraps of two-by-four lumber (check with someone building a house about getting the scraps, or buy the poorest grade two-by-fours at a building supply house), cut blocks of different sizes. Show a child how to sand the blocks. Next, arrange the blocks and decide what kind of buildings they might be: A tall one can be a business office building, a long one a ranch house; square ones can be grocery stores, big ones a school; and so on. Next, let a child decorate the blocks with paint. For example, the post office block could be red, white, and blue with a flag and a mailbox in the front. Let a child also make houses or apartment buildings representing his own home and those of his friends.

☐ **28. AROUND THE HOUSE.** The world is big—so is the world of blocks and cars. With a child, go from room to room of your house and assign each room a new name: the gas station, the shopping mall, the school, Aunt Sheila's house. In each room use blocks to build one of these buildings. Then, let kids run their trucks and cars from room to room and have pretend play in each room. You can be in that room reading or doing another activity, and when the transportation brigade comes, you can be the shopkeeper, gas attendant, aunt, and so forth.

★

SECTION 4: PAPER PLAY

FOR YOUNGER CHILDREN

☐ **29. KITCHEN PICTURES.** When a parent is working in the kitchen, a child can be creating a kitchen picture at the same time. Starting with a piece of cardboard, let the child draw a picture with crayons. Then, show him how to add texture and dimension to it by gluing on food items, such as macaroni, dried legumes, flour, and sugar. It takes very little of these food materials to make an interesting picture.

☐ **30. PASTE CHEF.** First show children how paste is made. Mix ⅓ cup non-self-rising wheat flour and 2 tablespoons of sugar in a saucepan. Over medium heat gradually add 1 cup of water and cook until clear, stirring constantly. Remove from heat and add ¼ teaspoon oil of peppermint or oil of wintergreen. Then tear colored papers into interesting shapes and use them to make a collage. These can be designs or pictures. Never ask "What is it?" or give orders such as "More blue" or "Work more slowly." If you make a collage at the same time, you can set an example by working carefully and enjoying your creation.

☐ **31. "MY MAIL."** When you sort out your daily mail, set aside the junk mail and let it be your child's own special mail. The large lettering and pictures will interest him.

☐ **32. FUNNY RAINBOWS.** With a piece of wax paper in front of a child, show her how to use a vegetable scraper on a crayon. As she scrapes different colored crayons, let the scrapings fall in various places on the paper. Next, cover with a second piece of wax paper. Carry this to the ironing board and give her a chair so she can help. (Place an old cloth underneath to keep the ironing board clean.) Show what pretty designs can be made by ironing the artwork with a *warm* iron. Let her do this herself, but watch carefully. Be sure to tell the child not to try this activity unless you're around.

☐ **33. RAINBOW CRAYONS.** Don't throw away those old, short crayons. Let your child peel off the paper and put them in a muffin tin that you've *heavily* greased. Put about ten pieces all of one color in a cup, or mix the colors for a rainbow crayon. Bake for 10-12 minutes at 275 degrees. Then cool and remove the crayon blocks, using a knife. They can be used as is or cut into a size convenient for little hands.

☐ **34. COOKIE CUTTERS.** Show children how to trace around cookie cutters, then carefully cut out the paper form. When a child has at least three cutouts (perhaps a tree, a bunny, and a gingerbread man), let him paste them on another piece of paper, color them, and draw a background, leaving a place at the bottom for a short story which he'll dictate to you.

☐ **35. WHAT DO YOU SEE?**   Draw a design of lines on a piece of paper, making a variety of large and small sections of crossing curved and straight lines. Ask a child what shapes she sees inside those lines. Let her color in the objects she sees. You will be surprised at what she finds. Then turn the paper upside down and see what else is hiding in the design.

FOR ALL CHILDREN

☐ **36. CHEAP PUZZLES.**   Save toy catalogs—they have many uses. Use pages from them, or full-page pictures from old magazines, to make puzzles. (You may want to paste them on blank paper first. If you don't, it's hard to tell which side is correct if pieces get turned over.) Give one picture to each family member, along with a pair of scissors. Each cuts his picture into six pieces (or more if children are older). Then everyone exchanges pictures and sees how fast they can put them together. Next, put all the pieces in the center of the table and let everyone work together to get all the pictures put back together.

☐ **37. BULLETIN BOARD.**   Make a family bulletin board for a wall everyone sees often (perhaps in the kitchen or the family room, by the dining table). Put a calendar on the board showing all the interesting things the family will do that month. Pictures, photos, home-chore lists, important phone numbers, invitations, schoolwork, and similar things can be displayed here. This is a much better headquarters than the refrigerator door, which should be kept for special announcements.

☐ **38. EXPAND-A-PICTURE.**   This is creative fun for all ages. Cut a full-page picture out of an old magazine. Don't let anyone see the entire picture, but cut it into as many pieces as there are family members present. Each is given a section to paste anywhere on his piece of paper. He then completes a drawing in any way he wishes with crayons or marking pens, adding people, scenery, and objects. It's fun to see the variety of ways the picture was expanded.

☐ **39. PAPER CUP PEOPLE.**   Let each participant make a styrofoam or unwaxed paper cup into a person. Invert the cups and draw a face and body on their sides. Position a large cutting board or piece of stiff cardboard at a gentle incline. Next, set each cup over a marble and let the paper cup people travel down the incline. Once you get the knack, have competitions. Change the slope for faster or slower races.

☐ **40. PLACE MATS.**   First, kids paste together two 8½-by-11-inch sheets of white paper, to form one 16-by-11-inch sheet that will become a place mat. Together, look through catalogs, magazines, and comics to find interesting pictures. Paste these on the paper. Be sure all loose edges are pasted down. Then, cut a piece of wax paper two inches larger than the place mat. Cover the pictures with it and turn the mat over and tape the edges of the wax paper to the back. Use these at supper as colorful place mats. To make them more permanent, iron the edges of the wax paper with a *warm* iron to fuse the wax paper to the pictures.

FOR OLDER CHILDREN

☐ **41. THE LIVING SCRAPBOOK.**   Buy an inexpensive scrapbook. Let a child print the name of the current month with a crayon and then paste in items contributed by the family. These might be a scorecard from a ballgame, a good school paper, a letter from Grandma, a recital program, photos, or a baby announcement. Let an older child write comments to go with the items. Add to the scrapbook each week, and let a different child be in charge the next month.

☐ **42. MAIL CARRIER.**   Run a loop of sturdy string from one room to another (bedroom to bedroom or family room to kitchen) and back again. Use a doorknob or chair back as the terminal around which the string goes. Test the loop of string by pulling on it to see that it moves smoothly. Then attach to the string a "mailbag" (a plastic grocery bag works well). Put a picture, a message, or a wrapped cookie in the bag. Gently pull on the string to send the mail to the other room. When you receive mail, you have to send some back.

☐ **43. HOW LONG?**   Everyone in the family writes a letter or draws a picture to send to a different faraway relative or friend. Write on the calendar the date the letters were sent and the date each person guesses he'll have an answer. See how close each person is.

☐ **44. NOTE CARDS.**   It's more fun to write thank you notes on handmade cards. Help a child gather flowers and leaves for pressing. Cut notepaper and put a thin coat of rubber cement where the flowers and leaves are to be positioned. Arrange the floral material. Then, put a piece of wax paper on top of the arrangement and put the stack of note cards under large books or in a flower press to flatten and dry for a few days. A child can also make gift tags and place cards for you this way.

☐ **45. CARD HOUSES.**   Using a deck of cards, show children how to make houses. Play games to see who can make the longest or tallest. See whose construction lasts the longest. A variation: Play together, taking turns adding one card at a time. Whose card makes it tumble? Or, put ten cards at each place at the supper table. No touching until eating is over! Then let each family member make something interesting with his cards: a design, a tepee, a house.

★

SECTION 5: ALL IN THE FAMILY

☐ **46. THE GUEST ROOM.**   On a weekend night, let each family member sleep in a different bed. It's fun to be in another's room! Parents, too! At breakfast the next morning, talk about where you slept and what was nice about the new room or bed or what needed improving in that room.

☐ **47. BIG BULBS.**   Purchase one or more big flower bulbs that grow well indoors. Amaryllis bulbs are ideal. Let kids name the bulb (Amy the Amaryllis, etc.). See how many days before the bulb sends up a shoot. Then measure the plant each day. Let kids keep a chart. Everyone can guess which day the first big bloom will open. If you have several bulbs, it can be a race.

☐ **48. BREAKING THE HABIT.**   Let TV be special at your house. When there's going to be something great for all the family to view, hang a sign on the refrigerator announcing the title and time. Occasionally, let each child invite a friend. Darken the room. Make popcorn. Talk about the show during the commercials. Also stop by the library and borrow *Breaking the TV*

Habit (Joan Wilkins, Scribner, 1982). It gives good ideas on enjoying TV while living life to the fullest. (See chapter 7, section 9, for more on TV.)

☐ **49. CANDLELIGHT NIGHT.**   Pretend you are colonists and spend an evening without electricity. Give safety rules concerning candles. With a candle in a lantern, go for a short walk in the dark outside. Eat, read, play games, and bathe by candlelight. Then be sure to extinguish all candles, making the last one to be blown out each person's bedside candle.

☐ **50. REPOTTING.**   Just as plants grow better when the environment is improved and the growing medium is revitalized, so do kids. Once a year work together to give a child's bedroom a new look. Don't spend money on this. Be creative by letting her put up new posters, relocate the bed, paint the bookshelf, and store tired toys and bring out others. A child's room is her castle (that's why a child should never be sent to her room as punishment). Give it a new look to make it a happy place to play, work, and sleep. When you've finished, inaugurate the new room by eating lunch there.

☐ **51. IN-HOUSE RACE.**   When kids have been sitting too long and outside play isn't a possibility, suggest an in-house race. Choose a color, such as green. Name the rooms that are part of the race course (try to use every room, plus the closets and bathrooms) and have the runner or runners go quickly from room to room, touching one green item. You run along, too. If just one plays, he counts up the green items found. If there are two or more, the winner is the first to touch a green item in each of the designated areas and return to the start.

☐ **52. INSIDE SLEEP-OUT.**   With sleeping bags or bedrolls, pretend the house is a forest. Let each family member choose a unique place to sleep "on the ground." Favorite places might be under the dining room table, in front of the fireplace, next to the dog, or in a bathtub. Play quiet music and provide a flashlight and a book for easy going-to-sleep.

☐ **53. CANDLE MAKER.**   Collect all the old candles you have. Let children choose the shapes for new candles, using dishes, cartons, and other forms that can withstand contact with hot wax. Affix to the bottom of the form a string that can be used as a wick, then carefully supervise the melting of the candles. Fish out the old wicks. Melt in a crayon to change the color of the wax. Cool slightly, then pour into molds. After the wax cools a little more, straighten the string wick or insert in the center a thin candle as a wick. When firm, remove from the mold and enjoy on the dining table or elsewhere.

☐ **54. PHOTOGRAPHER.**   Show how a simple camera works. With your help, let children take pictures of each other at play, with a pet, in a new outfit, and so on. When the pictures are developed, let each child write short notes about the photos and send these to faraway friends and relatives. Uncritically, show how their picture taking can be improved, such as by centering the main subject, by being sure the light comes from behind the camera, or by moving in closer.

FOR OLDER CHILDREN

☐ **55. THE HOUSE MYSTERY.**   Each family member has paper and pencil and lists various items in the house that appear in multiples: steps, light bulbs, potted plants, windows, doors, kitchen cupboards, drawers, coats in the front hall closet. Next, each person writes down his guess of "how many" are in each category listed. Then let each person become a specialist in one category and go around the house making a count of that item. When the counts have been made, see who had the closest estimates in each category.

☐ **56. KNOTS.**   First look in an encyclopedia or scout or camping handbook for illustrations on knot making. Together, select about five useful knots to learn. Then, provide each family member with a five-foot length of rope about one-quarter inch in diameter. Learn some of these knots: the clove hitch, for lashing things together; the square knot, for tying bundles and use in first aid; the bowline loop knot, for use in climbing or accidents; the two half-hitches, for tying a knot that is tight but can be easily loosened; the sheet bend or weaver's knot, for connecting two ropes. Learn just one at a time, waiting until everyone has mastered the knot. Then, for fun, do them in the dark some night to see how well you really know them.

☐ **57. NOSTALGIA NIGHT.**   Bring out an old scrapbook, a photo album, or some slides or movies. Decide some silly categories to look for: most adorable, worst clothed, strangest person, craziest pose. See how much everyone has changed! Let kids name the other people in the pictures. Do this several times each year but don't overdo it. About thirty minutes at a sitting keeps it fun.

☐ **58. VIDEO CAMERA FUN.**   If you don't have a video recorder camera, borrow one. First plan what your film will be: the story of one day, "This Is Your Life" for one person, or a made-up plot. Gather costumes, props, music, and actors. Talk about what you'll do but don't rehearse. Then take turns being director, actor, and cameraman. View your production and enjoy its flaws and high points. You'll do better the second time! (For other video camera ideas see chapter 7, section 9.)

★

SECTION 6: PET PALS

Pets provide opportunities for a child to be responsible, to express love and receive affection. Some children have fantasy play with their pets, talking to them—and listening to them. And a pet provides continuity and stability in a changing world.

☐ **59. SHOPPING AROUND.**   Rather than just surprising a child with a pet, shop with him before making the commitment. Investigate pets owned by friends and ask for suggestions. Go to the Humane Society or a pet store several times and look at the animals. Ask the question, "If you were getting a pet today, which one would you choose?" Pet-sit for another family to see how well children enjoy the work and play connected with a pet.

☐ **60. START SMALL.**   When choosing a child's first pet, start small, and start with an animal that can be touched. (This rules out goldfish!) A hamster or gerbil, or an older kitten, are good first pets. Dogs and ponies can come later. Before getting the pet, work together to make a list of what the pet will require: feeding, grooming, exercise, love. Talk about how these activities *must* fit into the daily schedule. Using pictures or words, make a reminder chart of what the child must do.

☐ 61. FISH, TURTLES, ANTS, AND BIRDS.   The first three are spectator pets. They are fun for a younger child to watch for a few minutes of the day. Older children may enjoy raising special fish varieties. Certainly you should consider these when your child wants a pet, but they do not provide the one-on-one companionship of other pets. They *are* a good test of a child's ability to care for a pet. Some birds make fine pets for older children who have the interest and patience to train and enjoy these beautiful feathered friends.

☐ 62. GUINEA PIGS!   These gentle rodents are wonderful for children, since they love to be cuddled and petted. Also known as cavies, they should be bought when about two months old. They live five to eight years. If your child likes to comb and groom, get the mop-haired Peruvian variety. Females mate as early as one to two months of age and are pregnant about sixty-five days, producing one to four babies per litter. Think ahead about other families who'll want the babies, and offer them at school, too. You'll need a cage, wood shavings, a sunlit place, food, and water. They enjoy companionship, so be sure they get plenty of attention.

☐ 63. KITTY LITTERS.   Having a litter of kittens may sound like fun, but remember, you have to find homes for all of them. Why not start out with just one kitten from your Humane Society. A kitten is *not* a pet for a toddler, who is apt to be rough or give it too much attention. It's a good pet for a kindergartner. The kitten will need a warm box, a scratching post (a good project for parent and child to make), a litter box, regular food and water, plus socializing and rest. Cats are playful and enjoy simple fun with a ball on a string, a small ball of yarn, or a toy that squeaks. As with dogs, consider neutering to avoid unwanted babies.

☐ 64. BEFORE YOU BUY THE DOG.   Read this book: *The Right Dog for You* (Daniel F. Tortora, Simon & Schuster, 1983). Remember that a dog will live about twelve to sixteen years, so the dog you choose will probably be the family dog for all the child's growing years. Choose a breed that ties in with a child's needs; different breeds have different temperaments and levels of activity, trainability, and sociability. Make at least four trips to the Humane Society or pet store to look at the dogs before making your decision to adopt or buy.

☐ **65. HOW MUCH?** With your prospective young dog owner, make a list of pet needs: bed, food, toys, flea repellant, shots, grooming, kennel care during vacations. Find the costs of these things at the pet store and at the vet and make a yearly total. Next, add up the time it takes (by day or week) to feed, groom, bathe, walk, and train a dog. Add to it minimum time for daily play with the dog. Consider the monetary and time commitments. A child who *really* wants a dog will not find this discouraging.

☐ **66. TWO TRICKS.** Divide the family into two teams. Each team selects a trick they think the dog can learn. Team members can practice the trick anytime with the dog. See which trick is learned first. Tricks can be to teach the dog to sit, lie down, shake hands, speak, roll over, jump over a stick, ring a bell, catch, or fetch. Don't pressure the dog by trying to teach more than two tricks at a time. But when two tricks have been learned, you can teach him two more.

☐ **67. RENT-A-HORSE.** At some time in childhood every child wants a horse. Owning a horse is very expensive. More than merely owning a pet, horse ownership can be a special way of life—very time-consuming, very costly. Riding, training, grooming, and showing can take all of a child's free time. Before you make such a commitment, check with your local stable or horse club to see about renting a horse for the summer. Let a child see what is involved in handling equestrian equipment and the horse's care and exercise. After the summer, talk about what she learned and if she is interested in continuing.

★

SECTION 7: DINING TABLE FUN

☐ **68. STARVING ARTISTS.** Cover the dining table with a plain paper cloth. Along with the silverware at each place, line up about five crayons. Don't give any rules, other than the invitation to draw and eat. Some starving artists will make mini-murals while others may trace around plates and glasses. Unless the paper gets spilled on too much, keep using it for several meals until all the white space is gone. Hang it on the bulletin board or the kitchen wall so everyone can see the art.

☐ **69. TV REPORTER.**   Tell only one family member about this idea. Help her make a fake microphone out of cardboard. Keep it hidden until the family is seated for supper, then introduce her as the "Inquiring Reporter" from your TV station. She can ask questions on school, business, how they like the food, what it's like to live in this house, what they'd change, and so on. If you want, record the interviews with a tape machine for playback later.

☐ **70. WHAT'S NEWS?**   In advance of supper, ask each family member to look through the newspaper and bring an interesting item to share at the table. Non-readers can choose a cartoon or picture. See how much you learn.

☐ **71. THE RESTAURANT.**   With one child as helper, plan to serve supper as if it were at a restaurant. Let him letter a simple menu and serve as waiter, seating the others. Serve soup, the main dish, and dessert, and, finally, set finger bowls on the table. The cook and waiter also sit at the table and ask how the service is and if the food is cooked just right. Present an exorbitant fake bill at the end of the meal.

☐ **72. WHAT'S IN A NAME #1.**   With the help of a library book on names and their meanings, look up the historical derivation of each family member's name. See how the name evolved and how it differs in various countries. One good book is *Name Your Baby* (Lareina Rule, Bantam, 1963). For instance, the name "Cliff" is from the Old English and means "from the steep rock," and a famous Cliff is Cliff Robertson. Share with children how you chose their names. Ask kids what name they wish they'd been given. Make up good (not mean) rhymes for each family member's name.

☐ **73. WHAT'S IN A NAME #2.**   Let each family member decide what he'd like his name to really mean. A parent should start. If your name is Steven, you'll pick out a quality to go with each letter: smiling, tough, enthusiastic, voracious, even-tempered, natty. Parents may have to explain some of the words, but that's easy vocabulary building. Then let a child come up with his own name-meaning. Everyone works together on the family surname. You may want to print these out for children to keep. Do it again in a year or so and see what new qualities are chosen.

☐ **74. ROYALTY SERVING.** When a new food is served at the table, anyone can ask for a "Royalty Serving," since being royal has rights. This is just one tablespoonful and is all that has to be eaten. Often, the next time around, the food is eaten in a normal-size serving without any comment.

☐ **75. TV CONVERSATIONS.** When the TV is on, conversation is off, so enjoy suppertime without TV competition. Instead, talk about what you've seen on TV. What made the show funny? Were the jokes at the expense of someone's feelings? How did it picture kids? Parents? Business? The law? What was dumb? What was interesting? What did we learn? Give recognition to those who give input to this conversation. (For more on conversations, see chapter 10.)

☐ **76. SURPRISE-GUEST SUPPER.** Plan a simple supper with a big casserole and salad. Each family member invites someone to come for supper at the exact same time and keeps the name of the guest a surprise. The conversation will be lively, with all the surprise guests.

☐ **77. WEIRD STORY.** Set a timer for five minutes. A parent starts making up a story with animals that talk, cars that fly, and other fanciful elements. After three or four sentences, the speaker points to someone else who must pick up the story and then point to another. When the timer goes off, that person points to another who must finish the story, tying up all the loose ends.

☐ **78. COSTUME SUPPER.** A few days in advance, tell the family that for a certain supper everyone will come in costume. Younger children may need some help. Children may borrow parents' clothes with permission. Make available old sheets, makeup, jewelry, crayons, and paper bags for over-the-head masks. Keep costumes a secret until dinnertime. Save the best costumes for use again.

☐ **79.. BAD MANNERS.** Rather than spoil a meal by harping on table manners, occasionally have a "Bad Manners Meal." Without letting others hear, tell family members what bad manners they may each represent: elbows on the table, talking with the mouth full, interrupting, reaching across the table, getting up without being excused, starting to eat before others. Sometime during the meal, each person must do his bad manners to see if he can get by unnoticed. Eating and conversation should continue as usual, but see who can catch another doing his bad manners act.

☐ **80. SUPPER-IN-A-TREE.** Give an ordinary day a twist by letting kids have supper in the low branches of a tree. Join them! Put an open bag on the ground under the tree and let each one see how good his aim is with used paper cups and napkins.

☐ **81. CANDLELIGHT SUPPER.** Kids never tire of candles, so eat supper by candlelight. First have candles in the center of the table, then vary this by putting a candle in front of each person at the table. Light these nightly. See whose burns the longest. Teach kids the way to blow out candles within cupped hands so as not to splatter the wax or knock a glowing wick onto the table. If candlelight suppers continue to be popular, consider buying a candle snuffer and a wick snipper.

★

SECTION 8: THE CHEF'S ASSISTANT

Let each child enjoy helping in the kitchen and learning to cook on his own. As a child becomes more interested in cooking, buy him a cookbook. Betty Crocker's *New Boys' and Girls' Cookbook* (Golden Press, 1965) is a good one. For outside cooking try the Girl Scouts' *Cooking Out-of-Doors* (Girl Scouts USA, 1960). Be sure to use the kitchen for non-cooking fun, too.

☐ **82. PHANTOM FISH.** *Gyotaku* means fish rubbing, which is an oriental art that is hundreds of years old. You will need a fresh fish six to eighteen inches in size and fairly flat (such as perch, bass, rockfish, or flounder), thick water-based ink from the stationery store, a small brush, a one-inch brush, and sketch paper or other water-tolerant paper. Follow these seven steps: (1) Carefully wash the fish with soap and water. *Dry well.* (2) Place the fish on some newspaper on your work surface. If the fins are wobbly, support them on clay and pin them in place. (3) Using a one-inch brush, paint a *thin* coat of ink on the fish, first applying it from head to tail. Leave the eye blank. Then, brush it again from tail to head so the ink catches under the scales. (4) Place the sketch paper over the fish and press it down firmly, being careful not to wrinkle or move the paper. (5) Remove the paper and look at the results. You can make more prints if you wish. (6) With a small brush, paint in the eye. (7) Thoroughly wash the fish under running water until it is clean—then prepare and serve it for dinner!

☐ **83. FABULOUS BREAD.** This special dough can be made into people, animals, baskets, and ornaments that can be painted and kept for many years. You'll need 4 cups of flour, 1 cup of salt, and 1¼ cups of water. In a big bowl , let a child mix the flour and salt and then add the water. When it is too stiff to stir, it is ready for kneading. Put some flour on a breadboard and on your hands. Knead the dough for about ten minutes, until it has the consistency of soft clay. Now shape the dough into figures or roll it out to a half-inch thickness and cut it with a cookie cutter. Place the items on a cookie sheet and bake at 350 degrees. Thin pieces will bake in thirty minutes, while thick ones take about an hour. After the objects are cool, they can be painted. When the paint is totally dry, they can be varnished for a clear finish. When storing, put them in plastic bags with a few moth balls to discourage bugs that might enjoy eating the artwork.

☐ **84. KITCHEN ARITHMETIC.** Teach these equivalents by actually letting a child test them with water and measuring spoons and cups.

3 teaspoons = 1 tablespoon
4 tablespoons = ¼ cup
8 tablespoons = ½ cup
16 tablespoons = 1 cup
2 cups = 1 pint
2 pints or 4 cups = 1 quart
4 quarts = 1 gallon

Even some parents don't know these, so let the kids test you, too!

☐ **85. CONTAINER PLAY.** Teach young children that all kitchen equipment isn't for play. Designate one shelf for a child's own supplies: plastic containers that fit one inside the other or that make a stack, a funnel for water play in the sink, a wooden spoon for stirring pudding, measuring spoons and cups, tongs, a spatula, a mold for making ice or Jell-O.

☐ 86. THE BAKERY.

On a Saturday morning, create your own bakery. In advance, select recipes and get ingredients. Plan to make cookies or a dessert, bread or muffins, and a casserole. Work in teams, seeing that each family member takes part in the making, baking, and cleaning up. Eat some of your creations, share some, and freeze some.

☐ 87. KITCHEN PUN FUN.

Copy this list (minus the answers) and see how many pun answers your kids can find in the kitchen:

Pun	Answer
Baseball equipment	Plate
Absorbing subject	Sponge
Medieval torture	Rack
Peacemaker	Scissors
Sad end of a ship	Sink
Cowboy territory	Range
Commentator	Potato
Things to adore	Door keys
When amazed, you're	Floored
Dance at a teen party	Mixer
Insincere flattery	Soft soap
Critics do it	Pan

☐ 88. FRUIT BOATS.

No matter what the season, fruit boats make a festive plate and are a project that kids love. Each fruit boat is an individual serving that looks like a sailboat. Start with a melon, such as a honeydew or a cantaloupe. Peel the melon and then let kids make long, boat-shaped slices (about one-eighth of a melon). Taking a little off the bottom will let the "boat" sit flat. Next, use a skewer to make a mast for each boat. Fresh bread thinly spread with peanut butter or soft cheese can be cut into triangles to make the sails. Carefully poke the "mast" through the sail, then stick into the boat. Now for the crew: Use a section of banana for the body, with grape legs, arms, and head affixed with three toothpicks. Let each boat sit in a sea of lettuce.

☐ 89. TABLE DECORATOR.

Let a child be the one to set the table and provide an interesting centerpiece. Show how silverware is placed in the order in which it is used, the piece to be used first being placed on the outside, farthest from the plate. Put napkins, forks, and salad plates at the left, and knives, spoons, glasses, and cups at the right. For little children, make a simple sketch of where the silverware goes and keep it in a kitchen drawer or on the bulletin board until it's mastered. For centerpieces consider using flowers, garden greenery with a figurine, an arrangement of small toy animals or dolls, a glass bowl with something interesting inside, or a child-made clay piece.

☐ **90. DOUGH FUN.**   When you're using pie dough or pizza dough, let kids have some pieces to cut into interesting shapes: animals, people, houses. Then "decorate" the pie dough with cinnamon and sugar, bake, and eat as a snack. For the pizza dough, let each child add her own favorite toppings, bake, and enjoy for lunch or supper.

☐ **91. "MY RECIPES."**   Provide a small box or extra file box for a child's own recipes. When he makes cookies or a casserole with you, copy the recipe and put it in his file. Older children can accurately make their own copies. Be sure to put a date on the recipe. Then, years later when the youngster goes off on his own, he'll take along this box of recipes he can make. These family favorites will remind him of home, and perhaps he will even be able to recall when he first made the recipe.

☐ **92. A FIRST SNACK RECIPE.**   This healthy snack is one kids can make with just a little help from you. These keep well in the freezer.

PEANUT BUTTER BATONS

¼ cup chunky peanut butter
¼ cup dry milk (do not reconstitute)
1 tablespoon honey
⅓ cup light cream
4 bananas, peeled and frozen
⅓ cup chopped peanuts

Put the first four ingredients in a blender and mix until smooth. Roll the bananas in this mixture to completely coat. Sprinkle with the peanuts and insert a flat stick. Freeze and enjoy!

☐ **93. A FIRST SALAD RECIPE.**   Let a child make one for each family member. On a salad plate, place leaf lettuce and top with a pineapple ring in the center. Peel a straight banana and cut in half. Place the banana in the center of the pineapple ring and press down slightly so the banana stands up like a candle. Make a flame for the banana this way: Use a vegetable peeler to get a strip of carrot about two inches in length. Loop it in half to represent the flame. Cut off the pointed top of the banana and replace with the carrot peel, pinching the peel at the top so it looks like a flame. Use a toothpick to affix it to the banana. Other fruits can be placed on the lettuce. (You can also omit the carrot and put a birthday candle in the banana and light it just before mealtime.)

☐ **94. A FIRST CANDY RECIPE.**   Here's a no-cook candy that a child can make with a hand mixer or a heavy spoon. Mix together 1 cup peanut butter, and 1 cup carob powder, 1 cup honey, 2 teaspoons vanilla, l cup coconut. Roll into balls or spread in a pan and cut into squares. Let the child share this concoction with friends.

☐ **95. COFFEE CAN SUPPER.**   Here's a unique main dish that kids can cook on the grill for an outside supper. For four people, use one pound of ground beef, seasoned with salt and pepper and made into four patties. Grease four very clean one-pound cans, such as coffee cans. Put into each can in this order: one meat patty, five carrot strips, two tomato slices, ½ cup drained canned corn. Top with salt, pepper, and a little butter or margarine. Cover each can very tightly with heavy-duty aluminum foil and place on a grill to cook about 25 minutes. While these are cooking, make dumplings, following the directions on a biscuit mix package. Then carefully remove foil from covered cans and drop about four spoonsful of dough into each can. Again tightly cover and cook 20 minutes more without reopening cans. Carefully open the cans (there will be steam and cans will be hot). Let each person eat from a can.

☐ **96. FIRST CAKE.**   This make-believe angel food cake is quickly made by children and toasted over the hot coals of a grill or camp fire. Use day-old unsliced bread. Cut off crusts and cut bread into two-inch squares. Put the bread on a roasting fork or green stick. Roll it in sweetened condensed milk and flaked coconut and toast over a fire until the coconut is brown and crunchy.

★

SECTION 9: AT-HOME ET CETERA

FOR YOUNGER CHILDREN

☐ **97. ALL-ALONE BOX.**   With a child's help, select some of her toys that are best played with alone. Put them in a basket or a carton that the child can color or decorate. Then put the collection on a top shelf or other out-of-the-way place. When there's an occasion when she has to play by herself for a while, bring out the All-Alone Box. Its novelty will hold her interest for a long time.

☐ **98. MAGNIFYING GLASS.**   Show how to hold and use a magnifying glass. Look at a woven fabric, breakfast cereal, hair, toes, a dog's nose, earth, a leaf, and someone's eye. See who can find the most interesting thing to look at.

☐ **99. BATHTUB SPECIAL.**   As a treat, let a child use the parent's bathtub for a long bath and playtime. Supply toys and inexpensive books, a big towel, bubble bath, and lotions. Bathtime is a special treat in a different location. Two toddlers can share the fun, but you'll want to control the splashing and be alert to safety precautions.

☐ **100. BALLS.**   Collect a variety of balls, large and small, and some containers (old cardboard boxes or kitchen pans and bowls). Let a toddler experiment putting one or more balls into the various containers. Then, using several balls under a carton, show how to make a carton roll. Show a child how to stretch out on a big ball and roll along on it.

☐ **101. BUBBLE MAKER.**   Make your own mixture of detergent and water or buy bubble liquid. You can use jar rings as blowers, blow through a real ring, or make rings out of lightweight wire. Practice making single and double bubbles. Make bubbles in the bathtub. See if the dog likes bubbles.

☐ **102. RAINBOW WATER.**   Experiment with making different colors of water by mixing food coloring and water in glass jars. (Wear aprons and immediately soak clothes with spills on them, as some colors don't wash out easily.) Add branches or flowers and put these colorful arrangements in each room. Remember that a little coloring goes a long way.

FOR OLDER CHILDREN

☐ **103. GUESSING WEIGHTS.** Put on a tray about ten different articles that you've weighed on a kitchen, postage, or bathroom scale: a book, an apple, a toy car, a letter, a ring, a pen, a dish, a shoe, a stone. Make a list of the various weights on a piece of paper. Let the family guess which weight goes with each object. Or, let them guess which is the lightest or the heaviest.

☐ **104. SOAP FRIENDS.** Give each child a large bar of inexpensive soap and a not-too-sharp knife. Let the sculptors keep secret what they are carving (a house, a car, a boy, a cat). See who can guess what the carving is. Use the soap sculptures in the bathroom. And don't waste the scraps: Tie them in cheesecloth and use them for washing in the bathtub.

☐ **105. TUNNEL.** Connect card tables to other tables and cover with sheets. When it's dark, crawl through the tunnel. Take turns being in charge. The person in charge can put strange objects in the tunnel, make eerie sounds, or reach in under the sheet with ice cubes, a feather duster, or a wet cloth. Then turn on the lights and have a race, using a timer to see who can go through the tunnel the fastest.

FOR ALL CHILDREN

☐ **106. SHOEBAGS.** No matter what your children's ages, buy a shoebag for each one. For baby, you'll tie the shoebag in the playpen and fill each pocket with baby toys. At first he'll only be able to reach the lower ones but as he pulls himself up, he'll be able to enjoy all the contents. Let other children find uses themselves. For example, when tacked on the wall, they make excellent repositories for small toddler toys. Older girls like them in the closet as a place to put ribbons, scarves, and socks. Boys and girls can put tools or art supplies in them. And of course, if all else fails, one can use them for shoes.

☐ **107. PICK-UP RACE.** When many toys are spread out, enlist the entire family for a pick-up race. Players get to guess how many minutes they think it will take. One minute? Eight minutes? Twelve minutes? When you say "Go!" everyone starts picking up *and* putting things where they go. (This means that things must be put away where they belong, not just put in a pile in the corner. The job goes faster when there are good storage places for toys.) Players may move faster or slower so as to be the winner, but other players will counter balance that. No prizes are won except the satisfaction of a job well done. After a few such races, kids will find that picking up isn't such a bad job after all.

☐ **108. THE BIG TEN FOR INSIDE PLAY.** Consider this list of ten great indoor activity toys that teach—toys that don't plug in, wind up, or need batteries. They run on imagination! You may want to buy one for your child's next gift occasion.

• For younger children: big building blocks, play dishes and pantry items, two or more puppets, sturdy rolling toys that can even be sat on, an easel, construction toys such as Lego, musical instruments such as a xylophone or a small but good toy piano, a cardboard or plastic playhouse, a family of dolls, a zoo or ark with many animals.

• For older children: a doorway gym bar, a simple camera, an easy-to-play musical instrument such as a recorder (not a tape recorder but an instrument), construction toys such as Lego, a microscope, a variety of cars and trucks that can be played with together, sports equipment, trivia games, a waterproof watch, box games such as Space Hop, Scrabble, Yahtze, Allowance, and Uno.

TWO

CAN CHRIS COME OUT AND PLAY?

 ackyards and neighborhood sidewalks can be great play places, but you can also enjoy many of these activities in a park. (Many of these games can be adapted for inside play on rainy or cold days.) Outside play provides healthy fun in almost every kind of weather, and it encourages independence and getting along with others. Without having to go other places to find it, there can be great fun right near home. Best of all, this kind of play has little to do with spending money!

★

★

SECTION 1: PLAYHOUSES FOR EVERY AGE

It's important that these construction projects be done with parent and child working together. No matter how young the child, the playhouse will mean more if she has helped build it. Through the years, the playhouse will be a place to play house, play office, a hiding place, a fort, a ship, a private place, a clubhouse—whatever the imagination desires. (For simple inside playhouses, see #610.)

☐ **109. "WEE HOOSE."**   The name of this playhouse recalls a Scottish toddler who loved to play outside. Using a tree or a fence as a sturdy beginning, build out from it a cardboard enclosure right on ground level. Use old cardboard boxes and sturdy tape. This temporary structure won't withstand the elements but is a good starter house. To make it last a little longer, cover it with a plastic tarp.

☐ **110. LOW HOUSE.**   Small children can enjoy a "tree house" just a foot off the ground. Using plywood, make a platform with twelve-inch legs. Use a sheet for the roof, attaching it to a tree and tying the corners out to the corners of the plywood. Let a child practice jumping off the one-foot platform, having lunch and rest-time in it, and using it to play games.

☐ **111. SPLIT LEVEL.**   Using the "Low House" as a base, add a second platform a few feet higher up the tree trunk and not directly above the "Low House." Be sure you securely fasten this higher platform to the tree and a nearby fence or support posts. Attach a rope or rope ladder and practice going down it with the child. In good weather, let this be an alternate location for doing homework or playing box games. (More ideas are given below for games to play with playhouses.)

☐ **112. THE MANSION.**   To the "Split Level" add a final level as high as safety permits. Firmly attach sturdy fishnet around this level so that the inhabitants are safe. The "Mansion" is only for those children who agree to abide by the safety rules: no jumping, no pushing. This can be a quiet retreat or a place to read, have a sleep-out, or enjoy some of the vigorous activities described below.

☐ **113. SPIFFY CONSTRUCTION.** Add to any level of the playhouse wood walls with window openings, a roof, and a door. It can be as simple or as elaborate as you desire. Don't make the house too finished at first; let the kids enjoy it in simple form. Then, when it gets a little boring, work together to add to it. Consider staining the wood or painting the house with good outside paint. Hang a bell near the ground that can be rung by those wishing to enter.

☐ **114. INTERIOR DECORATOR.** Choosing materials that can withstand being left outside, add simple furnishings to the house: a bench, a table, plastic curtains, a waterproof box for dishes, toys, simple games. A plastic-covered cushion like those used on lawn furniture makes a great place to rest and read. And why not top off the house with a flag or banner!

☐ **115. OVERNIGHT IN THE HOUSE.** Plan ahead for an overnight in the playhouse. Talk about safety factors. Be sure the sleeper can't roll out. A parent or older child can sleep in a sleeping bag on the ground below. You'll need bedding, flashlights, a bell to ring for help, a bedtime snack, and a book. After a child feels comfortable sleeping in the playhouse, let her invite a friend for an evening of play and a sleep-out.

☐ **116. CASTLE AND KING.** Two or more can play this game using the tree house and yard. Parents can play, too. The playhouse is the king's (or queen's) castle. The king is blindfolded and sits in the castle. The other players are knights who are trying to take the castle. Knights may come from any part of the yard, but they must come so quietly that the monarch doesn't hear them until they pound on the castle, making it their own. The monarch gets three challenges. (A challenge is when he points at what he thinks is an approaching knight and then quickly takes off the blindfold. If he hasn't pointed directly at the knight, he must put the blindfold on and the game continues.) If he uses up his three challenges the nearest knight becomes the new king. If he catches the knight on a challenge, the knight must go to the farthest corner of the yard, and the game continues until a knight captures the castle. Then he becomes king and the game starts over.

☐ **117. BINOCULAR TAG.** The entire family can play this at dusk. One player called the "Big B" sits in the tree house with binoculars. He covers his eyes while the others hide in the yard. He then looks only through the binoculars, trying to find a player and correctly name him. He issues orders to move one step left, right, forward, or back. Eventually he sees and identifies one player, then another. The last to be identified is next one to be the "Big B."

☐ **118. THE FORTRESS.** You'll need lots of old ping pong balls or other very soft balls for this. Divide the balls into two bags and divide the players into two teams. Half are defenders of the fortress and sit in the tree house with their balls. The other half are stormers of the fortress. The stormers start from one end of the yard toward the fortress. Each side throws balls, trying to hit the other side. When a player is hit by a ball, he and the ball go over to the other side. Eventually one side wins. Then they switch locations and play again.

☐ **119. TWO FORTRESSES.** If you live next door to another family, see about building playhouses in both yards. This opens up new kinds of play. Watch each other with binoculars. Pretend to be rival medieval fortresses. Be two whaling ships at sea. Practice throwing (for accuracy) soft balls or beanbags between the two, or play catch or rig up a string telephone. Plan a two-house sleep-out: supper and stories at one, sleeping-bag time at the other.

☐ **120. THE SINKING SHIP.** Play this on a warm day in lightweight clothes or swimsuits. You'll need a spray bottle for each player. The tree house is a ship at sea in a storm. One player, the captain, sits in the playhouse. She has a whistle. A string is placed on the grass about five feet from the playhouse (adjust its distance for the age of children). The other players are spouting whales and must stay behind the string. The captain blows the whistle once, and the whales try to hit her with water. (If she is hit, she becomes a whale and the player hitting her is now captain.) Whales must stop spraying and stand right where they are when the captain blows the whistle twice. Now she gets one chance to spray. If she hits a whale, the whale must join her in the ship. Then she blows the whistle once for whales to spray again. The game continues alternating in this way until the captain has all the players or the captain is hit and a new captain starts the game over.

SECTION 2: OTHER BACKYARD ACTIVITIES

FOR YOUNGER CHILDREN

☐ **121. SUPER SANDBOX.** Plan to build a sandbox over the course of several weekends. The first weekend get railroad ties and find the right location to make a rectangular box. (A rectangle is more fun than a square, as it allows for a mound or mountain of sand at one end—a real asset for imaginative play.) Sit on the ties and look around to see if this is the right location. Also go in the house to make sure that it is where you want it in your view. Consider your neighbors' views and the noise factor, too.

When you've found the right spot, dig out the earth six to eighteen inches deep, so the sand will be deep enough for play. The next weekend, sand the ties for slivers and fasten them to each other. Then line the depression with punctured heavy-weight sheet plastic to discourage plant growth but allow water to drain. Start gathering interesting plastic containers, molds, and tools (plastic kitchen scoops are great). The next week, fill the box with fine, clean sand purchased from the building supply yard. Fill it almost level with the ties and mound it six to ten inches higher in the center. Save some sand for refills after sand has been spilled out of the box.

Install hooks for a plastic drop cloth or tarp that will cover the sand and keep it clean. Supply small pieces of heavy plastic for making a lake in the sandpile (don't use clinging plastic film, for safety reasons). Don't forget to have the kids cover the sandbox at the end of the day or when not in use. You may have to teach kids to conserve the sand and to not throw sand at others or out of the sandbox.

☐ **122. SIDEWALK REMBRANDT.** This works on a patio, sidewalk, safe driveway, or even some basement floors. You'll need a small bucket and inexpensive paint brushes, large and small. Using just plain water as paint, start painting a picture of a person, house, or tree. When the kids see how it works, let them take over, seeing how big a painting can be made before the water dries and disappears. When it does, you have a fresh surface to begin again. Try writing names, too. Older children can write messages, do addition problems, or make cartoons.

☐ **123. DIGGING.** If you have a yard, set aside an inconspicuous section where kids can make dirt roads, run small trucks, dig tunnels and holes to China, or make a fort. You may want to help a child make a fence or plant low bushes around the private yard.

FOR ALL CHILDREN

☐ **124. SPRAY BOTTLES.** This is good summertime fun. Use small spray bottles with adjustable nozzles. The only rule is not to spray in eyes and ears! While kids are having great fun on a warm day spraying each other, you can participate by spraying thirsty plants with the hose. Remember that spray bottles are safer for kids than a high-pressure hose.

☐ **125. MINI-SPOTLIGHT.** Using a shiny object such as a pan, show children how to catch a beam of sunlight and direct it. You be the first to do it, reflecting the light on one child. That child has to perform something: skip, count to ten, say the alphabet, do a somersault. Then it is the child's turn to catch the light and direct it at someone else.

☐ **126. AIR SHOW.** Get the least expensive balsa wood airplane kits to put together. Then, have an air show in the backyard or nearby park. See which plane goes the highest, the farthest, can loop, stays aloft the longest, and survives a crash. You can expand this idea to include another family or the entire neighborhood.

☐ **127. PLANT FOOD.** Kids like to eat what they grow. Start small. Look at all the vegetable seeds at the store. Start with easy-to-grow lettuce, radishes, carrots, and beets. Let children prepare the seedbed, plant the seeds, label the four rows, carefully weed and water, observe, harvest, and then prepare their produce for eating. Another time, consider preparing more garden space for corn, squash, and cucumbers. A wonderful crop for kids is a strawberry patch. The plants look good, have pretty flowers, and they produce instant snacks (but remember to wash them first).

☐ **128. SCARECROW.** Every garden needs one, and making it is fun. Let each child contribute an old article of clothing. A scarecrow can be male or female. You'll need a pole or an old broom as a base. Stuff clothing with hay, dried leaves, or crumpled newspaper. Make a head from a stocking, use jeans and a long-sleeved shirt, and add accessories such as gloves, canvas shoes, a scarf, a hat, and even old jewelry. Give the scarecrow a name and let it sit at the dinner table before going out to work in the garden.

☐ **129. LIVING SCULPTURE.** It takes three to make living sculptures. A parent starts the game and then leaves it to the kids after the first round. One player is Michelangelo, who decides what is to be sculpted: a runner, an angel, a basketball player, a schoolteacher, a baby, a dog doing a trick. Michelangelo whispers this decision to one player and then takes that player's hand and swings her in a wide arc, saying, "Marble, do what I command!" When Michelangelo lets go, the player assumes the pose and holds it while Michelangelo swings the other player or players. As they hold their poses, Michelangelo inspects each sculpture and touches the best one. This player is now the new Michelangelo.

☐ **130. WAITING FOR A SWING.** When you first move into a house, plant two sturdy trees about eight to ten feet apart. These will become the trees for your old-fashioned rope swing. Depending on the trees and your growing season, you'll have to wait five or more years. Then, fasten a sturdy beam between the trees and drop the swing ropes from it. Make the beam as high as possible, so that the swing can go extra high. Older children will have to wait until the trees can take their weight; younger ones can swing sooner. Show kids how to pump so they don't have to be pushed. Make the seating board wide enough for two. Parents enjoy swinging, too.

☐ **131. SWIMMING POOL GAMES.** A backyard swimming pool is an investment that should be used often. These races can also be enjoyed at other pools around town: simple tag relay races, underwater and designated-stroke races, through-the-hoops race, paddling-on-a-float race, push-a-ball-with-your-chin race, one-arm race, feet-only race. Other games include the old favorites "Marco Polo," "Keep Away," and water volleyball.

☐ **132. AROUND THE POOL.** This game for all ages can be adapted to any pool. A parent or a large child is the leader and plays the game with smaller-sized children. In "Around the Pool," a player negotiates eight obstacles around the pool's perimeter, each worth one point. The leader makes the obstacles using his own body and the side of the pool. The players do not receive a point if they touch the leader while going through the obstacle. The obstacles are as follows:

1. Standing in the shallow end a short distance from the pool wall, the leader puts his hands on the pool edge. The swimmer swims between the leader's body and the wall without touching the leader.

2. Standing at the first corner, the leader makes a large "hole" with one hand on the coping and one leg on the wall. The swimmer goes underwater around the corner between the wall and the leader.

3. At the midpoint on the side of the pool, the leader puts both hands on the coping and both feet on the wall, making a "hole" for the swimmer to pass through.

4. At the second corner (at the deep end) the leader holds the coping and spreads his legs apart—one on each wall—to make an underwater "hole" that the swimmer must pass through, making a curve around the corner.

5. At the diving board, the leader holds the diving board with his hands and puts his feet on the wall, just under the water, forcing the swimmer to dive or flip over his legs.

6. At the third corner (at the deep end) the leader goes underwater and makes a big "hole" with his two arms, his hands just touching the wall, for the swimmer to pass through.

7. At the midpoint, the leader puts his back to the wall, holding the coping, and arches his back to put his feet on the wall. The swimmer must go through behind the leader's back.

8. Back at the shallow end by the corner stairs, the leader makes the most difficult form using his body and the steps, making the opening small and including a turn at the corner.

This may sound difficult, but it will become a family favorite.

★

SECTION 3: NEIGHBORHOOD FUN

FOR YOUNGER CHILDREN

☐ **133. BIG WHISTLE.**   When young children first go out into the neighborhood to play, parents need to know the difference between encouragement and interference. Free your child from overprotection by giving him a large whistle to wear on a cord. Tell him you'll still check on play regularly, but when you hear the whistle you'll come quickly.

☐ **134. CHALK TRAIL.**   Using chalk, help a child make a trail of arrows on your sidewalk and driveway and a short way down the street or even around the block. Don't just go in a straight line. It's fun to circle back or make a loop. Then invite a second child to go along, following the arrows.

☐ **135. SAIL BOATS.**   Make many little boats out of folded paper or big leaves. In a warm rain, dress in rainwear and go outside to sail these boats. Find puddles, little streams, or other safe places where water is moving. Standing safely on the curb, put each boat in the gutter and see it sail away. Bring along a bag and a stick to pick up any litter.

☐ **136. "DERANGEMENTS."**   Somewhat like flower arrangements, "derangements" is the title one youngster gave to her lopsided creation. This project can include one or more children. From your own yard, a neighbor's yard (with permission), or a vacant lot, collect flowers and weeds. Using bottles and jars, make unique floral "derangements," then deliver them as surprise gifts to neighbors and friends.

FOR ALL CHILDREN

☐ **137. HOPSCOTCH.**   With chalk, make a giant hopscotch on your sidewalk or driveway—or even in the garage. Get everyone in the neighborhood to try it. You can use small beanbags or pennies as well as stones, for tossing. Keep a big scorecard of how everyone did.

☐ **138. WALK AND TOSS.** When the family goes for a walk, or when a group of children plays outside together, try this simple activity that requires good aim. One person throws a small rock a short or long distance ahead. The other players toss their rocks, trying to get as near to the first rock as possible. As the group walks along, it will be easy to see which one is closest. Each player picks up his own rock, and the nearest one is the next to throw first. You can play this inside using poker chips or jar lids.

☐ **139. BEANBAGS.** Find scraps of sturdy material, such as old jeans. Let a child cut his own beanbag and help sew the two side seams, fill it with dried beans, and then sew it shut. Make extra beanbags for other kids in the neighborhood. This game teaches good aim. Start by throwing the beanbag into a wide circle. As kids get better, set up a target to hit, letting players stand about ten feet away. Next, try tossing beanbags into holes cut in cartons. The ultimate game has a large circle with several more circles inside and a bull's-eye. Assign a point value (five, ten, twenty and thirty) for the various circles and also a 40-point bonus for hitting the bull's-eye. Take turns tossing and keep score to see who gets to one hundred first.

☐ **140. PET SHOW.** On a sunny day, help your child plan a neighborhood pet show. Call other children and invite them to bring a pet and also one small wrapped prize. Set up categories depending on the pets: biggest, smallest, cutest, best behaved, most active, best trick. Using ribbon and cardboard, make these awards that can be presented to each winner and hung around the owner's neck. Each owner also gets to choose one of the wrapped prizes. Ask two senior citizens or neighbors to judge the event.

☐ **141. JUMP ROPE.** Invite another family to play jump rope together. It's good exercise for both generations. Do you remember these old jump rope rhymes?

• For beginners:

> I like milk and you like tea,
> I like the girls [boys] and the girls [boys] like me.

• For intermediates: The first jumper holds an envelope or paper and says:

Mailman, Mailman, do your duty;
Send my letter to an American beauty.
Don't you stop and don't delay,
Get it to her right away!

On exiting on the last word, the jumper must pass the letter to the next jumper who is entering without a pause.

• For the more advanced: This one is done with appropriate motions (turning, touching, crossing heart to show "I love you," pulling a light cord, waving).

Teddy bear, teddy bear, turn around.
Teddy bear, teddy bear, touch the ground.
Teddy bear, teddy bear, touch your shoe.
Teddy bear, teddy bear, I love you.
Teddy bear, teddy bear, turn off the light.
Teddy bear, teddy bear, say good night.

☐ **142. GUN-FREE #1.** More parents are wisely discouraging gun play, but that doesn't mean that exciting play activities have to stop. Good aim can be practiced with safe dart games, archery, or at the bowling alley. Strength can be promoted on a jungle gym. Tracking can be done by playing "Sleuth": One person or group starts out ahead of the other and leaves clues around the neighborhood; the others try to follow without being seen. A parent can also start adventurous play by suggesting a premise: "A truck is stuck in the desert sand. It's loaded with birthday gifts, a cake, and melting wax candles. It's your assignment to rescue the driver, the contents, and deliver the cake for the party. But a group of hungry kids is also trying to reach the truck." Let the kids take it from there. You'll be amazed at their creativity.

☐ **143. GUN-FREE #2.** In one neighborhood where gun play and BB guns were overly popular, parents got together and made a deal the kids couldn't resist. They selected a large toy they knew the kids would enjoy: an elaborate jungle gym. They gathered the kids and showed them catalog pictures of the new toy and offered to go together to buy it *if* they all turned in their guns. It would be put in the largest backyard and be accessible to all. The kids accepted the deal and went from killing games to healthier activities.

☐ **144. ARMY SURPLUS.** For active outside play, you'll find many good toys available at the Army surplus store—and they don't have anything to do with guns. Check out the bargain prices on items like pup tents, backpacks, and tools. Sometimes parachutes are available, and they are great yard toys when hung from a tree. They also can be hung from the ceiling of a child's room to give it a great new look.

☐ **145. BASKETBALL.** Too young to shoot baskets? Let kids practice their aim with a plastic clothes basket. Any kind of ball will do, the more the better: tennis balls, basketballs, baseballs, footballs, even the dog's ball. Divide the balls and put each child's initials on the balls he's to toss. Take turns tossing a ball into the basket from five to ten feet away (depending on age and skill). A ball that doesn't make it into the basket is "out." Continue taking turns until all the balls are "out." The winner is the last one to successfully throw a ball into the basket. Using a bench, raise the height of the basket and start over. See how high the basket has to be before no one can get a ball in.

☐ **146. WARM DAY.** Help children make lemonade and cookies. Let them make simple written announcements of a "lemonade social," giving time and place that day. Then the kids deliver the invitations to children and adults in the neighborhood. Help set up places to sit in the shade to enjoy conversation, lemonade, and cookies.

☐ **147. HOT DAY.** Cool off, using an inflatable swimming pool. See how many activities the family can enjoy in and around the pool. Let everyone sit in the pool for lunch. Take a rest and soak up a little sun. Read a book to children stretched out in the pool. With face masks, see interesting objects on the bottom of the pool. Make paper boats and have a race, blowing the boats to the opposite side. Put chairs around the pool and eat supper with feet in the water. Make a small bucket brigade to empty the pool water to thirsty trees. Let children take soap into the pool for an after-supper bath (don't empty soapy water on plants). With this much activity, you may have to change the pool water during the day and also start with clean water each day.

☐ **148. RAINY DAY.** Cut arm and neck slits in large plastic trash bags. Let kids add scarves or belts to make modish rain outfits. Boots and a hat complete the outfit. Make a raincoat for the dog, too. Now go for a walk in the rain. If the rain is very hard, take along an umbrella. Look at how cars drive, where water flows, how plants look, how the outsides of houses change. Find a place where water stands and, using a stick, see if you can free the water by making a channel. Tilt your head back and taste the rain.

☐ **149. COLD DAY.**   For outside play, help children plan a space adventure. Snow outfits look a little like space outfits. Wear helmets for an added touch. Let a wagon be the spacecraft and let children take turns steering it while following the directions of a blindfolded rider. Welcome them at the Space Station, where they get a cup of hot apple cider. Then, off into orbit near a hot planet—this is a fire in your outside barbecue (even though it isn't summer). Provide space balls (marshmallows) and space swords (sticks or forks) to toast the marshmallows. As it gets darker, give the spacemen a flashlight and let them play laser tag, the tag being made with the flashlight beam.

☐ **150. SNOWY DAY.**   During very cold weather, help kids design a large igloo in the biggest yard. Everyone helps by making snowballs. Make the tunnel just big enough to crawl through. Then, make the main room with higher walls. For safety, provide two boards and very heavy cardboard for the ceiling. Add some snow on top to finish. Using a hose with a spray nozzle, lightly spray the igloo so it will freeze and become more permanent in the cold weather. Several light sprayings will make it quite solid, but check each day to see that it isn't about to collapse. Let kids play, read, and snack in the igloo.

☐ **151. TOY EXCHANGE.**   Let each child look through her toys and select, with your OK, two or three that she is tired of playing with. Ask other families in your neighborhood to do the same. Get together and let the kids exchange toys. You'll be surprised at some of the choices! Do this twice a year.

☐ **152. SPORTS DAY.**   With another family, or with many neighborhood children, make a list of sporting events: broad jump, putting, shooting baskets, team hopscotch, tug-of-war, relays, croquet, obstacle course. Divide everyone into two teams and give handicaps for young children and non-athletic parents, if the teams aren't balanced. Provide time for practice before each event. Use a large piece of cardboard for the scoreboard and announce the score often. Have a hearty lunch ready and let losers serve lunch to winners.

153. PROGRESSIVE SUPPER. With three other families, plan a progressive supper. At the first house have the appetizer and play a game. At the second house, it's salad and a song. At the third house, it's a casserole and conversation. At the final house, it's dessert and storytelling. This is a great way for kids to get comfortable with the parents of their friends.

154. BLOCK PARTY. Choose the house in your neighborhood with the biggest patio or yard and the biggest driveway, family room, or garage. All ages participate, and each family brings a dish for supper plus slides or pictures. Before supper have three-generation relay races in the driveway. After supper outside and sharing of snapshots, gather inside the garage for slides, movies, or a rented video.

FOR OLDER CHILDREN

155. ROCKETS. One of the most exciting and educational outside activities for older, responsible children is rockets. Putting together a rocket kit and then painting and decorating the rocket requires skill and patience, yet it's interesting fun. Several kids can enjoy this activity together, and it makes a great afternoon for the whole family to watch the rockets being shot into the air. A large open space and a clear windless day are best. Using reasonable care, the rockets are fueled and sent aloft. Then they are retrieved and can be used again. Some rockets include special gimmicks, such as miniature parachutists who float down separately.

156. GLOOPERS. First make two or more Gloopers. You'll need a sponge ball (easily found at a variety store) and a long tube sock for each. Put the ball in the toe of the sock and tie a knot so it stays there. Next practice catching and throwing the Glooper. It should be thrown by holding the tail end and "winding up." Gloopers are good for catch, for funny softball games, for tag, and for other games that kids make up on the spot.

157. STILTS. Have fun walking on stilts. Start with short ones. Measure a child from the ground to armpit. Cut two smooth, sturdy poles about a foot longer than this measurement. Attach a footrest twelve inches from their ends. Show a child how to walk with poles under arms. Stilts have been used for centuries by people who live in wet climates. As children get better at stilt walking, you can use them for relay races and parades.

☐ 158. KITE DAY.
On a windy day get all the neighborhood adults and children outside for kite flying. Have hot chocolate and doughnuts to eat. Sometimes the cheapest kites are the best flyers. You could have prizes for the highest flying, the best homemade kite, and the most daring flyer. Before or after, discuss with children why a kite will fly, why it needs a tail, and how pulling on the string helps the kite gain height. Together, look up "Kites" in the encyclopedia.

☐ 159. LEAPING LIZARDS AND LLAMAS.
In this team game, the object is to see how far the group can jump collectively. Divide the group equally. One team is the lizards, the other the llamas. From a starting line, the first player on each team makes a standing jump. The second team member steps into the place where the first team member landed and makes his jump, and so on through all the players. See which team can jump the farthest. Then play again, letting each player make three hops or two backward jumps.

☐ 160. CAMP AT HOME.
Kids can have a great camping experience without officially going away. Plan a one- or two-week camp with six to ten kids of compatible ages and interests. Each parent volunteers to take a day and obtains a second "resource person," so that there are always two adults available. With child input, decide on activities: nature walks, leather tooling, boating, swimming, Indian lore, gymnastics, computer learning, fire building, outdoor cooking, trail following, singing, storytelling. Work out a schedule using parks, pools, basements, and backyards. Choose a camp name and scarf or T-shirt for campers to wear, and let campers choose Indian names for themselves. Let the last day include an overnight or an evening campfire supper with all family members present.

☐ 161. THE WINTER WALK.
Go for a family walk and look for things that begin with a letter of the alphabet. For example, select the letter s. You may find: snow, slush, slipperiness, sun, scarf, sapling, street. See who can find five. Then choose another letter. If you choose the letter m, look for mud, a maple, the moon, a machine, a mailbox, a man, a market, a monster, moss, and so on.

SECTION 4: WHEELS!

FOR YOUNGER CHILDREN

☐ **162. SURPRISE SAFARI.**   Young cyclers don't have opportunities to go far from home, so plan a safari: children on bikes, parents walking or roller-skating. Wear a backpack. Keep the destination a secret but give clues. When crossing a street say, "We are going to make our way carefully through the dangerous jungle." When you pass others on the sidewalk, say, "We see other natives on safari." When you see a dog or cat, say, "Watch out for wild animals!" When you get near a store, say, "Here is a watering hole." Make your clues fit your safari to the store, to a friend's home, to the school, or to a park, which is, of course, the wild game reserve.

☐ **163. SAFE DRIVEWAYS.**   When young children start playing on sidewalks and cycling alone, they may not be alert to the danger of driveways. To give your child a safe place for play, back your car out of the garage and park it across your own driveway, blocking access from the street. If your next-door neighbors with kids also do this, you'll have an even larger safe-play area.

☐ **164. CITY STREETS.**   If you have sidewalks safe for small cars and trikes, pretend they are city streets. Make some hazard cones out of orange construction paper and weight them down with rocks so they won't blow away. With cardboard and some sticks (or yardsticks) make all the traffic signs: slow, stop, no turns, four-way stop. Set these up along the sidewalks in front of several houses. With yellow chalk, mark the lanes, letting the road go on the sidewalk and up and down safe driveways. If there are enough children, make a green/yellow/red signal light and let one child control it, covering two of the colors with his hands to indicate stop, caution, or go. Other children can be police officer or gas station attendant (with a few tools to "fix" trikes at the mechanic's shop). This provides hours of fun and young driver education.

☐ **165. NEIGHBORHOOD BIKING.**   Let a young child learn the way around the neighborhood by cycling. Jog with her or ride your own bike in the street with her on the sidewalk. The neighborhood looks different and you'll both see more interesting details from a tricycle than from a car. Point out the homes of friends and neighbors, driveways to watch for, and nearby shops. Show a child just how far she may go on her own, but tell her that she can go farther when with you. Go several blocks from home, then let her show the way home with you following.

FOR OLDER CHILDREN

☐ **166. BIKE SAFETY.**   When a child is ready for a two-wheeler, help her plan her riding outfit. You may want to get her a new jersey in honor of the occasion. For new riders, insist on long pants and long-sleeved shirts. For all riders insist on a helmet and shoes (no sandals, no bare feet). Take pictures of her learning to ride. And, when she's mastered the two-wheeler, let her make one special long-distance phone call to a grandparent or cousin to tell about it.

☐ **167. NAME THAT BIKE.**   Teach pride of ownership no matter how old the bike. Let the child name the bike—after all, it's going to be a good friend for a long time. With decals or paint and a small brush, help him put the name on his bike. At the same time, inscribe an ID on the bike using a metal marker; many police stations have these to lend for marking equipment that might be stolen.

☐ **168. RENDEZVOUS BIKING.**   With at least two parents and two other cyclers, choose a park a few miles from home where you can picnic or play. Divide the group in half, a parent in each group. Using a map, choose two different routes to the park. Start out at the same time, one group following each route. Meet at the park for fun, then return home via the opposite route.

☐ **169. OLD-TIMES DAY.**   Pretend for a day that the car hasn't been invented. As a family, bicycle everywhere that it's safe to go: store, church, park, friends' houses. Time how long it takes to get to familiar places. Guess how long it takes by car. When you next go by car, note the time and see whose guesstimate was nearest right.

SECTION 5: OUTDOORS IN THE DARK

☐ **170. FOOTRACES.**   After supper, walk around the block or down the road and back. Pick out certain "destinations" for races, such as a light pole, a tree, a sign, or a driveway. Never put the destination across a street, driveway, or road. Start the youngest child first, then on up to the oldest. See who gets there first. Cheers for the winner. Then do it again, choosing another destination.

☐ **171. FIREPIT.**   A backyard firepit will be used for many years, and it is simple to make. With family help, it can be ready with one car trip and an hour's work. At a building supply store, pick out the least expensive brick to line a pit about three feet across. You may want to get some extra bricks and boards to make benches. You'll also need a bag of sand. At home, choose a place where a fire can safely be built. Dig the pit about eighteen inches deep at the center and sloping up to the edges. Line the pit with the sand as you set in the bricks, making as smooth a surface as possible. Make benches or use logs to sit on. Building just a small fire of wood or coals lets you cook wieners or marshmallows. It's great for parties but it's best just for evening talk and story telling.

☐ **172. STARGAZING.**   On a clear night, spread blankets on the grass and look up at the stars. Learn just one constellation the first time, starting with the Big Dipper. Next time, see who can find the Big Dipper. Then show a second constellation. Look for other things in the sky: airplanes, birds, UFOs?

☐ **173. FLASHLIGHT PLAY.**   Tell neighborhood children to come over at dark and bring a flashlight. In a safe backyard, play the usual games of tag, "Hide and Seek," and "Mother May I." For running games, set the flashlights on a patio table and point them toward the play.

☐ **174. KING OF THE FOREST.**   One child is the king of the forest—the lion. Let each other player decide for himself what animal he wants to be, as long as it's an animal that makes a sound (no rabbits allowed). Parents can be animals, too. The king of the forest stands in the center of the yard by a marker, while the others hide. Then, he roars like a lion, and the other animals must respond with their sounds. The king of the forest may take five giant steps any direction from the marker. Then, when he roars again and the animals respond, he tries to guess who is making one of the sounds. He says, for instance, "Michelle is the pig hidden by the fence." If he's right, Michelle must sit down by the marker; all the others choose new animals to imitate and the game starts again. The last animal recognized is the new king of the forest.

☐ **175. SILLY SONGS.**   Each player hides in a different place in the yard. A parent standing at the back door starts the song (to the tune of the camp song "This is table number one; where is table two?") A dad sings: "This is Daddy at the door; where is little Lisa?" Lisa must answer, "This is Lisa by a bush; where is Brother Paul?" And so it goes, each one telling where he is and calling for another. When all players have identified their locations, dad sings, "This is Daddy at the door, Lisa's by the bush." If that is so, Lisa is the next one to start the song standing at the door. However, players may change locations in the dark, in which case dad has to start calling around again. You have to remember where each one is hiding, and you have to have a strong voice to sing out in the dark.

★

SECTION 6: OUTSIDE ET CETERA

☐ **176. MIME TIME.**   If kids don't know about miming, read up and explain it to them. Play any outside activity (bike riding, tag, in the playhouse) but without talking—everyone's a mime. See how quickly certain hand signals and body signs identify what is wanted: sharing a toy, being "it," starting a new game, going inside to get a snack. Or play mime inside. See how long the family can manage without words. Make it short at the beginning, longer later. This can lead to one child's wanting to play the part of the mime, complete with a white face and white gloves.

☐ **177. OUTSIDE LIVING.** See if your family can live in the yard for twenty-four hours. Plan ahead, only permitting bathroom trips into the house. See who is the best organized for outdoor living. Get along without things you may have forgotten inside. Take the foods for all three meals with you outside. Fill the ice chest, use camp kits, cook in the firepit, engage in active sports, read and play games, and sleep in the playhouse or in sleeping bags.

☐ **178. TOP TEN TOYS.** Kids think these are the most fun to have outside: a bicycle, a rope ladder, a playhouse or tent, roller skates or skateboard, a wagon, a basketball and hoop, an inflatable jumping bouncer (like a trampoline), one of the new-style kites, a ring toss or horseshoe game, an inflatable pool. When it's gift-time for your child, consider one of these.

★ THREE ★

FASTEN YOUR SEAT BELTS

Time spent in the car with children can be either wasted, routine, or an enjoyable learning experience. Ordinary shopping trips, errands, visits, and short excursions are opportunities for togetherness in the busy weekly routine. And, these occasions provide training for longer car trips and other vacations. When you go in the car with just one child, you can make it an all-important one-to-one adventure.

★

SECTION 1: BEFORE YOU LEAVE

☐ **179. TALK FIRST!**   Kids don't like to be pushed into the car and rushed off to strange places. A few sentences in advance help to make a happy errand. Rather than shouting "Get in the car!" say, "We're running over to Grandma's because she cut her hand and needs a little cheering up" or "Mr. Johnson is coming for supper, so we have to hurry to the store and buy asparagus and grape juice." It's a compliment to children, even preschoolers, to assume they are interested in the reasons why things happen. Then, they're more apt to be helpful.

☐ **180. CHOOSE THE TIME.**   For young children, the best errand times are early in the morning, before they're tired or hungry, or after naptime. Don't yank a child from crib to car—give him some waking-up time. For schoolchildren, the best time is after school. Following their day of sitting at school, they will be better at sitting in the car if they have thirty minutes of vigorous play first. And it's nice to ask, "We need to run some errands; would you like to go now or in an hour?"

☐ **181. HOW TO ACT?**   Talk beforehand and again in the car about behavior. Should the child ask Grandma about her health? Does he have to be very quiet at the meeting? Is he to kiss Grandpa? If offered food, should he accept? What might he say when he leaves? What if he needs to go to the bathroom? Is the shopping trip going to include a stop at the toy store?

☐ **182. THE GOING SHELF.**   This is a requirement for every house with children! Make it a good-sized counter or shelf near the most common exit door. Anything that's going to leave the house is put on the "Going Shelf." This is the place for school lunches and lunch money, school books and projects, cookies for the Scout meeting, ballet shoes and piano lesson books, outgoing mail, clothes going to the cleaners, the file folder for a meeting, and any other item you've promised to take or return to someone. You'll save lots of extra trips by teaching kids to check the shelf before going out the door.

☐ **183. TWO MUSTS.**   Before leaving is the time for a snack and a trip to the bathroom. You may want to take along an easy-to-eat snack. See that children have a drink before leaving and that a baby bottle goes along. Don't ask children if they *want* to go to the bathroom. Just send them! Tell them this might be the one chance. (It's also a good time to wash off faces and hands.) If you must leave at a certain time, plan to spend fifteen minutes on the logistics of getting out the door with everyone and everything.

☐ **184. HOW LONG?** When will you return home? Let children know if the trip will take all afternoon and thus leave no time for play. Perhaps feeding the dog, leaving a note for others returning home, and making some supper preparations should be done *before* departure. Such tasks go faster when everyone works together. Sometimes homework can go along: a book to read for a report, spelling words to learn and be tested on, a topic that needs discussing.

★

SECTION 2: IN THE CAR

FOR ALL CHILDREN

☐ **185. STRAPPING IN.** Make it fun to use seat belts and car safety-seats. Start at the garage door and race to see who's first to be ready to go. Applaud the winner. Vary the seating arrangements and relocate car safety-seats regularly for new combinations. Make it routine for older children to help younger ones. Let the oldest (or youngest) give the "ready for blast-off" line.

☐ **186. WHO'S WHAT?** Give children an assignment. Depending on how many are in the car, let one be your navigator, keeping an eye out for street names, shop signs, and parking places. Another can be the safety engineer, monitoring the speedometer for a safe driving speed, watching for red lights, police cars and poor drivers, and seeing that doors are locked and passengers stay strapped in. If the ride is more than twenty minutes, let one be in charge of dividing some healthful snack evenly, giving out napkins for fingers and cleaning up afterwards. For longer rides, one child can be social director, organizing games and other car activities. Another can be in charge of songs or stories.

☐ **187. THE CAR ACTIVITY BAG.** Keep tucked under the seat or in the trunk an old flight bag or tote bag that contains toys to be played with *only* in the car. This keeps them special! Have toys for various ages of children, including a coloring book and crayons, a picture book or storybook, small dolls and animals for cooperative play, a tablet and a pencil, small automotive toys, children's card games, and a deck of playing cards. Most toys are for playing with while strapped in, but some can be for taking into Grandma's, using in the dentist's waiting room, and so on. Every few months, rotate new toys into the activity bag.

☐ **188. COMPARTMENTALIZING THE CAR.** If you have a stationwagon or van, it can be divided into activity areas. Perhaps the baby needs a quiet spot for a car-seat snooze. Noisy play can be far back in the vehicle. Those reading books can have the second row. Conversationalists can be in the driver's row. Sometimes just separating children makes for a more peaceful journey.

☐ **189. QUICK MINDS.** This is a game where the participants say the first thing that comes into their minds. The driver starts the game with a word such as "elephant." Someone will quickly say "trunk," and another person will answer "suitcase." The next may say "Grandma's," which may be followed by "cookies." It is interesting to see how one word leads to another and how very far the last word is from the first word.

☐ **190. THE MAGAZINE GAME.** Bring along an old magazine and let children tear out pages that show pictures of outside things: houses, trees, cars, flowers, birds, animals, buses, trucks, tall buildings. Have enough pictures so there can be three or more for each child. Turn the pictures face side down and let one child deal them out face down to each child. When the driver says "Go!" the children turn the pictures over and start looking out the windows to find the thing shown in each of their pictures. The first to find his three wins. When all the pictures are found, turn them over, mix them up, and start again.

☐ **191. ONE ON ONE CONVERSATION.** If possible, occasionally take just one child with you in the car. Or, let the others occupy themselves while you talk with just the one in the front seat. This time for private conversation can be very precious. You may learn some interesting things about your child when she's separated from the group. Don't quiz her; let her talk, and you listen.

☐ **192. CAR CHITCHAT.** Have a really interesting topic ready for discussion, something that will include all children. For example: "If you were mayor, what would you do for our town?" "What was the best gift you got for Christmas?" "What shall we do together this weekend?" "What's your favorite supper?" "What is the best party you've ever been to?" "How do you like a friend to act?" Let the kids do most of the talking.

☐ **193. SING ALONG.** See what songs kids already know and start with those. Then, add the old favorites, such as "I've Been Working on the Railroad," "God Bless America," and "I Love to Go A-Wandering." Let children introduce songs learned in school. You can buy an inexpensive songbook at a music store to keep in the glove compartment.

☐ **194. HOME AGAIN.** As you come down your street, tell each child what he's to carry inside. Parents shouldn't have to do all the toting! Little hands can carry little packages. The trip isn't over until the car is tidied and ready for the next excursion. Encourage this good habit when children are young, and continue it as they grow older.

FOR YOUNGER CHILDREN

☐ **195. ALPHABET AND NUMBERS.** When a child is learning his letters and numbers, let him find them along the roadside. An older child can help him play by okaying what he's found. Start with *A* and find it on a road sign, car, billboard, or building. Then go to *B*, and so on through the alphabet. Do the same with numbers, finding zero through nine on license plates.

☐ **196. WORDS I CAN READ.** When a child is starting to read, she is very pleased to find words along the road that she recognizes. Give her paper and pencil to keep a slash-mark tally of how many words she finds on this errand. Let her share the total and some of the words with the family at supper. Do this on several trips and see if she can get a larger total each time.

☐ **197. SUPER EYES.** The driver is needed to keep this game going. She names one thing that might be seen outside the car: a car with a dent in it, a child on the sidewalk, an ice-cream store, a black-and-white cow, a mailbox. The first child to see the item you've named gets the "bronze award" (this is just a way of helping him remember he's found one thing). Then name another thing to look for, and so on. When a child is a winner a second time, he gets the "silver award," and for the third thing he finds he gets the "gold award." Play as many times as necessary until all children get the gold.

☐ **198. SONGS AND RHYMES.**   You can do two things at once by keeping your eyes on the road and at the same time teaching nursery songs and rhymes to your children. Take it line by line and be patient. Start with "Baa, Baa, Black Sheep" or any other rhyme you know. Let a child show off at supper by sharing what he's learned. For a shy child, offer to say or sing the rhyme with him.

FOR OLDER CHILDREN

☐ **199. I'M GOING TO OUTER SPACE.**   This is a variation of an old game. One child starts by saying, "I'm going to outer space and I'm going to take with me an ape" (or anything beginning with the letter *A*). The next child *repeats that sentence* and adds to it something beginning with *B*. Continue from child to child all the way to *Z*. You can make the game harder by requiring that all words be selected from one category, such as foods, toys, tools, animals, or clothing.

☐ **200. LICENSE LETTERS.**   Decide on a category: names, foods, books of the Bible, movies, states, trees. Watch for license plates with letters on them. When a child sees a letter and is the first to name a correct word in that category, he gets a point. Let each child keep his own score honestly, the goal being ten. Change categories and play again.

☐ **201. LICENSE ADDITION.**   Some plates have only a few numbers, others have many, and some have both numbers and letters. Start looking for a license plate with only a number one (1) on it; it can have other letters, though. Then, look for a plate whose numbers *total* two, then three, and so on. See if you can find plates that add up to twenty or more.

☐ **202. HOW MANY MILES?**   Tell the children what stops are going to be made. Let each guess the total number of miles from garage back to garage. See who is the best estimator.

☐ **203. PINT-SIZED POETS.**   One child or parent makes up a first line of a poem. The next follows with a rhyming line. This child then starts the next two-line poem. Some examples:

> Sit on my knees / Unless you sneeze.
> I want to stop / 'Cause there's a cop.
> Dad read a book / About a crook.

☐ **204. CONNECTING WORDS.**   One child starts by saying a word. The next child or parent must respond with a word starting with the last letter of the preceding word, for example, z*oo*, *o*stric*h*, *h*a*m*, *m*oustache. The game is easy at the beginning but harder the longer you play, since repeats aren't allowed.

☐ **205. ODOMETER OGLING.**   One person, perhaps the driver, indicates a distant point along the car's path: a hilltop, a far building, or an intersection. Each child quickly tells how many tenths of a mile away he thinks it is. Watching the odometer, kids can see who is the best estimator.

☐ **206. MAP MASTER.**   If you have a detailed street map of your city or town, let children find where you are on the map, the destination, the best and most direct way to go, and an alternate route for coming home. Learning to read a map is one of the best skills you can teach future drivers.

★

SECTION 3: AT THE GROCERY STORE

Probably the most common errand for a parent and child is grocery shopping. When a child gets bored or cranky, he may turn on that old "I want" refrain, hoping you'll give in and buy some needless toy or candy item. Instead, you can use the ideas listed below to make the grocery shopping excursion educational fun. Other shoppers will thank you!

FOR YOUNGER CHILDREN

☐ **207. WALK/TALK/GAWK.**   These are the Big Three Grocery Rules:

> *Walk*—no running or pushing permitted.
> *Talk*—no crying or shouting allowed.
> *Gawk*—look but don't pester for things.

Teach toddlers this rhyming trio, and you'll find them reminding each other of it as they get older.

☐ **208. NAME THAT PICTURE.** Encourage children to recognize pictures and attach words to them. There are many pictures in the grocery store—on canned goods, cosmetics, paper supplies, and cartons. When children learn to recognize and name certain pictures, expand this idea by saying, "In this aisle we're going to buy applesauce. See if you can find the can with the applesauce picture on it."

☐ **209. TIED-ON TOY.** Try to shop when the baby isn't tired or hungry but take along a little bottle of juice just in case. Have a toy on a string and tie it to the child-seat, making the string short enough that the toy can't reach the floor. Keep the toy in the basket and offer it only if the child becomes fretful. Have a small spare toy in your purse (this beats letting your baby suck on your car keys).

☐ **210. ROLLING LUNCH.** A toddler will like having lunch during a grocery store excursion. En route, offer a simple sandwich made at home. While shopping, let him pick out a banana or other piece of fruit that he can eat at the check-out stand as soon as it's weighed. Buy a little container of juice for drinking while the car is being loaded. Save a cookie treat for the trip home.

☐ **211. REWARDS.** When children are very young, make it clear that grocery shopping is not a toy-buying excursion and that people who act up in the grocery store or plead for candy or toys get *nothing*. Reward goodness with a treat in the car on the way home or something special to do at home. Or, at the end of the shopping trip let a well-behaved child choose one food item: a new cracker, the flavor of ice cream he likes, a special fruit.

☐ **212. HOW MANY BAGS?** The check-out counter is boring for little children, so have them guess how many bags it will take to pack your groceries. Let the child count the bags as they go into the cart. Was this more or less than last week's total?

FOR OLDER CHILDREN

☐ **213. MEMORY TICKLER.** When a child can move around the market on his own, give him an assignment of getting one certain item on your list. Then give him two to find, then three. See how many things he can remember and find without coming back for reminders.

☐ **214. BASKET-PUSHERS.**   When your child wants to push the cart, walk in front of it so she won't get away from you—and also, if she hits someone it will be you! You may wish instead to push the cart and let the child organize items so as to get as much as possible into the cart. Show how to organize and stack, putting large or heavy items on the bottom rack, crushable and fragile items in the child-seat.

☐ **215. TEAM SHOPPING.**   Divide the shopping list into equal parts and divide the shoppers into teams, including yourself. Set a meeting place and see which team gets there first with all the items on their list. Remind team members to walk, not run. Be sure to compliment all helpers.

☐ **216. SACK LUNCH SELECTIONS.**   For children who carry lunches to school, it's important that they like and will eat what they take. Let a child choose different kinds of bread, new fillings, cottage cheese or yoghurt, and a variety of fruits and juices. Look over the possibilities and try new things each week.

☐ **217. MATHEMATICIANS.**   When there are several brands of the same quality, let children check to see which is the best buy per ounce (you'll let them judge the quality later). Show them how to read unit pricing, if it is available at your store. Have all kids guess what the total bill will be and see who's nearest. An understanding of food costs is part of growing up.

☐ **218. COUPON CHAIRMAN.**   Let older children take turns clipping food coupons for one month. Let them sort these into your coupon organizer, alerting you to expiration dates. When you make the grocery list, or while they are shopping with you, they can pull out coupons for items being purchased. At the check-out stand when coupons are totaled and deducted, pay the child 10 percent of the sum you get back.

☐ **219. HOW MUCH CHANGE?**   At check-out time, let one child watch the prices as registered by the cashier. If you pay with cash, let a child figure quickly how much change you should receive. Responsible children can take the keys and open the car and trunk to prepare for loading up. Let them return the cart only if they can do so safely.

☐ **220. UNLOADING.** Some parents like to put away groceries themselves, but kids can help by unloading the car, taking groceries out of the bags, and putting them on the counter near the pantry, freezer, or refrigerator. This helps them learn where things are kept. When kids are capable of putting the groceries away, divide the number of bags between the workers. See who is the fastest at getting the contents put away neatly in the right places.

★

SECTION 4: AT THE RESTAURANT

Eating out should be a treat for everyone—including the other diners! Use these ideas, plus some good advance preparation as described in section 1 of this chapter.

FOR YOUNGER CHILDREN

☐ **221. STARVE 'EM.** The fascination of being in a restaurant is usually sufficient to amuse a child while orders are being taken. Don't allow water and crackers to fill up young children, or they won't have any room left for the meal. Make this an absolute rule when kids are young!

☐ **222. LOOK AND FIND.** If a young child needs some activity, play "Look and Find." Ask him to find and show his spoon, his napkin, or the salt cellar. Have him point at the light fixture or the flower on the table. Tell him to watch for other little children, big trays of food, the person clearing the table, or things out the window.

☐ **223. LITTLE SACK.** Many folks go home from a restaurant, with a little doggy bag. But you may want to bring a little bag *to* the restaurant for the time when a toddler needs something special to amuse her. Have the bag tied shut with a ribbon; this will keep her busy getting it opened. Put one or two small toys inside. After she's emptied it, put a cracker or spoon in it and tie it up again. The possibilities are endless!

☐ **224. TWO PLATES.**   Ask for a small, empty plate to put in front of a young child and put her dinner plate out of her reach. Transfer to the small plate some of her supper and add more as she eats. This keeps the food fresh and the child interested. To have her try new things, put on her dinner plate samples of others' food. Then, transfer the samples to her small plate when she's ready.

FOR OLDER CHILDREN

☐ **225. THE RIGHT-HAND COLUMN.**   As soon as children can read, teach them to watch the right-hand or price column of the menu. If possible, give them a top price they should choose for their meal. (Also tell them that when in doubt, ask what the host is ordering and don't order anything more expensive than that.) Do they like a more expensive item a lot more than a less expensive one? See if they can find the least and the most expensive meals on the menu.

☐ **226. TOTAL COST.**   As everyone is ordering, let children try to mentally total the whole bill. See who comes nearest to the correct total. Let them see the bill and add it up again to be sure it's right. (This is best done during family dining. Tell kids we don't play this game when entertaining guests!)

☐ **227. PERCENTAGES.**   It's a good math lesson to let a child figure the tip for you. What is 10 percent, 15 percent, or 20 percent of the total bill? Show that 15 percent is 10 percent plus half of 10 percent.

☐ **228. BILL PAYER.**   If the check has to be taken to a cash register, let an older child do this. Before he goes, figure together how much change he should bring back.

☐ **229. NEW WORDS.**   Even the simplest menu has a new culinary phrase kids can learn. See if they can find Italian, French, German, Spanish, or Japanese words. Use the words again during the meal.

★

SECTION 5: GOING VISITING

Many children are unhappy or bored visiting adults. You can help by preparing a child in advance, telling him the purpose and length of the visit, and showing him how to participate.

FOR ALL CHILDREN

☐ **230. CONVERSATIONAL CLUES.** In the car, talk with each child about something she can tell while visiting: an event at school, a new toy, something she plans to do, a movie, a sport or club event. Start the tradition of thinking *in advance* of topics for sharing at social events—a good idea for parents as well as children.

☐ **231. THE OLD DAYS.** Old scrapbooks and photo albums are interesting for kids to see—especially if they include pictures of their own parents when young. Grandchildren should be encouraged to ask grandparents about the old days: what the world was like when they were young, the games they played, their favorite movies and TV, where they traveled, and the fads in clothes, music, and dance. Appreciation for another generation adds a new perspective to a child's life.

☐ **232. MY DRAWER.** Places you visit on a regular basis can have added excitement if the grandparent or friend establishes a drawer, box, or shelf for a child, in an out-of-the-way place. Here items are put in preparation for the young visitor—perhaps a toy, a picture, a game, or an old hat—whatever will be fun to discover when visiting.

☐ **233. AT CARE FACILITIES.** These visits are more difficult for children, since they cannot be as free in their activities and sometimes the friend or grandparent isn't able to be up and about. In advance, talk about the hospital or nursing home so the child knows what to expect. If possible, let the grandparent show a child the dining room, recreation room, and other rooms in the facility. Take crayons and paper along so that while adults talk, a child can make a drawing of something he has seen there. Provide time for a grandparent and a child to enjoy a game such as checkers. Ask what the grandparent would enjoy doing on the next visit. Emphasize the need to be quiet and well behaved for the other guests or patients. Remove any fear of the institution by explaining that the relative is there because they need special loving care, that the stay is a short one (if it is), and that the staff is there to make the patients or residents comfortable.

FOR YOUNGER CHILDREN

☐ **234. SHARING.** A child is proud when she has something to share. Let her bring along a bag with a picture, a drawing, or a toy to show. Encourage her to explain how something works and then let Grandma try it.

☐ **235. COOKIES AND LITTLE GIFTS.** A little child loves to take part in making cookies, cutting them out, and decorating them. A double batch will provide some for him to eat, some to share with the family, and some to share with a friend. Have him pack some in a box for taking to Grandpa. Let him tell how he helped make them (you may be surprised at his version of the recipe!). When a child has a gift for a grandparent, let him give it in his way and at his own time; let him have the fun of the surprise, the joy of giving, the fun of wrapping it and then watching someone unwrap it.

☐ **236. PETS.** If there is a dog or cat at the house you visit, talk about it in advance. If it is a friendly dog, let the child play with it, tell it to do certain tricks, and perhaps give it a treat. Teach the child to respect, love, and not abuse the pet. Without causing fear, point out safety measures in dealing with a strange pet and the danger signs that show a dog or a cat is becoming irritated. Enjoying the pets of others helps a child decide on the pet she'll choose, when that time comes.

FOR OLDER CHILDREN

☐ **237. FLOWERS AND WEEDS.** Let a child pick simple flowers or interesting weeds or branches before the visit. Then, let him arrange the items at the house for the pleasure of the recipient. Grandmas especially love this. If he can tell the names of the flowers and where he got them, that makes a good topic of conversation.

☐ **238. SHOWING OFF.** In a low-key way, children should be permitted to show off their accomplishments: singing, playing the piano, a new dance step, new or handmade clothes, reading aloud, mastery of a difficult spelling list. Grandparents usually take pride in children's abilities, so let the children shine.

☐ **239. GOOD DEEDS.** Start the tradition of having kids ask, "What could I do for you, Grandpa?" Kids like to be busy, and they can do such things as load the dishwasher, change a light bulb, thread ten needles, stack newspapers, sweep the sidewalk, or build a simple shelf.

☐ **240. NO COOKING.** So often grandparents feel they have to wear themselves out making a big meal. Occasionally let the kids cook supper at Grandma's. Bring the ingredients or stop at a deli or fast-food place en route. Let the kids clean up afterward, too.

★

SECTION 6: IN THE CARPOOL

The send-off for school should be cheerful and upbeat—no reminders to be good, no reprimands. Send kids off expecting a great day! On the way home in the afternoon, you'll learn a lot if you just listen.

FOR YOUNGER CHILDREN

☐ **241. GREETINGS.** Help children to learn one another's names and greet each other. As each one gets in the car, have all the others give a rousing "Hello, Nicole!" Do the same with good-byes as they leave the car, back home.

☐ **242. WAVING.** Let children cheer other folks on the street by waving to them. Passersby will be surprised, but they'll love it. See if the carpool kids can get someone to wave back.

☐ **243. NO SCRAMBLE.** The rush to get out can be made merry by selecting a different color each day of the week and saying, "Everyone wearing purple gets out first today." Or, say, "If you have an *A* in your name, you get out last."

☐ **244. WHAT'S LEFT?**   Start the system that the last one out looks on the car seat and floor for those leftover books, toys, and show-and-tell items. Give lots of praise to the one who finds something left behind.

FOR OLDER CHILDREN

☐ **245. WHO'S IN CHARGE?**   With the kids' help, find out who is the oldest child in the carpool. Let him have special privileges: sitting in the far back, being sure all books and lunches are taken, keeping the noise down. The next week, make it the second oldest, and so on until eventually each one gets a turn.

☐ **246. WEATHER FORECASTER.**   What will the weather be like at the end of the school day? Let each child guess and then after school see who was right.

☐ **247. QUIZ KIDS.**   To get kids talking, tell them they can ask you any question they want, and you'll try to answer. See if they can stump you. The one that does is the next one to be quizzed.

☐ **248. LISTENING.**   As children get older, the ride home from school will be taken up with conversation among the children. Just tune in; you'll be amazed and even pleased with what you'll hear! Some of these topics you may want to discuss further with your own child, at a later time.

★

SECTION 7: AT CHURCH AND OTHER QUIET PLACES

There are some events where children must conform to adult behavior and be seen and not heard. Looking around at the people and the new surroundings will occupy a child for a few moments. And, of course, you hope he will listen and learn. But sometimes you have to be ingenious! Even though you have talked about this experience in advance, you may need creative ideas to keep a young child occupied, quiet, and content.

☐ **249. THE NOTEBOOK.** When needed, bring out a small notebook and pencil. When the child gets tired of drawing in it, play copycat. You draw an X, O, or other simple symbol on a page. The child tries to copy it several more times on the page. Then give her a harder one—perhaps a triangle, a figure eight or a simple house.

☐ **250. LA, LA, LA.** Being quiet is difficult, so encourage your child to make sounds during the times when others are singing. If she can't read words or music, tell her to try "la, la, la." It will use up some of her energy, and she'll be more quiet when you sit down again.

☐ **251. SIGN LANGUAGE.** For use in church, teach a child five simple signs: A finger to the lips means no talking, hands together means pray, a beckoning finger means to lean in and listen to you, the OK sign means you like what the child's doing, and five fingers means church is almost over.

☐ **252. FIND THE NUMBER.** When all else fails, play this little hymnal game with your child, or let an older child play this with a younger one. Open your hymnbook at random. Kids on either side of you see the page number and quickly and quietly turn pages in their books until they have a match with you. Keep a score of who finds it first.

☐ **253. ONE GOOD IDEA.** At church and other meetings, there will be speakers who may not be addressing children. However, children should be asked to listen until they have heard one good idea that they can share afterward. By about age seven, this becomes a requirement. You'll find that when kids listen with the assignment of remembering, they often listen for long periods of time.

☐ **254. COMPLIMENTS.** Praise good behavior afterward! Occasionally reward it with a treat, such as a stop at the park or a ten-minutes-later bedtime. And don't forget to ask the child how you, as a parent, did. If you listened, share something you learned.

SECTION 8: AT THE HAIRCUTTER'S

This can be a scary experience for young children and thus an upsetting one for the stylist and other patrons at the barber or beauty shop. Try these ideas to get over this common problem.

☐ **255. THE BUILDUP.**   Before going to the barbershop or beauty salon, especially for the first time, prepare the child by giving the haircutter a buildup. Say, "Just like the pilot knows how to fly the airplane and the mail carrier knows all about mail, so the haircutter knows all about cutting hair!" Tell a child that he will be even more goodlooking after the haircut.

☐ **256. DOES IT HURT?**   Many children think that cutting something off their heads is going to hurt, like cutting a finger. They know scissors are sharp! You can show them that it doesn't hurt by cutting a fraction of an inch off your own hair (or cut some off of Brother's or the dog). Emphasize that there will be punishment, though, if they ever cut hair themselves!

☐ **257. HOLD ON.**   When perched in the chair for the haircut, give your child something to hold on to, so that her hands are occupied and she has a feeling of participation. Maybe she wants her teddy bear to see the haircut. Or, let her hold one of the clips used to hold hair out of the way, or a large mirror. Show her how she can see the back of her head. It helps if you stand directly in front of her and smile and talk. (Standing on one side may get her a lopsided haircut.)

☐ **258. STORYTIME.**   At home before leaving, start reading a short book to the child. Bring the book along and finish reading it during the haircut. This is probably better literature than what's available at the shop, and the desire to hear the rest of the story can quell any crying.

☐ **259. TAKE A PICTURE.**   When the deed is done, take a snapshot for the photo album. Let the child tell at supper just what it's like to have a haircut. This is especially helpful if a child has a younger sister or brother who'll be the next to have a haircut.

SECTION 9: QUICK EXCURSIONS

☐ **260. GO FOR A RIDE.**   The destination doesn't matter! Let your child choose to go by bus, subway, train, old-time streetcar, or ferryboat. Enjoy the sights and sounds; read the ads on the walls; watch the people and decide what they do and where they are going. Stop and visit a new neighborhood before returning home.

☐ **261. GARDEN SHOP.**   When buying plants for your yard, let a child pick an easy-to-grow plant, such as a pansy or petunia. Let him choose the place where it is to grow. As he gets older, he can choose more plants, until he has his own private flower garden to tend.

☐ **262. QUICK MUSEUM.**   Rather than spend a long time at a museum, make frequent, quick stops at a free museum. This way museums won't become boring or intimidating. If convenient, make your museum stop after a trip to the dentist, grocery, or other routine errand. Check to see if your town has a children's museum or a science museum with exhibits geared to children's participation.

☐ **263. TINY AIRPORT.**   Without going into the busy airport complex, find a good parking spot within sight of a runway of a small airport. Watch the takeoffs and landings. Pick out your favorite planes, the largest, the smallest, and so forth. See if the landings are smooth or bumpy. Count how many landings occur in a fifteen-minute period.

☐ **264. BEACH CASTLES.**   No matter how cold the water or the weather, it's fun to visit the beach. Dress suitably and bring along some sand toys and some bread. Make sand castles and canals. Then go for a walk and feed the bread to the beach birds. Collect shells and look for sand crabs. Bring along a thermos of hot chocolate.

☐ **265. BOAT HARBOR.**   Walk along the boats and read the names. Find the funniest name, and the smallest, biggest, oldest, and most interesting boats. Decide which one you'd like to own "someday." Look for boats that people live on, ski boats, boats that are for parties, boats that have commercial uses, and military ships. Count the sea gulls.

☐ **266. LAUNCHINGS.** Call a nearby navy base information number, or a shipbuilder, and ask the date of the next launching. Find out if the public is welcome. If so, watch an actual launching. Find out where the ship is going, the purpose of its voyage, and how long it will be gone. Afterward, look in the newspaper to see if the event was covered. Save the story for the family scrapbook.

☐ **267. THRIFT SHOP.** From family closets, select some clothing that can still be worn but that you no longer need. Take it to a thrift shop and donate it. Look at the amazing bargains. See who can find the most interesting thing to buy. This is a good place to find Halloween costumes. Teens might find out about volunteer work.

☐ **268. GARAGE SALES.** Along with church rummage sales, these can be fun with kids who understand the rule: If you break it, you've bought it. Let kids choose fabulous party clothes for the dress-up box at home. Budget-stretchers in clothes and toys are fun to find. Think about having a garage sale yourself or with another nearby family. If you do this, enlist kid-help and give them a percentage of the profit.

☐ **269. FIRE AND POLICE STATION.** Call first to find out when you're welcome. Then, have your child invite a few friends to go and see how these helpers work to make our lives more secure. Get to know at least one fire fighter or police officer, so you can send him or her a Christmas card. Kids might want to bake cookies for the staff. Write a thank you note for the visit.

☐ **270. UP IN THE AIR.** Check your yellow pages for places that give instruction on flying, hang-gliding, and parachuting. Watching these activities can be quite thrilling, and sometimes participants will be happy to talk to kids. Go and watch a hot-air balloon takeoff. Think about whether the family would ever want to take a balloon ride.

☐ **271. SHOPPING MALL.**   Since malls are growing in size, plan your trip with some rests along the way. Sit on a bench to watch the people, or stop for orange juice. Ask questions: "How many babies do you see?" "How many shoe stores are there?" "What do we see that is colored pink?" "If it were Christmas, what would you buy?"

☐ **272. IN THE DRESSING ROOM.**   It's difficult to shop for your clothes with child-help, but if it must be, prepare for the time in the dressing room. Surprise a child with a little bag of toys from home: a yo-yo, a book, a wind-up animal, paper and crayons. Also enlist his help in telling you the color he likes best—even which outfit is his favorite.

☐ **273. AT THE MOVIES.**   When it's time for a young child to attend her first movie, practice up at home by watching a movie on TV. Tell a child it will be long, that bathrooms are not convenient, that there will be limited snacking, and that talking is discouraged. Find out something about the movie in advance and talk about it. Help a child to maintain interest by having her look for animals or villains or comic characters. Talk about the movie afterward, retelling the good parts.

★

SECTION 10: SUITCASE LIVING

The fun of travel is increased by anticipation and organization mixed with flexibility. (Also read the in-car ideas in section 2 of this chapter.)

☐ **274. VISIT THE TRAVEL AGENCY.**   Before parents decide where the vacation will be, visit a travel agency and look at all the brochures. See the things that interest kids. Take home brochures on possible destinations and talk about them. Then decide on mountains, cities, or seaside, and going by plane, train, bus, or car.

☐ **275. SUITCASE LIST.**   Make a simple list of the contents of a child's suitcase. Put it in a pocket of the suitcase or duffel bag. When leaving a stop, kids should check the list to see if everything is packed. The most commonly left-behind items are footwear under the bed, clothing on a hook on the back of a door, items left on the bathtub ledge, and clothing mixed in with the bedspread. Make it a game to see who can find an item someone in the family was about to leave behind.

☐ **276. CAMERA KNOW-HOW.**   It helps if several in the family are camera-capable. Let younger children share an inexpensive camera for the trip. Before leaving, let kids shoot a roll of film to see how expert they are. Point out what made some pictures good and what would have made some pictures better. Show older children the fine points of your own camera. Look through travel folders and books of fine scenic photography to get tips on what makes good pictures.

Knowing how to take travel photos is important. Teach a child how to hold the camera (good and steady), how to set the exposure and distance to the subject, how to compose an interesting photograph (object centered, close enough to get detail, framing with a tree branch or doorway), how to handle bright sunshine (have it behind you and shining on the subject), and the importance of thinking just a minute about what is being taken. Many times, we see a sight from the car, plane, or train and snap it, then are disappointed with the result. Discuss proper techniques for taking pictures "on the fly" and through glass and explain that sometimes a good picture just won't result, so it's better to save the film.

On the trip, see that pictures include all family members—especially the family photographer, who often gets left out. When you return home, share your pictures, then put good ones up on the bulletin board before putting them away in an album.

☐ **277. EXTRA CREDIT.**   Before leaving, talk about the trip with your child and, if he's interested, talk with him and his teacher to see what part of the trip could tie in with schoolwork or serve as an extra-credit project. With this in mind, help the child gather ideas and material for his presentation. Snapshots, postcards, historical folders, a journal or notebook, artifacts, and souvenirs can be used to make the report interesting. But the report is not just a collection of things; the student's own observations are what's important. At a meal on the trip, encourage other family members to contribute ideas that the student might include. Remember that the project might be an oral or written report, or perhaps a written report with student sketches. Encourage work on the project along the way, so it isn't a burden to finish at home.

☐ **278. TRAVEL BAG.** Prepare a bag with essentials for travel: hand wipes, a plastic bag for rubbish, small emergency snacks, napkins, a deck of cards, little toys or books, small trays on which to eat or play, a pencil and paper, a flashlight, a first-aid kit, addressed labels for postcards, stamps, useful telephone numbers, maps, and, if needed, a foreign phrase book.

☐ **279. KEEPING THE PEACE #1.** Sometimes tempers get short on a long trip and kids frequently appeal to parents to settle matters. Designate one child as official peacemaker. All disagreements are referred to her for settlement. Change off about every hour. It's good practice in letting kids settle things on their own, knowing that each will have the job of peacemaker.

☐ **280. KEEPING THE PEACE #2.** When the trip is long, establish a daily complaint time. Have a little box or envelope. Complaints must be in writing (you'll have to write them down for non-writers). Consider them seriously and see how many you can settle. Happily, there will be fewer each day, since kids will learn to behave better so as to avoid having a complaint session when there are better things to do.

☐ **281. ON A PLANE.** Have a pre-packed flight bag or other small case filled with small, inexpensive, wrapped toys. Let a child choose one to open for each event on this list: takeoff, seat belt sign off, juice delivered, meal finished, game played, book read, certain ground items seen (farm, lake or stream, tall building, highway).

☐ **282. ON A SHIP.** As soon as possible, take a very complete walk around. Let children know where they have permission to be, what might not be safe, and where questions can be answered. Plan to have breakfast and dinner together each day; let older children enjoy the noon meal on their own. Sign up for the morning jogs. Plan daily shuffleboard contests. Let older children attend shows and movies even if you don't. Check to see if there is a youth program and insist that kids at least give it a try. In advance of leaving home, think of some costume ideas if the itinerary includes a costume night. Be sure to take any behind-the-scenes tours of the ship. Be with your kids for the first few departures and berthings of the ship, to point out things to watch for.

☐ **283. ON A TRAIN.** Permit responsible children to go certain places alone on the train. Suggest that they have a meal on their own one time and explain to them how to pay for it. Take turns sleeping in the upper bunk. Take a shower and see what a wild experience it is. When there is a long station stop, get out together and see what's new. Buy postcards and mail them at the next stop. Wake up early and watch the sunrise together. If the trip is uneventful, bring out some cards and board games or teach a child how to knit.

☐ **284. AT A HOTEL OR MOTEL.** Give everyone something to specialize in. These include checking out the recreational activities, getting ice and finding the vending machines, asking at the desk about nearby movies and restaurants, and giving bed assignments. Switch assignments the next night. Look in the drawers for free postcards and suggest they be used or put in the trip scrapbook. Be very firm about not taking things from hotels and motels except items that you are expected to use, such as soaps and shampoo. If the hotel or motel is a comfortable place to stay, ask for a list of its other locations.

☐ **285. ROVING REPORTER.** Take along a glue stick or paste and a large, brightly colored notebook with pages labeled for each day of the trip. Take turns being the "journalist of the day": the person who writes down the sights; pastes in ticket stubs, postcards, and place mats, and so on. Don't criticize spelling or lack of neatness—just let the writer tell what happened that day.

☐ **286. IF I LIVED HERE.** Stop in a small town. Pretend the family has moved there. Talk about the town as if you all know it: "This is the house I live in." (Everyone will pick a different one.) "This is the school I go to." "Here is where we play." "This is where I work." "This is where I buy shoes." Looking at a town from this perspective can be more fun than just whizzing past it on the freeway. When someone says, "This is where I eat," stop for a sandwich or ice cream. Ask the store owner what is special about the town and check out the suggestion before traveling on. Buy a postcard so you'll remember your adopted hometown.

☐ **287. RESTING TIME.** Travel is tiring and children as well as parents need some rest along the way. But pick the right times to rest: when facing a dull stretch of road, flying through clouds, or on a boring stretch of train track through the desert. There are times to be wide awake, seeing it all and taking it in. A child may be teased for sleeping through the high point of the trip. Parents can set a good example by determinedly napping at the right times. Show children how to settle down, get comfortable, take off their shoes, close the eyes (perhaps use an eye cover), really relax, and doze off.

☐ **288. CHANGE OF PACE.** Sometimes an auto trip goes so fast that the family needs a little time for a quiet activity. Be sure you take some simple fishing equipment along and know the law in the area where you are. Then pull off the road and find a stream or river. Go fishing! Those not interested can walk along the stream, talk, eat, rest, or read. You'll feel refreshed when you get back on the road.

☐ **289. MYSTERY MAP.** On a large piece of paper, make a map showing some cities and sites along the route for the day. Or you may use a spare map of the territory. Put the letter M (for Mystery Place) in a circle at several places along the way. This will give kids an interest in following the map and the road markers. When the kids note that you've arrived at a Mystery Place, share the "mystery": a stop to see something interesting or for a chance to play on a park's jungle gym, an apple or other snack, a new toy or game suitable for car play.

☐ **290. MAPSMANSHIP.** Explain how to handle a map, how to unfold and re-fold it properly, where north is and how to get oriented, how to hold the map in the same direction as the vehicle is traveling, and how to read road numbers, mileage indicators, and places of interest. Many maps explain points along the route, and a child can be delegated to read these aloud.

☐ **291. POLITE CONVERSATION.** The family will be having many meals together on the trip. Let each child practice the important art of conversation by bringing up topics for all to talk about and being prepared with something to speak of himself. Some topics that everyone enjoys are "What was the oldest thing we saw on this trip?" "What has been our best meal on this trip?" "Which hotel (motel) was the nicest?" " What was the high point, for you?" "What is the strangest thing we've learned?" "What new food did we discover?" "Who do we know who'd enjoy this trip?"

☐ **292. MEMORY NIGHT.** At supper back home, let each tell his favorite memory of the trip. You may be surprised at the things that stand out! Decide what places you'd return to again. Talk about other people you might recommend this trip to. Compare this trip with other trips. Share photos or show slides. Let one person make a list of the favorite memories, to be included in the scrapbook.

☐ **293. SCRAPBOOK SHARING.** When the last items are pasted in the scrapbook, let everyone relive the trip, then sign their names on the last page. Be sure to include photos. Put the scrapbook in the living room or family room where relatives and friends may enjoy it, too.

FOUR

THE GANG'S ALL HERE!

 child grows in both physical and social skills by taking part in group activities and lessons. These ideas introduce kids to the joys of achievement and good sportsmanship while also helping them understand that losing a game, or making a mistake at a recital, isn't the end of the world.

★

SECTION 1: SPORTS ACTIVITIES

Don't introduce children to organized sports at too young an age. It may be stylish to have a child in uniform, but the joys of unstructured outside play teach valuable lessons, too. Much time in an organized sport is spent watching, so it's important to learn how to observe as well as how to play.

FOR YOUNGER CHILDREN

☐ **294. JUNIOR SPORTS.** Let sports be part of each day's activities. With child-help, make a list of sports and put it on the bulletin board. See how many you can try in a month. For younger children these may include ringtoss, throwing and catching, gymnastics, swimming, croquet, climbing, and cycling. Practice sports at home. Make a simple balance beam, have a mat for tumbling and a tree or jungle gym to climb. Let a child practice hitting tennis balls off the garage door, throwing balls into a low basket, swinging a bat, and playing tetherball. At this age make it all fun, not work.

☐ **295. SPECTATOR SPORTS.** Start when children are young to introduce them to sports they can't play as yet. Buy a copy of a sports magazine, cut out pictures of various sports, and put them on the bulletin board. Go to a sports event at a local high school. Basketball, soccer, ice hockey, and volleyball are good fast sports to watch, a little more interesting for young children than baseball and football.

☐ **296. THE GOOD OBSERVER.** When a child first attends a game, explain in simple terms the object and show him how to yell, applaud or stamp his feet for his team. Bring along a thick cushion so he has a good view of the action. Explain the scoring and be sure to keep him up to date on the score. Encourage him to ask questions. Reward good behavior with a trip to the snack bar halfway through the game. Talk afterward to see what he's learned and if he'd enjoy going to another game.

☐ **297. THE BORED OBSERVER.** When a child begins to tire of the game, re-interest her by asking her to watch for certain plays and tell you about them, for example, when the basketball rolls around the rim, when the pitcher throws to first base to hold the runner, when the passer throws a long one, or when a goalie falls down. Give her a little tablet and a pencil to draw pictures of the game or players.

☐ **298. THE SLEEPY OBSERVER.**   When games are long, play "Can You Find It?" Have a child look for a player in green, an observer in red, a baby, a clock, a sign with a picture of food, and so forth. Let him note on a tablet how many of these he can find. Give a penny reward for finding ten, twenty, or thirty.

☐ **299. THE PARTICIPANT.**   Before letting a young child sign up for a team, let her watch the game a few times to be sure she sees that some team members sit on the sidelines, some play, some get dirty, and some fall down. After watching the game, talk about the sport and the skills she will need to learn. Talk about safety on the playing field, the need to wear the correct protective clothing, the way the referee watches for fouls, and other safety topics. Make certain she is eager to play the game, not just wear the uniform. Only when the child is certain that this is her current sport interest, should she be signed up for the team. Then, go to the games, cheer her on, and take pictures for the family scrapbook and sharing with relatives.

☐ **300. IT'S ONLY A GAME.**   Losing is hard, but celebrate just the same. Especially after a big loss, compliment players on what they did right. Champs don't always win, so celebrate *sportsmanship* at the ice-cream parlor, in the car, and back home. Does your child like and respect the other players? Does she feel that she's a good team player? What can she practice to improve? Talk about the good team plays, the scores, and the effort and exercise involved.

☐ **301. PICK A TEAM.**   Choose a high school team, maybe one an older relative or neighbor plays on, and become regular fans. Learn about the game, the cheers, and the team members. (Also see if some less-publicized sports can be watched: swimming, wrestling, archery.) Talk about the possibility of visiting the locker room and meeting some of the players. Read the game write-ups in the local paper. Put newspaper pictures of the game on the bulletin board. Consider buying a pennant or a team jersey.

☐ **302. BOWLING.**   Go to a bowling alley and observe good league play. Let each child pick a team and root for it. Decide if this is a sport the family might all enjoy. Ask if there are balls and shoes available for younger children, too. When you bowl the first time, make it just one or two games. If there is an experienced bowler on hand, let him give some tips before starting. Take home the score sheet. Plan to bowl again in a week and see how much better the scores are. Practice the proper way to hold and throw a ball, what steps to take, and special tips on hitting certain pins. Some of this practice can be done at home on a smooth floor with a soft ball, in preparation for bowling again.

☐ **303. OVER-THE-LINE.**   This game is similar to baseball except no bases are run. All you need is four or more players, a softball and bat, and a playground or park. All ages can play together: Older kids can team up with younger or less athletic players, or there can be, for example, two teens on one side and five little kids on the other. Extra outs can be allowed kids just learning the game.

Draw a line in the dirt with your heel from an imaginary third base to second base and from second base out to center field. Also draw a home run line or use a fence. Decide in advance how many innings you want to play. Each team at bat supplies its own pitcher. Each batter gets three underhand pitches to try to hit the ball over the line, and he stays at bat until he makes an out. If the ball drops in over the line, and is not caught, it's a base hit. If it's caught on the fly beyond the line or hits the ground in *front* of the line, it's an out. The defensive players must stay beyond the line to catch the ball. (Reaching over the line means an automatic hit.) All must keep track of which base the imaginary runners are at, because to score a run there must be four hits or a home run. As the game is learned, you can institute doubles and triples or make any rule variations you wish.

☐ **304. SKATEBOARDS.**   Require good safety precautions, including helmets and knee and elbow guards, when kids engage in this popular sport. When there are enough competitors, plan a neighborhood competition with points for various events: a difficult course, special maneuvers, a race down a straight run. Award a homemade plaque and hold the competition each month.

☐ **305. STEALING STICKS.** You need four or more players and ten sticks, five painted or tied with a string to differentiate them from the other team's five sticks. Divide players into two teams. Draw a line or place a string on the ground between the teams. The teams start ten feet behind this center line. Five feet back from each center line, place the sticks in a line. The object is to steal sticks belonging to the other team by crossing the center line, grabbing a stick and returning across the line without being tagged. Both teams play at the same time. A tagged player is a captive and must sit on the opposing sideline. Teams can call a time-out to trade a stolen stick for a captured player, if they wish. Players keep trying to steal sticks until one team gets all the opposing team's sticks or one team has captured all the opposing players.

☐ **306. GOLF.** This used to be the sport of wealthy older men, but now all ages and sexes enjoy it. Watch part of a championship match on TV. Then go to a driving range and let the entire family hit balls. Sink a cup in your lawn and practice putting. After these practices, go to a public course and try nine holes of golf. Non-playing family members can be scorekeepers, caddies, cart-drivers, and encouragers.

☐ **307. BADMINTON.** Here's a backyard game that provides plenty of exercise. The net and shuttlecocks are inexpensive, and the net can be lowered for younger players. Put up the net and get a family competition going. Play a few games after supper each evening.

☐ **308. VOLLEYBALL.** This is one of the best three-generation games. The rules can be very exacting or quite loose (the latter being called Jungleball). Start by teaching the basics of serving. Even young children can be servers, ball chasers, or linesmen. Next, practice spiking and setting. Invite other neighborhood families to play once a week in the summer. Teams can range from two players per side to as many as eight. Grandparents can play or be scorekeepers or referees.

☐ **309. SCHOOL TEAMS.** Aside from gym classes, children may want to play on a school team. Popular choices are soccer, baseball, football, swimming, basketball, wrestling, hockey, rowing, and sailing. Once the commitment is made, rearrange the family schedule so that parents and the family can support the game by attending or by talking about it at supper. Don't let sports separate family members at mealtime! Encourage a child to try several different sports during his school years unless he really excels at just one.

☐ **310. LITTLE LEAGUE.**   When a child joins league play, be sure that the fun doesn't go out of the game. Don't just take a passive, "I'll-bring-the-cookies" interest. Make the cookies but also get involved in finding the right league, team, and coach for your child. Be insistent on good sportsmanship by players *and* parents. Give your views to the coach in private and encourage him to let each team member play. Plan celebrations that include winners and losers. Find library books on the subject and encourage skills practice at home. And, when the child wants to go on to something else, don't force her to continue. This is *just a game*. Explain to her that she has made a commitment and should fulfill it, but that she can quit at the end of the season.

☐ **311. WATCHING GAMES.**   When it gets boring, let a child try these: (1) take a family survey on how many people are at the game and see who's nearest when the official attendance is announced; (2) keep a tally of the score and ask others what they think the final score will be; (3) choose his own MVP (Most Valuable Player); (4) look at the other spectators and pick out the youngest, oldest, wildest, or quietest.

☐ **312. WATCHING BASEBALL.**   Our national sport teaches many things, one of the most important being loyalty to a team through good and bad years. It teaches hope and optimism. It also teaches math, in computing earned runs and hitting percentages. And the very throwing of the ball—its torque and spin—is a physics lesson. Help a kid to keep score until the 4-6-3 double play is easy for him to score.

☐ **313. TV SPORTS.**   There are many exciting sporting events to be witnessed live on television. A parent's responsibility is to help the family find a balance between watching sports and doing other activities. With your child, look over the sports offerings for the week and choose one or two. Make it a family event. Pretend you're really there. Choose your team or player. Eat popcorn. Scream and cheer! During commercials, talk, write, knit, play a game—don't waste this precious time. And when it's over, turn off the TV and do something active.

★

SECTION 2: ORGANIZED CLUBS

☐ **314. PICK AND CHOOSE.** When autumn comes around, kids are bombarded with opportunities to join a variety of clubs. Discuss all the choices and let a child rate them in order of importance to her. Consider Camp Fire Girls and Boys, Boy or Girl Scouts, Boys' and Girls' Clubs, the YMCA, Indian Guides, church groups, Parks and Recreation activities, gymnastic centers, schools (music, drama, art, karate), sports teams, and library activities. Local newspapers and parenting publications will tell you about many more opportunities. Keeping some days free for unstructured play, let a child choose one or two groups. She should understand that she is committing herself for the season or the club year, often a six-month minimum. After that time and while the memory is still fresh, assess the group with the child. Let her decide whether to continue in the group or select something different. Some groups such as Camp Fire Girls and Boys and Boy and Girl Scouts may continue to be a favorite for many years, but there's no law against variety—after all, these are supposed to be enjoyable experiences.

☐ **315. START YOUR OWN.** If you don't find a group your child is eager for, organize a neighborhood club with other families. Plan just the activities that the group wants and include some challenges. Bring in outside leadership or take turns leading activities yourselves. While this is more work, it does bring parents and children together under different circumstances than school or church.

☐ **316. COMMITMENT.** Talk honestly with your child about what participation will entail: attendance at meetings, certain accomplishments, expenses, perhaps wearing a uniform, providing snacks, going on excursions, sales promotions, camping, holding office, parent help. If he is put off by such requirements, perhaps he would enjoy a less structured group. But once a child joins a group, the family should be very supportive and assume its share of the leadership, chaperoning, driving, and other responsibilities. In assessing the costs of being a member, you may want to offer a child an extra task or special project so that he can earn the dues or money for group expenses.

☐ **317. GROUP EXCURSIONS.** Consider visiting these businesses whenever a good-sized group of children is involved: (1) grocery store (ask your grocery store manager to take your group behind the scenes and tie this in with other activities such as menu planning, nutrition education, or serving a meal to parents), (2) power plant (see how gas and electric services are provided to your community), (3) telephone company, (4) large bank with a vault, (5) agricultural operation (farm, orchard, cattle- or poultry-raising facility), (6) fish hatchery, (7) dam or water filtration plant, (8) quarry or building supply yard, (9) train station and roundhouse, (10) large computer operation or store, (11) radio or TV station, (12) the post office. (Also check out the excursion suggestions in chapter 3, section 9.)

☐ **318. GROUP SALES.** When it is your child's turn to sell cookies, light bulbs, or some other fund-raising item, take time with your child to read about the rules, the goals, and the responsibilities entailed. Support your child's efforts but don't do the job for her. Let her practice her sales talk on the family first. Buy the product! Let her go to a good friend or relative next. Then, with success behind her, she's ready for selling to strangers. Talk about safety procedures in going door to door, especially the rules to go in pairs and not go inside houses. Suggest contacting neighbors and friends. Make a chart that will show her progress. Even if she isn't a big winner, appreciate her work and specifically talk about it at supper.

★

SECTION 3: THE GANG AT YOUR HOUSE

Here are some group games—some competitive, some not. For more ideas, you'll enjoy reading *The Cooperative Sports and Games Book* (Terry Orlick, Pantheon, 1978). (Group games suitable for parties are in chapter 11, section 2, of this book.)

FOR ALL CHILDREN

☐ **319. GROUP SNACK-AND-TELL.** When a group of kids first gathers for play at your house, get their attention with juice and crackers. Let them know some basic rules: no fighting, turns must be taken, toys must be handled with consideration and put away when play is finished. Tell them where the bathroom is located, where you'll be, and to ask before using the telephone. Also tell them you won't be always watching over them, but provide a bell for younger children to ring if they want your help.

☐ **320. CREATE-A-SNACK.** Creativity and nutrition combine when you let a group of children make unique snacks. Ingredients can include graham crackers, raisins, peanuts, marshmallows, banana slices, and peanut butter or honey as glue. Small houses, fantastic faces, even people are created. But remember, "What you make, you eat!"

☐ **321. OMBUDSMAN.** If the play gets out of hand, sit the group down for a story. Then, before returning to play, let them choose one child as the ombudsman. They'll like the word, which means an official appointed to investigate complaints and maladministration! Take turns at this job every half-hour. Be complimentary when play goes well.

☐ **322. WARNING BUZZER.** Find out when kids are due back home. About twenty minutes before, give them notice that there are only ten more minutes of play, then five minutes of pick-up-the-toys time and five minutes to get home.

☐ **323. THE CONVEYOR BELT.** Kids and parents lie side by side close together, face down on the carpet or grass. The "parcel" (a child) lies on his stomach across the upper backs and shoulders of the others. The conveyor belt people start rolling one direction, trying to stay together. The parcel gets a somewhat bumpy ride and when dumped off becomes the end person of the conveyor belt, and the first person of the conveyor belt becomes the next parcel. Larger parcels should be sure to support some of their own weight and not smash smaller conveyor belt kids. If there are many players, you can have a relay race using two conveyor belts.

☐ **324. THE DRAGON'S TAIL.** Draw a circle on the ground. All players stand on or just outside of the circle, and one person stands in the center of the circle—the dragon. A parent should be the dragon the first time to get the game going. Put a foot-long length of rope—the dragon's tail—on the ground within the circle. The players try to steal the tail without being tagged by the dragon. If tagged *inside* the circle, the player is frozen in that exact position until the next round begins. (These positions are often hard to hold since the person may be bending over to pick up the rope when tagged.) The first one to steal the tail (or the last one tagged) is the new dragon, and the next round begins.

☐ **325. SPACE LADDER.** This can be adapted for a large group of younger children or teens. Use a sturdy ladder. Have kids line up on both sides of the ladder and practice carrying it horizontally around the yard. The more kids, the easier it is to carry. When you have given safety instructions, it's time for one child to be the spaceman or spacewoman. The ladder is lowered so the spaceperson can climb aboard. First he can just sit as the others give him a ride. Then he starts moving "through space" (crawling) to the other end of the ladder. After each one has been in space, you can vary the activity by having the carriers raise the ladder higher in the air or by angling it. Older spacemen may want to carefully *walk* across the ladder.

☐ **326. BODY LANGUAGE.** One child starts the message by lying on the floor and forming a letter with his body (for example, an *I* or a *C*). Other children form letters alone or with one or more partners. Older children can make a message such as "I EAT PIE." (A curled up child is the period.) Or, divide into groups of three and make numbers. As the game proceeds, one child can be the director and tell the others what letters or numbers they must form. Groups can also form all the letters of the alphabet.

☐ **327. YEAR-ROUND HUNT.** It doesn't have to be Easter for kids to have a hunt. When a group of children are at your house, plan a nut hunt. While hunters wait in the kitchen, hide walnuts. Give each child a bag or basket and see who finds the most. Then show how to crack the nuts and eat them!

☐ **328. CRAZY DODGEBALL.** In this game, no one is ever out. Like dodgeball, the players line up on two sides of a line and throw soft balls at players on the other side. But in "Crazy Dodgeball," the hit player is not out; he continues to play but switches to the other side. Use half as many balls as players. Parents can play, too.

☐ **329. CANDLE RELAY.** Make a race course inside or outside, but *not* on carpet. Use chairs, toys, boxes, and other similar items as obstacles and show the route to all players. Start by emphasizing candle safety: tie back long hair, roll up sleeves. Then divide the players into two teams with one adult on each team to lead off. Teams start the relay race at opposite ends. Each first player is given a lighted candle, and he moves as quickly as possible through the course without letting the candle go out. When he has gone the length of the course and back, he hands the candle to the next on his team; continue the relay until all team members have played. Play it again using birthday candles, the first player lighting the next player's candle before he can start. Play it once more using just one birthday candle in a little holder; see if the whole team can finish the relay before the candle goes out.

□ **330. OBSTACLE RACE.** The group gathers in one room and is shown an obstacle course consisting of a bowl, a block, and a book placed in a line on the floor about three feet apart. Show where they will stand to start and let them study the locations of everything carefully. Then the players leave the room and decide who will go through the obstacle course first. Meanwhile, a parent removes the obstacles in the other room. Blindfold the first player and bring her into the room to the starting place. As she walks the course very carefully, gasp, scream, and laugh, to fool her. When she has finished the course, take off the blindfold. She'll be surprised—but happy to provide the sound effects for the next person to be brought into the room to repeat the blindfolded maneuver. The gasps and screams will get louder as you continue to the last player.

□ **331. SACK FUN.** Out of the least expensive sturdy fabric available, make large sacks, the smallest being three by five feet. Make a few huge ones, too. Old sheets are ideal, because kids can see through the material a bit and so don't feel closed in. You don't need to do more for this activity; it will take care of itself. Kids will try to see how many can get into one sack. Or they will try to hop or crawl in them singly or in a group (this teaches cooperation). They can also be used on grass for body rolling. Older children will use them for relay races.

□ **332. MERRY-GO-ROUND.** You'll need a pair of socks and a rope about six feet long. Put one sock in the toe of the other and tie the outer one to one end of the rope. In an open play area, the merry-go-round master lies on his back and starts to swing the rope in a circle, gradually letting out the length of the rope. The others join the merry-go-round one by one, jumping over the sock as it comes around. When all are in the circle, the game begins. The master varies the speed, and the riders must not get caught by the sock. If they do, they're out until the next game. The last rider becomes the new master.

☐ **333. PUSH-OVER.** The first two players squat on the floor side by side. Each hugs his knees with his arms. They *must* keep their hands clasped together. Now they try to push each other over. When one wins, another player joins the combat, until there is one left, who can defend his title if he chooses. Another version: All players squat in a circle and try to push others over. Eventually one wins, after a lot of laughter and shouting!

☐ **334. NEW MUSICAL CHAIRS.** This is a great game for holidays when several generations are present. Like the old game, there needs to be a circle of chairs, one for each person, and a source of music: a piano, a guitar, or a record player. The music is played, and when it stops, all sit down. Then one chair is removed. When the music stops, all sit down again, but this time no one is "out," because two must share a chair. The game continues, with chairless players sitting on a part of a chair or in the lap of another person.

FOR YOUNGER CHILDREN

☐ **335. WHOSE TURN NEXT?** Group play encourages the art of taking turns. When there's one toy that all want, help kids to understand first, second, third, and fourth users. Provide a simple timer for knowing when to switch.

☐ **336. A KNOTTY PROBLEM.** Six or more children and parents make a circle facing the center. Each one reaches toward the middle, taking the hands of two other people not next to him. Now, without letting go, try to untangle the circle. You're untangled when you have one large circle, a circle within a circle, or a figure eight. For variety, one player can be the director and instruct the others on what to do.

☐ **337. HUGS AND MUGS.** Players have to have happy mugs (faces) during this game! It's like tag, with two exceptions. First, players must smile so their teeth show. Second, while playing tag, a player is only safe when hugging another player. The one who is "it" can make huggers separate by counting to five and giving them a chance to run away. It's fun when a player being chased runs for someone to hug and suddenly that person hugs another player instead. It's wild but warm togetherness.

☐ **338. STAIRWAY BUS.** This works best with five or more kids. Choose one to be the bus driver and help her make some paper tickets. She sells these to the other children in exchange for different items they have (a shoe, a toy, a sweater) which are put in paper bags and loaded on the bus (the stairs). Then the bus driver sits on the bottom stair, the others lining up to get aboard. She can let one or several aboard, taking their tickets. They choose seats (stairs) on the bus. The others have to wait to board until she stops again. The bus driver pretends to drive and announces various stops: school, zoo, train station, toy store, ice-cream store. The riders can get off when they wish, taking one of the parcels with them, not looking inside. When all the riders have left the bus, they open their parcels and the one who has his own is the next bus driver. If no one has his own parcel, the same driver continues; if two have their own parcels, they are the next two drivers.

☐ **339. TOY TRADE.** Tell the neighborhood group to bring over toys they no longer want. Let each child choose a paper slip with a number. Starting with #1, children select toys. Let everyone play together with the toys. Some may want to trade toys again before going home.

☐ **340. A QUIET GAME.** All players lie down on the carpet and shut their eyes. A parent sits in the center and tells them to listen carefully and call out or raise a hand when they hear something. In advance, the parent has gathered some props, and after a silence, he makes various sounds: a bell ringing, a cough, a whistle, a kiss, a clap, a scratch of nails against sandpaper, a hum, turning pages, clicking teeth together, crumpling paper, a meow, paper tearing. Other sounds heard in the house may be included: a washing machine, a car noise, a dog barking, a door closing. Count how many different sounds the group heard.

FOR OLDER CHILDREN

☐ **341. MELON RELAY.** This is an outside game. You'll need two teams and two watermelons. The teams line up facing each other an arm's length apart. On each team, the first person sits, the next one stands, the next one kneels, the next stands on a box, and so on. Players may not move from their locations. At the word "Go!" the watermelon is quickly passed, or carefully tossed, to each player, going the length of the team. It continues to be passed from one end of the team to the other and back as many times as possible, scoring a point for each round trip. A dropped melon is returned to the start of the team, and they begin passing it again. As soon as a dropped melon breaks, everyone stops and takes part in a melon-eating race. The next contest is seed-guessing. All the seeds are left on the ground or the picnic table. Everyone gets a guess, and then the seeds are counted. The final event is hosing off players, table, and ground. Beware of seeds germinating into giant vines!

☐ **342. MOVING MAIL CARRIERS.** Give each player an envelope and a piece of paper. The player writes a short note about himself on the paper, seals it in the envelope and puts his own name in large print on the outside. All the envelopes are put in a heap, and each player takes one. Players make a circle, *holding hands* while also holding their envelopes under their chins. Players start looking for the person named on their envelopes. Without dropping hands, they try to get to that person and deliver the mail into his mouth. This takes cooperation, as the circle is being bent by others with the same intent. Every time an envelope is dropped or delivered, the players must pull outward back into a circle again. Don't tell the players in advance, but in this game the *last* player to receive his mail is the winner. He opens *all* the letters and reads them aloud.

☐ **343. BLANKETBALL.** Divide players into two teams and give each a sturdy blanket. Team members grasp the edges of their blanket and, first, practice tossing and catching a beachball in the blanket. Then the game begins. The ball is tossed in the air by one team, which then ducks out of the way as the other group comes in to catch the ball. The first team to score ten times wins. Here's a different version for stronger players: Put one player *in* the blanket to catch the ball and toss it back to the other team. This version requires the blanket holders to move swiftly.

☐ **344. THE SNAPPING GAME.** Players sit in a circle and are numbered in order. Number one starts the game by practicing the snapping routine: two slaps on the knees, two claps, a snap of the right hand, a snap of the left. When the group has mastered this sequence in rhythm, the real game begins. Player #1 starts the routine and when it gets to the right-hand snap, he says his own number at the same time. On the left-hand snap he calls another number. He must keep in time with the rhythm. Without stopping, the routine continues, and the person with that number answers: On the right snap he says his own number and on the left he calls any other number. Player #1 maintains the pace, speeding it up as players get better. When a player doesn't answer or answers incorrectly, the routine stops and that player goes to the "end" of the circle and takes that number. Thus some in the group get new numbers. Then the #1 player starts again. The object is to get to be #1—and stay there.

☐ **345. MINI-RELAYS.**   On separate tables or spread apart on a large table, place two bowls of dried split peas with two straight pins, two bowls of small beans each with two pencils, and two glasses each with three matches next to them. Divide the group into equal teams and make a start and finish line. The first player on each side starts the relay by running to the bowl of peas and spearing out three with the pin. Next she goes to the bowl of beans and lifts out three using the pencils. Finally she uses the two matches to lift the third match and balance it across the rim of the glass. Then she returns to her team and the next player starts. The team finishing first wins.

☐ **346. STRANGE BODIES.**   Give each player an 8½-by-11-inch piece of paper, a pencil, and a paper clip. Fold the paper into four equal horizontal sections. In the first section each player draws a head—any kind he wishes—making the neck lines just cross into the second section. Then all fold the first section back out of sight, secure the fold with a paper clip, and pass the paper to another player. This player starts at the neck and draws a body, making the bottom of the body go just into the third section. Then he folds the body and head sections out of view, and the papers are passed again. The legs are added by the next artist. Then the papers are folded and passed for the final time. This time, each player letters a name in the bottom section. It can be the artist's choice—someone present or well known. Papers are passed once more, then opened and shared. What strange-looking people!

347. MORSE CODE.
Kids will have fun learning to send messages with the "dits" and "dahs" of the Morse code alphabet. First, though, make it a neighborhood project to make a buzzer for each child. Your hardware store can supply you with a buzzer, wire, screws, and a spool. Next practice making the quick "dits," and then the "dahs," which should be three times as long as "dits." The space between letters should also be three times as long as a "dit." Provide each participant with a code chart (below) and start with very simple messages ("Come"; "Time to eat"; "This is Keith"). Kids can take turns sending, receiving, and decoding. Here's the alphabet:

A	dit–dah	N	dah–dit
B	dah–dit–dit–dit	O	dah–dah–dah
C	dah–dit–dah–dit	P	dit–dah–dah–dit
D	dah–dit–dit	Q	dah–dah–dit–dah
E	dit	R	dit–dah–dit
F	dit–dit–dah–dit	S	dit–dit–dit
G	dah–dah–dit	T	dah
H	dit–dit–dit–dit	U	dit–dit–dah
I	dit–dit	V	dit–dit–dit–dah
J	dit–dah–dah–dah	W	dit–dah–dah
K	dah–dit–dah	X	dah–dit–dit–dah
L	dit–dah–dit–dit	Y	dah–dit–dah–dah
M	dah–dah	Z	dah–dah–dit–dit

348. BALLOON BASHING.
Divide the group into two teams. Let each team work in separate rooms to make up six clues using the names of places inside and outside the house, such as "Polar bears love it" (the freezer), "Put your head on it" (a pillow), and "Builders like them" (blocks). Each team puts its clues inside balloons, which they then blow up. While one team remains in a room, the other team hides its balloon clues except for the first one. Each clue hints at the place to find the next clue. Then they give the other team the first balloon, and the timer starts. The team must break the balloon using palms of hands only. Everyone follows along as they look for the place of the next balloon clue. When they find the last balloon and reach the last place, the time is noted. When the first team is finished, the second team follows the other set of clues and tries to beat the first team's time.

★

SECTION 4: PIANO LESSONS PLUS

☐ **349. THE WHOLE ORCHESTRA.** Because there's a wide variety of instruments to choose from, don't fall into the trap of pushing a child into lessons on the instrument that *you* always wanted to play. If possible, attend an orchestra or band concert with your child and specifically listen to the different instruments. Go to a music store and ask for a demonstration of various instruments. Try to rent at first, or at least take advantage of optional trial periods before purchase. Encourage different instruments for different kids in the family, so that you may eventually have a home mini-orchestra.

☐ **350. BREAKING THE ICE.** The hardest part of instrument lessons is starting on a new assignment. When a child returns from a lesson, take time to look over the new work assigned. If possible, play the tune or hum or sing the melody. Then divide it into smaller sections to be mastered in the days to come. Perhaps the student will want to mark the sections for each of the days. It's much easier when there's a small part to work on each day.

☐ **351. "I SOUND GREAT."** Provide the practicing musician with a simple cassette recorder. She can play it back to hear mistakes, bad timing—and good playing. Let her decide if she wants to share a recording with the family or a friend or relative.

☐ **352. MINI-RECITAL.** Whether your child is a dancing bumblebee or a nimble pianist, let the entire family share in the progress. The evening before lesson day, have a three-minute recital of something new learned that week. Give much more praise than suggestions.

☐ **353. HOME BARRE.** For aspiring ballet dancers, make a barre, preferably by a tall mirror. This way the dancer can see how he looks and how perfect the positions are. An early morning before-school practice session can help a young dancer wake up mind and body.

☐ **354. PARENTS TOO.** It's fun for everyone when parents take lessons too. Sometimes the lessons can be joint ones. Find duets that you can play together: four hands at the piano, flute and organ, guitar and voice, cornet and sax, or piano and violin. You may have a budding family orchestra! Parents are never too old to learn new things.

☐ **355. HOW LONG DO I PRACTICE?**　A musician should use a timer, setting it for the allotted time, usually about thirty minutes. When the bell rings, he calls in Mom, Dad, or Big Sister and plays one more piece—his best piece, so that the practice ends on a high note.

☐ **356. RECITAL DAY.**　Keep things calm and happy on a recital or program day. In honor of the event, the performer gets his favorite food, he is relieved of some household tasks, and he's encouraged to take a little rest. Clothes should be ready, and he should feel comfortable in them. One final practice at home, then leave in time so there's no rush. Remind the child that mistakes aren't important and that few will notice if he just keeps going, does his best, and smiles and bows. The entire family should go to the event and be ready with praise at the end.

☐ **357. UNIQUE LESSONS.**　With your child, consider taking lessons on unique instruments: harp, cello, drums, organ, tuba, marimba. Consider taking other kinds of lessons: voice, drama, computer, tennis, diving. Before getting into these, it's helpful to talk with parents and children already involved. Ask about costs, time commitments, and practice.

★

SECTION 5: OFF TO CAMP

This is the ultimate group activity. Although you can't go with your child unless you're a counselor, you still can do many supportive things with him before and after this adventure.

☐ **358. CHOOSING A CAMP.**　Nowadays there are camps for computer study, camps for losing weight, camps for kids with drug dependencies, and many others. But unless your youngster *really* needs a specialized activity, let the first camp be of the old-fashioned variety, where horses, hiking, and water sports mingle in an environment of campfire-style camaraderie. Another year your child may want a more specialized program, but many kids prefer returning to the same camp year after year. In January, help your child send for camp folders, talk to other campers, and compare locations and prices. A big part of the fun is the anticipation and preparation for the time at camp.

☐ **359. ALMOST LIKE CAMP.** Avoid the homesickness problem by giving the prospective camper some practice being away from home, such as spending a weekend or longer at a relative's house. Learning to use camp equipment while at home, knowing what the family will be doing while she's gone, putting labels on camp clothes and trying them on beforehand, going to camp with a sibling or good friend, talking with other campers—these also make the transition easier. If possible, invite a seasoned camper to come and talk about the camp at snack time or supper. Before she arrives, help your child make a list of questions to ask her.

☐ **360. ONE SPECIAL THING.** Unless the camp prohibits it, let a child take to camp one special thing he can share: a card trick, a small toy, a funny story, a special tool, a magazine or a book. This gives him a link to home but also a way to share with new friends. It should not be an expensive item; just one that can give his self-esteem a boost. (A teddy bear or a "blankey" is not the right kind of thing to take. Make sure the take-along item isn't one that will get him teased.)

☐ **361. POSTCARDS.** Go to the post office and buy prestamped postcards. Help the child address them to her family, best friend, cousin, grandparents, and others. Then, when she has a spare moment at camp, she can write a short message. With her, make a little list of postcard topics, such as a new sport or activity, some interesting person, a new food, the scenery, a funny or exciting experience, and the camp location where she is sitting and writing. Explain that people like to hear about the little things at camp. Clip the list of topics to the cards and tuck into the luggage along with a pen.

☐ **362. SECRET NOTES.** Slip some sealed envelopes, enough for one each day, into the camper's duffel bag. In each one put some little message: a joke, a cartoon, a riddle, a poem, a photo of the dog, an item from the newspaper. Campers love to share these pepper-uppers with other campers. And they remind the camper that the family is thinking of him.

☐ **363. MENTAL HUG TIME.** Before the camper leaves, select a time, such as breakfast time or 9:00 or 10:00 P.M., that will be mental hug time. Tell her that the family will be especially thinking of her then and knowing she's having fun. She should similarly take a moment to think of the family and what they might be doing. Sometimes it works well to use the first star of the night as a reminder to think of the family.

☐ **364. WELCOME-HOME SUPPER.** The day the camper returns, plan a supper that doesn't include camp-style food! Have the camper bring all the things she's collected to the table. Talk about camp experiences. Enjoy her handicrafts and display them. Take pictures of the returned camper. Tell her about this special supper before she leaves, so she'll be thinking about what to share. Be sure to notice her tan, her self-assurance, or her new skills, and compliment her on these.

FIVE

THE WIDE WORLD OF BOOKS

 pen the doors of our world and the universe with activities that encourage reading. Start when children are young to have daily reading time rather than continuous TV time. And remember that *you* set the example. Research shows that parents who love to read have children who love to read!

★

★*Section 1:* Reading at home
★*Section 2:* Using the public library
★*Section 3:* Working with the school
★*Section 4:* Books to use together
★*Section 5:* Best-ever books

★

SECTION 1: READING AT HOME

As children grow, keep books moving through the house. Make reading a high-priority home activity. The ability to read and understand makes for better students and leads to better job opportunities and a lifetime of enjoyment.

FOR YOUNGER CHILDREN

For non-readers and new readers, check your bookstore and library for books with no words or just a few words. These give children a feeling of success as they learn the story told in pictures and "read" it to others in the family.

☐ **365. BOOK-OF-THE-DAY.** In the early morning choose a book a child has not yet read. Stand it on a shelf out of the child's reach but in a place where he'll see it often during the day. Put an interesting toy next to it. This is the first book for reading time that day. Change the book and the toy each day. If possible, use a toy that has a connection with the book.

☐ **366. THREE-D WORDS.** Use plastic clay to make three-dimensional words. Have a child roll different colors of the clay to pencil thickness. Then decide on a word a child really likes: bike, baseball, love, the dog's name. Using different colors for each letter, help her to form the letters, pinching the joints so they stick together. You can let these dry for a few days and then glue them on cardboard that the child has painted. They make a great plaque in a child's room, and she'll be proud of being able to read and write these special words.

☐ **367. BABY CHARADES.** When you come to a big word in a book, one a child may not understand, see if you can act out the word. This adds variety to the reading and increases the child's vocabulary more easily than telling the meaning or skipping the word. Say the new word several times and let him act it out, too. This way he's more likely to remember it. Let him share the new word with the family.

☐ **368. READING GAMES.** Play games in connection with reading to young children. Here's a nursery rhyme game called "Who?" To find the answer to the question, read the familiar rhyme shown in the parenthesis.

Who liked to garden? (Mary, Mary, quite contrary)
Who did something amazing at holiday time? (Little Jack Horner)
Who learns to be a musician? (Tom, Tom, the piper's son)
Who fell asleep at his work? (Little Boy Blue)
Who likes to play at night? (The Man in the Moon)
Who took a trip to see royalty? (Pussy Cat, Pussy Cat, where have you been?)
Who was interrupted while eating? (Little Miss Muffett)
Who lost her belongings? (Little Bo-Peep)
Who was a happy king and liked music? (Old King Cole)
Who didn't waste food? (Jack Spratt and his wife)
Who was very poor but also very kind? (Old Mother Hubbard)
Who had an accident while getting water? (Jack and Jill)
Who fell off a wall? (Humpty-Dumpty)

☐ **369. CHILDREN'S DICTIONARY.** Start the "let's look it up" habit early. Have a child's dictionary that gives simple meanings and has many pictures. When a child has extra time, let her turn to a page at random and pick out a word or picture she likes. Read the definition. Use the word in a sentence. See if she can use it in a sentence later in the day.

☐ **370. RHYMING STORIES.** For a change of pace, let non-readers participate by supplying the rhyming word in rhymed stories such as Dr. Seuss's. If it is a new book, the child will have the fun of guessing the word; if it is a familiar story, he'll have the satisfaction of quickly filling in the right word. A good book is *Read-Aloud Rhymes for the Very Young* (Jack Prelutsky, Knopf, 1986).

☐ **371. A NEW ENDING.** Before you finish reading a book to children, let them tell what they think the ending will be. Then finish the book and see whose ending comes closest to the author's. Help a young child write down her own improved ending.

☐ **372. WHAT HAPPENED AFTER.** When you come to the end of a book, make up an additional line beginning with "And the next day . . ." or "The next time this happened . . . " Let the child finish the sentence. This stretches a child's imagination and lets him practice being a storyteller.

☐ **373. FILL-IN-THE-BLANK.**   Help new readers by reading a book to them and then stopping at a word they know, letting them fill it in. Give lots of praise as children expand their reading ability. As you turn to a new page in a book, look at the illustration together and ask the child what he thinks will take place in the story.

☐ **374. TREASURE HUNT READING.**   Prepare this activity while children are at school or at play. It's good for beginning readers. Hide all the clues except the first one. When they come home, hand them the first clue. For example: Clue #1: Hang up your coat (they will find clue #2 in the closet); clue #2: Fido loves you (they will find clue #3 in Fido's bed). Continue, ending at the snack table or the book corner. Young readers will try hard to read clue words they don't know. And they'll be anxious to learn new words.

☐ **375. GROCERY STORE READING.**   Let a child who knows her alphabet point out letters she sees on products in the store. Then see if she can start with *A* and go through the alphabet. If she can't find a letter, write it on a tablet and go on to the next. Another trip, give the child a little tablet to write down any complete words she can read. Let her read her list at supper.

☐ **376. "IT STARTS LIKE."**   Play this little game with non-readers. Say a word, such as "ball" and ask a child to tell another word that *begins* with the same sound. At first you may give a hint, such as "It is something we read." When she's quick to answer "book," make the hints harder. Soon, give no hints at all.

☐ **377. ALPHABET BAG.**   Using a crayon, put a large letter, such as *D,* on a small paper bag. Look through an old magazine with a child, helping him find things that begin with *D.* You may have to help at first, indicating which page shows a dog, a dish, a doll, and so forth. As the child gets older, he will find appropriate pictures without your help. Cut out the pictures and put them in the *D* bag. Choose another letter and play again with a new bag. Let the child "read" the contents of his letter bags to other interested family members, or take it to school to share.

☐ **378. SISTER/BROTHER.** Some letters look alike. As a child is learning her alphabet, show her how these sister/brother letters are different: b and d, C and G, g and y, m and n, p and q, V and W. Write a row of one letter but put in one of the sister letters (C C C C C G C C). Let her find the G. Then read a book and let her find the sister/brother letters and identify them.

☐ **379. LIBRARY CORNER.** As soon as a toddler has books of his own, establish a library corner in his own room or the family room. It should have a shelf for his own books and a place for library books. Emphasize book care at this early age. On the wall hang a poster, including a picture he draws of himself reading. On it you can draw lines for his first list of books he has "read" and likes best. Later, add a small rocker to the corner as his reading chair. Keep this up as children grow, encouraging them to keep a list of books read.

FOR READERS

☐ **380. MUNCH MESSAGES.** Put little notes in school lunches. Everyone likes mail, so these munch messages will be read and shared! They don't have to be long: "Hi, Jessica, I know you'll do well in the relay race." "Dear Michael, I can't wait to see you after school, when we'll fly your new kite." Put in a new, harder word now and then. Encourage children to put good messages in each other's lunches, too.

☐ **381. THE OPEN BOOK.** Choose a place that gets lots of traffic: the front hall, the family room, the counter near the back door. Place an open book there, primarily a book of pictures and captions. Put a large paper clip on the page and turn the page each morning. Good books include *A Day in the Life of America* (Collins, 1986), an art book; *A World of Animals* (Bill Bruns, Abrams,1983); *National Parks of the West* (Sunset-Lane, 1980), *American Album* (Oliver Jenson, American Heritage, 1985); *Antarctica* (Eliot Porter, Dutton, 1978).

☐ **382. SECOND-GENERATION READER.** Suggest to a child a book that you read and especially enjoyed at his age. You can give him your old copy, a new copy, or borrow it from the library. Check the date it was published to see if it was a new book when you first read it. Don't discuss the book beforehand but let the child tell you what he liked about it. Then it's your turn to talk about why you liked it. On a trip, when the family has more time to read, share, and discuss books, take along some books suitable for two generations of readers.

☐ **383. LET'S MAKE A DEAL.** For every hour of TV watched, have a half-hour of reading. You may soon find that kids prefer reading to TV viewing. You can cover a lot more ground, learn more, and have greater adventures in thirty minutes of reading than you get in an hour of TV.

☐ **384. FIRST PERFORMANCE.** When a child has a short book she can read by herself, make a video recording of her reading it. Let each child have this privilege. You've recorded a very special moment in a child's life and one that the family will enjoy seeing in years to come. When a parent is away at storytime, the video can be played and the child can enjoy storytime with herself as storyteller.

☐ **385. MAKE A BOOK.** This is a project that a reading child can do for a non-reading sibling. Using an old magazine, the older child cuts out about fifteen interesting pictures. Have him paste them onto separate pieces of paper, leaving space at the bottom for a story. Then let him assemble the pictures in the order that fits the simple story he will write about them, using just about one short sentence per page. You may have to give some suggestions on the plot, but that isn't too important. Then let the older child present his book to the younger and read it to him. It may become a family favorite!

☐ **386. WORD BINGO.** Have kids draw a grid of twenty-five squares on sheets of construction paper, five squares wide and five high. Mark the center square "Free." Then, the players suggest words (easy words when playing with younger children, harder ones for older). Write each word on a three-by-five-inch card as each player writes it in any square of his chart. Take turns suggesting words until the charts are filled up and each word is also on a card. Now, make bingo markers out of cut-up paper or use buttons or poker chips. Shuffle the deck of cards and turn one over, announcing the word clearly. Players cover the word with a marker. Keep going until one player wins by having five in a row in any direction.

☐ **387. WHERE DO YOU READ?** Introduce variety into the places the family reads: by the fire, in a tree, in the bathtub, in bed, everyone on the parents' bed, at the beach, on the lawn, in a tent with a strong flashlight. See who can find a new and different place to read. Keep books in the car—for yourself and for kids—so that they're available when you're forced to wait for someone.

☐ **388. FAMILY BOOK CLUB.**   Give a name to your family book club, such as "The Eager Readers," "Peterson's Pages," or "The Big Book Club." Start a list of books read by each child. Give recognition for each ten books read and maybe a little prize for the most pages or books read in a month.

☐ **389. NEIGHBORHOOD BOOK CLUB.**   In the summer, when kids have more time, form a neighborhood book club. With other parents, set up a plan to share trips to the library, to exchange books among readers, and to keep a tally for each child and reward all readers at the end of summer. Let the kids name their club. The club can meet at different houses for reading and exchanging books. Check to see if your library has a book club.

☐ **390. BOOKPLATES.**   Bookstores sell inexpensive bookplates (the personalized ones cost more) that can be used by all the family. On a rainy afternoon, let family members bring to one room their favorite books, books they will always want to keep. Show where to put a bookplate in a book. On the bookplate should go the owner's name, address or phone number, and, if possible, the date the book was acquired, who gave it, the occasion, and so on. Include as much or as little information as you want. When good new books join the family, see that they get a bookplate.

☐ **391. SCRAMBLED WORDS.**   Make a list of nine words that all the players know and one hard new word. Write them in a list, scrambling the letters. You may want to make them all of one category, such as games, toys, foods, or animals. Make some easy (T C A—cat) and make some harder (E A E T H P N L—elephant). After you've made the first set of scrambled words, let the one who solved the most scrambled words make the next list for the others to enjoy.

☐ **392. BOOK CARE.**   Give a demonstration on how to open a new book: Holding the book with the spine on a flat surface, gently lay flat a few pages at front, then at the back. Continue this to the middle of the book. By handling a book in this way, the spine isn't cracked. Cover a well-worn book with shelf paper to protect it. With kid-help, make a bookmark for each family member, using thin cardboard, crayons, and a piece of yarn tied through a punched hole. Use this marker rather than turning down corners or laying the book down with the pages open.

☐ **393. OPINION TIME.** Encourage a youngster to talk about a book she's finished reading. Would she recommend it to someone else? What was interesting? What was funny? Would she like to read aloud a passage from the book? If you have time, let her tell the entire plot. This increases her skill in grasping a number of ideas and telling them in proper order. On her list of books read, let a child rank the book on a one to ten scale, ten being the best.

☐ **394. SUBSCRIPTIONS, TOO.** Good magazines make great gifts for great reading. Help a child choose one that ties in with his interests. Take a one-year subscription at first. Have interesting magazines available in the living room and family room. Good magazines include:

• *Highlights for Children*, 2300 West Fifth Avenue, Box 269, Columbus, OH 43215.
• *National Geographic World*, National Geographic Society, 1145 Seventeenth Street NW, Washington, DC 20036.
• *Ranger Rick*, 8925 Leesburg Pike, Vienna, VA 22184. (Publication of the National Wildlife Federation.)
• *Cricket*, 315 Fifth Street, Box 100, Peru, IL 61354.
• *Cobblestone*, 20 Grove Street, Peterborough, NH 03458.

☐ **395. IN THE CAR.** Keep family-owned books in a large protective envelope in the car. Have kids make a design on the envelope. As a change from conversation and games in the car, let children read aloud to you. This lets each one be a storyteller for the other children and also gives you insight as to how each child's reading is progressing. Don't fret over mispronounced words. This usually indicates a new word. Tell the correct pronunciation and ask about its meaning. Explain the meaning if others don't know it. Be sure to thank the reader!

☐ **396. THE PHONE BOOK.** Dull reading? Never! Let a child see how the book is organized, the importance of the pages at the front of the book, and how the book is alphabetized. Let her find the family listing and listings of other friends. Show how to look up services in the yellow pages. Look up a service you use (cleaner, restaurant, appliance repair) and see how many alternatives there are. If you have two telephone books, let two children race to find certain names or listings.

☐ **397. FIFTEEN-MINUTE BONUS.**   Bedtime may be eight o'clock, but be ready to give a fifteen-minute bonus for reading. This puts a priority on reading, makes it an enjoyable part of daytime activities, and encourages daily reading. It also serves as a pleasant, quiet activity that makes going to sleep easier.

FOR ALL CHILDREN

☐ **398. THE SUPPERTIME BOOK.**   Choose a book suitable for the ages of your children. At the end of supper, read just a chapter or a few pages of the book. Leave them wanting more! Make this a family tradition. As children become proficient readers, let them share in the reading, but remember that this is not a reading lesson but an enjoyable time together.

☐ **399. MY READING JOURNAL.**   When children are small, help them start a journal of books they have read. A parent can keep it going until the child is old enough to keep his own journal. You might want to give this book to a child who loves to read: *My Book About Books* (Barbara Burt, Telltales Press, 1986). This sturdy and wonderfully illustrated book has one hundred pages waiting for a child's entries and reviews. No matter how a book-reading record is kept, it should be a source of conversation and satisfaction for the child and the parent.

☐ **400. BOOKWORMS.**   Use construction paper to make the head end of a bookworm for each child. Make it about four inches in length. Tack these on the bulletin board and say nothing about them until asked. Then, with the kids' help, cut out additional curved sections for the bookworm's body. As a child completes a book, he writes the title on a curved section and pastes it onto his worm. Watch those worms grow! If you don't like worms, make a tree and add leaves for books read.

☐ **401. COMPARISONS.**   Read a book and then go to a movie (or rent a movie) and see the same story. What parts were left out? Where was the plot different? Did the characters and locations look like the ones in the book or as pictured in your mind? Which was better, the book or the movie? Books and movies for all ages include *Black Beauty, Pinocchio, Snow White, The Journey of Natty Gann, The Karate Kid, An American Tail, A Christmas Carol, Goodbye Mr. Chips, The Little Drummer Girl, Pride and Prejudice, The Wizard of Oz, Little Women, Mary Poppins, Alice in Wonderland,* and *The Adventures of Tom Sawyer.* Listings at your video store will give you other titles. You may want to see the movie first, then borrow the book for reading.

☐ **402. BOOK MOBILES.**   Some books will always be a child's favorites. Work together to make a mobile about memorable characters in these books. Let him draw the character, cut it out of colored paper, then help attach it with thread to a nice coat hanger. As more book characters are collected, firmly attach a second hanger to the first, and so forth. Let it hang over a child's bed, the characters moving slowly, reminding him of good books.

☐ **403. GUESS WHO?**   In the car, play a variation of the "Twenty Questions" game, using characters from books. Let children take turns giving yes and no answers about the characters they've chosen to be.

☐ **404. TUB BOOKS.**   Choose some inexpensive books for bathtub reading, just in case the book falls in the tub. Let a child relax and read for ten to fifteen minutes. Some children like to be read to as they bathe.

☐ **405. MAKE A MOVIE.**   Help a child pick out the important scenes from an action book. Let him draw these scenes on separate pieces of paper. If others in the family have read the book, they can contribute scenes, too. Add a blank piece of paper at each end and paste or tape the scenes together end to end like a reel of film. Cut two slots in a cardboard box, making the area between the slots the size of just one picture. Pull the first picture into place, then show one picture at a time in the framed opening. One child can narrate the "film."

☐ **406. A CHILDREN'S BIBLE.**   There are several fine simplified and illustrated versions of the Bible, suitable for young children. Go to a religious bookstore and look at these Bibles. Decide which one you'd like to own. For every good deed a child does and reports to you, put a coin in the "Bible fund." Earning the Bible this way is fun and makes it important.

★

SECTION 2: USING THE PUBLIC LIBRARY

☐ **407. STORYTELLING.** Plan a visit to the library to coincide with their storytelling time. That evening at supper, let a child retell for the entire family the story read at the library. She may wish to borrow that book another time to read it herself. Listening to storytellers helps a child become better at storytelling herself; it gives training in remembering the outline of a story, speaking clearly, and exercising dramatic ability.

☐ **408. MORE THAN BOOKS.** Encourage regular borrowing of books, but also investigate borrowing recordings and videos from your library. A nice change is a book on tape or recordings of children's songs from foreign countries. A child can listen while doing crafts, dressing, or cooking. These are also wonderful for times when a child isn't feeling well.

☐ **409. TIE-IN BOOKS.** With the help of the librarian, find books that tie in with such family activities as planting a garden, going on a plane trip, having a new baby, going to the zoo or circus. After reading a book about fire engines, visit the fire station. Reading tie-in books enhances the actual event. Reread some after the event, too.

☐ **410. HEAD START.** Before leaving the library, let a child read the first few pages in one or more of the books he'll be taking home. This head start serves to interest the child in the story, and he'll be eager to continue reading at home. At each library visit, look for different and interesting places to start reading a book.

☐ **411. LOOK IT UP.** Choose a topic such as clowns or gorillas. See how many places the subject can be found in different reference books. This broadens the family's knowledge on the subject and also introduces the use of many reference books. Start by looking up the word in different encyclopedias, then use the library's subject guide file and periodicals index.

★

SECTION 3: WORKING WITH THE SCHOOL

Visit the library at your child's school. See what might be needed and ask the librarian how you can help. At the right time, suggest some of these ideas.

☐ **412. BOOK TRADE.**   Set up a program that lets preschoolers bring to school a book they'd like to trade. Friday morning is a good trading day. Each child who has read the book puts his name inside the back cover. It's interesting to see which books get the most signatures. Any child bringing a book to the Book Trade can take one home.

☐ **413. BIRTHDAY BOOK.**   With the school librarian, set up a program that permits a child to give the library a gift book in honor of her own birthday. The librarian will have a list of wanted books at reasonable prices and with sturdy bindings, which can be ordered in advance. A bookplate with the child's name is put in the book, and it is presented in her classroom on her special day. After the birthday child has read the book, classmates get to borrow it before it goes into the school library.

☐ **414. BOOKSELLERS.**   This is a different way of giving a book report. Children read books of their choice and prepare a review for the class. The reviewer tries to "sell" the book he's chosen by enthusiastically telling about it, perhaps reading a paragraph, and sharing reasons why others would like it. Two children can compete in trying to "sell" two different books on the same topic.

☐ **415. PUPPET BOOK REPORTS.**   When several children have read the same book, let them give a book report using puppets as the characters in the book. They can act out one particular scene in the book or carry on a dialogue about the book. At the end of the report, the puppet characters should answer questions from the audience.

☐ **416. STORYTIME.**   If the librarian would like help, work with other moms and dads to provide parent storytellers for various age groups. There are excellent articles on how to tell stories, but enthusiasm, a little drama and creativity, plus practice will be enough to prepare you for this worthwhile school project. Costumes and props add interest. Let your children suggest stories and also let them watch your at-home rehearsal and give you suggestions.

☐ **417. INCENTIVE PROGRAM.** Ask local businesses or parents' businesses to give incentives for classrooms to read a specified number of books. The incentives might be an ice-cream party, an after-school movie, or a class trip to a business or park. Set up the incentive program so that the goal is challenging but reachable. Be sure to give credit to the businesses supplying the reward and let the class secretary write a note of thanks.

★

SECTION 4: BOOKS TO USE TOGETHER

☐ **418. FOR NEW PARENTS.** Communication starts with lullabies and nursery rhymes. For help, go to the library and borrow *Babies Need Books* (Dorothy Butler, Atheneum, 1980). Here are ideas for the brand new parent on how to begin the bond of shared communication from the moment the baby arrives. *The Baby's Catalogue* (Janet and Allan Ahlberg; Little, Brown, 1983) is a young child's answer to adult catalogs and also introduces five interesting but different families and how they like to read. It will be a longtime favorite. Even when a baby is young, read aloud each day. The sound of your voice and the rhythm of the reading will be interesting to the child and will help lengthen his attention span.

☐ **419. FOR READING ALOUD.** Some books come alive when read aloud, and Jim Trelease has gathered a wonderful list of them plus invaluable ideas in his book *The Read-Aloud Handbook* (Penguin, 1985). He tells how to make reading aloud one of the best parts of the day for both parents and children. Reading aloud is not just for young children. The ability to read aloud is important for both parent and child. It gives opportunities for growth in speaking effectively in front of others, in dramatic ability, and in other aspects of poise. With your children, look over the weekly schedule and set aside time for reading aloud each day.

☐ **420. WE'RE ALL ARTISTS.**   Hidden in each of us is an artistic sense that needs nurturing from babyhood onward. See that art is part of the nursery: good pictures, pleasing colors, mobiles, drawings or posters that are changed often. Read *Children Are Artists* (Daniel Mendelowitz, Stanford University, 1963) while your child is still an infant. You'll enjoy learning about the artist in you and how to support artistic talent in your young child.

☐ **421. GOOD MANNERS.**   Times have changed, but good manners are still in vogue. You can teach and share ideas on this subject with these books: *White Gloves and Party Manners* (Luce, 1965), for girls; *Stand Up, Shake Hands, Say "How Do You Do"* (Luce, 1977), for boys; and *What to Do When and Why* (D. McKay, 1975), for teens, all by Marjabelle Young and Ann Stewart.

☐ **422. PARENTING.**   After reading parenting books, share some of the ideas with your children. Decide which ones are worth a trial. For ideas read *I Saw a Purple Cow and 100 Other Recipes for Learning* (Ann Cole et al., Little, 1972), *Helping Children Learn Right from Wrong* (Sidney Simon and Sally Olds, Simon and Schuster, 1976), *Between Parent and Child* (Haim Ginott, Avon, 1969), *Your Child's Self-Esteem* (Dorothy Briggs, Doubleday, 1970), and *Six Weeks to Better Parenting* (Caryl Krueger, Pelican, 1985).

★

SECTION 5: BEST-EVER BOOKS

☐ **423. FOR PRESCHOOLERS.**   Here's a list of books to check off as you read them to your young child.

Title	Author
Bed Time for Bear	Sandol Stoddard
Brown Bear, Brown Bear	Bill Martin
A Child's Garden of Verses	Robert Lewis Stevenson
Corduroy	Don Freeman
Do Not Open	**Brinton Turkle**
George and Martha	James Marshall
Georgina and the Dragon	Lee Kingman

Goodnight, Moon	Margaret Brown
Peter Rabbit	Beatrix Potter
Spot Goes for a Walk	Eric Hill
The Story of Ferdinand	Munro Leaf
The Sweet Touch	Lorna Balian
The Velveteen Rabbit	Margery Williams
The Very Hungry Caterpillar	Eric Carle
When I'm Sleepy	Jane Howard
William's Doll	Charlotte Zolotow
Winnie-the-Pooh	A. A. Milne

☐ **424. FOR NEW READERS.** These books are ones that you can help your child enjoy. It's nice to take turns reading a page, so that reading isn't a struggle. Let your child check them off this list.

The Adventures of Albert, the Running Bear	Barbara Isenberg, Susan Wolf
All About Arthur	Eric Carle
Amelia Bedelia	Peggy Parish
A Bargain for Frances	Russell Hoban
A Bear Called Paddington	Michael Bond
Charlotte's Web	T. H. White
The Courage of Sarah Noble	Alice Dalgliesh
Curious George Flies a Kite	Margaret and H. A. Rey
Danny and the Dinosaur	Syd Hoff
Did You Carry the Flag Today, Charley?	Rebecca Caudill
Frog and Toad Together	Arnold Lobel
Gilberto and the Wind	Marie Ets
Harry and the Terrible Whatzit	Dick Gackenbach
Harry the Dirty Dog	Gene Zion
Hattie Rabbit	Dick Gackenbach
Horton Hatches the Egg	Dr. Seuss
Jennifer and Josephine	Bill Peet
Just the Thing for Geraldine	Ellen Conford
Katy and the Big Snow	Virginia Burton
Koko's Kitten	Francine Patterson
Little Bear	Else Minarik
Little House in the Big Woods	Laura Ingalls Wilder
Little Red Hen	Paul Galdone
Lyle Finds His Mother	Bernard Waber

Madeline	Ludwig Bemelmans
Miss Nelson Is Missing	Harry Allard
Mr. Popper's Penguins	Richard T. Atwater
Petunia	Roger Duvoisin
Uncle Remus Stories	Joel Chandler Harris
Why the Sun and the Moon Live in the Sky	Elphinstone Dayrell
Wolfhunter	Joel Kauffmann
Zamani Goes to Market	Muriel Feelings

☐ **425. FOR OLDER GRADE-SCHOOLERS.** Use this list for both kids and parents. If you haven't read these books, do so now so you can talk with kids about them.

The Adventures of Tom Sawyer	Mark Twain
All-of-a-Kind Family	Sydney Taylor
Along Came a Dog	Meindert DeJong
Andersen's Fairy Tales	Hans Christian Andersen
Angelita	Wendy Kesselman
The Baseball Trick	Scott Corbett
Beezus and Ramona	Beverly Cleary
Ben and Me	Robert Lawson
The Black Cauldron	Lloyd Alexander
Book of Nonsense	Edward Lear
The Book of Three	Lloyd Alexander
The Borrowers	Mary Norton
Bushbabies	William Stevenson
Caddie Woodlawn	Carol Brink
Call It Courage	Armstrong Sperry
The Call of the Wild	Jack London
Carry On, Mr. Bowditch	Jean Latham
The Cat Who Went to Heaven	Elizabeth Coatsworth
Charlie and the Chocolate Factory	Roald Dahl
Code and Cipher Book	Jane Sarnoff and Reynold Ruffins
Coyote Cry	Byrd Baylor
Cricket in Times Square	George Selden

Dear Mr. Henshaw	Beverly Cleary
Diary of a Young Girl	Anne Frank
From the Mixed-Up Files of Mrs. Basil E. Frankweiler	E. L. Konigsburg
Grimm's Fairy Tales	Jacob Grimm
Hailstones and Halibut Bones	Mary O'Neill
Henry Reed, Inc.	Keith Robertson
The Hobbit	J. R. R. Tolkien
Homer Price	Robert McCloskey
Hundred-Penny Box	Sharon Mathis
An Inheritance of Poetry	Gladys Adshead and Annis Duff
Island of the Blue Dolphins	Scott O'Dell
Johnny Tremain	Esther Forbes
Julie of the Wolves	Jean George
Just So Stories	Rudyard Kipling
King of the Wind	Marguerite Henry
Little Women	Louisa May Alcott
The Little Prince	Antoine de Saint-Exupèry
Mary McLeod Bethune	Eloise Greenfield
Mary Poppins	Mary Travers
Mrs. Frisby and the Rats of NIMH	Robert O'Brien
Night Places	Martin Bell
Peter Pan	J. M. Barrie
Philip Hall Likes Me, I Reckon, Maybe	Bette Greene
Pippi Longstocking	Astrid Lindgren
Rabbit Hill	Robert Lawson
Random House Book of Poetry for Children	Jack Prelutsky
Sarah, Plain and Tall	Patricia MacLachlan
Sing Down the Moon	Scott O'Dell
Swiss Family Robinson	Johann Wyss
Teetoncey	Theodore Taylor
Watership Down	Richard Adams
Where the Red Fern Grows	**Wilson Rawls**
The Wind in the Willows	Kenneth Grahame
A Wrinkle in Time	Madeleine L'Engle
The Yearling	Marjorie Rawlings

☐ **426. FOR HIGH SCHOOL STUDENTS.** Books are a great link between parent and child at this important time. See which of these books you haven't read and then read them along with your teen-ager. Ideas in these books can make for meaningful conversations.

Alice in Wonderland	Lewis Carroll
The Adventures of Sherlock Holmes	Arthur Conan Doyle
Anna Karenina	Leo Tolstoy
Autobiography of Benjamin Franklin	Benjamin Franklin
Brave New World	Aldous Huxley
The Call of the Wild	Jack London
A Connecticut Yankee in King Arthur's Court	Mark Twain
Cry, The Beloved Country	Alan Paton
Doctor Zhivago	Boris Pasternak
Don Quixote	Miguel Cervantes
Gone with the Wind	Margaret Mitchell
The Good Earth	Pearl Buck
Gulliver's Travels	Jonathan Swift
The Heart of Darkness	Joseph Conrad
How Green Was My Valley	Richard Llewellyn
Ivanhoe	Walter Raleigh Scott
Jane Eyre	Charlotte Brönte
The Last of the Mohicans	James Fenimore Cooper
Lord Jim	Joseph Conrad
Lord of the Rings	J. R. R. Tolkien
The Mill on the Floss	George Eliot
Moby Dick	Herman Melville
The Once and Future King	T. H. White
Pride and Prejudice	Jane Austen
The Red Badge of Courage	Hart Crane
The Return of the Native	Thomas Hardy
Robinson Crusoe	Daniel Defoe
The Scarlet Letter	Nathaniel Hawthorne
A Separate Peace	John Knowles
A Tale of Two Cities	Charles Dickens
Tales from the Arabian Nights	Richard F. Burton
The Three Musketeers	Alexander Dumas
Treasure Island	Robert Louis Stevenson

Twenty Thousand Leagues Under the Sea	Jules Verne
Uncle Tom's Cabin	Harriet Beecher Stowe
Walden	Henry David Thoreau
War and Peace	Leo Tolstoy
Wuthering Heights	Emily Brönte

WORK IS PLAY

ow to make and maintain a home is an important thing to learn when growing up. Don't feel you're being kind to kids by doing it all yourself and keeping them in the dark. Working *together* provides opportunities for child-input, companionship, and good conversation.

★

★*Section 1:* Home is more than a house
★*Section 2:* What makes a home tick?
★*Section 3:* Tools of the trade
★*Section 4:* Togetherness tasks for all the family
★*Section 5:* Togetherness tasks for preschoolers
★*Section 6:* Togetherness tasks for the grade school set
★*Section 7:* Togetherness tasks for teens
★*Section 8:* Incentives and entrepreneurs

★

SECTION 1: HOME IS MORE THAN A HOUSE

A team-feeling is built when members of the family understand and appreciate the contribution each makes. A home isn't a hotel but a loving headquarters from which all other activities grow.

☐ **427. PARENT FOR A DAY.**   Being "in charge" may seem easy. Let kids practice parenting by actually being a parent for a day (a weekend day is best). Let each child have a turn. In keeping with a child's age, decide what responsibilities will be included: giving wake-up calls, making meals, assigning household tasks, settling arguments, helping with homework, answering the phone, setting bedtimes, reading stories. Don't make it too hard, but don't make it easy, either. Let kids take on parental tasks such as laundry, baking, repairs, and cooking. A child with a driver's license can also drive carpools and run errands. A young child can be a parent by choosing clothes to wear, settling play arguments, giving others tasks to do, counseling on TV viewing, serving meals and snacks, and tucking others in.

☐ **428. IT'S OK TO SHOVE.**   Rearrange a room with the family's help. Solicit everyone's suggestions and try unique arrangements. Put away books and accessories and try others in their places. Switch some pictures around. Here's a new look at no cost.

☐ **429. THE "TO DO" LIST.**   No parent likes to hear "I forgot." Put on the wall in each child's room (or on mirrors or the family bulletin board) his "to do" list. When a child (or parent) is asked to do something that can't be done at that very moment, he puts it on his "to do" list. Encourage a child to accomplish these items on a regular basis. Never permit more than five items on the list. When a sixth is added, one must be completed and crossed off.

☐ **430. FAMILY CALENDAR.**   Enlist child-help to make a really big calendar each month. Put on it lessons, after-school activities, weekend events, church, social events with relatives, dates when parents are away, and so forth. Circle special fun events. Make sure there's something to look forward to each week. As children get older, this calendar keeps the "who is where" and "who needs the car" questions under control.

☐ **431. PAY UP.**   At the monthly bill-paying time, let children help. Let older children see how the water or electricity bill compares with another month's. Let them write the checks for you to sign. Younger children can stamp and seal the envelopes. Show kids how much was spent on groceries and eating out during the month. This procedure gives children some under-standing of family finances. Explain that blank checks must be kept in a safe place and never signed until fully filled out.

☐ **432. BALANCING THE CHECKBOOK.**   Sit around the supper table and let kids help you balance your checkbook. Show them how to account for checks, charges, deposits, and interest. Allow children to practice their addition and subtraction and arrive at the balance. Or, perhaps, teach them how to operate a simple adding machine. Point out that mistakes are usually made by the customer and not by the bank, but that occasionally even computers can make an error. Show how service charges can mount up.

Stress the importance of monthly reconciliation between checkbook and bank record. Explain how an overdrawn account results in a bad credit record, how bounced checks cost a stiff penalty fee, and how easy it is to record each check when written so that one always knows the exact bank balance. Show the difference between a checking account, a charge card, and cash, and how much easier it is to manage funds in a checking account than by cash. Explain the dangers of credit card purchases,which must eventually be paid off—plus the interest.

☐ **433. TV MANAGEMENT.**   With the help of a program guide, let family members give weekly input as to the best shows to see. Find some shows that the whole family enjoys and wants to view together. When only one family member wants to see a show, put his initials by the listing. Total up how much TV you plan to see in a week. For kids, no more than an hour a day is best, leaving time for a variety of activities. Don't permit a child to have a TV set in her bedroom; keep TV a high-quality, family-oriented activity.

☐ **434. EASY GROCERY LIST.**   Take the time to go to your usual grocery store and list by aisle number the most commonly bought items. Also do this for the produce, dairy, and meat sections. Leave spaces for write-in items. Next, make copies of this personalized preprinted list so you can put one on the bulletin board each week. Let family members know they should check off or write in items needed. Don't permit verbal requests, such as "Hey, I need toothpaste." Instead, remind family members where the list is. Save time by using the list and shopping just once a week.

☐ **435. MY OWN FILE.** A preschooler is ready for her own file folder as soon as she has something "important" to save: a letter from Grandpa, a school drawing, a program from the circus. Show her your file folders: for her and for each family member, one for the budget, for civic or social activities, for Christmas shopping, for letters to write, for bills to pay, for warranties. When you buy new file folders, get them in rainbow colors.

☐ **436. TABLE MANNERS.** Don't spoil mealtime with critical comments about talking with a full mouth or not using the right utensil. Handle this silently. The first of each week, decide what you want to work on, for example, no elbows on the table. Talk about it one time only. After that, outlaw words and use only "body language" to make comments. Just point to your elbow. It's more fun this way, no one feels "picked on," and manners improve. (See chapter 9, section 4, on table manners.)

☐ **437. REMEMBERING AND LISTS.** Rather than trying to remember everything, start the "write-it-down" habit early. Non-readers can be reminded with a picture. Give older children a little notebook for lists: friends' phone numbers, things to save for, birthday suggestions, funny stories, good thoughts. Have certain lists on the family bulletin board: the weekly grocery shopping list, approved TV shows, emergency telephone numbers, items that need repairing, and toys, tools, or books that have been loaned.

☐ **438. LET'S TALK.** Sometimes a youngster has something she wants to share, but you don't have time at that moment. Suggest that she share it at supper or with you alone at a special time. Kids don't like to be put off. And when you can't give a child an immediate answer to a problem, don't just say "later" but be specific: "after supper," "in a week," "tomorrow morning." Show the child you are sincere in wanting to have a serious conversation by putting it in red on your calendar. Then be sure you do it. Younger children like it when you give them an IOU for a talk time later in the day. Choose a good place for a one-on-one talk: in your bedroom, on a walk, in her room.

☐ **439. FAMILY MEETING.**   Once a weekend or once a month, gather the family together for a time of conversation (not about discipline). Talk about plans for the following week, a hoped-for vacation, or ways to improve family life. Serve apples and popcorn or another favorite snack. Let kids talk. Don't put anyone down. Do lots of listening. (For ideas about in-depth conversations see chapter 10.)

☐ **440. CHOICES.**   Give kids plenty of choices and encourage them to bring you choices when they want you to decide a matter. Start with very young children by letting them choose what to wear or what book to read. Then increase the number of choices. Give older children more complicated choices: one expensive shirt or two moderately priced ones, which night to stay up late, one two-hour TV show or two one-hour shows, which instrument to study, which club to join. Include kids in family choices: where to go on Saturday afternoon, what color to paint the house trim, whether to have a two-week vacation at the lake or one week in the big city.

☐ **441. A SECRET PLACE.**   Privacy should be respected within the family as long as the secrecy doesn't violate laws or family rules and morals. Kids should have places of their own where precious things will be safe. Sometimes it works to just tell kids that they should not go through the drawers and closets of others. But you may want to provide a lock for a cupboard or help a child build a sturdy box with lock and key.

☐ **442. GOALS.**   Once a year set personal and family goals. Let these come from each child with some parental input. Goals might be to get a dog, earn a specific sum of money, improve a grade, learn to ride a bike, or break a bad habit. Parents should make individual goals, too. Look at the goals the first of each month. Celebrate success and comment little on unfulfilled goals. Make family goals, too: to build a patio, to call Grandpa once a week, to walk the dog every day. Add new goals as others are achieved.

☐ **443. BOO-BOO BOX.**   Rather than make a big scene about possessions left in the wrong places around the house, encourage the family to put temporarily homeless items into the

Boo-Boo Box, a child-decorated box kept in the corner of the family room or laundry. When you can't find something, look in the Boo-Boo Box first. Once a week during chore time, a child can deliver the leftovers to family members.

☐ **444. WORDS I DON'T WANT TO HEAR.** Talk with children about acceptable language in family situations. Share phrases that you don't like to hear because they hurt family relationships. Let kids share words they don't like to hear. Parents should avoid saying: "You never do anything right." "Who do you think you are?" "I won't change my mind." "How many times do I have to tell you . . . " "I wish you were never born." "Shut up." And kids should avoid: "I'm telling." "I hate that food." "How come you never let me do anything?" "It's not my turn." "Shut up." Make a list and see if you can all get through a day without using any of these unpleasant words.

☐ **445. BAD WORDS I DON'T WANT TO HEAR.** Cursing and profanity are generally the mark of a limited vocabulary. When a child first uses profanity, don't overreact but don't let it pass. Help a child to choose *not* to swear, rather than to just repress the words in your presence. Teach him that swearing is not necessary in polite society and not done in his family. At the right time, tell a child the simple meanings of swear words. Explain that there are better words to describe each of these things, that exploding in swear words when one is frustrated or disappointed doesn't help anything, and that cursing makes others think less of you. Show how swear words are cruel, crude, senseless, or violate one of the Ten Commandments by taking God's name in vain.

It goes without saying that adults absolutely must set a good example by never swearing in front of children—or preferably never at all. A good many caring people have broken their own bad habit of swearing upon becoming parents; it's not such a huge sacrifice to make.

To help break the habit, place on the kitchen counter a jar with a slit in the lid. Fine swearers: twenty-five cents for kids, fifty cents for teens and parents. Use the fund for something special when the swearing has stopped. Suggest some alternative words: "Rats!" "Glitch!" "Kaflooey!" "Crash!" "Thunderation!"

☐ **446. WORDS I LIKE TO HEAR.** Many phrases give us a warm glow. Consider using these often: "You're right." "I have a surprise for you." "I'll consider what you want." "What a good idea!" "You don't have to clean up your room right away." "How nice you look." "You have my OK." "Well done!" "Good job!" "Congratulations!" "You are the greatest." "I miss you." "You can stay up late this time." "No one else could have done it as well." "What can I do to help?" "That's OK, you tried." "I like being with you." "Thank you so much." "I'm glad you're mine." "I trust you." "I love you." "I love you no matter what." Keep a list of these on your bathroom mirror and try to use some each day. Soon they'll be a natural part of your speech.

★

SECTION 2: WHAT MAKES A HOME TICK?

There's no longer "women's work" and "men's work" when it comes to division of household duties. Illustrate by example that both parents can do all sorts of tasks: Dads can wash dishes and diaper babies; moms can replace a faucet washer and change an oil filter. So go ahead and teach boys how to mop floors and girls how to cut the lawn.

☐ **447. DECK OF CARDS.** Take an old deck of cards and using the non-face cards, which have more writing space, write on each card (using marking pen or crayon) a task that needs doing weekly. Let kids contribute ideas of things they think should be done. Then shuffle the cards and deal them out. Depending on children's ages, you may want to deal more to parents or older children. It's OK to trade cards if the other person is willing. Each family member has a week to accomplish the tasks on his cards. Redeal them for the next week; this gives variety to chores.

☐ **448. POST AN AD.** When you have a *special* task that needs doing, "advertise" on the refrigerator door or other prominent place. Briefly outline the work and the reward or pay for it. Encourage others to post an ad when they have something they want done. Of course, most work doesn't have to have pay or a reward beyond a big "Thank you!"

☐ **449. IOUs.** Because everyone has different likes and talents, let each family member write down an IOU for a special task he's willing to do: wash the car, dust the book shelves, build a fire, fold laundry, make a bed, arrange flowers, serve a snack, play a game, rub a back. Let each person choose one of these IOUs that he can request be done at any reasonable time.

☐ **450. EXCHANGE IOUs.** When a family member is busy, she can ask another to make her bed or do another of her assigned tasks. But in receiving this emergency help, it's understood she'll do a task for the other in return. It's good to know that family members care enough for each other to fill in during busy times. Such IOUs can be oral or, better still, written down.

☐ **451. FIRST TOOL BOX.** For a child's third or fourth birthday, give him his own tool box. Each Christmas and birthday following, give him one tool of his own. To keep the tools straight, paint an identifying color for each child on his own tools. Then, when weekly repairs are done, the child is ready to assist, first by handing you the correct tool and observing, then by actually using the tool.

☐ **452. MY WORK SHIRT.** Everyone likes a special outfit. Using an old solid color shirt or an inexpensive new one and indelible marking pens, make a work shirt. First, let the child make her design on a piece of paper, then on the shirt. She may want to put her name on the back of the shirt. Designs can be of tools, stick figures, happy faces, a house with the family lined up in front, and so forth. Parents can have personalized shirts, too.

☐ **453. SHOW ME HOW!** Sometimes you have to show and then show again how a task is done. Remember, you've made a bed about eight thousand more times than a child, so your bed-making should be a lot better. When showing a child how to do a task, summarize by making definite points, such as "The two things to remember about emptying the dishwasher are carrying only one item at a time and being very careful of the sharp knives in the cutlery section." Be sure to let older children show younger ones how to do things. And find opportunities for the younger ones to show others, too. Patience at the beginning will save *you* work later on.

★

SECTION 3: TOOLS OF THE TRADE

Start with toddlers to teach respect for good craftsmanship. It isn't enough to merely "do" the job; it must be done properly. The project must look well, operate efficiently, and have a smooth finish. Living in an age of factory production, kids need to understand the virtues of handicrafts and the pride of a job well done. Your careful instruction, encouragement, and praise are essential! Teaching the use of tools demystifies many repair jobs, and it can save money, too. Here's how to start.

☐ **454. PLIERS—THE FIRST TOOL.** Children can learn to safely use a pair of pliers for removing small jar tops, nuts and bolts, or for grasping things that might otherwise slip from small fingers. Practice on an empty jar, a bolt in a piece of wood, or by pulling a string through a tight opening. Show how the pliers enable us to exert much more force than we could unaided and how we must use care not to apply too much force.

☐ **455. THE SCREWDRIVER.** The narrow blade is used to loosen or tighten screws. Demonstrate how it works on drawer handles, toys, or other repair tasks. Show how to firmly grasp the tool by its handle, using the other hand to guide and steady the blade. Show the difference between a common or flat screwdriver used for slotted screws and the phillips-head screwdriver used for the X-shaped screws common in automotive work. Discourage the use of the screwdriver for prying things open, since this bends and ruins the tool. Make a special point of teaching children never to run with tools or to insert any tool into an electrical outlet.

☐ **456. THE FAVORITE HAMMER.** Even the youngest child knows about hammers and pounding! But the hammer is much more than a mere blunt instrument; its major use is in driving nails. Teach the correct grasp with the three smaller fingers and the thumb holding the hammer, and the index finger along the shaft guiding its fall. As one strikes with the hammer, one also points straight at the nail with the index finger. This simple technique can eliminate many bent nails. Practice aiming, tapping lightly, and giving a hard blow to drive in a nail, and extricating them with the claw. Have a nail-driving contest including all in the family. See who uses the least strokes, who gets the nails in the straightest, and who doesn't miss the nail and mar the wood.

☐ **457. SAWS AND MORE SAWS.**   Use the proper saw for each type of material: the hand saw for wood, the coping saw for fine detail, the hacksaw for cutting metal. Show a child the many small teeth that provide the cutting action. Cutting is accomplished on both the push and the pull of the stroke. Uniform pressure should be maintained. Before starting a project, practice by drawing a line to show where the cut is to be made and then seeing how straight and accurate a cut the child can make. Saws should be hung when stored so that blades don't contact metal and become dull or bent.

☐ **458. TAPE MEASURE.**   Children may understand the use of rulers, yardsticks, and cloth tape measures, but parents should teach the use of a long metal tape measure. Accurate measurement is often the start of any workmanlike job. Here are good lessons in reading, in counting, and in adding inches and fractions of inches. Show where to place the pencil against the rule and how to draw a straight line and a right angle. Practice making measurements around the house: the length of a bed, the width of the stairs, the dimensions of the kitchen.

☐ **459. DRILLS.**   Drills are for dentists—and craftsmen, too. Kids love to drill holes for no purpose at all. Experiment with an old piece of wood. Show how to hold the drill to make the hole at the correct right angle, and how to avoid marring the wood. Show various drill bits and how to select the right size and insert the bit. If an electric drill is to be used, go over the safety precautions: how to turn it on and quickly turn it off, how to set the drill down, how to fasten down the wood to be drilled, and the wearing of safety goggles. Remind kids never to stand on a damp surface when using electrical equipment.

☐ **460. POWER TOOLS.**   It's best for a youngster to first learn to use hand tools, then later to step up to electrically powered ones. Many of the skills are the same, but hand tools require physical effort, produce results much slower (mistakes come more slowly, too), and give one the chance to observe more closely how the tool is working. But children soon want to use the power tools that you often use. So at the right time (when the child has strength and enough common sense to not hurt herself) explain how to hold and use them. Explain safety precautions; in fact, get out the instructions that came with the tool and go over the safety and usage rules. Emphasize the use of safety goggles, clamping down the work, and how to quickly shut off the power. Give careful supervision the first few times she uses the tool. Instruct the child in whether she may use the tool in your absence.

☐ **461. START A PROJECT.** When a child has mastered some tools and is interested in using them, work together on a simple project, such as a low bench, a bird house, or a bookshelf. Work slowly, letting the child do as much as he is able. Unless a child is eager, don't work on the project more than thirty minutes at a time.

☐ **462. OTHER TOOLS AND TALENTS TO TEACH.** In addition to understanding tools, kids should learn these additional skills: how to change a washer, how to determine the right wattage and safely change a light bulb, how to repair a frayed cord, how to use a plunger, how to reset a circuit breaker, how to lubricate a squeaky hinge. These may sound like work to you, but kids like doing these projects! Teach them well, so they can eventually do them for you, and later for themselves in their own homes.

☐ **463. LAUNDRY TOOLS.** Since laundry is forever with us, it might as well be pleasant. Get five or more inexpensive laundry baskets or build simple bins in the laundry area. Put the baskets where all the family can reach them. With words (or pictures for non-readers), label the bins: wash-and-wear, jeans and dark socks, bright colors, whites, hand wash, or whatever divisions you choose. Invite family members to turn in dirty laundry whenever they choose. (Explain that parents don't pick up dirty clothes; if they're not in the bins, they won't get washed.) Rather than having an old-fashioned once-a-week wash day, do a load whenever a basket is filled. See that older children know how to use the machines and also the use of prewash, bleaches, and softeners. (Keep bleaches out of reach of young children.) Explain that the improper use of bleach can permanently damage fabrics. Show how to care for wash-and-wear clothes and the importance of taking them out of the dryer immediately, to maintain their good looks. Encourage family members to read clothing care labels *before* buying clothes and again when washing them.

☐ **464. CLEANING TOOLS.** Since cleaning is no longer "women's work," *everyone* in the family needs to know how to keep a home bright and clean. Dusting, mopping, vacuuming, scrubbing, and scouring need to be demonstrated. Let children choose a task in which to specialize: Vacuuming Chief (includes changing the bag), Floor-Waxing Wizard, Dusting Director, Supply Chairman (supplies bathrooms with tissue, soap, toothpaste, clean towels; sees that kitchen paper towels are installed, pencils and tablets are at all phones, napkins are at the table, etc.) Show the use of specific cleaning supplies (cleansers, scrubbers, disinfectants, furniture polishes) so that kids are confident about their cleaning work.

☐ **465. KITCHEN TOOLS.** When children become interested in cooking, make a list of skills they can learn with your help. Post it on the inside of a kitchen cupboard door. Keep a separate list for each child since the older ones will learn more skills. The skills include the use of knives and parers, the mixer, the food processor or blender, the dishwasher, the food disposal, the cook top, cooking pans with special finishes, the oven, the microwave, and the refrigerator and freezer. Teach how to clean appliances. Expect cooks to leave the kitchen in better condition than they found it—a good motto for all family members.

☐ **466. SEWING MACHINE.** This useful tool is sometimes a mystery to everyone but Mom. Start with simple instructions and an interesting project. Don't start with mending or strips of fabric for practice; actually make something at the first lesson. A bag for balls or laundry can be made from a large rectangular piece of fabric. Show how to hem the sides together and hem the ends for a drawstring. Let a child make a simple nightie out of two pieces of flannel. Sew the front and back together at the shoulders and sides; leave arm holes unfinished and sew a drawstring neckline. When a child starts sewing from patterns, get an expandable file for labelling and sorting them.

SECTION 4: TOGETHERNESS TASKS FOR ALL THE FAMILY

Working as a team can be fun, yielding a wonderful sense of family togetherness that gives opportunities for talking, laughing, and learning.

☐ **467. WEED-FREE.**   Once or twice each year have a weeding contest. Use string to section off the lawn. Make as many sections as there are family members but make smaller sections for smaller children. Show the difference between weeds and grass. Show how to pull a weed to get the root. Then, give each one a bag and a section of the lawn to weed. After fifteen minutes, stop and count up how many weeds each has pulled; each one is worth a point. The biggest weed and the smallest weed are worth an extra point. Continue, in fifteen-minute intervals, until the lawn is weed-free.

☐ **468. PAINTING.**   Even the youngest child can help on a painting project, whether it is a fence or a wall. Old clothes and paint remover are essentials. Let younger kids do low, out-of-the-way spots; let older ones work on ladders; parents get the middle. When you've selected the painting project, let everyone guess how long it will take to do a good job. Try not to work more than ninety minutes at a time. Let younger children help with both the set up and the clean up. Talk about the proper use of the brush, the way to hold the brush so that paint doesn't run onto your hands, and how to avoid spills, how to mask off certain areas, how to clean brushes. You may want to buy some cheap small brushes for little children. When you're finished, have a family discussion as to how you did and what you might paint another time.

☐ **469. THE MESSY CLOSET.**   Each participant guesses how many minutes the project will take and writes down his estimate. Then, everyone helps remove the contents of the overflowing closet or cupboard. One washes shelves, one washes the floor, one cuts new shelf paper, and one installs it. Together decide what to toss and what to store elsewhere. One delivers those items and the cleaning equipment to their appropriate places; others put back the contents. Who was the best guesser? You may be surprised how quickly this job gets done and how much fun it is.

☐ **470. COMPOST PILE.**   Leaves, grass and other vegetable materials make a great compost pile and a good two-person job. First, make a cylindrical container from seven feet of four-foot-wide, 12–14 gauge wire fencing. Place leaves, grass, and garden and vegetable trimmings inside the cage. When it is eighteen inches in depth, add two inches of soil and a handful of nitrogen fertilizer. Keep it slightly moist and continue to fill. Every other week, mix and toss the contents. This is easy when done from a ladder. It is usually ready in about six weeks, but weather conditions and materials used may make this time vary. You'll know when it's ready when it is soft to the touch and has a good earthy odor. It's fun to spread, and you'll feel good about recycling garden debris.

☐ **471. FRONT DOOR CHAIRPERSON.**   The entrance to a home can be made inviting when two work together on front door beautification. This can involve the weekly care and watering of a plant at the door, or it can entail making a seasonal door decoration. Each week the porch and steps can be swept and the front door dusted or polished. Each month the hardware can be polished and the porch light washed.

☐ **472. ROOM-A-DAY.**   Who says the house has to be cleaned all on one day? Do it a room at a time. Spend just twenty minutes with as many helping as possible. One takes everything off furniture tops, another delivers items to other rooms, another dusts, another vacuums. Everyone sees how fast it can be done.

☐ **473. SHINY SHOES.**   Teaching a child about shoe shining also encourages good care of shoes. Perhaps a child will want to take on this job as a regular task or a special paid one. But you can't just turn a child loose with polish and shoes. The workbench is a good place for this project. Teach it in five steps: (1) spreading newspaper on which to work; (2) cleaning the shoes of dirt; (3) polishing the shoes, using the correct color and polishing the edges of the sole and heels only if appropriate; (4) buffing or putting on a polish coat; (5) cleaning up and returning shoes to owner's closet.

☐ **474. WINDOW TWINS AND TRIPLETS.** The sometimes tedious task of window washing becomes near-fun with kids helping. Work on one window at a time, using division of labor. It's easy to see if your work is really good when you do both sides of the window simultaneously. If there are two workers (twins), you take the top of the window, and the child takes the bottom. Do this inside and out. When you think it's clean, check each other's work for missed places. If there are three on the project (triplets), you'll probably do the outside and the kids the inside, working at the same time.

☐ **475. WET WORK.** Car washing is fun when done together on a hot, sunny day. Everyone wears bathing suits and gets soaked while completing the job. First, vacuum the seats, carpet, and trunk. Then turn on the water and let a short child specialize in tires, and another wash the top, another do the body, as another washes windows inside and out. Let one child climb inside and read a book aloud or to herself while others work. Be sure to alternate the privileged position of reader every ten minutes.

☐ **476. LET'S SWITCH.** Bed making can get tiresome so try switching for a few weeks. Let children make the folks' bed and parents make kids' beds. Surprise a child by putting an animal under the covers or a message where the toes go. Be prepared for things in your bed!

☐ **477. TRADING STAMPS.** Few folks like to stick the stamps in the books. Assign this job to a child with the understanding that one out of each ten books is hers. That way, when you obtain the item you're saving for, she gets a smaller item, too. Show her how to use a sponge to wet the adhesive, rather than using her tongue. Look over the catalog regularly and pick out items you'd both like.

☐ **478. HUMAN CHAIN.** Bringing in the groceries, filling the firewood stack, and doing similar tasks can involve the whole family in a human chain, carefully handing (or tossing) the items from one to another to accomplish the job quickly and have some fun at the same time.

☐ **479. GARAGE DAY.** When the job can't be put off any longer, have an official garage day. Even the youngest can help. Move everything out of the garage. Clean (sweep or wash) the floor. Let young children sit on a table and sort out nuts and bolts into tool boxes. Make shelving out of planks and concrete blocks. Organize items for recycling. Give to a rummage sale or throw away items that haven't been used in the last five years or items that don't have a future use. For a decorative touch, put travel posters on the walls. Before putting the car back in, set up a table and chairs and have lunch in this spiffy room!

★

SECTION 5: TOGETHERNESS TASKS FOR PRESCHOOLERS

Working *with* a young child lets you accomplish your tasks and still be together. At this age, work is really fun. Be sure to give praise for good work, talking more about what is done right than what is not. Why not applaud yourselves after each task!

☐ **480. WASTEBASKETS.** Show where the wastebaskets are in the house, omitting any that might have dangerous objects in them. Then, give the worker a large plastic bag and ask her to dump refuse into it. Explain that she should dump it and not pick it out, in case of sharp objects in the trash. She doesn't need to carry the bag; she can just drag it around. Help her put her findings in a rubbish can.

☐ **481. WASHBOWLS.** It's fun to play with water, so get the job of cleaning bathroom washbowls done at the same time. You need a little bench or sturdy box, an old towel, and a sponge or brush. Show your worker the washbowls to be cleaned. The first time show him how to turn water on and off, scrub, and dry with the towel. At the same time, you can be cleaning the rest of the bathroom or working nearby.

☐ **482. LITERARY LAUNDRY.** Show how to fold simple items. Make laundry time into book-listening time. Borrow cassette books from the library and listen as you work. It makes work go faster for both of you. Then, ask for the services of "Mr. (or Ms.) Speedy." Have fun running with stacks of laundry and delivering them to the right places in the house.

☐ **483. MATCHING FLATWARE.** Toddlers can take part in emptying the dishwasher by putting away the flatware as you do the other items. Show them the different sizes of forks and spoons and how to be careful with knives. They quickly learn to put the small forks with the small forks, the large spoons with the large spoons, and so on. This job gives them a good feeling of achievement.

☐ **484. HAND VAC.** Small vacuums are ideal for small children! Let your preschooler be in charge of certain vacuuming jobs that use the small vac: the car, the dog's bed, big chairs, around the edges of a room. Explain safety practices first, of course.

☐ **485. THE BROKEN TOY.** When a toy is repairable, let the child-owner participate in the repair job. This makes a child more careful and appreciative of his possessions and gives him the satisfaction of knowing how to fix things.

★

SECTION 6: TOGETHERNESS TASKS FOR THE GRADE SCHOOL SET

Working *with* a grade-schooler gives you opportunities to talk and also allows a child to appreciate the amount of work that goes into making home a pleasant place. Give more responsibility here and also be sure to give praise to good and willing workers!

☐ **486. SHINE ON!** When it's time to wash and shine the kitchen floor, let the team be a parent and a child. Divide the work: moving chairs and the dog bowl; getting out the pail, detergent, polish and mop; using the mop or the squeegee; putting on the wax and spreading it. Or, you can divide the room in half and see whose half comes out the shiniest. You'll find that kids are less apt to track in mud or leave spills on the floor when they've been part of the clean-up crew.

☐ **487. TUMMY BUFFING.** When floors need shining, let kids be human buffs! You might want to join them. Each person has a towel to lie on and a mitten for each hand. Scoot around on the floor, using hands only for propelling. Play Follow the Leader, going along the edges of the room. Play tag and see how fast the buffing gets done.

☐ **488. INVENTORY.**   Making a household inventory can be educational and fun, while also being very useful. In a large notebook, list the major items in each room. The parent may know the approximate value of each item, but let the child guess. It helps her understand the cost of home furnishings and other items of value. Work neatly, date the inventory and let the child cosign as inventory maker. Take photos of valuable items and label them to match the inventory. Store the inventory in a fireproof box or other safe place.

☐ **489. RAINBOW LOGS.**   This project, done by parent and child, gives joy to all the family. First, roll newspapers tightly and tie into log-sized bundles. Next, soak them for at least a week in this solution: For each gallon of water add 1 cup of salt and 1 tablespoon of copper sulfate (available at the drugstore). Thoroughly dry logs and then enjoy the bright green and blue flames for hours.

☐ **490. FLAG CHAIRPERSON.**   With one child helping, make a place to hang the American flag. You can make a pole and embed it in cement, or you can attach a flagpole holder to the house. Read about the history of our flag, when to fly it, ways to display it, how to care for it, and the rules of courtesy and respect. Let kids work together for a week as flag co-chairpersons, raising, lowering, and folding the flag. Consider spotlighting your flag so that it can be raised at night.

☐ **491. MEASURING.**   You can show a child how to measure without a ruler or tape measure. This is useful in many household tasks and when shopping. Measure your thumb and your child's thumb from the knuckle joint to the tip of the finger. This will give you an at-hand inch measurement. Do the same from fingertips to elbow. Then measure your step length this way: using a twenty-foot string or a tape measure, mark off two hundred feet on level ground or a sidewalk. Walk the course several times, noting how many steps you take. If you cover the course in one hundred steps, your step length is two feet. Now you can use your step length to measure distances, simply by counting steps. Measure some common household items using just fingers, arms, and steps.

☐ **492. OLD-FASHIONED POMANDERS.** To keep closets fresh, show kids how to make these good-smelling hang-ups. They also make great gifts. For each one you'll need a thin-skinned apple, *many* whole cloves, 3 teaspoons of cinnamon, 3 teaspoons of powdered arrowroot (available at the drugstore), a ribbon, and some plastic wrap. You may want to buy a quantity of cloves at a wholesale grocery. Start at the stem end of the apple and insert rows of cloves as close together as possible until the apple is completely covered. Then, roll it in the cinnamon and arrowroot, wrap it in plastic wrap, and let stand for two weeks. Finally, dust it off and tie on a ribbon, making a loop so the pomander can hang in a closet or bathroom.

☐ **493. WEEKEND CHEF.** First, talk about the elements of a nutritious lunch. Then, let your worker make lunch for the entire family each Saturday or Sunday for a month. Encourage creativity and be sure to eat what's set before you! While eating, talk about good lunches, so that you can shop for the right foods for the following weeks.

☐ **494. SCHOOL LUNCH CHAIRPERSON.** When grocery shopping, get lunch supplies for the week: bags, bread and fillings, fruits, cottage cheese, treats, napkins. Then, on a Sunday, let the school lunch chairperson make, wrap, and freeze all the sandwiches for the week. Yes, everything from tuna salad to peanut butter and jam! Don't add lettuce ahead of time. Then, on school day mornings, the worker quickly puts the elements of lunch in each box or bag.

☐ **495. BUG HUNT.** Once a month, give your helper a jar and together search the inside and the outside of the house for insects. Look for ants, spiders, worms, tiny mites under leaves, and flying creatures. Put bugs in the jar and identify them. (You may have to take them to the garden shop to find out whether the bugs are friendly or destructive.) For harmful bugs, talk about the importance of cleanliness and the use of insecticides and other safe methods of discouraging them. If you use insecticides, be sure to explain the necessity of careful application and definitely keep them out of reach of younger children.

☐ **496. MENU MAKER.** Plan a week of meals with the help of a child, letting him include his favorites. Let him make a shopping list from these menus and help with the marketing. Look at the register tape and find the most and least expensive items. Decide if there are good alternatives to expensive foods. Let another child help the following week.

★

SECTION 7: TOGETHERNESS TASKS FOR TEENS

In a few years this child will be on her own, so here's an opportunity for good work together and good conversation together. Stress the joy of achievement and the importance of thoroughness. Don't forget plenty of appreciation!

☐ **497. STICKER CUPBOARDS.** Using the popular stick-on notes, label cupboards, drawers, and closets that need to be cleaned. This is a job that you might want to pay for: twenty-five cents for a drawer, fifty cents for a cupboard, and so on. For example, write on the label, "Clean by next Monday for 35 cents." The plan works this way. The worker removes everything, washes out the area, and measures and cuts new shelf paper if necessary. A parent sorts out the contents, getting rid of the unwanted items. Parent and child together put the contents back.

☐ **498. TEAMS.** Team up a teen with a younger child to make sandwiches, wash a car, clean a room, or rake leaves. This helps the older child appreciate the younger, promotes conversation, and gives the older one the opportunity to learn how to be a good co-worker while also being "in charge" with kindness and patience. After two children have worked together as a team, talk with each privately to find out the strong points of the team. Occasionally have a team of three. If you need to have a team chairperson, be sure to rotate that responsibility.

☐ **499. SATURDAY OFFICE.** Sometimes a parent has to go into the office on a weekend. Take along a teen-ager, explain the assignment that makes the trip necessary, show how to unlock and get in, tell them who else might be there and how to act at the office, and point out any areas that are off limits. Give the child some interesting work that she can do (calculating, filing) and some routine work, such as making copies and collating. Allow her some freedom to look around the place. On the way home, talk about the job and her own job aims.

☐ **500. SURPRISE TEAM.**   When any family surprise is planned, like a hidden birthday cake or a surprise party, have a teen on your team. Explain why you are keeping it a secret and how to do so. Let him help with the shopping, pick up the cake, and join in the hoax of setting up a fake event as a cover for the surprise.

☐ **501. FAMILY HISTORIAN.**   Teens today are taking a greater interest in their roots. Let a teen work with you to put together a family history through pictures and words. Go back through the years to remember special trips, family homes, outstanding achievements, and funny happenings. Help the historian make copies of the family history for each family member. (See chapter 8, section 9, for more ideas on preserving the family heritage.)

★

SECTION 8: INCENTIVES AND ENTREPRENEURS

These ideas encourage kids to get tasks done and to think of ways to help on their own—the beginning of the entrepreneurial spirit!

☐ **502. WORK MOTTOES.**   Each month, put on the bulletin board an inspiring or humorous motto. Have the kids be on the lookout for mottoes and let them do the lettering. To get you started, here are some for the first few months: (1) "Wishing almost never makes it so, but wishing and working almost always does." (2) "There is no limit to the good you can do if you don't care who gets the credit." (3) "Diamonds are just little chunks of coal that stuck to their job." (4) "Footprints in the sands of time are not made by sitting down." (5) "When all is said and done, sometimes more is said than done." (6) "Never wrestle with a pig—you both get dirty and the pig loves it." (7) "If at first you don't succeed, try again. If at second you don't succeed, go play for a while, then try again." (8) "How come there's never time to do it right, but there's always time to do it over?" (9) "Experience is what you get when you didn't get what you wanted."

503. IT TAKES EVERYONE. Find in a magazine or newspaper a picture of a house, an active family, or another pleasant scene. Mount this on a piece of cardboard and then cut it into as many pieces as there are family members. Assuming that each family member has a few daily tasks, tell each one that when his tasks are finished he should tack on the bulletin board his part of the picture. As others finish their jobs, they will add parts to the picture. It takes everyone to finish in order to have a complete picture. Let kids find suitable pictures and change them every week.

504. THE WEATHER'S FINE. On separate pieces of paper, draw a picture of a thermometer tube for each member of the family. Color the ball at the bottom red and divide the remainder of the tube into seven sections, for the days of the week. Tack these pictures side by side on the bulletin board along with the list of who does what chores. When a child or adult has done his assigned tasks for the day he fills in one section using a red marker. It's good for kids to know that they aren't the only workers and that sometimes parents don't get everything done either. Before you can go on to the next day's work, you have to finish the previous day's tasks and fill in that section of the thermometer.

505. HOLIDAY CHARTS. Younger workers respond to the incentive of a seasonal chart that lets them add to a bulletin board picture when they have finished their chores. For example, for the month of February put on the bulletin board a cupid and cut out a supply of hearts. For each job done, a child gets to tack up a heart with his name and the task on it. Use different themes, appropriate to the month: for Easter, a paper basket and paper eggs to tack on top; for May, a May basket with flowers to add; for July, an American flag with stars to go in the corner; for September, a tree with colorful leaves to add; for October, a fence with many pumpkins to add on top; for Thanksgiving, a turkey with colorful paper tail feathers to pin on; for December, a Christmas tree with ornaments to hang.

506. ENVELOPE SURPRISES. Use up miscellaneous envelopes with this idea. Write on separate pieces of paper thirty different things your kids enjoy: a trip to the park, ice cream after lunch, staying up thirty minutes late, a bubble bath, calling Grandma, borrowing the family car for an evening, a movie and supper out. Seal these into separate envelopes and put them in a basket. The first child finished with daily tasks gets to choose and open an envelope. As the month proceeds, kids can trade envelopes. The child can ask for the reward at a mutually agreed-upon time.

☐ **507. COMMON GOAL.** Decide on something that the entire family would like: a small boat, a weekend trip, a new stereo. Set a one- to four-month goal for earning it, this way: Give each child three tasks to do each day and three additional ones for the weekend. Depending on the number of kids and the cost of the goal, assign a monetary amount to each task. For example, say you are saving for a $200 stereo the family will enjoy. You have two children who each do three chores a day and three extra each weekend. This totals a possible forty-eight chores a week, for which you will contribute fifty cents for each one completed. The more tasks completed, the faster the goal is achieved. You can keep track of the mounting sum on a chart, or you can actually put the money in a sealed container. Personal pride of accomplishment, peer pressure, and adult encouragement combine to get the work done. Parents should set tasks for themselves too, so that their part is more than just supplying the money!

☐ **508. WHAT THIS HOUSE NEEDS IS . . .** In early summer have a family talk about something the house needs: a patio, a newly painted front door, big pillows for the family room, better storage for games or toys. Let everyone contribute ideas on home improvement. Decide which ones are the most important. Work together to achieve some but also let a willing older child take on the responsibility for doing one on his own.

☐ **509. TO PAY OR NOT TO PAY.** Let's face it, money is often an incentive. Every child over five should have an allowance that just barely covers his expenses and also permits small savings for family gifts or a special treat. But the allowance should not be so big as to permit extravagances. The regular daily tasks assigned a child are done without pay, as part of family life. However, there can be a list of additional, paying jobs that a child may volunteer to do when in need of extra funds. Start such a list and post it on the family bulletin board so that it's always available for your entrepreneurs.

☐ **510. STARTING A BUSINESS.** Work with older children to start a business. This might be pet care for travelers, flower arranging, baby-sitting, rubbish hauling, car washing, lawn cutting and weeding, handyman jobs (minor repairs and painting), cupboard cleaning, helping at parties, making and delivering meals for senior citizens, marketing, gift purchasing and wrapping. Discuss responsibilities, expenses, skills, and other factors at the outset. Help the entrepreneur give a name to the business and publicize it among neighbors and friends.

SEVEN

SPECIAL SITUATIONS

ut of the ordinary occasions often bring out the best in both parents and children as they interact in circumstances that require persistence and creativity.

★

★

SECTION 1: WHEN IT'S SATURDAY MORNING AND YOU WANT TO SLEEP!

☐ **511. SATURDAY TOYS.** With child-help, select a box of really interesting toys and put it out of daily circulation. Then, after the kids are asleep Friday night, set it out for play the next morning. Place on the kitchen table the cereal, fruit, and dishes for the kids' breakfast so that they can easily serve themselves. When you're up and ready to do things together, have the kids pack up the toys, and you put them back on the high shelf. Change the toys each month or so.

☐ **512. CARD TABLE HOUSE.** Leave a card table and an old sheet in the play area. Tell children the night before that they may make a playhouse by putting the sheet over the card table. Suggest that it can be an igloo, a cave, a condo, a school—whatever they choose. Leave crayons or marking pens to decorate the sheet and blunt scissors for cutting windows or doors. This may become such a favorite activity that you'll want to provide a second sheet.

☐ **513. SATURDAY TRAIL.** Make a picture treasure hunt on three-by-five-inch cards (so you can use it over and over). Let the clues include the things you want kids to do: On the floor next to the child's bed put a picture of a mouth of teeth, which means brush your teeth; at the washbowl put a picture of a dog which means to feed the pets. In the dogfood bag put the next card: a picture of a bed, meaning to make your bed. Continue with pictures of a cereal bowl, clothes, a book—whatever your child can safely do on his own. Each time you use the cards put them in a different order and add one different card. About ten clues will get you an additional hour of sleep.

☐ **514. SATURDAY-ONLY VIDEO.** So that you know your kids won't be looking at mindless TV shows and commercials, provide a good video cassette for viewing. Set it up the night before so it is easy to start. Put a stack of crafts and games on the floor in front of the TV, so that kids can do two things at once.

★

SECTION 2: WHEN YOU'RE ENTERTAINING—WHAT TO DO WITH THE KIDS?

The answer is to include them in preparations and also provide activities for them.

☐ **515. THE COUNTDOWN.** Make two lists. The first is of all the things that must be done before the party: get house ready, set table, arrange flowers and games, make various foods. Ask children which ones they'd like to help you accomplish. Do many of these the day before the party and others the morning of the event. Then make a second list: the countdown to party time. This list will be a chronology of tasks to be done during the last two hours before the party. It might look like this:

> 4:00—Put meatloaf in the oven.
> 4:15—Kids' baths, with a story.
> 4:45—Get partially dressed, with kid-help.
> 5:15—Toss salad while children have light supper.
> 5:25—(Or earlier) Meatloaf out.
> 5:30—Finish dressing while talking to kids about party duties and guests.
> 5:45—Bring out prepared appetizers; put bread in oven.
> 5:55—Start microwave for vegetable; put ice in glasses.

Then note what must be done during appetizer-eating time: slice meat, put other items on buffet, pour water. This countdown takes the hassle out of last-minute work and makes kids feel involved in family entertaining.

☐ **516. MINI-PARTY.** Before the guests arrive for dinner, feed the children. As you prepare the dinner, set aside small portions for them. Ask how they like the party foods. You may find that the rice needs more spice or the cake requires whipped cream. If testing the supper isn't possible, prepare them a simple supper, such as macaroni and cheese with fruit salad. Surprise children by letting them have their supper on the "good" china.

☐ **517. VALET.** When you're getting dressed for your party or for going out, let a child be your helper. It's educational for him to see how Father chooses shoes to go with slacks or what jewelry and cosmetics Mother picks to go with her dress. Let him assist by bringing you certain items. This gives you the opportunity to talk before a time of separation.

☐ **518. DOORMAN.**   Let the oldest child be the official doorman, greeting the guests, taking their coats, and walking them into the living room or family room. Practice with younger children and give some suggestions as to what they might say. If possible, let them dress in keeping with the guests: jeans, suit, party dress, costume.

☐ **519. SERVING PERSON.**   While beverages are being served by older children or a parent, let a younger child serve the cheese and crackers. If a child has helped make the appetizer or knows what is in it and has tasted it, she can easily recommend it to guests. Older children can tidy up after the appetizers and put leftovers away and glasses in the dishwasher. You can hire children with later bedtimes to do the entire clean up. This lets them earn a little money while leaving you free to enjoy your guests and relax afterward.

☐ **520. SEEN, NOT HEARD.**   When your party is not a family event, work with children in advance to prepare an interesting evening for them. A surprise book from the library, a new cut-out activity book, a short list of approved TV shows, a game to play or a video cassette—these fill the time before bed. Make a little list of the possibilities. An older child can be in charge of the bedtime activities. Let older children take turns at being in charge so that you aren't bothered with petty grievances. For a very special party, you might have a relative or sitter take charge. Be sure to tell children that you want to tell about your party in the morning and you also want to hear what they have done. Give praise for good help and good behavior.

★

SECTION 3: WHEN A CHILD NEEDS SPECIAL RECOGNITION

☐ **521. PINK NOTES.**   Find bright pink note paper and envelopes (or any color that catches the eye). When a child has been especially good or thoughtful, write a short note and put it on his pillow. Pink notes increase a child's self-esteem and often get saved and reread.

☐ **522. GRAB BAG.** Keep out of reach a bag of inexpensive toys or collected giveaways. When you want to reward a child, let him close his eyes, reach in, and grab. These could be a marking pen, a yo-yo, a children's magazine, a coin purse, a little bag of nuts, or a bookmark.

☐ **523. BEDTIME CHIEF.** If you have more than one child, let one be in charge of bedtime, choosing the last game to play, the music for bathtime, a snack, the book to be read, and how many minutes (one to fifteen) they can stay up late. This makes her feel special.

☐ **524. A TOAST.** At mealtime, propose a serious complimentary toast about a child. Tell about his good qualities and good things done in the past. Toast with water or milk, clicking glasses together. See that you don't toast one child more than another.

☐ **525. SHARING.** Sometimes a phone call makes a child feel special. Encourage her to use the phone to share what she's doing with a relative or friend. She doesn't have to have done something in particular; just having the opportunity to talk makes her feel special. Let it be a one-on-one private conversation. And when a parent has to be working or out of town, a phone call to a child just to say you are thinking of her is very important.

☐ **526. JUST-BECAUSE PICTURE.** Make a quick sketch of a child and put it on the bulletin board or refrigerator. Don't worry about how artistic it is. Include the child's name, the dog, the boat he built, or whatever he's done recently. Put a big star or the word "WOW" on the picture. We all feel good when we see ourselves in a picture!

★

SECTION 4: WHEN A CHILD NEEDS TO BE CORRECTED

Today we realize that there are far better ways to discipline a child than to spank him. The object of discipline is to make a child *think* about what he has done and how he could act more responsibly. Spanking doesn't provide a good opportunity to think. It merely makes the child resentful and teaches him that hitting is a proper way of acting. While spanking is a quick form of discipline, research shows that it doesn't bring the right results in most cases, thus the parent has to spank again. More thoughtful means of discipline may take more time at first, but they are better at molding behavior.

☐ **527. THE "NO P/S" RULE.** How many children's arguments get escalated when one pushes another and he shoves back! Make a rule against pushing and shoving: No P/S! The one who pushes loses the argument, no matter what has happened before. If the other shoves back, he loses too.

☐ **528. THE CONTRACT.** Some children respond to business deals or contracts for behavior changes. Work on a large, lined piece of paper. First, decide what it is that you want the child to do: improve a failing grade, stop fighting with a brother, come home on time. Then, decide what you will do in return: cancel part of a punishment, return a confiscated favorite toy, permit a later bedtime. (You should use kid-input on this.) Now, write up the agreement as a contract: "I, John Jones, do hereby promise that if my daughter Lindsay will abide by the family curfew for one month, I will resume letting her use the family car one weekend night each week. Signed this twelfth day of May by . . . " Both parent and child sign the contract. Contracts can be simple or involved, depending on the child's age and the issue. But somehow, putting it in writing is often sufficient to correct the unwanted behavior.

☐ **529. THE THINKING BENCH.** This calms a toddler and lets her start to reason her way to better ways of solving arguments or problems. Have a small step stool or bench in the laundry room or kitchen. When a child is naughty, seat her firmly on the bench and set a timer for a few minutes. Say no more than that you want her to think about what she did and what she should have done. Stay nearby but be quiet. When the time is up, ask her to share her thoughts. Help her to verbalize what she should have done. Forgive and forget. Give hugs and send her back to play.

☐ **530. CHOPSTICKS.**   If you have a lawn, this idea will get it weeded and at the same time give a child quiet time to think over the wrong thing he's done. Using chopsticks and string, stake out a six-foot square on the lawn. Show the child the difference between grass and weeds and how to pull weeds to get the root. Fifteen to thirty minutes of weeding should give a child age five and upward the opportunity to think about correcting his behavior.

☐ **531. OPPOSITE CORNERS.**   When two kids argue, put them in opposite corners of the room, each facing her own corner. Set a timer for three to five minutes of quiet time to think about how they can settle the argument without parental intervention. Then, still not facing each other, let them talk of better ways of handling the matter. If they can't solve it themselves, step in with some ideas. You'll find that not having to face each other ends the problem of mean faces and intimidating body language.

☐ **532. A LITTLE NOTE.**   For the child who reads, a short note is sometimes more effective than other discipline. Express your disappointment in simple words, give some suggestions as to how he could do better, and encourage him to think about what he's done. Reassure him that you love him no matter what.

★

SECTION 5: WHEN IT'S TIME TO DISCUSS DRUGS

Eighty-five percent of kids over age ten try drugs, primarily marijuana and alcohol. Don't wait; start home education when children are young. Remind children often that you love them too much to permit even the smallest drug use. Be alert, aware, listening, compassionate, and, most of all, firm. Entire books have been written on this subject; these few ideas should get you started thinking about how to protect your child.

☐ **533. INFORMATION, PLEASE.** Communication is your most powerful tool in the drug war. Inform yourself first. Write to these sources for free information. Tell your youngster what you are doing and let him help address and stamp the envelopes. You will receive up-to-date, authoritative information for all age groups. Read it first, then share it with your youngster.

- Get Involved, Box 1706, Rockville, MD 20859.
- National Clearinghouse for Drug Abuse Information (NCDAI), P.O. Box 416, Kensington, MD 20795.
- National Federation of Parents for Drug-Free Youth, 8730 Georgia Avenue, Suite 200, Silver Springs, MD 20910.
- National Institute on Drug Abuse, 5600 Fishers Lane, Rockville, MD 20857.

☐ **534. A FIRST CONVERSATION.** Ask children what they know about drugs. Without asking for names, ask if they know kids who use drugs. Ask if they know why kids use drugs or what would make them use them. Make your disapproval very strong and include some facts from your own reading. Tell kids you'll do everything in your power to keep them safe from drugs.

☐ **535. A SECOND CONVERSATION.** Talk openly about the symptoms of drug use: lack of communication with parents, new and secretive friendships, mysterious phone calls, disrespectful and critical behavior, messy appearance, apathy, low grades, dropping out of extracurricular activities, need for more money, not feeling good, pink eyes or eyes sensitive to light, mood swings, and numbness. (These are usually associated with marijuana.) Point out that some of these symptoms don't appear immediately, but some often do. Talk about how these symptoms affect family life.

☐ **536. SETTING THE STANDARD IN THE HOME.** It's hard to convince kids of the damage done by smoking, alcohol, and other drugs if parents use these drugs themselves and sometimes let kids use them because it's "cute." Frankly discuss together any drugs that you or other friends' parents or other close friends or relatives use. Talk about groups that help people get off drugs and how much easier it is not to start. Sometimes kids respond to the challenge of stopping drug use if a parent agrees to stop his own harmful habit. Share the cruel facts on how drugs cause tremendous unhappiness and shorten lives.

☐ **537. START WITH PARENTS OF FRIENDS.** Since drug use often starts early, form a support group when kids are in about the third grade. With your youngster's help, make a list of fifteen friends and arrange a meeting of those parents. If possible, show a current film on drug abuse. Draw up some rules of behavior and let each family explain them to their kids. Meet again in two weeks to assess your progress and have regular meetings thereafter. Add families as your child makes new friends. As kids grow older, don't be vigilantes, but don't be taken in by denials of drug use. Say and mean these words: "If you see my child breaking the rules, tell me. I need to know."

☐ **538. IF THERE ARE DRUG USERS AMONG A CHILD'S FRIENDS.** Go a step further and start a larger parents group. You may wish to do it through your school's parent-teacher organization. Call on local educational and social agencies that can help with information and speakers. This parents' group can later consider other youth problems, such as suicide and the stress of homework, jobs, discipline, and getting into college.

☐ **539. FIND THE CAUSES.** One-on-one discussions with children can permit you to show them ways to solve problems rather than trying to escape them. Since boredom often leads to drug use, time spent with children by parents is an important factor both in the evenings and on weekends. Building a child's self-esteem combats both drug use and suicide (currently suicide is the second leading cause of teen deaths). Getting kids involved in community groups that have good adult leadership can provide wholesome activities, a feeling of self-worth, and drug-free friends.

☐ **540. REGAIN SOCIAL CONTROL.** Many parents try to please their children by providing a keg of beer or even drugs for kids' parties. Call the parents where a party is to be held. Ask these two questions: "Will you be there during the entire party? Are you serving liquor?" Encourage other parents to be good chaperones, seeing that kids don't leave the party and later return (often a sign of drug use). When your child entertains, require a written guest list and see that there aren't party crashers. Keeping parties small helps, too.

☐ **541. WHEN A CHILD IS ON HARD DRUGS.** Tell your child that the school and the community will help, but when it comes right down to it, the decision of being drug-free is his alone. State, however, that you plan to do everything in your power to help. Emphasize that drugs are dangerous as well as illegal. Tell the child that if necessary you will take a leave from your job to help him, or you will enter him in a treatment center. Emphasize how serious you think this is and how firm you will be because you don't want him to become addicted or insane or to die. Set guidelines for behavior and stick to them. Tell your child you will call the parents of his drug-using friends. You will separate him from other kids. You will see that he is always in school or where he says he will be. You will work to find out who the pushers are and notify the police. You will take away his driver's license until he's clean. You will take his credit cards and make him account for all his cash. You will insist on knowing where he is day and night and who he's with and what they're doing. Show him that you are serious. Plan on doing all this for at least a sixty-day period and then reevaluate. Most of all, love that child and *tell him so*.

★

SECTION 6: WHEN A CHILD ISN'T FEELING WELL

☐ **542. BELLRINGER.**   Supply a sick child with a big bell to ring when she requires your attention immediately. If it's a sick stomach, put an "upchuck bowl" on the night table to save cleanups. These give the child a feeling of security when you aren't right with her.

☐ **543. CHEERY PILLOWCASE.**   While confined to bed, let a child make his own special pillowcase. Use a tray covered with newspaper for a bed workspace. Talk about what he plans to design. Then let him decorate a plain pillowcase with indelible marking pens.

☐ **544. TUMMY TV.**   When a child feels like drawing, give her a very long roll of paper the width of a shoebox (or other similarly sized box). You may have to paste several pieces of paper together, or get a roll of butcher paper at the meat market. Ask the child to make a long continuous drawing. It can have a theme or tell a story. Put tabs at both ends of the drawing. Next, cut two widely separated, parallel slits in the shoebox bottom. Feed the long drawing through the slits from the inside of the box. Holding the tab, pull the paper through to show the drawing. Make up a story to tell as the pictures appear. Do it again and tell a different story. Later, the child may wish to add more pictures to her tummy TV.

☐ **545. SEWING CARDS.**   Make these with cardboard and colored yarn. Let the child outline a simple object: dog, house, himself, flower. With a sharp object, you punch holes at intervals along the lines. Then he uses the yarn and a blunt, large-eye needle or thin crochet hook to "sew" the picture.

☐ **546. WHO'S IN THE BED?**   While a child is sleeping, make Kleenex Kids this way: Wad a paper towel into a small ball, cover it with Kleenex (to make a head), and tie with a ribbon or yarn at the neck. On one, draw a face and glue on a collar or buttons. Give another an animal face. Make three or four more but don't draw on them. Hide them in the child's bed. When she awakens and finds the Kleenex Kids in her bed, she can take them apart to blow her nose or draw faces on the blank ones.

☐ **547. WHAT'S NEW.**   Each day a child isn't well, try to interest him in an activity that gets him back into his normal routine. These could be getting dressed for supper, doing some homework, making a phone call, playing with the dog, or helping a parent with a project. Don't let sick days become total TV days. As he gets better, ease him back into family life.

★

SECTION 7: WHEN THERE IS A DEATH IN THE FAMILY

☐ **548. A RELATIVE OR FRIEND.**   Let the child look at a scrapbook or photo album containing pictures of the relative, to remind her of all the good times. Talk about some of the things that happened in that person's life. Then ask if she'd like to draw a little picture of herself and that person enjoying some favorite activity. She could share this with a relative of the person that has died.

☐ **549. A CHILD.**   Talk about eternal life and the fact that this child continues to live and have interesting experiences. Don't tell a child that his friend has just "gone away." Be honest and use the regular and normal words. In daily conversation, talk about things they did together. Find out if the school would permit the planting of a tree in the child's memory. A helpful book you might want to read is *Last Week My Brother Anthony Died* (Martha Hickman, Abingdon, 1984).

☐ **550. A PET.**   Be honest; don't say the pet ran away or went to sleep (then kids will fear going to sleep). If kids want to know why, give an explanation. Say, "Sometimes a pet gets sick and cannot stay where it lives anymore. That's what happened to Chipper. But we're here and we're not leaving." Give a few non-morbid details, be non-clinical, and answer questions. Be very sympathetic. Reassure a child that he didn't do anything wrong. Perhaps you'll want to help the child plan a little memorial service. Read Genesis 1:20-25 and I John 2:25, or read Psalm 23. Let each person share a happy story about the pet. A good book about a pet cat that dies is *The Tenth Good Thing About Barney* (Judith Viorst, Macmillan, 1975).

★

SECTION 8: WHEN PARENTS HAVE TO BE AWAY

☐ **551. ENVELOPES.**   When you're going to be gone for several days, write a little message to children for each day. Put in reminders about things to do, like Scouts, Sunday school, tasks, TV shows, and a special note reminding them of your love and how happy you'll be to see them soon. Date envelopes for the days you'll be away and seal the messages inside. Put them on the kitchen table so they'll be opened each morning.

☐ **552. LATCH-KEY CHILDREN AND YOU.**   When children will be left alone at home from the end of school until a working parent comes home, the hours can be very boring and time-wasting. If possible, a parent should phone to be sure the child is safely home. Sometimes a schedule, worked out between parent and child, helps a child use the time alone productively, for example:

3:00—Puzzle and snack time
3:30—Exercise and outdoor games time
3:45—Homework
4:30—Preheat oven and set the table
4:45—Read a book
5:00—Watch TV (specify show)

A pet can provide needed companionship and be important to a latch-key child. An afterschool group activity can also help. If your child has any friends who are also latch-key children, be sure to invite them over for play sometime when you are home. Sometimes two responsible latch-key children will enjoy playing at each other's houses rather than each being in an empty house.

☐ **553. DESSERT WITH DAD.** (This works equally well when a mom is away all day and returns home after supper.) Let a child have dessert alone with Dad in the living room, dining room, or some quiet place. Talk about what happened while the child and Dad were apart. After that, go for a private walk. Let Dad read to the child as he bathes and gets ready for bed. Dad can give suggestions on what to wear the next day, read the bedtime story, and talk about things they'll do together on the weekend.

☐ **554. SURPRISE ACTIVITIES.** When a child has to amuse herself alone for more than an hour, prepare surprise activity cards. Make about ten cards, writing on each something the child would enjoy doing: read a book, make a snack, listen to a record, play with a certain toy. Fold each card and staple it shut. Put them in a bowl on a table and tell the child she should pull one out whenever she's bored or lonely. Talk about the activities she did when you return.

☐ **555. DO YOU PROMISE?** On the way to the airport, put the soon-to-be-away parent in the back seat with the kids. Parent and children start sentences with "Do you promise." A child will think of things like: "Do you promise to call us tomorrow night . . . to send me a postcard . . . to bring me a match-book . . . to think of me when you drink orange juice." A parent may say: "Do *you* promise to think of *me* when you drink orange juice . . . to think of me before you fall asleep . . . to draw a picture of something you did . . . to help Grandma make cookies . . . to give the dog a hug."

☐ **556. "WHAT I DID" LIST.**   Put a tablet of lined paper on the eating table. Let children list each day the important things they've done. Be sure to talk about these when you return home.

☐ **557. GOOD-NIGHT PHONE CALL.**   Check in with the kids by phone after supper and share something you've done. Talk about things you'll do when you return and remind them of *when* you are coming home. Ask about child activities. Give a little hint about something you'll tell tomorrow night when you call. This builds anticipation for your next call.

☐ **558. CASSETTE MESSAGES.**   Take time to make upbeat morning messages for your children. Record these and place the tape and player where children can listen to them in the morning. The tape should begin with "This is Monday" and end with "Now turn off the machine until tomorrow morning." Messages can be brief, funny, and slightly different for each day.

★

SECTION 9: WHEN TV TRIES TO TAKE OVER

If TV is taking away the time your family could be enjoying other activities, try these methods to regain control. But remember that the video camera is one of the good things about television. Now we all can be directors and producers, as the video camera takes its place in family life, in some cases replacing the ordinary camera. If you don't own one, rent or borrow one before buying so you can see if this is an activity your family will enjoy. Activities involving video camera use start with number 563.

☐ **559. MAKE A LIST.**   Set a reasonable number of hours each week for TV viewing (ten to twelve is plenty). Then, with the children, watch all regular shows the kids wish to see. Make a list of those you approve and explain your reasons for not okaying some. Let them use half of their TV time allotment on these shows. The other half can be on shows the entire family sees. Go over the TV program guide and pick out the most worthwhile programs. (One of the best ways to not over-watch TV is to turn it on for a specific program and turn it right off when the program has finished. TV should not be a continual background to all other activities.) Post the list where all can see it, look at it every few months, and keep it up-to-date. Point it out to sitters so that kids don't look at junk when you're not home.

☐ **560. CATCH THE NEWS.** But do it before or after supper. (TV *during* supper stops all good conversation.) Thirty minutes of news is all you need to keep current. Talk with children about world events. Let each family member choose a topic to follow each day of the week. See what is new on your topic. See how much more detailed the newspaper is on your subject. When a story is over, choose another one to follow.

☐ **561. TRY AN EXPERIMENT.** For a week or longer, live as if you didn't have a TV set. Listen to the radio for news, stories, and music. Use the time spent on TV doing more exciting things, such as having a family Monopoly night or a family-prepared Saturday morning breakfast. See how little you missed. When you go back to TV, you'll probably look at fewer shows! Some families have adopted the plan of TV on weekends only, except for educational specials. Encourage a child to write up this experiment for the school paper. Let her tell what she missed, what she did instead, and what she thinks about TV now.

☐ **562. CONSIDER A LOCK.** There are many devices for locking a TV so that it can't be turned on, or so that certain channels can be excluded. First try to turn off the TV when a program ends. Ask children not to turn it on except for a program from the approved list. If this doesn't work, explain that you'll be investigating a lock. If they still ignore your request, spend the money for the lock. The time saved from excessive TV viewing or watching inappropriate programs will bring the family closer together and will be worth the money.

☐ **563. A DAY AT OUR HOUSE.** On a weekend day, let each family member who knows how to use a video camera record activities at home: kids sleeping, breakfast, work projects, play, friends who stop in, errands, an excursion, cooking supper, reading, games, toy pick-up, bedtime. Look at "the day" and see if the time was spent doing interesting or boring things. If boring, plan to make some changes. Tape a similar show in a few weeks and see if the content has improved and also if kids are getting better with camera angles, panning, and other techniques.

☐ **564. HARD WORK AND PRAISE.** Use the video camera to record in some detail one work project: the building of a skateboard ramp, grass cutting and gardening, stacking firewood into a neat cord, baking and decorating a special cake, washing and polishing a car. Look at the tape with the workers and give lots of praise and appreciation.

☐ **565. FIRSTS.** There are many first-time events in family life. A videotape kept just for recording the first time something happened and added to from time to time makes memorable viewing and reminiscing for all the family. Here are some possible firsts for you to archive: first baby, first smile, first tooth, first steps, first day of school, first book a child can read alone, first bicycle ride, leaving for the first trip alone, first time to camp, first class in scouting, first party dress or long pants, first day after braces come off, first makeup-wearing occasion, first dance, first date, first time to drive the car. Include in each tape segment a view of the current day's calendar to "date" the event. Reserving one tape solely for family firsts and adding to it is a many-year project you'll treasure. When the kids are grown, they'll each want a copy of it.

☐ **566. FAMILY REUNION.** When visiting near or faraway relatives, get close-up video pictures of them and also record them at their homes and doing their favorite activities. Viewing this tape gives a child the feeling of closeness and a link to people he may not often see. If other friends and relatives have cameras, send one another regular taped sessions as a means of good communication. Best of all, the tape helps kids remember who's who in the family.

☐ **567. PARTY TIME.** A child's first party (and subsequent ones) can be captured on videotape. Make a list of the events you want taken and have a friend take the pictures without intruding on the activities. Be sure every child gets in the pictures. Just before the end of the party, show the film to all the partygoers, who will love to see themselves. (For teen party ideas using a video camera, see chapter 11, sections 1 and 2.)

★ EIGHT ★

LEARNING TOGETHER

So much learning can go on right within the home. There's no need to duplicate the work of the school. Rather, enrich a child's life by opening new vistas. Here are useful ideas for the preschool through high school years.

★*Section 1:* Vital skills
★*Section 2:* Computer basics
★*Section 3:* The three arts
★*Section 4:* The sciences and the outdoors
★*Section 5:* Civics and business
★*Section 6:* Supporting schoolwork
★*Section 7:* Religious training
★*Section 8:* Essential ethics
★*Section 9:* The family heritage

SECTION 1: VITAL SKILLS

These skills are not divided as to age, although some are for younger children. Use even the "younger" ideas on older children to be sure they haven't missed learning any of the skills.

☐ **568. USING THE DICTIONARY.** Each morning at breakfast, choose a word from the dictionary and use it at breakfast. Take turns at being the one who opens the dictionary and selects a word. Use it in a sentence. See who can remember to use the word later in the day.

☐ **569. USING THE ENCYCLOPEDIA.** Even before children can read, encourage the skill of looking things up. Take turns bringing one volume to the supper table. Older children can choose a topic to read about. Let a young child open it at random and point to an entry. Read about that entry and see what all the family can learn.

☐ **570. THINKING.** Encourage mental exercises and have fun with ideas from Reid Daitzman's book *Mental Jogging* (Marek Publishers, 1980). The 365 games have no right or wrong answers, but they increase the ability to solve problems. One exercise is to list ways to make a phone stop ringing. These might be some typical answers: Answer it; don't answer it; don't pay your phone bill; cut the cord; turn the volume control to off; blow up the utility company; remove the bell; go deaf; live on an island without electricity; hook the bell to a light. With the family, see what answers you get to the following questions: What are eight things to do in a dark room? What are five things you've never said to your brother or sister? What are six things you'd say to the president of the United States? What are seven things not to say to an Eskimo?

☐ **571. VISUAL PERCEPTION.** Use these activities to exercise visual conceptualization, a child's ability to learn through seeing. (1) Let a child help in the laundry by matching socks. (2) Point out different colors in her shirts and slacks; which colors are in both? (3) Give her a length of string and tell her to find five things shorter, five longer. (4) When cooking together, let her measure ingredients. (5) Place objects or toys on the floor. Let her put them in order as to size, then group them as to color. (6) When riding in the car, name an object such as a tree. Ask her to find things that are smaller and larger.

☐ **572. VERBAL EXPRESSION.**   Try these activities, being sure to make them fun, not tests. (1) Learn some tongue twisters together. See if you can say them better at breakfast or before bed. (2) Have a conversation about familiar things: a pet, a toy, a food. Ask a child not to give one-word answers but to make a sentence. Then see if he can catch you when you don't speak in a sentence. (3) Play "What's the Word?" Let a child give simple answers to these questions: What words tell how you feel? What words tell how you look? What words tell how food tastes? (4) Read stories without pictures to develop imagination. Fairy tales or brief news stories are examples. Ask a child what he "sees" in his mind when he hears the words.

☐ **573. MEMORY BUILDING.**   Try these brainteasers. (1) The Tray Game (fun for all the family): Put a few items on a tray. All look at it, then cover it. See who can remember the items. When older children are playing, put up to twenty-five small items on the tray and have them write them down after viewing the tray for a minute. This makes a good party game, too. (2) When reading a book with your child, open it to a page, allow only a glimpse, then close the book. Let a child try to find the page. (3) Print a list of five or more words. In a second column, print the same words in a different order. Let younger children match the words. (4) Read the newspaper together. Ask a young child to look in the headlines for three letters she knows. Play again looking for four or more letters.

☐ **574. MEMORIZATION.**   It may be out of fashion, but it's still useful and fun. There are things for all ages to memorize, from nursery rhymes and bedtime prayers to the Gettysburg Address, the Twenty-third Psalm, and "Casey at the Bat." Let each family member choose something to memorize; two sentences or four poem lines is the minimum. Put a copy of the selection to be memorized where it can be seen often: on the night table, on a bathroom mirror, on a bulletin board. See who is ready to share his memory work first. Don't comment on slipups; appreciate what each has achieved.

575. MOTOR COORDINATION. Keep these learning times enjoyable: (1) Write letters of the alphabet using dots and have a child connect them. (2) Let her practice cutting with a scissors on a zigzag or curve you've drawn. (3) Make a drawing of a circle, square, or triangle. Let the child "draw" these on a table or the floor using a long piece of string. (4) While on a walk, have a child walk backwards a certain number of steps, then sideways a certain number of steps. Then, call the changes more quickly: "Two backward, four to the left, one backward, three to the right." (5) Lay a rope on the floor or ground. Have a child walk on it, trying not to "fall off." (6) Sit in the middle of the room. Take turns naming something to point at. Go faster and faster, naming items from different sides of the room.

576. CREATIVITY. Today's world includes frozen meals, animated toys, recorded books, and computer chips. All a child has to do is learn to push the right buttons. Along with learning about useful technology, encourage creativity. (1) Give a child three very different toys, such as a doll, a small truck, and a musical toy, and ask her to use them *together* in a way that is fun for her. (2) Give older children four paper clips, a colored marking pen, and a piece of paper. See what they can create. (3) Begin a story about a woman who wants to get beyond a tall concrete wall. Ask what methods she might use. Some might be a rope, a ladder, ten people sitting on each other's shoulders, dynamite, a bulldozer, or just walking around the end of the wall.

577. SPELLING QUIZ. Let grade and high school kids and parents vote on these often misspelled words. You may want to have two teams, each with one parent. The ones everyone gets wrong can be put on a three-by-five-inch card on the refrigerator door. (Answers are at the end of this section.) Decide which is correct:

1. (a) accommodate   (b) accomodate
2. (a) inoculate   (b) innoculate
3. (a) commitment   (b) committment
4. (a) erect   (b) errect
5. (a) reccomend   (b) recommend
6. (a) inadvertant   (b) inadvertent
7. (a) proceed   (b) procede
8. (a) perogative   (b) prerogative

9. (a) liaison   (b) liason
10. (a) practitioner   (b) practicioner
11. (a) irridescent   (b) iridescent
12. (a) fourty   (b) forty
13. (a) consensus   (b) concensus
14. (a) embarass   (b) embarrass
15. (a) superseed   (b) superceed

☐ **578. FOLLOWING DIRECTIONS.** Learning to do exactly what is asked and doing things in a sequence can be challenging. Practice giving directions, making them more difficult each time. One order: "Put the envelope at Dad's place at the table." Two orders: "Deliver the shirt to Cosmo's room and bring me your towel." Three orders: "Have the dog practice his trick, give him a reward, and brush him." Four orders: "Brush your teeth, wash your face, comb your hair, and change your shirt." Afterward, check to see if the child followed the directions.

☐ **579. "THINGS I KNOW" CHART FOR PRE-SCHOOLERS.** When a child will be starting preschool, make her a chart of things you'd like her to know. Little by little, help her learn these, using a star or circle to show which ones she's mastered: her name, the meanings of "no" and "yes," bathroom etiquette, how to nap or pretend to nap, dressing herself, some numbers and colors, "please" and "thank you," how to sit quietly and listen, taking turns and sharing, how to treat books with care.

☐ **580. "THINGS I KNOW" CHART FOR KINDERGAR-TENERS.** Make a chart and let your youngster check off these items. Make sure he has also mastered those in the chart above. Include complete address and telephone number, left and right, throwing and catching, following directions, sitting quietly for longer periods of time, using scissors and paste, more numbers and colors, some letters, simple table manners, and safety rules. (See chapter 9, section 1, on safety.)

☐ **581. "THINGS I KNOW" CHART FOR FIRST-GRADERS.** Like the above two charts, make a list and let the child circle the skills as she masters them: how to tell time; the use of coins; how to speak in front of a small group; how to raise her hand to ask for the teacher's attention; how to make a telephone call; doing buttons, bows, and laces; putting on outside clothing; how to bring home assignments.

☐ 582. "THINGS I KNOW" CHART FOR GRADE-SCHOOLERS.

Here's a list for you and your child to work with during the summer before she starts school: how to look up words in a dictionary; how to use the phone book and a pay telephone; how to call 911; how to put out a small fire; how to cook a simple supper; how to repair a bike tire; how to clean and bandage a small cut; how to make an outline; showing politeness to elders, courtesy to peers, and kindness to those in need; how to pump gas at a self-serve station; how to write thank you notes. Some of these are necessary for school, others for this stage of growing up.

☐ 583. THINGS TO BE LEARNED DURING HIGH SCHOOL.

Challenge your teen-ager with this list and compliment him as he learns these skills for self-sufficiency: how to change a car tire, how to write checks and keep a checkbook, how to fill out a job application, how to cook complete nutritious meals, how to make a budget and stick to it, how to clean a room and a bathroom, how to care for and value his clothes, how to take care of his health and hygiene, how to talk easily and politely with the other sex, how to manage time and plan ahead.

ANSWERS TO SPELLING QUIZ: (1)a, (2)a, (3)a, (4)a, (5)b, (6)b, (7)a, (8)b, (9)a, (10)a, (11)b, (12)b, (13)a, (14)b, (15)neither, it's supersede!

★

SECTION 2: COMPUTER BASICS

While the computer is no substitute for good thinking and reasoning, it can perform many tasks accurately and quickly. See that a child's time is balanced between the computer and other activities. Be sure that computer games don't take over and crowd out other important aspects of work and play!

☐ 584. DON'T BE INTIMIDATED.

Most experts predict that we'll need to be computer literate within the next few years. A child can have a great advantage over his elders by being familiar with and fearless at the keyboard, starting in youth. If you have a home computer, permit kids to have some time at it, playing computer games and learning what the keys do. Teach respect for this high-tech device and teach your child that it cannot be handled roughly. Make a list of simple skills or the use of certain keys. Put a star by those the child has mastered. Keep computer sessions short and happy. Of course, food and drinks should never be allowed anywhere near the computer.

□ **585. BROWSING.**   Visit a computer store and see what particularly interests your child. Beyond computer games there are an ever-growing number of instructional programs, some geared even to the very young child. These teach eye-hand coordination, familiarity with the computer, and reading, spelling, and math skills. Select the programs carefully, preferably at a dealer where you can try them out before buying. Make the purchase an important occasion and don't buy too much at one time. Peruse the instructions with the child, then turn him loose. If you selected a program at the right skill level, the child should be able to continue without much supervision by you.

□ **586. FIRST LESSONS.**   Computer use teaches children and adults some valuable lessons. Bring out these lessons for your kids:

• The computer is not smart; it just obeys your orders. If you give it the wrong orders, you will get a poor result.
• The computer allows you to check your work on the screen as you do it. It's better to check frequently, to avoid errors.
• There is a relationship between cause and effect. When you touch a computer key, you can expect to see a result on the screen.
• Do good, careful work.
• The computer is fast. We humans need to raise our speed level in order to work in harmony with a computer.
• There is nothing magic or mysterious about a computer. It does exactly the work assigned to it by its program and the person at the keyboard. There is no cause for fear.
• When we think a mistake has been made, we should look carefully at our own work to see what error we've made and not assume that the computer erred.
• The computer is genderless and both girls and boys can and must become computer literate.

☐ **587. SPECIAL HELPER.** When you are using the home computer for some purpose, bring up a chair of the right height for the child to observe your fingers on the keyboard, your work on the screen, and any papers you are using. Explain just a few simple things at first, such as how to enter data into the program, how to correct mistakes, how to save your work, how to print a copy, and how to start up and close down the computer. Allow time for the child to observe. Be patient with her questions, and if you don't know an answer, admit it and look up the answer together. When you work on the same project again, let the child be your special helper. Soon she may be able to do it without you!

☐ **588. ASSISTANT TREASURER.** If you use the computer to write checks and pay bills, a child can help you with this task and, in so doing, grasp some fundamentals of money management, starting with the rule that we can't pay out more than we take in. While you are keying in data, allow the child to enter the date and the amount of the expense item. Let him help stuff, seal, and stamp the envelopes. Make the sessions interesting and happy; when the child tires let him go on to something else. Don't make it just solid work. When it's enjoyable he'll want to help you the next time.

☐ **589. KID P.S.** When you write a letter to a relative on the home computer, let a child add a few lines as a postscript. Show the child the format of a letter: the return address and date, the salutation and proper punctuation, the body of the letter and its layout on the page, the close and signature line, the place for any postscript. At first, the child might sit in your lap with hands just resting at the bottom edge of the keyboard. When she's ready, allow her to type a few words, and you do the rest. Later, let her type it all. Some parents encourage children's drawings on letters to grandparents, but also let her dictate a message to be typed in by you.

☐ **590. COMPUTER TALK.** Current articles about computers in newspapers or magazines make for good discussions. When your child is a bit computer knowledgeable, let her invite another interested child to come over to share information and computer time. Consider subscribing to a computer magazine for kids, but look them over first.

☐ **591. SCHOOL FEEDBACK.** Once your child starts using computers in school, you can expect some feedback. Take a lively interest in the school's program; inspect the school's set up; see how you can help your child to become confident in using the new keyboard and programs. Be sure that the teacher knows about your child's home computer interest. See if your child can teach you something new on a regular basis, letting you both grow in knowledge. Remember that kids love to teach parents for a change.

☐ **592. SUBTLE SPELLING LESSONS.**   When your child is ready to write something on her own, show how easily and accurately the computer's spelling checker works and how she can correct her work without having to recopy. Tell her to especially note the correct spellings, since the spelling checker is no substitute for learning to spell. Encourage using the spelling checker each time, since typographical errors can go undetected and detract from a good paper.

☐ **593. A PICTURE IS WORTH A THOUSAND WORDS.** Thus, many accounting and financial programs include a graphing facility. Learn how this works, then teach it to your child. Apply graphing to the family budget (or the child's allowance) and see how the budget was met or overspent last month. Help a child to use graphing to show how he spends his time, how his height and weight change, or how his grades go up or down.

☐ **594. STARTING LISTS.**   One of the easiest things to commit to the computer is a "to do" list. Start your own chores list and then allow your child to do likewise. The "to do" list is easy to keep current by making additions and deletions as work is completed. The print-out can be posted or carried about as one works. Also, a list of family outings and events can be printed up in fancy type and a copy given to each family member.

☐ **595. FAMILY "MAILBOX."**   When all the family is computer literate, you may want to do as many offices do: Provide a "mailbox" facility on the computer. Messages can be left and retrieved from the office mainframe. Much the same can be done on the home computer if the unit is located where all can have easy access to it and it is left running. Simply have an open file for each family member where telephone messages, school reminders, tasks, projects, and outings can be entered. (This is a big step up from leaving messages on the refrigerator door.) The items are deleted by the owner of the mailbox after he or she has seen them. The novelty of this method will encourage good phone messages to be taken.

★

SECTION 3: THE THREE ARTS

Encourage appreciation of the harmony of music, the joys of the written word, and the beauty in art.

FOR YOUNGER CHILDREN

☐ **596. POETRY BABIES.** There's something about rhyme that amuses and soothes babies. Whether it's time for feeding, bathing, or going to sleep, don't forget poetry. You may end up reading it to yourself, too. A good book to start with is *The Oxford Book of Children's Verse* (Peter and Iona Opie, Oxford University Press, 1973); it is easily borrowed, but you'll soon want a copy for the family bookshelf.

☐ **597. HOMEMADE ORCHESTRA.** Let a child help create three instruments for no cost. Make a drum out of an old metal pot and use with wood or metal spoons (or a kitchen whisk or whisk broom to make a different sound). For shakers, put dried peas or paper clips into covered plastic containers. For a stringed instrument, stretch elastic between nails on a board. Experiment with the sounds. Let a child sing a song and accompany himself. Play a recording and let the "orchestra" play along.

☐ **598. PLASTIC CLAY.** Save clay in tightly closed plastic containers. Work paint into dull colored clay for a new look. Several colors can be blended to see how new colors are made. Let a child decide if the object made is to go back into the container or to be left out to dry. If it is to be dried, give a child interesting things to decorate her creation with, such as sand, pebbles, old jewelry, or even cereal.

☐ **599. PAINT WITH . . .** Bored with paints and crayons? Let kids paint a picture with pudding (make several flavors) on a big platter. Eat it! Or paint with water and cotton swabs on blotter paper. When it dries, paint again. Or paint on the garage floor or sidewalk with ice cubes. Or let a child sit *in* the bathtub and paint it with watercolors. Let her shower it down later after everyone's admired it.

FOR ALL CHILDREN

☐ **600. FRAME THAT ART!** Children's art often deserves a better spot for display than the refrigerator. Mount pictures on box lids or cut a rectangle out of the lid and mount the picture behind the opening. To keep a picture very flat, use two pieces of glass or plastic, put the picture between them, and mount it with mirror clips. Use a wall in the hall or family room as the art gallery. Change pictures regularly. Store good work in an artists' portfolio, which has room for many years of work. Occasionally look back at the old work and show a child how she has improved.

☐ **601. MUSIC NIGHT.** Once a month, let each member of the family share about fifteen minutes of his favorite music. This can be from the radio, recordings, or tapes. Supper is a good time. First, listen to the younger children's music, then to the teens' favorites. Parents can play Golden Oldies, Gershwin, or Bach. Learn to appreciate the variety of music and musicians as you eat, talk, read, play a game, or do some craft project.

☐ **602. THE ART BOX.** Use a laundry basket with handles, a sturdy carton with a rope handle, or other suitable large container to make a box for the budding artist. With cardboard as dividers, make sections for pens, crayons, paints, brushes, paper, cellophane, stickers, apron, plastic drop cloth, and so on. Use envelopes for small items. Occasionally buy something new for the art box. It can be carried to various rooms of the house, but be sure to protect the carpet. Also take it on visits to grandparents.

☐ **603. CLAY PIECES.** Every schoolchild produces multitudinous clay items in the primary grades. Rather than just store them in the cupboard, make a display of them in a prominent place with a photo of the artist by her works. After a few weeks, store them, but bring them out in another six months or so, when a child has produced another masterpiece. This time, put the current work and the older work on the coffee table or another place where they'll be seen. Don't worry what your friends will say; they probably have many clay pieces, too, and just aren't bold enough to show them off!

☐ **604. WHICH INSTRUMENT.**   Make plans to attend a concert by a youth orchestra. Before going, look up orchestral instruments in the encyclopedia. Then see how many you can identify at the concert. Encourage attentive listening to pick out the different sounds they make. Point out how the violin bows must all be going in the same direction, how the orchestra members closely watch the conductor, and what the players do when "resting." Ask kids which instruments are the loudest, biggest, or most interesting to them. Would they like to learn to play an instrument sometime?

☐ **605. ART WALL.**   At a bookstore, find an inexpensive book of famous paintings. Cut it apart. On a wall in the family room or eating area, tack up several pictures at a time. Let each family member say what he likes or dislikes about the pictures. Share simple information on the subject, artist, and technique. Change pictures about every week.

☐ **606. SING-ALONG.**   Encourage vocal music. Let kids sing along with recordings, such as *Wee Sings*, ones the performer Raffi has made for young children, or recordings by current popular artists for older children. Kids can learn well-known songs from books such as *The Good Times Songbook* (James Leisy, Abingdon, 1974). Sing songs in the car, in the shower, before supper, and while doing the dishes. Compose songs for members of the family. Let a child write the words; you help with the music or vice versa. Surprise people with their own private song!

☐ **607. AIMING AT ARCHITECTURE.**   Start helping younger children recognize different home styles: colonial, French, ranch, contemporary. When driving, let them name the styles as you drive down residential streets. When in city areas, discuss building styles. Find out which buildings in your area have historic value. Visit them and learn about their preservation and about groups that work to save old buildings. Talk about the architecture of your present home. How does it differ from your own childhood home? Borrow an architecture book from the library to learn more.

☐ **608. MERRY MUGS.**   Visit a pottery craft shop and look at all the interesting greenware to finish. If kids don't have ideas of things they'd like to make, suggest mugs, which they can use each day. These can be for family members, parties, or gifts to friends and grandparents. Let a child first sketch her design on paper, then in paint on the mug. Don't forget to put a message on the inside bottom of the mug, such as "Hi," "All Gone," or "Want more?" And the artist should sign her work on the bottom. Return to the shop for firing, letting the child see the kilns if possible.

☐ **609. FABRIC COLLAGES.**   These may sound difficult but they're fun and easy for children of all ages. Collect scraps of fabric from friends and your own sewing remnants. Let children make collages by cutting and gluing fabric onto cardboard. Use cardboard of various sizes. Talk about cutting interesting shapes, using various textures, and combining interesting colors. The collage might produce a picture or simply a pleasing pattern of shapes. Frame some of the creations.

☐ **610. FABULOUS CARTONS.**   Don't throw away packing cartons; in fact, ask for some big ones at an appliance store. With marking pens, crayons, or paint, let children transform them into dollhouses, spaceships, cars, or igloos. Encourage kids to take time to make these really authentic by looking for pictures to copy from or let them be their own creative designs. Check at your local movers' for jumbo cartons that can be used as playhouses.

☐ **611. CLASSY SUPPER.**   Play a classical recording during supper. Start with ones like Grofé's *Grand Canyon Suite* or Mussorgsky's *Pictures at an Exhibition*. Go on to selections from Brahms, Beethoven, and Bach. Play the same music another night and see who can recognize it.

☐ **612. THE MURAL.**   Everybody takes part making a wall mural on a long roll of paper. Roll out paper on the ping-pong table, dining table, or floor so that each person has a three-foot section of the paper to work on. Agree on where the ground or floor level will be in the picture, and that a figure will be at least twelve inches in height. Then pick a topic (sports we like, our house in the morning, a picnic) and let each family member work on his own. When finished, look at your mural and decide where to hang it.

☐ **613. LOVE THOSE MUSEUMS!** When children first visit an art museum, the size of the building and the number of pictures can be overwhelming. Go for a short length of time, talk in advance, and keep the interest high by asking questions: "How does the person in this picture feel?" "Would you like to live at this place in the picture?" "What person is the center of attention?" "What colors do you like best?" "How many animals are in the pictures in this room?" "Are big pictures better than little ones?" "What picture do you like best?" Look at that favorite picture again before leaving. Sit down and look steadily at the same picture for a few minutes; do you see more in it now? Talk about the museum visit at supper.

☐ **614. DRAMA ON TAPE.** Start with a simple story that the entire family knows, such as Red Riding Hood. Assign parts, and collect needed sound effects. Let a parent or older child be the narrator. Without a written script, ad-lib the story. It can be fun and funny. Later you may want to write out a script and make your production more professional. Play the cassette back at supper or for grandparents.

☐ **615. CAR CULTURE.** Play music in the car, tuning to various stations or bringing along your favorite cassettes. Tell children the call number of your favorite station. Let them tell you theirs. If you have a pre-set push-button car radio, set a station for each family member. Teach children to identify ballads, folk songs, country and western, rock and roll, classical piano, and symphonic music. Ask questions: "Is the music fast or slow?" "Is it happy or sad?" "What instrument is playing?" "What do you think the dancer is doing?" "Is it a man or woman singing?" "Is the singer a soprano, alto, tenor, or bass?" "How does the music make you feel?"

☐ **616. TEXTURE PAINT.** Artwork takes on a new dimension when you add texture to a child's paint. Try sprinkling on these additives: buttermilk, sand, glitter, small cereals, cornmeal. Encourage a design that includes areas without texture and areas of different textures.

☐ **617. "TOGETHER CRAFT."** Depending on the ages of your children, select a "together craft"—one in which each family member can participate. These might be refinishing a chest, making a mosaic tile wall hanging, weaving squares for a TV lap blanket, or hooking a rug. Before buying supplies, go to a craft center or shop and learn about the craft, so that you know the skills required for successful completion.

FOR OLDER CHILDREN

☐ **618. MINI-THEATER.** Help your child and her friends make a little theater at home. Pick a place where it won't be in the way. Use a wire, bedsheets, and rings to make a curtain. Start with simple stories they know, such as Cinderella or Superman. Let kids assign parts, taking turns being the lead character. Older children may want to write scripts. Simple costumes and props can be added. Emphasize creativity, not professionalism, although the play can be shown to others if the actors wish.

☐ **619. CATE'S GAME.** This game points out words ending in "cate." Copy this list or read it aloud. See who first guesses the word.

> To teach (educate)
> To oil (lubricate)
> To rub out (eradicate)
> To foretell (prognosticate)
> To recommend (advocate)

Other words that you can define are abdicate, adjudicate, collocate, communicate, complicate, duplicate, deprecate, fabricate, implicate, imprecate, indicate, inculcate, locate, masticate, medicate, placate, pontificate, predicate, vacate, and vindicate. You may have to look up some meanings yourself!

☐ **620. FASCINATING WORDS.** Introduce children to homophones (words that *sound* the same but are *spelled differently*, such as "son" and "sun"), homonyms (words with the *same spelling* but a *different meaning*, such as fireplace "grate" and to "grate," meaning to rub). Take up these two interesting categories one at a time and keep a list of examples the family thinks up. The book *Two-Way Words* (C. Kurdna, Abingdon, 1980) will give you many ideas.

☐ **621. DIARY WRITING.** Urge your child to keep a diary. While it provides him with the opportunity to see what was happening a year ago, it is also a pleasant form of writing. Let the diary be private. Many come with a little lock and key. You'll find ideas on making writing enjoyable in the book *Free to Write* (Roy Peter Clark, Heinemann, 1987).

★

SECTION 4: THE SCIENCES AND THE OUTDOORS

Right at home are materials for scientific experiments. The library has books that tie in to a child's specific scientific interest, whether it is astronomy or electricity. A wonderfully educational book for kids eight to eighteen is *Science Experiments You Can Eat* (Vicki Cobb, Harper & Row, 1972), which lets you learn unique things—and eat the results!

FOR ALL CHILDREN

☐ **622. BATTERIES, BELLS, AND BUZZERS.** Show a child how to connect a bell or buzzer to a battery and a button. Let her decide how to use her invention: as a door bell for her room, in the hall where the buzzer can be used to call everyone to mealtime, outside as a "come inside" bell. One young inventor used it to announce when the bathroom was vacated; another set up a code to call each family member to the telephone. You'll think of many uses through the years.

☐ **623. SPACE ROCKS.** These look like they're from outer space, but you make them at home. Put some pieces of coal, coke, porous brick, tile, or cement in a bowl. Mix together 2 tablespoons of salt, 2 tablespoons of water, and 2 tablespoons of bluing (available at the grocery store). Pour it over the formation. The next day add 2 more tablespoons of salt *to the solution* in the dish (don't sprinkle on the top). The following day add 2 more tablespoons each of salt, water and bluing. Add a few drops of vegetable coloring or ink *to each piece of rock*. Keep in an open, dry area. If crystal formation hasn't started, add 2 tablespoons of household ammonia to the solution to aid the crystal formation. Watch the formations develop! Some will look like rosebuds, coral, or crystal. To keep it growing just add more of the original solution from time to time.

☐ **624. WATCH THE BIRDIE.** Help a child build or buy a simple bird feeder and place it where you can watch the birds eating.

Using a bird guidebook, or with the help of someone who knows birds, make a list of the birds that come to feed. Take photos of them. Visit a feed store and find out about the various seeds that attract different birds. Count how many different birds come to your feeder.

☐ **625. WEATHER RECORD.** With a child's help, install an outside thermometer. Let him record the temperature at the same time each day for a month. On this weather record he can also note if the day is clear, rainy, cloudy, or snowy; and if there is any wind, from what direction it comes, and about how strong it is. (You may want to consider purchasing a weather vane, too.) Keep the record and compare it with the same month next year.

☐ **626. RECORD-A-DAY.** Spend a quiet day in the woods, by the water, or in the mountains. Take along cameras, binoculars, a blanket, lunch, books, and games. This is a day for observation. Let children record the day on film from sunrise to sunset, showing the scenery, plants and animals, and activities. Take the same picture at three different times during the day: early morning, midday, dusk. Make a list of the sounds you hear in the morning, afternoon, and evening. List all the wildlife seen. Note when certain forms of animal life are more active. Find a place where birds and animals come for water. Talk of how you feel about having a quiet day outdoors.

☐ **627. SWIMMING NEEDLES AND COMPASS.** Show children how to make a needle float on the surface of the water. When they've mastered one of these two methods, let them share it at school: (1) Fill a bowl with water and place a piece of tissue paper on the water. Put the needle on it. When the paper becomes soaked with water and sinks to the bottom, the needle will still float. (2) Make two slings out of threads and lower the needle to the water, then carefully take the threads away as soon as the needle floats.

To make a compass, magnetize a needle by rubbing it on a strong magnet. Then, float the needle on water (see above). The needle then becomes a very sensitive compass. You can also place two magnetized needles on the water surface at the same time. They will slowly approach each other until they line up side by side.

☐ **628. THE SEED RACE.** Give each family member a pot in which to start morning glory vine seeds. First each should label the pot, then plant the seeds according to the instructions. Each person waters and cares for his or her own pot. See whose germinate first. As the plants grow, provide strings so the vines can climb upward in a warm sunny window. Whose vine will bloom first?

☐ **629. THE SPIDER WEB.** Getting close to a spider web takes away the fear and mystery of it. Find a spider web in your yard. Without disturbing the spider, let everyone in the family study the pattern of the web's construction and try to draw it on paper. Then read about spiders in the encyclopedia and in library books. Keep a daily journal on the web, noting when the spider is home, what is caught in the web, any damage to the web, and how it survives wind and water. Feel a short piece of web; is it sticky or smooth, strong or weak? Explain how the webbing is secreted from the spider's body and how it engineers the construction. See how long the web lasts.

☐ **630. MAGNIFYING GLASS FIRE.** Most every child who's owned a magnifying glass has tried using it to start a fire, so you might as well show your child how to do it safely. On a sunny day without wind, go outdoors with newspaper, magnifier, and a sprinkling can of water. Put the paper on a non-flammable surface, such as the driveway. Show a child how to angle the magnifying glass so as to direct and concentrate the sun's rays onto the paper to cause heat. Soon a brown spot will appear on the paper and shortly it will burst into flame. Let her put the fire out and start another fire, until she is satisfied with this little experiment. Impress on her the rule that she is never to play with fire or do this experiment without an adult and a sprinkling can.

☐ **631. TIDE POOLS.** Take a magnifying glass and see the fascinating life in tide pools and ponds. Look for many minutes at one pool but don't disturb the wildlife. Let children sketch what they've seen. Let each child pick out and follow her tadpole and see what it does and where it goes.

☐ **632. FOUND SEEDS.** Let children experiment with seeds they find in the garden: peach and avocado pits; seeds from foods such as squash, tomatoes, cucumbers, and citrus; the eyes of potatoes that have started to sprout. Some will not grow well but others may be prolific. However, the fun is in the collecting and starting of one's own seeds.

☐ **633. COLLECTOR'S BAG.**   When going on a walk or hike, take along a plastic bag for each child. Let them collect little treasures that they find (in keeping with the law!). Just before going home, let all display what they've found (a rock, a dead bug, a penny, a piece of seaweed, a colored leaf) and talk about good finds. Pick out some unusual rocks for a child's aquarium. Decide what is to go home, what should go in the rubbish can, and what should be left behind.

☐ **634. MATCHING TREES.**   Point out one kind of tree (for younger children make it a very common one). Examine it closely to see its bark, the shape and color of its leaves, and any flowers, fruit, or seeds, then see who can find another tree of the same kind. Next, choose a different tree but see who can also remember the previous tree. On the next outing, have kids point out and name trees they know, and begin the "lesson game" again.

FOR YOUNGER CHILDREN

☐ **635. ANT FRIENDS.**   Find some friendly ants. Put a very tiny crumb of the picnic lunch bread on the ground near them. Watch them discover it and take it away bit by bit. Do this *after* eating so you don't have ants joining you for lunch.

☐ **636. MAGNIFYING GLASS.**   With a magnifying glass let children take turns looking at bugs, leaves, soil, a blade of grass, a stone, or sand. See who can find the most interesting item to observe. Then encourage kids to carefully turn over rocks to see what's underneath. The wildlife is usually harmless, and it makes a child less squeamish when he can observe little critters this way. Be sure that children do not hurt the insects but merely watch them. Put the rock back after viewing.

☐ **637. OUTSIDE NAP.**   A towel or blanket under a nearby tree makes a great place to nap. Tell the child to shut his eyes and listen to the outdoor sounds. Ask him to remember all the different things he hears while he's napping. It's a good, restful change-of-pace.

☐ **638. TUMMY VIEWING.** Everyone stretches out in a circle on the grass, pine needles or sand with chin resting on the ground. This bug's-eye view of nature can be fun. Go around the circle and let each one tell what he can see, without lifting his chin off the ground. Keep asking each child until you've described everything within the circle.

☐ **639. MARGARINE DISHES.** Going to the beach is more fun if you take along some margarine cups or other expendable cartons or containers. These make excellent molds for sand building; they can be recessed as ponds or miniature bathtubs and are good for collecting water. An old flour scoop makes a sturdy shovel. Put these in a plastic bag for easy child-carrying.

☐ **640. FIRST SEEDS.** Using easy-to-grow seeds, help a child start them growing in the house. Put a wet sponge in a shallow dish. Let her put seeds into the holes in the sponge. Put it in a place where it gets light. Check each day and add water to the dish so the sponge stays moist but not soaking wet. Watch the seeds start to grow. If you want, you can later "plant" the sponge in the garden outside.

FOR OLDER CHILDREN

☐ **641. TRACKING.** Whether it is sand, soil or sod you're on, try tracking. Divide into two groups with an adult or older child in each group. The first group starts out about ten minutes ahead, leaving subtle signs as to where they have gone. (These signs should not harm the environment. They can be as simple as an arrow drawn in the dirt, a trail of pebbles or leaves, or small red markers to be picked up by the second group.) This second group tracks the first and if all goes well they meet. Set a time limit and have a rendezvous place if the two groups don't find each other.

☐ **642. MESSAGE IN A BOTTLE.** This is fun when you're at a small stream. Put a message in a *plastic* bottle and tape it shut. Let half the group go downstream. Launch the bottle in the stream and see how long it takes to bob its way to the other group. You can have races, too. Sturdy small boats can be used the same way. Remember to take all bottles and boats home afterward.

☐ **643. USING A COMPASS.** Buy or borrow an inexpensive compass and explain how it works: The needle is magnetized and points to the magnetic North Pole. Point out the eight principal points (north, northeast, east, southeast, etc.) around the dial. Also give the meaning of the abbreviations (NNE = north northeast, ENE = east northeast, etc.) around the dial and show where these are located. Show how to hold the compass flat and steady in the hand and how to sight along the needle's length toward some landmark. Try the game of "Distance and Direction": in turn, each player starts from the same spot and walks a specified number of paces in certain directions (start with four directions) and marks where he ends. Compare where each player ends.

☐ **644. BINOCULARS.**   Field glasses let everyone look at hills, boats, birds in treetops and other people. Show children their proper use and care. Explain how to focus. When everyone sits down to rest on a hike, bring out the binoculars and see what you can spot. Look at hands, feet, granola bars, and apples, too. Point out that looking through the wrong end makes objects appear to be much farther away.

☐ **645. WILDLIFE COUNT.**   On a walk, see who can find the most animals, birds, insects. Tell each child to pick up a fallen leaf when she sees some wildlife. Then just count each one's leaves at the end of the walk to see who saw the most.

☐ **646. EQUINOX AND SOLSTICE.**   First explain the words! The two days a year when day and night are of equal length are termed the equinoxes. The autumnal (fall) equinox is about September 23, the vernal (spring) equinox about March 20. The two days in the year when the sun is farthest from the equator are the solstices. The summer solstice is about June 21, the winter solstice about December 22. These dates are the longest and shortest days, respectively. In many traditions, including ours, these dates mark the beginnings of seasons. Show these dates on the family calendar and make them part of family tradition by having an event such as a summer solstice supper or a vernal equinox jog in the park. Kids can see if their friends know the meanings of the words.

☐ **647. LIVING IN THE PARK.**   Instead of a day in the country, try one in your own city park. Bring along such things as a hammock, croquet set, bat and ball, portable radio, and Frisbee. Also take cereal, fruit, rolls, and milk for the breakfast kickoff, and the fixings for a cookout supper. Conduct morning exercises, then games and relays. Buy lunch in the park from various stands. Then visit a park museum or an outdoor art show. After a short nap on the lawn, go for a midafternoon walk. Find fire pits and have a simple supper. After clean up, play circle games and tell ghost stories around the fire. You'll go home tired!

★

SECTION 5: CIVICS AND BUSINESS

Where better to learn how things work in the outside world than at home! Since television usually depicts business and government so poorly, this is your opportunity to show the good side of these important activities.

FOR YOUNGER CHILDREN

☐ **648. POLLING BOOTH.** When it's time to vote, take one child along. Let him see the process. Sometimes young children may go into the booth with parents. Tell a child about one issue or candidate that especially interests you. Let him watch some of the election results on TV to see if other voters agreed with you.

☐ **649. THE BANK.** When a child first receives gift money, start the tradition of spending part and saving part. Make a special trip to a savings institution to open her own savings account. Let her keep the record in her treasure box or in a special file folder. During the year, let her see how her money is earning more money. Suggest some savings goals but let her change her mind about what she's saving for.

☐ **650. THE PENNY POT.** Show children that even pennies count. Place a glass jar in the kitchen or family room. As family members get pennies, let them add them to the penny pot. After about a month, let a young child put them in stacks of five or ten, and then you make a total. Put them back in the pot and put a tape at that height indicating the amount of money inside. This way you can show a child how to judge the amount in the jar. Spend the money on something for the entire family: a movie, a book, a new ball.

☐ **651. THE LAW.**   Visit a courthouse (call ahead to get necessary information). Pick a non-violent crime case to observe for an hour. Point out the court reporter, bailiff, jury, and foreman. Listen to the testimony and decide what you would do if you were a jury member. Follow the case in the paper or phone the bailiff's office later to see how the case ended.

☐ **652. HOME OFFICE.**   With kid-help, organize the home desk area so that it is as efficient as a business office. Create file folders for each child, for family activities, for items awaiting an answer, for the budget, and so on. Supply the desk with paper and carbon forms, writing supplies, check-writing equipment, envelopes, and stamps. Make a list of organizational and time-saving home office items that you are considering buying. Maybe some can be gifts from kids to parents. Possible items are a return-address stamp, a paper punch, a tape dispenser, a calculator, an electric pencil sharpener, a stamp dispenser, a postage scale, a card file, a many-drawered unit to hold paper clips and rubber bands. Encourage responsible kids to use the desk.

☐ **653. THE BUSINESS APPROACH.**   Television so often pictures businesspeople as villains that kids often have false and negative impressions. Parents and children should watch for this TV stereotype, point it out to one another, and laugh about it, realizing that it is just a plot device to create a dramatic program. You can explain to your child that businesspeople are all around us and that they are our friends, neighbors, and acquaintances. At supper, talk about business friends and see how many different businesses they represent. Discuss the importance of business ethics.

☐ **654. THE STOREKEEPER.**   When driving to the store, tell kids some of the problems a storekeeper faces: how she must order products she hopes customers will buy, how merchandise must be displayed and advertised, how an inventory is made and how products that don't sell get marked down until they do. This is the real meaning of the phrase "clearance sale." Kids can understand that the storekeeper has to hire workers to label, explain, sell, display, restock, and collect for the merchandise. Parents can explain how the storekeeper (or any businessperson) has to pay taxes, such as sales tax, employee social security tax, and income tax. The many regulations, such as fair-trade requirements, environmental orders, and health and safety regulations, are all part of the costs of doing business and are eventually reflected in the prices that consumers must pay.

☐ **655. CAPITALISM TAUGHT.** Preteens (and even younger kids) can understand that a businessperson cannot stay in business unless he operates at a profit. The components of profit or loss can be discussed by the family. The cost of goods purchased plus rent, salaries, insurance, taxes, and other miscellaneous costs are all items that flow out. The price of goods sold to the customer provides the inflow of money. The difference is profit. What is a fair profit expressed as percentage of sales prices? Perhaps 10–20 percent? Most grocery stores make 2 percent or less! How do they stay in business on such a small profit margin? Only by selling an extremely large volume per month. Find among friends and neighbors a businessperson who is willing to share some of these basics with your family.

☐ **656. COMPETITION TAUGHT.** What does it mean for businesses to compete? (To offer better service, a higher quality of merchandise, a more convenient location.) Children are quick to compare one store to another. If the prices were the same, would you rather get clothes (or food or toys) at Store A or Store B? Why? Talk about service and loyalty. Point out newspaper advertising that compares prices. Find a product that is as good or better than a highly advertised one. Find out the costs of a newspaper ad or TV commercial and figure how much product must be sold to make it worthwhile.

☐ **657. ADVERTISING TAUGHT.** Find two new automobile ads in a magazine. See which ad draws the most enthusiastic response from family members. Show that price, while an important consideration, is not the only factor that helps us choose one car over another. Let the children point out how the ad sells the use of the vehicle, its safety advantages, the cost of upkeep, and its reliability and prestige. Pick a specific car and look for it when out driving. See if it looks as good as it did in the ad. Look in the newspaper used-vehicle section and see how the price of the vehicle changes with age.

☐ **658. SOCIALISM TAUGHT.** Through a movie, magazine article, or television program, a parent can start a discussion on life without competition—the life of socialism. Mention that in Russia, as an example, there are not several food stores to choose from, with varying prices and services, but only one. Without competition as permitted under the democratic system, no company or business has any incentive to improve prices or quality. And in Russia there are often shortages that no one tries to solve, for distribution is a government problem. Such discussions only scratch the surface, and children need to be repeatedly shown how free enterprise usually provides a better way of life for members of the community.

☐ **659. FOLLOW A STOCK.** Some economists say that the free stock market as developed in Western nations is the finest example of market forces at work. Our stock market (and bond market, commodity market, gold market, etc.) automatically adjusts and corrects prices between varying businesses and commodities, and reflects all differences by means of dollars. Show the stock market pages in the newspaper to your child. Let her select a company whose products she knows, such as Ford or General Foods, and pretend to buy one share, then watch its price weekly, perhaps keeping a chart. See how her investment grows over a six-month period. During times when the stock market (or the gold market or the grain market) is moving up or down in rapid jumps, help the child to understand the numbers. One share of stock in a certain company will give you annual dividends of $5 plus its growth in value. A bushel of wheat bought today for delivery next September will yield you a profit (or loss) of $3.50. Let kids see if "their stock" is mentioned on radio or TV programs that summarize stock market activity.

☐ **660. ONE ISSUE.** Before an election, find an issue that is of interest to kids: parks, schools, recycling. Listen for debates about it on TV. Find articles from the newspaper to share. You may want to attend a public forum on the issue. Let each family member decide how he'd vote. Talk about the result after the election and why the issue passed or failed.

☐ **661. LAWS IN THE MAKING.** Plan a trip to your state legislature. Write ahead for information and also write your own representative. Visit the representative's office, then sit in the gallery and see him in action. Count how many women legislators there are. See who is presiding. Via the newspaper, follow one of the bills introduced and see if it becomes law.

☐ **662. HOW TO REBEL.**   Help youngsters learn the right ways to rebel, whether against family rules or federal laws. Talk about demonstrations, petitions, voting initiatives, and letter-writing campaigns. Demonstrate how to disagree emphatically but not obnoxiously, and how to gather facts and present them in a winning way. Encourage kids to put some of these ideas into use at home or school.

☐ **663. WRITE A REP.**   Talk to kids about issues of national importance: education, peace, the draft. Using a list of Washington legislators (available in your newspaper), choose ones to write. Each family member can write a different legislator on a different subject. See what response you get. But be patient; you may not receive a reply for some weeks. Decide if you want to write again. Also decide if this legislator is representing your point of view most of the time. If so, make a small contribution from your family to his or her next campaign.

☐ **664. VOTE ON IT.**   Spend a week with the whole family voting on everything imaginable: what to eat, when to go to bed, what game to play after supper, what excursion to take, what TV show to see, what book to read aloud, who should feed the dog, who should pick up toys. Teach the proper way to make a motion: "I move that . . . ," then have a discussion, call for the motion, and vote with ayes and nays.

☐ **665. CROSS-COUNTRY TRIP.**   Plan a cross-country trip that you hope to make someday. Let kids look at maps and chart a route that includes the varied areas of America. Each week, "travel" along a portion of your route, looking at pictures of the land and talking about the interesting places you can visit. Divide into teams and research this information in the encyclopedia or at the library. Try to find a highlight for each state and major city. Your pretend trip could take you a year, but when it's over you'll know much more about the geography and history of our country.

☐ **666. THE AMERICAN'S CREED.**   In 1917 William Tyler Page, a clerk of the U.S. House of Representatives, wrote this simple creed, which many Americans have memorized (see below). Read it and discuss its meaning with your family. Find the lines in it that were taken from the Preamble to the Constitution, the Gettysburg Address, the Declaration of

Independence, the Oath of Allegiance, and speeches by Daniel Webster and John Hancock. Put a copy of it on your bulletin board.

I believe in
  the United States of America as a
  government of the people, by the people, for the people;
  whose just powers are derived from the consent of the governed;
  a democracy in a republic;
  a sovereign nation of many sovereign states;
  a perfect union, one and inseparable;
  established upon those principles of freedom, equality, justice and
    humanity for which American patriots sacrificed their lives
    and fortunes.

I therefore believe it is my duty to my country
  to love it;
  to support its constitution;
  to obey its laws;
  to respect its flag;
  and to defend it against all enemies.

☐ **667. FLAG STORIES.**   As a family project, learn the history of our flag. An encyclopedia or library book on the subject will help. Start with the Queen Anne flag used by the colonists from 1707 to the Revolution. Other flags are the Grand Union flag used by George Washington, the first official flag called Old Glory, or the Star-Spangled Banner. Younger children may enjoy drawing pictures of the flags. Learn about the stars on the flag and when the star for your state was added.

★

SECTION 6: SUPPORTING SCHOOLWORK

You may not be a schoolteacher, but you have an important job in preparing your child to learn all he or she can at school. Your own attitude toward learning makes a difference. An intellectual and inquisitive home environment will produce better students.

FOR YOUNGER CHILDREN

☐ **668. STARTING SCHOOL.**   During the summer before a child starts school, take a picnic and eat it at the school playground. Ask what he thinks school will be like and what he expects will happen. Talk about what he'll learn and some school rules. Try the playground equipment, then look in the school windows. Take a picture of him at his school. Ask him to draw a picture of the school. Let the child share his visit at the supper table. Then tell some of your school experiences. Invite for play a child who will be in his class.

☐ **669. PRETEND NAP.** Most preschools and kindergartens provide resting times in the daily schedule. Practice resting at home, especially with a child who isn't accustomed to napping. Tell her she does not have to sleep; she just has to pretend she's asleep. Suggest things to think about when pretending: a favorite story, what she wants for her birthday, a good snack, how many trucks she has, what the dolls are doing in the doll corner.

☐ **670. PRACTICE THE FIRST DAY.** Let a child select his first-day-of-school outfit. Help him figure what time he needs to get up to be ready to leave on time. Let him assemble what he's taking to school (food, money, show-and-tell item). Walk the route to the bus or the school, if possible. See how long it takes. At home later that day, have a pretend after-school snack. Start a school scrapbook and later let him put in it all the bring-homes from school.

FOR GRADE SCHOOL CHILDREN

☐ **671. DEAR TEACHER.** Teachers really appreciate this idea, which helps them get to know their students. Write a letter to the teacher, telling him about your child. Ask your child to suggest ideas to put in the letter: hobbies, goals, pets, travels, things she enjoys in school or may need some support in learning. Both parent and child can sign the letter.

☐ **672. STIR AND SPELL.** No matter what needs stirring or preparing in the kitchen, let young spellers bring their lists into the kitchen. Don't expect perfection right off. Ask a child how many he thinks he'll get right the first time through the words. Praise good work, keep stirring, and have him go over the list again.

☐ **673. THE GEOGRAPHY GAME.** Using a globe or a map of the world, one family member closes his eyes and points to a place. Who can name the country? What's the capital? What kind of government does it have and who heads it? Is it a free country or under a dictatorship? Do we know anyone of that nationality? What is the country famous for—products, people, scenery? Would it be a good place to live or to visit? Then look up that country in the encyclopedia and add additional facts to your mental storehouse of information. For additional information, write to the department of tourism of that country.

FOR ALL CHILDREN

☐ **674. HOMEWORK HAVEN.**   While homework is usually best done at a table or desk with supplies and reference books nearby, occasionally encourage homework or reading in some unique place around the house: on a parent's bed, on the stairs, on the patio, in the bathtub, in a low tree branch. Ask about the homework so a child knows you care about it and are aware of what and how she's doing and of the time it takes.

☐ **675. HALF-TIME.**   When there's more than forty-five minutes of homework, prepare a half-time break and share a bowl of popcorn or serve hot chocolate. Maybe go for a brisk walk around the block and talk about something totally different.

☐ **676. GREAT BOOK/DULL BOOK.**   When a youngster has a book report, let him share his report with the family at suppertime. Although every book isn't interesting to a child, encourage him to find something of value in it. Let him tell what was good, what wasn't, why he thinks the author wrote it, and whether he'd recommend it to siblings.

☐ **677. FORTY-EIGHT-HOUR RULE.**   When a child has a big report due at school, have her mark it on the family calendar on the date two days earlier. On this day, let her give the report or show off the project—sort of a "preview." Then, if needed, it can be improved the next day without the last-minute rush.

SECTION 7: RELIGIOUS TRAINING

Of all the kinds of home training, your way of sharing your belief in God and what He does for His children is one of the most important. Don't avoid the issue and say "the child can choose when he's older," for this only sets a child adrift in a difficult world without any anchor. Instead, start at a very early age to give him the tools for living adventurously by following God's laws.

☐ **678. ON YOUR WAY.** The ride to and from church can be educational fun. Pick out an object seen easily and often from the car (a traffic sign, a crossroad, another car). Then pick a topic (the Ten Commandments, the Beatitudes, the Lord's Prayer, Jesus' healings, books of the Bible). The game starts with the driver and goes around the car in order of seating. Suppose you have chosen traffic signs and the Ten Commandments. When someone sees a traffic sign the driver must say one of the commandments. At the next traffic sign, the next person must say another commandment. Continue until you have given all ten. If everyone gets stuck, someone can open the Bible and give a hint.

☐ **679. I BELIEVE.** Talk about your religion. What are its basic beliefs? How did your family choose this religion? Invite another family to go to church or Sunday school with you. Then go to their church for a visit. Ask them what their beliefs are. See in how many areas you agree. Don't let religion be a one-day-a-week thing; make it a part of everyday life. Institute some small observance at the breakfast table, perhaps the reading of a meaningful citation from the Bible. Include Bible adventure books with a child's other reading books. At supper, take turns saying a short blessing. Teach a child a simple prayer to say before bed. But most of all, teach your religion by the daily example of your behavior.

☐ **680. CHOOSE A FAMILY.** Talk about various families in the Bible. For starters, consider the families of Jacob, Joseph, Moses, David, Jesus, and Paul. How did the family members relate to each other? What did the fathers do? What was the place of women? Of children? Did the family support the work of their famous child? What was childhood like in those days? After you've talked about several families, let everyone choose the family they'd most like to be a part of and tell why.

☐ **681. WHAT WOULD JESUS DO?**   When children are old enough to have an understanding of Jesus' life and works, introduce the idea of using his life as a guide each day. Encourage the use of the question, What would Jesus do? For example, when a child refuses to share a toy, remind him that Jesus said to do to others as we'd like them to do to us (see Matthew 5:38-48, and Matthew 7:12). If a teen is concerned about being teased in high school, point out that Jesus walked right through the midst of his tormentors, unseen and safe (see Luke 4:16-18, 20, 28-30). If a pet has died and a child is inconsolable, remind a child that Jesus promises that they who mourn will be comforted (see Matthew 5:4). Parents may have to help younger children find answers to their problems in their Bible, but older children can find answers on their own.

☐ **682. CONTEMPORARY COMMANDMENTS.**   There's nothing outdated about the important rules for living given by God to Moses. Sometimes the words need explaining, but the situations for their use are the same. Take one commandment each week. Write it in large letters and put it on the bulletin board, refrigerator, or wall near where the family eats. After a few days, discuss its meaning for today's life. What present-day gods deter us from knowing the one God? Are there graven images today? What about swearing? How do we make the Lord's Day a special day? How do children "honor" parents? What does it mean to avoid killing, committing adultery, or stealing? Are we ever false witnesses? And is coveting OK if you keep it a secret?

☐ **683. A SIMPLE GRACE.**   At mealtimes, begin with a grace, said slowly and thoughtfully. Take turns choosing and saying the grace. You can read the opening verses of Psalm 103, verses 1-5. Here is another grace:

Dear God, we come together out of love for You and for each other. Thank You for the goodness of today and for this meal. Guide us and keep us in Thy loving care. Amen.

☐ **684. THE ADD-ON BEDTIME PRAYER.**   Little children can learn just the first two lines of this prayer. Then when they are about five years of age, they can add the next two lines and later the last four lines.

> The day is over, the world's at rest.
> Keep me safe, keep me blessed.
>
> Tomorrow help me learn and play
> Sharing love along my way.
>
> Thank You for my family too.
> Make them pleased with what I do.
> When in trouble, hear my prayer.
> Now to sleep, safe in Your care.

☐ **685. TEEN PRAYER.** As questions of self-esteem, peer pressure, and the future begin to confront kids, continue to share with them the idea of praying for God's guidance. Here's a prayer a young adult might like:

> Dear loving Parent of us all
> Guide me through the coming day.
> Give me strength to just say no
> When temptations come my way.
>
> Help me love when I see hate
> Let me know adventure too!
> Teach me what I need to know,
> But keep me safe in what I do.
>
> With You I know I'm not alone,
> So help me make an honest choice,
> Free from fear and angry words.
> Yes, I'm listening for Your voice.

☐ **686. "PRAY FOR ME."** A child feels very comforted when he knows that a parent prays for him daily. Talk with a child about the ways you pray for him—not with prayers that he get a certain toy or a certain grade on a test, but prayers for his growth in joy, wisdom, love, and other expressions of his God-given individuality. Tell a child that God has a special plan just for him. Encourage the child to tell you when something troubles him so that you can pray with him and for him. When a problem is resolved through prayer, be sure to talk about it with the child. Some children like to keep a little notebook entitled "Good Things God Does for Me."

☐ **687. BIBLE STORIES.** These are just as exciting as other books and deal with problems still existing today. Some good ones are Hanna-Barbera's The Greatest Adventure Stories from the Bible series, *New Testament Stories* (Norman Bull, Abingdon, 1984), and *See & Share Stories About Jesus* (Robert Kingsley, Abingdon, 1984). Share Bible stories at bedtime and other reading occasions. Make a list of Bible characters kids know and add to it. Start with these: Noah, Joseph, Moses, Deborah, Samuel, Ruth, David, Daniel, Jesus, Peter, John, Paul, the several women named Mary in the New Testament.

☐ **688. BIBLE AT BREAKFAST.** Along with conversation at breakfast, listen to the Bible. It's available on cassettes. Listening just five to ten minutes each morning can start the day on a positive note. Eventually you'll have heard the entire book.

☐ **689. TROUBLE.** Sometimes when a child has what seems to be an insurmountable problem, the only thing we can do is pray with him and for him. Here is an example of a simple togetherness prayer for parent and child:

> CHILD: Hello God. Help me know what to do.
> *PARENT: Dear heavenly Parent, show him the way.*
> CHILD: I try to live close to You.
> *PARENT: Keep him safe day by day.*
> CHILD: But the temptations are so big.
> *PARENT: But God is strong, the only power.*
> CHILD: And I have so much to learn.
> *PARENT: Be his Guide, share Your wisdom.*
> CHILD: Make me a part of what's going on.
> *PARENT: Reveal Your special plan for him alone.*
> CHILD: Let me feel good about myself.
> *PARENT: Enfold him in Your love.*
> CHILD: And let me show others I care.
> *PARENT: Let his light shine for all.*
> CHILD: I know You can help me through all this.
> *PARENT: With God, all things are possible.*
> CHILD: Way to go, right on!
> *PARENT: Amen.*

☐ **690. BOOKS OF THE BIBLE.** Help children become familiar with books of the Bible, telling a story from each of the sixty-six books (over the course of several years). Let a child put a tab in his own Bible at the stories he knows. Older children can find fifteen of the sixty-six books of the Bible hidden in the following paragraph. (Answers are at the end of this section.)

I love my Bible and once made some remarks about the hidden books of the Bible. This lulu kept some people actually looking so hard for facts and studying for the revelation. They were in a jam, especially since the books were not capitalized as usual. But the truth finally struck numbers of my friends. To others it was a real job. We hope this is a most fascinating few minutes for you, too. Yes, there will be some that are easy to spot. Others may require the wisdom of judges to determine the book. And, I must also admit it usually takes a few minutes to find hard ones. There will be loud lamentations when you see how simple it is. One parent says she brews tea while she puzzles her brain over these. How many did you find?

☐ **691. BIBLE EQUATIONS.** See how well kids know Bible stories and verses with these Bible equations based on numbers used in the Bible. For example: 7 = D. of C. Answer: Days of Creation. Some are more difficult than others. (The answers are at the end of this section.)

1. 7 = D. of C.
2. 40 = Y. in the W.
3. 3 = The T: F., S., and H. G.
4. 40 = D. of J. F.
5. 40 = D. after which N. opened the W. of the A.
6. 4 = S. of the H. C., N. J.
7. 12 = S. of J. or T. of the C. of I.
8. 10 = C. given M.
9. 9 = B. of J.
10. 20 = P. of S.
11. 12 = D. of J.
12. 150 = C. in P.
13. 3 = Y. of M. of J.
14. 70 = A. of J.
15. 1 = G.
16. 3 = P. under D.
17. 66 = B. in the B.

☐ **692. THE COMFORT BOOK.** Take a child to a stationery department and let her choose a blank book, the kind that has a cloth cover and empty pages for writing in. Start by writing one quotation in the book. Parent and child then add others through the years. Choose quotes from the Bible, poems, speeches, hymns, and songs. When the child is sad or sick or in need of comfort, the passages in this book will be important to her. Families have kept such books for decades and passed them down from generation to generation. A good first quotation is this one from the Bible: "Be strong and of a good courage, fear not, nor be afraid of them: for the Lord thy God, he it is that doth go with thee; he will not fail thee, nor forsake thee (Deuteronomy 31:6)."

☐ **693. A PARENT'S PRAYER.** Take time out to pray each day, keeping each member of your family in your thinking. Here's a prayer for the end of the day:

Dear God,
As this day closes and I look back on its joys and challenges,
let me be grateful for raising a child in a free country,
for the loving support of family, friends, and teachers,
for the progress my child has made in giant leaps of faltering steps,
for the realization that my most important gifts to my child aren't *things*, but *thoughts*.

And for the day soon unfolding, give me a comprehension of my child's precious uniqueness,
the patience and intelligence to show him right from wrong,
the humility to lead him and loose him,
the enthusiasm to live as an adventurous family.

Thank You for the fleeting privilege of guiding one of Your children.

Let me do it with joy, with hope, and most of all, with love.

Amen and good night.

ANSWERS TO HIDDEN BOOKS: (in order of their use in the paragraph) Mark, Luke, Kings, Acts, Revelation, James, Ruth, Numbers, Job, Amos, Esther, Judges, Titus, Lamentations, Hebrews.

ANSWERS TO BIBLE EQUATIONS: (1) Days of Creation; (2) Years in the Wilderness; (3) The Trinity: Father, Son, and Holy Ghost; (4) Days of Jesus' Fast; (5) Days after which Noah opened the Window of the Ark;

(6) Sides of the Holy City, New Jerusalem; (7) Sons of Jacob or Tribes of the Children of Israel; (8) Commandments given Moses; (9) Beatitudes of Jesus; (10) Pieces of Silver; (11) Disciples of Jesus; (12) Chapters in Psalms; (13) Years of Ministry of Jesus; (14) Apostles of Jesus; (15) God; (16) Princes under Daniel; (17) Books in the Bible.

★

SECTION 8: ESSENTIAL ETHICS

Honesty and responsibility are the traits parents most want in children. These are taught best by parental example and one-on-one conversations. Start with very young children to stress the importance of these traits.

☐ **694. BENDING THE LAW.**   Talk about the present-day tendency to make light of some laws: the speed limit, tax information, cheating on tests, petty theft, sexual harassment, under-age drinking. Be open about areas where you may be less than perfect, so that kids will feel comfortable about sharing occasions when they may be tempted to break the law. See if you can find concrete reasons to be strictly law-abiding and ways to make adherence easier. Come back to the topic regularly so kids will know it is important.

☐ **695. ONLY ONCE.**   Start early to use the phrase "I'm only going to tell you once." This promotes responsibility, because the child must listen and remember. It's her responsibility to remember, not yours to remind. To get started, tell kids that you're going to tell them only once to do certain things. At the end of the day, praise those who heard, remembered, and responded. Those who failed to remember must suffer the consequences by getting up earlier the next day to accomplish the work.

☐ **696. TOTALLY IN CHARGE.**   Select an area of home life that is important but not a life-and-death matter. For young children, it might be putting up and taking down the flag. For older children, it might be to wash the car twice a month. Explain that the job will not be done by someone else and that if she leaves it undone the family will suffer because of her irresponsibility. As a child gets older, loose her more and more from your reminding, letting her be totally in charge of more areas of her own life. Some of these may involve choosing club activities and carrying out associated assignments, doing school projects and regular homework, returning library books on time or pay the fine, writing thank you notes, and taking clean gym clothes and other items to school. A parent's responsibility is to support a child by providing the time to do these things and the self-supporting system for remembering without reminding.

☐ **697. THE DAY OF RECKONING.** Deadlines are an important part of life at home, work, or school. Certain things must be accomplished by set dates. Structure your system so that there is a regular review of deadline items, perhaps on Friday afternoons just before the weekend starts. The child's list will show him what remains undone. Your review with him will permit him to enter the weekend happily, knowing that he has done what is expected of him . . . or that he has some catching up to do at once.

☐ **698. TELLING THE TRUTH.** We want children to tell the truth, but when a child lies, the important question is not that she lied but *why* she lied. Be very calm when you discover a lie or other dishonesty. Take the child to a quiet place. Start a conversation by asking about what she was doing earlier, then move toward the time of the lie. Ask what she was thinking, what she was trying to accomplish. See if you can talk together about the lie and ways to accomplish her desire without the lie. When you have finished, state your strong disapproval of dishonesty and your faith and expectation that she will be honest.

☐ **699. TELL IT AGAIN, SAM.** When you hear something you don't believe is the truth, ask that the child tell it again, very slowly, remembering every detail. Or, if it involves an altercation or conversation between two children, let them act it out. Usually the falsehoods disappear under this close scrutiny.

☐ **700. WRITE IT OUT.** It's easy to tell a lie, but it's harder to write it down. When a child who is old enough to write tells a possible lie, don't dispute it, just ask him to write about it in great detail. You may find that the written form is nearer the truth. But you may find that he has buried the lie with truthful statements. Then take up what he has written and consider it little by little, agreeing with what is true and complimenting him on it. Question a statement you think is false. Since you have already agreed with his true statements, he may readily give up the false statement as a mistake.

☐ **701. LET'S PRETEND.** For younger children, use "let's pretend" to find the truth. Suppose a child has taken candy without permission and lies about it. Start by saying "Let's pretend it's an hour ago and you're very hungry. What could you do to have a snack?" When the child gives an acceptable answer, praise her. Next ask what would be the wrong way to act. Then ask the child if she'd like to tell you what happened. Be forgiving the first time, but don't let dishonesty become a habit.

☐ **702. MAKE SOME RULES.** When a child lies habitually, it's time to make some rules with him. These rules should be about lies concerning homework, play, breaking things, stealing, and all the other "I didn't do it" areas. Let the child help decide the consequences of breaking the rules. Make punishments greater if a child is caught in a lie than if he admits his mistake. At some quiet one-on-one time each week, talk with this child. Ask him to assess how he's doing at being more truthful. On a rating of one to ten (ten being the most truthful), how is he doing? Keep this up on a regular basis. (For more on ethics, see chapter 8, section 5, on civics and business and also see chapter 10, section 4, on problem-solving.)

★

SECTION 9: THE FAMILY HERITAGE

There are duties for both parents and grandparents in imparting accumulated wisdom about the past and sharing love within the expanded family. Whether your own parents are near or far, try to include them in family life. Let them bring their special abilities; let them reinforce your good ideas; let them present a different but positive point of view. If grandparents are far away, they may want to "adopt" nearby children and enjoy some of these activities. Here's a book full of ideas on bridging the generation gap: *Grandparents-Grandchildren: The Vital Connection* (Arthur Kornhaber and Kenneth Woodward, Doubleday, 1981). Borrow it at the library, read it yourself, read excerpts to your children, and let them comment on things they'd like to do with grandparents. Share it with grandparents so they can put some of the good suggestions into action.

☐ **703. FAMILY TREE.**   Use a long piece of shelf paper or other large paper. With children helping, make a family tree with children and their cousins at the *bottom*. Then work upward to your generation, then up to the grandparents, and so on—as far back as you can easily remember. Let children help with lettering and decoration. Put the tree on the wall where the family eats. Talk about the people on the tree: where they lived, their work and hobbies.

☐ **704. THE GRANDPARENT BOOK.**   Make a file folder called "Grandparents." Help your child put in it some notes on things she already knows about the grandparents: their home, careers, travels, sports, talents. When you're all together, encourage grandparents to share stories of their own youth, of when you were a child, and of exciting world events they've lived through. Old scrapbooks and photo albums can help. Show that grandparents can do more than baby-sit! Make them an integral part of family life, giving a different perspective to home, community, and world events. Let the child add to her grandparent book at each visit. There are fill-in-the-blank grandparent books available, but making your own can be fun. If you buy one, consider *A Grandparent's Book* (Milton Kamen and James Wagenvoord, HP Books, 1981).

☐ **705. THE SPECIALIST.**   Find a project, sport, or craft that a grandparent excels in (bowling, woodworking, sewing, guitar, etc.) Let a grandparent and a child have one-on-one opportunities to share in this activity. Sometimes a grandparent can specialize in transportation—being the regular driver to classes, parties, or Sunday school. The results are threefold: appreciation for a grandparent's skills, togetherness, and the closing of the three-generation gap.

☐ **706. ETHNIC FESTIVALS.**   Watch the newspapers for festivals given by one nationality; it doesn't have to be your heritage. When the family attends, you'll learn about the crafts, foods, history and music of another country and be able to compare it with your family traditions.

☐ **707. THE OLD NEIGHBORHOOD.**   Take children to a neighborhood where you grew up or lived earlier or where they were born. See the schools, stores, movies, and houses you remember. Or, visit an unfamiliar neighborhood in your town. Look at the houses, try ethnic food, and visit the shops and the park.

☐ **708. CASH.**   Parents should help grandparents with ideas on gifts that kids want. Discourage the giving of money; a gift that a grandparent has selected especially for this child is more meaningful. But sometimes a grandparent wants to give cash to a grandchild. Suggest doing it this way, to make a cash gift festive. Change the cash gift into one dollar bills. Have a balloon for each dollar. Roll up the dollar and push it through the neck of the balloon. Then blow up the balloons and tie them into a bunch with ribbon and a dangling card. This is much more fun to get than a check and the comment, "I didn't know what you wanted." (A caring grandparent *should* know what a grandchild would like.) The recipient can pop each in a unique way: run and jump on them or burst with a pin, a foot, a knee, the behind, the chin, both hands, or the forehead.

☐ **709. DANCE STEPS.**   Even the youngest child likes to step to music. Get out some old records and show the popular steps from your youth: the Lambeth Walk, the Twist, the Samba. Then do some simple folk dances like the polka or "Turkey in the Straw." See if you can involve grandparents, cousins, aunts and uncles in dancing together.

☐ **710. SING A SONG.**   Teach a foreign language song or have a friend do so: "Frère Jacques," "Aloha Oe," "La Cucaracha." Learn what the words mean in English. Try to use one or more of the foreign words in daily conversation.

☐ **711. PATRIOTISM TODAY.**   Make it part of your family heritage to love your country. We spend a lot of time talking about what's wrong with our country and seeing examples on TV. Start a list of what's *right* with our country. Let kids add to the list things they like about America, and their town, their school and home. Read all the verses of "The Star-Spangled Banner" and discuss how it came to be written. Learn "America" and "America, the Beautiful." Buy a flag and learn the proper etiquette of flag use. Raise the flag every day. Talk about American history in kid-terms; include its founding, its wars and peacetimes, and its inventors, artists, athletes, musicians, writers, and patriots.

☐ **712. PHOTO ALBUMS AND KID-CAPTIONS.** These don't have to be dusty old books filled with unknown faces! Each time you add pictures, briefly print the date, the event, and the identities of the people under each picture. Future generations will thank you! Keep the current photo album out, where the family can look at it regularly. The books become even more lively when you encourage kids to write comments along with the pictures. Sometimes the kid-captions are funnier than the pictures.

☐ **713. "THIS IS MY LIFE."** Thanks to inexpensive or free double sets of prints, you can now have extra pictures for the next generation. When children are born, start a "This Is My Life" photo album for each one. For the first few years you'll be putting in the pictures, but after that let the child keep the book current. When he establishes his own home, he'll have a good start on his own memorabilia, but you'll also have copies in your own album.

☐ **714. QUILT HANDS.** A heritage project is the making of a special quilt. It can even begin with a purchased quilt or comforter in a solid color. Write to *all* the relatives, asking them to trace their right hands on a piece of paper and send them to you. If they wish, they can send along a piece of fabric they like or that has special meaning for them. Using the paper hands, cut out fabric hands and baste them in a large circle on the quilt, fingers pointing outward, hands just touching. You may want to put a little batting behind the hands before finally sewing them on the quilt. Let sons and daughters help. Stitch the names beneath each hand and let helpers stitch their names on the back. It makes a wonderful family remembrance and can also be a gift to grandparents on a special anniversary or birthday.

☐ **715. A NEW HERITAGE.** Build family traditions that will become the heritage of future generations. Ask kids to tell you which things you do as a family that they will do with their children. Establish some "always things" in your family life. Start when kids are young to establish traditions, which might include always going to Sunday school or church, always eating supper together, always giving an end-of-day hug, always serving Mom breakfast in bed on Mother's Day, always having popcorn and apples for Saturday night supper, always adopting a needy family at the holidays, always shaking left hands after an argument, always sending Valentines, always reading a book at supper, always saying "I love you no matter what!" With family friends, talk about traditions and learn some of theirs. See if you want to add them to your customs.

★ NINE ★

THE GOOD LIFE

 Safety, exercise, nutrition, a sense of well-being—these necessities may sound boring, but they can actually be fun, with the ideas in this chapter.

★

★

SECTION 1: GOOD AND SAFE

Nowadays, unfortunately, we need to be extra protective of our children. It is important to be factual and serious without causing alarm. Try these ideas over a month's time and then go over some of them regularly. You may want to include these books and videotapes in your instruction:

Books:
• Mark Brown and Stephen Krensky, *Dinosaurs Beware!* (Little, Brown, 1984): on safety.
• Michael Pall and Lois Streit, *Let's Talk about It!* (R. & E. Publishers, 1983): on child abuse.
• Robin Lenett, *It's O.K. to Say No!* (Doherty Associates, 1985): on sexual abuse.
• Alan Garner, *It's O.K. to Say No to Drugs!* (Doherty Associates, 1987): on drug abuse.
• Oralee Wachter, *Close to Home* (Scholastic, 1986): on abduction.

Videotapes (available at video stores):
• "For Safety's Sake," Gary Coleman, New World Television.
• "Say No to Drugs," Gary Coleman, New World Television.

☐ **716. TELEPHONE ACTING.** Before permitting young children to answer the phone, have them "pretend answer." Let the child pick up the phone, but keep her or your finger on the button. You make the sound of the bell and let her answer the phone. Practice answers for when a child is alone in the house, when the parent is busy and can't answer, when the caller asks a child's name. Help her with the right answers until it is natural for her. Show her how to make outgoing calls to a neighbor and to Grandma.

☐ **717. 911 PRACTICE.** With a child's help, put the emergency number (911 in most areas) on each phone. Then practice making a call dialing the right numbers (the parent holds the button down). Also practice the conversation the child would have and see if he can give the address correctly the first time. Emphasize the importance of *never* using this number except in an emergency.

☐ **718. PHOTO DAY.** We are urged by law enforcement authorities to have current photos of our children available should they be needed for emergency identification. Do this for their protection but make it fun. Twice each year, take separate full-face pictures of kids and parents. Post them on the family bulletin board, then when you have the next set, put the old ones in the family album. You'll be surprised how much kids change.

☐ **719. OPENING DOORS.** Talk about what a child should do when the doorbell rings. Open the door? Ask who it is? Get an adult? Say nobody's home? Take a peek? Don't answer? Then have an actual practice by having another child or friend ring the doorbell. Do this several times until the child is confident about what you want her to do.

☐ **720. FIRE DRILL.** Go to each room, especially each bedroom, in the house. Talk about alternative ways to get out of the room to the outside in case of fire. Point out an object that could be used to break open a window. Show every family member where the smoke alarms are, how they sound when triggered, where the fire extinguishers are and how they work, and where the family will meet outside in case of fire. (Check extinguishers regularly to see that they are properly charged. Most fire departments will re-charge them for you.) Have a fire drill at least twice a year. Talk about what to do in case of other disasters (earthquake, tornado, tidal wave, flood, etc.) common to your area.

☐ **721. KNIVES.** Almost every child is fascinated with knives and wants to own one of his own. Emphasize that a knife is a useful tool—never a toy, never an object to be thrown or left lying around. Show how to open a knife, how to cut with it, and how to close it safely. Point out that a knife should be kept clean and dry. Show how to occasionally oil a knife. Let a child use a knife to whittle a twig for marshmallow-roasting or to peel an apple. When he's demonstrated good safety habits, let him save to buy a simple knife for himself, with the knowledge that it will be confiscated if misused. Some knives have a strong cutting blade plus other tools, such as a can opener and screwdriver, making them even more useful.

☐ **722. MATCHES.** One of the leading causes of home fires is children playing with matches. Keep matches out of a young child's reach. Also make it very clear that there will be major punishment if she is caught with matches. Under your supervision, show a child how to light a match and how to light a candle with it. Show her how to extinguish a match, how to be sure it is completely out, and how to properly dispose of the dead match. Let her light twenty to thirty matches in your presence, to take away their fascination. Have her light the candles on birthday cakes, start the fireplace blaze, and so on, explaining *when* and *where* matches are used.

☐ **723. STRANGERS.**   Without being scary, instruct kids *never* to go near a stranger's car, even if called by name, and never to accept a ride or candy or anything else from a stranger. Tell them to disregard the line "Your mother sent me to get you." Explain that the word *stranger* can include people whom he may have already seen near schools or stores, people who seem very nice and friendly. When a stranger tries to talk with a young child, the child should run as fast as possible to an adult (or older child if no adult is near) and tell what has happened. If you are divorced and your child is not to go with her other parent, tell the child kindly but firmly what the law has decided on her behalf. Also explain to children that someone—maybe even a relative—may try to touch their private areas, and that they should not be afraid to immediately tell you about it.

☐ **724. FIRST AID.**   Keep a supply of simple bandages within reach of young children. Show how to clean a cut under running water, and how to apply a bandage to a finger. Tell a child that you want to know when he has hurt himself, but that you also want him to know what to do if you aren't immediately available. Demonstrate how to stop bleeding by pressure or by holding the cut area high above the head. For a larger cut show how to bandage and bind with a scarf tied in a square knot. Also demonstrate the Heimlich hug for use when someone is choking. Show how to treat burns with cold water, how to treat dizziness by sitting with the head between the knees, and how to remove splinters with tweezers. Let children practice these under your supervision.

☐ **725. LOST IN THE SHOPPING CENTER.**   When entering a plaza, point out a store near where you enter. In front of this store will be the place you'll look if an older child gets separated. For a younger child, point out the security guards and the cashiers in the stores as people who will help. Tell them that they may be taken to an office to wait until you are notified and can come quickly. Occasionally play the game "Who would you ask to help you if you were separated from me right now?" until young children understand what to do.

☐ **726. LOST IN THE WILDERNESS.**   When hiking as a family, point out campground headquarters, trail indicators, and other landmarks. Have younger children hike between adults or older children. Create a family call (last name or "Hooray" or "Mush") and use it often to let you know that hikers are within shouting distance. Some families have a whistle to which everyone responds. No off-the-trail hiking alone for young children. Tell kids this is what wilderness experts suggest they do if they become separated from the group: Keep calm and conserve energy, stay right where they are, sit down in a sheltered place, and call or whistle at regular intervals.

☐ **727. WHAT IF?**   Before a child goes off to school, he needs to know what to do if you are late in picking him up. How long should he wait? Whom should he tell? Where should he go? Sew a little pocket in a child's jacket or backpack. Using foil, tightly wrap a coin to be used for a special telephone call, and use masking tape to secure the coin in the pocket. Put in with the coin two or three telephone numbers: parent, neighbor, relative, and also an emergency-only number such as 911.

☐ **728. SAFE FIRE MAKING.**   Practice building a fire and putting it out properly. The fire site should be on plain dirt, sand, gravel, clay, or rock, with the surrounding area free from anything that might catch fire. Show how to gather dry wood, including twigs and a few very dry leaves. Build a fire teepee style or crisscross style, using ample tinder. Show how to light the fire with your back to the wind. After using the fire, show how to put it out by sprinkling (not pouring) water on the embers. Stir the fire and continue sprinkling until only wet ashes remain. Turn over remaining logs and wet both sides. Then wet the ground around the fire. Next, cover the fire area with dirt so that it looks as if no one has been there.

☐ **729. SAFE DRIVING.**   When children are young, start to teach safe driving habits through word and example. A toddler loves a steering wheel on his carseat. Never let a non-licensed driver steer the car or sit in your lap while you drive! If you do, you're encouraging a child to break driving rules. Ask him to watch other drivers for courteous or dangerous driving. Let a grade-schooler play "If I were driving" and tell you when he thinks you should pass, slow down, change lanes, use a turn signal, or fill the gas tank—but don't forget to use your own judgment!

☐ **730. WATER SAFETY.** Teach young children to stay away from bodies of water, including swimming pools, unless you are with them. Also show them how to throw a life preserver or a rope to someone in the water, in case of emergency. In some cases, the person can be reached with a pole, a stick, or a shirt, but the family should practice these techniques. Show older children how to swim to the back of a victim and slide a hand across his shoulder and chest and under his other arm, so as to carry him while swimming to safety with one arm and doing the scissors kick.

☐ **731. THE TOGETHERNESS RULE.** Children under ten should always have someone with them when at home or when left in the car at a parking lot. When children go out outside after supper, two should go together. When sending a child on an errand, send along a second child or adult. When attending a movie and letting a child go for snacks or to the bathroom, send two. The togetherness rule is for safety and at the same time provides the fun of companionship.

☐ **732. UPSIDE-DOWN LEARNING.** Sometimes young children need practice in learning the numbers in their address or telephone number. To help, write the numbers clearly on a three-by-five-inch card. Let the child add a little picture to make it pretty, then pin the card on the child's shirt upside down. As she plays around the house, she'll look down and easily see the numbers. You'll be surprised how fast she learns.

☐ **733. TRUSTED HELPERS.** Talk about what firefighters and police officers do to maintain law and safety. Show how to identify them by uniform and motor vehicle. Let a child practice being a firefighter with a hose and a pretend fire. Let him play police officer, stopping speeding tricycles or holding back a child who is pretending to run into the street to get a ball. When you see a police officer walking on the street, introduce your child to him. This helps overcome the fear of a big person in uniform, wearing a gun!

SECTION 2: GOOD AND FIT

Start with young children to enjoy running, riding, ball playing and other healthy active sports as part of everyday life and not as an enforced regimen. These books are fun for parent and child:

- Barbara Isenberg and Marjorie Jaffe, *Albert the Running Bear's Exercise Book* (Houghton Mifflin, 1984).
- Mickey Herskowitz, *The Greatest Little Game* (Sheed and Ward, 1975).
- Barbara Burn, *The Horseless Rider* (St. Martins, 1979).
- Dennis Look, *The Joy of Backpacking* (Jalmar, 1976).
- William Berry, *Kids on Skis* (Scribner's, 1982).
- C. J. Maginley, *Make It and Ride It* (Harcourt, Brace, 1949).
- James Fannin, *Tennis and Kids* (Doubleday, 1979).

Look at sports books together and consider a variety of sports that teach self-discipline, concentration and relaxation. Consider learning a new sport each summer.

☐ **734. HOW TALL?**   Choose a place in the house, such as the laundry room or garage, where you don't mind making permanent marks on the wall. Use a tape or yardstick to mark out feet and inches on the wall. Then let each child and parent stand against the wall and mark his height with his name and the date. Do it once or twice a year.

☐ **735. POSTURE PRACTICE #1.**   The worst slouching goes on at mealtimes. It may look funny, but try this remedy. Each family member will have to sit in the same place for a month. Before the meal, hang a long thread from the ceiling over each chair, using a very small tack. Have drapery rings available. When each person is seated, ask him or her to sit up straight. Tie the ring to the thread so that it just barely touches the head and then snip off the excess. Do this for parents, too. Without being obnoxious, let family members remind each other when they've slumped and their ring is swinging free. Good lines for this are "No ringy-dingy, Jason" or, "Your halo is loose, Carol Lynn."

☐ **736. POSTURE PRACTICE #2.**   Play "No Hands" when book reading or homework is finished. Encourage the return of books, notebooks, or folders to their proper places by using heads, not hands. A family parade with books on the head is fun. See who can get all the way to her room or the bookshelf without dumping her book.

☐ **737. PRIVATE DRAWER.**   Give each child a drawer or a tray in a low bathroom cupboard to hold personal supplies: toothbrush and paste, dental floss, brush and comb, small bandages, cup, lotion, and manicure scissors when old enough to use them properly. Help a child identify his own towels and washcloth; label his towel bar if necessary. This reduces the sharing of items. Teens will appreciate having separate space for their own cosmetics, too. Larger families can give each child a plastic carrying tray that is kept in the bedroom but travels to the bathroom.

☐ **738. ALPHABETICAL TEETH.**   "How long do I brush?" is a common kid question. "Through the alphabet" is the answer. It usually takes a child several minutes to go through the alphabet naming something for each letter, for example, "*A* is for apple, *B* is for books, *C* is for cat."

☐ **739. TRAVELING TOOTHBRUSH.**   Some schools are now encouraging tooth brushing after lunch. If your school isn't, talk with those in charge. Your child doesn't want to be the only one at school with a traveling toothbrush! If brushing isn't possible, encourage a child to finish lunch with an apple or other crisp food that will loosen food particles collected on teeth. Then a child should have a good long drink of water to rinse the teeth. At home or on family trips, midday tooth brushing is much easier, so encourage it.

☐ **740. SMART SKIN.**   Make good skin care fun. Along with thorough washing at least twice a day, some kids find it fun to use a moisturizing cream or lotion on the face. They like to look shiny for the hour before bed! Let a child have his own container of a pure and simple lotion or cream. Hands, elbows, knees, feet, behind ears—these are all places for lotion. When children are to be playing in the hot sun, provide a sun-protecting lotion or oil. With a magnifying glass, let kids look at one another's skin. When they see pores and what's in them, they'll be more eager to care for their skin.

☐ **741. SAFE SHOWERING.**   Even toddlers can enjoy the fun of safe showering. If the floor isn't skid-proof, get a mat. Provide soap-on-a-rope. Shower time is a great time for singing, reciting, shouting, yodeling, hog-calling, and making animal sounds. The more enjoyable, the cleaner the child!

☐ **742. GRUBBY NAILS.**   Older kids may enjoy automotive work, painting, and other projects that result in dirt collecting on and under nails. Share this clean nail idea and suggest that kids try it just on one hand first, to notice the difference. Before beginning work on the project, use a *dry* bar of soap to rub the knuckles and palms. Then scratch the nails over the soap so there's actually soap under the nails. When washing up after the project, hands and nails so treated get clean quite easily.

☐ **743. THE A.M. GREAT EIGHT.**   Make a list of the things that must be done in the morning. Post it on the bathroom mirror so all the family can see it. These include bathrooming (an OK word for elimination), washing (showering/bathing), tooth brushing, nail brushing, leaving the bathroom neat, bed making, dressing, and hanging up pajamas. Start early to teach a child that there's no play or breakfast or leaving home until the A.M. Great Eight are finished. Some children may need a little chart to check off the elements of the routine.

☐ **744. THE P.M. GREAT EIGHT.**   Again, show what you want done in words or pictures posted in the bathroom. The P.M. Great Eight includes washing, tooth brushing, nail brushing, leaving the bathroom neat, clothes to the hamper, setting out the next day's clothes, bathrooming, and taking a drink of water.

☐ **745. LITERARY FITNESS.**   Introduce to kids these sit-down exercises, which can be done while reading or doing homework: (1) Arms extended sideways, make twenty circles with hands; (2) turn head ten times left and ten times right, going a little farther each time; (3) lift knees up, swing feet out, and point toes, fifteen times; (4) clasp hands behind back, arch back, lift chin as high as possible, then lower chin to chest, ten times; (5) extend feet and reach out to touch toes while seated, ten times. These movements will wake up the body and permit longer reading or homework sessions.

☐ **746. ROLLER-SKATING.**   Skating is a good togetherness exercise. When neighborhood sidewalks or roller rinks get boring, try skating in the park. Many parks have ample walkways where skating is safe, and it's a nice change from walking. Some parks have rules against skating, so check first. You may want to rent shoe skates. Show the basics of skating. Take along a short length of rope so a tired skater can be pulled. Carry a picnic lunch in backpacks and enjoy it at the halfway point or little by little at different locations along the way.

□ **747. JOGGING TWOSOME.** While one parent stays home with younger children, the other parent and one child take a weekend morning jog, followed by showers and a hearty breakfast. One-on-one togetherness builds family bonds. This is great for a working parent who doesn't see a child for an extended period of time during the week.

□ **748. SAFE CYCLING.** Plan a family cycle trip focused on bike safety. Let one family member have paper and pencil and be the scribe, writing down all the good ideas. Before leaving, talk about proper clothing and shoes. Stop cycling at regular intervals to collect ideas on these subjects: hand signals, passing, what to do when a car comes up behind, making a left turn, safe speeds, downhill runs, carrying packages, what to do when a bike goes out of control, changing a tire, and keeping bike in good mechanical condition. Let kids write up all the ideas for the school paper and you can also share them with the local paper as a feature on good places to ride safely in the community.

□ **749. CLUBS.** Use a health club, YMCA , or local pool to take part in family swim time. Some offer Jacuzzi relaxation, too. Visit several with the family before deciding which to join. Watch for sales on equipment and eventually have your own "fitness club" with a chinning bar, rowing machine, weights, cycle, and other equipment.

□ **750. WALKING VS. CARPOOLING.** Walking to school is great exercise and especially nice if a parent can walk part way. A child gets to think and to look around at the world as she walks. But if kids must be driven, consider starting early enough so that they can be dropped off a few blocks from school or at the far side of the playground.

□ **751. NATURAL EXERCISE.** A child's life can get so regimented that he doesn't have time for natural exercise. He doesn't need to take special classes if you provide these opportunities: climbing (teaches balance and strategy in selecting the next foothold), swinging (strengthens arms and legs, especially if pumping), jumping rope (good for breathing, teaches coordination), running games (increase endurance), swimming (provides low-stress exercise of whole body), cycling (strengthens shoulder and leg muscles), trampoline (teaches coordination, flexibility). Of all organized sports, soccer gives the greatest opportunity for exercise, since it has twenty-two kids constantly running, as opposed to sports entailing a lot of standing around or bench-sitting. Work out a schedule with your child for *natural* exercise each day.

FOR YOUNGER CHILDREN

☐ **752. BATHTUB FUN.**   Make it a rule not to leave a preschool child while he's bathing—not for one moment. See that your tub has a safety bar, keep the water level low, and have young children bathe at the end opposite the water faucets. Plastic boats and other toys are great for play. Show a child how to make bathtub waves that move boats slowly, how to slap the water to upset a boat, and how to blow a boat to the opposite end. Pour in some bubble bath and let a child make a cave in the bubbles and sail boats into it. He can also make himself a hat or a jacket out of bubbles. Take his photograph and put it up on the wall by the tub. A mesh bag hung on the faucets can hold tub toys so that they drip dry.

☐ **753. NAUGHTY NAILS.**   Start with toddlers and keep the habit going through the teens: Take care of fingernails each day. A nail brush and this little song sung to the tune of "Three Blind Mice" should do the trick for the young ones:

Ten naughty nails, ten naughty nails.
See how I scrub, see how I scrub.
They get so clean with a scrub of the brush,
And when I finish my mother won't fuss.
I scrub each pinkie with care, not a rush.
Ten clean nails, ten clean nails.

★

SECTION 3: GOOD AND NUTRITIOUS

Start early to show that nutritious foods can taste good. Read *Feed Me! I'm Yours* (Vicki Lansky, Meadowbrook, 1974), for many good ideas on creative food experiences for children.

☐ **754. WOW! SOMETHING NEW!**   When a new food or dish is going to be introduced at a meal, put a "WOW" sign on the refrigerator door that morning. Don't tell what the food is—let everyone keep guessing. Anticipation makes it more fun. When the new food has been tasted, take a poll and see how it rates on a scale of one (never serve it again) to ten (let's have it often). But don't give up if *you* think it's really good—try again with a slight variation to please the nay-sayers.

☐ **755. BACKWARD SUPPER.**   As a surprise, serve dessert first, then the meal (with the understanding that the peas won't be left on the plate). Do other things to vary eating procedures: Let a child sit at the head of the table, let the other parent or an older child cook and serve, eat lunch wearing blindfolds or with one hand behind your back, eat by candlelight, eat at an especially early or late hour, or eat an entire meal with fingers (including the peas). Kids eat better when mealtime is enjoyable.

☐ **756. FORCE FEEDING?**   Making kids eat when they aren't hungry and jamming down foods they don't like isn't wise. Try to maintain a three-meals-a-day, try-a-little-of-it routine. With a finicky eater, start a list of foods she *does* eat. Set goals for new foods and make a big deal when she adds one to her list. You will find that by serving a variety of foods and having her take a spoonful of each, your child will gradually accept some of the new ones. Be careful that snack time doesn't come so close to a regular mealtime that appetites are dulled.

☐ **757. DESSERT A REWARD?**   Don't withhold food as a punishment or give treats often as a reward. Good food is its own reward. Forget the line "If you're good you can have a piece of candy." But don't make sweets so forbidden that kids can't live without them. A tasty yet healthy dessert is part of a balanced meal. If you use it as a reward, you're saying it's the most important part of the meal. Keep mealtime an unemotional and pleasant experience. Don't provide a second dessert before bed. If you wish, dessert can be served later, say, an hour or so after supper, creating an additional time to be together. Let kids list favorite desserts. Then let one help you make a dessert while others in the family are cleaning up the kitchen after the meal.

☐ **758. MENU-MAKER.** Talk about junk foods versus a balanced diet. Let one child make healthful menus for a week. Other family members can give input. Let him make a shopping list from the menus, including nutritious snacks. Talk about what meals were especially liked and let another family member make menus for the next week. For variety, look in cookbooks for new ideas to go with the old favorites.

☐ **759. STICK OUT YOUR TONGUE.** Prepare this experiment for the family, perhaps with the help of one child. You'll need four cups: (1) 1 cup of water mixed with 1 teaspoon of salt, (2) 1 cup of water mixed with 1 teaspoon of sugar, (3) 1 cup of water mixed with 1 teaspoon of baking soda, (4) ½ cup of water mixed with ½ cup of lemon juice. Put a folded paper label under each cup to keep them straight, since they will all look alike. Using spoons, let each family member dip into cup #1 and try to identify it. Continue on with clean spoons to the other cups. See who can guess the four basic tastes: salty, sweet, bitter, and sour. You may want to bring a magnifying mirror to the experiment so each person can look at his tongue and see the taste buds (the bumps) that help us recognize these tastes. Talk about the importance of chewing carefully and really tasting food, rather than just gulping it down.

☐ **760. THE SCORE ON FOUR.** There are four basic food groups: (1) meat, poultry, fish, and eggs; (2) milk and dairy products; (3) vegetables and fruits; (4) breads and grains. Make a chart for each child with two spaces following the meat category and four spaces following each of the other three categories. Each day, let the child write in the spaces the foods in that group that she has eaten. See which ones are the most difficult for her to fill in. Help her investigate new foods and find foods she especially likes in each category.

☐ **761. WATER, WATER EVERYWHERE.** Start the water-drinking habit when children are young. Since the body is 90 percent water, it's important to drink about eight glasses a day to replace what is lost. These eight glasses are in addition to other liquids, such as juice or milk. Have a conversation about this with the entire family. Show how they can easily drink five glasses: a glassful first thing when getting up in the morning, after morning tooth brushing, after lunch at home or school to rinse out the mouth, first thing when coming home that day, and after evening tooth brushing. Now let the family figure where they can fit in the other three glasses. One answer is to drink a glass of water before embarking on a snack time. Another might be to serve a glass of water in addition to milk at supper. See that every family member has a bathroom glass (or that paper cups are available) and that kitchen water glasses are reachable for all. If your water doesn't taste good, consider buying bottled water and renting a cooler with a cold water tap.

☐ **762. MOST IMPORTANT MEAL.**   That's what teachers say about breakfast—a meal that can make a difference in a child's attitude and learning ability at school. So, that quick breakfast of sugar-coated cereal is out! Using the four food groups above, talk with kids about foods they can have at breakfast. This meal can include meat, eggs, hard cheese, or cottage cheese and yoghurt. Fruits are easy to include; you can serve vegetables by putting tomatoes, celery, and peppers in an omelet. And let grains be more than cereal; whole grain bread or toast, bran muffins, and hearty oatmeal are good too. Include kids in breakfast-making, and you'll find they eat eagerly. After all, it is the breaking of a long fast!

☐ **763. BREAKFAST SURPRISES.**   Breakfast doesn't have to be the same old things day after day. Let kids help make these nutritious day-starters: (1) peanutty toast (peanut butter on toast) with a fruit milkshake (banana, peach, pineapple); (2) raisin oatmeal cookies and cheesy scrambled eggs; (3) cereal sundae made of granola or cereal sprinkled on yogurt or ice cream; (4) grilled cheese sandwich and eggnog.

☐ **764. QUICK WAFFLE BREAKFASTS.**   When morning time is at a premium, consider waffles. No, not the expensive prepared variety loaded with preservatives. Instead, select a non-busy forty-five-minute time during the week and make a month's supply of waffles. Divide them for each breakfast and then wrap and freeze. Then make a list of toppings: fruit, syrup, yogurt, nuts, bacon. These are quick to fix and the bacon can be cooked, crumbled, and frozen in advance. The night before a busy morning, set out the waffles to thaw. Heat them in the toaster or oven and let kids choose toppings for a quick and nutritious breakfast.

☐ **765. CROCK POT BREAKFAST.** The smell of oatmeal, cooked overnight in the crock pot, will get most sleepyheads up. Let one child prepare the bowls, making each one different. On one there can be honey or blackstrap molasses. Another bowl can have canned, or fresh fruit chopped or slightly pureed in the blender. Also try oatmeal with yogurt, raisins or nuts. When each arrives at breakfast he chooses a bowl. Then, pour on milk or cream and enjoy.

☐ **766. THE NEW LUNCH PAIL.** With 85 percent of U.S. kids eating sack lunches, it's time for a new look for them. When school starts, kids often get new clothes, crayons, and notebooks. This year include a new lunch box, the insulated variety that keeps lunch fresh. Or get small packets of "blue ice" for use in existing lunch boxes. (It can be dangerous to leave some foods in a school locker for hours before eating, so the insulated box or the use of "blue ice" is wise.) Carefully label the inside of the box with name, address, and phone number. Talk about where the lunch box can be placed when packed so it's sure to get to school. Then talk about this family rule: Come home from school with both hands full. This means a lunch box in one hand, schoolbooks in the other.

☐ **767. THE NEW SACK LUNCH.** It's time to switch from lunches of mushy white bread, cookies, and chips. A wholegrain bread provides roughage and makes a tasty sandwich with sliced meat, tuna fish, or egg salad filling. Peanut butter and jelly is OK now and then. Include cottage cheese and a packet of herbs (kids like lemon pepper, Mexican spice, or salad sprinkles). Instead of a sandwich, try stoneground crackers and cheese wedges or a tomato stuffed with shrimp or tuna. A hardboiled egg with a spice dip is great. Include a fruit; apples, grapes, pears, and bananas travel best. A half melon filled with cottage cheese is refreshing. Plain yoghurt with sliced fruit to mix in at lunchtime is great. Consider making this unusual smoothie: Mix in a blender 8 ounces of tofu (a high-protein soy product), 1 cup of sparkling water, and 1 cup of frozen fruit (frozen berries from the supermarket are ideal), then pour into a thermos. Or, let kids make ahead many small meatballs. Cook and freeze them, then put a half dozen in the lunch pail with toothpicks for easy spearing. Add fruit and a granola bar, and you have a great lunch.

☐ **768. SNACK-HAPPY KID.** Snacking, or "grazing" as it is now called, doesn't have to mean candy and junk foods. It can be an opportunity for good nutrition. Let kids make these with your help: (1) Sliced cheese or meat looks good when cut into interesting shapes with cookie cutters. Pile the pieces on a wheat cracker. (2) Make "pupsicles" (small Popsicles) by freezing juice in an ice cube tray. Put a flat wooden stick in each when almost frozen. Store in a plastic bag in the freezer. (3) Even the youngest children can help cut up cauliflower, cucumbers, and other vegetables to make dunkers for dipping into yogurt or sour cream mixed with onion soup mix or herbs and spices. (4) A hearty after-school snack is a small baked potato with cheese sprinkled on top.

☐ **769. JUNK DRINKS.** Most soft drinks consist of water, flavoring, and sugar or a chemical substitute. Some drinks have caffeine, which is a drug. Others have additives to make them creamier or thicker. Read the labels on all the drinks at your house. Encourage juice drinking. A blender usually comes with a booklet of great juice drinks. One favorite is made with a banana, 1 cup of milk, 1 teaspoon vanilla, and six ice cubes. It makes a thick, delicious, nutritious drink. Don't blend it too long. Serve it immediately.

☐ **770. ENERGY LIFT.** It's interesting that most home accidents happen around three to four P.M., a time when energy and attentiveness are at a low point and spirits may need a little pepping up. Certainly a candy bar is fine now and then, but there are alternatives. Nature's own sugar-fix is fruit. Apples, pineapple slices, raisins (try the golden ones for variety), pears, peaches and grapes can be eaten almost anywhere—inside or out. Have these at an after-school "Snack and Tell" time when kids share the events of the day. When shopping, let kids pick out the seven fruits they'd like to eat each day of the week.

☐ **771. VEGETABLE HATERS.** Kids often turn away from vegetables because it's fashionable among their peers or because the vegetables aren't properly seasoned. Make a list of vegetables and let a younger child draw a picture of each one next to the word. Then prepare a variety of vegetables at meals, letting the child put a happy face on the list to show she ate that vegetable. Two happy faces show she *really* liked it. To get children to eat more than corn on the cob, consider providing these vegetable dishes: Celery stuffed with peanut butter, zucchini rounds (called flying saucers by the playschool set), zucchini or carrot strips with a soft cheese dip, cooked carrots whipped in a blender with cream cheese and stuffed in celery, cheese sauce over cooked chopped spinach, pan-fried onions, baked squash sprinkled with cinnamon and nutmeg, green beans mixed with strips of turkey pastrami, Brussels sprouts made into "round people" with toothpicks to hold their bodies together, frozen peas or corn (eaten with fingers—they're no colder than ice cream and they taste great that way).

☐ **772. WHAT'S FOR DINNER?** Less nutritious dinners are a result of failing to plan in advance. See if your children can correctly answer these five food questions: (1) How much protein should one have each day? A typical grade schooler needs about fourteen ounces. An egg is one ounce. You can ask children to weigh other protein portions on a food scale or to look at the weight on the package. (2) Are potatoes good or bad food? Good! Potatoes are high in vitamin C and are not high calorie unless you put on too much topping. Use butter and sour cream in moderation. Try cottage cheese or grated cheese on top, or mash with yoghurt and chives. (3) Is fish better than fowl or beef? Not necessarily. They can all be part of a balanced diet. Fish is lower in calories than fowl or beef. Remember this saying: The whiter the meat, the lighter the meat—lighter in calories, that is. (4) Is a salad necessary for supper? Yes, but it doesn't have to be just a heap of lettuce and dressing. Add peppers, carrots, julienne beets, celery, olives, raisins, nuts, canned corn, peas, and try an oil and vinegar dressing. (5) Are cake and pie good meal-enders? Yes, a dessert each day is fine, but alternate these baked goods with homemade gelatin desserts, tapioca and other puddings, and fruit and fruit desserts. Did everyone get five correct answers?

☐ **773. FAST-FOOD SURVIVAL.** It's fun to go to a fast-food place for hamburgers, fish sticks, fries, and a shake—occasionally. But if you find your family is there often, change the rules this way. A hamburger is fine, but it should be eaten with a salad from the salad bar consisting of at least seven different items (tomatoes, sunflower seeds, beets, etc.). When having chicken, ask for a skinless breast and then have a hot biscuit with honey plus a piece of fruit from home. Fish restaurants now have lighter batter, which tastes just as good. Fish and a salad is a better combination than fish and fries. When going for fast foods to be eaten in the car, take along your own beverages (milk and juices); they're much cheaper, often more nutritious, and you can have a greater quantity.

☐ **774. AFTER-SUPPER SNACKS.**   Whether it's homework, games, crafts, or TV time, a snack is sometimes nice. It doesn't have to be potato chips, cookies, or candy. One of the best is popcorn, but go light on the salt and butter. Kids love to make it! Have waxed cups on hand (like those at the movie theaters) and let the kids fill one for each family member. Nuts are another good choice, but both of these hard-to-digest foods should be chewed well. Buy them in the shell and let everyone crack and eat while doing other activities. For a nice change, have a plate of dried fruit: apricots, raisins, pineapple, peaches, or dates. Let evening snacktime be a time when one child takes requests from family members, serves them, and cleans up the kitchen afterward.

☐ **775. BEDTIME SNACK.**   It's a long time around to breakfast (the meal that breaks the long night's fast), so permit children a bedtime snack if they haven't snacked earlier. Younger children sleep better if they have a comfortable tummy at bedtime. Avoid empty calorie foods, such as potato chips and candy bars. Cheese and crackers or cheese and an apple with a small glass of milk are good choices. Be sure teeth get brushed after the snack. This bedtime snack has another purpose: It's a one-on-one time between parent and child, an occasion to talk and share love.

☐ **776. THE CHUBBY CHILD.**   Talk with children about body size. Don't praise thin bodies too much, but make it clear that pleasingly plump isn't as good as it sounds. Children who overeat are often sending messages. Research has shown that parents of fat children talked less to them, gave them less approval, and responded less to their behavior. And in the same research, slim children said that mealtime was more than foodtime, it was a time for interaction. Slim children ate less food at a slower rate and talked more to the group. The book *Don't Raise Your Child to Be a Fat Adult* (J. F. Wilkinson, Bobbs-Merrill, 1980) reports that one out of four American children is obese and that spending time with a child can help to slim him down: time talking, time showing interest in activities, time planning vigorous games and sports and carrying them out.

Encourage a chubby child to prepare a snack and sit down to eat it, rather than standing at the kitchen counter with a container of juice and a box of crackers, or walking around with a bag of chips. Parental encouragement and approval for improved eating habits is the single most important item in the success of a slim-down program with children. It doesn't have to be a diet, it can just be a new and better eating style. Don't wait; start it now.

★

SECTION 4: GOOD AND HAPPY

Many things contribute to a happy mental attitude. Some are as simple as knowing what parents expect, others are attitudes taught little-by-little over the years. Your most important gift to your child is self-esteem (ideas on this subject start with number 789). Sometimes a child feels frustrated and angry (ways to help begin with number 797). And in these changing times, you want children to be confident and informed about sex (read ideas 801 and onward). An open and understanding attitude on a parent's part will make for both a happy childhood and happy parenting years.

☐ **777. PARAMETERS.** Research shows children are happiest when they understand just how far they can go—what is acceptable or unacceptable in the family. When your toddler can talk, start a looseleaf notebook of simple rules (like not crossing the street), putting one rule on each page and letting her illustrate the rule with a drawing or a picture cut from a magazine. Add to the family rule book as she gets older, moving no longer needed rules to a section at the back of the book. Let older children join in making the rules and determining what happens when they're broken. Keep the notebook current, right up to the day a child leaves home for life on her own. You'll find that written-down rules are more effective than verbal ones.

☐ **778. GOOD FAMILIES DO FIGHT.** But they also know how to reconcile after an argument. Talk about ways to show that the fight is over. Suggest reconciliation lines that all family members can and should use after both sides have had their say, such as: "Let's talk about it next week." "How about making popcorn?" "That's enough on that topic, let's talk about . . ." "I see you feel strongly about this, but family peace means more to me, so I'll drop it." And remember the tradition of shaking with left hands to show that the argument is over.

☐ **779. NO CLIQUES.**   It's natural for family members to seek out certain other family members on a one-on-one basis. But cliques and "ganging up" on one person are damaging. When you see this happening, be quick to talk about it with those involved. Then organize games or work projects that change the pairs of children and parents to encourage a different one-on-one relationship.

☐ **780. PRIORITIES.**   With family input, make a list of the important events and chores for the month. Include things like soccer practice, a visit to Grandpa, and cleaning the garage. Number these starting with #2. At the top of the list, as #1, write: "Family Togetherness Time" and list some possible related activities. Look at the list often and be sure that the #1 priority is being accomplished along with the others. Make a new priority list each month, but keep the same #1.

☐ **781. MODERN ETIQUETTE.**   Times change, but these dozen are still good manners: (1) using "please" and "thank you," (2) thank you notes for gifts received and thanking others for being entertained; (3) proper introductions of friends to adults; (4) not interrupting or contradicting in the middle of a conversation; (5) promptness; (6) not snooping in the homes of others or picking up precious things; (7) standing when an adult visitor enters the room; (8) not starting to eat until others are ready and knowing which piece of flatware to use; (9) talking during a meal, but not with a full mouth; (10) keeping elbows off the table; (11) placing flatware at the four o'clock position on the plate when finished eating and staying at the table until the meal is over and one is excused; (12) passing food around the table, taking a proportionate amount, and passing the salt and pepper together. And for added compliments, teach kids to seat adults and open doors!

☐ **782. BEING A CHILD.**   Certain things can only be enjoyed when you are a child, so don't rush children into adult activities. Don't let being grown-up seem better than being a child. Don't push a child to learn to read as a toddler; don't plan his entire educational career before he starts kindergarten; don't shove children into beauty contests and designer jeans. There's just as much magic in toy cars as in getting a driver's license, just as much joy in make-believe dress-up as in getting pierced ears. If you need help in enjoying and appreciating the childhood years with your kids, read *The Hurried Child* (David Elkind, Addison-Wesley, 1981). Fight the argument "But everybody does it."

☐ **783. HAVING FUN.**   Good humor (but not teasing) is part of family life. Encourage kids to share funny stories. Outlaw groans that discourage humor and also outlaw sick humor and racial jokes. Tell a funny story, real or imagined. See who can retell it better. Share humorous cartoons and comics. Go to a funny movie or live comedy show and talk about what was funny. At large family gatherings such as Easter, Independence Day, or Thanksgiving, start the tradition of a joke contest. Appoint two or three people to be the "laugh meters" and have them choose the stories that get the biggest laughs. These get a prize. Be sure that you as a parent appreciate humor. Some adults are just aged children who have lost their love of humor—and that's "hardening of the attitudes." A good book to read is *The Laugh Book: A New Treasury of Humor for Children* (Joanna Cole and Stephanie Calmenson, Doubleday, 1986). Use books such as this as a jump-off for family humor.

☐ **784. A TIME FOR TWO.**   When the family consists of several children, everyday life may not provide one-on-one time between parent and child. It's important to find a portion of the day for these close times, and certainly at bedtime. You can also establish togetherness activities—something that you and only one child enjoy. These could be projects and crafts at home, or outside fun such as fishing, bowling, art gallery visits, jogging, or shopping—whatever interests both parent and child.

☐ **785. TIME-FOR-ALL.**   As children enter the teen years, homework and outside activities increase to the point where there might be no time for the family as a group. To keep the family together, you can decide early in the week that certain weekend hours will be spent together. Or, you can establish a certain night of the week as a family night. Some families find that a two-hour time on Thursday or Sunday evening is a good choice. Whatever you choose, start this time-for-all when children are young and keep it going through the teen years. Let family members take turns suggesting ways to spend this precious time.

☐ **786. GETTING ALONG.**   One wise mother, now a grandmother, made this rule: If you can't get along with your own brother or sister, you can't play with the kids on the block or friends from school. She explained that a child knows sisters and brothers best, so the child should be most able to be accommodating and understanding with them. Being successful in relationships with those we love gives us know-how in dealing happily with many other personalities. Love begins at home and radiates outward.

☐ **787. THE WHOLE PERSON.** Love your child for what he is. Be satisfied with a child who is a *child*, not a specialist in some adult field. Don't let schools label or categorize your child at an early age. You *may* have a math genius on your hands, but you also want a whole child, not a lopsided whiz who knows nothing about self-government, self-esteem, loving another as himself, or how to enjoy simple fun. Avoid attempts to push a child into advanced work until you feel the child is growing into a well-rounded individual. Value good work *and* good habits, good character, good motives.

☐ **788. SHARING AND NOT SHARING.** Not everything has to be shared by young siblings. Try this rule: If a toy or game is in the living room or family room, all children may play with it. If a child doesn't want to share a toy, it must be taken to his room and put away or played with there. When children start grade school, they can have unshareable toys in family areas providing they make it well known that no one else gets to use them.

☐ **789. "MY GREAT AND GOOD LIST."** To build self-esteem, help a child create a list of one or more good things she has done in the past. Put the list where the child can see it (her bed table or bookshelf is a good place). Make an effort to find good things to add to the list, no matter how small. Encourage her to add to the list, too. Look at it each night at bedtime and compliment the child on this growing list of great and good things. This is between parent and child and not for sharing with the other kids.

☐ **790. A SPECIAL-INTEREST COLLECTION.** Talk about collectibles. Let children start collecting things when they are toddlers. Go to hobby and collection shows and see what interests a child. Popular collectibles he might choose are stamps, miniatures, shells, cars, baseball cards, coins, bells, glass eggs, stuffed bears, dolls, music boxes, model planes, and rocks. When a child has a collection, ideas for gift-giving are easier too. Help a child to display his collection and share it with others. The special nature of his collection will also make him feel special.

☐ **791. TWO-WAY STREET.** Building self-esteem, showing appreciation, giving praise—we think that those are parent-to-child projects. But kids understand self-esteem better when they realize it's essential for every family member. To make the point that it's a two-way street, try this project. Draw a face on paper and put a crown on the head. Write under the picture the name of one of the children, for example, Alexandra. Tack her picture on the bulletin board and keep some stars handy. Anytime someone else in the family does or says something in praise of Alexandra, he gets to stick a star on her crown. Another week, put up a picture of a parent and follow the same idea, showing that parents need praise too. Continue until all family faces have had a turn.

☐ **792. GROWN-UP WORK.** Kids feel needed and responsible when you let them take over some of your duties. Let them pay the bill at a restaurant, give you the right change, and compute the proper tip. Or, let them put mail in the slot, address envelopes, or dial telephone calls. Older children can take on shopping, running errands, or paying for an extra little gift for someone. Little by little, loose them from your supervision, letting them take on things they are able to do and feel satisfaction in doing.

☐ **793. WATCH YOUR LANGUAGE.** In addition to avoiding profanity, parents have a special opportunity to build esteem with just the right words. No matter how exasperated you are, try not to say to a child "You never do anything right!" or any other line that lowers self-esteem. Practice saying these: "I'm glad you're my kid." "I love you no matter what." "We'll look back at this and laugh." "That was better."

☐ **794. HONORED GUEST.** Once a month or whenever the time is right, have a dinner in honor of one member of the family. He sits at the head of the table, is served first, doesn't have to help clear the table, and so on. Start the meal with a parent proposing a water or milk toast to the honoree. As in testimonial dinners, the others at the table say only nice things about the honored guest, such as "Cameron, we're so proud that you have a part-time job after school." Or, talk about a good grade, a speech trophy, a new haircut, or a story out of his past. Siblings try hard to do this, since they know they will be honored at another time. Although it will probably be a humorous mealtime, it makes the honoree feel good. End the meal with applause!

☐ **795. CHANGE "CAN'T" TO "CAN."**   When a child wants to try something and you must say that she *can't* do it, be sure to say what she *can* do. In this way, you don't leave her feeling helpless or useless. For example: "You can't jump off the roof, but you can jump off a low tree branch." "You can't sleep out in the park tonight, but you can sleep in the yard." "You can't go to a movie tonight, but you can go tomorrow or Saturday."

☐ **796. SING FOR JOY!**   Singing takes the anxiety out of situations and can also be a reassuring way to connect with another. For example, a parent cooking in the kitchen might sing out one line: "I'm working hard on things to eat." The child in an adjacent room sings back a rhyming line: "I like carrots, rice, and meat." A work song might go like this: "When we all work together we have lots of fun; when we all work together, we get the job done." The tune isn't important! Some families sing a hymn before supper. Parents often sing children to sleep. Let there be music around the table, around the piano, and in the car.

☐ **797. A SHOWER OR BATH.**   To help an angry child, remember that warm water soothes and the quietness of the bathroom brings peace. Depending on the child's age, stay with him or check up on him. Tell him how much you love him and how you'd like to help him concerning what made him angry. When the anger fades, talk about the problem.

☐ **798. POPPING BAGS.**   Suggest to a child that you both go and make a lot of noise before talking about the source of the anger. Take some paper bags (lunch bag size is best) and blow into them, filling them up. Using one hand to hold the opening tightly shut, see who can make the biggest pop by smashing them with the other hand.

☐ **799. PUNCHING BAGS.**   When a child feels like punching some*one*, substitute some*thing*. Beat the bed with a pillow, punch a beanbag chair, or throw balls at the garage door. Then sit down and talk, starting out with the fact that the anger didn't hurt anyone. Then talk about what caused the anger.

☐ **800. RUN AND WALK.** See how many seconds it takes to run around the house (or through every room of the apartment). Run again, seeing if the child can beat her own record. Then walk the same route hand-in-hand and talk about what's bugging her.

☐ **801. NO SPECIAL TIME.** Let a child understand that the differences in the sexes are not a mystery. Start with toddlers, using the proper terms for body parts and functions. No cutesy words and giggles. If sexuality is a natural part of family life yet private in some ways, you won't need to have one big "birds and bees" talk. Instead, you'll have many natural conversations as topics come up. Always be ready to answer questions clearly and simply. And don't broaden the topic with a big prepared speech; just answer the question asked.

☐ **802. GOOD BOOKS/GOOD IDEAS.** Consider providing books that give the facts on sex in kid-terms. From these will come some questions. Make it a practice to answer each one in short, simple terms. If the child is satisfied, then there is no need to elaborate. Questions about sex are different at each age. You are going to talk about it many times.

For younger children:
• Andrew C. Audry and Steven Schepp, *How Babies Are Made* (Time-Life, 1968).
• Martha Alexander, *Nobody Asked Me if I Wanted a Baby Sister* (Dial, 1971).
• Martha Alexander, *When the New Baby Comes, I'm Moving Out* (Dial, 1979).
• Sidonie Gruenberg, *The Wonderful Story of How You Were Born* (Doubleday, 1970).
• Sheila Kitzinger, *Being Born* (Grosset & Dunlap, 1986).
• Peter Mayle, *Where Did I Come From?* (Lyle Stuart, 1973).
• Lennart Nilsson, *How Was I Born?* (Delacorte, 1975).
• Guy Daniels, *The Beauty of Birth* (Knopf, 1971).

For older children:
• Evelyn Ruth Duvall, *Love and the Facts of Life* (Association Press, 1963).
• Life Cycle Center, *The Life Cycle Library* (Kimberly-Clark, 1981).
• Wardell Pomeroy, *Boys and Sex* (Delacorte, 1981).
• Wardell Pomeroy, *Girls and Sex* (Delacorte, 1981).
• Charlie Shedd, *The Stork Is Dead* (Word, 1982).

☐ **803. ANIMALS ARE EDUCATIONAL.** If you have hamsters with babies, a cat with kittens, or often-pregnant mice or bunnies, your child will soon have some questions about how animals get pregnant and how babies are born. You'll find the pets a big help in taking some of the mystery out of sex and birthing. Give factual answers. Explain how natural the process of birth is.

☐ **804. SEX EDUCATION IN SCHOOL.** Nowadays many schools have authoritative programs for grade and high school students. It is a parent's right to see an outline of these classes and the texts used. See that you have covered at home the subjects to be explained in school *prior* to the school discussions. Afterward, talk more to see what aspects were confusing or divergent from your own family ideas.

☐ **805. NO STORKS.** When Mother is pregnant, explain this to a young child when the mother begins to show (telling earlier sometimes makes the pregnancy seem *so* long to a child). Tell him often how much you love him and how parents can love two children—or twelve children. Let the child feel the baby move and listen to its sounds. Clearly explain that this is a safe, natural event and that mother will need some special care (no skiing), but she'll be able to do most things. Include the child in the preparations for the new baby, emphasizing how much you appreciate his help and how much you'll need it in the future. Remember to say that he was once a baby, and you're so glad he does so many more things now than the baby will do.

☐ **806. TV SEX.** While parents should try to shield children from sex scenes on TV, point out the differences between TV sex and married love. Talk about the fictitious and supposedly entertaining nature of TV and movie sex scenes. Talk about love, commitment, loyalty, marriage, and fidelity. See which of these are shown in a particular TV love scene. Don't forget to let a child see everyday caring and affection between parents. However, teach children early to respect your closed bedroom door.

☐ **807. THE BIRTH.** While it was popular for some years to have relatives, good friends and young children attend the birth of a new baby, many experts now feel that this is a close moment between wife and husband (or one close friend or relative). It helps the delivery to have less confusion and for the mother to be free of concern for the other children. Some children have had emotional problems from witnessing hard labor and difficult deliveries, and by being whisked away before an emergency Caesarean birth. But be sure a child sees the new baby just as soon as possible. Father might take the child out of school to see his new brother or sister—that's special!

☐ **808. PREMARITAL SEX.** Parents should start talking about the problems of premarital sex as soon as the grade school years. Don't let your own experience color what you expect of your child. Talk about pregnancy prevention, AIDS, venereal disease, abortion, and, most of all, abstinence. You may want to explain it this way. Sex is like a wonderful gift that has arrived in advance of Christmas. It will definitely be opened and enjoyed. Sex can be a beautiful experience, but it has to be experienced at the right time, with the right person. Another analogy: Would you want a child to fly an airplane? No, there are things that must be learned before that experience can be successfully enjoyed. There is nothing wrong with sex, but there *is* a right time for it. Keep the lines of communication open here by being frank and calmly answering all questions.

☐ **809. ANOTHER AUTHORITY.** Some parents don't have answers to sex questions or are too uncomfortable with the subject, and some kids don't believe what parents say. But there's still a way to educate. An outside authority sometimes can get the message across. Find factual magazine articles that cover the subject in a way that you approve of. Just put a paper clip on the article and leave it in a child's room. If he wants to talk about it after reading the article, listen carefully and answer questions. Sometimes a conversation with an authoritative person can be arranged: a minister, a counselor, a doctor, or an older friend. However you do it, see that your child is educated; don't ignore the subject and don't assume he knows it all. If you don't know the answers, it's time you got educated, too.

TEN

THE ROUND TABLE

alking around the supper table, by the fireplace, in the car, or on a walk gives young people opportunities to speak, to listen, to try out ideas, to express opinions, and to analyze different viewpoints. Research shows that children who are talked with and questioned grow the most, intellectually.

★

SECTION 1: HOW TO TALK MEANINGFULLY

☐ **810. TALK ABOUT TALK.** Start with some conversational guidelines. What do kids dislike about talking—sounding foolish? Being interrupted often? Starting an argument? Hostility to ideas. Being talked down to? Generalizations? Set down guidelines, which start with being a good listener (especially important for parents), waiting for a pause to pick up the conversation, letting everyone share the conversation time, asking questions, speaking as equals (no talking down), dealing in facts and feelings, and disputing politely. Choose casual and comfortable environments conducive to honest talk. Avoid serious discussions when anyone is angry, sleepy, sad, or hurried.

☐ **811. INTERRUPTIONS.** Researchers find that a good and spirited conversation includes interruptions. This is OK providing it's done equally, with no one person interrupting or being interrupted too often. Long monologues really aren't conversation anyway. Keep a scratch pad handy so that participants can make a quick note on something they didn't get to say or something they want to remember to add later. When talkers get used to occasional interruptions and find that they often help the flow of conversation, they don't mind.

☐ **812. AGREEING TO DISAGREE.** Face it, there are times when the family won't be in agreement. Set an example by showing your acceptance of another point of view. Emphasize the areas of agreement in the topic and talk about the differences, but don't make it a high priority to resolve them. Help talkers to find the "because" factor. Say, "Brian doesn't want a moose head on the wall in the living room because he thinks it's wrong to hunt animals." Or, "Samantha, is your negative feeling about the vacation because you don't want to leave Chipper in a dog kennel?" Show that respect for and understanding of another point of view doesn't have to mean that we accept that point of view.

☐ **813. A MODERATOR.** Let kids take turns being the moderator for family conversations. The moderator has these duties: to select a topic in consultation with others, to see that everyone gets an opportunity to talk, to help people disagree without being hurtful, to keep the conversation on the subject or to let it move to another topic with everyone's approval, to make a summary at the end of the conversation time.

☐ **814. HARMONY LINES.** Sometimes just a few words make the conversation run more smoothly and the participants talk more freely. Let all talkers remember these lines: "You really know a lot about this subject." "You put that very well." "I can see you feel strongly about this." "You're right!" "I like what you said." "I agree, but . . . "

★

SECTION 2: SIMPLE CHATS

Before embarking on round-table discussions, be sure you have opportunities for extended but casual conversations within the family on a daily basis.

☐ **815. TALK ABOUT TODAY.** Ask what was the best thing that happened today (or this week). What was the most exciting? The most fearful? What made you angry? What made you laugh? Such talk gives parents an opportunity to see how children react to everyday events and to help them keep experiences in perspective. If kids report nothing interesting about the day, it's an opportunity to plan some small event or adventure as soon as possible!

☐ **816. CHOICES.** Talk about "what if." If you could be anyone in the world, who would you be? If you had a thousand dollars, what would you do with it? If you could go back in time, what era would you choose? If you could be the parent in the family, what would be the first thing you'd do? If you could spend one day doing whatever you please, what would it be? Also discuss in detail one or two of the "what ifs" and see if you can make them come true.

☐ **817. TV TALK.** Television provides many good topics. What characters do you admire? If you could be a TV star, which one would you choose? Which commercials are good and why? How can you decide if a commercial is truthful? What is the purpose of violence on TV? Are the women on TV like Mom or are they different? What kinds of businesses and jobs are shown on TV? Are they shown honestly? Look at a TV show together and during the commercials and at the end talk about what's good or bad.

☐ **818. INVENTIONS.** Talk about things that weren't invented when you were a child—perhaps waterbeds, space shuttles, computers, or trash compactors. See which inventions kids think are very helpful and which are mostly cosmetic or frivolous. Talk about things you think will be invented when the kids are parents themselves. Consider an invention that you could use at your home. If it exists, put it on your "wish list."

☐ **819. DAILY PRAISE.** Chat each day with a child about something she's done well. Sometimes this is difficult, and the best thing you can say is "you were better behaved today than yesterday." Don't assume a child *knows* you appreciate and love her. Until it becomes natural for you, put the initials "DP" (for daily praise) in your personal calendar. If you've forgotten all day long to praise a child, you have a final chance at bedtime.

★

SECTION 3: JUMPING-OFF PLACES

Try these longer topics for in-depth conversations with older children.

☐ **820. PICK A TOPIC.** Start your round-table discussions with something important that doesn't directly concern the family. Talk in depth about just one subject. See that everyone is heard. Don't let parents take over. Sometimes announce the topic in advance, so all can be prepared. Or, choose a topic that no one knows much about; thus, everyone has to "bone up" a little. Talk about capital punishment, health foods, campus protests, and UFOs. Remember the line, "What do *you* think?"

☐ **821. FAMILY RULES.** Talk about the rules your family has. Are they necessary? How do they help? What rules will kids make when they are parents? Are there any new rules that the family needs? Which ones can be dropped? Do any of your rules relate to city, state, or federal laws? What laws directly affect kids? What are the hardest laws for adults to follow? What are unwritten rules? Just so kids can't say "I didn't know," write down the major rules your family has. Post them on the bulletin board. Bring them up to date regularly.

☐ **822. PRIORITIES AND VALUES.** Help children make choices as to what's important in their lives. Discuss these choices: Would you rather sleep Saturday morning or earn $10? Would you rather have a good but routine job and receive a weekly paycheck or do more exciting work but earn a commission? Would you rather have one fabulous party each year or three small parties? Would you rather volunteer as a hospital aide or help serve free meals to the homeless? If you could solve a problem, would you work on poverty, racism, drugs, world peace, energy, or major health disorders? In such discussions you may be talking about good and evil, wealth and poverty, right and wrong, pipe dreams and possibilities.

☐ **823. TWO-FAMILY TALK.** Invite another family that you know well for snacks and conversation. Pick a topic that is two-generation oriented and see if you can have a thirty- to sixty-minute conversation. Topics might be how to get the most out of living in this town, ways to save money, interesting vacations, learning to trust others, temptations old and new, or college life and benefits. If it goes well, have a talk another time with the same family, perhaps at their house.

☐ **824. ECONOMICS FOR KIDS.** Talk about money and its uses. What was the most expensive item in our supper? Do we spend more on food or housing? Which costs more, getting dental braces or a new bicycle? Who earns more, a teacher, a minister, a senator, or a truck driver? Share a simple household budget, showing what percentage of earnings goes for food, home rent or payments, clothes, entertainment, college funds, electricity, and other expenditures. Consider ideas on improving family economics. Decide to make some changes and talk about them again later to see if they are working.

☐ **825. DATING.** Well before kids get interested, talk about dating. Then talk about it again when kids start to date. Suggest interesting things to do on dates. What kinds of things can you talk about so you get to know the other person? Discuss why some people are popular and others don't seem to be. What would each family member look for in a close friend? What's current dating etiquette? Why do people go steady? Is going steady an invitation to sex? Is this a good idea? How can you break off a relationship? How do you get over a relationship? Let kids suggest and you add ideas on things they would never do when on a date. Talk about the family home and how it can be used for fun with a date or with a group of friends.

☐ **826. RACISM.**   See who can name all the races of humans. What race are we? Whom do we know of other races and nationalities? What are the stereotypes of ethnic groups? How do books, movies, and TV show people of other races? What are cultural differences? Do these affect people today? How can we get along with people of other races? What can we do to get to know families of another race? What is our church doing? What is our town doing? What would it be like to be part of a multiracial family? How can racial disagreements be settled before they reach the violent stage? See if there are people of other races that you can get to know and have as friends.

☐ **827. HEROES.**   Base this conversation on a news clipping about a local hero. Who are the heroes in history? Who were Bible heroes? Who were the heroes in literature? What are some heroic professions? Do some heroes remain nameless? Has someone in the family done something heroic? Are heroes role models? What causes people to be brave and strong? Encourage family members to put pictures of people who do heroic deeds on the family bulletin board. Do you know someone who has done something heroic? Find out how and why they did it.

☐ **828. DILEMMAS.**   Take turns presenting dilemmas. Encourage kids to give honest answers. Don't criticize any answer, just give alternate solutions and keep the conversation going. Here are some to start: What if you found a wallet with money and ID in it? What if you found a $10 bill on the sidewalk? What if the bank put extra money in your account? What if you saw someone shoplifting? What if the soda machine returned extra coins to you? What if someone asked to copy your test answers? What if you were asked to deliver a mysterious package to another kid? What if you worked in an office that had supplies you could use at home? What if you were small for your age and could get into the movies for child-prices? Would you stop at a red light at a deserted corner at midnight? What if you see a policeman accepting money from a driver he's pulled over to the side? What if you are driving in a parking lot with a friend who damages a parked car? What do you say if the friend asks you to be quiet about it, but then the owner comes back and asks if you saw anything? Remember, these are discussions, not tests!

☐ **829. BULLIES.** Talk about bullies: the ones who try to bully physically and those who try to bully mentally. What is intimidation? How can one fight back effectively? When should one stand up for one's rights? When should one separate oneself from the situation? Do we bully other family members? Can a family member speak up when his viewpoint is unpopular? Do we bully each other by playing favorites? Do we bully each other by using cruel, snide, or cynical remarks? How can we get our way without being a bully? Are peacemakers respected? Make up some mock scenarios and let kids and parents act them out so they can practice their responses.

☐ **830. LOVE AND SEX.** This discussion will be repeated at different times during a child's growing-up years. Sometimes it will be better as a one-on-one conversation. Parents can start when children are young with these topics: What do we mean by the word "love"? Whom do we love? How are boys different from girls? Why are some things private? What do you do when someone tries to touch your private areas? What kinds of love do we see on TV and in books? Later you'll want to talk frankly about body changes and puberty, premarital sex, pregnancy and prevention, AIDS, fidelity, and the marriage commitment. (Also see chapter 9, section 4, on sex.)

☐ **831. DREAMS.** Everyone dreams, but many often forget what they dreamed. An interesting conversation time can center on dreams: what one remembers, how real events weave in and out of dreams. Find out about REMs (rapid eye movements). Do most people think dreams have any connection with life, or are they usually fantasies? What can one do about scary dreams? You may want to look up the subject in a reference book.

☐ **832. "HELP ME!"** A child should feel comfortable asking family members for help with personal problems. Sometimes a child will want to talk only with a parent, but sometimes the entire family can give suggestions. A discussion of the problem and possible solutions makes everyone feel better. "How can I help you?" is such a nice offer for a parent to make to a child. Encourage discussion of problems in relationships, physical development and ability, schoolwork, and future plans and dreams. When you don't have the answers, help a child find someone who does.

☐ **833. MAKING CONVERSATION.** Discuss what makes another person fun to talk with, questions that keep the conversation going, and body language to use when talking to others. Below are some questions a person might use to initiate conversation with people of different ages. You may want to act out some of these discussions. Tell family members to report back when they've actually used some of the questions.

• With younger kids: Who is your best friend? If you could have just one toy, what would it be and how would you play with it? What time of the day do you like best? (Adults should avoid asking kids: Have you been good? Do you like TV?)

• With older kids: What feelings do you get when you listen to music? Has the women's movement affected your school? What fashion trends are your favorites? (Adults should avoid asking: When are you going to wear real clothes? What do you want to be when you grow up?)

• With young adults: What's the greatest time-saver in your busy life? What's the most important thing you've read lately? How do you fit sports into your schedule? (Avoid: How many children are you going to have? Do you smoke marijuana?)

• With senior citizens: Who was the most famous celebrity you ever met? Do you see trends or cycles in government (or in clothing, economics, entertainment)? Our weather's been bad, but what's the worst storm you remember? (Avoid: How are you feeling? Have you made out your will?)

• With the bereaved: I know you have a lot to do, so how could I help you? Do you remember that wonderful afternoon we all had together? Everyone cares about you; do you know you're a survivor? (Avoid: You'll soon forget your grief. It's all for the best.)

• With businesspeople: How have computers changed your business? What qualities do you look for in employees who want to move up in your business? If you were to start over today, would you choose the same field? (Avoid: What do you do all day long? Can I give you a suggestion?)

☐ 834. TEN COMMANDMENTS OF CONVERSATION.

Discuss these rules for successful conversational exchanges. (1) Thou shalt have at least three topics of interest to talk about at a social event. (2) Thou shalt have an ace-in-the- hole question for a time when the room becomes interminably silent. (3) Thou shalt not give monologues but let other people talk too. (4) Thou shalt look pleasant when thou talkest, avoiding scowling and other body language that intimidates. (5) Thou shalt not be afraid of a pause in the conversation; it provides a time to react to and think about what has been said. (6) Thou shalt treat another's topic tenderly, disagreeing with grace, not putting the other person down. (7) Thou shalt read newspapers, magazines, and books so that you talk with facts, not rumors or gossip. (8) Thou shalt work to include all members of the group, not leaving out one sex or age. (9) Thou shalt plant clues in your conversation for others to pick up and ask about. (10) Thou shalt remember that conversation is at least 50 percent listening.

★

SECTION 4: PROBLEM-SOLVING DISCUSSIONS

☐ 835. THE LIST.

Start with young children to solve problems rather than allowing them to continue. Some problems just go away if you ignore them for a while, but when one persists, it needs to be dealt with. Make a list of problems *you* must solve. Talk with your spouse about them and decide which ones are for parents only and which involve the children. Talk with them about the difficulties you plan to settle. Let kids add their problems to the list, too. Then take them up one at a time. Try to find the solution to a major problem and cross it off the list each month.

☐ 836. FIVE STEPS.

When the family has gathered for the first time to solve a problem, introduce these five steps—steps you'll use often: (1) Gather facts; (2) state the problem concisely; (3) list the alternatives; (4) carefully consider each alternative; (5) make a decision for now.

Good books about this topic are: *Raising Brothers and Sisters Without Raising the Roof* (Carol and Andrew Calladine, Winston, 1983) and *Problem Solving Techniques in Childrearing* (Myrna Shure and George Spivac, Jossey-Bass, 1978).

Here's an example of how to use the steps:

1. Facts: Karen returned home at 1:00 A.M. last night. The curfew is 12:30 A.M. She's been late before. Dad was very angry. Karen got angry, too.

2. The problem: The parents don't want this to happen again. Karen is afraid of being punished severely.

3. Alternatives: Never let Karen go out again. Get rid of curfews. Put an alarm clock in Karen's purse. Make the curfew earlier. Make the curfew later. Punish her date. Make her come in earlier next time, by as many minutes as she was late. "Campus" her one night for every fifteen minutes late. Make a flexible curfew, say 12:15 to 12:45 A.M.

4. Talk over each alternative and rule out those that are unacceptable. Consider the remaining ones.

5. Plan to try two or three of the possible solutions over the next month to see how they work.

☐ **837. BASIC SKILLS AND ASSUMPTIONS.**   Ask yourself, Do I really want this problem solved, or do I just want my way? Do the children have sufficient understanding to help solve this problem, or should the parents solve it alone? Is this the time to solve it? Are the family members rested and calm? If so, go ahead with the five steps, remembering that you are an independent fact-getter, a nonjudgmental and loving negotiator. Start early to use the term "negotiate" with your children.

☐ **838. FEELINGS, TOO.**   Facts are important, but feelings are too. As you hear others talk about a problem, also encourage them to share their feelings. How did they feel before the problem occurred? How do they feel now? What would make them feel happy or satisfied? From the understanding of feelings, you may be able to bring about a solution that just facts wouldn't indicate. Encourage kids to consider feelings—theirs and others'.

☐ **839. WITH YOUNGER CHILDREN.**   Your problem-solving session will be shorter, but it should still follow the same five steps listed above. Younger children can often explain a problem to you by acting it out; in that way they may reveal more facts.

Some children like to put the problem or argument in the mouths of puppets or other toys. You can also ask a child to make up a story about a friend who had this same trouble. This defining of the problem is the hardest part. Next, you'll want to suggest some solutions and let the child suggest some, too. Make them many and varied, make some funny, then start eliminating them until you get down to the final ones. These deserve careful consideration before the decision is made. Don't hesitate to let a child change the decision and try another acceptable alternative. When the problem is solved, be very congratulatory about it.

☐ **840. WITH GRADE SCHOOL CHILDREN.** The same five steps are used, but often you have to stop all the action to get a problem-solving session going. This age is good at the five-step process since they like being sleuths and gathering the facts. They're also more inventive in suggesting solutions. A parent can be more specific in telling a child exactly what behavior is expected of him. You will find kids are very careful in selecting from the alternatives. Start using the five steps on a minor matter so that they are familiar when you get to more difficult problems. At this age, you may find that they solve some predicaments on their own using some or all of the steps.

☐ **841. EVERYONE'S A WINNER.** When a decision has been made, it should be satisfying to all parties. There shouldn't be a winner or loser, but just adjustments in behavior or activities. Make the process challenging but fun. Adjourn when you're about to lose your temper or when anyone else is mad or feeling tense or picked on. Pick up the discussion at some better time. Take time to go over the decision later to see how it's working. And don't forget the praise!

☐ **842. PLAY GAMES.** Some in-car or around-the-table games help children practice problem-solving and negotiation. Ask kids some "How would you feel if . . . " questions and let them ask you some, too: "How would you feel if someone broke your best toy?" "How would you feel if you were complimented on a job you didn't do?" "How would you feel if you were wrongly accused?" Also ask kids "What would you do if . . ." questions: "What would you do if you didn't want to play the game?" "What would you do if someone hit you?" "What would you do if you broke something precious?" If you contemplate a situation and the solution before it occurs, then a proper result will come more naturally.

ELEVEN

CELEBRATE!

 ere are new views of birthdays and holidays and new ways to celebrate and share the joy. Party planning isn't just for moms. You'll find it's more fun when the family works together. And don't depend on the calendar; you can have a party *any* day.

★

★*Section 1:* Parties for all ages
★*Section 2:* Games for all ages
★*Section 3:* Around-the-year celebrations
★*Section 4:* The best-ever Christmas
★*Section 5:* Make your own holidays

SECTION 1: PARTIES FOR ALL AGES

FOR YOUNGER CHILDREN

☐ **843. THE BIRTHDAY CROWN.**   With child-help, fashion a sturdy cardboard crown and cover it with foil. Add glitter, foil, or cellophane "jewels" to it, so that it is really elegant. Put it on the night table in the birthday person's room after he's gone to sleep the evening before his birthday. The next morning, he may wear it to breakfast and anywhere else he chooses. Keep the crown for the next birthday person.

☐ **844. DANCING DOLLS.**   Using a very long piece of sturdy white shelf paper, fold it accordion-style in about eight-inch widths, making about eighteen folds. Then, let a child draw the outline of *half* a boy or girl on the top paper in the stack. The figure should have an arm and hand extending to the folded edge of the paper. (You may want to refine the silhouette a little, since this is going to be with you for many years.) Now using a big pair of scissors or a very sharp knife, cut through the paper following the outline, being careful not to cut where the hands join. (You may remember this from making paper dolls.) The child takes the top piece and you take the bottom, carefully opening it into a long line of dancing dolls. The first doll gets a number on it corresponding to the child's birthday age. He then uses marking pens to put face and clothes on that paper doll corresponding to how he thinks he looks today. String out the dancing dolls across the fireplace or the stairs—wherever they'll be seen. Save them and each year bring them out a few days before the birthday. Let the birthday person number and decorate the next doll.

☐ **845. PRACTICE TIME.**   A few days before the birthday party, let a child practice some of the skills she'll need to make her guests glad they came. You pretend to be one of her guests. Ring the doorbell and let her open the door, invite you in, and show the way to the party room. Put one of her toys in a box and have her pretend to open a gift and say something about it. (And what does she say if it's something she already has?) Let her practice the end of the party, walking you to the door and thanking you for coming and for the gift.

☐ **846. TAKE-HOME BAG.**   Provide a small paper bag for each child attending the party. Before the party, let your child make a drawing on each bag. As the guests arrive, have crayons or markers available so each can put his name on his bag or draw another picture. The bags are put around the party room so that when a guest wins a prize or has a favor, he can put it in his own bag.

☐ **847. MANY PRIZES.**   Everyone likes to be a winner, so rather than having a few expensive prizes, have many inexpensive ones. In a game, the winner will get a prize, and all other participants will be awarded a small treat such as a sticker, gum, or a balloon. When buying prizes, look for ones that provide many prizes for one price, such as balloons. Good inexpensive prizes are pipes and bubbles, yo-yos, good comic books, bubble bath, sugarless gum, crayons, marking pens, chocolate kisses, small cars, and colorful stickers.

☐ **848. WISH LIST.**   Go with a child to a toy store and see which toys really interest her (rather than just giving in to TV-advertised toys). Younger children like things that move, so look at toys that roll or stack. Help her make a wish list that includes a variety of toys of different prices. You can use this list in purchasing her gifts and to help friends and relatives who ask for suggestions.

☐ **849. GOING-TO-A-PARTY GIFT.**   Let a child take part in the purchase of his gift to another child. As you browse, let him choose by himself three possible gifts. Then help him decide on one. Show him how to wrap it himself, perhaps in the paper of the Sunday comics, and also make his own card. You will find that the gifts he selects may be ones he'd enjoy himself on a gift occasion.

☐ **850. THE BUSY BOX GIFT.**   Call a local print shop and ask if they have leftover paper (they usually do and usually throw it away). Get various colors and shapes and stack it carefully in a nice sturdy box, which you decorate with the recipient's name. Let your child do the rest of the box decorating. Add paste, crayons, small scissors, a small stapler, and so on. Although it doesn't cost a lot, this Busy Box will be a very popular gift.

☐ **851. PIRATE PARTY.**   The invitations show a pirate ship and tell kids to wear costumes. Put a pirate flag on the backyard climbing apparatus and attach sheets to make great sails. Have gold coin chocolate candy on the eating table. The pirate's parrot can be a piñata. (If you can't buy one of these inexpensive gift holders, make one out of a sturdy bag.) Let each guest be blindfolded and try to hit the suspended piñata to break it open. Make treasure maps that lead to "hidden treasure" (prizes). Play "Walk the Plank," seeing who can walk blindfolded the length of a narrow plank on the floor.

☐ **852. CABBAGE PATCH PARTY.**   Each guest brings a favorite doll, Cabbage Patch variety or not. Awards are given for the cutest, best dressed, best smile, nicest hair, most lovable, chubbiest, most humorous, and so forth. In advance, help your child make the awards out of ribbon and foil, with a pin to affix to each doll. Guests introduce their dolls and make statements about the dolls' characters to "judges" (two parents), who later let the party person announce the winners. After lunch (which could include stuffed cabbage or coleslaw), children can make baby commercials. Divide the group into pairs. Let each team draw from a hat the picture of a product; you'll find plenty in just one baby magazine: diapers, baby food, a crib or rocker, a toy, shampoo. Give the pairs ten minutes to prepare their commercial, which can include dolls, a song, a poem, a skit—whatever they wish to employ to sell their product. Then they present their commercial to the group, which votes on the best. It's also fun to photograph these with a polaroid camera so that the photo can be taken home.

☐ **853. PARK PARTY.**   Plan a party in the park for active children. On a large piece of poster board, make a scorecard of the participants and the events: going down the slide feet first, head first, backward, in twos; swinging ten times; going through the tunnel or across the bars; taking part in a relay race. Paste on small stars for each event tried and big stars for each event completed. Hang balloons in the trees. Put all the gifts on one picnic table, food on another. When gifts are to be opened, let kids take turns choosing a package to be opened. The chooser must hop (or skip) from the gift table to the birthday child. The last event is to pick up all the trash and leave the park looking beautiful.

☐ **854. GIFT IDEAS.**   Go shopping (without buying) so the child can make a wish list that has gifts of various prices on it—including not just toys but also books, sports equipment, and clothes. Suggest some longlasting gifts such as a microscope or telescope, a rocket kit, a cassette player, or a certificate for an instrument of his choice. Use this list when friends or relatives need suggestions.

☐ **855. NEW PRIVILEGES.**   Parents should have a private meeting time with the birthday child. Give him new privileges and responsibilities: an increased allowance, a later bedtime, a larger clothing budget, a later curfew, more use of the family car, greater discretion in making his own choices, new areas of complete responsibility. Base these on age and past performance but be sure to make some changes each year. Make this meeting an important birthday event.

☐ **856. BEFORE THE PARTY.**   Talk about party rules, then write them down together so that there can be no misunderstanding. These rules can serve for all parties but should be discussed and modified for each event. Here are some ideas: A party is by invitation only. Those invited are not to bring guests without prior OK. Parents get to look at the guest list. Except on a special occasion, the number on the guest list should not exceed the number you can comfortably feed and entertain in your home. Once a party has started, there's no leaving and returning. An adult chaperon will always be on hand. Music will not be so loud as to disturb the neighbors. The party will end with a certain event at a certain time. Guests will have a safe way to go home. No alcohol will be served. No smoking or drug use will be permitted. Clean up of the party will be finished by the child by noon the next day.

☐ **857. THE SIMPLEST PARTY.**   If a youngster wants to have a party without much preparation, let it be a potluck party. Each guest brings part of the meal and the group prepares it together in the kitchen: salad, stuffed hot dogs, veggies and dip, apples, milk shakes. After the potluck, show a good rented movie or play a trivia game. Stop the movie about twenty minutes before the end. Serve popcorn and hot chocolate or sodas and let everyone guess how the movie will end, then see who's right. After the end of the movie, play music and talk.

☐ **858. OLYMPICS PARTY.** Help plan a party featuring many different sports: croquet, horseshoes, badminton, shooting baskets, Frisbee throwing, volleyball, relays, two-legged races, tug of war. Divide the guests into at least three teams. Let each team choose a country and a song (which doesn't have to relate to the country—it should just be a short peppy song others know). Make Olympic gold, silver, and bronze medallions out of foil and ribbon. Do one event at a time, awarding the prizes and singing the winning team's song after each event. Serve Olympic-size sandwiches and make-it-yourself sundaes.

☐ **859. CRAFT PARTY.** This works well for children about eight to twelve years old. Everyone takes part in making things.

• *Cooked Dough*. Let the group mix up a big batch: 3 cups water, 1 cup salt, 4 tablespoons alum, 4 tablespoons oil, 4½ cups flour. Bring the water and salt to a boil; you can add food coloring at this point. Remove from the heat and add the alum, oil, and flour. Knead well. See who can make the most fantastic object.

• *Scenic Paperweights*. Provide a small baby-food jar for each participant. You'll also need a box of moth flakes, Duco brand cement, and plastic figures or ceramic items and water. Glue the figure to the lid of the jar. Let it dry while you're doing another activity. Put 2 tablespoons of moth flakes in each jar, then add water almost to the rim. Put glue around the *outside* of the jar's rim and the *inside* rim of the lid. Screw the lid on the jar and don't turn it over until the glue has dried thoroughly. Then turn it over and watch it snow!

• *Crystal Spheres*. Mix ½ cup of Dawn brand detergent with 5 cups of water. Add a dash of glycerin for staying power. Mix well and place in a big, flat tray. Then let the kids fashion large wire hoops from coat hangers. Wrap the wire with cotton string or yarn to hold more of the solution. Go outside and make gigantic bubbles by dipping the hoops in the tray.

The food for this party can be in keeping with the crafts theme: make-it-yourself sandwiches and sundaes.

☐ **860. PIG PARTY.** Invitations should feature a pig and ask those attending to dress in pig-pink. The word "yes" is never said during the party; "oink" is used instead. Plan relays that are done on all fours. The refreshments should include a pig trough made by you and your child. Buy one or two long sections of plastic gutter at a building supply store. (This will be a favorite so it's worth the money—it's even useful for adult parties.) Be sure to get end pieces so that you have what looks like a very long dish. Thoroughly wash the gutter, then fill it, allowing about eighteen inches per eater. Put in scoops of ice cream with toppings. Yes, supply spoons for eating! The trough can also be used in other ways: space out groups of ten grapes in the trough and race to see who can guzzle them up first without using their hands. Or, fill the trough with popcorn and place it on the floor so that many can reach it at one time.

☐ **861. HORSE PARTY.**   For horse enthusiasts, this party can be fun and utilizes horse equipment, but it isn't necessary to invite a real horse. Guests come in jeans or riding clothes. Each guest chooses a horse name and uses it all through the party. Write these names in large print on name tags so everyone can see them. Serve lunch from a saddlebag and let the guest of honor sit on a saddle. Have lots of awards on hand for the games; these can be prepared by you and your child in advance and should look like horse-event ribbons. Out of foil and a large jar, make the loving cup for the overall winner. Games can be relays and jumping contests, but the favorite will be the hurdles. Before the party make simple hurdles out of lightweight wood posts, and poles or plastic sprinkler pipe. The poles should rest on pins on the posts, so that they fall off when a foot catches on them. Put in several sets of pins so that hurdles can be raised. Place the hurdles around a track. For practice, let the horse-guests compete with the hurdles low. Then raise them for each event. The hurdles are so much fun that you'll use them often, so you may want to invest the extra time in making them more permanent. This is a party where you'll definitely want to take pictures.

☐ **862. ITALIAN PARTY.**   This is ideal for kids who like to cook and can follow directions. Rewrite the following recipe on numbered three-by-five-inch cards, putting only a part of the directions on each card. Don't tell what the finished dish will be, but let kids go into the kitchen one by one and do what it says on the card. This recipe will feed eight. Assemble the following items before the party:

Broccoli—2 big stalks
1 medium-size onion
8 oz. can of peeled tomatoes
1 lb. lean chopped beef
2 cups water
Salt and pepper
¾ lb. of pasta (shells, bows, or elbows)
2 tablespoons of olive oil
1 loaf of crusty bread
Butter and parmesan cheese

Also assemble two large cooking pots, foil, a colander, table settings (including bowls), small ice-cream bowls, a tureen, an apron, potholders, and a small pan for melting butter. You'll also want spumoni ice cream in the freezer and apple cider or grape juice on ice.

The cards should say:

1. Fix the broccoli: wash, then peel the stems and cut into small pieces. Cut the head into spoon-size florettes.
2. Dice the onion. In the large pot, lightly brown the meat and onions in the oil.
3. Add to the pot: broccoli, the can of tomatoes, 1 tablespoon of salt, ½ teaspoon of pepper. Cover with two cups of water and bring to a boil, then immediately turn to low. Start heating water for pasta in the second pot. Tell the person with card #5 to go to the kitchen in twenty minutes.
4. Turn on oven to 350 degrees. Melt butter in a small pan. Slice bread and dip one side in butter. Sprinkle with cheese. Reassemble loaf and wrap in foil. Put in oven.
5. Check the broccoli for doneness. In the second pot, cook pasta according to directions on package. Check broccoli as pasta cooks, turning it off when tender. When pasta is done, drain it in the colander and rinse.
6. Take drained pasta and add it to the broccoli mixture. Taste and add salt if needed. The consistency should be like a thick soup, so add water if needed. Turn burner to low.
7. Set the table with napkins, utensils, and bowls. Put servings of spumoni in small bowls and put back into the freezer.
8. Fix beverages. Put hot bread on a plate and main dish in the tureen. Call everyone to dinner.

This dish is called Minestra and is a Sicilian recipe. Letting each guest work at putting it together is a party in itself. You'll get many comments along the way! You can show a good Italian movie after supper.

☐ **863. MYSTERY PARTY.** Older teens enjoy these packaged parties that test creativity. Check your game store for a mystery game kit. The kit supplies invitations and suggestions for costumes that the eight mystery characters can wear to the party. A tape is supplied that starts the who-done-it. Usually there are two acts, and characters answer questions in keeping with their role. You don't know the solution for about two hours; it's a suspenseful and exciting party. You might want to serve refreshments at the midpoint or just have snacks all during the game. Party and game shops have a variety of these games, which can usually be reused.

☐ **864. NEW INVENTIONS PARTY.** Everyone brings a toy or game and gets to tell what they like about it. Then, they tell how they would like to *change* it. After everyone has had a turn, give out paper and pencils for drawing or describing a picture of a toy or game that hasn't been created yet. Have each guest search your house for an invention that is (in his estimation) either the most or the least useful to a family. Play word games such as Scrabble and make the game prizes inexpensive items: batteries, marking pens, colored drawing paper, small notebooks, magnifying glasses, and other items for the inventive mind. For food, provide pita bread and a variety of fillings so kids can invent their own sandwiches.

☐ **865. ROCK STAR PARTY.** Each guest must dress as his favorite star and be prepared to lip sync a recording by that star. The party room should have colored lights and a fake microphone. Prizes are awarded for best costume and best singer. Set up small tables facing your "stage" and have snacks and soft drinks available, then finish the evening with dancing.

FOR ALL CHILDREN

☐ **866. PLANT A TREE.** If a child's birthday falls during the planting season in your area, present the child with his birthday tree. Pick a small tree, about the same height as the child. Carefully select the right spot and plant it together. Measure tree and child the next year. This becomes his own tree, and he should care for it as needed. Remind him that in the years to come when he returns to his old homesite, "his" tree will always be a reminder of the good years of growing up.

☐ **867. CHOOSE A BIRTH DATE.** What's so magical about the actual date on which a child was born? For a child, it's the celebration that counts: the friends, the party, the gifts, the cake, being the center of attention. Children born near Christmas often get cheated out of their fair share of gifts and excitement. This is important to the birthday person, so let her choose another date at a less busy time. Doing so also spreads out the gift-giving times for parents! For a December baby, consider the half-year birthday date. June is a great time to have a party!

☐ **868. JUNGLE PARTY.** Guests dress as Tarzan, Jane, or a jungle beast. Decorate with green crepe paper, paper flowers, and some live plants. Outside, hang ropes from trees for swinging. Have a hand-over-hand rope climb, which can be used for a contest. Also have a Tarzan call contest and award prizes for the best costumes. Serve food on mats on the floor or ground. Make it all finger foods: pineapple, papaya, banana bread, skewered meat sticks.

☐ **869. VIDEO PARTY.** This requires a team: the camera operator and the interviewer. Each guest will be interviewed as he arrives at the party. But prior to each interview, the interviewer secretly asks a question on camera. Then, with the camera *off*, he asks the guest a different question. The cameraman then turns the camera *on* for this answer. This mismatch of questions and answers can be very humorous. For example, the interviewer secretly says on camera, "Hello, Lisa, I'm the inquiring reporter. Could you tell our audience the proper way to behave in church?" Then, with the guest present but the camera *off*, he asks, "How do you apply your makeup so beautifully?" *Then* the camera comes on and records the answer. Other question combinations are (1) "How would you describe your best friend?" and "What does Godzilla look like?" and (2) "What makes an interesting conversation on a date?" and "What were the most difficult questions you've ever been asked on a test?" Keep the video camera going during lunch, taking extreme close-ups of people eating. Then, divide into teams of two and see which team can make the most unusual pose for the camera. Finally, after you have at least a half hour on tape, sit down together and play it all back.

SECTION 2: GAMES FOR ALL AGES

☐ **870. EYES AND FEET.**   This is actually three games. Hang a sheet in a doorway and cut a slit in it the size of an eye. Divide the players into two teams; put one behind the sheet and one on the other side. One person behind the sheet puts one eye up to the hole. Those on the other side of the sheet get one try to identify the eye and if they guess correctly they get a point. Then the next team member does the same, and as correct guesses are made, the process of elimination makes it easier. When the first team finishes, it's the other side's turn to try for a higher score. Next play it by cutting the hole slightly bigger and guessing mouths. The game can also be played by raising the sheet about six inches off the floor and guessing stocking feet or bare feet.

☐ **871. THE LABYRINTH.**   You'll need a little prize for each player. Wrap these and attach each to a different color piece of sturdy ribbon or yarn at least fifteen feet in length (longer for older kids). Attach a Popsicle stick to the other end. Put the prizes around one room—under chair legs, in a closed drawer, under heavy couch cushions—covering all sides of the room. Then take the attached ribbons and lay them across the room. As you lay each ribbon, weave it around the others. Bring all the Popsicle stick ends to one spot. Players choose a stick and then start winding up the ribbon, ducking under and around the others as they work to reach their prize. The game can also be played outside between trees, climbing bars, or bikes. Make the tangle of ribbons easier for young children, harder for older ones.

☐ **872. HOW YOU'VE CHANGED!**   In the party invitation, ask each guest to bring his baby photo. Place these around the room with a number by each. Everyone gets to look at the pictures during the early part of the party. Then give each person paper and a pencil to list the numbers and after the number the name of the baby. Give a prize for guessing the most right and also for the most wrong (don't tell this in advance). This game can also be used for a family reunion.

☐ **873. LEAN-TO.**   On soft carpet or grass, divide the group into pairs. Space the pairs a good distance from each other for safety.

The partners face each other, placing the palms of their hands together, then each takes a few steps backwards so that they are leaning on each other to keep their balance. When all the pairs are in this position, say "Go!" At the same time, each tries to push his or her partner back into a standing position without either one of them moving their feet. It's hard! The first to do it wins.

☐ **874. WHO'S WHO?** Using magazines that feature people, music, sports, or news, cut out pictures of well-known personalities. Give each picture a number and pin the pictures around the room. Give players paper and pencils to write down the first name, last name, and occupation of each. This means there are three correct answers for each picture. Each correct answer is worth a point, so with twenty pictures, a perfect score is sixty. You can vary the game by pinning the pictures to the backs of the players and having them ask yes-or-no questions of the group as to who they are.

☐ **875. HAND HOCKEY.** Divide players into two teams and have them stand in a line facing each other with outstretched hands, palms up and little fingers locked together. The first player in line is the referee, the last player is the goalie. The object is simple: to pass a penny down the line from referee to goalie. The only rule is that each player must keep the two little fingers tightly locked together. The penny goes back to the referee if it falls on the floor or fingers come apart. As soon as the penny reaches the goalie, it's a point. He carries it back to the referee and the penny starts down the line again. Five points makes a winning team.

☐ **876. NOAH'S ARK.** This game works equally well for younger or older kids. Before the party make a card (about six-by-nine-inch size) for each player. On one side put the name of an animal (easy ones for younger children, harder ones for teens). On the other side at the top, put a number and the words "Sketched by." Pass out the cards so that no one sees the animal name except the recipient. Then give the players about ten minutes to do a really good job of drawing that animal on the "Sketched by" side, and signing the work. The cards are then collected and then handed out around the room and players are given numbered papers on which they write the name of the animal drawn. Prizes are awarded for the most correct answers and also for the person who drew the animal that was identified correctly the most times.

☐ **877. YOU'RE THE ONE.**   Teens like this game since it breaks the ice. One guy sits on a stool and is blindfolded. He is then told that he is searching for (the name of one of the gals at the party) and he must identify her by her hand. Each gal puts her hand in his, and he decides if it's the one. If he's correct, the guys' team gets a point. Then it switches, and a gal is blindfolded and must identify a certain guy by feeling the noses of all the guys. Again, award a point if the guess is correct. Continue alternating until everyone has had a turn to guess. The side with the most correct guesses wins.

☐ **878. ARF.**   One player, called the dog trainer, is blindfolded and given a yardstick or pointer. The others sit in a circle behaving like dogs. The trainer turns around three times, then points and says "Speak!" The person pointed to must bark like a dog. The trainer can ask the dog to speak again. If the trainer can identify him, that player becomes the trainer. After the next dog trainer is blindfolded, the dogs should switch their positions.

☐ **879. BALLOON VOLLEYBALL.**   Play inside or out. Put down a tape or string to divide the teams. A good-sized balloon is tossed between the players, who try to keep it from landing on their side. Depending on the age and number of players, make rules concerning how to hit the balloon: hands only, heads only, feet only, or any other part of the body. A team gets a point each time the balloon touches the ground on the other side. A variation is to require that the balloon be moved only by blowing it.

☐ **880. WHISTLE TAG.**   You'll need an inexpensive whistle for each player. The whistles are tied to the waists of each player so that they hang down to about the back of the knees. A circle of chalk or string is made so that players are inside and somewhat crowded together. The room is slightly darkened. The object is to blow the whistle of another person without her tagging you first. But you can't be tagged if you're standing up straight. So players move stealthily about standing upright, trying to quickly stoop and blow the whistle. When a player is tagged (while not standing up) or when a player's whistle is blown, she is out and sits at the edge of the circle. You'll have two winners, since it is almost impossible for the last two players to blow each other's whistle.

☐ **881. MAGIC QUARTER.** This works best with two teams each having three to six players, one of whom is the captain. The players are seated closely around a card table, each team using two adjacent sides. A quarter is given to Team One, and they put their hands under the table and pass it around until the Team Two captain says "Now!" at which point all Team One members must place their hands on the table, palms down. They can do this by bringing the hands up slowly over the edge of the table or by bringing the hands down quickly with a bang on the table to cover the sound of the coin hitting the table. Team Two players look at the hands and decide together which one has the quarter under it. The object is to find all the hands *without* the quarter. They guess one person at a time, and the hands are turned over. If they don't turn up the quarter until the last hand, they win and it's their turn to have the quarter. If they turn up the quarter too soon, it is hidden again by the same team.

☐ **882. CANDLE LIGHTERS.** You'll need a stopwatch, two sturdy beach balls, and two dripless candles. Divide the group into two-person teams. The stopwatch is started when the team members are handed the two beach balls. Each must sit on a ball and balance with feet off the floor, only using hands for support. Then when both are balanced, one is handed a lighted candle and the other an unlighted one. As soon as they get the second candle lighted from the first, the watch is stopped and the time noted. Other teams try to beat that score, and the shortest time wins.

★

SECTION 3: AROUND-THE-YEAR CELEBRATIONS

JANUARY

☐ **883. NEW YEAR'S DAY.** Plan a three-generation open house in the afternoon during TV bowl games. Borrow TVs so games can be seen in several rooms. Serve football game foods like softdrinks, popcorn, hot dogs, or pizza. Reserve one room just for talking and non-football games. Kids, parents, and grandparents should each invite friends. If there are real football enthusiasts, have a contest to see who is the best guesstimator. For a prize, give an interesting calendar for the new year.

☐ **884. RESOLUTIONS DAY.** After the excitement of the holidays is over, have a day when you gather to discuss resolutions or goals for the coming year. Decide first on ones for the entire family, for example, to share good news each day, to have a day of rest each week, to do something adventuresome each weekend, to communicate with relatives regularly, to eat dinner together each night, or to read every day. Then, each family member works on individual goals: to learn a new sport, to make a new friend, to improve a grade, to contribute a new idea at the office, to get rid of a bad habit. Write all these down. On the first of each month, bring them out and see how you're doing. Keep it up for the year and count up how many resolutions worked.

☐ **885. LAST DAY OF CHRISTMAS.** Celebrate the end of the Christmas season on a weekend day. Take the tree down, but make it a happy event with all the family helping. Serve the last of the Christmas cookies and play Christmas carol recordings one last time. Have a tablet and a pencil handy so that family members can write secret messages about the holidays, and tuck them in the boxes with the decorations so they'll be found next December when the season comes 'round again.

☐ **886. TWELFTH NIGHT.** In England this holy day is celebrated January 6, twelve days after Christmas. You can give it a special meaning at your house. Let it be the night you talk about interesting things to do in the coming year. Too often parents just "announce" what weekend excursions are going to be, without finding out what the entire family would enjoy doing together. Use a map and draw a circle, making a fifty-mile radius around your home. Note all the interesting things on the map: parks, historic places, towns, lakes. Start a Twelfth Night list of some weekend activities, near and far. If kids don't have much input, encourage them to think about it and check with friends, then bring it up again. At supper on Monday each week, all vote on the next weekend's activity. Keep the list going through the year.

☐ **887. MARTIN LUTHER KING DAY.** This newest holiday deserves family attention. From an encyclopedia read a summary of black history, starting in Africa. Then read a book on black history in America. Your librarian will help you find good books. Take turns reading aloud parts of speeches by Martin Luther King, Jr. Consider how your family or your church could break the separation between the races and have activities and make friends with people of all colors. See how the newspaper covers the event before and after the holiday.

FEBRUARY

☐ **888. GROUNDHOG DAY.**   This falls on February 2 or thereabouts. The entire family gets up with the sun and goes outside as pretend groundhogs. Like the famous groundhog or woodchuck who carries on this European custom, look to see if you cast a shadow. If the day is sunny and you can see your shadow, you should be frightened and go back to bed, since there will be six more weeks of winter. However, if the day is cloudy and you can't see a shadow, be happy that spring will soon be coming. Put the prediction on the family bulletin board and see if it comes true.

☐ **889. VALENTINE'S DAY.**   Let children make and decorate an old-fashioned Valentine's box a week in advance. Encourage the making of handmade cards. Put cards and small gifts inside. You may want to write a "love letter" to each child, telling him all the ways he's special to you. On February 14 open the box at supper, sharing some of the cards but letting some be private. Make this a red-and-white meal. Serve red Jell-O, white chicken, red beets, white potatoes, red and white cake with pink milk. Maybe everyone will want to dress in red and white. Talk about Saint Valentine (look him up in the encyclopedia) and discuss how we can be as caring about others as he was.

☐ **890. VALENTINE'S DAY TEA PARTY.**   Invite daughters, moms, and grandmoms for an afternoon high tea. Party dresses are in order. Before the party help kids make a heart-shaped background for picture taking. To give a formal touch, select classical records as background music. Make a fancy tea table with finger sandwiches and small cakes. A pretty pink punch bowl can be the centerpiece of another table. Let brothers serve as waiters. You'll be surprised at how well children like a formal event.

☐ **891. PRESIDENTS' DAY.**   February 12 is Lincoln's birthday; February 22 is Washington's. These are usually honored on the third Monday of the month. Using shelf paper, make a time-line of the years from George Washington through Abe Lincoln. Put in the important dates in both these presidents' lives and add other historic dates between. Hang it on a wall draped with red, white, and blue crepe paper. So that children understand what life was like in those years, play the "Can You?" game: Can you think of a game played barefoot? Can you name a book that was written then? Can you name a toy that was popular then? Can you guess what Lincoln would have had for supper? Can you pretend to be Lincoln and read by candlelight? Can you think what President Washington wore to bed? Can you tell what might happen if you chopped down a cherry tree? Can you describe the weather when Washington was at Valley Forge? Can you picture the crowd at Gettysburg? Can you name the play Lincoln was watching when he was assassinated? Can you imagine what it is like to be a president?

MARCH

☐ **892. SAINT PATRICK'S DAY.** Irish or not, green is the theme. The night before, help kids find green things to wear. A little green food coloring in the scrambled eggs, served with ham, makes Dr. Seuss's famous *Green Eggs and Ham* breakfast. Slip something green into the lunchbox: celery, a green apple, green cookies. For supper, have a green tablecloth or napkins, green leaves (or green pine branches) in the center of the table, and think up some green foods and have the kids help prepare them: green water or milk, green mashed potatoes, green vegetable or salad, cupcakes with green frosting. Ask one of the kids to find out who Saint Patrick was and share this at supper.

☐ **893. BEST FRIEND DAY.** Select a date near the end of the month and honor friendship on this special day. A few weeks in advance, let each family member choose and invite a best friend. Plan a few simple activities: a hike, a movie, supper by the fireplace. Make a best-friend card to give at the end of the day.

(Please note that Easter is listed in April, although it is sometimes in March.)

APRIL

☐ **894. APRIL FOOL'S DAY.** Set the table for supper *under* the table, and all eat on the floor. Color the milk or water blue. Bake nuts in a cake and give a prize for finding the most. Hide a big alarm clock in the room and set it to go off during supper. Have a funny face contest at supper. Secretly reset a clock and see who notices it. Encourage each family member to do a prank that isn't mean or dangerous. Play crazy old records on the phonograph in the evening. Short-sheet beds for bedtime surprises. Tuck something unusual under each pillow: a rock, a baby tooth, a silly photo, a Canadian coin, the comics.

☐ **895. PATRIOTS' DAY.** A few states still honor this holiday commemorating the Battle of Lexington and Concord, fought April 19, 1775. This battle between British troops and American patriots marked the start of the Revolutionary War, which brought freedom to the colonies. Supper is a good time to talk about the founding of our country. Read Ralph Waldo Emerson's poem "Concord Hymn," which contains the well-known lines: "Here once the embattled farmers stood, / And fired the shot heard round the world." See how many patriots the family can name. Name some present-day patriots.

☐ **896. THE EASTER TREE.** Like a Christmas tree, an Easter tree is a daily reminder of the beauty of the season. With kid-help, cut a large branch and spray it with clear varnish or paint. Stand it in a pot using clay or stones to keep it in place. Everyone makes permanent Easter eggs by piercing both ends of an egg with a large needle and blowing out the contents (which can be used for scrambled eggs). Decorate the eggs and glue ribbons to them so they can hang on the tree. Put your tree in a place where you'll see it often. At the end of the season, store your decorated eggs in egg cartons for safekeeping until next year. You can even store your branch for next year.

☐ **897. EASTER STORYTELLING.** In the weeks before this date, read those passages from the Bible that tell of the last days of Jesus' ministry. Let kids join in reading of the miracles, the healings, the triumphant journey into Jerusalem (read this on Palm Sunday), the preparations for the Last Supper, what went on at the meal, and what happened when Judas betrayed Jesus in the Garden of Gethsemane. Continue with Jesus' trial, the crucifixion, the days in the sepulcher, the resurrection morning, and Jesus' meetings with his followers before his ascension. (You'll find all these stories at the ends of the books of Matthew, Mark, Luke, and John.) No one can say that these stories aren't filled with adventure!

☐ **898. EASTER HUNT.**   A new kind of Easter hunt! Along with the traditional eggs and chocolates, hide elements of a good breakfast. Wrap these in plastic or foil with name tags, so that each family member gets one of each: a sliced orange or apple, a piece of coffee cake, a soft-boiled egg and a spoon (it will stay hot in its shell if you wrap it in foil), a small container of juice.

MAY

☐ **899. MAY DAY BASKETS.**   Save half-gallon milk containers during April so that you'll have waterproof inserts for your baskets. Cut them down so they are approximately six inches high. On April 30, find a field where you and your children are welcome to cut blooming weeds and wild flowers. Pick armloads and bring them home in pails of water. Next, weave one-inch strips of construction paper into long rectangular pieces large enough to wrap around the milk containers and give a basket effect. Glue in place. Then cut the flowers' stems and divide them into the cut-off milk containers. Fill containers with water. Make decorative paper handles for the baskets, then deliver them to friends and neighbors in honor of May Day.

☐ **900. MOTHER'S DAY.**   Let this be the traditional no-cooking day for Mom. Dinner out is fine, but meals cooked by others in the family are more special for her. (Just remember to clean up the kitchen afterward!) Start with breakfast in bed, the entire family gathering together. If Mom works at an office, surprise her with a plant to brighten her desk. If Mom's at home, plan time to give her a manicure or other special treat during the day. Have a celebration in the evening, doing just the things that Mom likes best.

☐ **901. OTHER MOTHER DAY.**   A few weeks before Mother's Day, talk with the family about other good mothers you all know. Choose one and plan a surprise event for her Mother's Day. This can be as simple as sending her a card or giving her a ticket good for free baby-sitting. Or, you can make a surprise visit with cake and beverage in the afternoon. More elaborate ideas are dinner out, flowers, casserole of the month (a different casserole delivered each month, made when you're making one for the family), or offers by kids to do tasks or run errands on a regular basis.

☐ **902. MEMORIAL DAY (Decoration Day).** This is celebrated the last Monday of the month and is a day to recognize those who have died defending the United States. Some families make trips to cemeteries to place flowers on family graves. If you do this, take the time to talk about these important people and their contributions to the family and community. Turn the focus away from death to a commemoration of the lives of the departed. Another idea is to attend a ceremony at a military cemetery. This can be very impressive if a child has background information about the veterans being remembered. Make this more than just another day off. Talk about living our lives in such a way as to make a difference to society so that we will be remembered by the good we accomplished.

JUNE

☐ **903. FLAG DAY.** If you don't own one, buy a flag. Learn the history and traditions of flag use (from the Scout handbook or the encyclopedia). In good weather, have a child put the flag out each morning and bring it in at night. Check with your town or nearby mall and see if they put up many flags on holidays. If not, get the idea started. Talk about the pledge to the flag, what it meant when it was written, and what it means today.

☐ **904. FATHER'S DAY #1.** With another family, plan this day as a total surprise to the fathers. After church, gather with the other family and present the dads with matching T-shirts in honor of their day. Using a large car or van, go off on an adventure (you might want to blindfold the dads). Depending on your destination, take along equipment for fishing, hiking, or softball. Spread a picnic lunch, enjoy the out-of-doors, then off for pizza and a movie. Before tucking Dad in for the night, gather in the parents' bedroom for a cup of hot chocolate and chat about Dad's dad and Dad's granddad.

☐ **905. FATHER'S DAY #2.** In the week before his special day, present Dad with an "It's Your Choice" certificate, signed by all the members of the family. This entitles him to a day of his choice: what he wants for breakfast, what he wants to do, what he could use as a gift. Let kids help make the day come true. This is a satisfying day for dads who don't like surprises.

☐ **906. SCHOOL'S-OUT DAY.** Even children who just love school enjoy a change of pace when school is out. On the last day of school, plan a "School's Out" celebration. Excuse kids from non-essential chores. If possible, pick them up and also some of their friends when school ends. Go for ice cream. Talk about the best memories of the school year. (Don't talk about grades until tomorrow!) Have an outrageous suppertime: Make pointed dunce caps for everyone; serve foods that can be eaten with fingers; outlaw the mention of certain words like school, teacher, book, grades, class. Make up stories about strange or funny adventures you plan to have this summer. Let kids stay up as late as they wish and sleep in the next morning. When you *do* talk about grades the next day, be sure to be very appreciative of the things a child has accomplished, and don't overemphasize a poor grade. There will be time enough during summer to give a scholastic pep talk.

☐ **907. SUMMER CALENDAR DAY.** After school's been out a few days, make a ten-week calendar of the summer. Put on it the known events: vacation, camp, visits, parties, church, lessons. Talk about other things to do and put these on the calendar in the weeks where there's room. Be sure each week has something fun. Put the calendar on the bulletin board for everyone to see.

JULY

☐ **908. INDEPENDENCE DAY.** Have your own parade if there isn't one nearby. A few weeks before, go to everyone on your block or street and suggest an 11 A.M. parade followed by potluck hot dogs, salads and ice cream. Everyone can participate. Decorate bikes, wagons, wheelchairs, baby strollers, and cars with crepe paper and flags. Pets can parade, too. Wind their leashes and collars with ribbon and streamers. Choose grade-schoolers to be Miss Liberty and her court, dressed in white sheeting and carrying torches. Let the parade be led by the kid who owns a drum, bugle, or baton.

☐ **909. JULY 25.** Have a "five months to Christmas" party. Bring out a Christmas decoration for the living room or family room. Put up the train and play with it. Start the Christmas list and let everyone give ideas on what they *might* want. Eat turkey (even turkey hot dogs). Make a batch of Christmas cookies, decorate them, and eat them. Wish everyone a "Merry five-months-to-Christmas!"

☐ **910. FAMILY DAY.** Join the movement to make this a worldwide commemoration of the family. Already several states have set aside by statute the first Sunday in August. Kiwanis International promotes August 2 each year as Family Day. No cards, no gifts, no commercialization, just a low-key joining together for a family-centered celebration. While many take the family for granted, others are victims of broken families, so gather your family so that you can take note of your blessings and renew your appreciation and love for one another.

☐ **911. SCHOOL PREP DAY.** Back-to-school shopping is a good opportunity to share the excitement with your child. Mark on the calendar a separate time when you can shop with each child alone, while someone looks after the others. Go to a nearby shopping plaza and get the school supplies, then any new clothing items needed. End at the child's favorite fast-food stop. Talk about her hopes and plans for the coming school year. When home again, let her make a display of her purchases for everyone to see.

☐ **912. CARNIVAL DAY.** When the summer days get long and boring, help kids plan a carnival day. One or two parents and ten or more kids can have a lot of fun with this. First, talk about different carnival events: tossing rings over bottles, face-painting, guessing weights, throwing balls through a hole in a board, a safe dart throw, lemonade and cake stands. Next, let kids decide which activity they want to work on and how any profits will be divided. Each gathers the necessary equipment for his booth. The place is the next decision; a big front yard is best. One child can make signs announcing the carnival, which can be displayed at street corners. Go to a discount store and get lots of inexpensive prizes, balloons, and small candy items. A few days before the event kids can make reminder flyers telling the time, date, place, and events at the carnival. These can be delivered to each house in the neighborhood and to other friends and relatives. Setup should be done on the morning of the event, using card tables, umbrellas, a few chairs or benches for comfort, and balloons and crepe paper streamers for a festive look. Keep prices very low so that kids and parents will play the games and buy the food.

☐ **913. PETS' DAY.**   Choose a day to honor all the pets in the neighborhood: fish, birds, cats, dogs, hamsters. Make this their official birthday each year. Give cats and dogs bows and put streamers on fishbowls and bird cages. Then plan a yard picnic with the pets as guests. Serve sandwiches and pet treats. Talk about when you got them, the things they've learned, and what you hope they'll learn to do in the coming year. Let them show off their tricks!

SEPTEMBER

☐ **914. LABOR DAY.**   Sometimes this day is a sad holiday, signaling the end of summer vacation. Make it special by combining labor and play. Decide on one large labor project for the morning, such as fence painting or garage cleaning. Start early enough to be finished by noon. While working, talk about various types of jobs and what they entail. Explain the labor movement to kids so they understand the work of unions and trade associations. Then, celebrate in the afternoon by playing until sundown.

☐ **915. NEW HORIZON DAY.**   Meet with each child separately and discuss his financial needs. If you haven't done it on his birthday, set a new allowance and a new bedtime. Change it to a later time than last school year (usually about fifteen minutes later). Talk about what he plans to do in the coming school year and what after-school activities he'd like to join. Encourage his hopes and assure him you'll do all that you can to *help him* make them happen.

OCTOBER

☐ **916. CHILD HEALTH DAY.**   This is usually observed the first Monday of October. During the long summer, some families slip into careless eating habits. With the family read parts of chapter 9 of this book. Decide on several improvements you can all make in nutrition and fitness. Actually write them down and put them on the bulletin board. See how soon you can make some changes.

☐ **917. COLUMBUS DAY.**   This is usually the second Monday of October. There are many myths and also many true adventure stories about this famous explorer, who was so sure of the world's being round that he risked his life to discover the New

World. Using an atlas or globe, trace his journeys across the Atlantic. Read about his discoveries in the encyclopedia or from library books. Make an Italian or Spanish supper in his honor.

☐ **918. GRANDPARENTS' DAY.** Just as important as Mother's Day and Father's Day is the day honoring grandparents. Telephone calls, cards, useful gifts, and celebrations are in order. If grandparents live nearby, grandchildren can make a book of coupons for services they are willing to perform: cutting the lawn, bringing out porch furniture, shoveling snow, gift-wrapping, running errands. These are often more welcome than gifts.

☐ **919. HALLOWEEN.** Grade-schoolers like to have a scary Halloween party. Let them make invitations featuring ghosts and goblins. Ask kids to come in costume. Have the house lit with candles. Sit in a circle around one candle and start a scary story, letting each one add to it. In the story, each child can also make a sound effect (scream, meow, moan, wind, footsteps, sigh, sinister laugh; let him give his sound effects whenever he wishes. As the story gets near the end, blow out the candle and finish the story in the dark. Have a punch bowl like a witch's cauldron. (Make it smoke by putting dry ice in the bowl and pouring the juice over it.) Make cookies shaped like cats and witches. Play "Witch's Broom." Blindfold one guest, and have her stand on the bristle end of the broom and then walk the length of the broom. Those who do it without falling off win. Go trick or treating *inside* the house. Let other friends and parents be in each room of the house. With the house dark, let teams of two kids carry a flashlight and go from room to room, knocking on the closed door as if it were a house door. Plan some surprises in the rooms. Play "Pin the Tail on the Black Cat." End the party on a positive note, so that kids know that Halloween is fun and not to be taken seriously. Bobbing for apples is a good last event.

NOVEMBER

☐ **920. VETERANS' DAY.** Call a nearby veteran's hospital and find out what you can do to be helpful: collect interesting books and magazines for reading, make tray favors, bake cookies. A few days ahead, work on the project so that it is ready to deliver on the holiday or the day before. While the family is working together on the project, talk about the holiday and how it started. Explain the importance of the eleventh day of the eleventh month at the eleventh hour. If *you* don't know about the history of November 11 and Armistice Day, look it up in the encyclopedia.

☐ **921. THANKSGIVING DAY.**   With relatives or other families, plan a potluck feast with everyone sharing in the cooking. Kids can prepare a skit about what they think the first Thanksgiving was like. Let this be the entertainment after the big midday feast. Then, using a truck, have a late afternoon hayride on country back roads or in fields. Return home for a new Pilgrim tradition of piñata-bashing. If you can't find a piñata, make one out of two paper grocery bags (one inside the other for strength), tied and hung from a tree or in a large wide doorway. Fill the bag with wrapped candy, blindfold each person, and let him take a swing at the bag with a stick or small bat. After collecting all the candies, have a simple pick-up supper of turkey sandwiches and fruit.

DECEMBER

(See the next section for Christmas ideas that will make the holiday meaningful and fun.)

☐ **922. HANUKKAH.**   For many people, the Jewish holiday of Hanukkah is the most important holiday. This is also called the Feast of Lights or Feast of Dedication. The word "Hanukkah" can be written "Hannuka" or "Chanukah" and means feast. The celebration begins on the twenty-fifth day of the Hebrew month *Kislev*, lasts eight days, and usually occurs in December. It celebrates the Jews' defeat of Syrians about 165 years before Jesus' time. The Jewish festivities were held in the temple in Jerusalem, which the people were cleansing of desecrating Syrian idols. They could find only one cruse of undefiled oil to use for their holy lamps, but miraculously, the lamps burned for eight days. The leader, Judas Maccabaeus, proclaimed the festival which is still held today. Gifts are exchanged and charitable contributions are made, but most important, the eight candles of the menorah (a ceremonial candelabrum) are lighted, one each day to the eighth day. If you would like to know more about this holiday, read *The Hanukkah Book* (Marilyn Burns, Scholastic, 1981) or *The Jewish Holiday Book* (Wendy Lazar, Doubleday, 1977).

SECTION 4: THE BEST-EVER CHRISTMAS

Here's a month of Christmas ideas to add to your December calendar. There's at least one for each day of this busy and important month. Choose the ones that best fit your family and add your own traditions. Remember to make it a time of love and sharing, not a commercial production. Build memories through togetherness times.

☐ **923. DECEMBER 1.** Start by reading the Christmas story from Luke 2:1-18 and Matthew 2:1-10. If you have a crèche (manger scene), let the children put the characters into the manger scene as they are mentioned in the story. Select a large "Christmas Candle" to light each night this month. You may want to read just *part* of the Christmas story each Sunday, adding to your crèche the pertinent characters, starting with Mary and Joseph going to Jerusalem, next the shepherds, animals and angels, then the baby Jesus, and finally the three kings.

☐ **924. DECEMBER 2.** Call a social services agency, your church, or other service group and find out how you can adopt a needy family for Christmas by providing clothing, toys, canned goods, and perhaps a small tree. Explain the project at supper. Share what would be involved and ask your family if they'd like to do it. Talk about what each child could contribute in the way of clothes and toys. Ask children if they would like to share a small amount of their savings or allowance to buy new toys, too. Call this project "the Christmas Family."

☐ **925. DECEMBER 3.** After school, let children make a special Christmas-morning coffee cake. Put just one pecan in the coffee cake. (The person who gets the nut on Christmas morning can be first to give his gifts.) Wrap and freeze the coffee cake. Here's the recipe:

> 2 cups flour
> 3 teaspoons baking powder
> ½ teaspoon salt
> 4 tablespoons melted butter or margarine
> 1 egg
> ⅔ cup milk
> 1 can of pie apples or drained peaches

Topping: 2 tablespoons sugar mixed with 1 teaspoon cinnamon and 4 tablespoons melted butter or margarine.

Sift first three ingredients into a bowl. Add the next three ingredients and mix with a large spoon until blended. It will be like soft dough. Using a spoon, spread in two round 8- or 9-inch pans or one rectangular 9-by-13-inch pan. Arrange the fruit on top, pushing it into the dough. Add the topping. Don't forget to hide one nut in the dough. Bake at 375 degrees for one-half hour.

☐ **926. DECEMBER 4.** Make ornaments out of wood or plastic thread spools, old earrings and other discarded jewelry, shiny paper, ribbon, styrofoam shapes, glitter, spray paint. (If you don't have such supplies on hand, a visit to a craft shop will give you ideas.) Choose one to give to a neighbor or shut-in; let the others be the centerpiece on the dining table until tree-trimming day.

☐ **927. DECEMBER 5.** Visit the library and look at books about Christmas. Borrow some, including one to read aloud at supper. Choose Charles Dickens's *A Christmas Carol* if kids haven't heard it. Start to read a few pages each night.

☐ **928. DECEMBER 6.** Take one child Christmas shopping today (or tonight, when the lights and decorations look so much prettier). Specialize in finding gifts that must be mailed. Wrap them and write notes to far-away friends and relatives.

☐ **929. DECEMBER 7.** Be a Christmas Angel! Put everyone's name in a bowl on the supper table. Each draws a name and then does a good deed in secret for that person between now and Christmas Eve. Don't tell whose name you drew! Who can guess their angel? Also look in the newspaper and see all the special activities for Christmas. Together choose a concert or special event the family would enjoy and put it on the calendar.

☐ **930. DECEMBER 8.** It's Christmas Tree day! First, though, call a neighbor or relative to see how you can help him or her with the shopping, a meal, package wrapping or mailing, or even getting a tree. Go as a family to help that friend and end up at the Christmas tree lot. Let each one find "the best tree." Pick one by vote, take it home, and stand it in a cool place in a bucket of water.

☐ **931. DECEMBER 9.** Make Christmas wrapping paper for special gifts. Use plain white paper, such as butcher paper, and poster paint. To make designs, dip washable kitchen tools (like a potato masher, whisk, or fork) in paint and "print" on the paper. As background music for supper, start playing Christmas recordings. See who can name the carol first.

☐ **932. DECEMBER 10.** Make Christmas cookies with all the family helping. Let each person be a specialist in one kind. Show younger children how to roll out dough, cut, and decorate. Try the recipe shown below, guaranteed to please chocolate lovers. Store and freeze most of them, but eat and share some now. Look at a TV program guide and let each family member choose a Christmas special. Enjoy the cookies when you watch one of the shows together.

BUMPY BROWNIES

> 1 package German-chocolate cake mix
> ⅔ cup evaporated milk
> ½ cup melted butter or margarine
> ½ cup chopped nuts (optional)
> 1 package caramels (about 50), unwrapped
> 1 6 oz. package chocolate chips

Using a mixer, blend the cake mix with only ⅓ cup of milk, the butter, and the nuts to make a dry batter. Pat *half* of this mixture in a greased 9-by-13-inch pan, working it over the entire bottom of the pan. Bake 6 minutes at 350 degrees. Set aside to cool.

Melt caramels in ⅓ cup of evaporated milk using low heat, or melt in the microwave. Stir vigorously with a spoon to combine milk and melted caramels. Spread over cake layer.

Sprinkle chocolate chips over mixture. Crumble the remaining cake mix over the top and press down lightly.

Bake 20 minutes at 350 degrees. (It will appear slightly unbaked in the center.) Cool; refrigerate for an hour to let it set up. Then cut into squares and freeze or keep hidden in a tight container in a cool place.

☐ **933. DECEMBER 11.** Everyone helps to get the Christmas cards out. Kids can make their own with colored paper, wrapping paper, stickers, stars, and crayons plus a personal message or picture. These special cards can go to relatives, friends, and teachers. Parents and older children can write notes on the family cards. Then everyone seals and stamps. If there's a mailbox nearby, mail them this very night. Don't you feel great when this is done!

□ **934. DECEMBER 12.**   After supper, pile everyone in the car and go for a drive through different neighborhoods. Count Christmas trees in windows. Look at outside decorations. Practice familiar carols in the car. Then stop by the home of friends or relatives and pretend to be old-fashioned carolers by singing a song at their door. (You may warn them you're coming.) Maybe they'll serve you hot chocolate and a cookie! If their tree and decorations are up, get some ideas for your own home.

□ **935. DECEMBER 13.**   Absolutely finish Christmas shopping with the help of all the family. If a gift is to be purchased for one child, the second parent or an older child can do other shopping with that child. Let younger children (who aren't old enough to shop alone) help in selecting gifts for others. "Sell" them these gifts at a greatly discounted rate, as low as a few coins for the youngest. Don't forget items for the Christmas Family (December 2). Celebrate with a fast-food supper and let everyone share memories from Christmases past.

□ **936. DECEMBER 14.**   Everyone helps unpack the Christmas tree decorations and the train. One child checks that lights are in working order. Everyone helps trim the tree: putting hooks on ornaments, adding icicles or garlands, making the train work. Be sure to serve Christmas cookies and juice and have Christmas music playing. You may want to have on hand a new ornament each year for each child to unwrap and hang. Buy these the previous year at the after-Christmas sales.

□ **937. DECEMBER 15.**   Make the house beautiful! Let children decorate their own rooms using extra family decorations, ribbons, and fresh-cut greens. If they wish, let them hang their own empty Christmas stockings on their room doors. The eating table, the front door, and the top of the TV set all deserve festive touches. Talk with the family about buying one new decoration each year. What would it be? Where would it go? If you have time, go and get it this very night. And don't forget to put a red bow on your pet and see that he has a Christmas stocking, too.

☐ **938. DECEMBER 16.** Let this be a quiet day. Talk about the meaning of Christmas, the coming of the Christ-child, and his message of love. At night, bundle up in warm clothes and go out in your backyard or to a park and look at the stars. Talk about the Star of Bethlehem.

☐ **939. DECEMBER 17.** The family wraps all gifts today. Make it clear that anyone caught peeking in packages loses a package. Enjoy the wrapping time by letting a spouse or older child read to you. Be sure there are small items to put in stockings (thank you note paper, candy, an inexpensive toy, cosmetics, a new pen, a tool). Don't hide packages unless absolutely necessary. Put them where you can all enjoy looking at them.

☐ **940. DECEMBER 18.** Share the beauty of your home today. Let each child invite a friend for a simple casserole and salad supper. (Parents should invite a friend, too.) Let the kids make Christmas placemats out of construction paper or shelf paper, using crayons or marking pens for the Christmas designs. Dessert is ice cream with the Christmas cookies made earlier this month. Enjoy the tree, and the decorated rooms, the train. Get good new ideas by asking the friends about their traditions. Have a candy cane hunt to end the evening. Friends get to take their placemats home.

☐ **941. DECEMBER 19.** It's nostalgia night. Bring out old scrapbooks, photo albums, slides, and movies. If grandparents are nearby, let them enjoy this backward look. Talk about Christmas when you were a child. As you talk, gather the items for the Christmas Family (December 2). Everyone helps pack the food, clothing, and used and new toys. Wrap all the toys as gifts. Be sure to mark items, for example, "toddler toy," "size 10 sweater."

☐ **942. DECEMBER 20.** This is the day to make your deliveries. Everyone helps load the car with the things for the Christmas Family (December 2), cookies, and packages to deliver to family and friends. Don't forget little remembrances for the mail carrier and other service people.

☐ **943. DECEMBER 21.** At supper, make a list of all the relatives, senior citizens, and friends who would enjoy a Christmas phone call. Let each child think of one or two things she could share on the phone. Then, make those telephone calls during the inexpensive calling hours. Save the calling list for next year.

☐ **944. DECEMBER 22.**   There's always a special Christmas movie playing at a close-by theater, or, for those with video recorders, there are great Christmas movie classics to rent. Afterward, make sundaes.

☐ **945. DECEMBER 23.**   Kids help make the Christmas cake. Use your own recipe or white cake mix. Divide the batter in half and mix green food coloring on one half, red in the other. Bake and, when cool, frost with white icing. Decorate with Christmas candies or colorful sprinkles. If possible, get a head start on some of the other cooking for the next day.

☐ **946. DECEMBER 24.**   Plan ahead to have this day the major cooking day (so Christmas Day is free.) If entertaining relatives, invite them for Christmas Eve. Divide the work, letting children set the table and put out serving utensils, platters, carving knife, and so forth, make the salad, and prepare vegetables. Talk about the Christmas Angels (December 7) and see who had a good deed done by one of them. Remember to thaw the Christmas morning coffee cake (December 3). Go to a Christmas Eve church service. Before bedtime hide new pajamas for each family member in his bedroom. Let everyone get in pajamas for the hanging of stockings—non-Santa believers, too.

☐ **947. DECEMBER 25.**   Let the morning be a wild time of opening the little gifts in the Christmas stockings. Then serve that Christmas coffee cake (December 3) with a selection of juices. The person who finds the nut can be the first to give his gifts. Stress the "giving" part of this day. Savor the gifts and appreciate the giver; let all watch as each one opens a gift. Starting this when children are young makes for a happier morning of gift-opening— not an event that's over quickly with the child having no idea of who gave him what. For an afternoon break, take a walk around the block or take a short nap. Hold back one gift for each family member—something small, such as a book, that can be tucked under the pillow to sweeten the end of this special day.

☐ **948. DECEMBER 26.**   Let children invite friends to come over and bring their favorite new toy. Since kids are on vacation let them sleep by (or even under) the Christmas tree in sleeping bags.

☐ **949. DECEMBER 27.** It's time to write thank you letters. Make it fun by having everyone bring note paper and supplies into one room. Play "Stunts" as you write. When someone finishes a letter, she is entitled to ask anyone else to do a stunt: somersault, head stand, ten push-ups, twenty jumping jacks. Small children can draw thank you pictures, which a parent or older child can letter for them. Schoolchildren should write one sentence for each one year of their age, fifteen lines being the maximum. Don't correct spelling; it's the thought that counts.

☐ **950. DECEMBER 28.** Go with the family to the year-end sales at the shopping centers. See if you can find bargains in wrappings, ornaments, or even the first gift for next Christmas. In the car, talk about all the Christmas activities. Listen to hear what was good and what can be dropped next year.

☐ **951. DECEMBER 29.** Make a scrapbook of all the things that have happened this year. All year long, have a box into which you toss kids' schoolwork, sports scorecards, programs, birthday cards, travel mementos, your Christmas card, photos—anything that describes the events of the year. Let kids help paste these in the scrapbook. Then, with a marking pen, write short explanatory notes. Let kids write comments, too. Reserve the last page for the signatures of those who have helped to put the book together. Look at "the year that was" together and talk about all the things you've done.

☐ **952. DECEMBER 30.** It's "Thanks to Parents" Day. Let kids take over the house for a day, assigning tasks, making most decisions, preparing the "Seven-Can Supper," and finishing the day with activities of their choosing.

THE SEVEN-CAN SUPPER

> 1 can chicken soup, undiluted
> 1 can chicken or tuna, drained
> 1 can sliced mushrooms, drained
> 1 can green peas, drained
> 1 can sliced water chestnuts, drained
> 1 cup milk
> 1 can chow mein noodles

This supper is easy to make using one large pan. Combine the first five ingredients in pan. Stir together over low heat and gradually add milk. Keep stirring over heat but don't boil. When ready to serve, remove from heat and add noodles. Stir and serve with a salad.

☐ **953. DECEMBER 31.**   Let each child select toys that can be put on a top shelf now and brought out in February, when they'll seem like new toys. Have a safe family-style New Year's Eve party—perhaps a progressive supper with other families. Plan two-generation charades that all can play. Have noisemakers and decorations. Using shelf paper, make a big banner welcoming the new year. Celebrate every hour by turning on a radio to hear the New Year welcomed in New York, Chicago, Denver, and finally Los Angeles.

★

SECTION 5: MAKE YOUR OWN HOLIDAYS

☐ **954. HAPPYDAY.**   When a child has had some great disappointment, talk together about it, then plan that day or the next day as a "happyday"—his own private holiday. Together make it simple or elaborate. Let the child select something special to do, excuse him from some of his tasks, serve cake with candles at supper, and let him stay up thirty minutes later at night. Don't fill the calendar with "happyday" celebrations, but when one is needed, it provides a warm family feeling.

☐ **955. ABC DAYS.**   Sometimes the summer vacation seems long. At first it's fun, and a trip is great, but often there's an empty month. This is when you start twenty-six consecutive days of fun called the "ABC days." This idea can be adapted to the age of the kids. For younger children, learning the sound of the letter is also part of the day (long *A*, short *A*, hard *C* as in "cut," soft *C* as in "cereal"). But the main fun comes in the creativity of making the letter part of the day's activities. For example, on "*Aa*" day, bake an *a*pple pie, go on an *a*dventure, visit the *a*quarium, and eat an *a*rtichoke. On "*Bb*" day, *b*uy *b*right *b*ubble gum and try to *b*low *b*ubbles at the *b*each in a *b*athing suit. Letters *Q*, *X*, and *Z* are exciting days. You may have to look in the dictionary to find ideas, but you can drink a *q*uart of milk after a mock *q*uarrel, play a *x*ylophone and learn about *x*erography, and plant *z*innias when the sun is at its *z*enith. After all, the sky's the limit with this idea!

□ **956. ARBOR DAY.**   This is celebrated in different months in various states and Canada. So, choose a good planting time for your area and have your own celebration. In an encyclopedia, look up the founders of Arbor Day: J. Sterling Morton, naturalist Luther Burbank, and tree-planter Birdsey G. Northrop. Go to a nursery and see various trees. You don't have to plant a big tree; fingerlings are fun, too. Teach how to care for and protect trees, the importance of never removing the protective bark, and how wind can affect the shape of a growing tree. Even discuss safe tree climbing. Encourage tree planting in your town and at school.

□ **957. JUST BECAUSE DAY.**   Involve children in working with you to make a surprise party for someone outside the family. Let the honoree think she is just coming over to visit or have a meal. Invite some of her friends as a surprise. Make a cake with her name on it. Take photos of the party. Present a card or a little gift, such as a photo album, to show how much you appreciate the person. This can be done for a teacher, a minister, a neighbor, a senior citizen, a teen-ager, or a young child. Everyone likes to be honored!

□ **958. FIFTH SUNDAY.**   Four times a year, a month contains a fifth Sunday, and this can be a time to do something together. Note the fifth Sundays on your calendar and make them very special. Along with Christmas and birthdays, Fifth Sundays can become a tradition. Everyone should give ideas as to what special thing will occur. With church as the beginning of the day, go on to new adventures. Some possibilities are climbing a small mountain, painting a needy person's house, going on a boat ride, and going to two movies but having a meal in between.

□ **959. ADOPT A HOLIDAY.**   Choose a holiday from another country and read up on it. Find someone of that nationality and invite him over for the holiday. You may want to celebrate a different one each year. Choose from: *Cinco de Mayo* (May 5 in Mexico), Saint Andrews' Day (November 30 in Scotland), Bastille Day (July 14 in France), Commonwealth Day (second Saturday of June in England, in honor of the monarch), Liberation Day (April 25 in Italy), Constitution Day (May 3 in Japan). You can also celebrate those special weeks that are regularly promoted: National Bird Week, Mardi Gras, Pickle Week.

TWELVE

LOVE IN ACTION

Here's the greatest gift to a child: love—learning to love others and feeling much-loved. It's especially important that dads talk about and show love, too. In return, you'll find that kids can be caring! Here's how one third-grader described a loving parent: "Love is what I get at home on the day I wear a yucky purple shirt to school, I miss the bus and have to walk, I get hiccups during my book report, someone steals the good stuff out of my lunch, and then on the way home I step in something. Still, Mom gives me a hug!"

★

"Love does not consist in gazing at each other but in looking outward together in the same direction."—Antoine de Saint-Exupéry

★

SECTION 1: LOVE-TOUCHES

Start early to hold, hug, and touch a child. Don't be afraid to show your love. Let it be natural, and continue love-touches as a child grows.

☐ **960. EVERYDAY TOUCHES.** Make occasions for touching and holding children in loving and proper ways. Walk hand-in-hand, give hello and good-bye hugs or friendly slaps on the back, use the "fireman's carry," have lap-sitting for storytelling or hair brushing, or sit shoulder-to-shoulder in a family circle.

☐ **961. MORNING SQUEEZE.** At breakfast, hold hands around the table. Starting with a parent, send the message "I love you" around the table by squeezing the next hand three times. Then squeeze four times for "Have a great day!" Then get going!

☐ **962. THE LOVE CIRCLE.** First thing in the morning, last thing at night, in the dark when camping out, just before someone leaves on a trip—any togetherness time can be a time for a love circle. Stand in a close circle. Putting your hands behind the people on either side of you, grasp the hands of the next person. This weaves the group together. Move close, move back, stand on tiptoe, sit on the ground, but don't let go.

☐ **963. TRIPLE HUG.** Parents can scoop up a small child into a three-way hug. See if you can get all noses together! Kisses all around!

☐ **964. SEATTLE HUG.** Teach this when children are small. It's a good way to hug such people as aunties, brothers, and ladies at church. (1) Face the person and smile. (2) Take hold of their upper arms (that way you can control how close you get). (3) To avoid noses meeting, go to the right of the other person's face. (4) Brush cheeks or give a light kiss. It's friendly, sanitary, and easy to do, and you might get your preteen son to hug Auntie Roslyn if he's been practicing all his life!

☐ **965. ALOHA SANDWICH.**   Try this Hawaiian way of holding hands. Each person places his or her hand atop another's, making a big stack of touching hands, and eventually using both hands of each participant. It pulls you close together. Some families do it once a day, after breakfast or supper.

★

SECTION 2: LOVE VOCABULARY

☐ **966. "SIGN LOVE."**   Show children the international hand sign of "I love you" (see illustration on the opening page of this chapter). Let them "sign" love as they leave for school or return home from play.

☐ **967. RILY.**   This is an acronym for "Remember I Love You." Put it on notes and letters or say it over the phone or as kids go off to school or play. Encourage kids to use it when they may not feel comfortable using the actual words. Have them check to see if friends and relatives know the secret meaning of "RILY."

☐ **968. DISARMAMENT.**   With kid-help, make a list of "fight-ing words" and post it on the family bulletin board. These are words that start fights or are hurtful. Every family's list will differ, but these might be some comon ones: "I hate you." "You stink." "I never want to play with you again." "You're a baby." See if the children can get through a day without using these words. Then try for two days, and so forth. Soon the words may not be used at all.

☐ **969. WORDS OF LOVE.**   Help your child use love-words by setting an example. Say such things as: "I love to be helped." "I like what you're doing." "I love being loved by you." "You are so precious to me." "I love you all the time." "I care so much for you." "I loved being with you today." Make love a common word, so that kids aren't startled when you say it. Sometimes, too, you have to say, "I love you too much to let you do that."

☐ **970. LITERARY AND TV/MOVIE LOVE.**   When reading with children, note how characters express love and caring. See what words the characters use or what they do. Point out some examples; let kids find others. Also comment on characters that aren't kind and loving. When a child sees a love scene on the screen, talk about it later. What words were used? Was it a nice kind of love that showed how people care for each other? How else did characters show they cared for each other? Did love make a difference in the story?

★

SECTION 3: LOVE DEEDS

☐ **971. JUST BECAUSE.**   It doesn't have to be a holiday to give a little gift. On no occasion at all, slip a small item under a child's pillow. It needn't be expensive; sometimes it's just a give-away that comes in the mail. Parents may find that they get "Just Because" items under their pillows, too.

☐ **972. WARM FUZZIES.**   This is a popular name for notes of love and encouragement from parent to child. Warm fuzzies can be as long as a sonnet or letter, or as short as the phrases "I love you, Laurie" and "Things will be better tomorrow." Leave one in a drawer, on a mirror, or under the bed pillow. You'll find that children will treasure these private loving messages.

□ **973. SEPARATE BUT EQUAL.** When there are several children in the family, sometimes one appears to be good and another bad. One child may bring home many stars or awards from school. Another may be a star soccer player and have a lot of friends. Another may not yet have found her area of excellence. But a parent has to love each child equally, although it may be shown in different ways. It's very important for a child, especially one who doesn't get much public acclaim, to be told that you love him, and told this in front of other family members. You will always love your children, but you will love them for different things. It may be easier to love an always good child, but you can say to a challenging child: "I love you because you make me *stretch* as a parent." "You make me grow." "You're a great guy—don't hide it."

□ **974. "HELP THE ONE WHO'S BEHIND."** So often the family is rushing to get out the door. Getting dressed, feeding the dog, gathering things to take along—it's wild. Teach family members to shout "Help the one who's behind." When everyone else calls back "Who's behind?" the one in need of help shouts his name. It's fun to come to the rescue!

□ **975. SECRET FRIEND.** Explain to the family the importance of doing nice things and not taking credit for them. Parents start the tradition and soon kids follow. Secret-friend deeds include putting a supportive note or cartoon in a lunch bag, making someone else's bed, and putting a flower on the table, taking out the trash without being asked, and tucking a granola bar into a briefcase. You may want to anonymously exchange names and see who can do a good deed for the other person without being found out.

★

SECTION 4: LOVE BETWEEN KIDS

□ **976. CRYING BABY.** Start when children are young to encourage expressions of love and caring. When a baby is crying, ask an older child to comfort the baby, hug her, and entertain her, for example, "Scotty, will you please give the baby some love?" As children grow, continue this idea of giving loving support to a sibling. Be especially appreciative when this happens. Learning to be a caring person is a great lesson.

☐ **977. WATCHDOGS.** Encourage kids to take an interest in the activities of their siblings—to become sensitive watchdogs. When they see a way to help, or when you suggest one and they do it uncomplainingly, give lots of praise. For example, you might say: "Matthew has a big test tomorrow. Why don't you see if he'd like you to feed the dog and set the table for him. I'm sure there will be a time when you might need extra help." Or, a child might see that the Sunday paper is spread over the floor and just pick it up without being told. That's a real watchdog! To do the loving, helpful thing should be natural; it doesn't need a chart or a reminder or a reward.

☐ **978. "I'D LOVE TO!"** Popularize this phrase as a family saying. Start out encouraging it during children's play together. Tell them to let you know when they've said it. Being agreeable is a sign of caring. Use it yourself when asked to do something. Another good phrase is "No problem." When asked to do something, a "No problem" reassures and melts away the task. Parents can show the way to use these phrases.

☐ **979. CHANGE THE ENVIRONMENT.** Sometimes conflict comes when siblings are getting bored. You can return the children to more loving relationships by changing the environment. This could involve taking the same game or toys to another room, turning off the TV and turning on music, or introducing some new element to play. When a parent does not respond to kid's arguments with shouts but rather speaks kindly, softly, and calmly, the situation changes more easily. Use the phrase "I love you both too much to let you do this."

☐ **980. SHARING AND CARING.** Make opportunities to share. Let children cut one cupcake in half. Show how to use a timer so that everyone gets to use the favorite toy. Make a little chart and use different colored stars for achievements: red for doing chores, green for reading a book, silver for nutritious eating, and a larger gold star for sharing and caring, for showing love.

□ **981. ASK FOR ATTENTION.** Sometimes what seems like an unloving attitude is a cry for attention. Teach children to *ask* for attention when they need it, and in turn be sure to give 100 percent attention in response. This helps to recognize a child as an individual rather than as just part of the group called "the kids." When you visualize a child as caring and competent and successful, you treat her that way and she responds. In your daily unstructured time with a child, make sure that the greater part of it is spent doing things the child wants to do. Paying attention to a child as an individual pays big bonuses in child-to-child relationships as well as parent-to-child ones.

★

SECTION 5: LOVE BEYOND FAMILY TIES

□ **982. COOKIE MAKER.** When a friend isn't feeling well, or when there are newcomers or senior citizens in the neighborhood, let a child help make cookies and then go and deliver them. Or, when there's a new student at school, take cookies and go to visit that family. Parents can talk and kids can serve the cookies; this breaks the ice in conversation and makes it easier for a child to show he cares.

□ **983. BORROW A BABY.** Caring for a baby can be fun and educational, and "borrowing" one for a few hours lets another parent have some free time. Be sure your family members understand the needs of the baby. It's a wonderful way to show the other busy parent that you care. Of course, you'll be on the scene, but let your own child help as much as he's able. You'll both have fun doing it.

□ **984. GET-WELL KIT.** Help a child put together a get-well kit for a relative or friend. Depending on the age and sex of the recipient, put in some of these items: a book, cartoons, *TV Guide*, a pen and a pencil, stationery to write thank you notes for flowers and gifts, cologne, a granola bar, a small toy or truck that can be played with in bed, a small mirror, a sports magazine, crossword puzzles, other little puzzle games, nail polish, a cassette of music or words. Let the child choose and pack the items and help unpack it for the recipient. Encourage your child to take along some other things to share: a good school paper, a recent photo, a game they can play, a book he is reading.

☐ **985. SHARING SUPPER.** Once a month plan to share a simple supper with someone who doesn't have many friends. This could be a senior citizen in your neighborhood, an older relative, a new friend from church, or a foreign student. If she wishes, let your child do the inviting. Then work together to make the meal and clean up. Help the child find conversational topics and some activity, such as a game, to share after supper.

☐ **986. WHAT CAN WE DO?** Don't always supply the idea for a loving deed. Let children think of kindly things to do. Say: "Grandpa isn't feeling well; what do you suggest we do?" "The neighbors don't seem to know anyone yet; what could we do?" "Children are starving in Africa; what could our family do to help?" Help youngsters see that love and the ability to put that love into action is a solution to many problems.

☐ **987. NEIGHBORHOOD CARING.** See if you can find in your neighborhood someone who needs extra loving care. It might be a lonely child, a senior citizen, a shut-in, or a handicapped person. As a family, talk about what you might do to show you care. Consider rendering these services: reading, going to a movie together, grocery shopping, writing letters, yard care, package wrapping and mailing, hair or nail care, auto repair or washing, a simple supper, a daily phone call for a few weeks.

☐ **988. FEED THE BIRDS.** Caring goes beyond people. In the cold of winter (and other times, too), let a child take charge of providing food for hungry birds. A shelf in a tree or on a high pedestal, or an inexpensive bird feeder, works well. Some table scraps plus bird seed will keep the birds coming back for more. Talk about caring for birds and animals as opposed to killing them for target practice. Be supportive of your local animal care agencies. When you go to the zoo, ask to speak to the bird keeper to get new ideas on how to care for "your birds."

☐ **989. LOVE CASSETTE.** Make a tape to send to a far-away friend or relative, or to one of the kids' friends who's moved away. Tell the latest news, jokes, successes and failures, what the pets are doing, movies seen, and so forth. Make the tape just like a friendly chat and help kids overcome self-consciousness. Show how to use the pause control to stop the tape while you think of the next thing you want to say. Kids like to end tapes to grandparents with a chorus of "We love you!" or "RILY!" (See section 2 of this chapter.)

☐ **990. COUNTRY CARING.** Reach out beyond family, friends, and neighborhood. Talk about others in need of loving in our own country. Decide what your family could do through a service project. By contacting your local Social Services agency, you can find a project that will fit your family. It may mean distributing clothes, serving meals at a shelter, collecting blankets, delivering dinners in a "Meals on Wheels" program, or giving a program at a care facility. This is not a project just for parents but one for the entire family.

☐ **991. ADOPT-A-CHILD BY MAIL.** One of the best family outreach projects is the adoption of a child through one of the agencies that provide care for overseas children and some nearer home. The contribution will be a modest sum each month, but more important is the exchange of letters. Ask for a child similar in age to your own. You may want to have an English-speaking child. The letters you receive will give you clues about your adopted child's way of life, education, and interests. In compliance with the agency's guidelines, you may be able to provide books or other gifts for the child's birthday or a holiday. If you adopt an overseas child, find out all you can about his country through library books. Be sure to pin the child's picture on your bulletin board. Some of these relationships continue for years, and your family will have the joy of having made a real contribution to another's life.

☐ **992. ADOPT-A-CHILD FOR REAL.** No matter how many children you have, you may want to consider adopting one more. Not every family has the time, temperament, and money for more kids, but if you think you do, talk over the project, first with your spouse and then with the other children. Slightly handicapped or minority children are in greatest need of a loving permanent family. You might want to be a foster family first. The red-tape involved in both of these projects can make it frustrating and difficult, and it will mean more work for parents than for the children, but the benefits for the whole family can outweigh the problems.

☐ **993. DO YOU LOVE ENOUGH?** Ask yourself these questions and then talk about the meaning of them with your children. Do you love enough . . .

to carry on without others' appreciation?
to see the problem separate from the person?
to persist in love when you are rebuffed?
to reach out to the other person even when he's wrong and you're right?
to put aside the hurts of the past?
to forget the wrong when the lesson is learned?
to love the seemingly unlovable?
to forgive and then forgive again?
to make the word *love* an active part of your vocabulary?
to make deeds of love your vocation in life?

★

SECTION 6: MEMORIES OF LOVE AT DAY'S END

☐ **994. ROOM SERVICE.** Surprise a child when she's getting ready for bed by bringing a tray with milk and a cracker to her room. Sit down and chat about the day. She'll feel very loved to have you "waiting on her" with this treat.

☐ **995. WHATSOEVER THINGS.** Too often a family gives all its attention to problems, forgetting the good things that happen during the day. Before an older child goes to bed, or in tucking in a young child, talk about something good that happened during the day, something beautiful that you saw, or something nice that was said. Take your clue from the Bible (King James Version), Saint Paul's words in Philippians, chapter 4, verse 8: "Whatsoever things are true, whatsoever things are honest, whatsoever things are just, whatsoever things are pure, whatsoever things are lovely, whatsoever things are of good report; if there be any virtue, and if there be any praise, think on these things." A child going to sleep thinking on these "whatsoever things" will rest peacefully.

☐ **996. THE ESSENTIALS.** There's no hassle at bedtime if you tell a child that there are only three reasons he may get out of bed.

First, though, provide these essentials: (1) advance preparation, including getting ready for bed, going to the bathroom, and having a drink of water; (2) a story or conversation, short or long; (3) soft music from the radio if he wishes; (4) a bell at the bedside to call parents in case of emergency; (5) a hug and a kiss; (6) reassurance: "All is well," "I love you," "See you in the morning," "It was a good day," or "I'll check on you in a little while." Then, the only three reasons he may get out of bed are (1) he doesn't feel well, (2) the house is on fire, or (3) he would like to be punished.

☐ **997. ROCKER TIME.** A rocker is often connected with love. If you don't have one, consider purchasing one when you have money to spend on furnishings. It's where a parent comforts a young baby, holds a toddler, and reads to a young child, and where older sister can hold baby brother for his bottle. If possible, keep up the rocker routine, sitting in it for storytime or conversation as children get older. Rocking and reading is great fun for older kids. Encourage older kids to sit and rock from time to time, rethinking the happy memories attached to the family rocker.

☐ **998. BEDTIME STORIES.** Reading books at bedtime is a given. But also consider the creation of memorable family legends. When a child is young, make up stories with her and friends as characters. Include some repetitions as you tell more of her story another night. For example, the story can begin the same way: "One day when you were flying along in your space ship." or "It was at that point that I asked my faithful companion Bucky the beagle what he would do." Mingle facts with fantasy in your family legends. Use family history and interests and make other family members into characters such as "Grandpa, the king" or "Cousin Carrie, the President of the U.S.A." A good book for young children is *Baby's Bedtime Book* (Kay Chorao, Dutton, 1984). Toddlers will like *Goodnight Moon* (Margaret Brown, Harper-Row, 1977).

☐ **999. "TRIPLE T" MEANS TUCKING IN.** Really tuck in a child. Bring the covers up around his shoulders and make them snug around his body down to his toes. This kind of hands-on cuddling is similar to snuggling a baby. Kids love it, especially if you make it fun. Youngsters look forward to Tuck-Tuck-Time, then a kiss and to sleep.

☐ **1000. NO MATTER WHAT.**   Love is not withheld because a youngster has been disobedient or lazy or has disappointed you in some way. If the day has put a strain on parent-child relationships so that you haven't found the time to verbally express your love, bedtime is a perfect opportunity. Try love messages such as these: "You are so special to me." "No one could ever take your place." "You make me happy in so many ways." "I may not always *like* some things you do, but I'll always *love* you." "I love you no matter what!"

★

SECTION 7: THE LAST WORD

☐ **1001. THE FOREVER CLUB.**   When children are young, start the Forever Club and keep talking about it through all their growing-up years. The Forever Club makes a bond between parent and child that can't be severed by thoughtlessness, arguments, hurtful activity, distance, marriage, new responsibilities, or even death.

The Forever Club is your family's mental storehouse—a storehouse you build day by day with activities that guide and teach and amuse. It isn't composed of monumental happenings as much as daily togetherness and love.

When a new baby joins the family, induct him into your Forever Club. You will always know and love him even though there are times you will not be with him or know what he's doing. You will remember his smile and his pout, his hand in yours, his special way of talking, his likes and dislikes, his tragedies and triumphs.

Good club members must be ready to let other club members try new things. The older club members must be ready to loose the younger ones. *Loosing* has nothing to do with *losing*. Loosing means that you know that your child is cared for by God and thus is loved and satisfied, happy and protected. Therefore, you can be unworried and at peace. You *loose* your child when he takes his first step . . . or the first time he plays outside alone . . . or crosses the street without you . . . or starts school . . . or stays overnight at a friend's . . . or goes to camp alone . . . or attends a movie with pals . . . or goes on that first date . . . or borrows the car . . . or leaves for a career or college . . . or sets up a home and business away from yours. That's *loosing* a club member. But, you can never *lose* a club member. After all, your bond is forever: always your baby, always your beloved, always your eternal friend, always your child.

Book 1 Index

(Activities indexed by idea number, not page number)

Roller-skating, 746
Room arrangement, 50, 428
Round table discussions: art of making conversation, 810-14, 820, 833; bullies, 829; choices, 816; dating, 825; dreams, 831; family rules, 821; economics, 824; first conversations, 815-19; helping one another, 832; heroes, 827; inventions, 818; love and sex, 830; moral dilemmas, 828; praise, 819; priorities, 822; problem-solving, 835-42; racism, 826; supper talk, 815; television, 817; with another family, 823
Royalty serving, 74
Rules, 777-79, 781, 786, 821

Safety: bicycle, 166; books on, see chapter 9, section 1 introduction; in the car, 729; child identification, 732; fire drill, 720; fire making, 728; first aid, 724; knives, 721; lost child, 725-26; matches, 722; opening doors, 719; photographs for, 718; strangers, 723; telephone, 716-17; Togetherness Rule, 731; trusted helpers, 733; in the water, 730
Sales, group, 318
Sandbox, building of, 121
Saturday activities, 511-14
School: homework, 672, 674-77; lunch chairperson, 494; preparing for first day, 668-71, 911; School's Out Day, 906; support of, 668-77
Scrapbooks: family, 41, 951; travel, 293; when visiting, 231
Seattle hug, 964
Self-esteem, 521, 524, 526, 787, 789-96
Sewing machine use, 466
Sex education: through animal observation, 803; books, 802; family discussion, 830; pre-marital sex, 808; in school, 804; use of correct words, 801; use of other authorities, 809; when mother is pregnant, 805, 807
Sharing, 335, 788, 980
Ship travel, 282
Shoe bags, use of, 106
Sickness: activities for recovery, 547; cheery pillowcase, 543; get-well kit, 984; Kleenex Kids, 546; sewing cards, 545; tummy TV, 544; use of bell, 542
Sidewalk painting, 122
Singing. *See also* Music

—for reassurance, 796
Skateboarding, 304
Skills. *See also* Computer; Tools
—for preschoolers, 579; for kindergartners, 580; for firstgraders, 581; for grade-schoolers, 582; for high-schoolers, 583; basic, 568-83; dictionary use, 568; encyclopedia use, 569; following directions, 578; homemaking, 86, 89, 91, 462-66; measuring, 491; memorization, 574; memory building, 573; motor coordination, 575; reasoning, 570; spelling, 577, 592, 672; verbal expression, 572; visual perception, 571
Skin care, 740
Sleeping. *See also* Bedtime
—in different places, 46; inside sleep-out, 52
Snack-and-Tell time, 319
Snacks, 320, 768-70, 774-75
Soap carving, 104
Solstice, explanation of, 646
Space adventure, 149
Space rocks, how to make, 623
Special situations, 511-67
Spelling, 592, 672
Spider webs, 629
Sports activities: preparation for, 299; school teams, 309; spectator, 295-98, 301, 311-13
Sports Day, 152
Sportsmanship, 300
Spray bottle play, 124
Star gazing, 172
Stationery, making note cards, 44
Stilts, 157
Storytelling: bedtime, 998; Bible, 687; Christmas, 923; creative, 576; Easter, 897; weird, 77
Strangers, dealing with, 723
Swimming pool activities, 147
Swing, how to build, 130

Table: decorations, 68, 89, 889, 896, 926, 937; manners, 79, 436, 781; setting, 89
Taking turns. *See* Sharing
Tasks: for all the family, 467-79; for preschoolers, 480-85; for grade-schoolers, 486-96; for teens, 497-501; bill-paying, 431; car washing, 475; checkbook balancing, 432; closet cleaning, 469; front door chairman,

Book 2

1001 MORE Things to Do with Your Kids

TO

Chris, Carrie, and Cameron

who were the guinea pigs for

many of these ideas and who now

pass them on to the next generation

CONTENTS

ACKNOWLEDGMENTS

In collecting this second book of 1001 kid-tested ideas, many good friends have been helpful. My appreciation for their creative suggestions goes to:

Linda Bargmann, Debi Brewster, Gloria and Robert Brewster, Mildred Corruccini, Clifford Douglas, Marty Fraser, Lynne Grantham, Nancy Gruber, Piper and Bruce Hunter, Diana Jackson, Barbara Kerbox, Melissa Kinder, Sheila Kinder, Connie King, Carrie Krueger, Diane and Cam Krueger, Robin Brewster Okun, Elieth Robertshaw, Judy Strachan, Cathy Turrentine, Diana Usrey, and Donna Walker.

DEAR READER

ow exciting to be spending time with your youngster, having fun, but also learning together! Being a good parent, a creative parent, isn't a painful process when you take a little time each day to be WITH your child.

Ten years ago when I started to write *1001 Things to Do with Your Kids,* friends wondered how I could ever come up with so many ideas. With our own youngsters, nieces, nephews, plus input from my lectures at schools and parent groups, it was easy! And the book became a best-seller for my publisher and was a book club selection.

A few years later, a woman spoke to me after one of my lectures and showed me her dog-eared copy of the book in which she had checked off every idea! "More, please" is what she said. And as other readers echoed her request, I knew it was time to start collecting new ideas. And so, this time with the help of friends, relatives, children—and now grandchildren, too—I created and tested the next 1001 ideas. There are a few of the same subjects, but always with a unique twist. So here's an all-new collection for you and your family.

While this book is loaded with fun things to do together, it also has a serious side. You'll find things to do with your child in order to get chores done, to discipline thoughtfully, to support education and culture, and to teach virtues—those important traits that comprise an intelligent, responsible, and caring youngster.

You may think I have left out certain topics. That's because they have been fully covered in the first book (or in another of my ten books). I do suggest that you have a copy of the first *1001 Things to Do with Your Kids* as a handy cross-reference.

This is not a book that tells you what you must do, but rather what you can do. We didn't do all these fun things in a short space of time—and neither will you—so pick and choose the ones you think you and your kids will enjoy. But remember, you have just a few years before your kids leave home, so get started!

In front of each of the 1001 ideas is a little box. It's mainly decorative, but you can put a check mark in it as you complete that activity—as my friend with the dog-eared copy did. So, to her, and to the thousands of families who enjoyed and benefited from *1001 Things to Do with Your Kids*, here are 1001 MORE things!

— *Caryl Krueger*

ONE

A WONDERFUL DAY

SECTION 1: OH, WHAT A BEAUTIFUL MORNING!

SECTION 2: AFTERNOON CONNECTIONS

SECTION 3: DINNERTIME DELIGHTS

SECTION 4: EVENTFUL EVENINGS

Weekdays don't need to be dull! Having fun with your child, as well as working and learning together, doesn't have to wait for the weekend. Here are ideas to give highlights to weekdays, so that you can enjoy every day with your youngster. Even if both parents work away from home, these morning, afternoon, and evening connections are vital.

SECTION 1:
OH, WHAT A BEAUTIFUL MORNING!

❑ **1.** **WAKE UP TO MUSIC.** If most everyone in the family gets up at about the same time, play stirring music to get the family moving. Recordings of marches, Tchaikovsky's *1812 Overture,* rap music, or even yodeling will cover up the groans of, "Do I have to get up?"

❑ **2.** **INDEPENDENCE DAY.** By the time a youngster is four, she can have an alarm clock and be responsible for getting up on time. (If she doesn't, make her bedtime earlier until she does.) Tell youngsters what you expect them to do independently before they leave for school. If necessary, make a list and put it where they can't miss seeing it.

❑ **3.** **TICKLE TIME.** Start the day with a smile by giving a quick tickle to another family member as you pass one another during the morning rush.

❑ **4.** **UP-AND-AT-'EM FIVE.** Encourage kids to shout a number (one through five) as they finish the before-breakfast essentials: (1) the bathroom stop, (2) dressing, (3) bed-making, (4) room-tidying, and (5) their morning chore, such as feeding the fish. When you begin to hear many shouted fives, it's probably time for breakfast.

❑ **5.** **THE ABSOLUTE ESSENTIAL.** Teachers report that kids who skip breakfast do not learn as readily as others. For this reason, insist on a hearty breakfast at your house. Find out what kids like to eat and see that it is available to them. Make breakfast easy, especially if kids have to prepare it themselves. Save the fancy breakfasts for the weekend. Don't let your youngster suffer academically because his stomach is growling!

WHAT GOES ON AT BREAKFAST?

Beyond good nutrition, breakfast is a necessary time of connecting after the long separation of sleep and before the long separation of school and work. Breakfast conversation should include: each person's plan for the day, telling when the family will be together again, inspiration, news, confidence-building (especially on test or report days), and expressions of love.

❑ **6.** AVOID CONFUSION.   First, talk about today: getting to school and work, getting home, places to go after school, errands to run, kids to pickup, who will start dinner, and any scheduled evening events. Also go over things that a child needs to take: toy, school project, lunch, money, books, Scout cookies, homework, report, gym shoes, and so forth. It helps if you have a "going shelf" near the door where such things can be placed and easily seen.

❑ **7.** WHEN WE MEET AGAIN.   Because the family is going to be separated for many hours, it's important to establish connections from the present (morning) to the future (when we'll see each other again). This may be after school, at supper, or several days hence after a business trip. Let kids tell you about what they want to do when you are together again. And, in turn, tell them how much you are looking forward to hearing what happened while you were apart.

❑ **8.** GOOD WORDS FOR THE DAY.   Two books that can be helpful at the breakfast table are the Bible and the dictionary. Read a verse from Psalms or another inspirational passage. Then, let a child open the dictionary at random and point to a word. (Word-a-day calendars can also be used.) Read the word and a simple definition. See who can use the word during breakfast. Then see who can use it at supper.

❑ **9.** NEWS OF THE DAY.   Although your TV is definitely off during breakfast (so it won't cut down on family communication), a parent can hear the current news by listening to a radio while dressing. Choose a news tidbit in keeping with your child's age: "The World Series starts today."

"Soccer balls are on sale at the Emporium." "It rained two inches at Grandpa's." "Last night the city council approved money for the new school."

☐ **10.** CONFIDENCE-BUILDING.   While the day may be merely challenging for adults, it can be intimidating for kids. Breakfast talk should build confidence so kids set out ready to succeed. Consider your child's activities and use lines such as: "Your friends will like the dinosaur you're taking for show-and-tell." "Your book report sounded great last night and I know you'll give it easily." "I like what you're wearing today." "Take a deep breath before the physics test—you're well-prepared." "The cookies you made for Scouts taste great and they'll love them." These reinforce a youngster's feeling of self-worth.

☐ **11.** ALL-IMPORTANT LOVE.   As you part, your love for one another should be the send-off. Don't fail to hug, kiss, and verbalize your love each morning to each family member. One family holds hands around the table and gives three squeezes meaning "I love you," then four squeezes for "Have a great day," and finally two squeezes for "Let's go!" Good parting lines include: "I'm proud you're my kid." "Always remember that I love you." "You're very special."

☐ **12.** THE BEST THING.   Even if breakfast is a brief meal, take time for family members to share "The best thing I'm going to do today." (One gradeschooler said "The best thing is coming home!") Listen to these "best things" and do remember to add your own hopes for the day.

☐ **13.** BREAKFAST TRANSLATIONS.   Most everyone has learned another language or picked up a few foreign words. Gradually introduce these at mealtimes. Say "danka" ("thank you" in German) or "bon voyage" ("happy travels" in French) or "por favor" ("please" in Spanish). Soon, words such as sayonara, au revoir, and aloha will be common terms at your house.

❏ **14.** SURPRISE MESSAGES.   While watching evening television, or at some other time, encourage family members to write little notes on small pieces of paper. (Preschoolers can draw a simple picture.) Keep these in a kitchen drawer and occasionally tuck one in a lunch box or coat pocket. The message can be brief: "I'm looking forward to supper with you and hearing about the Brownie meeting." Or, "Let's play catch." Ask at dinner if anyone got a surprise message and who they think was the author.

❏ **15.** CAR POOL CAPERS.   Don't waste driving time—use it for fun and subtle education. Avoid corrections and confrontations. For young children, sing songs, teach rhymes, tell a familiar story and let them be the sound effects. With gradeschoolers, let them add up numbers of license plates or play "I'm going to Mars and I'm taking an APE." (Each person repeats the line and adds something with the next letter of the alphabet.) Use car pool time to listen, too, since you'll learn what kids are thinking.

SECTION 2:
AFTERNOON CONNECTIONS

❏ **16.** MYSTERY JAR.   For after-school fun, place a jar with a message inside on your kitchen counter. Let kids know they are to check the mystery jar after school. Put in a note that says, "Fruit sticks in the freezer" or "How many doorknobs are there in this house?" or "Graham crackers are yummy in the tummy." This starts the homecoming on a happy note.

❏ **17.** THREE BIG REASONS.   If kids will be home alone after school, a working parent should make a phone call home—a short call, but with three purposes. First, it reassures the parent that all is well (the school child has returned home). The second reason is an opportunity to talk with the youngster and inquire about afternoon activities (not TV, but inside or outside play followed by chores or homework). And the third reason is to tell the child how much you care for him and what time you'll be home.

❑ **18.** **AN IMPORTANT NUMBER.** Of course parents' work numbers are posted at home and the school also has them on file. But the time a youngster usually needs the number is when she's at a friend's, the library, or an after-school activity. Find a good place to put your business number: on the inside of her notebook, taped inside the lunch box, on a card in a coat pocket, or on something your child is sure to have with her at all times.

❑ **19.** **A "COOL" HOMECOMING.** If you pick up your child at school, avoid asking if he behaved himself and what he did that day. Just let the youngster talk as you listen. And if you must ask questions, make them casual ones such as, "What shall we do after supper tonight?" Over a snack, your youngster will probably reveal what you need to know about the day's events.

❑ **20.** **TOGETHERNESS SNACKS.** Surprise your youngster by joining her in a snack time held in a different location: her room, your bedroom, porch, under a tree, living room floor, or in the attic.

❑ **21.** **CHANGE-OF-PACE.** Kids have spent most of the day sitting down. So, the first after-school activity shouldn't be a sedentary one. The diligent student may want to do homework, but encourage a change-of-pace activity such as playing outside with a friend, bicycling to the park, making brownies, or working on a craft or hobby. With your youngster, make a list of change-of-pace activities and do one for at least thirty minutes each afternoon— together with you or on his own.

❑ **22.** **CHORE TIME.** Chores done at nine at night can be miserable, but tasks done in the late afternoon can actually be fun. As your child does a task, do some work yourself and see who finishes first: Can he set the table faster than you can make a salad? Can you open the mail faster than he can provide food and water for the dog? Until doing chores becomes easy for a child, this little competition is a quick way to get them done.

THE GANG'S ALL HERE

As family members return home for the day, it's time for AIR, a three-step welcoming, so important after the long time apart. Like a breath of fresh air, AIR provides a gentle transition from the busy day and takes just a few minutes. At the same time it rids the family of weary and hungry feelings, omits pestering for attention, and expresses your loving interest.

❑ **23.** *A* IS FOR ACKNOWLEDGMENT. We all like attention, so let your first moments be ones of joyful acknowledgment complete with a greeting, kiss, hug, lap-sitting— not a torrent of words but a renewal of the parent/child and parent/parent love relationship.

❑ **24.** *I* IS FOR INTEREST. This important sign of caring need not be a lengthy dialogue. In fact, link the interest to a later time by saying, "Did you go on the field trip? I want you to tell us about it when we have our juice." "Did you get a new piece of music at your lesson? Let's play it together after supper." Such easy questions involve no arguments or judgments, but promise a portion of your time later. Show your interest by being sure that the "later time" truly comes. Kids recognize when "later" means "never," an indication of no interest on the part of the parent.

❑ **25.** *R* IS FOR RELAXATION. How can you take time to relax when everyone is starved? It may sound elegant, but serve part of the meal and call it the appetizer course. Tailor this food to the age of your child and remember that a small amount can suffice. Consider a banana sliced in milk, crackers and cheese, cucumber sticks in yogurt, juice and a graham cracker, or even a salad. Then sit down in a place different from your dinner location and eat this together. Listen, munch, listen, talk, listen, smile, listen, appreciate.

SECTION 3:
DINNERTIME DELIGHTS

THE SUPER SUPPER SETTING

Dinner is a meal eaten at a table, without the TV on. (When the TV is talking, no one else can talk. Listen to the news on the radio before supper since radio news provides more facts than TV news in the same amount of time.) There are certain elements that make the meal something to look forward to, rather than a boring ritual. Try these to enliven this bonding time.

❑ **26.** **NO LITTLE RED HENS.** Supper preparation is a great one-on-one time. While other family members are doing chores, reading mail, tackling homework, one parent and one child can be the supper team. A very young child can set the dining table and then draw at the kitchen table. A parent can stir-fry while testing a child on spelling words. A teen can make a salad while having a heart-to-heart talk with a parent. Don't prepare dinner on your own; let it be a joint event, adding to the happy time you spend with your kids.

❑ **27.** **SET THE TIME.** When kids are young, establish the routine of eating dinner together. If commuting and team practices cause a later dinner, give at-home kids part of the meal (such as the salad) early, and then sit down together as a group. Insist on dinnertime together and weekly reaffirm your plan by saying, "Our family will eat together at 6:30!"

❑ **28.** NOT AN EAT-AND-RUN EVENT. Dinner should take about thirty minutes. Young children can be given toys in the high chair or put in a playpen next to the table until they learn to stay seated. Since the cook has taken time to prepare the meal, family members should be appreciative and know that it is rude to leave early.

❑ **29.** TAKE A NUMBER. If the family eats in silence or is one where everyone talks at once, put numbers in a bowl and let family members draw for talking order—just sharing something brief before more conversation later. Parents should be sure to contribute from their day: an interesting work project, a challenge, new things learned. Try to keep dinner talk from getting too serious—if someone has a big problem, make time to discuss it after dinner.

❑ **30.** CURRENT EVENTS. Keep kids informed on important happenings in the world outside the family. Young children may listen and ask questions, while older kids can contribute. Encourage them to bring to the table a clipping from the newspaper—even a picture or cartoon. Play down the negative stuff but talk about an election, a scientific discovery, a new business in town, a sports event, and so forth. Ask questions such as, "What do you think about that?" and "How will it affect us?"

❑ **31.** UPCOMING EVENTS. Early in the week, focus the dinner talk on one event that will take place on the weekend. Let everyone help choose the family activity and be sure to put it on the calendar. (You may want to keep a list of possible activities on the bulletin board.)

❑ **32.** VIOLINS PLAYING? Hardly, but do have a music background for dinner. Let kids choose an all-music station or play their own recordings. To be fair, each family member should have a dinner with his choice of music and be prepared to share a few facts about it. Choose music without intrusive lyrics so as not to compete with your own talking.

ADDING FUN TO DINNER

☐ **33.** THE CONTINUING BOOK.   At first, kids may think this is a dull idea, but I suggest you try it anyway. Choose a book of interest to kids of varied ages, and one they haven't read. Read for just ten minutes as youngsters finish eating. (Parents read until kids are teens and wish to help.) If you need ideas, look at *The Read-Aloud Handbook* by James Trelease (Penguin: New York, 1985).

☐ **34.** KID AMBIENCE.   Let your child make the dining table a special place with no-iron napkins, a flower or object in the center of the table, and candles. Let the child choose the place: in the dining area, around a family room table, on the patio table, and occasionally on a picnic table.

☐ **35.** MORE THAN "YES," "NO," AND "NOTHING." Meaningful conversation at the dinner table sometimes needs a boost if it's to go beyond those three words. With preschoolers, you can ask a zany question like "What would happen if we had our mouths on the back of our heads?" Older kids and parents can discuss more serious issues like "What should be done about all the wasted food in the world?" Such impersonal questions will warm up kids to talking and soon they may share more personal topics. And when this happens, all should remember that the purpose of dinner conversation is to learn about one another, not to criticize.

☐ **36.** SEATING ARRANGEMENT.   While it may be customary to sit across from children at the table, sitting next to them is better since it takes away the "teacher is looking at you" feeling. Even if you are a small family, let youngsters make place cards (from painted clay or colorful paper) and then take turns making the seating plan.

☐ **37.** WHERE ARE WE EATING TONIGHT?   A parent or older child looks up the name of a country or city in the encyclopedia. Then as dinner begins, she says "We're eating where it is SO windy, a place where there are Cubs, where a cow perhaps started a fire, where Carl Sandburg wrote a famous poem, and where a main street is called Michigan Avenue. Where are we?" (The answer is Chicago.) Make the descriptions of other countries and cities harder or easier depending on the kid's ages.

❏ **38.** FACE MATS. Like place mats, face mats are placed on the dinner table. Youngsters can use art paper or shelf paper and draw the face of each family member. Although the drawings may not be too accurate, encourage elements that help identify the person (a smile, a missing tooth, a tie, blue eyes, a pony tail). The kids can then place these around the table wherever they choose.

❏ **39.** TORTILLA MESSAGES. A creative mom puts mystery messages on tortillas when they're part of the meal. From a slice of cheese, she cuts out letters or numbers and places a code message on top of each burrito, enchilada, or chimichanga. No hints are given and the family has to guess what the symbolism might be. For example, it might be the age of the youngest child, each person's initials, school grade levels, Dad's age, the telephone area code, the number of pets in the house, the month of the year—sometimes it's easy, sometimes hard, but it's always conversational.

❏ **40.** SEVEN CAN SUPPER. Here's an easy meal that older youngsters can make all by themselves and serve to parents. In a saucepan, put a can of chunk tuna or chicken (can size depends on family size). On top of that add these five canned ingredients (the first three drained): sliced olives, sliced water chestnuts, peas, chicken or mushroom soup, and milk (a soup can full). Heat and gently stir. Just before serving, add a can of Chinese crisp noodles.

❏ **41.** GOOD NEWS. School-aged children hear plenty of bad news from the TV set. Balance that with good news this educational way. Tear the newspaper into single pages (choose a page from various sections). Place one page at each place at the table. During the meal, call a moratorium on talk as each person scans his page for an item of good news. Then resume talking as each shares something positive he's read.

❑ **42.** **DELIGHTFUL WORDS.** When the family sits down to eat, share a few of these special words to describe the day, the food, or the family: awesome, incredible, bodacious, outstanding, exceptional, spectacular, imaginative, terrific, superb, remarkable, fantastic, marvelous, astonishing, phenomenal. It sounds silly, but "sweet talk" does wonders for those end-of-day attitudes.

❑ **43.** AKA. Those initials stand for "Also Known As" and it's a game you can play at dinner. Explain to kids that they can have a new descriptive name such as Munching Michael or The Queen of the House, or Superkid, or DEE-lightful Dad. Give kids awhile to choose their AKA and then let each announce who he is. Use these AKAs for the remainder of dinner and the evening.

❑ **44.** TIRED TODDLER. When a young child gets bored with the meal and others in the family haven't finished, give him a whipped cream dessert! On his tray, put a big glob of low-fat whipped topping (or yogurt) and let him finger paint with it. Of course, he'll lick his fingers but a busy baby is a happy baby.

❑ **45.** AFTER THE LAST MOUTHFUL. Avoid the stampede from the table through cooperative cleanup. Everyone from toddler on up should have an assignment. Each can carry his own dishes to the kitchen sink. Parents and teens can put away leftovers. The person with the best sense of organization can load the dishwasher, or a teen can wash and a younger child dry the dishes. A toddler can stand on a stool and wipe the counters and table clean. And a young child can sweep the floor. With this joint activity, the cleanup is over in less than ten minutes.

SECTION 4:
EVENTFUL EVENINGS

After dinner, parents and kids usually have individual things to do, but first take a short time for a family activity. Whether you spend twenty minutes or an hour, this special time brings family members together before homework and the bedtime routine.

FOR BABIES AND PRESCHOOLERS

❏ **46. FINGER GAMES.** It's comforting for a parent and child to be close, and for finger games you'll want the child in your lap. Start with "This Little Piggy," "This Old Man," and "Teensie Weensie Spider." Then graduate to "Patty Cake" and learning to count to five. With a marker, make little faces on your fingers and let these tiny people talk to your child.

❏ **47. EXPLORATORIUM.** Surprisingly, many kids don't really know how to play with their toys—they just toss them around. Get down on the floor and explore just one toy—the little train, the doll in the bed, the jack-in-the-box. Illustrate the train sounds, talk to the dolly, act surprised when Jack pops up. Then combine two toys—for example, let Jack surprise dolly. If you use different toys each night, your child will learn creative ways to play.

❏ **48. LITTLE FINGERS, LITTLE CRAFTS.** Don't feel you need to buy an expensive craft kit—make a simple one with your child. Punch big holes in a piece of cardboard and show how to lace string or yarn through the holes. Or, draw together on plain paper with crayons (you don't need coloring books yet). Explore the good feeling of soft clay. Don't try to figure out what a child molds with it; any shape is fine.

❏ **49. MUSIC MAKERS.** Put dried peas into a plastic container and tape it shut. This is the child's instrument. Yours is two wooden spoons to beat time. Make up a short silly song such as "This is our song, so sing along!" After you have the song and instruments going, see if you can march down the hall to your music.

❑ **50. SIMPLE GAMES.** Put a long string on the floor and see who can walk the length of it without falling off. Have a doorway chinning bar and practice hanging from it. Play with all the balls in the house by sitting on the floor with legs outstretched and rolling the balls back and forth.

❑ **51. WHERE SHALL WE GO?** Ask questions and let the child show you the answer. A parent may ask, "Where can we read?" (A child leads to the bookshelf and a rocker.) "Where can we find rain inside the house?" (A child leads to the shower.) "Where can we find ice?" (A child leads to the freezer.) Vary this by hopping, skipping, or crawling to the destination, or carrying a child piggyback.

❑ **52. QUICK PLAYHOUSE.** Throw a sheet over a card table and put a book, toy, dishes, a rattle, and so forth, underneath. Then you and your child move in—except you pretend to be a baby and the child the parent.

FOR GRADESCHOOLERS

❑ **53. BOX GAME WEEK.** Uncle Wiggly, Scrabble, dominoes, checkers, chess—you no doubt have a shelf full of games at your house. It only takes fifteen to thirty minutes to play a game (or part of a game such as Monopoly) in the time after dinner. Have a box game week when family members choose six or seven games to be played one each night after dinner. Applaud the winners for their skill and also applaud the losers for their graceful good sportsmanship.

❑ **54. OUT OF THE HOUSE.** A change of place gives a boost to the upcoming quiet evening activities (homework, chores, reading, bedtime preparations, and TV). So, leave home for an after-dinner walk, a visit with neighbors, a quick trip to the park, bicycling around the block. Some families also work in a visit to the library or a thirty-minute swim at the Y. Don't just drift from dinner table to TV; plan a change of scenery.

❏ **55.** KIDS IN CHARGE.   Start the tradition of letting youngsters be in charge one night a week. One family does this each Thursday when kids take over before supper, choosing what and where to eat, what activities follow dinner, what TV programs to watch, what books to read, and whether bedtime is postponed fifteen minutes for good behavior. Occasionally being in charge helps youngsters to accept supervision when parents are in charge.

❏ **56.** BE A SPORT.   Throw balls in baskets, practice hitting baseballs, and catching footballs. Sink a can in the backyard and practice golf putting. Hit tennis balls against a wall. Do tricks on the jungle gym. Play table tennis. Work out with an exercise video.

❏ **57.** SHARE A CRAFT.   You can work side-by-side on different projects or together on the same project. Consider woodworking, sketching, sewing, porcelain painting, pottery-making, stamp or coin collecting, furniture refinishing, flower arranging, collage making, gourmet cooking, soap carving, model train building. If you don't have any ideas, you'll find lots at a craft store.

❏ **58.** QUICK BAKING.   Don't serve dessert with dinner but prepare something with kid-help that can be eaten later in the evening. Make pudding, brownies, cupcakes, or fruit cobbler. For an unusual treat, mix together nuts, canned mandarin oranges, and vanilla cookie pieces in a little melted butter and brown sugar. Served warm, this ten minute production may become a favorite.

FOR TEENS

Be realistic! Your after-dinner time with teens is going to be short—perhaps just twenty minutes, but it can be a pleasant change in the hectic schedule. School nights are not usually social nights, so kids should be at home. Of course, they need to complete homework and then they'll want TV and telephone time—but only after a little togetherness with the family. Try these quick ideas.

❑ **59.** GET PHYSICAL. Right after dinner, take just fifteen minutes for something active: jogging, cycling, shooting hoops, or Ping Pong. It's okay if your teen is better than you are!

❑ **60.** GAMESMANSHIP. Spend time playing a game the teen enjoys: backgammon, chess, poker, grown-up card games, and box games. Chess can be played over several nights' duration by just putting a poker chip or coin under the last piece moved.

❑ **61.** SPEEDY WORK. If you work on a project together, you may be able to cut down on Saturday tasks. Change the oil filter in the car, work on constructing a bookshelf, clean a closet, sew on buttons. Such jobs done together increase a youngster's self-esteem because you show that you need him.

❑ **62.** POPCORN PROJECTS. Evenings at home are ideal times for munching popcorn. Make it interesting by working with kids to make a gallon or more of homemade popcorn. Then experiment with toppings: garlic salt with chili powder, or cinnamon and sugar, or powdered sugar with brown sugar. Or, look in a cookbook for how to make caramel corn.

❑ **63.** KICKING-BACK TOGETHER. Read while your youngster reads. Look at a TV show together and comment on it. Listen to music together. Most every teen has some evening kick-back time. Try to coordinate your activities so you can be together. One family has what they call "Ten minutes in the dark" when they just sit outside together—no conversation needed.

❑ **64.** PLOTTING FOR FUN. Discuss family and teen entertaining. Plan parties and discuss foods, games and activities, whom to invite, music, costumes if any, and a time schedule. Including a teen and asking for advice show your respect and confidence in her.

❑ **65.** HOMEWORK SNACK. Don't be a pest, but drop in at least once during the homework session. Bring a tray with juice, cookies, or crackers and cheese to share. Ask if you can be of any help—not doing the homework but proofreading, testing, finding supplies, hearing a report. This keeps you in touch with both the academics and the teen.

THE BEDTIME COUNTDOWN

Depending on the age of your children, you may tuck them in bed, or they may kiss you good night as you go to bed. Still, a regular bedtime routine is very important as a loving and calming activity.

❑ **66.** SING THE TOYS AWAY. When it's time to pick up toys, teach youngsters this song (to the tune of "Three Blind Mice") and see if the toys are in their places after two, four, or six times through the song: "Pick up toys, pick up toys. Some are girl's, some are boy's. They all have a home and I'll put them away. That way I can find them the next time I play. Pick up toys, pick up toys."

❑ **67.** BEDTIME TAG. If you have trouble heading youngsters toward their beds, a parent can introduce bedtime tag. It's just like any other game of tag and can be played inside the house in winter and in the yard in summer. Designate an area for the game. The parent will do the tagging and when a child is tagged, she's the first to start getting ready for bed. You can also make it two or three tags before a child is out and must start the bedtime routine.

❑ **68.** THINKING DEEP THOUGHTS. Family members scatter to various parts of the house (the basement, under the dining table, in a box in the garage, in the shower stall) for a quiet five minutes of thinking on just one topic. A parent whistles or rings a bell at the end of the five minutes and all gather in one place to share the mystery of where they've been and what they thought. For example: "I was in the bathtub thinking about summer at the lake." "I was at the desk thinking about paying bills." "I was on the kitchen floor hugging the dog."

❑ **69.** SOOTHING SUDS.   While teens usually prefer a morning shower, younger kids enjoy a warm bath as a prelude to good sleep. Even though soaking in water is delightful, it is also a time for occasional bathing lessons: how to wash ears safely, how to give a good shampoo, how to brush fingernails and toenails, how to carefully wash the tummy button and private parts.

❑ **70.** NO DRIPS.   Kids love popsicles but they can be a sticky mess. Why not let them drip in the bathtub? Give little children their dessert treat in the tub, then scrub them up and get them ready for teeth-brushing and bed.

❑ **71.** BATHTUB BOATS.   Show young children how to fold paper into small boats for floating in the tub and moving with fingers or toes. Add other bathtub toys on top of the boats and see what it takes to sink them. Wring out the wet boats and roll them into tiny balls for tossing into a floating cup. Then, as the tub drains, see who can "score" by tossing them into a nearby wastebasket.

❑ **72.** BATHTUB STORM.   Storms will be less intimidating for little kids if you recreate the storm right in the bathroom. With the youngster in the tub and washed, start slowly with rain (coming from a sprinkling can). Then make "thunder" sounds by knocking on the side of the tub or beating on a toy drum. Make "lightning" by going over to the wall switch and turning the lights on and off. (Of course, never let anything electrical near the tub.) Then tell the child it is time to come in from the storm and safely wrap him up in his towel.

❏ **73.** **BODY STICKERS.** Let little kids be nude for awhile before bed and have fun with stickers. Show him how to put a sticker on the end of a finger and wave with it. Then on toes and wiggle them. Hide one on the palm of her hand and play peek-a-boo. Put one on her tummy and tell her to push her tummy in and out. One on a cheek can be puffed in and out. Then remove all stickers (restick them on a favorite stuffed animal) and jump into pj's.

❏ **74.** **HOW LONG TO BRUSH?** Good habits start early, so (several times weekly) brush your teeth alongside your kids. Research shows that brushing is less thorough on the side you hold your brush—right-handers do the poorest job on the inside right, lefties on the inside left. While kids think that they know how long two minutes is, a timer will accurately inform them when they should be finished.

❏ **75.** **FLASHLIGHT NIGHT.** For the thirty minutes prior to bedtime, give each family member a flashlight. Turn out all other lights. See what fun it is to find the cookie and milk snack, lay out clothes, take a bath, read a story—all by flashlight. It can be reassuring and allay fear of the dark to have a nonlit flashlight on the night table.

❏ **76.** **TOO OLD TO READ TO?** How about letting your kids read to you something that interests them? You'll learn more about your child from their choices. And, the reading often leads to good conversation at bedtime.

❏ **77.** **LITTLE BAGS HELP.** Thank goodness for plastic bags that zip shut and let us see what's inside! Before bed is a good time to tidy the bedroom and plastic bags can really help. Use them for barrettes and hair bows, jewelry, crayons, puzzle pieces, small toys, game pieces, and even those mystery items that will later find their way to their proper home.

❏ **78.** **MY DAY.** Take photos of your child: getting up, dressing, having breakfast, going to school, doing homework, eating dinner, playing a game—whatever activities are most common to his day. With his help, paste the photos onto heavy paper and make into a book called "My Day." Place it on his night table and before bed look through the book to see which activities were part of this day.

❏ **79.** **BEAR BASKETBALL.**   When you put a toddler to bed, place many toys and animals in the crib—and one bear. You can teach hand-eye coordination by showing him how to drop the toys into a large basket placed next to the bed. When the game is over, let him choose his three favorite soft toys to go back into the crib.

❏ **80.** **READY FOR A NEW DAY.**   Help a youngster get a head start on the next day by preparing the night before. Let youngsters select their clothing from a section of acceptable school clothes in their closet. At the same time, used clothing should be picked up. Encourage kids to gather in one place (your "going shelf") books, homework, projects, show-and-tell items, lunch money, and items for after-school activities.

❏ **81.** **THE CHAIR PERSON.**   There's usually a chair in a child's room. Use that as the place to make a chair person: a laid-out collection of clothes for the next day. Let her lay out the underwear, pants or skirt, and top she plans to wear in the morning, placing it like a real person in the chair with socks and shoes on the floor in front. The chair person will remain seated all through the night, waiting for action the next morning.

❏ **82.** **SUMMARY OF THE DAY.**   Before tucking kids in, gather the entire family in one bed (kid's or parents'). See if the group can recount the events of the day: "We got up." "We ate breakfast." And so on, right up to "We put on our pj's," "We played this game," and "Now we're going to sleep."

❏ **83.** **60 PERCENT TO 0 PERCENT.**   Although a magazine survey showed that 60 percent of children under ten are afraid of the dark and being alone, this can be reduced by parent-child conversation that calmly talks about nonexistent monsters and ghosts, storms and disasters, fierce animals and insects. Talk about darkness being just the absence of light—and permit a night-light if that is comforting. See that activities and stories before bed are calming and not fearsome. Place a bell on the night table and let your child practice ringing it to summon help, but not for trivial needs. Some youngsters like to have a radio on—it makes them feel less alone. Tell your child that you will be close by and check on him regularly—and do so. (These are brief nonconversational checks.) Read poetry and let the soothing rhythms bring sleep. Don't lie down with a little child, but occasionally sit nearby to help a youngster triumph over night fears and grow in independence.

❑ **84.** **NO MATTER WHAT.** Whatever the age of your child, whatever has happened during the day, animosities should be erased at bedtime. For unsettled problems, set a time to discuss them (tomorrow evening, Saturday morning). With sleep followed by school and work, you are entering a long period of separation from your youngster, so be sure to express your love.

❑ **85.** **LOVE LINES.** Put your love into words: "I'm so glad you're my kid." "We can do anything together." "Remember, I love you." "I love you no matter what." "You're very special to us." "You were really good today." "Today was better than yesterday, and that's great." "I'm proud of you." "I'll check on you in a little while."

❑ **86.** **WHEN PARENTS ARE AWAY AT BEDTIME.** Sometimes a parent can't tuck in a child, but there are still ways to connect. Make a cassette of bedtime songs, a story, and prayers so that a child can hear your voice. For a child who reads, a note on the pillow is comforting. Or, name a doll or animal "Daddy's love buddy" or "Mommy's kissing pal." When you are home, include the doll or animal in the bedtime routine and when you're going to be away, be sure the doll or animal is sitting right on the bed pillow. When parents are not present, the sitter needs to follow the traditional bedtime routine, which can be explained as part of the instructions.

❑ **87.** **RELAXED RAG DOLLS.** In preparation for sleep, there need to be relaxing activities—not games of tag or jumping jacks. One family has an interesting ritual. The child lies flat on the bed like a rag doll and the parent lifts one of the "doll's" legs, seeing how limp it is. Then the parent drops it with a thud. Then the other leg and each arm is tested to be sure it is truly a limp rag doll. Finally the covers are pulled up and the parent kisses dolly goodnight.

❑ **88.** **JUST PRETEND.** You can't force sleep, but you can encourage resting time. First, see that bathroom and drink-of-water needs are satisfied. At bedtime (or naptime) suggest that a young child stretch out and hug a favorite toy. Say that it is okay to talk to that toy or sing to it. Grade-schoolers can listen to soft radio music. However, there is to be no getting out of bed (except for emergencies). Be strict on this. Tell the pest that keeps getting out of bed that for each time you have to put him back, he goes to bed ten minutes earlier the next night. Suggest that he just *pretend* to sleep—he doesn't actually have to sleep—and as we all know, pretending sleep usually brings sleep.

❑ **89.** **BEDTIME BLESSINGS.** No matter what the age of a child, bedtime prayers can include blessings for others. One family does it with the notes of a simple scale. On "do" a parent may start by singing "Goodnight and blessings on all." Then a child can go up one note to "re" and sing "Bless Grandpa." Then blessings can be asked for each other family member, a person taking an exam, a sick friend, the dog, and so forth. It's fun to see if you can go from "do" through "re, mi, fa, sol, la, ti" and up to "do."

❑ **90.** **NEW BABY'S PRAYER.** As you put your little one to bed, here is a prayer to say:

Little babe, so small, so dear,
We're so happy you are here.
Now it's time to say goodnight.
Everything will be all right.
I hold you in my arms so tight,
So rest until the morning's light.
Close your eyes and have your rest,
Little one, so sweet, so blessed.

❑ **91.** **TODDLER'S PRAYER.** This new prayer is for a young child: Little girl (or boy), I hold you near. With God you're safe from every fear. My kisses send you on your way, So let sweet sleep now end your day. When morning comes with clouds or sun, You'll be refreshed for happy fun. Now rest secure within our love, And blessings on you from above.

❑ **92.** **KINDERGARTNER'S PRAYER.** Here's a prayer your child can learn: Playing time has been such fun, And book reading now is done. It's time for me to go to bed, Pretty angels round my head. God's messengers are at my side. Safe in His love I now abide.

And don't forget to end your day with a prayer for yourself!

TWO

LET'S PLAY!

SECTION 1: THE CHILD-FRIENDLY HOME

SECTION 2: THE INSIDE SCOOP

SECTION 3: RIGHT IN YOUR OWN BACKYARD

While youngsters can play alone or in a group at school, playtime with just a friend or two can be the best. The shared intimacy, the stress free and casual camaraderie of playing with a friend is an important part of childhood and teaches lessons in how to have fun, be creative, and get along. See that your home is child-friendly—from the toddler years right through the teens.

SECTION 1:
THE CHILD-FRIENDLY HOME

❑ **93.** NOW IS THE TIME. Plan to have friends of your youngsters at your house this very week. Of course it's nice when your youngster is invited to another's house but be eager to have kids play at your house. Make the effort, make the time, make the arrangements, even pick kids up or walk over to get them. Urbanization of neighborhoods and more households with both parents working outside the home won't silence the sounds of childhood if you create a comfortable gathering place.

❑ **94.** FOOD AND FUN. Be prepared with snacks—not junk foods, but nutritious and appealing things to eat or prepare. While kids snack, take this opportunity to briefly talk with your child and her friend—then just listen and learn. Hungry teens especially associate a good time with good eats, so be prepared!

❑ **95.** ROTATING TOYS. Play at home can get boring with the same toys, so a month or so after Christmas or a birthday let your youngster select some toys that can be stored in a box on a high shelf for play in a few months. Some parents rotate toys with the start of each season. It's like "Christmas in April" when the stored box is opened.

❑ **96.** PLAY PLACES FOR YOUNGER KIDS. No matter how small your house, create a place where kids can play without worrying about breaking something or being underfoot. The child's own room or family room is ideal, but one dad created a carpeted area in the garage and put a low portable fence around it. This cool spot was a favorite on hot days. Toys should be handy and kept on shelves or in boxes or bins. See-through plastic bins are nicest, "banker's boxes" will do, and one family created a wall of pegboard and hooks with see-through plastic grocery bags for each kind of toy or game.

❑ **97.** PLAY PLACES FOR TEENS. As kids mature, they want more privacy from parents and younger siblings. Help them make a place for listening to music, reading magazines, and talking together. Furnish with big pillows or beanbag chairs, a low table for food, and a radio or CD player. While you may be comfortable with a closed room door when there are kids of the same sex together, when there are boys and girls together this rule should apply: A brick in the door and two feet on the floor!

❑ **98.** KID INPUT, PARENT GUIDELINES. Ask youngsters what you can do to make your house an interesting place for their friends. Keep these points in mind:

- Once you've greeted the friends, don't intrude on play. When a child has a friend over, she doesn't need you as a playmate.
- Ask what time the friend should go home and remind him about fifteen minutes ahead so that there is time for cleanup.
- Don't be a grouch. Loud music or a few crumbs on the floor beats worrying about where your child is and what she's doing.
- Be prepared with ideas, but hold back, giving playmates the opportunity to create their own fun.
- Let kids settle their own disagreements as much as possible. If you think arguments are caused by boredom, suggest a change in activity.
- Never discipline your child in front of a friend. If possible, wait until the friend goes home. If you must say something, call your child into another room and talk quietly.
- Be grateful—your child has a buddy! Be sincerely pleasant to the friend and compliment her on something. Say you hope she'll come and play another day.
- Make play even better. After your youngster has had a friend over, ask him what was good about the time together and what wasn't enjoyable. Talk about how to make play even better the next time.

SECTION 2: THE INSIDE SCOOP

❑ **99.** MARBLE MANIA.   Gather many marbles and many cardboard tubes. You can start with a few, but you'll want lots, so ask friends to save them from gift wrapping paper and kitchen towels and wraps. Your youngster is going to make a tube raceway, starting at a high point (such as a kitchen stool) and going down gradually to the floor. Cut some tubes in half lengthwise so you can see the race course. Connect the tubes using masking tape or duct tape, remembering that the upper tube should always feed into the next lower tube. At first, it's fun to just watch the marbles go down the chutes. But there can also be races, starting two marbles at a time or seeing which one rolls the farthest at the end. If you want to get fancy, create a fork in your racecourse or make a trapdoor hole that some marbles will whiz over and others will fall through. You can even expand your tubing to cover several rooms.

❑ **100.** WRITE ON YOUR BACK?   Why not? Back writing can be a fun activity when kids are wearing bathing suits but have tired of the water. Using washable pens, line up kids (and adults) train-style and practice writing a word on the back in front of you. Everyone then tries to figure ·out what his word is. When you get the knack, write short messages and concentrate harder!

❑ **101.** MIRROR FACES.   Sit in front of a large mirror with one or more children (sitting on a bathroom counter in front of a wide mirror works well). Quickly announce an expression such as "happy." See whose face is the happiest. Let that person name the next look: sad, laughing, afraid, sleepy, winking, angry, crying, pouting, ugly, beautiful, dreamy, silly.

❑ **102.** BOISTEROUS BEANBAGS.   Play on the floor with your youngster and some beanbags. Throw them at each other's toes. Show how to balance them on the head.

Put one on your stomach and watch it move when you laugh. Lie on your back with feet in the air and balance one on each foot. Stand up with your head back, put one on your nose, and try to walk.

□ **103.** EGG CARTON FUN.   See who in the family can find the best use for clean egg cartons. Let kids put snacks in them for no-mess eating. For breakfast, soft boil eggs and put one in each carton with toast squares in some of the pockets. A child's desk drawer can use one to hold clips, rubber bands, keys, and so forth. Do the same for kid's stuff in the bathroom: bows, clippers, pins, and so forth. For a teen, the carton can be used in a drawer for holding earrings. In the garage, let kids sort different nails into the pockets. The carton can hold beads or buttons for crafts. Place one in a family room cupboard for all those mysterious little toy parts you find.

□ **104.** RAINY DAY LIFESAVER.   Can a large trash bag be an interesting toy or gift? Here's how to make a toy in a trash bag. Using a very large disposable aluminum turkey-roasting pan, cover the bottom with sand or cornmeal and place the pan in the bottom of the flattened trash bag in order to catch any spillover. Supply a collection of inexpensive toy soldiers, planes, motorcycles, trucks, cars, animals, and fencing—whatever you can find. Stimulate a child's imagination by helping her to create a situation (a man parachutes into a field and lands on a cow's back . . . . Davy gets a new motorcycle and decides to ride and ride until he runs out of gas). Then see what happens as roads are made and people go into action. When play is over, store everything in the trash bag until next time.

□ **105.** THE BALL MYSTERY.   This is a game kids of all ages can play. And depending on age, you'll use three to six empty cans of the same size. Remove the lid and label, be sure there are no sharp edges, wash and dry them. Set them out on a table, then hide a small ball under one of them. Quickly move the cans around, then see if the youngster can find the ball. Next, let him hide the ball and you try to find it. It's a game kids enjoy showing to friends.

❑ **106.** HIDE THE TIMER.   Younger kids will enjoy this fast-moving game played throughout the entire house. While youngsters stay in one closed room, a parent hides a timer (the kind that continuously rings or buzzes, set for about two minutes). Kids race to find it before it goes off. The one finding it is the next to hide it.

❑ **107.** INVISIBLE WRITING.   Place lemon juice in a shallow dish. Cut the point off a toothpick and show a child how to use it to write a secret message on paper: ("Dessert in the refrigerator." "You can stay up late." "Let's play Monopoly.") When the message is thoroughly dry, pass it around the dinner table to see if the mystery message can be read. Then, show how it can be read with a flashlight (or with a parent holding it near a lighted bulb or placing the paper by a heater) as the heat makes the writing appear.

❑ **108.** APPLE PUZZLE.   Teens or parents can do the cutting with a sharp knife, going around the apple's circumference in a zig-zag manner, making many similar Z-shaped cuts. Be sure the knife point is reaching the core. Then pull the two pieces apart. A young child can try to make it fit back together. For older kids, cut apart several apples, and using a stopwatch, see who can reassemble the apples the fastest. Be sure to eat the apples afterward.

❑ **109.** PUDDLE JUMPING.   Kids will enjoy jumping over imaginary puddles. Using old newspapers or grocery bags, show kids how to rumple them into "puddles"—some flat, some puffed up, some narrow, some very wide. When they've made about twenty, they can deliver them to strategic pathways in the house as well as in front of the refrigerator, toilet, and television. Put some together in a hall to make it nearly impossible to get past without stepping in the puddle. One child is the first leader and he announces that the jumping will be with two feet together, or by stepping backward, or hopping, or swinging arms in circles as you walk. A leader can also give commands such as "Get a grape from the refrigerator." Finally have timed races to see who can leap all puddles the fastest. At night and with all the lights out, see who can avoid the puddles.

❑ **110.** **BOX TRAIN.** Help a child line up a row of cardboard cartons (without tops or with the tops tucked in). Connect them with duct tape to form a train and attach a rope at one end. Let her collect dolls, animals, trucks and other items that need to be transported by train. The child is the engineer and uses the rope to take the train through the house. It's also a novel way of picking up toys at the end of the day.

❑ **111.** **SAME BUT DIFFERENT.** A parent thinks of popular books, movies, or television shows and translates the title into other words. For example, "The Three Little Pigs" becomes "The Trio of Small Porkers," "Beauty and the Beast" translates to "Gorgeous and the Creature," and "Sesame Street" is "Seedy Avenue." After challenging kids with a few of these, let them think up some themselves.

❑ **112.** **MIGHTY MEGAPHONES.** For two children you'll need two gallon-sized plastic milk jugs. A parent can easily cut off the bottom of each. Now they become megaphones so kids can broadcast to one another and to parents, [shouting into the top hole].

❑ **113.** **WINDOW WONDERS.** Let kids choose used bright colored crayons and remove the paper wrapping from them. On a work surface covered with newspaper, give each youngster a piece of wax paper about eighteen-inches long. Show how to use a grater or peeler to grate one color of crayon onto the wax paper, then another. Push each color of shavings into an area about two-inches square and at least one-quarter-inch deep. Overlapping colors will produce new colors. Place a small hardware "nut" near one edge of the shavings (to be used later for hanging). Cover the shavings with another piece of wax paper and top with a piece of newspaper. Help the youngster run a warm iron over the newspaper for about ten seconds. (Peek under to be sure the shavings are melting.) Remove the newspaper and wait until the crayons are completely cool and hard. Peel the crayon creation from between the layers of wax paper. At this point it can be trimmed if desired. Thread a ribbon through the nut and hang in a window for all to admire.

❑ **114. IT'S IN THE BAG.** Fill a bag with a dozen ordinary objects such as a key, brush, ball, comb, pencil, toy car, penny, ring, clip, bottle opener, hard candy, or bolt. With two or more participants, let the first one reach into the bag and draw out one item and begin the story, using that item in a sentence. For example if the key is pulled out of the bag, the story might begin: "Once upon a time a bad king locked a beautiful princess in her room and threw away the key." The next person draws out an item (for example, the brush) and must continue the story: "All day long she played with her pet lion and used her own brush on his mane." Continue in the same way and see the imaginative twists and turns in the story.

❑ **115. DOLL MANNERS.** An easy way to teach children good manners is to have a pretend meal with a doll or animal in attendance. Together with you, set a little table and provide juice and cookies. Let the child teach the doll, with a little help from you. Some Mom lines: "Does Dolly have her napkin in her lap?" "Ask her if she'd like more juice." "What did she say when you offered her a cookie?" "Do you think she's finished eating and has asked to be excused?" In this way, you are not directly teaching or correcting the child, but the message will still come through.

❑ **116. HOMEMADE PHONE.** Show a child how to put his fingertips lightly on his neck and feel the vibrations when he hums. This is the basis for the homemade phone. You'll need two metal cans with the tops safely removed and a hole made in the center of the bottom. (Be sure the top edge and bottom hole aren't sharp.) Cut a piece of string that will reach the length of the hall or other long area. Draw the string through the can holes and knot it, connecting the two cans with their open ends toward the string ends. Let each youngster take one can and move apart until the string is taut and not touching anything. One child speaks into his can while the other puts the cup to her ear to listen, experimenting with how softly they can talk and still be heard. Point out how different the sound is from normal conversation.

❏ **117.** SHELLS AND ROCKS. What youngster doesn't have a collection of miscellaneous rocks and shells! Help him make something decorative by embedding them in plaster of Paris—available at any craft shop. Use pie pans as a form for making an interesting wallhanging (glue a hook to the back), or cut down yogurt containers to make forms for personal paperweights. Prepare the plaster according to instructions, then place the rocks and shells in an appealing arrangement.

❏ **118.** JUST LIKE REAL LIFE. Young children enjoy pretending and you can help by providing some supplies. To go along with their toy dishes and cookware, provide an unused picture cookbook and some recipe cards. To add to fun with a toy telephone, give them an outdated phone book. When riding in the car, provide road maps and a small purse with an expired driver's license. For a desk or table, share an old typewriter or adding machine—it's still fun for kids, even if it doesn't work perfectly.

❏ **119.** ARM WRESTLING. For kids of about equal strength, arm wrestling can be fun. Sitting at a table and clasping one opposite hand, at the signal the participants try to push each other's arms down to touch the table. Three downs make a win.

❏ **120.** BACKWARD WRITING. Let kids try to write a simple sentence backward and then hold it up to a mirror to see the message. It probably won't be readable. Then show the trick: look in the mirror while writing, not at the paper. Then let them write messages to family members or friends.

❑ **121.** MATCHING PAIRS. This game can teach concentration to kids from age four and up. Using a deck of cards turned face down in several rows on a table, the object is to turn over two matching cards (two fives, two queens, and so forth). If no match, replace them face down. If a match, you keep those cards and take another turn. For older youngsters, use a full deck. For the youngest, start with a total of ten cards (five matching pairs) and when they master it, add more pairs.

❑ **122.** STILTS. When kids wish to be taller, you can actually show them how to make that happen. For each youngster you'll need a pair of cans (large juice cans or coffee cans) with one end removed. (Be sure there are no sharp edges left.) On each can, make marks on either side one inch down from the closed end. A parent should use a hammer and nail to punch through the can at this point, and then widen the holes with a screwdriver. Now cut two pieces of rope that are three times the length from the child's knee to the floor. Let kids thread the ends through the holes from the outside and tie knots on the inside. Help the youngster (who is wearing rubber-soled shoes) up onto the can top, standing on the ball of the foot. With this mastered, hand her the ropes and steady her as she takes her first straight-legged steps. Soon it will be easy!

❑ **123.** TOOTHPICK TOWN. A box of round toothpicks and quick-setting glue are all that's needed for a toothpick town. It makes a unique centerpiece for the table. Help a child cut the pointed ends off the toothpicks. Now you're ready for construction. With uprights and cross pieces you can make a fence and then build a miniature log cabin to go inside the fence.

❑ **124.** MYSTERY BOOK. Let kids cut out magazine pictures that they like, then paste these on every other page of a spiral notebook. On the blank pages, cut out a portion of the page to make a little window—some large, some small. Then when you "read the book" together, see if the youngster can identify the mystery picture by looking through the window.

□ **125.** **WHO'S GOT THE BUTTON?** In olden times, button collections were popular, and nowadays they're popular again. Provide kids with a glass jar and a variety of buttons (you can ask friends for some, too). At first kids will find it fun to sort them into colors and shapes and count them. Then, they can make a display by sewing them onto a piece of fabric that can be framed for a wallhanging. Or, they can be glued to a piece of painted plywood and framed. Also teach kids how to play "Tiddledywinks" with buttons.

□ **126.** **MEGATOWN.** Who says you must play with just one toy at a time? Some of the most creative play comes when kids combine several toys: train, Hot Wheels, a doll house, small figures and animals, and toy buildings. (Don't be concerned about the relative proportions of cars and figures—it doesn't matter in this kind of play.) Encourage the building of Megatown on a floor area where it can be played with undisturbed for several days or weeks. Create a city, suburbs, park, school, zoo, and so forth. Help kids create Megatown scenarios: a race between cars and trains, the arrival of friendly aliens, a dog elected mayor makes up new laws, the animals escape from the zoo, and so forth.

□ **127.** **LANDSCAPING WITH SHEETS.** When kids are playing with cars and trucks, it helps to have roads and highways, hills and valleys. Provide old sheets and show youngsters how to use marking pens to draw roadways on them. To make hills, crumple newspaper into a mound and put it under the sheet, pressing it down firmly. Then cover the mound with uncrumpled newspaper to make a smooth surface and replace the sheet. Now you have a hill that vehicles can roll down on their own. The nice thing about landscaping with sheets is that when play is over, they fold up nicely for another day.

❑ **128.** SING ALONG.   Don't be hesitant about learning the words to kids' favorite songs—as long as the words are acceptable! And do teach kids your favorite songs, or those of your parents and grandparents. Nowadays many schools don't have money for music classes, so it's up to you to teach singing. Borrow a songbook at the library to find the words of old-time favorites and patriotic songs. At the type-writer or computer, let each person key in the words of a song or two. Make sufficient copies and take them along on your next excursion for a car sing-along.

❑ **129.** PILLOW PUPPETS.   When a youngster needs a soft cuddly toy, help him make one out of a pillowcase. Stuff the case with fabric scraps, foam rubber, or anything clean and soft. Then, tie it shut to form the neck. With marking pens, let him draw a face and hair on the case. He then stands behind his big puppet friend and talks for him. The pillow puppet makes a good naptime companion—a child will talk to him and easily fall asleep.

❑ **130.** FABRIC FOLKS.   Let kids draw a figure of themselves on a sturdy piece of cardboard about twelve-inches high. Then, get out your scrap bag, scissors, and glue. Show them how to cut out clothes for the figure and glue them in place: hats, shirts, pants, mittens, shoes. When playtime is over, put the fabric folks in a folder to keep them safe for another day.

❑ **131.** LITTLE HANDS, BIG CARDS.   It's difficult for lit-tle children to hold the cards for games—in fact one of our sons always took his cards to another room to sort them. That's when we invented the card fan holder. Cans such as Crisco or some snack foods have plastic lids. Using two lids of the same size, place them with the flat sides together and staple them as near the middle as possible. Put tape or a sticker over the staple. Now cards can be sorted and played easily if the child places them between the two lids.

❏ **132.** **BARTER TIME.** Go over the toy shelves with children, selecting good toys they no longer play with. Suggest the same idea to other families in your neighborhood. Then arrange a barter time when each child has a card table of toys on an area of your lawn. Show how two-way and three-way trades work and how to barter for one big toy with three little ones. Bartering doesn't cost anything and teaches good lessons about negotiating and value.

❏ **133.** **NO LAUGHING.** With a group of two or more kids, have them sit facing one another or in a small circle. Set a timer for three minutes and see who can sit that long without talking, giggling, or laughing. Participants can make funny faces at one another, as long as they are silent. It's harder than it sounds!

PAINTING PROJECTS

❏ **134.** **CREATING PAINT.** With kid help, make finger paint. In a large pan, mix one cup of cold water with one cup of flour. Let the child stir it until it is smooth. Next, the parent adds three more cups of cold water and cooks the mixture over medium heat, stirring constantly until the mixture bubbles and thickens like gravy. Reduce the heat and cook one minute more. Pour the mixture into four bowls. Let kids add a different food coloring to each bowl and stir. Cover the bowls with plastic wrap until cool. Then paint!

❏ **135.** **PAINT PRECAUTIONS.** Paint can permanently stain, so work outside or in a play area. Provide aprons or big T-shirts for artists, and cover surfaces with newspaper. A good first project is making wrapping paper and a matching card. This saves money, and the wrapped gifts look unique and festive.

❏ **136.** **MAGICAL WRITING.** Show kids how to use up those white crayons that come in every box. Let a child write a simple message using white crayon on white paper, and then ask someone to read it (which can't be done). The child then presents the reader with any color of watercolor paint. When he paints quickly over the surface of the paper, the mystery message appears, revealed in magical white writing.

❏ **137.** INK SPOTS. This project uses ink and paper and requires a covering to protect the work surface. Fold a piece of white or colored paper in half. Open it, put a drop of ink in the crease, close it, then massage it. When dry, the paper can be refolded as a greeting card or hung as art work on a bulletin board.

❏ **138.** POTATO DESIGNS. Cut a potato in half for each child. Then, with a blunt knife or other safe tool, let the youngster cut a design or letter into the cut end. This becomes a stamp that can be dipped into various colors of paint and printed on paper. By rinsing the potato stamp, you can use it for several colors. With a little guidance, kids can now create artistic note paper and wrapping paper, using the potato stamps, as well as sponges and kitchen tools such as whisks and mashers. Print on paper that can be folded to use for letter writing. Don't throw away large drawings; instead use them to wrap gifts to and from kids. These uses save money and encourage art.

❏ **139.** GLASS DOOR ARTISTS. It's fun for kids to paint sliding glass doors. Cover the ground with newspaper for drips. Let kids use spoons to put the paint on the glass doors and let fingers do the arranging. (When tired of the painting, kids can wash it off with soap and a hose.)

❏ **140.** WHAT SHALL WE PAINT? Walk through the house and let kids find things they'd like to paint such as the bookshelves in their room or an old wagon. Set up an outside painting area. Find all those miscellaneous spray cans you have in the workshop. Show kids how to safely use spray paint and clean the nozzle afterward. Use a light spray of a second color to cover any irregularities.

❑ **141.** ROLL IT ON. Here's a drip-free way to let kids paint. Save used roll-on deodorant bottles. Pry off the ball at its base (a parent should do this with a screwdriver). Rinse the bottles and fill each with one color of slightly diluted liquid tempera paint. Put the ball back on and let kids roll away. And, when they've finished, replace the caps to keep the paint fresh.

❑ **142.** PUDDING PAINT. To celebrate the end of a painting project, make pudding paint. Just make a batch of chocolate instant pudding according to the directions. Have kids sit at a table with clean hands and a clean piece of paper in front of them. They then dip their fingers into the pudding and paint away (licking their fingers when they have finished their masterpiece).

KITCHEN FUN

❑ **143.** WHAT'S GOOD ABOUT LIMA BEANS? Some kids don't like to eat them, but most all will enjoy growing them. Provide a glass jar and some paper toweling that has been slightly dampened. The paper towels should be stuffed in the jar so they touch the sides. Then, the youngster inserts some lima bean seeds between the towels and the glass and places the jar in a sunny window. The seeds are interesting to watch as they sprout. Keep the paper towels moist until the seedlings outgrow the jar and then plant them in pots or in the garden.

❑ **144.** MAGIC MUD. Give your youngster a cup of cornstarch in a bowl and also a cup of water. Let her add the water gradually until the mixture is like bread dough. Then, show her how to roll the mixture into a ball. Now, watch the ball carefully as it will magically dissolve to liquid!

❑ **145.** PRETZEL SUCKERS. Sometimes it's hard to get kids to eat fruit. Work together to make these tantalizing snacks. Insert small pretzel sticks into banana chunks, pineapple pieces, or grapes. You won't be able to make enough!

❑ **146.** **IN A PICKLE.** Although pickles can be made from many fruits and vegetables, show kids how to make Thunder and Lightning pickles.

THUNDER AND LIGHTNING PICKLES

4-5 large ripe cucumbers   3 pints of ice water
⅔ cup salt   3 sprigs dill
1 tablespoon white mustard   2½ cups vinegar
2 teaspoons grated horseradish   ⅔ cup water
2 medium hot red peppers   ¾ cup sugar

Let kids peel cucumbers, cut in half lengthwise and scoop out seeds, then cut the halves in thirds lengthwise and then cut the thirds in half. Place in ice water, add salt, cover and let stand overnight. The next day, drain well. Divide the dill, mustard, horseradish, and peppers between two sterilized jars. Heat the vinegar, water, and sugar, add the cucumbers and boil gently five minutes. Then pack the pickles into the jars to an inch from the top. Add the boiling solution to a half inch from the top. Seal for storing, but put some in the refrigerator for immediate eating. This recipe will make two quarts.

❑ **147.** **MYSTERY BISCUITS.** When it's time to use up leftovers, let one of your kids help you make mystery biscuits. Any refrigerated biscuit dough will work, but the roll-up crescent variety works best. Don't tell others what's inside! It can be a half hot dog, chicken pieces, lunch meat, tuna fish, olives and onions, ground beef and taco sauce, broccoli or other veggies, cheese, even peanut butter and jam if used sparingly in the very center. Roll them up and bake according to package directions.

❑ **148.** **MOUSE SALAD.** Youngsters can prepare a squeaky salad as you make the remainder of the meal. Give them: canned pear halves, dried apricots, string licorice, whole cloves, mini-marshmallows and toothpicks cut in half. You can pat the pears dry and set them out on the work surface, with the hollow side down. Kids insert toothpicks in dried apricots and attach two at the midpoint of each pear as perky ears. Then, they cut two mini-marshmallows in half and use a clove to push each into the pear as a nose and eyes. Each mouse is then put on the salad plate and a coil of licorice is laid out for the tail.

☐ **149.** TONGS RACE.   When you're busy in the kitchen, you can keep young children busy and improve their coordination at the same time. Gather twelve small toys, or use twelve small items found in the kitchen. Show how tongs can pick up these items. Then, place a muffin pan in front of the child and let her put one item in each cup. Once she gets the knack of using the tongs, use the kitchen timer to see if she can put the twelve items into the cups in one minute. Then see if she can take them out and put them back in two minutes. She'll want to do it again and again as she gets faster.

☐ **150.** NOT-HOT HOT DOG.   For children too young to work over a hot stove, work together to prepare a not-hot hot dog. Using a long hot dog bun, put peanut butter on one side and jam on the other. Then, instead of the wiener, put a banana inside. It looks like a hot dog and it's a lunch your young child can make with just a little help from you.

☐ **151.** BASTER PLAY.   Water and kids go together and your young child will enjoy playing with your baster as you prepare supper. All you need are two bowls of water (put a little gravy coloring, juice, or food coloring in them to make it more interesting). Then, let your youngster go to work squeezing the bulb, watching the colored water come up the glass tube, and then emptying it.

☐ **152.** LITTLE RESTAURANT.   Even if your family is small, let one child create a family restaurant. Help him set up the table with a special cloth and napkins. Provide him with an apron and menus (which he letters by hand or on computer). Make family members wait outside the room, and then seat them and present the menu. The first course gives a choice between soup or shrimp cocktail. If anyone orders the shrimp, the waiter goes into the kitchen and returns to say that it isn't available. The main course choices can be stewed buffalo with okra or the dish that you really plan to serve. (You can also use up many one-portion leftovers by putting them on the menu.) While others are eating the soup, the waiter and cook prepare the plates and then remove their aprons and join the others. However, at the end of the meal, the waiter puts his apron back on and offers dessert: a choice of ice creams and toppings.

❑ **153.** MONSTER DOUGH. Creatures from the deep or outer space are fun to make from this no-cook (and inedible) dough. Combine 1 cup of salt with one and a one-fourth cups water and two teaspoons of cooking oil. Show kids how to knead the mixture until smooth. Then divide it into several small bowls, color each with food coloring, and mix well. If it is sticky, add flour; if it is dry add droplets of water. Use the creations as decorations at the dining table.

❑ **154.** REGULAR PLAY DOUGH. Make this easy recipe and enjoy modeling fun with your kids. Mix together in a saucepan: one cup of flour, one half cup salt, one half cup water, two teaspoons cream of tartar, one tablespoon of vegetable oil, and a few drops of food coloring. Heat and stir until a ball begins to form. Cool before using or store in an airtight container in the refrigerator until modeling time.

❑ **155.** EDIBLE PLAY DOUGH. Measure two cups of peanut butter, two cups of powdered milk, and three tablespoons of honey into a large bowl. Let your youngster mix it all together. If it is too sticky, add more powdered milk, one spoonful at a time. You can add chocolate bits, nuts, raisins or other edibles. Next, prepare a clean surface for dough play and be sure all hands are clean. Kids will make interesting objects they can later eat.

SECTION 3: RIGHT IN YOUR OWN BACKYARD

❑ **156.** **AIRBORNE AEROBICS.** See who can keep a soccer ball in the air for the longest time without touching it with hands or letting it touch the ground. Count how many times each player bounces the ball off her helmeted head, shoulder, thigh, or feet. Give players three turns and average their scores to determine the best juggler.

❑ **157.** **MARVELOUS MUD.** When rainy days continue on and on, still permit outside play—in the mud! Establish some clothes that you don't care about and let the kids wear them with boots. Create a mud pond in an old kiddie pool. Set it out on a rainy night and the next day show kids where they can scoop up dirt and take it to the pool. You can be sure they'll want to play in it. Spoons, pails, funnels, and old strainers make slimy fun. With less water, kids can create roads for small cars or mud mansions (like sand castles). Of course, there can always be mud pies created in old pie tins and allowed to dry.

❑ **158.** **POPCORN HIDE-AND-SEEK.** Kids love finding a person (or a gift) by following a trail of popcorn through your yard or the park. Occasionally make a fork in your trail—one fork being a dead-end so that seekers must go back and follow the other fork.

❑ **159.** **AN EASY CATCH.** It's discouraging when balls bop kids or pop out of their small hands. Teach the technique of catching by using a partly deflated beach ball. Stand behind the child and guide his arms and hands as you show tossing, as well as catching, by making a cradle to catch the ball.

❑ **160.** **WINDMILLS.** It's quick and easy to make a windmill or pinwheel. Using sturdy paper, cut a seven-inch square. Draw lines across the square from opposite corners. Cut on the line from each of the four corners to about three-fourths inch from the center. Take one corner of each of the resulting triangles and glue or staple it to the center. Using a short straight pin, make a hole in the center and then push the pin through, affixing the pinwheel to a narrow straight piece of wood or stick. For safety, be sure the sharp end is firmly in the wood. Now a youngster can run with it and watch it twirl.

❑ **161.** DIGGING TO CHINA. Create a place for kids to dig in the backyard—some spot that is visible from the house but not too prominent. Small shovels or trowels will encourage digging and the excess soil makes a mountain next to the hole. While kids won't dig straight through the earth to the other side, look at a globe to learn what place is on the other side. A digging area can provide fun with cars, trucks, and boats, and does make bath time a nonarguable event!

❑ **162.** RELAXING TOY. When you think that your budding gymnasts need a quiet activity, here's one that is fun and fascinating. Provide each child with a plastic liter-sized soda bottle with the label removed. Let him fill the bottle halfway with cooking oil, then a few drops of food coloring, then the remainder of the way with water. Put the cover on tightly and then take the bottle outside and stretch out on a lounge chair or blanket. Show the youngsters how to slowly tilt the bottles back and forth, watching the tidal wave inside build. It teaches that oil and water really don't mix, and it also provides quiet fun.

❑ **163.** WHEEL RACE. Make two racing prods—one for a parent, one for a youngster—by putting a cross piece on the bottom of a three-foot long piece of lath (or other wood the size of a yardstick). The cross piece forms a "T" at the bottom. Now find two large wheels from an old wagon or trike. Using the racing prod, see who can push their wheel the farthest. Kids usually excel over parents.

❑ **164.** CALL A MOOSE. With a shoelace and a round can from potato chips, you can create the "call of the wild." (Save up these round cans so a group of kids can each have one.) Discard the plastic top and punch a small hole in the bottom. Tie a knot in one end of the shoelace and thread the remainder through the hole and out the bottom. Dip the lace that hangs out from it in water. Then, run your fingers down the lace as if squeezing the water out. The resulting sound will either bring moose to your backyard or send the dog into hiding!

❑ **165.** GOOP. This wonderful substance is made indoors but best played with outdoors.

> ### GOOP
>
> | 8 ounces of white glue | food coloring |
> | water | 20 Mule Team Borax |
>
> Combine glue, three-fourths cup water, and food coloring in one bowl. In another bowl, mix one-fourth cup water with one tablespoon Borax, and add this to the first bowl, stirring until it forms a Goop ball. Remove the ball. Again combine one-fourth cup water with one tablespoon Borax and mix it into the glue mixture, stirring until another Goop ball forms. Keep repeating the process until the glue mixture is gone. Then knead all the Goop balls together. Now you're ready to play by pulling and patting the Goop into strings and unique forms. Store the Goop in an airtight container.

❑ **166.** HOMEMADE RAIN GAUGE. Using a test tube, help a child affix it to a stake. Place it upright in a low traffic but open area of the yard. After a good rain, listen to the radio and find out how much rainfall was measured. If it was five tenths of an inch, mark that spot on the gauge with tape and pen. From this he can figure the markings for less or more rain. See how accurate this gauge is compared to the experts. Find out how much rain is normal for your area and how much rain has fallen thus far in the "rain year."

❑ **167.** WEB WATCHING. Locate a spider web in the yard. Don't disturb it, but observe how it is anchored and how big it is. Look at it each day to see what the spider is catching. What does the spider eat? How fast does it eat? Does the spider ever leave the web? Consider giving your spider a name.

☐ **168.** FACES IN THE CLOUDS.   When kids need a quiet moment in the middle of outside play, provide a blanket for a relaxing activity. Lie down with them and look up at the clouds. Describe what you see in a particular cloud—a face, a mountain, a bus. Everyone will see something different. Look for cloud formations and make up a story, for example: one cloud (perhaps the bus-shaped one) is trying to go up a hill (the mountain-shaped one) and runs out of gas. You can also pretend that clouds are islands and that you are swimming from island to island across the sky. See how fast the clouds change, offering new creative story shapes.

☐ **169.** DOLL BOUTIQUE.   Most little girls like to dress dolls. Help make a doll boutique in the backyard. Invite your daughter's friends to bring fashion dolls to the boutique. Show how flowers and leaves can be made into doll apparel gluing leaves and petals to material. For example, a hollyhock blossom hat, a chain of daisies as an elegant stole, rhubarb leaves as a skirt. Snapdragon blossoms make excellent shoes. Your child's creativity may amaze you.

☐ **170.** GIANT BUBBLES.   Don't cry over spilt expensive store-bought bubble liquid. Make a giant container of your own by mixing two cups of Joy dishwashing liquid (somehow this brand works best) with six cups of water and three-fourths cups of light corn syrup. Pour one cup in a large shallow bowl. Store the remainder, tightly covered. Using a large coffee can or juice can, cut off both ends. Hammer the cut edges until they are smooth. Dip either end in the solution and wave back and forth, forming giant bubbles.

☐ **171.** SLIPPERY SLIDING.   A slight grassy slope and an old shower curtain can provide good exercise and fun. Cut the shower curtain in half lengthwise and lay both pieces on the slope, the upper piece overlapping the lower one. With everyone in swimsuits and a hose for dribbling water on the slide, there can be running, jumping, and sliding fun for all ages.

❑ **172.** LEAPING BOXES.   You'll want sturdy crates and lightweight kids to enjoy jumping fun. Start with just one small crate and see who can leap the farthest from it. Then, add a second larger one and let kids leap from one to another. Gradually add crates until kids can have a contest to see who can leap the fastest from one to another, off the end one, and back to the first.

❑ **173.** POTPOURRI.   Show youngsters how to collect the petals from dead rose blossoms at your house (or from neighbors who give permission). Set them on trays until they are completely dry. Then, using a large pail, crush the rose petals with an "essential oil" (available at craft shops). Package the potpourri in squares of net for immediate use in drawers, or in pretty, tightly sealed jars for gifts.

❑ **174.** TODDLER TUMBLES.   When small children are out playing on asphalt or cement, knees can easily get scrapes. Avoid "Owees" this easy way: buy a pair of tennis wristbands and slide them on the bare knees. They'll also pay for themselves when the toddler wears them over long pants since there will be fewer tears to mend (and fewer tears to shed).

❑ **175.** HARE AND TORTOISE BIKE RACE.   On a safe driveway or sidewalk, chalk two parallel four-foot wide lanes about twenty-five feet in length. (Older children can have a longer race course.) Two riders start cycling down the lanes as slowly as they can, keeping their feet on the pedals as they stay within the lines. The last cycler to cross the finish line is the winner.

❑ **176.** TWENTY MINUTE WEED CONTEST.   Using strings, divide the lawn with a section for each youngster and adult. Draw names out of a bag and let each person choose a section. Then, in just twenty minutes, everyone pulls weeds (being sure to get the roots). See who pulled the most, the biggest, the smallest, or the most unusual.

❑ **177.** MANY SPRINKLING CANS.   Save gallon-sized milk containers until you have enough for a group of kids. Punch many holes in the bottoms of the jugs. Let kids take them outside and use a hose to fill them with water. Then they can give plants, grass, and their own feet a drink.

❑ **178.** CRAZY CROQUET.   If you don't have a croquet set, find one at a garage sale. Of course, the regular game is fun, but crazy croquet can make your yard a neighborhood favorite. Choose objects that the ball must go under, over, around, or through: a lawn chair, a tree, a child's wagon, a plastic container with both ends cut off, a hose, and so forth. Use the wickets (but bent metal clothes hangers are a good substitute) at the entry and exit of each obstacle and number them so that players go in order, one shot at a time, a second shot if mastering the obstacle. If you have a slide, start the game there by having players start their balls at the top, which should then go through a wicket near the bottom.

❑ **179.** GIANT HOPSCOTCH.   This is an extended form of regular hopscotch, except make it like a trail, down your driveway, and then along your sidewalk. Mark some squares for the left foot, some for the right foot. Put in plenty of two-foot resting spots. When they tire of it, let kids wash it away with a hose.

❑ **180.** ROLLING RACE.   In a yard or park, find a small grassy slope for active fun. (This also works on a sand dune.) Show kids how to lie on one side and start rolling down the hill (you may have to provide a gentle push for little ones and promise to catch them at the bottom). When the fun of rolling begins to fade, have simple races, then a relay where the roller runs back up and tags the next person to start.

❑ **181.** CHALKTOWN.   On a safe driveway, help kids sketch out a large transportation system using white chalk. Show how to draw highways, small roads, airports, and railway tracks. Using green chalk, add trees, fields, and mountains. With blue chalk make rivers flowing into lakes with docks. Using red and brown chalk, draw houses, and sky-scrapers. Next, collect many toy cars, planes, boats, animals, and people from toy bins in the house. Place these in your setting with boats crossing the lake, police chasing a car, planes taking off, farmers in the field, families in the houses. Several children will enjoy Chalktown for many days (a car can drive over the chalk)—until the rain washes it away.

☐ **182.** TAKE AIM! Place two foot-long sticks in the ground about a foot apart. Make a line about ten feet back from the sticks. Each player stands behind the line with a frisbee and tries to roll it between the two sticks. Give players five tries and keep score if you wish to select a winner.

☐ **183.** KID GARAGE SALE. Suggest that kids and their friends clean out their rooms and family rooms, gathering clean out-grown clothes and usable unwanted toys, books and games. Set up card tables with signs marked twenty-five cents, fifty cents, one dollar. Let one youngster, who adds well and can make change, be in charge of each table, putting the money in a fanny pack. A parent can oversee one table or the entire project. If you have lots of young participants, consider a table with lemonade and cookies for sale. This event is good training in salesmanship.

☐ **184.** WHAT'S IN THE YARD? From your own garden, gather blossoms from flowers and leaves from trees. Place them carefully between wax paper and then under heavy books. When they are dried (after about two weeks), make a plant identification book. Use a dab of glue to affix them to a page and label the page with the name of the flower or tree. Ask friends and neighbors if you can search their yards for plants not found in yours. See how quickly kids learn the names of the specimens.

☐ **185.** BUGGY GARDEN? You can keep insects off plants without using poisons. Help a child to plant a bug-free vegetable garden by using fireplace ashes around the edge, and planting marigolds and nasturtiums (which repel insects) next to the veggies. Your garden shop can give you other poison-free suggestions.

❑ **186.** TALK TO THE FLOWERS. Develop conversational skills by taking a walk with little kids around the yard (or down the street). You set the example by chatting to plants and creatures, and then let the kids take over. "Hello daisy, we're taking a walk and like your yellow flowers." "Hi there ant, where are you going?" "Greetings fence, how many gates do you have?" "Bye grass, sorry I stepped on you."

BALLOON FUN

Balloons can be fun, providing you follow certain precautions. Keep balloons away from babies and toddlers who might put them to their mouths, break them, and suck them into their throats. The following ideas are such fun that even sophisticated teens and parents will want to join in the action.

❑ **187.** BALLOON BARBER. For each participant you'll need an air-filled balloon, a safety razor (or bladeless razor for young kids), and shaving cream (one or two cans for a group). Each person is given a handful of shaving cream, then he sits down on the ground with the balloon between his knees and lathers the cream over the entire balloon. Then the razors are passed out and the "shaving" begins. The aim is to get all the lather off the balloon without popping it.

❑ **188.** BALLOON VOLLEYBALL. Divide kids into two teams and place a string or net between two trees or poles. Fill several heavy-duty balloons about one-third full of water and then fill with air. (This makes a balloon that flies erratically.) A balloon is thrown, rather than hit, from one side of the net to the other. The game is played like volleyball and ends when one side has eleven points.

❑ **189.** LADDER SPLAT. Everyone loves to see dropped things go "splat." The object is to make the biggest splash. Kids fill many balloons with water to the same size, using a watering can with pointed spout or a small hose nozzle. A ladder is placed on patio or driveway and each player tosses a balloon to the ground with as much force as possible. Scorekeepers quickly outline the splat with chalk and put the youngsters initials inside. (Turn the ladder each time to provide a dry area.) The winner gets to pick up all the balloon fragments!

❑ **190.** SPACE BALLOONS. Help kids to build a giant slingshot to catapult water balloons into space—or at least across the yard. Fill many balloons with water and put them in boxes or bags for easy transport. Establish a firing line and an area beyond with a finish line. (Important: when someone is in that area, no one is permitted to launch a balloon.) Using rubber tubing available at a hobby shop, cut two ten-foot pieces and connect them with a large plastic kitchen funnel. (Drill a hole in each side of the funnel and tie the tubing with a small tight knot inside.) If you don't have a funnel, experiment with other receptacles, such as plastic milk cartons with one end cut off. Two youngsters, standing well apart, hold the ends of the tubing, while a third youngster puts a water balloon in the funnel and pulls it back. When he lets go, the balloon sails toward the finish line. Practice this several times before having a competition.

❑ **191.** BALLOON KEEP-AWAY. Provide each player with a pie pan. The group sits in a close circle and an air-filled balloon is launched. Each player uses her pan to swat the balloon away. If it can be hit again, the game continues. If the balloon hits the ground, the nearest person is out. If it hits a person, the person that hit the balloon is out.

❑ **192.** COOL-OFF TIME. For a wet and wild ending to an afternoon of balloon fun, gather all the surviving balloons and fill them with water. Using a very fine needle, poke a small hole in each balloon so that there is a slow leak. Then let kids start firing them at one another. The object is to keep tossing them at others until the balloons run out of water.

<u>THREE</u>

FOUR SEASONS FUN

SECTION 1: SPRING

SECTION 2: SUMMER

SECTION 3: AUTUMN

SECTION 4: WINTER

These ideas that tie in with specific holidays and the seasonal weather will help to build wonderful year-round family memories.

SECTION 1: SPRING

❏ **193.** THE FIRST SPRING TREE. Even before spring has sprung, you can help kids make a spring tree right inside your house. Start with a scouting expedition to find a small dead tree or a large branch. Your tree should be pruned into a pleasant shape and then scrubbed. Spray paint the tree in a pale color or with clear polyurethane to give it a shine. Depending on its size, plant it in a basket or pot filled with sand or plaster of Paris. Now it is ready to be decorated with tissue flowers, Easter eggs, felt birds, or other objects that say "Spring is here!"

❏ **194.** READY, AIM, FIRE. On the first day of spring, celebrate by bundling up and eating outdoors. Plan an easy-to-eat meal and let family members sit in a tree or on the jungle gym at home or in the park. Put large paper bags—weighted with a rock—on the ground at varying distances. As the meal progresses, let each person try to fire his refuse into the bags—no prizes, but cheers for good shots.

❏ **195.** JAPANESE DOLL DAY. Early each March, Japanese girls enjoy a centuries-old celebration by displaying their elaborately dressed dolls. Let your daughter also celebrate by inviting friends to a doll party, using paper doll invitations. Have a doll fashion show and tea party.

❏ **196.** APRIL FOOL FOOLERY. Encourage family members to do clever pranks (never mean or dangerous) on this humorous holiday. Get a plastic bug collection at a party store—cockroaches encased in plastic ice cubes will wake up soda drinkers! A fake mouse in the cupboard is fun. Or, put a small paper cup of water on the top of the bathroom door to provide a surprising shower.

❏ **197.** SPRING FLOWER CONTEST Put each family member's name on a popsicle stick or other marker. Then walk around the yard together looking at all the budding flowers, each person putting his marker by the plant he thinks will bloom first. This helps youngsters become aware of the coming of spring.

❑ **198. EDIBLE BIRD NESTS.** Let kids make this spring snack for themselves or for a party. First, they crumble three large shredded wheat cereal biscuits into a mixing bowl. Then, stir in a half cup of shredded coconut, two tablespoons of brown sugar, and a half cup of melted margarine. Using a muffin pan, line the cups with small pieces of foil, then press the mixture into the bottoms and up the sides. Bake them for ten minutes in a 350 degree oven (or until toasty crisp). When cool, let kids lift out the foil nests and remove the foil. When ready to serve, add the "eggs": green and red grapes, melon balls, cherries, even jelly beans, and Easter candy.

❑ **199. A CELEBRATION OF FREEDOM.** Passover is the Jewish celebration commemorating the Exodus from Egypt. The name comes from a devastating plague that passed over the Israelite homes. Today it is celebrated at a feast called a Seder, which has commemorative foods and the reading of the Passover story. If your family is invited to this feast, certainly go. If not, educate your children by sharing newspaper stories about it.

❑ **200. KEEPSAKE EASTER EGGS.** A few weeks ahead of your big Easter party, assign each guest the name of another guest so that a special Easter egg can be made. If guests don't have their own ideas, suggest these: cutting an oval in one side of the egg and drawing a scene inside, covering an egg with thread or fine ribbon, or writing a short letter or poem around the egg. Prepare egg-viewing on a prominent table or shelf by lettering the guest's name on a cardboard collar that holds the egg. After everyone has admired them, put them on the table as place cards.

❑ **201. LOOK-ALIKE EGGS.** Exchange names within the family or a larger group. Then, using indelible markers, each person makes an egg to look like that person—match hairstyle, eye color, and so forth. Then have a guessing contest as to the identity of each egg.

❑ **202.** **HAIRY EGGHEADS.** Give everyone in the family a "good hair day" by making eggs with "hair." Using nail scissors, carefully cut off the top of the egg, saving the insides for cooking. Put a pin hole in the bottom. Then wash and dry the eggs. Next, using indelible markers, let family members put facial features on each egg. Fill eggs with soil and a small quantity of quick-germinating grass seed. Use an egg carton as your growing area. Water gently, cover with plastic wrap, and put in a sunny area. When grass sprouts, remove the plastic wrap. In about ten days, the eggs will have a bushy mane, ready to trim, tie in a ponytail, cut Mohawk style, or braid. Make each finished egghead a collar of cardboard on which to stand.

❑ **203.** **SYMBOLS OF EASTER.** No matter what your religion, teach kids the meanings of Easter symbols. White lilies are symbols of purity. Rabbits and chicks represent springtime and new life. The cross is the symbol of Jesus' victory over death and is displayed in Christian churches. It is also recreated on biscuits called hot cross buns. Candles, which are often extinguished on Good Friday to symbolize the darkness of the Crucifixion, are then relighted Saturday evening. The Easter Parade, which originated in New York, highlights springtime clothing and fabulous hats. Egg hunts go back to a German folktale that credits the Easter rabbit with laying eggs for good children. The lamb was the Jews' sacrificial symbol at Passover and later the Christian symbol for Jesus' sacrifice. Colored eggs came from Mesopotamian Christians who used them as symbols of Easter joy.

❑ **204.** **EASTER BREAKFAST.** Using a cookie cutter, cut the center out of a piece of toast—one for each guest. Kids can toast the centers and frost with cream cheese while a parent puts the toast frame on the skillet, breaks an egg into the opening, and then fries toast and egg on both sides. In advance, let youngsters prepare two or three kinds of melon balls and place them in a bowl inside an Easter basket for a festive table centerpiece.

☐ **205.** HELP BUILD A NEST.   In the spring, birds are looking for materials to use in making their nests. On a tree or shrub where you have seen birds, let kids hang colorful bits of yarn, tiny pieces of cotton, and short pieces of thread small enough for birds to carry away. When you see the birds regularly going back and forth to a particular spot (a knot of branches or twigs), you can assume they have a nest there. Do not disturb the nest! When the eggs have hatched and the babies have flown away, only then look at the nest and see which of your materials went into the making.

☐ **206.** PREPARE FOR HALLOWEEN NOW.   Why pay for pumpkins when you can have the fun of growing your own? At the garden shop, look at the pictures on the seed packets and choose the ideal shape for your jack-o'-lantern. Plant the seeds in an area where you don't have other precious plants, since pumpkins have the habit of taking over the territory. Pumpkins don't require much tending—just sun and a little water.

☐ **207.** SPRING TREASURE HUNT.   Make a backyard hunt by drawing simple pictures on pieces of paper (a fence, hose bib, rosebush, garage door, tree, deck, sandbox, and so forth). Retaining the first picture as the first clue, place the others. (For example, give the child the picture of the fence, and at the fence place the picture of the hose bib.) At the last clue, place a little surprise in a plastic bag buried in the ground or well-hidden. Do a different set for each child, or let young kids search together as a group.

☐ **208.** GO FLY A KITE.   Spring breezes make great kite-flying days. (Kite-flying is over 2000 years old and was started by the Greeks and the Chinese.) On a day when you see flags swaying or leaves fluttering, buy inexpensive kits and work together to assemble them. Choose a site away from streets, power lines, and trees. Have your child hold the kite about forty feet downwind of you. As you walk backward letting out string, the child holds the kite high and then lets it go. Now it's time to let the youngster be the pilot as the kite soars.

❑ **209.** BACK FENCE COLLAGE. With kid help, cut up miscellaneous colored paper, comics, and wrapping paper into various shaped pieces and place them in a bag. Then attach a large piece of paper to the fence. Let kids reach into the bag for one piece and then glue it in place, gradually putting together a collage. When finished, you can lay the paper flat, brush additional glue on it, and shake glitter over the collage.

❑ **210.** MAY BASKETS. On May Day, honor the old Roman tradition of secretly delivering flowers to friends. Early in the day, or the evening before, collect wildflowers, garden flowers, and assorted greenery. Let them sit in a pail of water for an hour or more. For each bouquet, you'll need a container that can be made ahead of time: fancy shopping bags or colored construction paper cut into a piece at least ten-inches square and twisted into a cornucopia. Decorate the paper with ribbons and glitter. To form a handle, make holes on opposite sides of the cone and run a twenty-four-inch ribbon through the holes, tying it on the inside. Just before delivering, kids arrange the flowers against the greens and tuck them firmly in the cone. Now you're ready to "ring and run" as kids place them on the doorknobs of friends and relatives.

❑ **211.** MAKE A MAYPOLE. You'll need a sturdy pole in the ground, or you can put a pole through the hole in the center of a heavy umbrella table. Next, cover a long wrapping-paper tube (larger in diameter than the pole) with colorful paper. For each youngster, cut an eight-foot length of crepe paper streamer and staple one end securely to the inside top of the tube. Staple a flower to the loose end and put the tube over the pole. With sprightly music playing, kids pick up the loose ends and move around the maypole. Then divide the group in two and let half go one direction and half the other direction, ducking under or going over the streamers.

❑ **212.** CINCO DE MAYO.   In 1862 the Mexicans expelled the French forces, and even today on May 5, there are celebrations of this event on both sides of the U.S. border. (Don't confuse this with Mexican Independence Day that is September 16.) Make your own fiesta, choosing from the huge variety of Mexican foods. The decorations can be red, white, and green streamers (the colors of the Mexican flag). Play mariachi music in the background. Buy a piñata or make one out of cardboard and tissue paper. You can even cover a box with strips of colorful paper. Fill your piñata with candy and hang it by a sturdy rope from a tree branch. Using a bat or pole, blindfolded kids each get one swing. Watch the scramble for candy when it finally breaks!

❑ **213.** MOM'S OWN WEEK.   Rather than just a one day celebration, make the Mother's Day celebration last an entire week. Dad, or another adult, can help a youngster make a booklet out of seven envelopes stapled together and each labeled for a day of the week. Inside each envelope is a promised good deed such as: making lunch, reading poetry to her, cleaning out a closet, watching a sibling so she can have a long bubble bath, and so forth. In last of the seven envelopes can be a letter of love to Mother.

❑ **214.** DAUGHTER EXCHANGE.   If you're tired of hinting about a Mother's Day gift, this idea lets you go shopping and still be surprised. With a friend who also has a daughter (or son), agree on the amount of money to be spent. Then go to the mall and exchange daughters. It's fun to shop with the other girl and help her buy what her mommy would like.

❑ **215.** MOM'S GARDEN GIFT.   Dad helps the kids plan this gift—a garden they will plant and care for, and from which Mom can just reap the rewards. At a garden shop choose one flowering plant for instant beauty, one tool, and a selection of seed packets of vegetables and compatible flowers. Arrange these in colored tissue paper in a basket. Make a card that tells that the family members are giving their time and effort to start and maintain the gift. Each message should be specific: "May planting, love Cliff" or "Watering twice a week, love Mark" or "June weeding, love Jamie." At the back of the basket add a homemade wood sign that reads "Mom's Garden," which she can place in her special garden.

☐ **216.** THE EYES HAVE IT. As the sun grows brighter, show kids how to glamorize their sunglasses in preparation for summer. You'll need trimmings such as felt and pipe cleaners, beads, glitter, and small buttons. Help kids cut flowers and leaves from felt and glue them onto pipe cleaners that you twist around the ear pieces. Try a row of beads over the top of the frame, or glue glitter all the way around the frames.

☐ **217.** INTERNATIONAL SWING DAY. This celebration originated in Korea but can be carried on by your children. It's a day of outside fun featuring swings of all sizes, some for two people. If you don't have a swing, consider hanging one from a tree. Hang bells nearby so that swingers can ring them with their toes as they swing.

☐ **218.** WRITE ON! High school graduates like to collect signatures of friends. Suggest a new way to do this using a light colored T-shirt or light blue denim jacket. Friends sign, using a black felt-tip marker. Back home, the teen can go over the signatures with fabric paint. It's a memorable outfit for informal school events or the last day of school.

☐ **219.** FATHER FLIPS! Actually it's Dad's pancake breakfast that flips. Help youngsters prepare the batter, then let them be creative about the pancakes for Father's Day breakfast. Make some in shapes (and others must guess what they are) or add strawberries or blueberries to some. One family puts in M&Ms, pushing them in just after flipping them to the second side.

❑ **220.** SURPRISE PARTY FOR DAD. In advance of Father's Day, go to a T-shirt shop and get a shirt for Dad that says "King for a Day." Then plan a surprise picnic in the park (secretly putting all the party items in the car trunk). On the big day, suggest that the family go for a ride, ending at the park where you have arranged to meet another family. The dads are given their shirts and join in multigenerational games such as egg tossing, two-legged or sack races, and tag using water balloons. Tug-of-war can be the last event before lunch and gifts.

❑ **221.** GIFTS FOR DADS. Let kids choose their own gifts to give. Present them at a picnic, the ball game, or the intermission of a play. Good ideas are: a new cap, a soda mug, sports equipment, barbecue tools, magazine subscription, electric tool, jazzy socks, or handmade coupons good for a home-style car wash, garage cleaning, lawn-cutting, or other service.

❑ **222.** ROYAL END TO FATHER'S DAY. Whatever activities you enjoy together during the day, see that the end of the day is royally suitable for the king. Kids can settle Dad into his comfy chair with the Sunday paper or his favorite TV program. Then help kids make a drink called "The King's Ambrosia." In a blender, whip up a small can of drained sliced peaches and add a half cup of orange juice and one teaspoon of vanilla. Just before serving, add two scoops of vanilla ice cream and blend until thick. Serve with two straws just in case Dad wants to share.

❑ **223.** END-OF-SCHOOL HONORS. Your child may not have received straight A grades, been given a letter for outstanding sports achievement, or been class president. Even so, appreciate progress—no matter how small—and do attend those final assemblies. Start when kids are young to celebrate success—this doesn't mean you reward shoddy work, but you do emphasize an area of improvement. You can do it with words ("Imagine, you're finishing sixth grade—you're halfway to your high school diploma" or

"Wow, your D in math moved to a C!"). Or you can do it with action by planning an end-of-school surprise: a trip to the skating rink, a special movie, a beach picnic.

❑ **224.** END-OF-SCHOOL DISPLAYS. Let your child help to display his best work. Frame a piece of art for the wall. Or cover the coffee table with all those clay pieces made in previous years. Read an outstanding paper at supper. Write or telephone grandparents with some special news or send them an outstanding essay paper or drawing.

SECTION 2: SUMMER

❑ **225.** JELL-O TOSS. Follow the package directions for making Jell-O Jigglers in a flat baking dish. When the gelatin is set and you're ready to play, cut into one-inch squares. For outside fun, young children can toss squares into a pail, seeing who has the best aim. For older kids, form pairs standing three feet apart. Give each player three cubes and see who can toss the cubes into the other's open mouth. Or, kids can climb a tree or play equipment and aim at various targets.

❑ **226.** MAKE A POND. In just one day, your family can create a scenic backyard pond—a great idea for a family with older kids since it could be a hazard to younger ones. Place the pond (which is not for wading) where there are bushes behind it and where it is easily seen from the house. Obtain a pond liner or a wide piece of heavy duty black plastic. Use a hose or string to "draw" the outline in keeping with the size of your liner. Then everyone digs. Use a plank across the hole to be sure the edges are level. Slope the hole toward the middle that should be at least one-foot deep. Check the pond bottom for protruding rocks, then cover it with damp sand. Next, spread the liner, letting it come up and over the rim. Be sure that excess material is folded down flat. Fill the pond to a desired level and make any rim adjustments. Then, trim the excess liner at the rim, leaving enough to tuck under rocks for a natural appearance. Push some rocks partly into the water for a realistic look and then landscape with small plants. It's a summertime project your family will be proud of year-round.

❑ **227.** **FLASHY FIREFLIES.** Show children how fireflies communicate by sending blinking signals. An enjoyable outdoor game can be played by all the family on a moonless night in a large yard or a park. Each person will need a flashlight and a partner. With their partner they create a signal consisting of short and long flashes. Partners go to opposite ends of the play area and all flashlights are off until the game begins. At this point, partners start flashing and when they recognize their partner, they run to meet each other. The first partners to find each other are the winners and the game begins again.

❑ **228.** **SPONGE TAG.** Using string, make a large circle in which players wearing swimsuits must stay. Place a pail of water at the edge of the circle and put a large sponge in it. The person selected to be "it" grabs the sponge and throws it at someone. The person who was hit dunks the sponge in the pail and tries to hit someone else. For rowdy fun, provide several pails of water and every player with a sponge.

❑ **229.** **POPCORN RELAY RACE.** For a party or backyard fun, let kids make a big batch of popcorn. Next, show each participant how to make a pair of popcorn holders. Poke a hole in the center of a paper cup and push a sturdy rubber band halfway through the hole. Place a paper clip on the end of the rubber band inside the cup and pull the other end until the clip is at the bottom of the cup. The rubber band will hold the cups in place on top of the players' feet. Divide the group into two teams and let the captain fill each player's cups with popcorn. Place a shallow box for each team about fifteen feet from a start line. When the whistle blows, the relay begins with the first member of each team racing carefully to the box and emptying his cups in it, spilling as little as possible along the way. The runner returns to the start line and tags the next team member, then goes to the end of the line to refill his cup. After three minutes, the popcorn in each box is measured (a large measuring cup works well) and the team with the most wins.

❑ **230.** **BUBBLE CIRCLE.** On a nonwindy day, put a thin paving stone in the bottom of a plastic wading pool. Then fill the pool with bubble liquid (see #170 for the recipe) just to the place where the top of the stone will stay dry. Have a youngster stand on the stone as you lower a hula hoop over his head and into the bubble liquid. Raise the hoop and a big bubble circle will form. Don't forget to save the bubble stuff for use another day.

❑ **231.** **POLAR BATH.** At bath time, provide kids with a big bowl of ice cubes. After they're clean, they can float the cubes in the tub until they've cooled down and are ready to get out and dry off.

❑ **232.** **JULY 4 BIRTHDAY.** Since Independence Day marks the birthday of the United States of America, think of a birthday gift that the family could give to the country. Some suggestions are: planting a tree, writing a congressman with a good idea, offering to paint over graffiti, cleaning up the street where you live, or approaching a business that might provide food or funds for a party at a veteran's hospital.

❑ **233.** **NEIGHBORHOOD PARADE.** For Independence Day—or just any day—let kids organize a miniparade by going around the neighborhood and getting volunteers. The parade can consist of decorated bikes and wagons, strollers with pets or babies riding, and kids dressed as clowns or the parade flag bearer. Drummers and other instrumentalists can also march. For a truly big parade that might go to a park, go down the town's main street with decorated golf carts, bikes, and horses with the town fire engine leading the way. The traditional ending is an ice-cream social.

❑ **234.** **COOL KIDS.** On hot days, there can be a constant procession of kids coming to the kitchen for cold drinks. With kid help, fill plastic soda bottles or water bottles with favorite drinks, leaving space at the top. Cap and put these in the freezer. Then, when you head out for fun at a picnic, beach, or park, you have big refreshing drinks that stay cold for many hours.

❏ **235. SQUARE PUMPKINS?** Kids can give a pumpkin a creepy new look by teaching it to grow into a square. When a pumpkin first begins to form, very carefully slide it into a gallon plastic milk carton without breaking it off the vine. As it grows bigger, it will fill the carton. When it's ready to be picked, just cut the carton away, revealing the unique shape.

❏ **236. FREE AT LAST.** Youngsters who have the summer off from school enjoy the initial freedom, but usually, after a few weeks, the novelty wears off. This is the time to talk together about some goals for the summer. These could include a building project such as a sandbox, tree house, fire pit, fence, or bookcase. Or a physical fitness goal such as learning to ride a bike or do a certain number of push-ups. Or it could be a learning goal: how to tie shoes or tell time. Or an educational goal such as reading a specified number of books. After conversation, write up each family member's summer goal (parents included), and post it. Then don't nag, just encourage.

❏ **237. CORN DOLLS.** For each doll you'll need the husks from one ear of corn and some lightweight string. Holding the husks together, turn down the top two inches and tie them to form the head. Halfway down, tie the waist line. Pull out a piece on either side as an arm and tie near the end for a wrist. At the lower end, separate the husks into two legs and tie each ankle. Kids can put a face on the corn doll with markers.

❏ **238. PVC=PRETTY VIGOROUS CHALLENGE.** Gather together leftover lengths of PVC pipe from neighborhood garages. Also collect old Ping Pong balls (or any balls that will fit through the pipe). In a big sandbox or at the beach, kids can create hills and mountains. Lay the pipes on the slopes, some connecting, some with roads between them. Kids will develop their own races as the balls follow the tube tunnels.

❑ **239.** BASTILLE DAY PARTY. On July 14, celebrate the 1789 storming of the French prison that was the beginning of the end of the monarchy. French Independence Day at your house can feature a French cafe supper: French bread served with fruits and cheeses, or cheese fondue. Drink sparkling grape juice and top it all off with crepes (little pancakes) with French vanilla ice cream. Have one person research a few French phrases that can be taught to everyone.

❑ **240.** PARENTS DAY. Traditionally the fourth Sunday in July, this day is unlike Mother's Day and Father's Day because no gifts are involved. It celebrates the spirit of good parenting. At breakfast, talk about the qualities necessary to be a good parent (love, patience, intelligence, humor, honesty, self-worth, creativity, responsibility) and the qualities necessary to be a good child. (Are they the same? Are there some that a youngster can do without?) You'll no doubt come up with a few more. Then celebrate together by switching roles for the day.

❑ **241.** COOL JUMPING. While jumping rope is great exercise, it can also make you hot. Cool down by adding a little splash and dash to the game. All you'll need is a long (about twelve foot) cotton clothesline, plus large plastic glasses. Fill each glass to the top, then players (each holding a glass) jump into the turning rope and make four jumps before jumping out. After all players have done this, compare the glasses—the youngster with the most water left is the winner. You can also play with teams, the second player on the team jumping in with the first and taking the cup as the first jumper goes out.

❑ **242.** SAND CANDLES. Let kids collect sand from the beach or the sandbox—about one quart per youngster. Place the sand in bowls and mix in just enough water so that an interesting hole, about the size of a cup, can be made in the sand. In a double boiler, the parent melts paraffin or old candles and a crayon for color. Suspend a wick or string from a dowel placed across the bowl top. Pour cooled wax into the sand mold to about a half inch from the top. (If you don't have a wick to suspend over the mold, you can wait until the wax is setting and then place a candle in the center.) When the wax is completely cool, remove the free-form candle from the sand.

❑ **243.** KIDDIE KORRAL. What do you do with a wading pool that's sprung a leak in the bottom? If it's beyond repair, it can become a safe play area for a baby. With a comfy blanket on the bottom and an interesting collection of toys, it provides a play place as parents garden or do other tasks. And, it moves easily from place to place.

❑ **244.** CAMP WILDERNESS. There's no need to drive to a campsite when you can create "Camp Wilderness" right in your own backyard. With other parents, choose a day when all the neighborhood kids can sleep out together in your secure backyard. For supper, invite the other parents to bring food for the grill and help set up tents and games. After eating together, the host parents take over for twilight fun and bedtime snacks. Don't count on a lot of sleep as there will be screams and laughter as stories are told. Insist that no one leave the area and that emergencies or other problems are reported to you. In the morning, mix up a big bowl of blueberry pancake batter and let the campers prepare their own on a griddle on the outside grill. Afterward, let everyone pitch in to clean up and then send the happy (but sleepy) campers home.

❑ **245.** BORED PETS. Veterinarians say that pets who learn new things stay young longer. And on long, warm summer days, pets can get just as bored as kids. Suggest Pet School and let kids see how to improve the life of their pets. Fish can have a larger bowl and more interesting landscaping. Hamsters and guinea pigs can "go free" in a tiled bathroom for awhile (close the lid). Cats will benefit from a homemade carpeted maze to play in and scratch. Dogs can learn a new trick, practiced each day with praise and rewards.

❑ **246.** **SUMMER STORMS.** Power outages and fierce storms won't upset your family if you prepare for them in advance. In a sturdy box, let kids pack the supplies and place them in the basement or other safe place (such as the car trunk in case you are caught away from home). Supplies can include a flashlight and a radio with extra batteries, a first-aid kit, sweaters, blanket and pillow, some long-lasting well-sealed snacks, water, a book containing many stories, and a deck of cards for various games. Check and update the contents yearly.

❑ **247.** **NIGHTTIME PICNIC.** On a night when kids can sleep late the next morning, plan a picnic supper after the sun has set. Young children may require a cracker and cheese snack at their usual eating hour, but save the main dish and dessert for a candlelight supper. Kids can make the plainest backyard look wonderful with a colorful table cloth, a few flowers, and candles on the table and in far corners of the yard. The cozy atmosphere is conducive to good conversation.

❑ **248.** **METEOR SHOWER.** Watch your newspaper in August for the annual Perseid meteor shower—usually a three-day event that peaks in the early morning hours. Choose a night with the least moon and pick a place in the yard free from other lights. Get comfortable on lounge chairs or blankets, face northeast, and start counting. Sometimes you'll see dozens in just one minute—a display that appears near the constellation Perseus. And don't forget to wish on these "falling stars."

❑ **249.** **MINIATURE GOLF.** Create your own miniature golf course in your backyard. Yes, you will have nine round holes in the ground, but they'll fill in or grow over quickly when you tire of the game. You'll need at least two putters (available at thrift shops), balls, eighteen poker chips, and nine sixteen-ounce cans to be sunk in the ground. Place two poker chips on the ground to show the starting place—from between the chips—for each hole. Here are some of the obstacles: a shoe box with a hole on either side, a sand trap made by piling some sandbox sand around one hole, a bunker made of rocks with just a few openings through them, a hula hoop laid flat that must be shot into and out of, a series of coffee cans to go through, a hole (the can) elevated with soil so that one must play up to it, a series of five wire "doors" (made from hangers) to shoot through, small branches and leaves to serve as the rough, and a water hole made by sinking a very large container of water into the ground immediately in front of a hole.

❑ **250.** NATURE PAINTS. In your own backyard there are natural colors just waiting to be used. Let kids draw a picture outside, using just a black marking pen for the outline. Then, go hunting for colors to rub on and fill in. Use grass for green, geranium blossoms for red or pink, and dandelions for yellow.

❑ **251.** MINI-MEALS. In hot summer weather, appetites may need a little less food and more encouragement. The answer is minimeals, foods kids will enjoy helping to prepare. For breakfast, make tiny pancakes, just one and a half inches across. Alternatives are mini-muffins, mini-sausages (cocktail size), and doughnut holes. For lunch, cut sandwiches into fourths or sixths and watch them disappear. Serve with bite-sized cheese cubes and small crackers, tiny pickles, grapes, or cherries. For dinner, serve chicken wings or drumettes. Vegetables can be peas and panfried new potatoes. Dessert can be mini-sundaes served with just one mini-marshmallow or chocolate chip on top.

❑ **252.** TREASURE BOXES. A good project for a summer day is to make a treasure box—a private place for a youngster to keep that special bird feather, rock, or baseball card, safe from curious siblings and parents. Help a youngster select a sturdy carton such as the kind that envelopes or copy paper come in. Or use a plastic container with a lid. Get a padlock at a hardware store. Collect small magazine pictures, photos, wrapping paper, stickers, stars, beads, orphan earrings, nuts or small nails, and a penny. Then with glue, affix the paper items first, then the dimensional ones. For a final touch, line the inside of the box with a soft fabric. If you wish, a clear lacquer finish will make the outside surface more durable.

❑ **253.** WATERMELON LANTERNS. Kids can make watermelon lanterns for an inviting nighttime table setting. Cut the top of a melon and let younger children use a melon ball tool to scoop out the insides. Next, older youngsters who can handle knives make the lanterns by carving small designs into the sides. Place small candles in jars and put inside. Serve bowls of summer fruits topped with sherbet along with kid baked cookies for a very special dessert for family and friends. The lanterns can be saved for another night by wrapping and refrigerating them.

❑ **254.** SOLAR SNACK. On a hot day, show kids how to use the sun's rays to cook a snack. Glue a big piece of black construction paper to a big piece of heavy-duty aluminum foil. When the glue is dry, roll up the paper like an ice-cream cone, foil side in. Now you're ready to cook. In a small glass dish that will fit inside the cone, crack an egg and top it with cheese. Or, cover a few slices of apple with cinnamon sugar. Put plastic wrap tightly over the top and put it in the "oven." Prop the cone with the open end of the oven toward the sun and let your snack cook for about twenty minutes.

❑ **255.** COOL SAILING. Making boats of ice is fun; sailing them in a tub or wading pool is even more fun. Make ice boats this easy way (all should be identical in size for fairness). Use a pint-sized milk carton filled with one and three-fourths cups of water with a little food coloring in it. Push the "mast" made of a wood chopstick into the water through the carton opening. Place the carton in the freezer for next day fun. When ready to race, make a sail out of colored paper, then cut the carton away and staple the sail to the mast. Now, place the boats in the water and see how they sail. As the ice melts, some may tip over, sails may fall off, but the winner is the one to outlast the others.

☐ **256.** NEW SCHOOL YEAR, NEW ROOM.   While you can't give a youngster an entirely new room, together you can give it a new look. Consider what the needs will be for the new school year—a bigger study area, storage for sports equipment or an expanding hobby, or some new clothes. Give the room a new arrangement, bag up outgrown clothing and toys for charity giving, expand the work area with board-and-brick shelves or a desk wing made of a piece of wood with file drawers underneath. Consider new window coverings that you can make together. And, if the carpet is worn, cover it with a bright area rug. Let youngsters hang interesting things on the wall: posters, sports equipment, a bulletin board, a full-length mirror. Make a sign for the door announcing whose room it is.

☐ **257.** FASHION WARDROBE.   Don't just set out to the mall to buy kids clothes without a plan. Let them first search a week's worth of newspapers and cut out ads for clothes they'd like to own. Encourage them to compare the prices. Is there a style that looks especially good on their body shape? What colors do they like? How much money can be spent? From this information make a shopping list and, when you return home, see how your purchases compare with the pictures.

☐ **258.** LABOR DAY SURVEY.   While enjoying the picnic or barbecue on this holiday, talk about labor—different kinds of work. Let one youngster make a list as each person tells about his or her job and the jobs of relatives. See if jobs held by one generation affected the professions of the next generation. Do any of those present have the same profession? What careers do the adults think would be best for each youngster? What do the kids think of these suggestions?

☐ **259.** LABOR DAY STREET PARTY.   Bring all the parents and kids together for a potluck party. With your kids, hand deliver the invitations and when folks RSVP, ask them to bring a casserole, salad and rolls, or dessert. Play these three games. *(1) Target practice.* Hang a series of targets such as pie pans, hula hoop, and metal cowbell from a clothesline or tree branch. Everyone gets a chance to hit the targets with three tennis balls. *(2) Guess your weight.* Make one person Professor Guesser who whispers his guestimate to each person stepping forward to be weighed on bathroom scales. If the professor isn't within five pounds, the person gets a candy prize. *(3) Tug-of-war.* Put a knot at the middle of a sturdy twenty-foot rope. Divide everyone into two teams at opposite ends, with kids at the front and adults at the rear. Draw a line on the ground and start the game with the knot above the line. Now everyone starts to pull and when one whole team is pulled across the midline, the other team has won.

SECTION 3: AUTUMN

❑ **260.** NEW BEDTIMES. Although it's technically still summer, Labor Day signals the start of fall. Let this day also remind you that your youngsters are starting a new school year and deserve new bedtimes. (Bedtimes should be thoughtfully set and strictly enforced since teachers complain that many students are too sleepy to function in the morning.) Discuss a bedtime with each youngster and take into consideration her ideas as well as how quickly she fell asleep under the old schedule. Kids that can't get going in the morning definitely deserve earlier bedtimes. Don't let the end of a TV show influence the decision. It may be easier to put several children to bed at the same time, but unless you have twins, each should have her own special time.

❑ **261.** HARVEST MOON. Each autumn there is one moon that is very special. Called the harvest moon, it occurs nearest the autumnal equinox of the sun, about September 23. The moon rises at the same time for several nights and shines with such brightness that farmers in northern climates can work late into the night to bring in the harvest. Check to see when it will be harvest moon in your area and sit outside to watch it. Let kids make Swiss cheese sandwiches in honor of the moon, and corn on the cob to honor the harvest.

❑ **262.** APPLE TIME. Autumn apples can be made to last by including the family in a project to dry them. (They make tasty treats for lunch boxes or snacks.) Everyone peels and cores the apples and one person slices them into rings about an eighth-inch thick. A younger child can dip each ring in a mixture of three parts water to one part lemon juice so the apple doesn't turn dark. Another youngster can lay them out on paper towels and cover them with another towel, patting them dry. Now they can be strung through the holes and hung in a sunny window for seven to ten days until dry and chewy. Or, they can be put on a cooling rack placed on a baking tray and dried in a 150 degree oven for four hours.

❑ **263.** BIKE DAY. Before the weather changes, choose a weekend day when all activities are done with bicycle transportation: marketing, errands, team practices, and excursions. You will need helmets for all and safe child seats for those too young to peddle. Plan a safe route to a picnic location and let everyone carry part of the load: food, blanket, hats, and so forth. In advance, call a friend who lives along the way and stop there for liquid refreshment. If you make Sunday a bike day, think how smashing you'll all look cycling in to church!

❑ **264.** SANTA'S WORKSHOP. Before the garage gets too cool for comfortable work projects, set up Santa's workshop—a garage area where the family can work together on craft gifts. Find a project that can involve all ages. A good one is making candleholders from wood stairway spindles—something easily available at a lumber store. These will need to be cut in segments, sanded, drilled to hold a candle, painted or lacquered, then wrapped along with an appropriate candle, and tagged for giving.

❑ **265.** AUTUMN WALK BRACELET OR BELT. Before going on a walk or hike with kids, provide them with an adhesive bracelet or belt. Use adhesive-backed paper (such as Contac) and make a strip about two-by-eight inches for a wrist or a strip long enough to go around the child's waist. On the nature walk, collect and affix only fallen items—leaves, blossoms, bark, seeds, and sand or dirt. Back home, they can go on the bulletin board or dining table as a remembrance of your autumn walk.

❑ **266.** SIGNATURE PUMPKINS. In early September while pumpkins are still growing, show your youngster how to write her name on a pumpkin with a ballpoint pen. Then, with a sharp pen tip or letter opener, go over the writing, breaking the pumpkin skin. As the pumpkin gets bigger, so will the signature.

❑ **267.** DENIM NOTEBOOK. School notebooks take on a new look when you and your child dress them in jeans. Using an old pair of jeans, cut a piece that is two inches larger than each dimension of the notebook. Wrap the book in its new covering, fold the extra material inside, and glue it down.

❑ **268.** SCHOOL LUNCH SEMINAR. Stifle brown bag boredom by having a conference with kids concerning a school lunch that goes beyond peanut butter and jelly. Consider these alternatives and let kids vote on which ones to try. Fruits: a melon scored for easy eating and a container of cottage cheese, cherries with yogurt dip, grapes frosted with egg white and dusted with sugar. Veggies: tomato stuffed with tuna fish, carrots with low-fat salad dressing dip, lettuce spread with peanut butter and tightly rolled. Main dish: chili or soup in a thermos, triple decker sandwich, chicken legs, precooked meatballs, hard-boiled egg with salsa dip, and that peanut butter sandwich with sliced banana or bacon inside. Dessert: oatmeal cookies and a small container of frosting with spreader.

❑ **269.** PIE-PLEASER DAY. Honor pies of all kinds on one special day planned by the kids. It can be apple or peach pie for breakfast, lunch of triangle-shaped fruits and sandwiches served in a pie pan, pizza pie for dinner, and a light custard pie for dessert.

❑ **270. COLUMBUS QUIZ.** On Columbus Day, see who can answer these five questions correctly. (1) What was his native country and what country did he sail for? (Answers: Italy, Spain.) (2) How did he navigate? (Answer: By dead reckoning—he knew just enough celestial navigation to measure the latitude from the North Star.) (3) Was he trying to prove the world was round? (Answer: No, educated people already knew that. He was trying to find a short route to the Orient.) (4) How did King Ferdinand and Queen Isabella help him? (Answer: She did not give her jewels; the royal treasurer advanced $14,000.) (5) What were the names of his three ships? (Answers: Nina, Pinta, Santa Maria.)

❑ **271. AUTUMN LEAVES.** Show kids how to turn green leaves red. Cut about five green leaves into pieces and place in a jar. Cover with rubbing alcohol and then mash them a bit with a spoon. Seal the jar with plastic wrap and a lid. Then fill a large bowl with hot tap water and swirl the jar in it until the alcohol turns dark. Cut a strip about an inch wide from a white coffee filter, placing one end in the mixture and the other end over the jar lip. In a few hours, you'll see the autumn colors that are normally hidden by the green chlorophyll.

❑ **272. AUTUMN MAZE.** When there are leaves covering the lawn, use a leaf rake to make a pathway like a maze (with dead ends) for kids to follow. For each child, hide a wrapped granola bar or other snack for them to find under a pile of leaves at the end of the maze.

❑ **273. PUMPKIN TOWER.** Kids carve three pumpkins (one small, one medium, one large) using any design they choose. Set aside the tops of the large and medium ones. Place a large candle in each and then stack them, largest on the bottom, where they can be seen and appreciated indoors or out. They can also be carved to make a pumpkin man: the top one as the head, the middle one the body with carved buttons, and the bottom one with carved legs and feet.

❑ **274. TRICKS TO MAKE A TREAT.** Of course there is always pumpkin bread, but there is another treat that can be made when it's pumpkin time. Let kids take out all the seeds from a moderate-sized pumpkin, rinse them, and then dry them on paper towels. In a bowl, mix three tablespoons of salad oil and one-fourth teaspoon of salt or garlic salt. Toss the seeds and then spread them on a cookie sheet. Bake at 250 degrees for an hour, but be sure to stir them every ten minutes. When cool, kids will gobble them up!

❑ **275. NONSPOOKY HALLOWEEN AT HOME.** Increasingly, families are getting together for nonscary home-style parties rather than encouraging candy-begging in the neighborhood. Decorate with bales of hay (or corn shocks) and pumpkins. Have a costume contest. Along with the usual pumpkin carving contest and apple bobbing, have a pumpkin relay race. Divide the group into two teams and give each a similar-sized small pumpkin. Participants crawl to a designated line and back, pushing the pumpkin with their foreheads. Also hang sugar cookies (instead of apples) on strings from the ceiling. (Poke holes for the strings as soon as cookies come out of the oven.) Kids must eat an entire cookie, keeping their hands behind their backs. Serve hearty country food such as chili, and end the evening with simple square dances or line dances.

❑ **276. PROGRESSIVE HALLOWEEN PARTY.** Preteens will enjoy a neighborhood costume party when four families within walking distance share the work. Each neighbor and youngster prepares food and a game. The first house: a punch bowl cauldron (dry ice makes it smoke) and a selection of board games. The second house: chips and dips with sodas, then bobbing for apples in a kiddie pool. The main course can be at the next house with hot dogs in pita bread plus a salad of orange Jell-O containing black raisins.

Then all can also play the dance game called limbo. The final stop can be decorating prebaked round cookies to look like pumpkins, followed by music and dancing.

❑ **277. AUTUMN PARTY GAMES.**   Younger kids can play "Witch's Broom" in which they are blindfolded and walk on a broom from bristle end to handle. Gradeschoolers might enjoy dancing with apples tucked under their chins, passing them on to one another. Or, light just one candle in each room of the house. Divide the group into pairs, each thinking of a trick as they hide. One couple doesn't hide but goes trick-or-treating. They look for hidden pairs and when they find one, the hidden pair demands the trick they've thought of. Then, the four start out looking for another pair, and when they find them, all four must do that next trick. And so it goes until the last couple is found—and they are given the prize.

❑ **278. SAME COSTUME, DIFFERENT LOOK.**   Each invitee to the party is told to dress as a pumpkin. Some will make a big orange bag out of inexpensive fabric with holes for neck, arms, and legs. The bag will be stuffed with newspaper. Another may paint her face like a pumpkin and wear an orange hat with a green felt stem. Remember to take a photo of all the various pumpkins and give each one a prize (fattest, funniest, most original, seediest, skinniest, and so forth).

❑ **279. PUMPKIN PRINTING.**   After Halloween and before your jack-o'lantern turns moldy, use the rind to make stamps. A parent can cut the rind in squares, circles, moons, diamonds—whatever shapes kids want. Next, provide tempera paint for dipping and paper to print on. The pumpkin stamp can be used many times, rinsed, and used in another color to make pictures, designs, note paper, and wrapping paper.

❑ **280. LEAF PRINTS.**   Show kids how to sponge paint on the underside of a freshly picked leaf that has distinctive veins. Then place the leaf on a piece of paper and cover with a second piece of paper. Apply gentle pressure and then remove the top paper and leaf. The remaining leaf print can be used as a place card or for writing paper, or made part of a book of prints.

SECTION 4: WINTER

You'll find many winter holiday ideas in my books *101 Ideas for the Best-Ever Christmas*, as well as in *1001 Things to Do with Your Kids*.

❏ **281. STRESS-FREE HOLIDAYS.**   There are many components to the holiday season: traditions, family gatherings, connecting with friends, gift giving, personal reflection, and spiritual renewal. Allow time for your children to enjoy each aspect of the holidays. Plan fewer but more meaningful events. Talk about your family traditions—keep some, throw out some, establish new ones. Let each family member light a candle at dinner each night and follow this with a moment of thoughtful silence. Make the days ones of excitement, caring, fun, and wonder.

❏ **282. FIRESIDE FUN.**   Teach kids how to lay and light a fire as well as what to do if a fire gets out of hand. Demonstrate the use of a fire extinguisher and how to call 911. Enjoy an outdoor campfire (perhaps after a wintry hike) with everyone in warm clothes. Show how to safely extinguish both indoor and outdoor fires.

❏ **283. GOOD DEEDS.**   Without any advance hints, bring up the subject of good deeds. At dinnertime, ask family members if they can suggest some good deeds and then jot down their ideas. Continue the discussion by asking what good deeds tie in to Thanksgiving, Hanukkah, Christmas, or New Years. When you have a fairly good list, discuss which ones might be meaningful to do as a family.

❑ **284.** FIRESIDE SUPPER. Save on heating bills by eating an occasional supper by the fire. Start with a bowl of fruit soup (pineapple, peaches, raisins, pears, cinnamon, and nutmeg in juice) served warm. Next have a "pile on" potato. This is a baked potato that you top with cheese, sliced hot dogs, sour cream, chili, and so forth, and serve in foil surrounded by a napkin. In between bites, place it in your lap and it will keep you warm. Serve cookies, warm from the oven, to end the meal. This menu can also be popular for a teen party. You'll find that winter fireside suppers are conducive to warm feelings and good conversation.

❑ **285.** WISH LISTS. Each family member writes out a list of things he would enjoy receiving as gifts. Of course, he won't receive all the things on the list, but some suggestions can be saved for birthdays. Post the lists on the bulletin board so that family shoppers can get some good ideas and also share some with grandparents.

❑ **286.** ROLL THOSE CANDLES! At a craft store, let each child choose a sheet of beeswax. Also purchase candlewick cording. Cut the sheet into four rectangles. Next, the youngster lays a wick (about an inch longer than the beeswax) across one side. Roll up the beeswax tightly, starting at the side with the wick. A cluster of candles makes an attractive decoration for the table or mantel.

❑ **287.** GRATEFUL CHAIN. Starting early in November, family members share at supper what is meaningful to them as well as especially good things that happened during their day. Cut construction paper into strips and write the remembrance briefly on the paper. Then, make it into a link, using glue or a staple. Attach the next one to the first and gradually your "grateful chain" will grow so that it can be hung above the table, down the hallway, or up the stairway.

❑ **288.** GRATEFUL TREATS. A parent makes a gift tag for each person who will attend the Thanksgiving dinner. Then kids prepare a two-part treat for each guest: along with a piece of candy, they add a note that says "I'm thankful for you because . . . ." The note and candy are wrapped, the tag put on the outside, and then distributed during dessert.

❑ **289.** ALPHABET BLESSINGS.   This familiar game has a new twist when each letter represents something for which the family is grateful. Go around the table from A to Z. It might start: "I'm grateful for applesauce . . . babies . . . candy." See who can recite all twenty-six!

❑ **290.** WILDERNESS FEAST.   While you're cozy indoors enjoying a huge meal, there are birds outside who would enjoy a feast of their own. Help youngsters prepare seeds and bread, placing them off the ground so as not to attract rodents. If it is freezing outdoors, place a pan of warm water nearby to provide a quick drink.

❑ **291.** COUNT-YOUR-BLESSINGS CAKE.   For holiday dessert, make and frost a cake. The family gathers around to finish trimming the cake with M&M-type candies, adding one as they name a blessing. You'll be surprised at how many candies adorn the cake!

❑ **292.** FANTASY CANDLES.   Here's a craft that kids will enjoy making and giving. You'll need two pounds of paraffin or that same quantity of candle stubs, a quart milk carton, a long taper (narrow candle), and plenty of ice cubes. First, let kids put the ice cubes in a sturdy bag and hit them with a hammer, turning them into midsized chunks. An adult or teen should supervise melting the paraffin (carefully over water or in the microwave) since wax can be flammable. One child holds the taper in the center of the carton, another scoops the crushed ice around it, filling the carton. Next, the adult pours the melted wax into the carton and as it runs down through the ice it makes a crackling sound. (You can make the candles in various heights and colors if you choose.) When the wax is hard, tip the carton to drain away the water, then carefully peel away the carton. When you light the taper, the show begins since the ice has caused unique pockets in the paraffin, revealing imaginative light.

❑ **293.** GINGERBREAD HOUSE.   From sturdy cardboard, fashion a small house with windows, door, and a roof. Using a mix, make gingerbread in a loaf pan, then slice it and let it dry overnight. Next, kids affix the gingerbread to the house with frosting. Provide decorator frosting tubes to fashion shutters, roof shingles, and a sidewalk. Use coconut for snow around the house. Tiny candy canes set in frosting or marshmallows make a fence, and other candies can be used as colorful decor. Use it as your holiday table centerpiece.

❑ **294.** HAPPY HOLIDAY SHOPPING.   Divide the list between adults and teens and let younger kids decide with whom they wish to shop. Go to special stores featuring sports equipment, computers, jewelry, clothing, or hardware, and let kids see what treasures and bargains they can find. Punctuate the shopping with a stop for yogurt or a cookie. Ask youngsters what they see that they'd like for themselves (and pass along these ideas to those shopping for them). For wrapping, use the colored comics with red ribbon—letting each shopping team work in a separate room. Kids are proud to have input in shopping rather than just being told what they are giving.

❑ **295.** GREETING CARD MAGIC.   Don't just toss incoming Christmas cards in a heap. Talk with your family on how best to display them. Here are ideas that your youngsters can carry out with a little basic help from you. Hang a sheet on a wall and then pin the cards to the sheet. Or, place an attractive hook in the ceiling (you'll use it each year) and attach to it about seven wide ribbons reaching to the floor plus about two feet more. Attach a weight to each ribbon and then move it outward so that the ribbons form a conical tree. As cards arrive, pin them to the ribbons.

❑ **296.** AUTOMOTIVE PICNIC.   Go for a wintry ride to see all the outdoor Christmas decorations in your area. Plan a special car picnic to eat along the way. Let kids make hot cheese-filled biscuits as parents cook skewers of cubed meat, small onions, boiled potatoes, and brussels sprouts. (Wrap these in individual foil packages.) Prepare individual thermos bottles of hot soup. And, of course, provide a small bag of Christmas cookies for each child. Let kids observe the creativity of the displays and see what ideas they'd like to use next year.

❑ **297.** WHAT'S INSIDE CHRISTMAS? Play this word game with children about age eight and up, or you can form teams of an adult with a child. How many words can you make using the letters of CHRISTMAS? For example: mist, cat, this, chair. (You can also play using other holiday words such as mistletoe or fireplace, and other holidays such as Halloween, Independence Day, and Valentine's Day.)

❑ **298.** POPCORN SNOWMEN. Everyone loves marshmallow treats so let kids make these for decorations, table favors, gifts, or family munching. In a large mixing bowl, put fifteen cups of popped popcorn. In a saucepan, melt one stick of butter and twenty ounces of marshmallows, stirring until melted. Pour over popcorn and mix well. Making the balls for the snowmen is easy if you coat your hands with butter and work on wax paper. Make three sizes of balls and stack one on another. Give them pretzel stick arms, also eyes, mouth, and buttons made of colored candies. Add a scarf made of red string licorice or fruit leather. If trimmings aren't sticking, affix them with a little white frosting.

❑ **299.** FAREWELL CIRCLE. At the end of a Christmas party, family reunion, or other large gathering, close the evening with a candlelight song. Use short candles and put a foil collar around them to take care of drips. Form a circle in the dark and let each person light the candle of the one next to him. Then sing a closing song ("Silent Night," "Goodnight Ladies," "Auld Lang Syne"). At the end, go around the circle, each person blowing out his candle until it is dark.

❑ **300.** TRAVELING DINNER. Most everyone knows someone who can't get out, yet would appreciate a home-made holiday dinner. Make it a nice gift by purchasing a large inexpensive tray and letting youngsters make a place mat and favor. When preparing your holiday meal, share generous helpings of everything plus a sampling of Christmas cookies. Place a small wrapped gift on the tray (note cards, aftershave, silk flower, and so forth). Let kids deliver the tray.

❑ **301.** RECYCLING GREETINGS. Sit around on the floor and look at all the cards received. Separate the photo cards and put them on your bulletin board to remind you of those friends. Let each family member choose a card he thinks is most beautiful and then write a note to the sender. Cut illustrations off cards, thread them with yarn, and save for next year's gift tags. Finally, cut in half the picture from twenty cards and shuffle them. See who in the family is fastest at matching the two halves.

❑ **302.** A FAMILY NEW YEAR'S EVE PARTY. Make it a potluck event with guest families bringing foods tied in with the time zones: chowder for the East Coast, salad and corn for the Midwest, a beef dish for the mountain states, and lemon pie for the West Coast. Kids and adults can play the resolution game. Each person writes a resolution including the word "because": "I plan to go on a trip to Paris . . . because I adore French men." Or, "I plan to lose weight . . . because my wife says I'm starting to resemble Santa." Collect the resolutions and cut them in half just before the word "because." Then, put the halves in separate bowls. Each person takes a turn drawing one from each bowl and then reading them together as a unique and often humorous sentence.

❑ **303.** END OF THE YEAR STORY. Each January, start a very simple diary of family highlights in a small notebook kept at the dinner table. Note two or three highlights each month, for example: January 5—snow is two-feet deep; February—Molly is second in speech contest, Dad gets a new office; March—Grandpa visits. Then, as the year ends, make a final December entry, perhaps what you'll do New Year's Eve. Then on New Year's Day, read it together and marvel at all the accomplishments of the previous year.

❑ **304. POLAR PICNIC.** Let kids gather the trappings for an indoor winter picnic on the living room floor: ice chest, thermos, paper plates, checkered tablecloth, and a big blanket. Everyone should wear shorts and sunglasses. Tasty food can be prepared with kid-help: hot dogs, hamburgers, fried chicken with side dishes of potato salad, cole slaw, or fruit salad, and apple pie. Fill the thermos bottles with pink lemonade. To complete the theme, toss rubber horseshoes, have indoor relays, and an obstacle race.

❑ **305. LOVE LETTERS.** A love letter from one family member to another makes a novel Valentine's Day gift. Provide kids with special paper and help them construct a simple sincere letter. There are six parts. *(1) Place and date in the upper right corner might say:* "Written while watching you play," or "written while sitting by the fire." The date can also be whimsical: "February—St. Valentine's month" or "Ten days before THE day." *(2) The salutation.* This can be more sentimental than just "Dear Max." How about: "Dear Marvelous Max," or "To my first precious child," or "To someone who changed my life." *(3) The first sentence.* Share a reason for writing: "I know you'll get lots of silly Valentines, but this is a serious one." Or, "Sometimes I don't tell you how much you mean to me." *(4) Give an example of something that happened between the two of you:* how a youngster tidied the kitchen when you were tired. Or something a person said you'll always remember— whatever links you together. *(5) The reiteration.* Say it again: "I'll always love you." "You've made me happy." "I'm glad you're my kid." *(6) The close and signature.* Get poetic: "You're forever-lovin' Mom." "Your number one fan, Dad." "Still in love after twenty years." A few stickers, an envelope filled with glitter and sprayed with after-shave, and you've got a real love letter!

❏ **306.** GIVE A HAND TO GRANDMA. Little kids can make Valentine cards by tracing around their hands with red markers on white paper. A parent can draw a large heart around the hand print. Mount the paper on cardboard and put the child's name and year on it. Grandmas will save these each year, seeing how the hand prints get larger.

❏ **307.** SECOND CHRISTMAS. Keep the spirit of the holidays alive. Celebrate again in February or March when spirits need lifting. Enlist kid-help to plan a festive one-day event, complete with a few decorations and an inexpensive gift for each person. Stuff a turkey and teach kids how to carve. Play holiday music as you eat Christmas cookies.

❏ **308.** LEAP DAY. Every four years you get an extra day—February 29. Make it unique by discussing with the family something special to do. Encourage your child's school to have a special Leap Day discussion on how to make the time at school better and safer. At home, suspend most rules and routines. Don't cook. Put bowls of chili in the refrigerator for family members to heat and eat when they please. Place a bowl of fruit on the counter along with crackers and cheese and a plate of cookies or brownies.

<u>FOUR</u>

AFTER SCHOOL FUN

SECTION 1: GOOD SPORTS

SECTION 2: EXTRACURRICULAR, NOT EXTRA STRES

SECTION 1: GOOD SPORTS

❑ **309.** NO EXCUSES. Living in a small apartment, the lateness of the hour, no one to exercise with—those are just excuses that can be overcome. Get a chinning bar and install it in a doorway so that the family can always enjoy a healthy stretch. Before kids' bedtimes, flip off the TV and do somersaults, handstands, and jumping jacks in the living room or hall. Have hand weights for all to use and get an aerobics video (suitable for kids and parents) as "someone" to exercise with.

❑ **310.** THE TERM GAME. See who in the family can explain the meaning of these sports terms: balk, free throw, bunker, cast, slalom, sinker, double axel, pirouette, left hook, eight ball, audible, Fosbury flop, mogul, formula one, wedge, touchback, spike, lure, suicide squeeze, and forehand drive. Could anyone identify all twenty?

❑ **311.** GO FOR THE GOAL. In a large yard, make a playing field about twenty by fifty feet with a chalk goal at each end. Play like a regular soccer game but make the rule that for goal attempts the ball must enter the goal area on the ground. The first team with five goals wins.

❑ **312.** JOIN UP. Membership in a "Y," sports club or gymnasium will encourage your family to be more active. Ask friends about facilities they enjoy. Visit them with your youngsters. See which appeals to the majority. Then join up and vow to really get your money's worth.

❑ **313.** SPORTS NIGHT. If you have trouble finding time to get out to walk daily or play tennis, set aside one night a week for an hour of active sports with the family. Write it clearly on the calendar so that everyone will take part. It can be going to your gym or club, or it can be fun in your own backyard (playing catch or doing tricks on the jungle gym) or in your driveway (shooting hoops or hitting balls against the garage door) or walking, jogging, skating, or cycling around the neighborhood.

❑ **314.** THE FAMILY THAT PLAYS TOGETHER. As kids get older, investigate the many "togetherness" options available in the sports field so the family can enjoy active time together. The top rated all-family sports are: bowling, in-line skating, mountain biking, tennis, and horseback riding. Talk with youngsters about going water rafting together, or taking golf lessons. These joint activities can be excellent bonding experiences.

❑ **315.** SPORTS CHALLENGE. Issue an invitation to another family with youngsters of similar ages to yours. Divide into fair teams but not along family lines. Let each team create a name for themselves (Mason Street Monsters, Awesome Olympians, and so forth) and select a team captain. Plan six to eight events in keeping with kids' ages. Some might be: around-the-house team relay, dodge ball, croquet, shooting baskets (have a ladder for short kids), obstacle race, or rope climb. Play in the morning, serve hot dogs and lemonade for lunch, and then relax in the shade.

❑ **316.** SOCCER BALL STEALING. Make two teams of two. One team stands in the center of a double chalk circle (two rings, two feet apart) with the other team between the chalk circles. These players pass the ball between themselves while staying between the chalk lines. The two in the center try to reach out and steal it. With a stopwatch, determine the pair who can steal it the fastest.

❑ **317.** EASY FISHING. Take kids to a trout farm or other fishing farm and let them see what it's like to catch a fish. Teach them how to bait a hook, cast, reel in the fish, remove the hook, even clean the fish. If they aren't turned off by this process, take them out for a real fishing trip and afterward, teach kids how to cook the catch.

❑ **318.** BACKYARD VOLLEYBALL. Of course there are official rules, but you don't have to heed them for backyard volleyball as long as the game is fair. All you need to start is a rope between two trees and a ball. Set the rope a suitable height for the players. You may eventually graduate to a net and even take the game to the beach for sandy fun.

❑ **319.** INTRODUCING TENNIS.   Draw a chalk line on the driveway about fifteen feet from and parallel to the garage door. With racket and ball, play a game with your youngster, taking turns hitting the ball to the door and returning it. Then move the line back ten feet more and show the backhand stroke and how to serve. When your youngster has some confidence, take her to the park for a real game.

❑ **320.** OKAY CROQUET.   While backyard croquet may not flex many muscles, it does teach strategy and helps to perfect aim. It's a great after-supper all-family game in the summer. If children are young, make it just a two-ball game with a parent teamed with a child.

❑ **321.** FORE!   You can't play golf until you can connect with the ball. Start by taking the family to a driving range at a time when it isn't too busy and you can all be next to one another. Show how to hold the club, swing, follow through, and of course "keep your eye on the ball." When a youngster gets a good feel for the swing and is consistent with his aim (and doesn't keep missing the ball), enjoy golf at a par three course. For truly interested beginners, buy used clubs at a sports store. Golf is no longer an elitist game and it's good exercise.

❑ **322.** MINIATURE GOLF.   While this game is mostly for fun, it does have value in teaching putting skill. Make teams of an adult or teen with a younger child so that everyone has a chance to win. Miniature golf courses are often part of fun centers that also feature batting cages, bumper boats, and video arcades. So, if you go, take along lots of quarters!

❑ **323.** CUSTOM SPORTS GIFT.   When there's a golfer in the family, let kids customize golf balls as a special occasion gift. Purchase a package of balls and a bag of tees. Next, cover the work surface with newspaper and decorate the balls with permanent marking pens, adding names, pictures, and short encouraging lines. Then, go to work on the tees, adding colorful stripes to them.

❑ **324.** **HOME BATTING CAGE.** Many recreation areas have a batting cage that lets players safely hit balls. You can make one in your own backyard by purchasing a large amount of inexpensive fish netting and hanging it from trees to form a barrier for balls. And, when parents are busy, it is a good one-person activity.

❑ **325.** **ICE RINK.** Flood and freeze part of your backyard as an ice rink. With kid-help, shovel snow into a barrier around an area and then use a hose to fill it. Do this on a calm night so that the ice freezes smoothly. This also works on a vacant lot with neighbors pitching in to do the work.

❑ **326.** **OUR TEAM.** Choose a spectator sport that's of interest to the entire family (football, baseball, soccer, basketball) and attend some games. Read the daily newspaper columns that detail the team's successes or failures. Get to know the players. Take an interest in trades. Enjoy a game via TV or radio so as to keep up-to-date every day. At a sports shop, purchase a team shirt or cap for each family member.

❑ **327.** **TWIRL THAT TOWEL.** The newest sign of enthusiasm by sports spectators is towel waving. At a sports event when there is an occasion to celebrate, it is waved high and twisted in the air. There's no need to buy a costly team logo towel for this occasion. With youngsters, select older hand towels and dye them the team color. Make a sufficient number so that they can share them at the game with their friends.

❑ **328.** **TRIATHLON.** Athletic activity within the family should promote good sportsmanship and personal achievement as opposed to mere competition. A family triathlon is fun and can accommodate kids of varying ages. Start on bikes, riding in a safe area to a predetermined destination where there is a red ribbon for each to claim and return home. (Young children can be given a head start.) Participants go immediately to event number two, which is the obstacle course: climbing through a tube or box, up a rope, and then running around the outside of the house to a table. On the table is event number three: guzzling a can of pop or juice.

BICYCLE EXERCISE—
WITH HELMETS OF COURSE!

❑ **329.** BICYCLE RELAY. Divide cyclers into teams of two. For a flag relay, make a wide straight course of at least 100 feet with a start and finish line. Place a team member at each end, standing next to his bike. Give the rider at the start line a "flag" (handkerchief or colorful piece of fabric). At "Go," she starts for the opposite end. As she crosses the line, she hands the flag to her teammate who then mounts and rides back. The first one to across the line is the winner.

❑ **330.** BARREL RACING. You may not have barrels or cones, but find good-sized objects such as cardboard boxes and place them on your race course, close enough together that it takes skill to cycle around each one. With a stopwatch, make it a race against the clock.

❑ **331.** CURVY CYCLING. This competition is for teen cyclers—wearing helmets and knee pads. Make a race course with start and finish lines. Using chalk, draw two parallel curving lines the length of the course. Being timed with a stopwatch, each participant tries to see how quickly she can negotiate the curvy course. You can also make a race course with obstacles to cycle around or over: crumpled newspaper, cones, pails of water, a hose placed across the course, or a series of boxes.

❑ **332.** RIDE AND TIE. This is somewhat like the famous races combining walkers and horseback riders. You'll need teams of two and one bike for each team. Plan a course about two miles in length in an uncongested part of town. You'll need some adults to monitor six trees or poles along the route that are tied with a red ribbon. Each team begins at the starting line, one walking, one riding. When the first ribboned tree is reached by the rider, he leaves the bike and starts walking in the direction of the next tree. Soon the walker arrives, picks up the bike and rides on to the next marker where they trade again. Win or lose, it's very good exercise.

SECTION 2: EXTRACURRICULAR, NOT EXTRA STRESS

Certainly we want the best of everything for our youngsters—but don't give it to them all at one time. Too often, parents plan an after-school schedule for kids that fills in every moment until dinner, and sometimes even after. School, coupled with sports and other organized activities, can exhaust a child and stress a parent. Plan together how to spend the free time—with emphasis on the word "free." For a happy balance, try these ideas.

❑ **333.** GROUPS ARE GOOD. Extracurricular activities bring social, physical, and emotional benefits for most every child. And, they're beneficial for an only child or an overlooked child from a large family. Discuss with your youngster what she hopes to attain by being part of a group. Being on a losing team teaches the importance of good sportsmanship, a desire to try harder, and grace in defeat. Being on a winning team teaches good sportsmanship, team spirit, the reward of diligence, and generosity in victory. Setting up a camping tent teaches ingenuity, self-sufficiency, and the ability to follow directions. Being the treasurer of a group teaches math and honesty. Being the president teaches leadership and humility. Not being an officer teaches how to follow and how be a team player. Earning badges or beads teaches the feeling of achievement and the willingness to investigate a spectrum of subjects. Playing in a recital teaches memorization and poise. Training a horse teaches precision and patience as well as care for an animal. Unless you plan to let your child grow up to be a hermit, she'll need to know how to work effectively with others. A group activity can be a useful microcosm of society that teaches valuable character traits while expanding her knowledge base. So, in choosing activities, encourage one that especially involves interaction with others.

❑ **334.** **NO PRESSURE DECISION.** You and your youngster know the time needed for homework, leisure, family activities, and sleep. And you certainly know better than coaches and club leaders whose job it is to encourage participation. Each autumn have a family discussion as to which extracurricular activities are really important. Consider the time commitment, the cost (uniforms, instruments, costumes, dues, excursions, and equipment) as well as the benefits (fun, education, physical activity, new skills). Only then, make your decisions.

❑ **335.** **A DUO COMMITMENT.** Most extracurricular activities require commitment from both parent and child. Consider this before you sign up. Is the parent committed to being supportive: attending events, arranging transportation, providing funds? Is the child committed to a time period such as the entire school year or at least a semester? Since benefits aren't always immediately apparent, establish the concept of giving the activity a fair try (a minimum of three or four months) and then deciding whether to continue. A team may seem exciting when the uniform comes, but rather boring a few months later. Club friendships can take time to flourish. So, before joining up, fully discuss the youngster's commitment required by the organizers of the activity, as well as the commitment required of you as parent.

❑ **336. HOW MANY ACTIVITIES?** Having an organized activity every day is actually harmful for a child. Certainly there are special times when there may be extra practices, but a life of solid structure and relentless routine can stifle creative and spontaneous thinking and play. With your youngster, go over the possible activities for an unstructured day: backyard play, play with friends, play with a pet, reading by the fire, working on a craft. Two or three days a week of organized activities provide a good balance. If both parents work, boys' and girls' clubs offer a safe place for after school play (unstructured time) and organized activities (structured time).

❑ **337. NOT FOR BABIES.** While three-year-old ballerinas and soccer players look cute, wait until age five before starting most group lessons and sports. Don't let a child start too early and get burned out on an activity he might really enjoy later. Also, pushing a child into physical and social situations too soon can be physically and emotionally damaging. Although you will consult with your child, you are still in charge and just because the neighbors have a toddler violinist doesn't mean you have to have one, too! Learn to say "no" when life and activities are just time-fillers. Some activities are grand at age four, others at age fourteen.

❑ **338. WHO PAYS?** For many activities there will be an initial charge for membership or dues plus the cost of equipment, books, craft supplies, or instrument rental. Even if parents can afford to pay all of the cost, let a youngster contribute a small amount, such as ten percent. When a kid has an investment in the activity, she is more apt to work to get the most for the money.

❑ **339. PRACTICE NOW!** That can be one of the most dreaded phrases of childhood. So, when considering lessons or teams, be up front as to the time commitment for practice. Tedious batting practices, hours on the piano bench, or the work involved in earning badges are considerations when choosing an activity. Since you as parent take care of the costs and transportation, the child should be willing to do the needed practice. List the pros and cons of an activity, with practice time definitely a part of the decision. Before a youngster can hit a home run or have a lead in *The Nutcracker*, there are hours of learning involved. Don't let activities become unpleasant nagging sessions. If practice is to be at home, set a minimum time (like 30 minutes) and let a timer be the watchdog.

❑ **340.** RAINBOW OF CHOICES.   The decision won't be just between soccer and Scouts. Consider all the options, taking into consideration the activities that close buddies enjoy. Consider banjo lessons, crafts classes, reading classes, gymnastics, magic clubs, swim lessons, computer clubs, foreign language clubs, and rocketry groups, even the unusual such as harp lessons and mountain climbing lessons. Remember, that there is always next year for those activities not chosen this time. And unless you have a child prodigy, you don't need to insist on piano lessons for ten continuous years. Tell your child, "You won't know if you like something until you really try it." But remember, don't force a child into an activity just because that was your own childhood heart's desire.

❑ **341.** ARE YOU A FREELOADER?   At-home parents often complain that working parents are freeloaders when it comes to helping with kids' activities. The jobs of chauffeur, coach, chaperone, scout leader, cookie-drive chairperson, costumes maker, and such are difficult to fairly divide. When a child is considering an activity, talk about your possible input. If you work outside the home, talk with the leaders so that they know you are willing to help in some tangible ways such as Saturday activities, providing food, making costumes or scenery on weekends. Don't just beg off entirely. This puts your child in an uncomfortable position, and there are many benefits to your really striving to take part when possible.

❑ **342.** CHEERING SECTION.   Don't be among the missing when your daughter hits a home run or your son makes first class in scouting. Be sure the whole family takes part in the cheering section!

❑ **343.** **TIME ALONE.** Spontaneity and unplanned fun are parts of the fleeting joys of childhood. Educators and psychologists worry that rigid routines are producing passive robots and pressured kids. Give a youngster time to explore on his own in a safe environment. Don't permit your child to become a puppet with others pulling the strings. Be sure your weekly plan makes time for creative aloneness. Don't let your child live with a daily schedule of school, organized activity, dinner, homework, chores, television, and bedtime. Let some of the adventure of the weekend days filter into the weekdays. Lessons learned when alone include how to make do with what is at hand, how to combine several games and toys into a greater game, how to repair what is broken, how to be content without outside stimulation. Diligence, patience, and creativity are exercised in time alone, and you may hear those wonderful words "I did it myself!"

❑ **344.** **GOOFING OFF.** A youngster's free time diminishes with every passing year. Time to "goof off" is soon gone. Encourage totally zany activities and safe adventures at your house. Not everything has to be a grand learning experience. At the end of the week, ask kids what was the craziest thing that happened during the week. You may be surprised at some of the responses.

FIVE

GOING PLACES

SECTION 1: THANK GOODNESS IT'S FRIDAY

SECTION 2: EATING OUT WITH STYLE

SECTION 3: TRIPPING ALONG

SECTION 1: THANK GOODNESS IT'S FRIDAY

At last the weekend has arrived bringing free time for the family. Still, there is so much to do! Of course there are errands to run and home projects to tackle, but the real focus of the weekend is family. (Make quick work of work by reading chapter 11—"Can Chores Be Fun?") Because your home is probably your biggest investment, give it good use by planning some events right there. And, you'll also want to take the time to enjoy family-oriented excursions. Here are ideas for both.

❑ **345.** NOT FROM ABOVE. Each Monday (sometimes the gloomiest day of the week), talk about the excursion possibilities for the next weekend. Don't just announce (as if you are king) what the family will do. Listen to suggestions—even take a vote if needed. Keep a list of places to visit and add to it regularly. And ask other families how they spend their weekend togetherness times.

❑ **346.** FRIEND-FOR-A-DAY. Acquaintances can become friends when they spend time together. Plan ahead with your youngster for him to have a Saturday with just one friend. Start that day right after chore time. Talk about possible things to do: cycling, making a tree house, knapsack lunch, an art or craft project, taking photos, game time, dinner with the family, listening to music, and stopping for ice-cream cones when taking the friend home.

❑ **347.** OVERDONE OVERNIGHTS. The frequency of "overnights" is giving them overexposure. They should be a *special* treat and parents and kids should work out a plan for them in advance (even though it may not be exactly followed). Depending on ages, from one to six friends can be invited. Begin the event with a make-your-own-pizza supper, followed by a vigorous outdoor activity such as volleyball. Then it's time for a chosen-in-advance video and dessert. Roll out the sleeping bags and turn on the music for conversation and pillow fights. In the morning, kids do a total cleanup while parents make stacks of pancakes. Then, don't let the event drag on—send the sleepyheads home.

☐ **348.** THE WAKE-UP PARTY. This variation on a slumber party starts at 7:00 in the morning when guests arrive in their pj's, carrying their pillows. Trays with pancakes, sausage, and juice are ready to take to the bedroom, plus a gooey coffee cake for midmorning. Activities include hair style and manicure changes, a pj fashion show, and pillow decorating. Using white pillowcases and indelible marking pens, each guest decorates a case, then everyone writes messages on the others' pillowcases.

☐ **349.** SUNRISE EXCURSION. Even though it may be tradition to sleep late on Saturday, go on a sunrise excursion. Plan to be on a hilltop facing east at dawn and take binoculars and breakfast with you. Get your lawn chairs in place so that you see the first glow before the curve of the sun explodes on the horizon. Have a guessing game as to how many minutes it will take for the full circle of the sun to appear. Serve a sunrise breakfast of round foods in yellow and orange colors: slices of oranges, bagels with cream cheese, granola cookies, plus lemonade to drink. On the ride home, let kids draw pictures of the sunrise or see how many words they can think of that rhyme with the word "sun."

☐ **350.** AMATEUR ARCHITECTS. Check out a book from the library about different styles of architecture. On neighborhood walks, teach kids to look for the different styles: ranch, Georgian, colonial, southwest, and so forth, indicating the special features of each. Note the different kinds of roofs—both the style (gable, mansard, hip) and the material used. Then look up houses/homes in the encyclopedia to see examples of residences in various parts of the world.

☐ **351.** HOUSE SNOOPING. Unless there is a "No Trespassing" sign posted most owners don't object to neighbors walking through a house under construction. If the owners are on hand, welcome them to the neighborhood and ask permission to look around. With youngsters (not toddlers) and after warnings about open stairways and nails, visit a newly framed house. Determine the floor plan for the house and how it would suit your family. See the views from the various rooms. Decide which bedrooms are for kids and which are for parents.

❑ **352.** **YEAR-ROUND CHRISTMAS.** Many shopping plazas feature year-round Christmas stores. Visit one as a family and pick out just one new decoration for the coming holiday. Older youngsters and adults can find good ideas for handmade ornaments and might then get an early start on their projects.

❑ **353.** **TO THE TOY STORE.** What more exciting place for a child than the toy store. But it doesn't have to be a "Buy this for me!" occasion. So that you aren't panicked when birthday party invitations come, keep on hand one or two gifts. Let your child pick out toys she herself would like—that way you know the gifts will be winners. Also, in advance of a birthday or Christmas, have your youngster show you toys and crafts she would like. This way you can note brand names and prices for your own information or passing on to a relative or friend.

❑ **354.** **SIMILARITIES, DIFFERENCES.** Visit a church different from your own. (Youngsters may go to Sunday school, parents to church.) Stay for the fellowship time afterward. On the way home, see how many similarities there are between this church and the one you attend (prayers, hymns, Bible stories). Then see how many physical differences there are (architecture inside and out, vestments of those officiating, traditions such as kneeling). As you visit other churches, note the wide variety in the services but especially the things you have in common.

❑ **355.** **WISE SHOPPERS.** Involve kids in reading product labels at the market. Show them how to find calories as well as fat, sugar, and salt content. When choosing a snack, let them compare products and serving sizes to determine what a normal amount might be. When home, let youngsters package their snacks in serving-sized plastic bags so that the entire amount isn't eaten at one sitting.

❏ **356.** MUNCHING MESSENGERS. Let gradeschoolers help speed your grocery trip. Give them two or three items to find and bring back to you for approval. Eventually you will be able to divide your list in half. Another day, ask each assistant shopper to find one new item that would be tasty to try (if it fits the budget). As a reward for good help, buy a bag of munchies for your messengers to enjoy on the way home.

❏ **357.** GOING VISITING. Going visiting was a welcome diversion in decades past, one worthy of revival. Let kids take part in planning a social visit. First, select someone who would enjoy a one hour get-together. Next, make the call and say that you'll be bringing refreshments. Let kids make cookies or a cake and punch. Then, talk about what one does during such a visit, other than eating. What can a youngster share in conversation? Is there something he can bring along to show? Would he like to take a photo? Also describe the end of the visit—thanking the person and saying good-bye.

❏ **358.** WAITING ROOM WAITS. Most waiting rooms have truly ancient and boring magazines for kids. In your car, keep a portfolio of paper games (like follow-the-dots), stickers, paper and crayons, crossword puzzles, small books, and other interesting activities so that waiting time isn't a total waste. These can also be used in the car when waiting at the park for the ball game to end or waiting at the train station for the commuter.

❏ **359.** EXCURSION CHAIRPERSON. Most newspapers have a special section devoted to weekend activities: concerts, movies, special events. Each week, one youngster can peruse the section and come up with a good suggestion. (If it turns out to be a dud, don't grumble, there's always next week.) The chairperson plans when to leave, the route, car seating arrangement, food to take along, and amusements for travel time.

❑ **360.** **CULTURE? NO WAY!** Don't be afraid of introducing kids to museums and concerts. At least once a month, select an enriching excursion. (See chapter 6 for ideas.) Advance preparation (listening to a symphony recording, reading about famous painters) will make all the difference in enjoying the event.

❑ **361.** **EVENTS THAT COST.** When you have to pay for tickets (to the ball game, circus, ice show), make the selection far enough ahead so that you can read up in advance. Check the team statistics, learn the players names and positions, read the review of the circus and talk about all the varied acts. Ask, "If you could be in the circus, which act would you choose?" Look up ice skating in the encyclopedia and read the descriptions of all the special moves. If the ice show has a specific story, go to the library and read a book about the plot.

❑ **362.** **ANCIENT BASKETS.** Gather long grasses from a prairie or other untended roadside area. While they are still pliable, show a child how to weave them into a mat or basket. Keep this handwork on the dining table and watch how it dries and changes in color. Use the mat as a coaster, and use the basket (with a jar inside) to hold wildflowers.

❑ **363.** **YUCKY SNAKES.** While you may not want reptiles as pets, youngsters need to know which ones to steer clear of and which ones aren't harmful. Visit a pet store and look at more than just the puppies and fish. Often the store owner will be willing to remove a snake from its habitat and show how it can be held and stroked. Since snakes are the most feared of all reptiles, this demonstration diffuses some anxiety. Get to know the snakes indigenous to your area (the library will have a good picture book) and discuss the proper action should one turn up in your yard or on the trail.

❑ **364.** HOT AIR. Hot air balloon companies offer fabulous and expensive rides into the sky. But, it also can be fun to just observe the takeoffs and landings. Look in the yellow pages for hot air balloon companies. Call and find out where and when they will be taking off (usually early morning or late afternoon). Go and observe the noisy excitement. Kids may want to start saving for such a trip.

❑ **365.** FARMER-IN-THE-DELL. Most areas have an open-to-the-public farm, a place for hands-on petting or the picking of fruit or pumpkins. Go to see the animals, then pick apples or cherries, and when back home, enjoy a family project of making a pie or two. The eating is extra special when you've made it yourself!

❑ **366.** RINK-WATCHING. Even the youngest kids enjoy a visit to a roller skating or ice skating rink. When merely rink-watching, pick out one person to especially watch—see when he slips up or where she makes a good move. Or, observe an ice hockey team in practice. When kids are old enough to try their own skills, make skating a special treat. At the same time, you may rediscover your own skating skill.

❑ **367.** VEGGIE FARM. Ask the manager of a vegetable store to tell you where you can see locally grown vegetables. Call ahead for permission to visit to see how many different veggies are grown at one farm. Find out who in your family has eaten the most different vegetables. Buy seeds and grow some vegetables that your kids like. Let them do the planting, weeding, harvesting, and preparing. Lettuce, tomatoes, carrots, corn, and radishes are favorites, but also plant a vegetable not as familiar to your family.

❑ **368.** FABULOUS FIFTY CENTS. Visit a garage sale or thrift shop. Give each youngster fifty cents and turn him loose to locate a useful or fun bargain. Display the items at dinner that night, and then put the fabulous finds into use.

❏ **369. LLAMA NOT LAMA.** While a lama is a priest in Lamaism (a form of Buddhism), the llama (pronounced the same) is a South American animal related to the camel but without a hump. It is kept as a beast of burden and valued for its soft woolly hair. Llama farms often welcome visitors, and youngsters enjoy seeing these unique animals that are also kept as pets. You can find a llama farm in the yellow pages of the phone book. Call first before visiting.

❏ **370. OSTRICHES AND EGGS.** While you're tracking down unusual animals, consider a visit to an ostrich farm, a newer and profitable business. These nonflying birds, originally from Africa, can run really fast. Be sure to see the eggs and young birds and find out how they are marketed. On the way home, talk about the saying that ostriches hide their heads in the sand and thus think they are invisible. That's why a person who doesn't face facts is said to be an ostrich.

❏ **371. A IS FOR ASIA AND ABACUS.** Many cities have stores and markets featuring Asian products. Visit one and admire the beautiful porcelain items. View the unusual foods and find something you've never seen before. Often there is a department with toys and clothing, too. But one thing not to miss is the abacus. This ancient Chinese device, also used in early Greece and Rome, can be used to add, subtract, multiply, divide, and calculate square roots and cube roots. Consisting of rows of beads in a frame, it has been adapted to teach arithmetic to blind children. Ask for a demonstration and consider buying one just in case your adding machine or calculator malfunctions! It also makes an interesting conversation piece when left on a living room table.

❏ **372. SWITCHING YARD.** At many railway yards, you'll find a fascinating area called a switching yard. Call in advance and you'll be welcome to see how freight is handled, tracked, and how the freight cars are sorted and made into trains. Read the variety of names on the freight cars. See how many different uses they have (hauling grain, oil, animals, and so forth).

❑ **373.** SMALL AIRPORT.   Take a picnic for eating on the lawn of small airport. Watch the variety of planes parked, taking off, and landing. Go in the building and see all you can see—some small airports have an observation area where you can clearly see the planes and even hear the control tower talking with pilots.

❑ **374.** THE LISTENING HIKE.   All family hikes don't need to be through the woods or up the mountain. Plan one for a relatively flat area with some open fields. Sit under a tree for lunch. Then, suggest a listening time: everyone stretches out and shuts eyes. Identify sounds such as birds, planes, crickets, dogs, cars, streams. Make up a story about some of the sounds: "Once upon a time, there was a hummingbird who wanted to be a jet plane. . . ." Let each one suggest a sentence or two as the story develops.

❑ **375.** MOO TO YOU.   Many dairies welcome visitors. See how cows are fed, washed, and milked. Find out how milk gets from the dairy to the grocery store without spoiling. See how many different products the dairy produces. If there is a sales room, take home a dairy product you may not have tried before.

❑ **376.** CARE BEAR SURPRISE.   When hiking with the family, younger kids sometimes become grumpy and tired. To keep them excited about the destination, explain that care bears live in the clouds and keep their eyes on the hikers. And, they reward them with a small candy bar or little toy when they reach the top of the hill. Of course, the surprise has to be at the hilltop but you can manage this by letting one parent go ahead, supposedly to scout out the area, leave the surprise, and then help look for it when all arrive.

❑ **377.** **WANNA BEE?** Look up beekeeping in the yellow pages and call to see if you can visit a bee farm. Learn how honey is made and how bees toil from sunrise to sunset (hence the term "busy as a bee"). You will see the bees' pollen baskets and learn how some bees have the jobs of caring for young bees while others clean the cells of the comb. There are over 300 honey varieties so try a new one for eating on toast, in hot milk, or mixed with chocolate sauce.

❑ **378.** **ON THE ROAD AGAIN.** On the outskirts of most towns is a truck stop. Go there for lunch one day—the grub will probably be hearty and good since eating well is a highlight of a trucker's day. See the facilities for resting and showering. Look at the big rigs and see how many have self-contained sleeping units. Do you see any women drivers? A trucker may actually talk to you and tell you about the load being hauled.

SECTION 2: EATING OUT WITH STYLE

❑ **379.** **GRACIOUS EATING WITH ONE COMPLAINT.** Since eating out is more expensive than eating at home, and it should be viewed as a treat for the entire family, don't rush through the meal and don't permit kids to spoil it with whining and arguing. In advance, tell them that going to a restaurant is special and requires their best manners. Also announce that they only get one complaint ("He kicked me" or "I don't like this food") and after that it will be ten minutes earlier to bed for each complaint. That usually reminds kids to solve problems amicably.

❑ **380.** **NO WASTE.** When going to a restaurant, insist that youngsters select some nutritious elements in the meal. With a hamburger, suggest a salad, rather than fries. Do not ask the question "What do you want?"

rather phrase it "What will you eat?" It's money-saving and food-saving to order kid-sized portions, divide an order, or take home leftovers to eat later.

❏ **381.** CULINARY CONVERSATION. Use these questions that focus on food. What is the specialty of this restaurant? What items on the menu sound tasty yet are nutritious? Is there an entree that no one in the family has ever tried? Looking at the right hand column, what is the most expensive dish on the menu? If we could make this food at home, which item would you choose? Who is the most uniquely dressed person in the restaurant? What is she eating? (Remind kids not to stare.) What do you think her profession is? What do you think our bill will be?

❏ **382.** GOURMET VOCABULARY. See who knows the meaning of strange words on the menu. You can also take along this list of terms for a quiet guessing game while waiting for the food: braised, consomme, bearnaise sauce, prawns, torte, fromage, poisson, linguini, crepe, roulade, knackwurst, mit schlag, bisque, borscht, chateau briand, chutney, Creole, escargot, goulash, mousse, paté, sukiyaki, sushi, sweetbread, tripe, wiener schnitzel, Yorkshire pudding. When back home, you may want to look up the ones that no one knew.

❏ **383.** WHAT'S THE TIP? An easy way to show kids how to figure the correct tip to leave (about 15 percent unless fabulous service) is to double the tax. For example, if the bill is $40 and the tax in your area is 8 percent, you'll see a tax of $3.20 on your bill. Double $3.20 is $6.40, so leaving $6.50 is usually acceptable. This is good math practice for kids.

❏ **384.** NOT ALWAYS DINNER. When you plan to eat out over the weekend, it doesn't have to be dinner. Consider having a hearty breakfast eaten at a restaurant that features things kids like (such as a pancake house). Go to a buffet-style restaurant for lunch. Look at how people pile their plates high with food. See if you can observe wasted food. Have popcorn at a six o'clock movie and then go out for a light supper afterward.

❑ **385.** FOOD SPIES. If you buy food at a fast-food stop, young children might enjoy eating in the car near the take-out window. They can watch the cars as they pass through and guess what the driver has ordered and see if he immediately starts to eat it. Or, eat inside and see if everything is eaten with fingers and if there are more adults than kids eating. Or, visit a grade school during lunchtime and wander past the rows of tables, observing what's being eaten. At the grocery store, look for folks who eat as they shop.

❑ **386.** FARMERS' MARKET. Instead of buying lunch, stroll through a farmers' market where the many free samples offered will probably satisfy hunger. Let kids buy something interesting to take home for dinner.

SECTION 3: TRIPPING ALONG

❑ **387.** GO WITH A PURPOSE. Travel can be more than just getting away from a busy life and relaxing. See that your family trips combine some education with the fun. For example, if you are going to Yellowstone Park, read up on geysers before leaving. While en route to Philadelphia, have the family read together the Bill of Rights and the Preamble to the Constitution. Before enjoying Disneyland, learn about the cartoon business—yesterday and today. If going fishing, visit a bait shop and ask the salesperson to explain lures and the types of fish they attract. Share the purpose with kids by saying, for example, "We're driving to New Orleans and on the way we're going to listen to the style of music called the blues."

❑ **388.** CONVERSATIONAL CAPS. Before leaving home, buy a plain white cap or hat for each family member. Take along sturdy thread and needle, and a tube of glue. As you travel, you'll find patches, pins, small figures, decals, and other items that can be affixed. The caps will be conversation pieces along the way and mementos of the trip.

❑ **389.** **LEAVE THE DRIVING TO SOMEONE ELSE.** Families are finding alternatives to expensive travel modes. Buses offer these advantages: the entire family can enjoy gazing out the large windows, the opportunity to walk around in the bus and at rest stops, no traffic jams or getting lost, onboard bathrooms, large comfy seats, bring-along snacks whenever you want them, and sometimes interesting people to talk with. Start with a day trip to a family-oriented destination. You may like bus travel so much that you decide to make a circle tour of the country at a bargain price.

❑ **390.** **MAP IT OUT.** When traveling by car, don't permit map ignorance in your family. On a map showing your town and also your destination, mark the route. Let youngsters take turns being your skilled navigator. A good navigator always knows the mileage to the next town (math), possible educational stops en route (history), highest mountains nearby (geography), and town populations (reading). The navigator also chooses the next rest or meal stop (intelligent analysis).

❑ **391.** **AMUSEMENT CENTER.** Buy an inexpensive shoe bag and attach it to the back of the seat (in front of the kids). Let them choose some items for the many pockets, but you should put in some surprises. Tailor it to the ages of the children and the length of the trip. It's an orderly place for paper and crayons, finger puppets, small cars, doll and doll clothes, the comic section of the Sunday paper, granola bars, sunglasses, a bottle of water, a map, postcards and pen, small puzzles, and games.

❑ **392.** **WHIP OUT THE PROJECT.** A teacher often gives an assignment to write a report about a family trip. This can be a bore to do when back home from the vacation. So, make plans to get the report finished while on the way. Take along the necessary paper, pen, and laptop desk, and let the entire family give input for the report. It can also be used as a permanent travel journal.

❑ **393. GET SMART WHILE SITTING.** Whether on plane, train, bus, or in the car, there are bound to be some dull stretches with nothing going on. One of the best brain teasers is the book *Brain Quest for the Car* by Gold (New York: Workman Publishing, 1995). It is ideal for gradeschoolers and older kids and their parents. It contains over 1000 interesting questions and answers about Americana, plus score pad and pencil. These are not trivial, but worthwhile facts.

❑ **394. SEDENTARY SCAVENGER HUNT.** Before leaving on your trip, work together on a computer to make a list of things you'll see along the way. List types of buildings (factories, barns, skyscrapers), makes of vehicles, products advertised on signs, states on license plates, types of animals, names of department stores and food franchises, and scenic objects such as lakes, picket fences, and snow-capped mountains. Make several copies for each person so you can play several times. The object is to be the first to find and check off each item on the list. You'll hear "Cow on the right" and "Jeep in front of us." No, the driver may NOT play!

❑ **395. INDELIBLE MEMORIES.** Provide a T-shirt for each family member and also a piece of heavy cardboard that fits inside (to use as a portable desk). Take along a set of indelible markers. During the trip—in the car, at the picnic table, before bed—each person draws something connected with a good event that day. It could be a train ride, a deer, a snowy mountaintop, a banana split, a clown. Gradually the shirt will become a hand-created memento of good times.

❑ **396. NOTABLE NOTEBOOK.** In advance of the trip, help each youngster make a special game notebook. You'll need a three-ring notebook with vinyl page protectors, some zip-lock type plastic bags, dry-erase markers, and a small cloth. First search through magazines, coloring books, and activity books for interesting pages to color, bingo games, follow-the-dot pictures, mazes, and workbook pages. Put each of these in a page protector so that the game can be played, then wiped clean, and played again. At the front of the book, insert through the rings a bag with the markers and cloth so that these essentials stay with the notebook. Put in some blank pages for writing letters or taking notes and for other pencil and paper games.

❑ **397.** THE STORY AROUND YOU.   While riding in the car, tell a story round-robin style. (Each person adds a sentence in each round.) However, the sentence must include something the storyteller can see. First person: "I was sitting in the car when one of my shoes suddenly spoke to me!" Second person: "I was so surprised, I almost drove into a road sign." Next person: "But, I was saved by a cow I saw dancing by the fence." And so the story goes, round and round.

❑ **398.**   ADJECTIVE STORY.   Make one copy of this story before leaving on a trip. Without revealing the story line to the family, ask each person to suggest an adjective (descriptive word) that you fill in, in the order given. Then read aloud for lots of laughs. Adapt this story to your family and your own trip.

> **The True Story About Our _____ Trip**
>
> On a _____ day, the _____ (your name) family set out for _____ (destination). In the car were _____ (name), _____ (name), and their_____ parents. Mother drove the _____ car and the others sat around reading _____ books and eating _____ food. Finally they got to their _____ destination. Here they got out of the car. _____ (child's name) said it was a _____ sight. _____ (child's name) thought it was a _____ day. The parents said it was worth all the _____ money that the _____ vacation cost. They all agreed that it was truly a _____ trip.

❑ **399.** DON'T RUSH.   Travel doesn't have to be a scramble from place to place. Each day choose a place to sit down and talk. At the Grand Canyon, imagine how explorer John Powell felt in the 1800s as his boat sped down the gorge. In a town, talk about what looks new and what looks old and notice the ages and races and activities of the townsfolk. At a beach, imagine what it would be like to be washed upon the shore after a shipwreck. At the zoo, imagine and describe a conversation between two animals. At an amusement park, decide what new kind of ride you'd like invented.

❑ **400.** TRAVEL CONNECTIONS.   Everyone in the family can play this car game consisting of words connected with travel. It starts with the word "car." The next person must come up with a travel word beginning with the last letter in "car." So she might say "restaurant." The next would say "train" and the next might say "nachos." Now when someone uses a word that doesn't seem to have a travel connection, the game stops while he explains: "I plan to eat nachos the next time we stop." And so the game continues with some far-fetched and funny connections.

❑ **401.** TRAVEL COLLAGE.   While a scrapbook or photo album can be a good memento of a trip, a travel collage can bring back memories and serve as wall art at the same time. When traveling, save picture brochures, maps, photos, ticket stubs, samples of unusual soil or sand, postcards, travel stickers or decals, and so forth. Back home, buy an inexpensive frame at least 18 x 24 inches in size. On cardboard, paste a map as the background and artistically arrange and glue on top of it all the other mementos of the trip.

❑ **402.** VANITY PLATES.   Often while traveling you'll see license plates that have a message in them. See who can find the most unique. And, while looking at plates, keep a list of states shown on them. Count how many states you find on your trip. You can also add up the numbers on the plates of the car just ahead of you. See who can find the biggest total on one plate.

❑ **403.** HOME VACATION. Plan a vacation near home, saving the cost of travel to a faraway place and thus the cost of overnight accommodations. Make a list of interesting places within a hundred mile radius of your house. Let kids vote on which destinations they might like. Then plan together the complete vacation day: on the road an hour before breakfast, midmorning arrival at the destination for activities and lunch, late afternoon departure with dinner on the way home. Let kids take turns planning a home vacation and choosing one friend to take along.

SIX

IS YOUR KID CULTURED?

SECTION 1: CULTURE WITH A CAPITAL "M" FOR MANNERS

While manners are now greatly relaxed compared to a few decades ago, there are still some basics every youngster should know that go well beyond "please" and "thank you." Teaching these principles at home will help make good manners automatic when kids are out on their own. And, don't forget to praise the well-mannered child, showing that you value responsible and poised behavior.

❑ **404. AT THE TABLE.** Don't let mealtimes become nagging times. On Monday, choose one aspect of good table manners, explain it, encourage it, and tell the family to be alert to it all week long. The next Monday, talk about how everyone did, and introduce a new idea. See how many of these basic table manners your kids know: starting to eat when all are seated or served (or a parent picks up his fork), keeping elbows off the table, eating with the mouth closed, not talking with food in the mouth, using utensils correctly and knowing which to use, passing common dishes around—not across—the table and asking permission to take some on the way, passing salt and pepper together, coping with a bone or other inedible objects, covering a cough or sneeze, placing utensils at the "four o'clock" angle on the plate when finished, and asking to be excused. Occasionally have a bad manners meal when family members try all the bad manners imaginable. This will be fun, but it will make bad manners so memorable that good manners will become more important.

❑ **405. NEW FOODS.** When children are young, have them try new foods. They can ask for a very small portion when eating out. At home, they can have a "royalty serving" (about two tablespoonsful), which should be eaten. Explain that it is bad manners to make derogatory comments about the taste or appearance of food.

❑ **406.** **INTERRUPTIONS.** Doorbells and phones ringing can be very disruptive during a meal. Each week assign one youngster to handle these. Unless an emergency, callers should be asked if they can call back or a message should be taken so the call can be returned. Letting the answering machine take the call is another option. If it's kids who are telephoning or ringing the doorbell, encourage your youngsters to tell their friends that the family eats between 6:30 and 7 (or whatever the time) and that they aren't available then.

❑ **407.** **FAMILY FRACTIONS.** Just how many french fries or how much salad should one take from the serving dish? It's a matter of fractions. For example, if there are four people in your family, the first person may take up to one-fourth, the second person may take one-third of what is left, the third person can take one-half of the remainder, and the last person can have all that is left. Show youngsters how to figure the appropriate amount and they'll never embarrass themselves or cause an argument by taking too much.

❑ **408.** **INTRODUCTIONS.** Although it's a current fad to call everyone by first names only, insist that your youngster know and use the last names of friends when introducing them to you. As soon as nonfamily members enter your house or car, they should be introduced to a parent. Younger people are introduced to older people: "Chris Smith, I'd like you to meet my dad, Mr. Cooper."

❑ **409.** **TWO IMPORTANT WORDS.** Teach kids that it's almost impossible to overuse the words "thank you." On some occasions, a thank-you on the spot is sufficient, such as when a youngster stops in at a friend's home and the parent gives him a soft drink. A phone call of thanks is acceptable after a casual meal. However, a party, a planned dinner, or a gift still require a written thank-you.

❑ **410.** **NO RESPONSE.** Countless gift-givers complain

about kids not responding to gifts received. At age three or so, start the habit of thank-you notes for gifts. Until the child can write, it can be a drawing with the parents lettering "Thank you Aunt Amy" on the paper. But, when a child learns to write, the thank-yous are their own work—perhaps you'll address the envelopes. Teens are expected to write promptly—good practice for when they're on their own.

❑ **411. NO THANKS, NO GIFTS.** When a parent got tired of nagging her grade school son to write thank-you notes for birthday presents from friends and relatives, she came up with this effective solution. She collected the gifts and was about to put them in a box on a high shelf when her son asked what she was doing. She calmly replied, "These aren't really yours until you've said 'thanks' for them." The son wrote his thank-you notes that very day. Another parent says that he and his son place the opened birthday gifts in the center of the table so he can look at them (but not touch them) until the task is completed.

❑ **412. YOU LOOK PRETTY.** When kids get compliments, their response is often embarrassment and head-hanging. Encourage kids not to belittle themselves or express shyness, rather, show them how to accept compliments graciously. Help them to respond by practicing these lines: "It's new. Thank you for telling me." "I worked hard on it, so I'm glad you like it." "What a nice thing to say!"

❑ **413. MANNERS AT FRIENDS' HOMES.** You hope your child is a good guest, and he will be if you talk together about how a guest should act. Ask what he expects of a pal playing at your house—then he'll understand what he should do at his friend's house: never snoop in private places, never touch precious objects, wipe feet when coming inside, ask permission to use the phone, never ask to stay for a meal, help to put away toys and games when finished playing, and say good-bye and thank you when leaving.

❏ **414.** CONTRADICTING AND INTERRUPTING. In family conversations, we're usually so casual that several people are talking at once, or arguing a point. This makes it hard to remember to be more polite in public. Kids should be taught not to monopolize conversation but to give others the opportunity to speak. And, unless it is extremely vital, they should not contradict.

❏ **415.** ENTERTAIN BACK. When your youngster begins to get party invitations and is invited to go on excursions or trips with other families, explain the obligation of "entertaining back." Of course, if your child finds that he doesn't enjoy the company of that person, it can stop there. But, if he wants to continue the friendship, he should remember to return the favor. Continually being entertained by others and accepting invitations without reciprocation is very rude and should be discouraged. There's no need to entertain back in the same manner—a fancy meal at another's house can be paid back with popcorn and a movie.

❏ **416.** SAYING "NO" POLITELY. You are training your youngster to refuse alcohol, cigarettes, drugs and other controlled substances. And, you are teaching her to refuse to take part in cheating, or in shoplifting and other petty crimes. But, also teach her what to do when a group is misbehaving: speeding, trashing, or abusing others. Remind kids to always have at least a quarter on hand so they can call for help, to separate themselves from the mayhem, or to ask you to come and pick them up.

❏ **417.** LET'S DANCE. Some kids seem to have natural rhythm and good moves. Others border on the clumsy side. Start when children are young to teach them to dance. If you don't know current dance steps, ask others to teach them, or get them lessons. There are many occasions in life when knowing how to dance is important, and when a child has this skill, she is much more socially comfortable.

❏ **418.** MANNERS ARE NOT SEX-RELATED. Being male or

female does not excuse youngsters from being kind and caring. Practice these with your youngster: seating someone who may require it, holding a door open for others, offering an arm or a hand to someone, and helping others to get into today's smaller cars.

❑ **419.** CONVERSATIONAL MANNERS. Teach young children to take an interest in others by asking questions—that's the start of good conversation. Show the difference between showing interest and prying. Before a child has dinner with another family, talk about some topics he might share (as well as some things not to be mentioned).

❑ **420.** DON'T REWARD RUDENESS. Impolite habits and unacceptable language are often learned from older siblings or peers who encourage this behavior because they think it is mature or funny. When your child is boorish, don't laugh, but also don't explode since that rewards rudeness with extra attention. Rather, talk to the child (and the older offender if you know who that is) and say that such conduct is offensive, and can be punishable if it continues.

❑ **421.** FORMAL FAMILY DINNER. Every few months, practice all the best manners imaginable by having a formal dinner. Set the table with good china and linens and appropriate silverware. Let family members dress up for the occasion. Serve something special such as turkey, salmon, or beef with all the trimmings. Have sparkling cider for toasts. Eat by candlelight as family members practice their conversational techniques along with good table manners.

SECTION 2: ART FROM THE HEART

Feel insecure at an art museum? Does modern sculpture look like lumps of clay? Read on for ideas to interest your youngsters in the art world.

VISIT AN ART MUSEUM

❑ **422.** **BEFORE GOING TO A MUSEUM.** When youngsters are four or older, it's time to visit a museum. Call in advance to find out about free days, availability of strollers, use of cameras, and places to eat. Take a maximum of three or four kids. First, visit your library and borrow some art books, but don't ponder each page. Let kids look through them at their own pace. Then, announce the date for the excursion, put it on the calendar, and refer to it as a great privilege.

❑ **423.** **ON THE WAY TO THE MUSEUM.** Talk about colors and what colors are each child's favorite. Ask what artists draw with: crayons? pencils? oil paints? Ask who can remember something from a picture in the art book: a boat? a flower? a child? Explain the four museum rules: no running, no shouting, no touching the art work, and have fun.

❑ **424.** **BEFORE ENTERING THE MUSEUM.** Sit on the steps for a snack. Explain that the paintings are very precious so there will be guards to protect them and also to help people. As you enter the museum, look at the architecture, say hello to the person on duty at the door. Then, to save backtracking, visit the restrooms now.

❑ **425.** **SELECTING "MY PAINTING."** As a quick first stop (you'll come back later), visit the museum gift shop to look at the postcards of paintings that are on display in the museum. [Ask in which rooms these paintings are displayed.] Let each youngster and parent choose a postcard (her "personal painting") and purchase it. Using string or ribbon that you've brought along, make a small hole in one corner and let little children hang the card around their necks; others can keep it handy in a pocket.

❑ **426.** **VIEWING PICTURES.** Don't sign up for a tour—that's too regimented for this first visit. And remember, you don't need to see every room in the museum. Leave some for another time. Choose rooms that seem most interesting or least occupied. Move at a leisurely pace and don't give a running commentary—just look and listen to kids' comments. Remind each one to be on the lookout for his post-card picture. Then, after some viewing, ask a child to find a picture with his favorite color. Have them look to see if happy pictures have bright colors and mysterious pictures dark colors. Don't skip the modern art. Ask what the artist might have felt when he painted the picture. Does the painting's title give a clue?

❑ **427.** **WHO PAINTED THESE PICTURES?** Show where most artists sign their works and read a few of their names. Show how the artist's name and other information about the painting is often posted next to the picture. See if it gives any further information about the artist, ownership, date painted, and if for sale, the price. Look for paintings by Rembrandt, Picasso, El Greco, Monet, Renoir, Wyeth, Cassatt, and Seurat.

❑ **428.** **WHAT'S THE PICTURE ABOUT?** If you're with school-aged kids, sit down on a bench in one of the rooms and give each child a paper and pencil. See how many different subjects they can list: a storm, a family eating, a child watering flowers, Jesus, landscapes, rich people, buildings, battles. Compare the lists.

❑ **429.** **AM I IN A PICTURE?** Look for people and animal paintings. Are there paintings of children? old folks? soldiers? angels? dogs? sheep? cows? moms and dads? Encourage each youngster to find a picture he thinks he could fit into or would like to be a part of—as a warrior, queen, horseback rider, and so forth. Let everyone point out places that look interesting for play, living, working, or visiting.

❑ **430.** **"IF I WERE A MILLIONAIRE" LUNCH BREAK.** After about an hour of viewing, take a restroom and lunch break. Talk about a picture that each youngster would like to take home if he could afford the (most likely expensive) price. Why does he like the picture—because it is beautiful? big? funny? sad? Do others like the same picture? Is it the picture on his postcard?

❑ **431.** AFTER LUNCH LOOKING. Before heading for home, help kids to find their postcard pictures (the information desk can help). Return to favorite paintings and make note of the painting's title and the artist's name. If permitted, photograph each youngster with his favorite painting. If photography is not permitted, do take a photo of the group outside so that this excursion can go in the family memory book.

❑ **432.** GIFT SHOP INVESTIGATION. Return to the museum shop and investigate books, games, and other artistic gifts. Listen for kid comments that may give you ideas for birthday and holiday gift-giving. Consider the purchase of an item that would be useful in your youngster's art education.

❑ **433.** KEEPING THE MUSEUM VISIT ALIVE. Back home, put the postcard pictures on the family bulletin board or let children send them to grandparents, telling about the excursion. Talk about favorite paintings and what made them special. Encourage an art project at home but don't suggest what to draw, rather just see what your youngster creates. Display the finished pictures. Now that the museum is no longer intimidating, plan a followup trip. As children grow older, discussion on technique, historical art, religious art, patrons, the Masters, and so forth can be part of the experience. A tour led by a docent will also be valuable.

ART IN THE HOME

❑ **434.** BOOKS TO BORROW OR BUY. Put an art book on a table or pedestal that everyone passes. Open it to one page, and turn a page each day. Some books you will want to look at together or read include *The History of Art for Young People,* by H. W. Janson and Anthony F. Janson (New York: Abrams, 1987), *The National Gallery of Art* by John Walker (New York: Abrams, 1984), and *Children Are Artists* by Daniel M. Mendelowitz (Stanford Univ. Press: Stanford, Calif., 1963)—an old but wonderful book.

❑ **435.** WALL OF ART. Rather than having kid-art on the refrigerator, stacked on the counter, or being sneaked into the rubbish, create a wall of art in a hallway. With youngsters, go to a frame shop and ask to see their least expensive, slightly damaged, or poster frames. Let each child choose one. Back home, help them frame their best artwork and then hang all the frames in a group with some at adult eye level and others at kid eye evel.

❑ **436.** HOME ART GALLERY. Hang sturdy string or a clothesline at eye level across a child's bedroom or the family room. Let him clip to it his latest art projects. When the line is full, let family members pretend they are at a museum and comment on their favorites.

❑ **437.** TELL ME ABOUT IT. Parents want fingers on hands, chimneys on houses, and hair that isn't green. This kind of intrusion or "improving" of kids' art can be discouraging. Rather than asking "What is it?" say "Tell me about it." Suggest youngsters show and explain their latest art work to the entire family at supper, or to friends who come by.

❑ **438.** KITCHEN EASEL. As soon as kids are old enough to color or paint, invest in a simple easel. Put it in the kitchen (where spills are easily cleaned up), provide the artist with an apron or big T-shirt as a cover-up, and let the child paint as you prepare dinner. This allows you to supervise and encourage, and subtly brings you and your youngster together on a regular basis.

❑ **439.** OUTDOOR ART FAIR. Make good art a part of your home atmosphere. Visit a fair at a school or park.

Look at the pictures and prints. If reasonably priced, let a youngster select one for her own room or give her a painting or art object as a gift.

❑ **440.** **BREAD PEOPLE.** Cut the crusts off bread slices—several slices per child. Show youngsters how to knead the glob until it feels like clay (older, coarser bread may need a few drops of water added). Now it is ready to be molded much like clay. It makes a good activity to do on a tray while traveling in the car. Afterward, it can be put outside for the birds.

❑ **441.** **WHAT'S INSIDE?** When youngsters are old enough to handle a knife for soap carving, have them envision the object that is hidden inside the soap (famous sculptors do this before they begin chipping the marble). Then, show them how to cut away the soap to reveal the object inside. (Tie up soap scraps in netting for use in the tub.) Display the finished product and when the artist is tired of it, it can be used at bath time.

❑ **442.** **PAPIER-MÂCHÉ.** This is the French word for pulped paper that can be made at home and used for modeling. Supervise the cutting of several newspapers (regular newsprint, not colored or glossy) into one-inch wide strips. In a large bowl or pail, cover the paper with water and let soak overnight. The next day divide the mass—a portion for each child. Knead the soaked mass and squeeze out the excess water (using a strainer or sieve works well). Then mix in ordinary paste. Now it is ready to be molded into small objects and dried. Or, it can be used to make a mask, doll's head, animal, or a relief map. As it hardens, it becomes durable and can be easily painted.

❑ **443.** **ROLLING PIN ART.** This requires an old rolling pin that you tightly cover with string, wound around (close or far apart) or glued in a design. Glue the ends of the string in place and let dry. Cover the work surface with newspaper and then plain poster paper. In an aluminum tray that is large enough for dipping the rolling pin, pour thick poster paint. The youngster makes a print by rolling the dipped rolling pin on the paper. If you have two rolling pins and two trays of paint, you can roll a second design across the first when the first is dry. The paper makes nice place mats, wrapping paper, or wall decorations.

❑ **444.** COLORFUL COLLAGE. Abstract or representational art work can be made using the collage method. (The term comes from the French word meaning to paste or glue.) It teaches the use of color, proportion, and materials. Torn paper collage is a good way to begin. Colored paper, tissue paper, wallpaper, magazines and even newspaper can be combined for a pleasing effect. Cardboard or canvas board is the base for pasting down the various elements. This art form lets the artist try the placement of the elements before gluing them into place. As proficiency increases, objects such as buttons or leaves can be added. Collage is a good all-family art project.

❑ **445.** SAND PICTURES. Show kids how to mix sand with powdered tempera paint (one-quarter cup sand mixed well with two teaspoons of dry paint). Put the colors in shakers or spice containers with most of the holes covered with tape to limit the flow of the sand. Affix a picture hook to the back of a sturdy paper plate. With a pencil, kids can sketch on it a simple picture or design. Next, they start with the background color by spreading glue on the desired area, then shaking on the sand mixture. Excess sand is then shaken onto a paper towel and returned to the shaker. Follow the same procedure with the next colors until the picture is finished. It dries quickly and can be hung almost immediately.

❑ **446.** RAINY DAY ART. On a drizzly day, get the family together for this simple art project that has great results. Everyone is given paper to use on a tray or cookie sheet. Using washable markers or colored chalk, each makes a picture or design. As soon as there is a misty rain, set the trays outside for just a few minutes. The colors will bleed together to form an interesting painting. Bring the paintings inside and dry them on newspaper before hanging.

❑ **447.** **TUBE BRACELETS.** Show kids how to make the popular eye-catching bracelets worn by both gals and guys. At a pet or aquarium store, buy a package of standard airline tubing and a package of connectors. Let kids decide the bracelet length—usually about seven inches. Attach a connector at one end and then fill the tube with glitter, sand, sequins, tiny nuts and bolts, even paper and fabric scraps. Use a toothpick to poke the items in the tube, leaving about a half inch at the end. Then firmly push this end into the connector. It's the style to wear several and they can even be used to hold a house key by pushing the tubing through the hole in the key.

❑ **448.** **POTATO BEADS.** Girls will really enjoy making these necklaces out of real potatoes. A parent should peel and cut a large raw white potato into three-fourth inch chunks. Kids then poke each chunk through the center onto a kabob skewer, being sure the chunks don't touch. Set them on a cooling rack to air dry, turning them every three days for a total of two weeks. Now the chunks are hard as rocks and can be painted with acrylic paint to look like turquoise. Let them thoroughly dry before highlighting with dabs of black paint wiped off with a paper towel. The black will stick in the crevices for a natural turquoise look. The "beads" can then be strung with needle and fishing line.

❑ **449.** **MACARONI JEWELRY.** Girls can make necklaces and bracelets, boys like to make head bands and belts. All you need are lengths of yarn, dry macaroni, and Cheerios. To make threading easy, put glue on one end of the yarn and let it dry. While Cheerios come in colors, you can make colored macaroni this way: Mix a half cup of rubbing alcohol with a little yellow food coloring and immerse noodles, then dry on newspaper covered with wax paper. To make green, add blue food coloring to the mixture and repeat the process. You can also start with red food coloring for red noodles, then add blue for purple noodles. Alternate cereal and noodles for interesting designs.

❑ **450.** LUNCH BOX ART. Let a child turn her lunch box into a game. Using acrylic paint on a plain plastic lunch box, paint on the grid for a tick-tack-toe game. Inside the box, place two colors of paper clips (to represent the X's and O's) in a film canister. Friends will enjoy lunching and playing together.

❑ **451.** FELT BOARDS. This creative toy can be played with at home or in the car, and it makes a fine homemade gift from a child to a friend. Check your fabric scrap bag for pieces of felt, or go to a craft or fabric shop and buy remnants or small pieces in about eight colors. Have at least one-half yard each in green and blue. Using a sturdy dress box as a base, create a background of blue sky and green grass inside the box. Glue these in place. Then let kids cut out many objects and shapes: house, tree, dog, sun, parent, child, wagon, and so forth. Also cut circles and rectangles that can be used to make up figures, being sure that there are some small pieces for eyes and mouth. These felt cut-outs will stick to the background and let kids make pictures and stories. The lid of the box keeps all the pieces inside when play is over.

❑ **452.** ART AT SCHOOL. Many schools have cut back on teaching art or may just permit drawing as a diversion without any professional input. Call or visit your school to inquire about the art program. Art appreciation is just as important as art "doing" so encourage and help the teacher plan field trips to museums (art, sculpture, photography) and the display of good art at the school. Art teaches history, design, zoology, anatomy, architecture, botany, costuming, perspective, and more. At school meetings, voice your opinion on the importance of art instruction.

SECTION 3: ALL THE WORLD'S A STAGE . . .

☐ **453.** LIVE THEATER. Television, movies, and picture books cannot match the magic of live theater—seeing Peter Pan fly across the stage or Beauty dancing with the Beast. A school play, youth theater, or summer theater may not be as grand as Broadway, but still, take children to plays several times each year. Live theater requires a youngster's commitment of mind and body as she follows the words and the action and is drawn into the plot. The characters are real people she cares about. It is as different as seeing a live circus or looking at a picture book about animals.

☐ **454.** SHADOW PLAYS. Hang a sheet in a doorway and place a floodlight about eight feet behind it. Let kids play between the sheet and the light, acting out nursery rhymes and scenes from familiar books. See if the audience can guess who the actors are portraying.

☐ **455.** THE PLAY'S THE THING. Rig a curtain near one side of a room and create a stage. Let kids begin by recreating favorite stories—allowing them to play the lead parts and a parent playing all the other parts. Fairy tales and cartoon movies are a good place to start. As youngsters take an interest in plays, they can create costumes and simple scenery. And if they get really good, they can charge a dime for spectators! Libraries have books of simple plays for all ages, but some of the best plays are made-up spur-of-the-moment ones. Encourage this kind of creativity by suggesting a situation or plot line.

☐ **456.** HAND PUPPET THEATER. Take a very large box, remove both ends, and cover one end with a long piece of fabric, attached only at the top. Place the box on a table with the open end toward the audience, the curtained end to the back. Puppeteers bring their arms up under the fabric, which shields the kids from the audience, and they speak the words for the hand puppets. Suggest familiar stories such as *The Three Bears* or *Pinocchio*. As they get more proficient, youngsters can each manage two hand puppets and make up some stories on their own.

❑ **457.** MARIONETTE THEATER. String puppets are more expensive than hand puppets but offer a wider range of movement. There are kits for making string puppets but they can also be purchased ready-made. The homemade stage can be a sturdy box with the top side and the audience side open. Help youngsters write a short play that can be acted out by the puppets. Invite neighborhood kids to view the show.

❑ **458.** AUTO THEATER. When on a long drive, create a play inside the car. First, state a premise suitable to the ages of the children: a princess needs to find food for her hungry people, or a rock band suspects trouble at a school concert. Then get volunteers for parts: princess, farmer, magician, band leader, troublemaker, class president. Without rehearsal, start the dialogue (it helps if a parent begins). Let actors speak when they choose, interrupt one another, give sound effects, and see how the plot turns and twists.

❑ **459.** THEATER AT SCHOOL. Although school productions can be corny and even boring, they do serve a good purpose. Parents should promote theater at school and all the family should attend the plays and pageants from preschool through college years. School theater encourages poise and participation as well as the skills of memorization and public speaking. It also introduces to young audiences the skills of sitting, watching, listening, learning, and appreciating.

❑ **460.** FAMILY PLAY READING. The library has excellent plays that you can borrow. When children read well, borrow a play, assign roles among family and friends, and have your own play-reading evening. While it is enjoyable to just read plays—from Euripides to Shakespeare to Neil Simon—this activity can be expanded by purchasing mystery play kits at a game store and having a party. These kits include ideas for the characters, certain lines of the script, clues, and even suggested refreshments for the intermission.

☐ **461.** THEATER LINGO. Explain to youngsters the difference between producer and director, and the meaning of these theater terms: plotting, prompters, blocking, flying scenery, On and Off Broadway, summer stock, tragedy versus comedy, Greek theater, Kabuki, Theater of the Absurd, and Theater-in-the-Round. Discuss the roles of famous actors such as Tallulah Bankhead, Helen Hayes, Sir Alec Guiness, Orson Welles, Sarah Bernhardt, Marlon Brando, and Katharine Hepburn. See who in the family can name a play written by these famous playwrights: Anton Chekhov, George M. Cohan, Sir Noel Coward, Gilbert and Sullivan, Lillian Hellman, Victor Hugo, W. Somerset Maugham, Arthur Miller, Harold Pinter, Thornton Wilder, and William Shakespeare. You'll find that this is a good education for you, too.

☐ **462.** TONGUE TWISTERS. Speaking in front of family and friends and not being shy or embarrassed is a good first step toward being able to speak in public. Parents and kids can take part in a weekly tongue twister event—perhaps at supper on Mondays—and see who really excels by the end of the week. Start with "Peter Piper," "She Sells Seashells," and "Theophilus Thistle." Be quick to laugh at your own mistakes.

SECTION 4: MEET YOU AT THE MOVIES

☐ **463.** KID MOVIES. Probably the first movie your child attends will be a movie made just for kids. Prepare your youngster by seeing that he is rested, fed, and has a cushion to sit on. If it is a classic, summarize the plot in a simple way. Reaffirm that it is a movie, not real life, and that if it is scary, he can shut his eyes. Take along a blanket in case he wants to curl up and sleep. After the movie, talk about what was funny, exciting, or interesting.

❑ **464.** AGE APPROPRIATE. Don't be pressured into letting your youngster attend movies that you don't approve of. If there's nothing appropriate to see, rent a video and pretend you're at the theater. Line up the chairs, darken the room, serve popcorn and sodas, and enjoy the show. Nowadays movies come out fairly quickly on video and you can save a lot of money by just being patient. As with a regular movie theater experience, talk about plot, characters, violence, stereotypes, and so forth when the movie is over.

❑ **465.** ART FILMS. By the time kids are preteens, introduce them to some of the fine classical films—those that may not be at the multiplex theater but rather at a small theater that shows art films. Pick ones with authors and actors who are respected. Encourage the reading of other books by the same authors.

❑ **466.** ACADEMY AWARDS. Create an interest in more than just the best films and actors. When the nomination list comes out, talk about all the various categories that will be honored. See as many of the films that you feel are appropriate for your youngsters. Then have a party on awards night—a simple dinner with friends of all ages who enjoy movies. Let the participants vote in all the categories and see who is the best at assessing greatness, then present awards of your own.

❑ **467.** BE A REVIEWER. Don't take a friend's word about what films to see. Read newspaper reviews for additional ideas. Some publications have a weekly listing of all movies with ratings plus comments on aspects of the movie that parents should be aware of (violence, sex, profanity). Make a thoughtful family decision rather than just choosing the movie with the biggest first-week viewership. When you and your kids have seen a movie you especially enjoyed, encourage others to go.

❑ **468.** LIGHTS, CAMERA, ACTION. Video cameras let everyone be part of a movie—writer, director, cinematographer, actor. Show kids how to use the camera and then encourage them to make a mini-production. You may have a future Spielberg under your roof!

SECTION 5: TAKE NOTE OF MUSIC

❑ **469.** BABIES LOVE MUSIC. Before kids know the difference between rock and Rachmaninoff, surround them with music. Play joyful music first thing in the morning. Play marches during play time. Play soothing music at naptime and bedtime. Sing to children and teach them to sing. When riding in the car, play music tapes they enjoy. And turn on the radio to a music station as background for conversation or snoozes. Easy-to-operate toddler cassette players make useful gifts.

❑ **470.** HOME INSTRUMENTS. Long before you consider buying a piano, let youngsters play with small instruments. Create a special bin so that all the instruments are readily available: cymbals, sticks, triangle, drum, harmonica, castanets, bells, and tambourines are a few that you can inexpensively buy. After showing how each are played, let kids accompany recorded music that has a good beat. Suggest they march to the music. Finally, encourage kids to make up songs to sing as they accompany themselves.

❑ **471.** INSTRUMENTS TO MAKE. Let kids make their own instruments and then record their music. Here are five they can make with a little help from you. *(1) SHAKERS.*

Pour one-quarter cup of dry beans into an empty container the size of a pint water bottle. Screw the cap on tightly and shake. *(2) RHYTHM STIX.* Cut the spoon end off of old wood utensils. Tie on a bright tassel for the end of each stick. Then show a child how to make rhythm by hitting the stix on a turned-over pie plate. *(3) BODY BELLS.* You can buy "jingle" bells cheaply at a craft store. String them on a pipe cleaner for wrist and ankle bells, attach them to a ribbon for waist bells. *(4) DRUMS.* Collect empty soup or vegetable cans, wash, remove labels, and let kids spray paint them. (Be sure there are no sharp edges.) Cut shelf paper or paper bags into circles and attach over the open end of the can with rubber bands. Use the eraser end of unsharpened pencils to beat out a rhythm. *(5) BOUNCING BUTTONS.* Help kids sew buttons to the tips of the five fingers of a glove. Show how to tap the finger buttons on the thumb button for a bouncy click.

❑ **472.** BOTTLE SCALE. Obtain eight identical bottles and place them in a row. Fill each one with water, using a small amount in the first, then more and more with the greatest amount in the eighth one. To make a music scale, start with the first bottle by blowing over it. Then, tune the second one a tone higher by adding or deleting water. Continue until you have do, re, mi, fa, sol, la, ti, and do.

❑ **473.** MUSIC LESSONS. Encouraged by a parent or the desire to play in the school band, a youngster may opt for lessons on a musical instrument. Within reason, let her choose her instrument, and consider renting it at first. The commitment should be for at least six months; after that time she can quit or choose another instrument. No matter what she chooses, she'll learn to read music. This exposure to music should be pleasant, not forced, but parents should be insistent on a specified amount of practice time. The entire family should attend programs and recitals.

❑ **474.** MUSIC WITH AN ATTITUDE. By the time kids are in school, they begin to form opinions about music styles. Be open to listening to various kinds of music as long as the words are not offensive. Have music with supper each night, taking turns playing favorite music. And since you listen politely to their music, kids will do the same for the music you choose. See that you have in your home collection at least one recording in each of many categories: symphonic, ballet, opera, musical comedy, choral music, dance music, rock, ballads, soul, country and western, reggae, and so forth.

❑ **475.** BANNED AT YOUR HOUSE. Let your kids know that they may not spend their money on music that has destructive values. In her book *Raising PG Kids in an X-Rated Society* (Nashville: Abingdon Press, 1988), Tipper Gore says: "We should be deeply concerned about the obvious cumulative effect of this cult of violence that has captured the public's imagination and pervaded our society. Few parents realize how much the angry brand of music that is part of it has presented suicide, glorified rape, and condoned murder. The message is more than repulsive—it's deadly." Let your youngsters know that you are just as concerned about the music they listen to as the television or movies they see.

❑ **476.** A SYMPHONY FULL OF INSTRUMENTS. Schools often have trips to hear a local symphony. Beforehand, find pictures of instruments in an encyclopedia and read a little about each. Encourage your youngster to listen for particular instruments: a harp, the tympani, glockenspiel, French horn, or double bass. Also introduce him to the protocol of reading the program notes, listening without conversation, and applauding at the end (not between movements).

❑ **477.** LISTEN FIRST. There are many symphonic pieces that will interest kids: the *1812 Overture*, which features cannons; *Grand Canyon Suite*, which makes grand musical pictures; *Peter and the Wolf*, which tells a story; and *Pictures at an Exhibition*. Other ones with special appeal are *The Sorcerer's Apprentice, Afternoon of a Fawn*, the *Alpine Symphony*, and *Also Sprach Zarathustra* (the theme used for *2001: A Space Odyssey*). You can borrow these from the library.

❏ **478.** WHO WROTE THIS STUFF? A cultured person is acquainted with the names of classical composers. From this brief list, let each youngster choose "her composer." Look up the name in the encyclopedia to find facts. Find among your own recordings (or borrow one) a composition by the composer and listen to it together. Some names are: Johann Sebastian Bach, Ludwig von Beethoven, George Bizet, Frederic Chopin, Claude Debussy, George Handel, Wolfgang Amadeus Mozart, Gioacchino Rossini, Jan Sibelius, Richard Strauss, Peter Ilich Tchaikovsky, Giuseppe Verdi, and Ralph Vaughan Williams.

❏ **479.** THE VOICE AS AN INSTRUMENT. See who in the family can sing the highest and the lowest notes. Explain the voice ranges (soprano, mezzo-soprano, contralto or alto, tenor, baritone, and bass). Encourage singing in the shower with high notes like chirping birds, and low tones like frogs. Using a dictionary, see who can define one of these vocal music terms: *a cappella,* aria, recitative, duet, *appoggiatura,* and *basso buffo.*

❏ **480.** FIRST MUSICAL. Classic musicals are always being revived on Broadway and in theaters across the country. Summertime is a great time to attend a musical comedy production. To help understand the words, listen to a cassette of the songs before attending. Musical comedies make good listening in the car, and you may hear some of the family singing right along. Encourage your school's music department to put on a popular musical and be sure to support it.

❏ **481.** FIRST OPERA. The majesty and pageantry of an opera production far outshines the opera plot. However, before taking a youngster to an opera, definitely read the plot and discuss the historical context. Tell what language it will be sung in. You may find that there is superscript (the words in English shown above the stage) and this is some help. Opera stars are often showcased on television, so look for these programs as an introduction to the opera world.

❑ **482.** MUSICAL TERMS IN DAILY LIFE. Painlessly introduce musical terms by incorporating them into family conversation. For instance, instead of saying "Come quickly," say *"allegro."* For slowly, use *"largo." "Con brio"* means with great liveliness. For "Speak loudly" (or softly), say *"forte (or sotto) voce."* To pick up toys, say *"vivace,"* which means with lively speed. When a child is about to take too large a helping of ice cream, say *"non troppo,"* meaning "not too much."

❑ **483.** DINNER MUSIC. It may not sound quite as lovely as the roving violinist in a fancy restaurant, but you can have your own dinner music at the table when eating is finished. Give out bells, kazoos, drums, spoons, and glasses so that each person has an instrument. Choose recorded or radio music with a lively beat. Let one person be the conductor and indicate when an instrument should be played and how fast or loud. This idea is also fun for an all-adult dinner party.

❑ **484.** SAW MUSIC. A single-handled carpenter's handsaw is now looked upon as a serious instrument. The saw has been played at elegant weddings and with symphony orchestras. This old-time music maker is one that you can introduce to a gradeschool youngster. With the saw handle between your knees, use one hand to flex the long blade (cutting side down) and the other hand to run a violin bow across it. With practice you can get various tones, even a scale. The music can be ear-assaulting or hauntingly beautiful.

❑ **485.** PATRIOTIC SONGS. While most youngsters know the national anthem, "The Star-Spangled Banner," use car time to teach other patriotic songs. Find them in song books and create your own song sheets. Learn these songs: "America," "America, the Beautiful," "God Bless America," "I'm a Yankee Doodle Dandy," "The Navy Hymn," and the songs or hymns of other military units. Tell kids that the word patriotism comes from the Greek word *patris,* meaning fatherland.

❑ **486.** FAVORITE HYMNS. Many hymns are common to all faiths. You will find these in hymnals, and many encyclopedias have the words that you can copy: "Abide with Me" by Henry Lyte and William Monk, "A Mighty Fortress Is Our God" by Martin Luther, "Blest Be the Tie that Binds" by John Fawcette, "Faith of Our Fathers" by Frederick Faber and James Walton, "Glorious Things of Thee Are Spoken" by John Newton (who also wrote "Amazing Grace") and Joseph Haydn, "Nearer My God to Thee" by Sarah Flower and Lowell Mason, "Onward, Christian Soldiers" by L. Sabine Baring-Gould and Sir Arthur Sullivan, "Rock of Ages" by Augustus Toplady and Thomas Hastings, and "The Battle Hymn of the Republic" by Julia Ward Howe. Many of these hymns have interesting stories with them and knowing the background will make them memorable.

❑ **487.** "MUSIC HATH CHARMS." That saying is overlooked by many schools who have weak or nonexistent music instruction. While bands and choral groups are popular, one of the most important school classes should be music appreciation. Don't let this education slip through the cracks—talk to the principal and superintendent at your youngster's school, write letters, attend meetings, and encourage the PTA to allot some of its funds to underwrite such a class.

SECTION 6: DANCING—WITH TWO LEFT FEET

❑ **488.** TODDLER TWO-STEP. As soon as a child can walk, show him how to move to music. He'll be happy to mimic you. Then take him in your arms and dance. Play dance music during his activities. When it's time to pick up toys, play fast music to encourage speed.

❑ **489.** FIRST LESSONS. While tiny ballerinas are adorable, don't start dance lessons too young and before muscles are ready to be stretched. About age five, consider dance lessons such as ballet or tap for both boys and girls. It's good training in being graceful and poised.

❑ **490.** THE DREADED COTILLION. Many youngsters learn from friends how to dance. But in order to really make your youngster a confident dancer, you may want to consider enrolling him in a cotillion—an organized dance class for boys and girls. These teach current dances plus how to waltz, fast-step, tango, and so forth. At the same time, they afford opportunities to learn the etiquette of dancing and to make friends. When the kids return home from each lesson, let them share what they learned with others in the family.

❑ **491.** FIRST BALLET. Since many kids think attending a ballet performance is going to be boring, start with something intriguing. A good first ballet is *The Nutcracker,* which is performed many places during the Christmas holidays. In some areas, local ballet students perform with the professional company. The ballet is usually shown on television, and seeing it there doesn't dim the excitement of the actual production. Children as young as three will find it fascinating to watch the live production—provided they've had a nap before attending.

❑ **492.** MORE THAN BALLET. Check your newspaper for dance programs at theaters and colleges that feature modern, jazz, or tap dancing. Choose one that has interest to your kids and go early enough to read the program. Exposing them to various kinds of dancing may intrigue them into wanting lessons.

❑ **493.** DANCING IN THE DARK. Parents often don't get time to dance together. Before a child's bedtime, turn the lights low and put on some of your favorite dance music. Let your youngster watch you dance together, then a parent can dance with a child, and finally, all three dance together.

SECTION 7: A WAY WITH WORDS

Speaking distinctly and correctly is one of the leading signs of a cultured person. Learning should start early and continue through the teen years when bad habits tend to creep in. Two good ways to promote correct speech are to speak accurately yourself and to encourage reading.

❑ **494.** NIX THE BABY TALK. Let the baby do baby talk, but parents should just smile at the cuteness and speak correctly. However, don't discourage early speech by correcting children. Certain mispronunciations often linger until first grade—don't emphasize them, they'll probably go away. Encourage young children to speak by listening to what they say and then asking questions that require more than a yes/no answer.

❑ **495.** DOES YOUR CHILD KNOW THE BASIC VOCAB-ULARY? Although "mommy" and "daddy" are usually the first words, beyond those is a basic vocabulary that if learned could make home a more peaceful and efficient place. These twenty-four words/phrases should not only be taught, but clearly understood: yes, no, maybe, please, thank you, now, later, today, tomorrow, come, sit, stop, help, ask, tell, share, give, follow, quiet, pick up, left, right, hello, good-bye. Kids who understand these few words are a joy to their teachers, too!

❑ **496.** SIX FAULTS YOU CAN CORRECT. Borrow a simple grammar book at the library and tackle these problems for your kids and yourself. *(1) Troublesome pronoun.* If you incorrectly say "Give the paper to Dad or I" (instead of me), you can expect your child to say "He and me want cookies" (instead of he and I). Go over the simple rules of pronouns as nouns or objects. *(2) Vile verbs.* Knowing the proper use of lie-lay, teach-learn, bring-take, says-said and others will increase kids' confidence in both writing and speaking. *(3) Non sequiturs or run-ons.* In Latin, non sequitur means "It does not follow." Children often think so rapidly that words spill out randomly, such as "I fell off my bike and when is supper?" Permitting this in speech will carry over into writing. *(4) Happy agreement.* The pronouns have to match. For example, "Each one took their cookie" (each one is singular and thus "their" should be "his" or "her"). Or, "Everyone must mind their manners," but since the pronoun "everyone" is singular, the possessive pronoun must be singular—as in the first example. *(5) Adverbs and adjectives—not the same.* Of course adjectives modify nouns and adverbs modify verbs telling how, where, when or to what degree. Thus it is correct to say, "That is a good story. She told it well!" "He walked slowly." "It was a slow day." *(6) Sound alikes.* Principle/principal, capital/capitol, counsel/council, who/whom/whose, and its and it's. Grab your dictionary and with your youngster look these up. Here's a start: "It's" is always the contraction of "It is." "Its" is always the possessive of "it" even though, unlike other possessives, it has no apostrophe.

❏ **497.** **OFTEN MISPRONOUNCED WORDS.** Start with "becuz" and "gotta" and "wanna." Sloppy speech in early years is hard to cure. Say "nuclear" instead of "nucular," and don't sound the "L" in calm, balm, Psalm, palm. And, remember that "both" means "the two" so never say "the both" (as in "the both of them were hungry), which would mean "the the two."

❏ **498.** **STREET SLANG.** Profanity, trash talk, and slang are words usually used to show anger or frustration, or to hurt. Often the words are meaningless on their own. Such inappropriate terms, originally used to shock or get attention, are unfortunately now so common they've lost even that value. Kids pick up these words from peers, but if a parent also uses them, the parent should unlearn them. An educated person doesn't need them, and parents should take a strong stand against their use. Help a child find real words—better words to express feelings.

❑ **499.** **PHRASES THAT HURT.** Talk about hurtful words: fatso, four-eyes, stupido, and so forth. Name-calling, as well as sarcasm, insisting on having the last word, muttering insults, and being officious ("Get out!" "Bring it!" "Shut up!") are all signs of a person's losing control. Show kids how to handle the frustrations that bring on these phrases and thus gain control. Play-act alternate ways of speaking when upset and calm ways of responding if these words are directed at you.

WORD FUN

❑ **500.** **BURIED WORDS.** A monster is going to bury all the words in the world except five. Everyone lists the words she wants to save, followed by a reason why that word is important. Then share the lists and see if any words appear on more than one list.

❑ **501.** **SOMERSAULTING WORDS.** Don't hesitate using colorful language with kids—practice at mealtimes and on car rides. Choose words that have unique sounds: whoosh, bumptious, smithereens, marshmallows, cantaloupe, gypsies, caterpillars, abracadabra, murmur, giraffes, curmudgeon, dillydally. Then, when kids know the meanings of the words, let them make up funny sentences such as "The curmudgeon hit the cantaloupe and smashed it to smithereens." "Caterpillars murmur for marshmallows."

❑ **502.** **RAMBLING STORY.** Someone writes a sentence to start the story and then passes the paper to the second person who adds another sentence. The paper is then folded down so only the second sentence shows. Others continue to add sentences, only seeing the preceding one. It makes a great story when read aloud.

❑ **503.** **A BIG DEAL.** Reading leads to good speaking. When your child is responsible enough to have her own library card, make it a special occasion. Talk about it in the days ahead. Make the trip one for just parent and child. Let her sign up for the card, borrow some books, and then go out to buy a special wallet or purse in which to keep it.

❑ **504.** **CHARACTER SWITCH.** Switch characters between books. For example, if you've read to a child the story of Pocahontas and the story of Cinderella, reread the story but put the other character into the title role. Does Cinderella lose a moccasin? Does Pocahontas stand up to her wicked stepsisters? The switch brings lots of conversation and laughter.

❑ **505.** **READ AND POINT.** Start word/picture associations when reading to young children. When you read the sentence "The dog came running" have your youngster point to the dog. Point to the "d" in dog and emphasize it as you say it. You're not teaching reading, but just the connection of the oral word with the written word and with the picture.

❑ **506.** **ANALYTICAL READING.** When a youngster has finished reading a book and has enjoyed it, talk about what made it special. Was it the exciting main character? the twisting plot? the description of the mysterious setting? the odd way a character spoke? Start when kids are young to analyze the importance of words in writing, as well as in everyday conversation, a politician's speech-making, school debates, and essay-type examinations.

❑ **507.** **TOP TWENTY GRADE SCHOOL CLASSICS.** Although *1001 Things to Do with Your Kids* listed many books youngsters should read, here's a list of what many consider the top twenty. See how many your kids have read.

The Adventures of Tom Sawyer	Samuel Clemens
Aesop's Fables	Aesop

Alice's Adventures in Wonderland	Lewis Carroll
Andersen's Fairy Tales	Hans Christian Andersen
Anne Frank: The Diary of a Young Girl	Anne Frank
Anne of Green Gables	Lucy Montgomery
The Arabian Nights' Entertainments	Andrew Lang, editor
A Christmas Carol	Charles Dickens
Don Quixote of La Mancha	Miguel de Cervantes Saavedra
Gulliver's Travels	Jonathan Swift
Heidi	Johanna Spyri
Just So Stories	Rudyard Kipling
Little House in the Big Woods	Laura Wilder
The Little Prince	Antoine de Saint-Exupery
The Phantom Tollbooth	Norton Juster
Pinocchio: The Adventures of a Little Wooden Boy	Carlo Collodi
Tales from Shakespeare	Charles and Mary Lamb
Treasure Island	Robert Louis Stevenson
The Wind in the Willows	Kenneth Grahame
Wizard of Oz	L. F. Baum

❏ **508.** **TOP TWENTY HIGH SCHOOL CLASSICS.** How many of these great books has your teen read?

The Age of Innocence	Edith Wharton
All Quiet on the Western Front	Erich Maria Remarque
The Ambassadors	Henry James
Babbitt	Sinclair Lewis
The Bridge of San Luis Rey	Thornton Wilder
Emma	Jane Austen
Ethan Frome	Edith Wharton
The First Circle	Aleksandr Solzhenitsyn
For Whom the Bell Tolls	Ernest Hemingway
The Forsyte Saga	John Galsworthy
The Great Gatsby	F. Scott Fitzgerald
Human Comedy	William Saroyan
Les Miserables	Victor Hugo
Look Homeward, Angel	Thomas Wolfe

Moby Dick	Herman Melville
My Antonia	Willa Cather
1984	George Orwell
A Passage to India	E. M. Forster
Sons and Lovers	D. H. Lawrence
Vanity Fair	William Thackeray

❑ **509.** **BUILD A LIBRARY.** Some books are worth keeping forever, even though they've been read many times. Start a library shelf for each child. Add to it by buying good books at a garage sale or getting hand-me-downs from friends. As kids get older, box up some of their favorites to keep for their own children.

❑ **510.** **CHAPTER BOOKS.** While it is easy to whip through a quantity of kiddie books, when a child enters kindergarten, consider starting on books with chapters. This has many benefits for kids up to about age eight (when they often prefer to read on their own). First, it is a continuing story from night to night—something eagerly looked forward to as the plot develops. Second, just one chapter book usually has as much reading value as a few dozen kiddie books, so you save money, and bookshelf space, too. Third, you're reading good classical literature (such as Laura Ingalls Wilder's *Little House* series or *Little Britches* by Ralph Moody). Chapter books often tell of good times in the past and are historically interesting as well as entertaining.

❑ **511.** **THE BOOK BUNCH.** In a neighborhood of grade school kids, parents can take turns driving the weekly library trip with several young readers. The library often has a week night or Saturday story hour, kid-friendly computers, and a thick-carpeted room for lounging and reading. One parent can set up the schedule for the "Book Bunch," which means that a parent only drives once a month, allowing the other parents special time with their other kids or spouse.

❑ **512.** POETRY POSSIBILITIES. In poetry, each word is carefully selected to create the mind-picture as well as the rhythm or rhyme. Include poetry reading as part of your youngster's education in words. A good basic book to borrow or buy is *The Oxford Book of American Light Verse,* edited by William Hamon (New York: Oxford Univ. Press, 1979). You'll find the full poem of "Take Me Out to the Ball Game" by Jack Norworth, songs by Oscar Hammerstein and Cole Porter, "The Village Blacksmith" by Henry Wadsworth Longfellow, as well as "A Visit from Saint Nicholas" by Clement Moore.

❑ **513.** SILLY STORY. Ask kids to suggest adjectives (descriptive words) that you will write as a list of about twenty—words like silly, crummy, sloppy, yummy, darling. Next, take a simple story that a child can read (*Red Riding Hood* or *Goldilocks and the Three Bears*) and ask the youngster to pause before each noun (a person, place, or thing). At that point, you'll read the first word on your list. So, the story becomes: "One day (silly) Red Riding Hood put on her (crummy) coat and took a (sloppy) basket of (yummy) food to (darling) Grandma."

❑ **514.** THE BOOKWORM. Encourage reading year-round by helping each child make a bookworm. The worm is composed of links of construction paper with a large piece at the beginning showing the worm's smiling face. When the first book is finished, the youngster writes the book name on a link and attaches it to the head. Then as more books are read and links are made, the worm gets longer and longer. Soon it will be so long that it can be hung from a curtain rod, strung across the breakfast nook, or cascaded down the stair railing. With several children there can be several worms. Young children will get a link for each book, gradeschoolers who read chapter books will get one for each chapter or twenty pages.

❑ **515.** PHOTO-JOURNALIST. Look through your latest snapshots and choose ten to be laid out on a table. Give family members paper and pencil and invite them to study the pictures and then write a fictional story about them. You'll be surprised how creative and unique each story is.

❑ **516.** **DEAR AUTHOR.** When a youngster has particularly enjoyed a book, encourage her to write a letter to the author, in care of the publisher shown in the front of the book. She should tell specifically why the book appealed to her. Most authors will respond, and a letter from a "real" author will be treasured.

SEVEN
LET'S GET TOGETHER

SECTION 1: BUILDING MEMORIES TOGETHER

SECTION 2: PARTY TIME!

SECTION 3: GETTING TOGETHER WITH GRANDPARENTS

SECTION 1:
BUILDING MEMORIES TOGETHER

It doesn't take money to build family memories. It's often the little things that count—little things that are fun and loving—and will probably be passed down to the next generation.

❏ **517.** MY HOW YOU'VE GROWN! Once a year, on a memorable date such as New Year's Day, measure the height of each family member. You'll need a painted one-by-four piece of lumber that is seven feet in length. Start by writing on it the length in inches when a baby is born. Then, measure each year and put the date by the height. Parents should be measured, too. Keep your height gauge in the family room, nailed to a door frame so it can be easily removed if you move.

❏ **518.** THE FAMILY BANNER. With input from all family members, design your own family flag that can fly outside your door or on a backyard pole. You'll need a piece of sturdy fabric and indelible fabric markers to draw objects or faces, or to make a design. Kids like the flag flown for a birthday or when friends are invited over. It can also be taken to the park or beach to identify your family's area.

❏ **519.** TIME CAPSULE. Plan a family party to prepare and bury a family time capsule to be dug up in ten years. Ask relatives and good friends to bring personal items, newspapers, and photos to share. In advance, help kids dig a hole and obtain a sturdy metal or plastic container. Each person tells about his item for the capsule as someone takes a video to record the event. Finally the capsule is wrapped in plastic and buried. Be sure to mark the location with a rock or stake. And remember to have a party ten years later to dig it up!

❏ **520.** YOU'VE COME A LONG WAY BABY! Each year, make part of a quilt for a youngster's sixteenth birthday celebration. It will consist of large squares of fabric, four panels across and four down. Make just one panel each year, decorating it with something symbolic of that year. The first year might be a teddy bear, the second year a swing, and so forth. Just before the birthday, add the sixteenth panel, the filling, and backing. It makes a memorable gift that a youngster can hang on a wall, cuddle up with, or save for his own child.

❑ **521.** LITTLE SURPRISES. Many families build memories around traditions that seem fairly insignificant. One family has a special tray that food is served on when a child isn't feeling well and must eat in bed. Another warms a big bath towel for the birthday person's use. A son occasionally puts a flower on his mom's computer. Another family is known for April Fool's Day pranks. Another has a once-a-year totally-backward-meal-day—steak for breakfast and pancakes for supper. And for a family living in a warm and humid climate, a happy tradition is putting clothing in the freezer overnight for a refreshing start of the day!

❑ **522.** HAND PRINTS IN CEMENT. When you move into a new home or are remodeling a house, there may be wet cement. (If not, get a bag of ready-mix.) Before the cement dries, let each family member put his hand print in the cement (the dog can make a paw print). Then write the name under each print and date your masterpiece. As years pass, it's fun to see how hands grow!

❑ **523.** FIFTH SUNDAY. Make a holiday (no work, all fun) on the four days a year that are fifth Sundays. Mark the date on the calendar well in advance and plan to do something unique—something no one in the family has done before. If you need suggestions, the weekend editions of the newspaper or a travel book from the auto club will give you ideas for local events and destinations you may never have heard of.

❑ **524.** SAME PLACE, DIFFERENT TIME. Each year, take

a family portrait (ask a friend to take the photo) in the same place. Choose the front door, the fireplace, by a tree, or by the family car. Be sure that family members are in the same place in each photo to permit easy comparison as the years pass.

❑ **525.** NAME THE HOUSE. Each home has some distinctive feature that can be used in giving the house a name. Have a contest to select a name for your house (Mountain View, Pink Palace, Remodeler's Dream, Hunter's Hideaway, Smith's Retreat). Consider putting a sign on the house with the name, or using the name on computer-made stationery.

❑ **526.** MY BUDDIES. What fun to look back at photos of childhood chums! When your youngsters—toddlers to teens—are together with their friends, take plenty of candid shots, but also have kids pose so you can get a good picture of each face.

❑ **527.** TWO FOR ONE. When getting family photos developed, take the double print option. Let each youngster keep her own photo album while the parent keeps the family album. Divide the photos—one set for the family album, the others among the kids. Together relive the events while you fill the albums. Don't forget to put a date and place on each page and identify nonfamily members.

❑ **528.** MY HOUSE, MY ROOM. In the autumn, just before school starts, let kids try on their new school clothes. Then, take a picture of them in their bedroom and another on their bike in front of the house. It will be interesting to see how the house, the room, and the child changes each year.

❑ **529.** MEMORABLE TREAT. Enlist the help of grandparents who may have enjoyed a taffy pull in their youth. One family makes it a yearly summer tradition, now enjoyed by the fourth generation. Here's their recipe:

TAFFY

1½ cups sugar	2 tablespoons butter
¾ cup light corn syrup	2 teaspoons lemon juice
⅔ cup water	4 drops of yellow food
½ teaspoon salt	coloring
1 teaspoon vegetable	
glycerine (found at a health food store)	

In a large pan, combine the first five ingredients and mix well. Then cook and stir, removing it from the heat when a candy thermometer reads 250 degrees. Now, stir in the butter and coloring and pour onto a greased flat pan. So that the edges don't harden, occasionally use a metal spatula to fold over the sides until the mixture is cool enough to touch. Then brush on the lemon juice. Now it's time to butter hands and gently stretch the taffy until it is elastic. At this point you can actually pull it into a rope. When the pulling fun is over, cut the rope into small pieces for munching.

❑ **530. MEALTIME MEMORIES.** When the family eats together regularly, meals can be one of the prime memory building times. Monthly (or on a regular basis), inquire about what mealtime events were the most fun. It may be the meal where the kids planned the food, or the night when awards were given for doing chores that month, or when everyone came in costume. Or, it may have been "Bad Manners Night" when everyone tried to break the rules of mealtime etiquette without being noticed. Perhaps it was when the final chapter of an exciting book was read. (You'll find more on this topic in *1001 Things to Do with Your Kids*, ideas #68 through #81.)

❑ **531. HUNTING TRADITIONS.** Don't let the Easter egg hunt be your only hunt. Make happy memories by creating various occasions for a hunt: at a birthday, always hide one gift and let the receiver find it by searching for it as others give "hot," "warm," "cold," or "freezing" comments; at Halloween have an in-the-house hunt for candy as an alternative to the door-to-door method; at Christmas when there is an unwrappable gift such as a bicycle, create clues that lead to the gift. For sandbox fun, bury biodegradable packing popcorn and give a prize for the first child finding twenty-five of them.

❑ **532.** BABYHOOD PRESERVED. Set aside one of your baby's special little outfits plus a soft toy or small rattle. Make a copy of the birth certificate and select one or more baby photos. When the child is about five, work with her to make a memory box. At a frame shop, buy a deep frame that will accommodate and protect the items (some even come with Velcro to affix the elements to the backing). Make a pleasing arrangement with the certificate or announcement in the back, photos, clothing, and so forth on top. Use glue or Velcro to hold it to the backing, then finish the framing. When the youngster moves to her own home, let her take her memento frame as a reminder of her babyhood.

❑ **533.** MORNING GREETING. Start the tradition of a unique greeting and encourage the phrase to be the first words exchanged each morning. It can be "good morning" in another language such as *"bonjour"* (French), or "Up and at 'em" said with a high five.

❑ **534.** JOKATHON. Family reunions can be very nostalgic. Add humor to large gatherings of relatives by having a joke contest. Let folks know in advance that there will be prizes for the funniest story. Help your children practice their joke-telling skills so they can compete.

❑ **535.** BIRTHDAY BREAKFAST IN BED. Even if it's a school day, have everyone gather in the bedroom of the celebrant for cereal and a cupcake with a candle on it. The cake can come at dinnertime, but this tradition starts the day right.

❑ **536.** IF THEY WRITE A BOOK ABOUT YOU . . . Who knows which family members will become famous! Help future biographers by keeping a family diary. It can be as simple as a loose-leaf notebook kept at the dinner table. The first person finished eating can note highlights of the day or week. Just a few lines written regularly provide an interesting resource.

❑ **537.** ELECTION PARTICIPATION. Let kids have memories of your regular participation in local and national elections. Include them by sharing the sample ballot, reading some of the propositions together, and deciding on how "the family" should vote. And, let a youngster go to the polls with you so he can see how the system works. Make election day a special day by having dinner in front of the TV and watching the early returns.

❑ **538.** CHRISTMAS MANGER. A wonderful Christmas memory is the assembling of the family crèche, little by little, on the Sundays before Christmas. Start the first week of December by reading the story of Mary and Joseph and let kids place those figures in the scene. The next week read about the shepherds, and let the kids add them. Next, read about the kings, and put them in place. On Christmas Eve, read about the birth in the manger and place the animals and baby Jesus.

SECTION 2: PARTY TIME!

Be original and help your youngster plan a really interesting birthday party right at home, rather than at some restaurant or expensive amusement center. If you love parties, you'll want to read my book *The Family Party Book* (Nashville: Abingdon Press, 1996), which will give you hundreds of ideas for parties, games, prizes, and foods—for children, teens, and adults, as well as for reunions. The party themes described below are given in detail in the book. Here are highlights from that book as well as some new ideas.

❑ **539.** THEMES FOR PRESCHOOLERS. This age loves make-believe so plan a party with your child that has some magic to it and lets a child use her imagination. Possibilities are: Pirate Party, Dress-Up Tea Party, Mother Goose Party, Teddy Bear Picnic, Snowball Party, Artist Party, Princess Party, Animal Party, Circus Party, Fairy Tale Party, Train Party, Ballerina Party, and Wizard of Oz Party.

❑ **540.** THEMES FOR GRADESCHOOL PARTIES. These more active parties will be winners: Safari Party, Olympics Party, Clown College, Make a TV Show (video) Party, Old MacDonald's Party, Western Party, Penguin Pool Party, Hobo Party, Mall Party, Castle and Kings Party, Dinosaur Day, Space Mission, Cowboy Round Up, and Let's Go Fishing Party.

❑ **541.** THEMES FOR TEEN PARTIES. These themes provide opportunities for conversation, music, and dancing: Karaoke Party, Time Capsule Party, Pancake Party, Wild and Wet Party, Sweet Sixteen Party, Schools Out Party, Backward Progressive Dinner, Baked Potato Supper, Full Moon Dance, Pentathlon Party (described below), and South Sea Island Party.

❑ **542.** TWO GENERATION PARTY. It's a pentathlon—five different games in one night. Divide the guests into teams of two and make a scoreboard to keep up-to-date on winners. First place gets ten points, second is seven points, third is four points, and the other teams get one point for participating. Some games will require both on the team to play, some just one playing and one as coach. Each game is played for twenty minutes, then a break for sports snacks and sodas, then rotate to the next game. Choose five games from this list: Jenga or pickup sticks, Velcro ball, Scrabble, golf putting into a circle of string, dominoes, darts, Monopoly, hearts, Ping-Pong, or checkers.

❑ **543.** HOLIDAY PARTIES KIDS LOVE. Plan holiday celebrations with your youngsters and include other families. Some occasions and parties are: New Year's Day—Resolution and Football Party; Valentine's Day—Candy-making Party; St. Patrick's Day—Irish Supper Party; April Fool's Day—Pranks Party; Easter—Neighborhood Egg Hunt; Mother's Day and Father's Day—Surprise Parties; Independence Day—Old-Fashioned Picnic and Games Party; Halloween—Hayride and Square Dance Party; Thanksgiving—Potluck Party; and Christmas—Caroling Party.

❑ **544.** A BACKWARD PARTY. Send invitations that are written backward (it's easy if you write it out first and then copy each word from the end to the start). Ask guests to come with their clothes on backward. Serve the birthday cake first, then open packages, then have the other food, and end up with games done in a backward way (run an obstacle course or relay race backward, or play the Ballooney Sandwich game described below). End the party with each guest backing out the door.

❑ **545.** WELCOME TO THE NEIGHBORHOOD. Get to know new neighbors at a weekend barbecue/potluck party. On cardboard, make a large drawing of the neighborhood, showing where everyone lives. Provide name tags that also list hobbies or careers. Let your youngsters plan outdoor relays for everyone and some for kids only.

❑ **546.** GRADESCHOOL GRADUATION PARTY. Guests come dressed as kindergartners in ruffly dresses or short pants, hair bows or slicked down hair, and carrying lollipops. Play little kids games such as "Mother, May I" or "Simon Says." If possible, contact school friends before the party and videotape each of them telling a unique but true story about one of the graduates. Play the video at the end of the party.

❑ **547.** HIGH SCHOOL AND COLLEGE GRADUATION PARTIES. The theme can be "Welcome to the Real World." Invite friends and relatives for a sit-down meal of steak and beans—symbolic of the feast-or-famine days ahead. From old slides and photos, prepare a video production called "This Is Your Crazy Life." Gifts should be useful in the real world the grad is entering: cookbook, alarm clock, bus pass, tie, appointment book, downtown area map, quick energy bars, a broom, and so forth.

❑ **548.** SPARE GIFT. Don't get flustered if your youngster gets a sudden invitation to a birthday party. Keep a unisex gift on hand, such as a game. Always let your youngster, if over age five, do the wrapping and card writing, and if under five, do it together.

❑ **549.** PARTY GIFT FAVORITES. A recent survey showed these toys as the top ten favorites of younger children: kitchens and kitchen dishes and foods, small racing cars, a working watch, hop ball, small Barbie-type doll or action figure with clothes and equipment, sleeping bag, set of wild animals, telephone, Etch-a-Sketch, and easel with paper and paints. When visiting a toy store, look at these items and ask your kids how they rank on their own wish lists.

❑ **550.** A UNIQUE GIFT. A memorable gift for child or adult is an American flag. You'll find them in a wide range of prices at a flag store (listed in the yellow pages under "flags"). You can also buy a flag of a person's native country. Include a pole and wall bracket, along with a booklet on flag protocol. As you wrap the gift, talk with your child about flag history, and look it up in the encyclopedia if you don't have all the answers.

GAMES

❑ **551.** CAPTAIN HOOK. Mark out the boundaries of a large rectangular play area and choose one player to be Captain Hook. He stands in the middle of the play area with other players inside the boundaries. On the word "Go," Hook chases any player and attempts to tag him with one hand. A tagged player hooks (holds) onto Captain

Hook's hand and they continue to tag other players using only their free hands. As tagged players are added to the two ends of the line, all must be sure to hold hands at all times. Players may not run through the line of hooked-together players or outside the boundaries. The last player to be tagged becomes Captain Hook for the next game.

❑ **552.** SONG STUMPERS. While having refreshments, encourage kids to call out the name of a song and see who can be the first to sing the opening line. This is fun when several generations are playing together.

❑ **553.** WEIRD WORDS. Give each guest a small card on which is written an unusual word (keyed to the age of the group) such as clumsy, dribbled, crimson, stingy, bionic, bagpipes, superfluous, dilapidated, statuesque, medicinal, bothersome, ticklish. The object is to work the word into the conversation without it being noticed. After about thirty minutes, have each person reveal their weird word and when (or if) they used it.

❑ **554.** TELL THE TRUTH. With a group of twelve or more, each person writes down something that no one else knows about him. These papers are put in a bowl and then each person selects one. Going around the circle, the person reads the statement and gets one guess as to who has written it. For example, a guest says "Molly, are you the person who climbed in the fountain by the court house?" If it's not Molly, the game moves to the next person who reads the statement he has and tries to guess who wrote it. Sometimes you'll go around the circle several times but as the field of possibilities shrinks, guesses are finally correct.

❑ **555.** PENNY HUNT. In the yard, scatter one hundred pennies. Give a bag to each child and see who can find the most in five minutes. Count up the pennies and if it does not total one hundred, send the hunters out once more. They get to keep what they find.

❑ **556.** **TUNNEL RACES.** At a fabric store, buy a twelve-foot length of stretchy black tube material (usually seamless jersey), an investment that will last for years. Play relay races through it, or make teams of a parent and child going opposite directions and having to pass each other inside the tunnel. It helps if an adult holds each end of the tube.

❑ **557.** **BALLOONEY SANDWICH.** Make a start and a finish line and blow up a number of large balloons. Pair off into teams of two (one adult and one child or two kids). The pairs make a ballooney sandwich by standing back-to-back with a balloon between them. They must keep the balloon off the floor, not using their hands or holding hands, as they shuffle from start to finish. Dropping or popping a balloon means they start over.

❑ **558.** **BE A STAR.** Hand prints in cement are a big attraction in Hollywood as they will be at your party. Have as many large cardboard boxes as guests. Cut the box sides down to about the three inch point. Line up the boxes on the patio or grass. Get bags of ready-mix quick setting cement and prepare according to the instructions. Put it in the boxes (about two inches deep) so that it is still wet when the party begins. As guests arrive, have a spotlight on the boxes and ask the "stars" to make a hand print and sign their name for posterity. These boxes of cement will set up sufficiently so that the guests can take them home at the end of the party.

❑ **559.** **HUMAN CONVEYOR BELT.** At least eight youngsters lie down on carpet or grass, close together side-by-side and face up. At the command "Go," they turn together to the left, then roll face down, then continue the same direction until face up, all the time remaining tight to the person next to them. Practice this until they can do it without separating from the youngsters next to them. Now load the conveyor belt with human cargo. One child lies down at one end across the other bodies. As the kids now begin to roll, the "cargo" moves along the belt until deposited at the other end. Let everyone have a chance to be the "cargo."

560. **STRING MAZE.** This is fun for kids only or kids and adults. In advance, lay one string from the doorway of a room, under and around furniture to a hidden place. Tie a candy bar or prize to the end of the string. Do the same thing again, starting at the doorway and going a different direction but crossing the first string. Continue with new strings until you have one for each player. Then the group gathers at the door where each is given a string and told that she may not let go of it under any circumstances. However, she must carefully wind up the string and find the prize at the end. There will be lots of climbing under and over strings, a lot of laughing, and a few arguments over who is making a hopeless knot.

561. **"I WENT TO THE MALL."** Ten guests sit in a circle and each is given a slip of paper with one word or phrase written on it. These are the words to be handed out in this order: fan, rocker, scissors, sewing machine, tight shoe, itchy new shirt, horse, sunglasses, perfume, and cuckoo clock. The first person begins by saying, "I went to the mall and I bought a fan" and he starts fanning himself. All the others must also fan themselves. The second person says, "I went to the mall and bought a fan and a rocking chair." She starts rocking **AND** fanning as do all the others. So it goes around the circle, each one adding their purchase and indicating their motion: fan with the left hand, rock the entire body, cut with the right hand, sew using the left foot, tap the floor with the right foot, squirm shoulders because of the itchy shirt, move up and down like a horse, blink because of the sun, sniff perfume, and say "cuckoo-cuckoo." It sounds silly, looks silly, but it is possible!

562. **THE COACH'S NIGHTMARE.** Prepare for a simple basketball game in a gym, backyard, or driveway with a basketball hoop. Announce that there will be two teams—girls versus guys. The girls will be dressed normally. However, provide the guys with their basketball outfits: women's long dresses, high heels, and boxing gloves (or have each one tie one hand behind his back). Get the clothes at a thrift shop. The game will be a nightmare, but a funny one.

❑ **563.** EGGPLANT EXTRAVAGANZA. This relay race, which can be played indoors or out, will need a start and finish line, two poles or yardsticks, and two similar eggplants. Divide the group into two teams. The object is to start at the line and use the yardstick to push the eggplant to the finish line where the next team member takes over. It sounds easy, but participants soon find that when it comes to rolling, an eggplant has a mind of its own.

PARTY FOOD

❑ **564.** FEEDING YOUNG KIDS. Keep young children involved in preparing the party food. A bakery (or your home bread machine) can make bread in bright colors, resulting in intriguing sandwiches. Another hearty dish is a pig in a blanket—a hot dog wound in refrigerated crescent dough (with a little catsup and cheese inside) and baked. Skewered fruit chunks can be assembled by kids. Forget plates and serve food in baskets. Sprinkles are a favorite and can be used on ice cream, cake, and even hot dogs.

❑ **565.** EATS FOR GRADESCHOOLERS. Let kids assemble their own submarine sandwiches. For dessert, make clown cones by scooping a ball of ice cream and adding coconut hair, candy eyes, cherry nose, and an orange segment mouth. Freeze the ice cream until very hard, and top with a pointed cone just before serving. Make a cake look like a train by cutting a sheet cake into rectangular sections, frosting these, piping on windows and doors, and decorating with candies and licorice for the smokestack and other details. For a safari party, find canteens and backpacks at an army surplus store and use them to hold buffalo burgers and jungle juice.

❑ **566.** HEARTY FOODS FOR TEENS. Pancakes with many toppings (fruits, nuts, syrups, ice cream, yogurt, chocolate chips, marshmallow creme, whipped cream) provide opportunities for fun. Make-your-own pizzas can work in a similar way. Provide an interesting nonalcoholic punch bowl with this make-ahead recipe: For each gallon of apple juice, add one quart of milk, one-fourth teaspoon nutmeg, a half teaspoon of cinnamon, and two teaspoons of vanilla. For serving, pour it in a punch bowl and (again for each gallon) stir in a twelve ounce container of whipped topping. They'll love it!

❑ **567.** **CAKES WITH CHARACTER.** Have older children prepare, bake, and frost a cake. Then, let them start the tradition of placing a nut in it (even if you buy a cake, tuck one pecan between the layers). The person who finds the pecan gets a little prize. Other traditional items to hide and find in cakes are a ring (the finder is the next to be married), a penny (the finder will receive unexpected money soon), and a yellow button (the finder might get kissed under the next full moon). For cakes (except birthday cakes), make them look beautiful by decorating them with edible (nonpoisonous) flowers that you have rinsed and dried. Let kids use geranium leaves with nasturtiums, daisies, or snapdragons. Or, make a candy-decorated cake with small pieces of candy in the filling and others arranged on top.

SECTION 3: GETTING TOGETHER WITH GRANDPARENTS

Don't let get-togethers with relatives consist only of big meals with adult conversation. Provide opportunities for youngsters to interact with grandparents and others. You'll find many ideas in my book *The Ten Commandments for Grandparents* (Nashville: Abingdon Press, 1991).

❑ **568.** **ONE-ON-ONE.** Encourage a grandparent to have an activity with just one youngster at a time. It can be an overnight, a trip to the ball game, a shopping excursion, or picking and arranging flowers. When two are together there are wonderful opportunities for both fun and bonding.

❑ **569.** FAMILY HISTORY. Provide time for your youngster to work on a family tree with a grandparent. Make it a family photo tree, showing each name and if possible, a picture. (You may have to write and ask relatives for their photos.) Or, work together to record a family audio history or make a photo album from pictures that have been long stored in a shoe box. Let grandparents take kids to see the grandparents' old neighborhood—the house they lived in, where they went to school, where they worked—and have lunch in a restaurant where they used to eat.

❑ **570.** PHONE VISITS. Let a youngster make the weekly phone call to a relative. But first, make a list together of things to share—from school and play, or from parent's work, and activities. It gives the relative a different perspective from your usual call.

❑ **571.** GOSSIP AND TRUTH. Kids hear stories about relatives—some true, some not. Find something especially good about each relative and tell your youngster. When you plan to be with relatives, encourage kids to ask them about their youth, work, family, and traditions. Even though some relatives may have more "sterling" character traits than others, let your youngsters make up their own minds about relatives.

❑ **572.** TRADITIONS. Ask your preteen what "firsts" are important: first earrings, first long dress, first car, or a first communion or bar mitzvah. Then, talk with a grandparent about being a part of the tradition. Some will want to buy that long dress, contribute 50 percent of the cost of the used car purchase, or take part in the religious event. It's an important link between the generations.

❑ **573.** ROUND-ROBIN. When youngsters are old enough to write good letters, show them how to start a round-robin letter among cousins and other relatives. Four to six is an ideal number. (Each participant will write a letter and perhaps include a photo, then send it off to the next who will add her letter and send it on.) Help make a list that includes the order the letter is to go, and the address of each participant. See how long it takes for the letters to come back.

❏ **574.** REUNIONS. Great memories for kids come from family reunions. Gradeschool and high school youngsters can help plan the get-together, whether it's one dinner or a long weekend. Let one youngster set up a mailing list on the computer. Another can plan kids' games and adult/kid relay races. Everyone coming brings a dish for the meal. For everything you need to know about big reunions see *The Family Party Book* (Nashville: Abingdon Press, 1996).

❏ **575.** STORYTELLING. Encourage grandparents to tell family history stories to kids—they can be even more exciting than fiction! A globe or old photos can be used as props. Stories of life in another country, life during a war, or life without television can be quite fascinating. Kids also enjoy stories told about olden times. Let the grandparent name the stories: "The Legend of the Lost Brother" or "Why Sparky the Dog Got His Picture Taken." These stories can also be told on audio cassettes and sent by grandparents to faraway grandchildren.

❏ **576.** BEDTIME STORIES. A grandparent who is a good storyteller can record tales for toddlers to listen to as they fall asleep. One grandmother has alternated familiar kiddie songs with stories and poems. While not ready for prime time, she is a star to her grandchild.

❏ **577.** TALENT SHARING. Initiate a conversation among you, your children, and your parents to see what talents of interest to kids can be shared by the grandparents. Here are some: how to drive a car, enjoying the outdoors, cooking and baking, auto repair, photography, sewing and knitting, painting, workshop projects, computer, sports, music and dance lessons, and religious training. You may be willing and thankful to let the grandparents completely take over one or more of these activities.

❑ **578.** A VERY SPECIAL TRIP. One of the nicest and most memorable connections between grandparent and child is a special trip, often in honor of a youngster's twelfth birthday. Ask your parents if they would enjoy doing this for each child, and if so, have them prepare a list of possible trips for the child to choose from. (The choices could be a sailboat trip, a weekend at Disneyland, a visit to the Grand Canyon, a trip to Hawaii, or even the grand tour of Europe.) Help the youngster make the choice well in advance so there is plenty of time for anticipation. Prior to the trip, spend ample time talking together about sight-seeing, foods, clothes, manners, souvenirs, and the keeping of a journal.

❑ **579.** GRANDMA'S CAMP. Busy parents are happy to support this idea. Overnight at Grandma's Camp takes on a special flair since it takes place under the stars. (But if the weather changes, it can still be in sleeping bags in the living room.) Food is cooked outside, served in a mess kit, and breakfast is always blueberry pancakes.

❑ **580.** GRANDPA'S SECRET GARDEN. One grandchild is taken in on the conspiracy to plant a mysterious garden with Grandpa. Together they buy seeds, prepare the soil, plant, cultivate, weed, and eventually harvest. No one else knows what has been planted until it blooms or produces.

I LIKE . . . YOU LIKE

Exchanges of gifts between grandparents and kids can be boring—or memorable. (Grandparents who don't really take the time and make the effort to know youngsters just send a check. In turn, kids often give grandparents whatever their folks buy.) Change this impersonal approach by helping kids find out the things their grandparents enjoy (gardening magazines, tools, candy and nuts, card games, a football team, sweaters) and then shop with them for a gift that ties in. Help grandparents learn the interests of their grandchildren (books, trucks, video games, cycling, birds, doll houses, sewing, CDs, sports team caps) so that they can choose gifts with appeal.

581. GRANDPARENTS DAY. Of course there can be gifts and a dinner for this holiday that is the second Sunday in September. But when grandparents are not nearby, kids can prepare a very special memory. Each grandchild fills out a paper headed "Ten Extraordinary, Marvelous, Wonderful, Fabulous Things About My Grandparents." Illustrate the list with drawings and mail to arrive on time. The grandparents will read and reread them, maybe even frame them—and certainly feel loved.

582. THE PINK GRANDMA. Let young children do their own gift shopping as much as possible. Be handy for guidance, but respect a child's choices and help him stick within his budget by shopping at a 99 Cent Store. One young boy wanted only pink gifts since he knew that was Grandma's favorite color. His mother turned him loose with his five dollars and this is what he bought: a pink fly swatter, a pink dust pan, pink nail polish, a pink guardian angel pin, and his favorite choice, which he named "the most beautiful gift," a glistening pinkish/copper colored scrubbing pad. Grandma especially enjoys cleaning with it!

583. FINGER FOOD FUN. Surprise grandparents by having a meal without silverware. Everything served is to be eaten with fingers. Let kids help plan the foods that can include: chicken, pizza, kebabs, spareribs, fried shrimp, fried potatoes, carrot sticks, corn on the cob, apple slices, melon balls, cookies, brownies, and ice-cream cones.

584. GRANDMA SAYS . . . that you can tell much about a person by looking at their hands. That's why she gives each grandchild, at about age four, three grooming tools: a small nail brush for scrubbing the undersides of nails, an emery board for smoothing rough nails, and a nail whitener pencil. She demonstrates the use of each and knows that because they have their very own, they will get used more often—especially when she's coming to inspect. With your kids, look at one another's hands and see if they would pass inspection.

❏ **585.** **FABULOUS FRAMES.** Let kids make picture frames for gifts to grandparents. And, of course, kids will put their own pictures inside these frames made of cardboard. At a stationery supply store, get the sturdiest cardboard available. Using the photo as a size guide, a parent cuts two pieces of cardboard two inches larger all around than the photo. Then cut an opening in one piece a half inch smaller than the photo. Now the youngster is ready to decorate this second piece with paint, ribbons, pennies, shells, buttons, or puzzle pieces glued to the frame. Next, tape the photo in place on the backside and add the second piece of cardboard as a backing. A small easel can be made of the excess cardboard.

❏ **586.** **FOR SOMEONE WHO HAS EVERYTHING.** One gift that kids can give is the gift of love and appreciation. Help kids write an alphabet-of-love card for a relative. Following each letter of the alphabet, put a word that decribes the recipient. For example: A—affectionate. B—boisterous. C—clever. D—daring. And for X and Z consider X-tra special and Zany. Using a dictionary may help!

EIGHT
THERE'S A BIG WORLD OUT THERE

SECTION 1: GROWING UP GRACEFULLY

SECTION 2: MANAGING MONEY

SECTION 3: A SHRINKING WORLD

SECTION 4: THE FUTURE IN YOUR HANDS

SECTION 5: GETTING ALONG WITH OTHERS

SECTION 6: LIFE WITH AND WITHOUT TELEVISION

SECTION 1:
GROWING UP GRACEFULLY

Parents need not fear the preteen and teen years if they prepare for them with their children. And the important word here is WITH. Don't wait until the teen years to discuss the four D's: dating, driving, drinking, and drugs.

DATING AND SEX

❑ **587.** DATING REQUIREMENTS. Before a youngster starts to date, talk together about your "need to know" concerning certain facts. These are: the full name and phone number of the date, the means of transportation, the destination or destinations, and the time he or she will be home. Be insistent that no youngster goes out the door without sharing this information.

❑ **588.** ASKING FOR A DATE. When asking for a date, a youngster should ask well in advance and give specific information as to the event. And, kids should learn how to graciously turn down a date or calmly accept a "no." Sometimes a youngster will ask a friend to call on his behalf, however, if a youngster isn't mature enough to make the call himself, he isn't old enough to date! A little role playing at home will help kids to get over their shyness and will help the one responding to the question.

❑ **589.** WHEN MAY I DATE? In your family rules, which you have in written form, specify the age for solo dating (sixteen is quite common). You won't be pestered at age eleven if the rule has been known all along. Your rules might state: At about thirteen, it's acceptable for a boy to come over to study; at thirteen it's okay to attend chaperoned preteen parties, which are not really dates; by fifteen there can be double dating—with you or another parent driving.

❑ **590.** WHO MAY I DATE? Set basic standards before dating begins. Don't permit your youngster to date kids you do not know anything about. School dropouts, out-of-town visitors, one with a gang affiliation should be ruled out. Also, let your kids know that they are to date youngsters about their own age—a two-year difference being the max.

❑ **591.** POPULARITY AND PRESSURE. These are just two topics of interest to preteens. *Girltalk—All the Stuff Your Sister Never Told You* by Carol Weston (New York: Harper Perennial, 1992) has a casual style that will bring parents and daughters up-to-date information on relationships with each other and with boys, etiquette tips, meeting new people, and all the other topics that can be worrisome. It's a good book to read together—a little at a time each evening.

❑ **592.** IT TAKES GUTS. Give your youngsters support in saying no to silly, stupid, or illegal behavior or fads such as randomly picking up a stranger, cutting classes, shoplifting, using alcohol or drugs, tattooing and body-piercing, drag racing, or doing graffiti or vandalism. Some of these activities are considered fun on dates. While it takes courage to go against the crowd, saying "no" actually garners respect. Teach your kids lines such as "I'm too busy for that," or "No thanks, I'll pass," or "Sorry, catch you later."

❑ **593.** IT'S WRONG! So much education on the subject of sex is based on a parent's view of what is right and what is wrong. While a teen's obedience to these standards is essential, knowing the **reasons behind** the obedience are important when there is great peer pressure. Parents should start early to go beyond "It's wrong!" and provide facts to support your own values. When you provide kids with this ammunition, they may in turn share it with peers.

❑ **594.** STRAIGHT SCOOP. To share accurate information, a parent often needs the backup of some straightforward facts. For parents of teens who want to replace myth and misinformation concerning puberty, sex, contraception, sexually transmitted diseases and more, the book *How Sex Works* by Elizabeth Fenwick and Richard Walker (New York: Dorling Kindersley Inc., 1994) offers a good opportunity for discussion together. Parents might want to read the book before the teen does. It includes actual questions from teens with answers from the professionals.

❑ **595.** **PARENTS' RIGHTS.** Rather than letting clinics subvert family relationships by secretly counseling kids on morally important matters, it is up to parents to actively participate in this counseling. In a society where most schools will not give a child an aspirin without parental consent, parents should have the minimal right to be notified (not asked for permission but notified, even if after the fact) when a minor daughter is receiving a drug related to sexual activity or having an abortion. It is not only a right, but a duty to be your youngster's mentor.

❑ **596.** **THE THIRD CHOICE.** Teach your youngsters that there are not just two choices: contraception or pregnancy. The third choice is abstinence. Parents should not complacently accept the inevitability of today's rate of teenage sexual activity. Read Kristine Napier's book *The Power of Abstinence* (New York: Avon, 1995). Then initiate a discussion on the subject.

❑ **597.** **WHY NOT PREMARITAL SEX?** Explain to kids that early sex experiences have bad results: one-third of all abortions are done for teens; babies born to teen moms are more likely to be brain damaged or retarded; venereal disease is epidemic and can cause sterility or death; and there are more attempted suicides among pregnant teens than girls of other ages. Also discuss the fact that a girl labeled "easy" has a difficult time shaking that reputation and regaining respect. Locker room talk isn't a myth nor is the burden of living with guilt. This is brutal information, but it's part of your parental job to share it and then talk about it together.

❑ **598.** **AIDS.** Your goal isn't just to help your youngster avoid HIV infection, it's to help him make smart decisions. Start a conversation by taking a cue from the media that gives plenty of information. If you feel a youngster is (or is going to be) sexually active, you must be **very explicit** concerning the dangers ahead. Go beyond what is taught in school by ordering, reading, and discussing the free booklet *Aids Prevention Guide* from the National AIDS Clearinghouse, P. O. Box 6003, Rockville, MD 20849-6003. It's written specifically for parents.

DRIVING

❑ **599.** NOT AUTOMATIC. The car may be automatic, but permission to drive isn't. While the law states an age when kids may drive, the level of maturity varies in teens. Let driving be a privilege granted only to responsible kids. Let them know in advance what you expect in the way of grades, integrity, and responsibility.

❑ **600.** MORE THAN DRIVER'S ED. Don't count on kids learning it all in school. See for yourself by sitting right next to your youngster and observing driving habits during the period she has her learner's permit. Give her many opportunities to drive so that you both have confidence when she starts to drive alone.

❑ **601.** DRIVING TABOOS. Start with gradeschoolers to inform kids about bad driving practices such as driving without a license, cutting off another driver, drag racing, picking up strangers, speeding, and drunk driving. Also point out tailgating, failing to use the lane change indicator and check in the mirror, speeding through intersections on the yellow light, and even leaving keys in the ignition and failing to lock the car. When out together in the family car, point out these bad habits in other drivers.

❑ **602.** FIRST OFFENSES. You'll make your point about safe driving practices if you come down hard on the first offense—taking the car without permission, getting a ticket, or other infractions. It won't harm a youngster to do without the car for a month—he'll think twice about his actions the next time. Although it is grim information, tell kids that an accident can change the life of another family, of himself, and your family.

❏ **603.** REWARDS. Start slowly when allowing a youngster to drive on her own. When she has exhibited good driving practices for about six months, she can then drive others. Compliment her when she's been responsible and increase the number of times she can borrow the car.

❏ **604.** A CAR OF MY OWN. At about age thirteen, let a youngster know that only when he has his license and proved his abilities as a good driver will you consider the purchase of a car for him. However, he can start a car fund for the future. Talk about the cost of buying a vehicle, insurance, and maintenance. Set up a plan where the parent (or grandparent) will pay half if the youngster earns the other half of the cost with a part-time job. You may want to provide opportunities for earning extra money at home during this time.

TOBACCO, ALCOHOL, AND DRUGS

❏ **605.** A GIRL WITH A CIGAR? An increasing number of girls are taking up smoking, even cigar smoking. Despite devastating health damage, smoking is an expensive habit that makes for smelly breath and clothing. Tell them the truth: the majority of boys prefer girls who don't smoke. If you smoke, make it clear to your kids that you don't approve of anyone smoking and you wish you could stop. Make it clear that it is easier to just not start than to quit. One smoking grandfather feels so strongly about this that he pays for a year of college for any grandchild who does not smoke.

❑ **606.** POT PRESSURE. Kids often believe the myth that marijuana is harmless, but three decades of research have disproved that. Inform your kids that today's grass is ten times stronger than that smoked a generation ago. While a few youngsters might not show a reaction, others get drowsy or act drunk, have impaired judgment, reduced attention span, vision problems, reduced learning ability (due to brain cell impairment), and severe loss of motivation. And, the drug stays in the system, decreasing resistance to infections and damaging lungs far more than cigarettes. The need for drugs is a sign that the youngster is not willing to face up to challenges in a mature way. It's a cry for your help.

❑ **607.** COCAINE, PCP, LSD, AND HEROIN. Get the facts and share them with your kids—**don't be timid.** Start by describing these four temptations. Cocaine (coke) is a powerful and expensive stimulant that can last for days, then cause intense depression, resulting in a craving for a new high. PCP (angel dust) is cheap and deadly, causing hallucinations, mood disorders, paranoia, hostility, brain damage—the symptoms sometimes recurring years after use. LSD is an unpredictable drug that can cause severe psychotic symptoms (some users believe they can fly and jump out windows), "bad trips," and mental damage that can last forever. Heroin, an expensive hard-to-kick drug, requires a "fix" several times a day. Addicts suffer from chills and nausea as well as liver damage and hallucinations. Withdrawal is painful and often not effective. Because addicts often share unsterilized needles, AIDS is spreading through the heroin-addicted population. The methadone program that supplies a synthetic narcotic free of charge has had some success. In order to support these habits, many users turn to stealing that further complicates their lives.

❑ **608.** JUST ONE LITTLE DRINK. With alcoholism affecting kids as young as ten, start your education early. Explain the dangers. Auto accidents caused by drunk driving are the leading cause of teenage deaths. Alcohol use is a crutch for those who think it relaxes them, gives them confidence, or helps them forget troubles or fall asleep. It is actually a depressant and even those who drink in moderation gradually require more frequent and stronger drinks to get a lift. Few people can say that they drink less and less as the years pass.

❑ **609.** KEEPING CLOSE. The best way to protect kids from drug use is by maintaining good and open communication, remaining actively involved with them and their friends, giving them opportunities to increase self-esteem, and expressing high expectations for their achievement in school and career. However, once drug involvement has begun, it is important to seek professional help immediately through school counselors and other professionals.

SECTION 2: MANAGING MONEY

A recent Harris poll found that 88 percent of high school students said they had "learned everything they know about money from their parents." Whether parents have been good or bad examples in the past, they can now learn financial skills and instruct kids how to avoid financial pitfalls.

❑ **610.** THE SAVING RATIO. Starting when children are young, encourage them to save 10 percent of their income—income being allowance and gift money. Take them to the bank and go through the procedure of opening an account. You may want to start the account with a gift of $100 since there are often benefits of having an account in three figures. Nowadays, you may not be dealing with a kindly investment officer, but rather with an impersonal ATM. Show kids how these machines work. When statements come, and at earnings time, be sure to show kids what their money earns. Help them determine both long-term and short-term goals. Delaying gratification and saving for something is great financial training.

❑ **611.** MATCHING FUNDS. Parents (and grandparents) can make matching fund deals with youngsters. Perhaps the teen is considering the purchase of a first car, a 4-H animal, or ski equipment. In order to encourage saving, offer to "go halves" (pay for the second half of the investment) if the youngster saves for the first. But remember to treat all your young savers to the same special deals.

❑ **612.** BAD EXAMPLES. Keep a watch out for investment scam stories in newspapers and on TV. Teaching your child to be wary of the promise of amazing returns is the foundation for savvy investing. Show how a credit card account charges interest and how instant gratification can cause big trouble. And, if you have made injudicious investments, "fess up" since this bad example will be especially meaningful.

❑ **613.** NO SECRETS. By the time kids can add and subtract, take them into your confidence concerning your budget and investments, but explain that this information is to remain within the immediate family. When you decide on an investment (a home, car, bond, and so forth), go over the finances and show exactly where the money comes from, where it goes, and what the long-term result will be. Sometimes this shared analysis will help *you* to see the nonmerits of the investment.

❑ **614.** BUDGETS AND ALLOWANCES. Having money and learning how to budget it should be taught when youngsters first receive an allowance. Talk about how it must last (one week for young children, two weeks to a month for older ones). Remember that an allowance is given for being part of the family. Work together to make a list of what the allowance should cover and total up this amount. The list can include school lunches, bus fares, school supplies, entertainment (such as CDs and movies), church contributions, special purchases (wants that are more expensive than parents are willing to buy), and money for gifts to be given that month. For other spending needs, provide the opportunity for kids to earn money.

❑ **615.** THE CLOTHING BUDGET. Entirely separate from the allowance is a youngster's clothing budget. In the late summer, before school begins, sit down with each child and look over all the clothes and shoes. Get rid of things that are worn out or do not fit. Make a list of bottoms that need tops and vice versa, as well as under and outer apparel. Make a guesstimate of the total cost and then deduct one-fifth (to increase your effort to make good buys). This figure is a six month budget, and if there are "must have" fad items, provide opportunities for the youngster to earn the money, or put the item on her wish list for a birthday or holiday.

❑ **616.** CREDIT FREE. Early in a child's life, establish as a general rule that one saves first, and buys second. Credit cards can be a handy and useful tool but only when the account is paid off monthly. Show your child a charge account statement, look at the interest charged on an unpaid balance, and figure what it would cost to not pay the bill. Share facts on the dangers of abusing credit cards—and set a good example yourself.

❑ **617.** TALK ABOUT RISKS. Although a bank savings account pays a small amount of interest, the purchase of a stock might bring attractive returns—or big losses. Explain the concept of a mutual fund and look at the component companies. What does your youngster think of Levi Strauss or Nike as an investment? Teach kids to be alert to the daily Dow Jones Industrial Average announced on television, and what, if anything, it means to the family.

❑ **618.** PRETEND PURCHASE. As a learning experiment, let a youngster pick a stock that is attractive to her and make a pretend purchase of 100 shares. Show her how to keep a log of its ups and downs, splits, and dividends. Then after one year, compute the profit or loss.

❑ **619.** TICKER TAPE VISIT. Teens can learn from a visit to a stock broker's office. (Just watching the ticker tape is fascinating.) Or, if you're nearby, visit a stock exchange.

❑ **620.** GET SMART. Depending on age, your child will enjoy one of these two items: a video for gradeschoolers called *Piggy Banks to Money Markets* (Los Angeles: Price Stern Sloan, 1993) and *Learn to Earn* by Peter Lynch and John Rothchild (New York: Simon and Schuster, 1995, a book for older kids. Watch, read, and learn together.

❑ **621.** A REAL INVESTMENT. If you are inclined to buy a stock yourself, sell your youngster one share of the stock. Choose a company that has appeal to kids. As they get older, young people may appreciate a safe and conservative investment gift as a college graduation or wedding remembrance.

❑ **622.** THE MIRACLE OF COMPOUND INTEREST. With pencil and paper, show youngsters how compounding interest can make a difference. As an example, say that you put 100 dollars in an account where you earn 5 percent interest. At the end of the year, show that you have earned $5.00 without doing anything but leaving it in the bank. At the end of the second year, what would you have? You'd have $5.25 more, making a total of $110.25. Now, how long must you leave the money in the account to double it? This shows kids the importance of shopping around to get the best interest rate and then letting the money work for them.

❑ **623.** THE MONEY JAR. For many of us, going out to eat is a treat. To make it more affordable, use the money jar method. On a counter in the kitchen or family room, place a large glass jar with the lid taped in place. Have a slit in the jar top that will accommodate coins. Excess change, money from recycling, fines for using profanity, and other donations all go in the jar. Counting it is fun for kids and it makes the going-out event more appreciated.

❑ **624.** CAR WASH ENTREPRENEURS. Earning money takes a twist with this multiactivity project. With grade and high school kids (your own and their friends), choose a date well in advance for a car wash. Advertise it with flyers and posters created by the youngsters. While some kids do the cars, others occupy the car owners with twenty-five cent lemonade, a bake sale, and mini flea market. Afterward, discuss the money earned, divide it up, and see if it was worth it.

❑ **625.** HOLIDAY HELPERS. Many folks welcome extra help during the busy holiday season and enterprising youngsters can easily earn extra cash. Help your youngster create an attractive flyer offering services such as package wrapping and mailing, snow shoveling, Christmas tree purchasing. During the year, there are opportunities beyond babysitting and lawn cutting: dog washing and walking, putting up screens, replacing batteries in smoke detectors, house cleaning, or making minor repairs. Show how a youngster can key her services to seniors as well as busy young families.

❑ **626.** ZILLIONS. Teaching kids to be wise consumers is a project of Consumers Union in their magazine *Zillions*. Because children between ages eight and twelve have more than $17 billion at their disposal, they need to be knowledgeable in the face of media hype and peer pressure. There are interesting stories and facts on bikes, sports equipment, snack food, "hot" clothes, in-line skates, boredom busters, and many other topics related to spending. Ask for a copy at a newsstand or library and you may decide to subscribe.

❑ **627.** PENNY PEBBLES. Sometimes homes are surrounded with landscaping that includes two different colors of pebbles. One grandmother found that some of the red gravel had got mixed with the green gravel. Since neither she nor her husband liked this bend-over work, they hired their young grandchildren to put the colored gravel pieces back where they belong. For this task they paid a penny per pebble. Since their grandkids enjoyed the project, the grandparents now keep a list of other tasks such as polishing silver, dusting baseboards, cleaning kitchen drawers, cleaning hanging light fixtures, and running sprinklers.

❑ **628.** SATURDAY VISIT. Let your child visit your workplace for half of a day so she can see how you earn a living. Let her be useful by making copies, filing, cleaning out a drawer, and so forth. On the way to the office, talk about how you got this job. On the way back, talk about your plans for future work. Ask your youngster what she thought were the interesting or boring parts of what you both were doing.

❑ **629.** KIDS READ *THE WALL STREET JOURNAL?* Why not—it's a great learning experience. Start gradeschoolers reading the page one column "What's News?" and, as they get older, read and share other short stories of interest. Help them understand terms found in articles: supply side, gross national product, balance of trade, Dow Jones Average, NASDAQ, Federal Reserve, and so forth.

SECTION 3: A SHRINKING WORLD

History, geography, politics all touch us as well as the world around us. Prepare kids for the world of tomorrow by talking together about these important subjects.

❑ **630.** IF I WERE PRESIDENT. Someone about the age of your child will grow up to be president of the United States. Initiate a discussion and ask, "What do you think that youngster is doing now? If you were going to be president, what subjects should you study? If you became president, what would you try to accomplish?" Don't be judgmental: you can learn from a child's imaginative answers.

☐ **631.** WHERE IN THE WORLD ARE YOU? Obtain a globe (better than a world map) at a garage sale or buy one of the inexpensive cloth ones that fit over an inflatable ball. It doesn't matter if it isn't totally up-to-date—that gives you an opportunity to talk about recent changes. Play this game: One person looks at the globe and picks out a place name while the others aren't looking. She announces the name "Zanzibar"—or whatever—and all youngsters start searching for it. After one minute, parents are permitted to look, too. The first to find the place is the next to choose, but eventually make sure everyone has a turn.

☐ **632.** CHANGE THE LOCATION. While reading or telling stories to children, change the locale to something unusual. For example, the story of the three bears could take place in Russia; the *Cat in the Hat* might be in South Africa; or *Heidi* could live in Mexico. Wherever you choose, let the child find that place on a map or globe and, as the story develops, you can change the story further to suit the geography of that area.

☐ **633.** WALL CHART. Since many youngsters have a poor knowledge of historical chronology buy *The Wall Chart of World History* by Edward Hull (New York: Dorset Press, 1988). This fold-out book contains a wealth of information in pictures and words, and the fourteen connecting panels trace history in a time line from the biblical times to the current times. It's a good springboard for conversation, questions, research, and school projects since it shows what was going on concurrently throughout the world at any time.

☐ **634.** DATE CONTEST. Have a family contest to see who remembers the importance of the following twenty dates:

230,000,000 B.C.	Age of dinosaurs begins
A.D. 0	Approximate date of birth of Jesus
476	Approximate date Rome falls, which ends ancient history and begins medieval history.

1000	Approximate date Leif Eriksson explores North America
1215	Magna Carta signed
1271	Marco Polo travels to Orient
1300–1600	Renaissance
1440	Gutenberg invents movable type for printing
1492	Columbus lands in America
1564	Shakespeare writes during reign of Elizabeth I
1620	Plymouth Colony established in America
1776	U. S. Declaration of Independence
1815	Napoleon Bonaparte defeated at Waterloo
1860s	Lincoln is president, U.S. Civil War
1903	Wright brothers' first airplane flight
1914–17	World War I
1939–45	World War II
1944	First digital computer
1946	Television era begins
1969	Man walks on the moon

❏ **635.** FOLLOW ONE TOPIC. Talk about national and world issues that are historical in nature and will affect the future: orphans in China, Middle East peace, pollution, the two-parent workforce and day care, drugs, apartheid, terrorism, and so forth. Let each youngster choose one topic to follow in the news. After about six weeks, see what new facts each one has to share.

❏ **636.** FLAT MAP. Show kids what a small world it is. Attach a flat world map to a wall and use pins to locate your hometown, where you've vacationed, where relatives live, where you go on business, where there are conflicts in the world, where relatives have fought in wars, and where certain food products are raised.

❏ **637.** **PEN PAL.** When a child writes well enough to communicate—usually by age eight or nine—ask if he'd enjoy a pen pal. You'll be able to locate one through your school, place of worship, your overseas contacts, or a pen pal club. Such connections make "foreign" seem friendly.

❏ **638.** **STAMP COLLECTING.** Stamps give glimpses of the world since they show landscapes, historical sights, flags, and famous people of many nations. Visit the post office to see stamps and a collector's shop to see many more. If kids are interested, obtain a beginner's stamp book. While you can buy beautiful stamps of many countries, start with a small selection, and if this becomes a child's collectible, purchase more philatelic supplies.

❏ **639.** **POSTER DECOR.** Visit a travel agency with your youngster and ask if there are any excess posters you can have. Let her use them to decorate the family room or her bedroom. Talk about the scenes and identify the countries. Decide which country the family would like to visit.

❏ **640.** **THE GEOGRAPHY OF A TRIP.** When taking a major trip with the family, don't just concentrate on historical sights and local foods. Prior to the trip, spend a little time each week learning about the size and terrain of the area, the climate, business and industry, political history, dialects or language, and interesting products to buy.

❏ **641.** **NOT A PARTY.** Rather than emphasizing party affiliation, talk with kids about political priorities—what you and they believe government should do. How are these goals realized (or not) in your country and in other countries? Can your family take part in local politics and problem solving, or write letters to state and federal officials? Encourage full participation in government, starting with being registered to vote.

SECTION 4: THE FUTURE IN YOUR HANDS

Tune in with your kids to the world of science, discovery, and the concerns for the environment. Borrow this book from the library and you may want to own it: *Science As It Happens* by Jean Durgin Harlan and Carolyn Good Quattrocchi (New York: Henry Holt, 1994). It's a wonderful collection of family activities for children ages four through eight.

❑ **642. SCIENCE IN THE KITCHEN.** Encourage an inquisitive spirit with simple experiments in the kitchen. These include mixing food coloring to make new colors, seeing how yeast makes bread rise, watching how clear gelatin solidifies a liquid, heating a small amount of water with salt in it and letting it evaporate to form salt crystals, making paste from water and flour.

❑ **643. EARTH DAY.** Each April, the world celebrates Earth Day—an opportunity for families to show appreciation for the environment. Start by clipping newspaper articles and noting local observances. Of the many options, choose one as your family's cause, whether it is reclaiming a park, combating graffiti, or planting trees, and set aside time to work on it this week.

❑ **644. CONSERVATION AT HOME.** Let kids organize home recycling (cans, glass, plastic, paper) and also the recycling of possessions no longer in use. Go for a trash walk (with gloves and bags), cleaning up your neighborhood. Look critically at your own property and beautify it. Support legislation that protects the environment. Even scrutinize your water and energy bills and see what steps the family can take to conserve.

❑ **645. SCIENCE IN THE WORKSHOP.** Show a child how to string empty thread spools to make simple pulleys for hoisting small toys. Create an inclined plane from pieces of wood, then roll cars down it to see how steep the plane can be tilted before the car tumbles off. Demonstrate how a spirit level shows a flat surface or a vertical one, and how the two form a right angle.

❑ **646. LIFE BOOK.** Help a youngster appreciate the variety of plant life—trees and flowers—by making a life book. Go on walks and carefully collect, identify, and then press various specimens. See how many trees and flowers grow right in your own neighborhood. Let the child encase the dried specimens in plastic or glue them on paper to make a book that can be easily added to.

❑ **647. STAR QUESTIONS.** Encourage interest in the heavens by looking at the stars on a clear night. Ask kids: "Do you think there is life on other planets? What is the brightest star? The largest star cluster? Is there a star that blinks?" (You may have to look up these answers.) For a second session, have a star map so you can identify the Big Dipper (Ursa Major, the Great Bear), the Little Dipper (Ursa Minor, the Little Bear), Polaris (the North Star), Venus (Earth's sister planet), and the Milky Way (our galaxy).

❑ **648. UNDER THE SEA.** Marine biology is a popular subject and one that immediately interests kids. Visit a public aquarium, then go to the shore to look at tide pools, and eventually enjoy snorkeling and scuba diving for a closer look at marine life. Let your youngster create a realistic fish tank (not just a bowl of goldfish) and learn how to maintain it.

❑ **649. MOON WALK.** Show kids the progression of the phases of the moon. Before bed, go out and see what phase the moon is in. Make it a tradition to go for a "moon walk" on the first night of each full moon.

❑ **650. FOR 3-6 AND 7-12.** The National Wildlife Federation now has a magazine for three- to six-year-olds, and it's as creative and fun as its *Ranger Rick* for seven- to twelve-year-olds. It's called *Your Big Backyard* and features games, stories, plenty of pictures plus a monthly poster, all keyed to children from three to six. A twelve-month subscription is just $15, from NWF, P.O. Box 777, Mount Morris, IL 61054-8276.

❏ **651.** **TINY LIBRARY.** Bookstores carry pocket-sized books that identify birds, insects, flowers, and trees. Offer to buy one for a youngster who is interested in one of these fields. Give a small reward for identifying five birds (or flowers, and so forth), then ten, then twenty-five. Show your interest as you learn together.

❏ **652.** **BUG SEARCH.** There are many little creatures right in your own backyard. Help kids overcome fear of harmless bugs by carefully observing them. Arm kids with a big spoon or hand spade, a shallow box, and a magnifying glass. Look in buggy places such as dark corners, the underside of leaves, sidewalk cracks, and under rocks. See who first finds a bug and can carefully lift it with the spoon into the box for observation and identification. After viewing it through a magnifying glass, put the bug back in its home. Another day, provide kids with a garbage can cover to place in the garden in a cool or shady spot. Leave it for forty-eight hours and then carefully turn it over. Investigate, identify, but don't harm the little creatures who have moved in. You will see worms and other insects just as you can when turning over a rock when on a nature hike.

❏ **653.** **BUTTERFLY BABIES.** In the spring, show your child the miracle of metamorphosis by preparing a little home for a caterpillar and watching it turn into a butterfly. Read in an encyclopedia about the stages of life, from egg to caterpillar to pupa to chrysalis to butterfly. Cut the top from a half-gallon milk carton and cut windows in each side. Tape fine gauze over the windows and rubber band a gauze square on the top. Provide food (leaves) and moisture (cotton dipped in sugar water.) Now go outside—it won't take you long to find a caterpillar marching along. Carefully move it into the carton, taking along the twig or leaf where you found it. You will see it shed its skin, form a chrysalis, and usually in a few weeks, there will be a butterfly. Watch it hatch. Now it's time to place your butterfly house outside and remove the top so the butterfly can go free.

❑ **654.** **BRING THE OUTDOORS IN.** Don't let indoors be devoid of the wonders of nature. A piece of driftwood combined with pine cones makes an interesting centerpiece. A shell collection can be on a fancy plate in the living room. An interesting rock makes a good paperweight. Field flowers and weeds, daisies and dandelions make attractive bouquets. Each week ask one youngster to bring an interesting nature item inside and place it in the middle of the table so you can admire it and talk about it at dinner.

❑ **655.** MINI-GREENHOUSE. Help kids cut the bottoms off gallon-sized plastic milk jugs. At the nursery, let a youngster choose some tomato plants for his garden. Cover with the jugs to enhance the growth and also to protect the plants from unexpected frosts. On warm days, the jugs can be removed for a few hours.

❑ **656.** PET ROCKS. Use a fishbowl to display the interesting rocks youngsters collect. At the library, look for a book on rocks and identify the finds. Use big rocks as bookends. And, if a youngster really enjoys rock collecting and displaying, consider a gift of a tumbling machine—the kind that polishes rocks to show off their true beauty.

❑ **657.** CRICKETS TELL THE TEMPERATURE. Crickets are known as the songsters of summer, but their chirping can also indicate the current temperature. Test them this easy way. In the evening, go to a quiet grassy place where the family can listen for cricket calls. Explain that crickets chirp for several reasons: to warn others of danger, to protect their territory, and to attract mates. As the weather gets warmer and their metabolism rises, their chirps come more rapidly. Once kids are attune to the chirps of a cricket, have them count the number they hear in a fifteen second period. Then, add forty-two to this figure and you will have a somewhat accurate air temperature. So, if they hear twenty-eight chirps in fifteen seconds, add forty-two to that and see if the temperature is 70 degrees.

❑ **658.** TRACKING. When hiking, divide the group in two, each with an adult. The first group starts out ten minutes ahead of the second group, the first leaving clues as to where they are going (rocks in the shape of an arrow, a little pile of leaves, a flower on a trail marker). See if the second group can arrive at the same destination. Have some pre-agreed meeting place should your tracking not be particularly adept.

❑ **659.** FIELD GLASS TAG. In a forest preserve or tree-filled park, play tag without running. In the center of the designated area, indicate with sticks two places where "It" can stand. All the others hide where they can see one of the two sticks, but where they themselves can scarcely be seen. "It" has binoculars and can move only between the two sticks while looking all around through the binoculars. If "It" sees a person, she calls out that person's name while pointing that direction. If she's guessed right, the person says "Yes," and becomes the new "It." If she's guessed wrong, there is silence and she must start looking again.

❑ **660.** THE RAIN MAKER. How does the rain get into the clouds? Show how with this experiment. The child heaps ice cubes into a small foil pan. The parent heats a small amount of water and then pours it into a large, clear canning jar and places the pan on top. The air right under the pan is cold as it is high in the sky. Let the child shine a flashlight into the glass to see the rising water vapor and a cloud forming under the pan. Peek under the pan to see the droplets condensing on the bottom side. Replace the pan and keep watching together until the droplets become heavier and then fall back into the water like rain falling from a cloud. In almost the same way, water is picked up from the earth and as it cools in the sky it condenses into droplets.

❑ **661.** TIDEPOOLS. Small bodies of sea water provide safe living places for many aquatic animals. Plan a visit to tide-pools in your area. Bring along mats or cushions so kids can lie down and look right into the water for small fish, moss, and sand crabs. Stay in one location for many minutes so that shy creatures will come forth.

❑ **662.** GETTING BATTY. Bats need not be fearsome, even though youngsters should be taught not to play with them. Still, when they appear at night, swooping through the air, you can give your family a chance to see them a bit closer. Bats don't see objects, but they do hear objects that break into the cone of sound that they create by their high-pitched squeals. So, when something enters that cone of sound, the sound bounces back to the bat. Try tossing peas into the air in front of or behind a bat. The bat will pursue what it thinks is a moth or other snack. Bats are smart enough, though, to soon realize that you're playing a game and they will quit.

❑ **663.** RAINBOW GARDEN. First talk about rainbow colors and help a child to draw a rainbow on paper. Next, choose a plot of ground where the youngster can make a rainbow flower garden. Prepare the soil, cultivating it into six parallel arches about one foot wide and about six feet long. Visit a garden shop to pick out seeds of six varieties having the same growing conditions. If using young plants, you'll need about six of each. Here are suggestions in rainbow colors: red carnations, orange nasturtiums, yellow marigolds, green fern, blue dwarf delphinium, purple African daisies.

❑ **664.** DOLPHIN LISTENING. Ask: "Are sounds louder in air or water?" Let your youngster listen to scissor blades opening and closing. Then fill a large bowl with water.

Have her press one ear against the bowl as you open and close the scissors in the water. She will find that the water carries sound vibrations better than the air and they will sound much louder. Explain that in this way dolphins hear noises from one another under the water.

665. IT'S ALL IN YOUR HEAD. Have a child listen carefully as he hums a tune. Then ask him to press his ears shut with both hands. Ask him to hum again. He will find that the sound is louder coming through the bony parts of the head than it is coming through the air. Show how to touch the jawbone while humming and feel the sound vibrations.

666. SPRING READING. At the library borrow one of these three books to read and enjoy with your children—including teens. The first two books are by the same author, Sharon Lovejoy, and evoke memories of a much simpler childhood: *Sunflower Houses* (Loveland, Col.: Interweave, 1991) and *Hollyhock Days* (also Interweave, 1994). The third is *Nature Crafts for Kids* by Gwen Diehn and Terry Krautwurst (New York: Sterling, 1995). The latter features fifty unusual projects using nature's materials.

667. SWEET TWEET. Help youngsters learn about local birds with *The Audubon Society Field Guide*—available for various regions (New York: Knopf, 1993) or *The National Audubon Society Interactive CD ROM Guide to North American Birds* (New York: Random House, 1996). The excellent pictures and descriptions will show youngsters how to quickly identify local birds and how to keep a list of birds the family has seen.

668. FOLLOW THE SUN. Help a youngster chart the sun: the time it rises, the time it sets, the path it takes overhead. At a garden shop or garage sale, buy a sun dial and place it in the yard so it can tell kids the correct time.

669. FOREVER FLOWERS. Take a walk with kids and choose small flowers and leaves to decorate a bookmark.

Arrange them between paper towels and press under heavy books for about two weeks. Then, help kids cut a piece of heavy white paper to a two-inch by seven-inch size. Using a small paint brush, spread glue over the backside of the pressed flowers. Then arrange them, glue side down, on the paper. Let the glue dry, then cover the entire bookmark with adhesive-backed clear plastic. Punch a hole in one end and tie a colorful piece of yarn through it.

❏ **670.** WHAT'S INSIDE? When a toy or appliance breaks and is no longer repairable, let kids take it apart and see what's inside (with the understanding that a broken item is **never** plugged into an electrical outlet). This helps to demystify mechanics and physics. A parent can give input as to the purpose of the inner workings.

❏ **671.** BIRDS AT YOUR WINDOW. To bring birds to your window sill, let your youngster make this attractive bird feeder. First, he should take a pine cone and spread it lightly with peanut butter. Next, put it in a paper bag with about a half cup of bird seed. Close the bag and shake it until the bird seed adheres to the peanut butter. Now place it near a window and observe how many different birds come to enjoy it. See who can identify some of the birds.

❏ **672.** SPIDER WEB ART. Let kids locate a spider web in the yard and observe whether it is occupied. When no spider has been seen for three days, the web can be collected. First, lightly spray the web with hair spray on both sides. Using a piece of black construction paper, touch the middle of the paper to the center of the web. The hair spray will cause it to stick to the paper. Gently detach or cut the web from where it is anchored on the branch. Again spray the web with hair spray. Now you are ready to observe fantastic workmanship.

❏ **673.** CRYSTAL MAKING. A parent heats one cup of hot water as a child measures a little more than a half cup of sugar. Pour the water into a heat-proof glass container (such as a small canning jar) and let the child add a half cup of the sugar and then a bit more until no more sugar will dissolve in the hot water. Tie a length of string to a pencil and balance it across the top of the jar with the string hanging straight into the solution. Place the container where it won't be moved but can be observed. Depending on the size of the jar, the water will evaporate in a few days or a week. The sugar will form crystals up the string.

❑ **674.** **WORM FARM.** Most kids find worms fascinating and although you can buy a ready-made farm, it's more fun to make your own. Cut the top off a one gallon plastic milk container. In the bottom, put two inches of dirt, then two inches of organic matter (grass clippings, leaves). Then repeat this procedure, being careful not to mix the layers. Moisten the layers until damp but not soaking. Next, move in the earthworms. You can find these in your garden or buy them at a tackle shop. Put them on the top layer and watch them dig in. When you can't see them, cover the top with cardboard and put the container in a dark place such as a closet (no, the worms won't escape). For the next few weeks, watch through the container sides as they multiply. After a month or so, turn them loose in your backyard to aerate the soil.

SECTION 5: GETTING ALONG WITH OTHERS

The important skills of building friendships, handling relationships, and making decisions are ones that are taught gradually at home throughout the years. Here's how to get started.

❑ **675.** **FINDING FRIENDS.** Initiate a conversation with kids about friendship. Ask: "What is a friend? Are your friends just like you? How are they different? Do you have friends of different ages, different ethnic backgrounds?

Why are friends important? Can you trust friends? What is your responsibility when a friend has bad habits? What happens when a friendship ends? Who is your current best friend? Why are you a good friend?" Then talk about places where new friends can be found.

❑ **676.** THE LANGUAGE OF FRIENDS. Although friends should be able to be frank, show kids that certain actions and phrases can destroy a relationship. Lazy youngsters who never want to do anything or try something new aren't much fun as friends. Gossipy kids who are always talking behind someone's back and telling you all that's wrong aren't real friends. Spoiled kids who always want their own way and complain that no one pays attention to them make poor friends. Bossy kids who deal in name-calling, sarcasm, getting the last word, and giving orders to others are not fun to be with. Ask kids how they themselves stack up in these categories.

❑ **677.** NO GRUMPS. Most everyone has something they could complain about, but people who constantly talk about small problems are depressing to be around. Teach kids to bring up problems with the aim of settling them, not just talking about them. Discuss the signs of a cheerful person and see how many of the signs you and your child exhibit.

❑ **678.** YOU NOT ME. Encourage youngsters to become vitally interested in other family members—their school or office work, sports interests, challenges and triumphs, and small things, too. It gives others a good feeling. We get along best when others care about us, celebrating our victories and comforting us when we're down. Play this little game: ask family members to find out something good about another family member during the day—any time up to dinner. Then at dinner, ask each one what they've learned.

❑ **679.** I PROMISE. Don't say those words lightly. In dealing with others, both inside and outside the family circle, our word is important. Talk about the words promise, pledge, vow, oath, contract. Ask: "Which of these already exist in the family (for example marriage vows or a contract to purchase the house). What does the Pledge of Allegiance mean?" See if each person can come up with a promise she plans to keep this week.

❏ **680. SHARING WITH FRIENDS.** When a young child is coming to play at your house, talk with your child about his own toys. Let him put away any toy he is not willing to share. Or, start the play by dividing toys into two groups, one for each child. Trade later.

❏ **681. ACCENTUATE THE POSITIVE.** Praise is great and it's easier to get along with others when we're appreciated. Find something to praise each youngster for each day. Ask kids to look for things they can appreciate in other family members—and **tell** them. When you accentuate the positive ("That was great the way you mowed the lawn"), you can also include a secondary message ("Do remember to lock the garage when you put the mower away") which is acceptable in this context.

❏ **682. HOLD THAT TONGUE.** Regrets and feelings of guilt can come from speaking thoughtlessly. Tell youngsters that you will try counting to ten before shouting or criticizing, and that you want them to practice the same control. Then speak softly and persuasively. The way you say something, the tone and volume, and your body language can be more meaningful than the words. Teach kids—and yourself—to make good use of phrases such as: "That was nice." "Can I help?" "I really need you." And use nonjudgmental phrases such as "I think . . ." or "It seems to me. . . ." Think of the words you use with your family as words that help them achieve their dreams.

❏ **683. JUST SAY "YES."** People who constantly say "no" or "I don't want to" can be a drag. Prepare a series of questions as a practice: "Will you jump off a building? Will you give me some help tonight? Will you play a game with me? Will you smoke a cigarette? Will you give me half your cookie? Will you give your best friend your homework to copy? Will you take five dollars from Mom's purse? Will you show me how to solve a computer problem?" Talk about the importance of saying "no" to bad ideas but trying very hard to say "yes" to good ones.

❑ **684. REVOLT.** Talk with youngsters on how to disagree when they feel strongly about an issue. Show how responsible revolt and the convictions of just one person have brought about many important changes. It takes courage to believe in an unpopular opinion and it takes persistence to bring about change within the confines of the law. Work together to make changes in the home as well as in the community.

❑ **685. NEARER THE GOAL?** When your youngster is facing a big decision—to take an advanced placement class, to find an after-school job, to join a club, to take part in a time-consuming sport, to spend all his savings on a vehicle, to apply to a particular college—help him to look at it in relation to his goals: "Does this decision get me nearer to my goals?" If not, suggest he think twice about doing it. This helps a youngster to keep focused on long-term success, not short-term gratification.

SECTION 6: LIFE WITH AND WITHOUT TELEVISION

By the time a youngster finishes high school, she will have viewed about 15,000 hours of television—mostly with little benefit. Too often, watching TV takes the place of more valuable activities—physical play, reading, talking as a family. This chapter will help you balance television time with togetherness time.

❑ **686.** WHAT NOT TO DO WITH KIDS. Don't let them become inactive and lazy "couch potatoes." Don't let them do homework with the TV on. Don't let TV cut off family conversation and take up the time you can use for joint activities. Don't let the TV program guide rule your house! Take this "Couch Potato Quiz" and have your kids do the same. Answer these questions yes or no:

(1) Do your children do homework in front of TV?
(2) Do you eat with the TV on?
(3) Do you need the mere sound of the TV to feel comfortable and not alone?
(4) Are you depressed if you miss the end of a show—or an entire show?
(5) Do you ignore conversation because the TV talks louder?
(6) Is the TV program guide your favorite reading?
(7) When friends stop in or when you entertain, do you leave on the TV?
(8) Do you sit through a show but afterward realize that you don't really remember much about it?
(9) Have you committed certain commercials to memory?
(10) Does TV viewing increase your apathy about violence and world problems?
(11) When you think about relaxing, does TV viewing come first to your mind?
(12) Do you find yourself falling asleep in front of the TV?

More than three "yes" answers indicate that you're a candidate for couch potato and you may want to rethink your free-time activities.

❑ **687.** THERE'S MORE TO LIFE! Could your family exist without TV? When there was a power failure, one family found that TV was not the core of family togetherness. Someone remembered that their boom box ran on batteries, so, by candlelight they listened to CDs and the news of the storm. They had such an enjoyable time in the dark that they plan to do it again—even without a power failure.

❏ **688.** THE ON/OFF SWITCH. The national average for TV on-time is forty-five hours per week. In some homes the television is on, talking mostly to itself, every hour of the day. Teach kids that television viewing should have a purpose, and to turn it on when a chosen show begins and turn it off afterward. Many families find that an inexpensive portable radio is a handy alternative and much quicker at reporting breaking news. You can enjoy the latest news while cooking, the ball game while doing repairs or garden work, music while reading or doing homework.

❏ **689.** SELL THE TV. Yes, that's a definite possibility. This is a cold turkey approach and families who have done it report that there have been profound changes in their young people (and often in the parents, too): better grades, increased physical fitness, new skills. Ask kids what they would think of selling the television set. Listen carefully to their reasons for keeping it.

❏ **690.** MAKE GOOD RULES. If the above suggestion brings cries of revolt, sit down and work out some rules. Cover how much television may be viewed per day, when to view (after homework and chores), what programs are approved or disapproved (actually make a list and post it), no TV with mealtimes, no cheating when parents aren't home, no week night TV if a grade falls to an unacceptable level (such as C minus). Breaking the rules should result in no TV at all for the next week.

❏ **691.** IF NOT, WHAT? You can't replace something with nothing. When you decide to take control of television viewing, be ready with enticing activities to take its place. Outdoor sports equipment, a new indoor game, the introduction of a hobby or collection, a pet—discuss the possibilities and let your youngster choose what she will enjoy on a regular basis. One teen I know got into shortwave radio communication and no longer has much interest in television.

❏ **692.** PLUGHUGGERS. If you need a strong means of controlling television viewing, consider the V-Chip or devices such as plughuggers, which lock onto a power cord with a key, preventing use of the television (or any other device such as a computer). Nintendo also makes a lock that prevents the insertion of game cartridges. Before spending ten to thirty dollars for such devices, talk with kids about being more responsible—but if you get nowhere, lock it up.

❏ **693.** SEX EDUCATION? Although we teach children that television life is not real life, children accept many of the TV values as real and justifiable. The average youngster hears and sees about 16,000 references to sexual intercourse on TV each year and few are within the context of marriage. The impression is that "everyone does it." This means it is important for a parent to monitor viewing and explain the vast difference between TV and reality. Either **you** will teach sex education or television will do it for you.

❏ **694.** THE VIOLENCE FACTOR. The National Institute of Mental Health reports overwhelming scientific evidence linking television violence to aggressive and violent behavior in children. These kids are more pessimistic, less creative, and use violence as a first, not last, resort. Even toddlers who watch cartoons with mock aggression are abnormally cruel to playmates and pets. Other research has shown a connection between violent television and disobedience and lack of trust (kids start believing the world is a mean and fearsome place). Exposure to violence blunts emotional reactions and makes people less caring. Don't be part of the 75 percent of parents who set no limits on the TV their kids watch. Be alert to the fact that prime time TV averages five acts of violence per hour.

❏ **695.** A NEW TRADITION. Create a television hour (or less) when the family can watch together. Say no to programs with the wrong values, and yes to channels with good programming. Choose just one program to see. Rotate the choice of the program among family members.

❏ **696.** SATURDAY MORNING TV. One of the so-called benefits of television is that parents get to sleep in on Saturday morning as kids look at cartoons of rabbits bashing one another over the head. Cartoons typically subject children to twenty acts of violence per hour. Instead, provide a quality video for each Saturday morning, plus a toy box of "Saturday only" toys that will occupy kids until parents are on hand for the day's activities.

❏ **697.** TV TIES TO VIOLENT PLAY. When children watch TV that features action figures, they soon want to buy those toys. And, if parents permit this, they will soon be mimicking the violent actions seen on TV in their play at home. Start when kids are young to tell them you won't permit toys connected with violence in your home—no guns, no tanks, no terminators, no toys that blow up. It won't be easy and you may have to endure some whining, but explain to your children that you want their play to be positive, not negative.

❏ **698.** COMMERCIAL TALK. Yes, we know that commercials pay for the programming but you're not required to give them your undivided attention. Instead, mute the commercial and ask questions or go over the plot or point of the show. You could also discuss the commercials and the ways they entice viewers to use the product advertised.

❏ **699.** USE THAT VCR. Be the master of your television set by taping shows you want to see and then watching them at a convenient time. Teach youngsters how to run the VCR (or maybe they'll teach you). Then, when you sit down to look at the program, you can fast forward through commercials, thereby cutting about fifteen minutes from an hour show. You can save money by taping good movies and viewing them as a weekend treat or in the summertime when new TV shows are limited.

❏ **700.** THE LIBRARY CONNECTION. If a program's topic is of special interest, find library books on the subject or other writings by the same author. Suggest these for reading before or after the program.

❑ **701.** GET MORE SLEEP. Every night between 11 and 11:30, three million children are still watching late night adult programming! Don't permit TV sets in kids' bedrooms. Encourage eight hours of sleep, and more for younger kids.

❑ **702.** THE CRITICAL EYE. Being picky isn't always bad. If you find yourselves in the middle of a bad program (and you just have to know how it comes out), make the best of it. Let one viewer look for stereotypes of women, races, blue collar workers or business people, and personal beliefs. Let another tally violent or gratuitous sex acts. Also monitor the glamorous use of drugs, alcohol, and tobacco. A parent with a tablet can make note of phrases not to be used in the home. Viewing with a critical eye will help to avoid TV trash another time.

❑ **703.** A CHIP FOR A SHOW. Here's a way to encourage kids to think about what they are viewing rather than just looking at any program that comes on. Every Monday, give each youngster fourteen poker chips (or some other kind of marker that can't be reproduced). Each one is worth thirty minutes of television. Apart from shows you've ruled out, they can "spend" a chip on any program. At the end of the week, buy back unused chips for twenty-five cents each.

❑ **704.** MAKE SPECIALS TRULY SPECIAL. When there is something truly worth time and full attention, build it up in the days beforehand. Serve dinner or snacks as the family watches together. During commercials, talk about how this show is special. Occasionally invite friends to join you.

❑ **705.** INVESTIGATE CHANNELS. Don't stick to just the major networks. There are other worthwhile programs out there. Sometimes just viewing the politicians in their deliberations is illuminating and humorous. Encourage kids to go beyond MTV—way beyond—and discover all that TV has to offer. Be willing to look at a show on a new channel once or twice before ruling it out.

❑ **706.** Q IS FOR QUALITY. Encourage family members to view the best TV this way: for one week, let each one read the guide and choose what he thinks will be the best quality programs. View these together and talk about them later. This often results in the choice of an educational show over a sitcom—and with hope that may become habit-forming.

NINE

VIRTUES

The issues in this chapter are fundamental to a youngster's well-being and maturity. You will find it challenging and enjoyable so don't skip over it.

SECTION 1: VIRTUES AND THE FIVE Cs

While it may seem like hard work to instill virtuous behavior in children, this teaching is one of the most important things you do WITH your children. It is not taught in a moment; it is taught by example, through stories, through consistent moral living.

There are countless lists of "The Virtues" and you will decide for your family which ones are most important to you. Theologians believe that Paul was among the first biblical writers to list virtues when he wrote in his letter to the Philippians to think about things that are true, honest, just, pure, lovely, and of good report. Other scholars have listed faith, hope, love, loyalty, temperance, courage, prudence, humility, trustworthiness, and responsibility. My list is slightly different, but is inclusive of the same ideas. Now it's up to you to talk about them and teach them.

❑ **707.** THE FIVE Cs. One family decided that these five concepts were what made their family tick: *cooperation, communication, compliments, commitment, and compassion.* They put a list of these on the refrigerator and tried to live them. Soon they noticed that when there was disobedience, disappointment, or disagreement (the three Ds) in the family, one of the five Cs had been broken. Talk about the five Cs and see if you find they are the answer to the three Ds.

SECTION 2: HONESTY

❑ **708.** HONEST TALK ABOUT HONESTY. Start a discussion on honesty by asking which of the following would be acceptable behavior for the average person? (1) Tax evasion (2) Keeping money found on the street. (3) Falsification of credentials. (4) Bringing home office materials. (5) At a store when given too much change, keeping it since they charge big prices. (6) Using crib sheets at school. (7) Plagiarizing or buying reports for school. (8) Using an older sibling's report as your own. (9) Parents being unfaithful to their vows. (10) Telling little white lies. (11) Telling little white lies so as not to hurt someone's feelings. (12) Telling the truth, but not all of the truth. (13) Shoplifting. (14) Lying about age to buy alcohol or tobacco. (15) Buying and using drugs. (16) Not buying, but using drugs given to you. (17) Exceeding the speed limit. (18) Exceeding the speed limit on a lonely road. (19) Pretending to put money in the church collection plate. (20) Sneaking out of the house.

❏ **709.** **MAKE IT EASY.** Don't play district attorney by grilling and trying to trap a child. Make an environment where honesty is valued and mistakes are not magnified. When you think a child has done something wrong, explain that punishment is always less when the truth is told immediately.

❏ **710.** **GET TO THE CAUSE.** If you can determine the cause for the dishonest action, you can probably find the cure. Talk with your youngster to see why he cheated in the game, why he took money from your wallet, why he got drunk when he'd promised he wouldn't drink at all. When you find the cause, talk together about alternate ways to solve the problem or challenge.

❏ **711.** **NO PROMISES.** Never make a child promise that she will never tell another lie. Rather, encourage her to try very hard not to lie. Show her that she should be honest because it is the right thing to do, not out of fear or because of what others may think. And let her know that although some dishonest actions go undiscovered, those wrongs will be eventually recognized and punished—hence it's smarter (and less embarrassing) to be honest at all times.

❑ **712.** DOUBLE STANDARD. Parents should avoid teaching that dishonesty or shoddy ethics is okay under certain conditions. While you may say "Never tell a lie," do you sneak short twelve-year-olds into movies at half price? Or, do you quickly pocket a five dollar bill you find lying on the sidewalk? Or, do you bring home office supplies for use at home? Play "what if" with your kids (make up stories that give them a choice for doing right or wrong) and let them do the same for you.

❑ **713.** "BUT EVERYONE ELSE DOES IT." Parents hear this argument often and need to respond firmly. Because everyone is doing wrong, doesn't make it right. Explain that just as different families look different, have different jobs, and have different ways of behaving, your family is unique. You have set standards and made rules for what you believe is best for the family, and it is your right to ask that these be followed. Use the statement: "I love you too much to let you do that."

❑ **714.** HONEST TODDLERS. Start when a child is young, as soon as she can recall a shared experience, to let her retell what happened. Praise her if she can tell exactly what happened. Say that this is the truth, that this is honest. If she states something that truly did not happen, gently say that it is not exactly the way it happened. Speak with admiration about telling the truth, but make a big distinction between the truth and imagination or make-believe.

❑ **715.** "I TRUST YOU." When children are young, introduce the word "trust" and use it often. Say: "I trust you to put away the train." "I trust you to take one cookie from the jar." "I trust you to take fifty cents from my wallet." Choose occasions where children will find it easy to be trustworthy, and as they get older, show your confidence by increasing their opportunities for independent honesty.

❑ **716.** "YOU DON'T TRUST ME!" When youngsters say this, it usually stems from the fact that the youngster has deceived the parents earlier. So, trust has to be re-earned. Much of parental distrust comes from their not knowing what kids are doing, due to lack of communication. Tell youngsters to talk about their activities so they won't seem mysterious to the adults. Thus, when a teen honestly volunteers information, parents will become more trustful.

❑ **717.** LOYALTY TO ONESELF. Talk about how one can be true to one's own beliefs about himself. A youngster must have faith in his own abilities and the strength to not compromise his standards. Discuss together what these abilities and standards are and how both youngster and parent can work together to support them. If one is loyal to oneself, he does not give in to peer pressure. Talk about ways to battle negative peer pressure that can erode an honest person.

❑ **718.** LOYALTY TO HUMANITY. Here are some ethical questions for discussion: What is our responsibility for others in the family and the community? How can we be "our brother's keeper" and still take care of ourselves? Does this kind of loyalty take money? What are the attributes of a loyal friend? What can one do when a friend has a problem? How can the loyalty of just one person benefit many?

❑ **719.** LOYALTY TO ONE'S NATION. Encourage kids to be honest about their feelings toward their country rather than dishonestly following the herd. Ask: "What are the benefits of our homeland? What benefits do other countries offer that ours does not? If you could live elsewhere, where would you choose to live—and why? If one is going to live in a country as a loyal citizen, what are the opportunities and responsibilities?"

❑ **720.** TAKE AN HONEST STAND. Discuss with the family current community issues of importance, as well as voting, serving in civic groups, and working for political candidates. During a campaign time, consider working together for a candidate. Or, take a stand on an issue that is important to your family and write a letter to the newspaper.

❑ **721.** **INTEGRITY IN GOVERNMENT.** Let youngsters see the law and government in action. Arrange a visit to a court in session or a meeting of the city council. Quietly listen during the session and afterward ask kids for their opinions. How is the law upheld? Do those in power seem responsive to the people? Would you like to be in law or government? What would be the advantages and disadvantages? What education would be required or useful? Share newspaper articles about law and government rulings that affect kids.

❑ **722.** **HEROES.** Talk about people that are admired for their integrity. Include some historic figures such as George Washington, Thomas Jefferson, Patrick Henry, Sitting Bull, Abraham Lincoln, Eve Curie, Teddy Roosevelt, Amelia Earhart, John Glenn, Mother Teresa. Why were they heroic? Were they patriotic? Brave? Angry? Innovative? Ask: "Who in public life today might become tomorrow's hero? Are there as many women heroes as men? Are most heroes famous? How can one be a quiet hero?"

❑ **723.** **FEELINGS.** Someone has said, "The baggage of unethical living is a big load to carry through life." In a nonjudgmental way, ask kids how they feel when they've been honest and how they feel when they've been dishonest.

SECTION 3: RESPONSIBILITY

When a youngster is successful at doing something, she feels in charge and her self-esteem soars. Here are some ways you can teach responsibility and improve self-worth, thus helping kids to be diligent and self-governing.

❑ **724.** **GOOD, BETTER, BEST.** During growing-up years, a youngster has many chances to excel, causing some parents to constantly push kids toward higher and higher achievements. But it is also acceptable in some areas to do a good job (as opposed to a better or best job). Some things don't really make a difference. Talk with a youngster about the skills most important to her and focus on these.

❑ **725. DISAPPOINTMENTS.** Mastery is a slow succession of many small gains, and along the way there may be some setbacks. Teach a youngster to learn from disappointments, then shrug them off and move onward. Use the phrase "Don't let that stop you!" and encourage the phrase "I won't let this stop me!"

❑ **726. TO DO OR NOT TO DO.** Let kids know what you expect them to do and what happens if they don't do it. (See chapter 10 on the subject of rules and punishments.) Do not remind, do not threaten, do not restate the punishment. Just be quiet and let the child make the choice—and accept the consequences. This leads to a self-disciplined young adult, prepared to make good decisions.

❑ **727. STIMULATING INDEPENDENCE.** Step-by-step teach your child to master his environment, to become independent of reminders, to be ready to make decisions. Use these lines to encourage independent action: "You can handle this." "You want me to think you don't know how to do it, but I think you do." "I'll be nearby if you should need help." "How do you think this should be handled?" These lines show a respect for a child's growing intelligence and ability.

❑ **728. STIMULATING INTERDEPENDENCE.** A child doesn't live alone on an island, so cooperative behavior is a parent's aim. Working with others can increase self-esteem. Encourage a youngster to take part by using these lines: "We need your input at the family meeting." "You can come with us if you'd like. We'd enjoy that." "It will go faster and better if you help make the cookies." "You had a problem like this before, so sharing how you solved it can help us all." "We're in this together."

❑ **729.** **EARNED, NOT GIVEN.** While you can't hand a child self-esteem on a platter, you can provide daily opportunities for him to earn it and for you to recognize it. Set tasks and goals you know he can achieve, then move on to more difficult ones. Always verbalize the successes: "Wonderful, you did it!" "How great to do it by yourself." "It was hard to do, but you hung in there."

❑ **730.** **DAILY SUCCESS.** Make a child's environment such that he feels successful more times in a day than he feels unsuccessful. Arrange the house, his room, and play areas to make dressing easy, toy pick-up easy, hand washing easy, helping in the kitchen and garage easy. This way he'll try to do more things on his own and add to his success list.

❑ **731.** **NO NITWITS.** Never make a child feel stupid when she doesn't immediately accomplish a task. If possible, explain the "how to" only once. When you constantly tell a child how to do something, you make her feel inadequate. Rather ask: "You got the first part right, what comes next?" or "Could you think of a better way to do this?" The feeling of respect that comes with success brings an important sense of security to a child.

❑ **732.** **PERSISTENCE PAYS.** Part of self-government is the ability to be diligent—to refuse to give up. When a child is engaged in an age-appropriate activity—learning to ride a bike, finishing a homework assignment, practicing for a recital—there may be setbacks along the way. This is when a parent needs to encourage, to remind of previous challenges and triumphs, and to build on those successes. Help a child make a list of accomplishments (learning to tell time or getting an A in spelling), add to it, and refer to it when persistence is waning.

❑ **733.** **GIVING UP.** Many things worth doing are not accomplished on the first try. Tell your youngster how many times he fell when trying to learn to walk—yet he did learn. Share the fact that there are some things that need not be learned at present. Don't let a youngster feel guilty about setting the two-wheeler aside for a month or repeatedly getting a C grade in math. Praise him for trying and show that while he didn't get the usual reward for diligence, there will be a time when he **will** succeed.

❑ **734.** SELF-CONTROL. While we don't teach a youngster to bury emotions, we do teach that there is usually a time and place for exhibiting them. Anger is the most common symbol of loss of control. Demonstrate various ways to assuage angry feelings: breathing deeply and counting to ten, leaving the room, tearing yesterday's newspaper in half, beating a pillow on the bed, throwing a ball against the garage door, taking a shower, going for a walk. When you see anger building, suggest one of these, and then talk about the cause when everyone is calm.

❑ **735.** THE "GOOD" CHILD. So much of parental attention is focused on the child who seems to be marching to a different drummer and not getting it together. How important then to also spend time in praise for the child who finds it easy to be responsible, who has good self-esteem, and learns quickly. At day's end, verbally tally all the good things a child has done, and tell him how much you appreciate his goodness. Don't compare or label kids—love them equally.

❑ **736.** RESPONSIBLE PET OWNERSHIP. Too often, parents get a pet because they think it will "teach" responsibility. Before adding a pet to the family, show youngsters what is involved and how they will be accountable for another living being. Obtain library books on care and feeding, and seriously consider the time commitment and the costs. A youngster who wants a pet should take the responsibility to feed, train, groom, and clean up after it. Emphasize the fact that the commitment to an animal can last for many years.

❑ **737.** CHOICES. Give kids the opportunity to make many choices so that they feel self-governing in many areas: what to wear, what to purchase with savings, whom to play with. For some choices, add the word "or": "You may buy one forty dollar shirt or two twenty dollar shirts." "You can choose to come home on time, or come home late and stay home all next weekend." "You may make three five-minute phone calls or one fifteen-minute one." With your child, make a specific list of things he can choose totally on his own and a list of things reserved for parent/child consultation.

SECTION 4: OPENNESS

Having good communication with youngsters makes family life much more harmonious. Starting early to talk regularly and honestly together will keep the lines of communication open during all the growing-up years.

❑ **738.** NO-MATTER-WHAT. From toddler years onward, remind kids that you love them "no matter what." You may not always like what they do, but you love them. So, encourage a child to share problems and mistakes. Hearing about them is better than being kept in the dark. You stifle this sharing if you react with thoughtless punishment, shouting, or ridicule. Say this often: "It's okay to tell me, because I love you no-matter-what."

❑ **739.** LISTEN EARLY. Parents often don't find their young child's communication very illuminating, hence they tend not to listen. Thus, when the kids get older, they no longer bother to communicate. Take a vital interest in the explanations and descriptions of a child's activities from babyhood onward. Make it natural to talk with them in an enthusiastic and appreciative way. And don't hesitate to ask "Is there anything I should know?"

❑ **740.** WEEKLY UPDATE. When teens suddenly clam up, parents can be frustrated because they don't know what is going on. You imagine that bad things are happening. Establish a weekly update session—each Sunday at dinner or other convenient time. With a calendar in hand, go over the past week's events and then the upcoming week, noting activities of each family member. Ask kids to elaborate on the events, times, places, and activities, as well as any problems.

❑ **741. COMMUNICATION KILLERS.** Family communication is turned off with lines like: "Shut up." "What a dumb idea." "Quit arguing!" "Not now, I'm too busy." Better lines are: "Let's find a time to talk." "How's that going to work?" "Who should settle the argument—you two or me?" "That sounds like a good idea—I want everyone to hear all about it at dinner."

❑ **742. FIVE TOPICS.** Kids who chatter away endlessly at home, sometimes become silent in public. Practice with them responses to compliments and ordinary questions. Then, when going to a social event, take time beforehand or in the car to help a youngster think of five things he can share: a school project, a sport or hobby, a movie or TV show, something funny that happened, or an excursion. If youngsters can't think of five things that are going on, it's time you enriched their lives!

❑ **743. PUT IT IN WRITING.** While watching TV or at some relaxing time, write short notes on paper of a distinctive color. (At one house they're called pink notes.) These can be as short as "I was proud of you at the game" or "Your hair looked good this morning" or "You're special!" Put them on pillows and in pockets or lunch pails. Encourage kids to write pink notes, too.

❑ **744. SILENT COMMUNICATION.** Occasionally a youngster will clam up and refuse to talk, perhaps going into her room and slamming the door. To diffuse the situation it's time for "under the door messages." Compose a message of love to the child and include the hope that she'll write back. Slip your note under her door, then go to your room, shut the door, and read or do some busy work. If you don't get an answer in fifteen minutes or so, try again.

❑ **745.** A CONFIDENTIAL JOURNAL. Sometimes kids like to communicate with themselves. Take youngsters to a stationery store and show them the blank books that can serve as journals or diaries. Encourage them to write as often as they like, perhaps daily, and put a date on each entry. To get them started, suggest the first entry: "Today we bought this journal that will record all the wonderful things that will happen to me." Tell kids you will never, never read their journal without their consent.

SECTION 5: OPTIMISM

Expecting good, being cheerful, and having a sense of humor: these comprise a healthy point of view for both parents and kids—and at the same time, they make for a happier home.

❑ **746.** WATCH YOUR EMPHASIS. Parental example is important. If you go ballistic when a glass of milk spills, your child will give small mistakes the wrong perspective and think that these events are important failures and occasions for fearfulness. (Your better reaction would be to teach him how to clean up the mess and place his glass in a safer place.) When every small mistake brings shouting, followed by tears or guilt, a child develops a pessimistic and cautious attitude that overshadows the happy times.

❑ **747.** LINES TO OUTLAW. Don't let your youngsters become accustomed to pessimistic statements, which they may have picked up from you. Outlaw "Nothing ever goes right." Quickly counter with a mention of things that have gone right. The same goes for these: "There's not a thing I can do." "I'm so upset, I'll never be happy again." "The world's a mess." "This is hopeless."

□ **748.** LINES TO LOVE. Teach optimism by expressing hopefulness as a part of daily conversation. Use these lines and teach your youngster to use them: "That's not so bad." "I had trouble learning that, but I finally got it." "It's not the end of the world—let's try again." "I know you'll do it." "Let's work on it together."

□ **749.** SOUND OF LAUGHTER. Borrow from the library a book of jokes suitable for children. Tell one at each meal. Encourage kids to tell "clean" funny stories and to laugh— even if the laugh is on themselves. Have a "jokathon"—a contest to see which family member can tell the funniest story. When there is laughter, it's hard to be pessimistic.

□ **750.** IN THE DUMPS. Here's a comforting proverb to share with a youngster who is struggling with failure: *Rejection, mistakes, and failures are the ideal stepping stones to success.* Then talk about what can be learned from the failure. Keep close to a child who is depressed. Show how pessimism is contagious and not beneficial. Find some small thing to be hopeful about, and build on it until the dumps have gone away.

□ **751.** THE REWARDS OF PATIENCE. While it is difficult for a loving parent not to fulfill a child's wishes immediately, the virtues of optimism and patience are a contributing factor in the development of a well-adjusted and optimistic child. A Columbia University study reported that children, as young as four years of age, who were able to wait the longest for a reward (toy, trip, candy), were able to handle stress more competently than less patient children. Delayed gratification resulted in youngsters with higher test scores, a more optimistic outlook, and the ability to cope with frustration.

❑ **752.** **THERE IS A WAY.** Reassure a youngster that there is usually a way to accomplish his dreams. Somewhere, somehow, the good things will come if he has patient hope. And, when something good eventually happens, be sure to remind a youngster that indeed there is a way.

SECTION 6: FAITH

A parent should set the example of a strong faith. This wholehearted faith in a supreme being is essential in these changing and often chaotic times—but this doesn't always come naturally. A child should be given the opportunity for religious study that will introduce her to the inspiring religious writings of the past. Many of these time-tested precepts are invaluable as the basis of a strong family life.

Children may ask about seeing God. The following ideas may help, and can be adapted to the age of your child. You can actually have these three experiences or talk about them to make a point. Although the word *God* is used in this chapter, you can use whatever term you choose for the Supreme Being.

❑ **753.** **AT THE SEASHORE.** See the waves whipped by the wind, whipped to a froth, and crashing on the shore. You do not actually see the wind, you see the result of the wind. In the same way, you cannot actually see God, but you can see the results of God's activity in your life—in God's caring love for you. You can see love between parents and children. You can see love when a firefighter saves a child. You can see love when someone does a good deed. When you see love, you see God.

❑ **754.** **IN THE WOODS.** Listen to the rustle of the leaves on the trees. You cannot see the wind causing this, but you see the result of the wind. In the same way you can hear God's angel messages talking to you in the form of good ideas. Be quiet and listen.

❑ **755.** THE WIND'S TOUCH. When a breeze is blowing, you can feel its touch against your cheek. You cannot see the wind, but you feel the result of the wind. In the same way you can feel God's presence with you when you are alone or afraid. You are never separated from your God who always loves you.

IDEAS TO PROMOTE FAITH

❑ **756.** MAKE A CHOICE. Perhaps you were raised in one religion and your spouse in another, or perhaps you had absolutely no religious training at all. It is difficult for a child to have faith, comfort in difficult times, and a feeling of purpose without religious training. Visit various places of worship and investigate their childhood education. Listen to the speakers, observe traditions, ask about basic beliefs. Discuss the choices with kids, select one that you are most comfortable with, and attend as a family.

❑ **757.** WHAT'S IT FOR? When a child is a toddler, start to talk about God. Tell him he is a child of God. Show him how to talk with God by praying. As children grow older, help them find an explanation for the universe and its consistency, for life, for death, and for life after death. Such basic reasoning and teaching leads the youngster to see the significance of what he does here, rather than to feel that life has no value or plan.

❑ **758.** SUNDAY IS OUR "DAY OFF." That argument is often heard, but it's not beneficial to a strong family life. A weekend that includes a religious observance is a weekend that has added value. When kids are small, tell them that attendance at Sunday school is a "given." And when you leave church for your picnic or dinner at Grandma's, ask kids what they have learned that will be useful in the coming week. Don't let religion become a one-hour-a-week routine—make it meaningful for the entire week.

❑ **759.** THE RIGHT START. While many families say grace

at dinner, it is also a nice tradition to start the day with prayer. Holding hands around the breakfast table for a moment of silent prayer and then a short audible prayer reminds youngsters of God's place in their lives. You can also read a portion of the Bible each weekday morning as kids eat breakfast. For young children, a children's Bible may be more understandable.

❑ **760.** ONE-A-WEEK. The Bible contains many useful and comforting verses that are easy to memorize. Put a new one on the bathroom mirror each Monday and see how quickly it is learned. Here are a few for starters: Matthew 5:48; 2 Timothy 1:7, 4:7; Proverbs 15:1; Psalm 34:4; Numbers 6:24-26; as well as verses from Psalms 23, 91, and 139, the Commandments in Exodus 20, and the Sermon on the Mount in Matthew 5 and 6.

❑ **761.** BIRTHDAY DEEDS. Starting with preschoolers, establish the tradition of doing a good deed on your *own* birthday. Because much attention is placed on receiving gifts, make the day memorable by doing something for someone else. Tell a youngster the night before her birthday that she should think about her birthday good deed. And, when she blows out the candles on the cake, she can share what she did that was caring to others.

❑ **762.** TRANSLATE THE COMMANDMENTS. While these may seem like irrelevant teachings to kids, the Ten Commandments are applicable to today. See if kids can "translate" them into modern terms. For example, "Thou shalt not steal" might become "Thou shalt not shoplift." "Honour the Sabbath day" becomes "Go willingly to Sunday school." "Thou shalt not kill" could become "Thou shalt not glorify the torture and killing seen on TV." Or, "Thou shalt not even *think* killing thoughts."

❑ **763.** THE TIME LINE. On a family room or bedroom wall, affix a long piece of plain shelf paper. Turn this into the Bible time line, divided into Old Testament and New

Testament. Each time a Bible story is learned, draw the character on the time line and write the name of the story. For example, in the Old Testament there will be notations for Noah, Abraham, Isaac, Deborah, Jacob, David, and so forth. In the New Testament section there will be Mary and Joseph, Jesus, disciples, Mary Magdalene, Paul, and John. If in doubt about the order, a Bible dictionary will give you the dates.

☐ **764.** WHO DID WHAT? See if your youngsters can match these Bible characters with a special thing they did:

Moses	Killed Goliath
David	Healed people
Daniel	Received God's Commandments
Jonah	Was an early missionary
Noah	Fathered the tribes of Israel
Ruth	First recognized Jesus after crucifixion
Jesus	Was safe in the lion's den
Mary	Was David's grandmother
Paul	Got swallowed by a whale
Mary Magdalene	Was Jesus' mother
Jacob	Built an ark

☐ **765.** BIBLE AS HISTORY. These following words are part of history and yet are still meaningful today. You may know some and have to look up others, but first see how many your kids are familiar with: baptism, Gentiles, gospel, Holy Spirit, Jerusalem, Torah, psalms, Pharisees, Pentecost, patriarchs, Passover, Messiah, apocalypse, atonement, Babel, communion, and sacraments. If you and your kids know at least a dozen, you're Bible smart.

☐ **766.** OTHER BELIEFS, OTHER BELIEVERS. Tolerance and understanding reduce strife in this world. Do your children know the similarities as well as the differences between Christian and Jew, Protestant and Catholic, Hindu and Moslem, atheist and agnostic? Help them gain a basic understanding of the great religions of the world: Christianity, Judaism, Islam, Confucianism, Taoism, Buddhism, and Hinduism. And they should be conversant with the names of well-known religious figures: John Calvin, Francis of Assisi, Martin Luther, Muhammad, the current pope, Billy Graham, Mary Baker Eddy, Joseph Smith, John Wesley, and others.

❑ **767.** BIBLE CHARADES. When children begin to be familiar with Bible stories, it can be fun to play Bible charades. It works just like the regular game, except all characters are biblical. No words, no props, just action. For David facing Goliath, pretend to pick up stones, then vigorously throw one. For Lot's wife turned into a pillar of salt, walk forward, then turn backward in horror, and freeze. For Peter walking on the water, walk carefully, then sink to the floor with hand outstretched. For the three kings coming to Jesus' birth, walk majestically, pointing and looking upward. You can easily think of many more.

❑ **768.** BIBLE CONCENTRATION. Using three-by-five cards, write paired words on the cards, then cut them in half. Some paired words are: Moses/Commandments, Noah/Animals, Eve/Apple, Jonah/Whale, David/Lyre, Daniel/Lion, Jesus/Beatitudes, and Paul/Missionary. Make ten to twenty pairs depending on the age of the child. Then place them in several rows face down. A player turns one over and then tries to choose a match. If they match, he collects both cards and gets another turn. If they don't, he returns the cards to face down and the next player takes a turn. The winner is the one with the most cards.

❑ **769.** FAMILIAR QUOTATIONS. Like the old-time game of Authors or Go Fish, this game consists of Bible quotations written out on cards and cut in half. Deal out the cards, then take turns asking for the half you don't have. For example, if you have the half quote that says, "Do unto others" you would ask another player, "Can you give me, 'As you would have them do unto you'"? The other player must give it up if he has it. (If he doesn't have it, the player that does will probably ask you for your half when it is his turn.) You can keep asking as long as you are successful, but when you get a "no," the next player takes his turn.

❑ **770.** JOURNEY TO THE PROMISED LAND. Young children like board games where they move a marker from a starting point to a finish while avoiding pitfalls along the way. On cardboard, make a road from Egypt to the Promised Land. Mark the road into many squares and put some pitfalls along the way such as "Red Sea," "no food," "giant people," "breaking the commandments," "lost in wilderness," and "stopped at Jericho." All the markers start as slaves in Egypt and move, at the throw of a die, out of Egypt across the Red Sea through the wilderness and on to the Promised Land. If one lands on a square that is a pitfall, he must go back four squares. A Bible or children's Bible will help you in making this enjoyable game.

❑ **771.** PERSONAL NATIVITY. At Christmas, assembling the manger scene (holy family, shepherds, kings, animals) can be a family activity. However, go shopping with kids and buy an inexpensive manger scene for each. This is their own personal nativity that they can assemble in their own room in their own way.

❑ **772.** EVERYONE'S HOLIDAY. Don't limit your children's experience with religious holidays to just your own tradition. With the help of books or friends of other religions, learn about one new celebration each year. Twelfth Night, Passover, or the Swedish Saint Lucia's Day are just some possibilities. Talk about your new celebration with accuracy, respect, and reverence.

❑ **773.** DRAW A SYMBOL. With paper and pen, show kids how to draw symbols of other religions. Draw the cross or Bethlehem Star of Christianity (five points). Draw Judaism's Star of David (six points). Draw the Star of Islam (also five points). Once kids can see the differences, let them make a design, using all the symbols, as a sign of harmony between religions.

❑ **774.** **TRAVEL SIGHTS.** When on a trip with youngsters, don't overlook religious lessons. Check ahead to see what unique churches, synagogues, or tabernacles are in cities where you'll visit. Go to at least one on every trip and learn together. Talk afterward about the similarities and differences with your own religion.

❑ **775.** **MISSION POSSIBLE.** Just as many companies publish their corporate mission, each individual can make a statement of purpose and then focus on ways to reach those objectives. In his book, *The Sales Bible* (New York: William Morrow, 1994), motivational expert Jeffrey Gitomer urges each person to write out his own mission. This is heavy stuff, but worth the effort. Kids of grade school age upward can answer these questions on paper: Define yourself—who are you and how are you different from others? Who or what are you dedicated to (family, football, making money, and so forth)? Define your services to others. How can you strive to get better, to grow? What is the example you seek to set? What are the ideals you live by, or seek to live by? You and your family members are writing this out *for yourselves,* not others. Don't be embarrassed to flatter yourself. Write your mission with pride and a spirit of adventure. Make a copy, sign it, and put it where you will see it. Then try to live it every day.

SECTION 7: HUMILITY

Kids need a parent's example as a person grateful for the help of others, and humble enough to express it. Humility also includes modesty and the ability to apologize—useful qualities in family life.

❑ **776.** **NOT BETTER THAN OTHERS.** A humble person does not think of himself as superior in every way. Explain to your child that no one likes a snob or a racist. Help him recognize where he excels, but also where he still has work to do. Make it a practice to find something good in everyone with whom he comes in contact and think about how many others contribute to this life.

❑ **777.** AND YOU HELPED. When a youngster or parent is lauded for an achievement, make it a practice to express humility by giving credit to those who helped. See if kids can recall something in their day that succeeded because another person helped.

❑ **778.** IT WAS NOTHING. Don't let kids demean their achievement by false humility. It really was something! Give kids the gracious words to accept the compliment in a humble way and then to tell something about how it was done.

❑ **779.** NOTHING TO BE GRATEFUL FOR? Sometimes parents have to subtly remind kids of all they have to be grateful for. They might say "I'm grateful to have a job." "I'm grateful for this house." "I'm grateful for you kids." Then kids should be encouraged to think of the things they're grateful for. "I'm grateful I can read." "I'm grateful for my old bike." "I'm grateful we don't have broccoli often." Once youngsters learn to think this way, they'll find many important things they can be grateful for.

❑ **780.** THE GLAD GAME. For little children who are occasionally cranky, play the Glad Game. Hold the child in your lap and start "I'm glad I have a lap. I'm glad you know how to sit. I'm glad you're sitting in my lap." This silly beginning should help the child overcome his crankiness and perhaps he'll share some things he's glad about.

❑ **781.** SORRY OR NOT. It takes humility to say you're sorry when you've done something wrong. It's a worthy lesson to teach yourself and your children. But, it takes even greater humility to apologize when others *think* that you've made a mistake when you honestly believe you have not. Help kids to say "I'm sorry you feel that way." "I'm sorry your feelings are hurt." "Even though we disagree, I still love you."

SECTION 8: LOVE

So you aren't a huggy-kissy person? You can learn to be! So you don't have time to care for anyone but yourself and your immediate family? You can make time! It's important to set an example of love and outreach for your children.

❑ **782.   RANDOM ACTS OF KINDNESS.**   Mottoes like this are often skin-deep but this one has merit. It means that our kindness doesn't have to have a reason. We don't have to be shoved into it. Explain this concept to children and let them create random acts on their own. You will find that, without reminding, they are kind to a younger sibling, offer to help a neighbor, give part of their allowance to a charity, and offer to work "for free." Be sure you praise these random acts!

❑ **783.   HUGS.**   Starting with the very young, teach a variety of hugs: arm hugs, knee hugs, head hugs, and (of course) body hugs. A symbol for a hug can be made by clenching a fist (closing your fingers) and then taking the thumb of the same hand and tucking it behind the first finger. It looks a bit like a little person being hugged. Make hugs a part of your family greeting and parting. It is said that hugs are practically perfect since they are low energy with high yield, pesticide free and inflation-proof, nonfattening, nonpolluting, nontaxable and are fully refundable!

❑ **784.   CARD BOX.**   Sending a greeting card is a sign of loving care. Let youngsters send a photocopied letter to all relatives and close friends, asking them to tell their birth date and year, and if married, their wedding date and year.

Let them compile this into a month-by-month list, showing the names, dates, and years. (That way you'll all know when a youngster is five or sweet sixteen, or when adults have a special anniversary.) With list in hand, go shopping at a discount card shop (or make your own cards) and write on the envelope the name of the recipient. Make monthly dividers and place the cards and list in a shoe box. On the last week of every month, get out the box and address the cards. Be sure that each family member signs his own name, and if he chooses, writes a message.

❏ **785.** COUSIN CONNECTION. As soon as youngsters enjoy talking and telling stories, set up a connection with a distant cousin. Provide cassette tapes and let youngsters make a tape in private (the conversation is less inhibited), telling about her latest activities. This can also work between a grandparent and a faraway grandchild.

❏ **786.** CONTINUOUS BONDING. For many years it was thought that a parent only bonded with a child right after birth. (Officially, bonding is a deeply felt affinity for another that establishes ongoing mutual attachment.) Now research shows that bonding can take place later as well as early in a child's life. Holding a child close and telling her that she's a precious part of your family will help to strengthen the bond with very young children. But, close-together activities such as hiking or doing a craft together while talking about his important place in the family, can strengthen the bond with older kids. So, on a regular basis, keep the family bonds strong with both words and deeds.

❏ **787.** WHAT IS LOVE? It's wanting the best for another. It means liking someone as well as loving them. Love is built on joint experiences, not just physical attraction. Tell your youngster how you and your spouse met and fell in love. Tell them that the teen years are often filled with puppy loves but although these are usually fleeting, they are useful in recognizing the real thing when it comes along.

❑ **788.** **SERVING TOGETHER.** Start the memorable tradition of regularly helping others. It is easy to do this at a shelter where your family can come and serve meals to the homeless or disadvantaged. Your social service agency or church can put you in touch with such a shelter. Prepare kids in advance for what they will see; remind them to be polite. Afterward, have a frank talk about the experience.

❑ **789.** **THE BLESSINGS OF OUTREACH.** When a youngster is old enough, help her connect with a group that can use her talents. She can be a mentor or tutor to a younger child, read to a senior citizen, make tray favors for a hospital, volunteer at a recreation center, collect donations for the homeless. On a regular basis, a project of just two hours will bless her with new friends, new talents, new insights, and an increased understanding of the goodness and peace that really exists in this world.

❑ **790.** **SIBLING HARMONY.** Each of your children is distinct and lovable in unique ways. Emphasize this, especially when there is a new baby. Say "I hope you will help the baby grow up into a nice person like you." "I know he's little, but you have such good ideas, so can you think of a way to include him in your play?" Be sure to give each child special opportunities not afforded the others. Reward harmonious play. Choose toys that require cooperation and cut down on sibling rivalry—toys such as building sets or a playhouse.

❑ **791.** **FORGIVENESS.** Whenever a child does something wrong—no matter the magnitude—set an example of forgiveness. If it was a big mistake and you must punish the child, end the discussion with "I forgive you." If it was something small, just say "That's okay, I forgive you."

❑ **792.** **LOVE NEVER ENDS.** Children will grow up and move out, but your love goes right on forever and ever. They will always need your love and support. Plan to be in touch each week, and end each conversation with "Remember, I love you."

TEN
RULES TO LIVE BY

SECTION 1: LAW AND ORDER

SECTION 2: RULES FOR A HAPPY HOME

SECTION 3: WHAT HAPPENS WHEN . . .

SECTION 1: LAW AND ORDER

Much of the chaos in home life is caused by a lack of orderly systems for taking care of routine duties. These ideas will help you and your youngster cut through the boring stuff and get on to the fun.

❑ **793.** MANAGING TIME. Show a youngster that there is indeed time for both homework and play. Together, make a list of estimated times for everything in his day. For example, sleep, nine hours; getting up and going to bed routines, one hour; school and travel, seven hours; home meals and snacks, one and one-half hours; chores, a half hour; after-school play/lessons/sports, two hours; after-dinner family activity, a half hour; homework: one and one-half hours; television, a half hour; before-bed reading, a half hour. This shows that everything *can* be accomplished.

❑ **794.** SKILLS TO TEACH. The home is a happier place when each family member is self-governing in certain basic behaviors and skills. See which of these fourteen skills your youngster has already learned and which ones are still to be mastered: to get up when the alarm goes off; to accomplish the morning routine before breakfast or play; to eat nutritious meals; to remember what must be taken to school or activities; to keep a list (rather than try to remember) of things a parent has requested; to take care of clothes and toys; to understand priorities (what must be done first, what can wait); to care for important papers and money and jewelry; to throw away junk; to write down phone messages and put them in a designated place; to return telephone calls; to be aware of all family events; to accomplish chores without being reminded; and to get homework assignments completed on time.

❑ **795.** THE MOTTO. Here are wise words to teach your kids. When they are old enough to write legibly, have them letter this motto on bright paper for posting in their bedrooms, the playroom, or on the refrigerator door. The motto is: *Don't put it down, put it away!*

❑ **796.** KID OFFICE. Being a student with a full social life requires a business-like environment. When a child starts back to school, see that he has a work area of his own: a desk or table with shelves and drawers handy. Using paint or nail polish, show him how to code his own tools: ruler, tape, stapler, scissors, pencils, pens, markers. Also supply clips and rubber bands, tablets and paper, envelopes, and a small card file so he can make cards for friends' phone numbers and addresses.

❑ **797.** FANCY FILES. Files are no longer a dull manila color. At a stationery store, let a youngster choose her own color of folders. Back home, work together to set them up. Her files could include: instructions and warranties on games and equipment, report cards and special school papers, budget and savings account information, letters received/letters to write, ideas on hobbies and collections, pet information, clubs and other activities, ideas and clippings about places to go, and so forth. While these are few compared to your own files, they provide good practice in keeping papers under control.

❑ **798.** BIG BULLETIN BOARD. A bulletin board in a youngster's room can be both decorative and useful. A calendar on the bulletin board lets him note music lesson dates, due-dates for reports, sports practices and games, parties, and other events. While some of this may be on the family calendar, keeping a record of his own obligations encourages responsibility. Work with a youngster to make a bulletin board that is attractive and shows photos, awards, and memorabilia.

❑ **799.** "KEEP DRAWER." Some things seem too precious to throw away. Provide a little-used drawer (or a box on a closet shelf) as a "keep drawer"—a place for a program from a play, a sports award ribbon, photos, postcards—all those things that could cause clutter or get misplaced. At the end of the year, let a youngster choose what to toss, what to put in the yearly scrapbook, what to put in an attic keepsake box.

❑ **800. YEARLY SCRAPBOOK.** Looking together through scrapbooks of childhood years can be pleasant and bring back good memories. Make an annual scrapbook and each year look over the scrapbook made five years ago. See how appearances have changed, what each youngster accomplished, what events were highlights. Things to put in the family scrapbook include: play and sport programs, awards, newspaper clippings, photos, postcards, special birthday cards—all those things that made family life special.

❑ **801. BAG DAY.** Once a month, or as needed, give each family member a sack and turn them loose in the house to find things that aren't where they belong. (Sometimes it's fun to count up each bagful.) Next, dump the items onto a table and sort them by rooms—things that go in the play-room, the garage, a bedroom, and so forth—and place items for one room in one bag. Then let kids choose which bag they'll take in order to return the items to their proper homes.

❑ **802. COLLECTORS.** Some kids love to pick up stuff others might call junk. If it's not harmful or unsanitary, help the collector find places for these treasures. Bottle caps look good inside a large jar. Feathers can be stapled to an old leather belt and hung on the wall. Rocks can be displayed in a prospector's pan on a shelf. One mother of a collector kid has given him a set of matching jars, all from apple sauce, which sit in a row on a shelf—one for pebbles and beach glass, one for sand, one for spark plugs, one for pennies, one for pogs, one for sports pins.

❑ **803. MY PLACE, YOUR PLACE.** Family members need to feel that each has an area just their own. This can be a desk, half of a bedroom (or an entire bedroom), a bathroom, a den, or even a special chair. Help kids to understand that they don't invade your space and you don't look through theirs without asking permission. For a baby, a playpen gives a sense of independence and security, since considering the baby's size, it's comparable to an adult enjoying a cozy nook. See that all family members have places where they can happily be on their own.

SECTION 2: RULES FOR A HAPPY HOME

To live together harmoniously and efficiently requires some basic "givens"—rules that everyone understands. These rules should cover safety, play, family living, use of the car, dating—whatever areas might cause problems.

❑ **804.** **RAINY DAY ACTIVITY.** Work together to make a family rule book. Find pictures in magazines to illustrate the points. Don't leave any behavior to conjecture—be specific: We never play with matches. We don't talk to strangers. We don't take the car keys without asking. Review the rules yearly so that they continue to be age-appropriate.

❑ **805.** **PRIVILEGES.** In the back of the rule book, answer some of the "When can I . . . ?" questions. You will need to think these through yourself and then consult with your family. Here are some possibilities: At age five you may cross the street alone. At age nine you may go to a movie with friends. At age twelve you may have your ears pierced. At age thirteen you may go out with a group of kids at night. At age fourteen you can wear makeup. At age fifteen you may go on a double date. At age sixteen you may go on a date.

❑ **806.** **RESPECT FOR AUTHORITY.** Show your child that you love her and will always treat her fairly. In return, she is to respect you and do her best to please you. This desire to do the right thing is a form of preventive discipline.

❑ **807.** **MY MAIL BOX.** Busy families sometimes fail to relay phone messages and other important information to family members. So that there can be no confusion, let each family member create his own box for mail, phone messages, and reminders. Decorated shoe boxes lined up on a desk or counter make a good home post office.

❑ **808.** **YELLOW RIBBON.** Just as police use a yellow tape to mark an area that is off-limits, so parents can show young children places they are not to be. Buy a roll of bright yellow ribbon and string it wherever you don't want kids to be at the present: in the kitchen, by the fireplace, near workshop tools, in a closet where gifts are hidden, by your computer area. It can be tied in place or just laid on the floor. Teach kids that they can be near you, but that they mustn't cross the line into the cordoned-off area. Occasionally let kids use the ribbon to make their own private play area.

❑ **809.** **WITH, NOT AT.** One of the best ways to have responsible kids is to have a dialogue—a conversation *with* them rather than just lecturing *at* them. This dialogue should be more about good behavior than bad. Before a youngster goes to a birthday party, a wedding, or an overnight at a friend's home, anticipate things that might happen and discuss ways to handle these challenges. Let the dialogue come from the youngster, with the parent filling in the missing details.

❑ **810.** **THE FAMILY MEETING.** A once-a-week forum is a good place to consider both rules and gripes, and can also be informative regarding holidays, trips, and parties. Handle such questions as "How can we all get to breakfast on time?" "Who took the keys and didn't put them back?" "Let's make new bedtime rules now that it's summer." In a democratic atmosphere, kids feel comfortable bringing up requests and even asking for arbitration over disagreements. At these meetings there should be a pact that everyone will remain calm—no raised voices, no hurtful remarks. The setting should be pleasant—perhaps by the fireplace with popcorn and apples to eat.

SAFETY RULES

❑ **811.** MATCH FASCINATION. For young kids who seem intrigued with matches, sit together at a table with matches and a bowl of water. Show how to light a match, striking it away from the body. Let each youngster light and extinguish at least twenty matches—sufficient to bring on boredom. Then give the rule: Matches are only to be used in the presence of an adult.

❑ **812.** FIRE EXTINGUISHER FACTS. While most every house has a fire extinguisher, few family members know where it is—and more important, how to use it. A recommended location is under the kitchen sink since many fires originate in the kitchen. Let youngsters practice removing the extinguisher from its holder and showing how they would use it.

❑ **813.** SHARP TALK ABOUT KNIVES. Train kids in the proper use of knives. Using a table or butter knife, let preschoolers spread butter on toast. As they get older, graduate them to cutting beans, slicing celery, dicing hard-boiled eggs. Teach older youngsters how to carve a roast. A good gift for a preteen or teen is a Swiss army-type knife.

❑ **814.** GUNS KILL. Many people now keep guns in their homes, and even if you don't, your kids may play at homes that have guns. Question other parents about guns at their houses. Guns need to be locked up (not left in night table drawers where kids can find them) and the key must be well-hidden. Not permitting toy guns for play will lessen the danger of an accident. Talk about guns and establish these two rules: Never touch a gun. If another youngster has a gun, immediately leave the area and report it to a parent or other adult.

❑ **815.** **SOMEONE'S AT THE DOOR.** Practice with younger children just what you want them to do when the doorbell rings. Are they to open the door? Are they to ask who is there? Are they to get an adult? What if they are alone? Actually play-act the procedure with you outside the front door and the child inside.

❑ **816.** **SOMEONE'S ON THE PHONE.** Although kids love to answer the phone, it's best to do it yourself until a child is able to take a message. If a child is alone, he should be sure to not reveal that fact. Play-act (actually using the phone and holding down the button) so that the child can practice saying "Mom is busy but will call you back." Pretend to be the caller and ask: "Is your Dad there?" "When will he be home?" "Is anyone with you?"

❑ **817.** **STRANGER SITUATIONS.** A stranger might approach a child on the street or from a car at the curb. Again, play-act the proper response (actually do this outside with a neighbor in a car). The stranger/neighbor asks the child to come over to the car (the child refuses). The stranger/neighbor offers candy (the child says no and runs off). The stranger/neighbor says that the parent has sent her to pick up the child (the child says no and runs away). The stranger/neighbor tries to grab the child (the child runs away screaming).

❑ **818.** **THE OTHER PARENT.** Clearly explain to children that when parents divorce, there are laws that must be followed by both parents. (Most "missing" children have been abducted by "the other parent.") Gently tell kids that they are not to go with the other parent before getting your OK and, if that parent is insistent, they are to scream for help or run to another adult. If there is danger of abduction, alert teachers, neighbors, and nearby friends. These measures must be taught, but do so in a serious but matter-of-fact way to lessen the fear.

❑ **819.** MANDATORY SEAT BELTS. While everyone knows they should strap in, passengers become more lax with increasing age. When the family gets in the car, make it a race to see who gets his seat belt fastened first. Call out "First done," "Second done," and so forth. Never make exceptions, which can be tempting when you are going a short distance or have a large group of kids to transport.

❑ **820.** WHERE ARE YOU GOING? When a child of *any age* leaves the house, she should tell exactly where she is going and when she will return. If parents are not home, this information should be written and placed where it will be seen. Your rules should also state that if she leaves the destination to go somewhere else, she must telephone home or your office with that information.

❑ **821.** CURFEWS—A MUST! With kid-input, set reasonable coming-home times. These might be 5:00 from after-school play, 8:00 on a school night, 11:00 on weekends, with exceptions for special occasions. Make the time clear: the curfew is 11 P.M. At 11:01, the youngster is definitely late. At 11:15, you will start calling other parents. At 11:30 you may wish to call the police. Let kids know how serious you are about this matter. (Punishments for breaking curfews are in the next section.)

RULES FOR PLAY

❑ **822.** DISAGREEMENTS. As much as possible, let kids work out their own disagreements, as long as the argument doesn't become physical. If you intervene, ask participants to sit down and quietly think what has happened. Ask each to tell her side. Then ask if they would like you to settle the matter (they usually don't) or can they settle it and continue play.

❑ **823.** PUPPETS TELL WHAT REALLY HAPPENED. When it is difficult for a child to admit guilt or misbehavior, bring out the puppets—one for the parent, one for the child. The parent puppet starts by asking what is going on.

The child puppet usually tells just some of the facts. The parent puppet asks that the story of what happened be told again. (A second telling usually is more detailed than the first.) The parent puppet can say, "Little puppet, I want you to think really hard and see what else you can remember" or "What would Scott (the child) like you to tell me?" This usually brings out all the facts.

❑ **824.** THE FAIRY QUEEN. When kids playing dress-up or house begin to bicker, join in the game by becoming the fairy queen. If possible, wear a crown, a white scarf, or other elegant item from the dress-up box. With your fairy wand (this can be a yardstick wound with ribbon), make queen-like pronouncements instead of ordinary discipline. For example: "The queen wants everyone to speak kindly." "The queen will divide the toys and announce when they are to be exchanged." "The queen does not want to put anyone in the dungeon." This less-personal discipline very often works.

❑ **825.** SNACK ATTACKS. Sometimes kids get in trouble for eating candy or cookies—especially just before meal-time. Solve the problem by working together to make a snack bin for each youngster. You can use any kind of covered container labeled with the child's name. Put in packaged nutritious snacks—some salty, some sweet—that you approve of. Two a day should be the max and you should put in enough to last one week. There are just two rules—you can't eat another person's snacks and you can't snack in the hour before a meal. Then, put the youngsters on their honor, with the knowledge that the snack container only gets filled once a week.

RULES FOR LIVING TOGETHER

(Also see chapter 6, section 1 on the topic of manners, so essential for living together.)

❑ **826.** LITTLE WORDS FOR LITTLE FOLKS. Teach toddlers the spoken words of good manners: please, thank you, I'm sorry, excuse me. If a child asks for something without the word "please," or accepts something without saying "thank you," prompt him the first few times with the words "What do you say?" But quickly drop that line. Just ignore the request without "please" and quietly take back the given item if there is no "thank you."

☐ **827.** BORROWING AND RETURNING. It's good manners to ask before taking another's possessions. And it is very good manners to return the item promptly and in good condition. While it is good to share within a family, don't permit borrowing when the borrower does not show proper care for the item. If borrowing goes on outside the family, create a "borrowed" list for the family bulletin board. Show the date and who borrowed things like garden tools, kitchen supplies, toys, books, and so forth.

☐ **828.** CLOSED DOORS. A closed door is a message. It says: "Knock first." A closed door can also say: "Come back later." All family members over age four are entitled to some private time. This can be in the bathroom or in one's own room. However, parents should be alert to what is going on if the door is closed for long periods of time. And, when kids of opposite sexes are in a room, the door remains open.

☐ **829.** OOPS, I BROKE IT. Teach kids to "fess up" to mistakes. Things do get broken or spilled or lost, so make it a family rule to immediately admit what has happened. Don't accept any lame excuses such as "the cat did it."

☐ **830.** BEDTIME PEST. When a young child is ready for bed, be sure that she's had a bathroom trip, a drink of water, a story, and hugs and kisses. Then, unless you want a bedtime pest, explain to her that there are only three reasons for her to get out of bed and come to you: (1) She is sick and you will tend to her in her room. (2) The house is on fire or there is some other emergency you should know about. (3) She has not had enough punishment today and is asking for more. This system usually cures the pest.

❑ **831.** **BABYSITTER TREATS.** Some kids act up when a sitter is to care for them—they either cry or they are disobedient. Make a night with a babysitter into a special night. Call it "Popcorn Night," "Monopoly Marathon," or "Fudge Sundae Night." And, give the sitter the option of extending the bedtime by fifteen minutes for kids who don't cause trouble. Soon kids will be looking forward to having a sitter and planning what games and activities to do together, rather than just watching TV.

❑ **832.** **THE NAP FAIRY.** Young children who fight naptime (and still believe in the tooth fairy) should be told about the nap fairy who brings a little treat to kids who rest without argument. When sleep comes, the parent can place a small item on the foot of the bed.

❑ **833.** **RHYMED RULES.** For children under seven, family rules can be learned more quickly when they rhyme. Teach these to your youngsters:

Come when called the first time: When Mom or Dad calls my name, I come as fast as a speedy jet plane.
Being excused after a meal: We eat together for family fun, and ask to be excused when we're all done.
Coming in from play: I wipe my feet when I come in the door. That helps me keep mud off the floor.
Manners: "Please" and "thank you" are easy to say. How many times have you said them today?
Sharing: I have so many, many toys, I love to share with girls and boys.
Helping: "Can I help?" are words I can say. When work is done there's time to play.
Responsibility for a pet: I pat my doggie in a gentle way and remember to feed him every day.
Strapping in: In the car there's one way to be: Seated and belted means safety for me.

Crossing streets: When crossing a street, a hand I hold. That's the rule till I'm five years old.

Talking with strangers: I do not talk with strangers I see. This rule for safety is important to me.

Fighting over toys: If I argue about toys and don't act right, the toy is put away, out of my sight.

Snacks: When I get hungry and want a treat, I ask permission before I eat.

Taking turns: Taking turns is the way to talk. Speak one-at-a-time and please don't squawk!

Bathroom etiquette: After using the toilet, the thing to do is wash my hands and dry them, too.

Hitting: Hitting hurts and makes me sad. I remember what's right so I won't be bad.

TV viewing: Once in a while I see TV. But only if the program is good for me.

Picking up toys: When finished playing at the end of the day, I quickly put my toys away.

Clothing: My clothes never get thrown on the floor, just in the wash or in my drawer.

When it's bedtime: When I am told it's time for bed, I don't argue or shake my head.

Getting ready for bed: Before I go to bed each night, There are four things that I do right: Go to the bathroom without a fight, brush my teeth so they'll be bright. Wash my hands with all my might, give a hug and say "good night!"

Staying in bed: When I'm tucked into my bed I say my prayers and rest my head. I don't get out of bed and play. I think about the fun today.

SECTION 3: WHAT HAPPENS WHEN . . .

When family rules are broken, there is often need for punishment. These ideas will help impress on young people that they are responsible for their actions.

❑ **834.** **KEEP YOUR PERSPECTIVE.** Don't punish for every little infraction. Pick your occasions in order to make a point. Overlook minor wrongs with a laugh or a comment "That's silly." You want to teach youngsters that some things are very important and others less important.

❑ **835.** **SPANKING.** Although spanking is still one of the most common forms of punishment, decades of research show that it is less effective than other means (explained below) for making sure that the mistake is not repeated. When your youngster can understand, about age three, explain that you will discipline him in various ways, but spanking will not be one of them. (Spanking teaches a child that hitting another person is an appropriate response and he will use it with friends or even with you.) Spanking does not focus on the problem and how to correct it.

❑ **836.** **TAKE YOUR CHOICE.** When kids act up, tell them firmly that they have a choice to make. "It's your choice to nag me about wanting candy and be punished as soon as we get home or it's your choice to help me in the grocery store." Or, "You can choose to take toys away from Brian and then be punished, or you can choose to play happily." Leaving the decision up to the child is a first step toward self-government.

❑ **837.** **WHEN AND THEN.** When giving children options, state them when possible as "when . . . then" statements. For example don't say "Barry, you can't go to the park until you have cut the grass." Rather, state: "Barry, when the grass is cut, then you can go to the park." It is important not to stress choices negatively, and to put the more attractive activity second, as in the above example.

❑ **838.** **EITHER . . . OR.** Leave some decisions up to youngsters by stating it this way: "You may either stay up late tonight or you can stay up late one night this weekend. You decide." This empowers the youngster to make the decision.

839. **FRIENDLY CHOICES.** When you are working out a problem with your child, give the child a choice. As an example, Peter has lost his bike, which is essential to his paper route and to getting to school. Start by asking Peter what should be done. (Peter's usual response will be "I don't know.") Next, offer a solution that requires the child's help: "We'll help you buy a new one and you can help pay for it." When Peter rejects that idea, state that it's a way for him to take responsibility for where he leaves his bike. In a firm and friendly tone, give him a choice of walking to school and pulling a wagon on his paper route, or paying three dollars a week for the bike. (This is a plan you can both live with.) Give the choice once. Expect the youngster to test you. Stand firm, remain friendly.

840. **BAD BEHAVIOR BY PARENTS.** When a parent nags and scolds, the child gets attention and feels the power of keeping parents busy with him. When the parent gets angry and then gives in, the child feels the power of getting his way. When the parent gives vengeful punishment, the child rebels, figuring that he has been hurt so he can hurt back. When a parent gives up correcting a child, the child figures the parent doesn't care about him anymore. Working together, you and your youngster can stop this vicious circle!

841. **LISTEN AND AGREE.** When a child comes to you with a complaint or tale of woe, listen carefully and **agree with his feelings.** Child: "Hank pushed me down on the cement." Parent: "That must have hurt." Child: "I got a D on my paper and the guys think that's funny." Parent: "That must disappoint and hurt you." The child hopes you will have a solution, but you must remember that the problem is his, and he has to find a solution. Certainly you will help but not take the lead. By listening and agreeing with his reaction, you are not condoning what happened, you are creating an atmosphere for discussion and solution.

842. **WHAT IS PUNISHABLE?** Here are some examples. For very young children, you'll need to discipline for: ignoring rules, acting mean to friends, breaking things on purpose, tantrums, and failing to share. For gradeschoolers: breaking rules, forgetting chores, failing to do homework, and continually getting bad grades. For older kids, the same plus: cutting classes, getting a traffic ticket, being disrespectful, and taking part in dangerous and illegal activities. Punishment helps kids to remember the right things to do.

❑ **843.** WHAT ABOUT APPEARANCE? What kids wear does not have to become a discipline question. Kids can follow modern trends without being dirty or sloppy. With kid-help, divide a youngster's closet and shelves into sections: clothes suitable for school or casual events, play and work clothes, and clothes to wear for family events, church, and social occasions. Don't be swept along into buying expensive clothes. Don't comment on school clothes unless they are totally tacky, too revealing, or have gang connotations.

❑ **844.** WHAT ABOUT HER ROOM? One of the biggest points of contention in the family is the status of a youngster's room. The words "Clean up your room" echo around the world. Set a minimum standard of cleanliness (no food items or clothes on the floor) and then be sure that there are adequate shelves/boxes/drawers for a youngster's possessions. It should be a family rule that the room is tidied up once a week so it can be cleaned (by youngster, parent, or cleaning person). This includes changing the sheets, dusting, and vacuuming or mopping. If the room is not tidy for cleaning day, this is an occasion for discipline. (One mom charges her teen ten dollars an hour to tidy and clean it.) How the room looks the remainder of the week is the child's business since the room is her private domain.

❑ **845.** WHEN TO PUNISH? As soon as possible, unless your anger is out of control, or the offense is so serious you want to think about it for awhile or consult with your spouse. Sometimes a working parent is told of disobedience at school or hears of it from the babysitter, and so must deal with it after-the-fact. Still, do it as soon as possible.

❑ **846. WHERE TO PUNISH?** Home is best. Punishment in public is difficult and often compounds the problem by adding humiliation. If away from home, you may be able to find a quiet place. If not, you can say "I can't discipline you here, but believe me, you will be punished as soon as we're home." Then follow through on your threat.

❑ **847. WHO PUNISHES?** Unfortunately in many busy families it is no one! Corrections should be made by both parents so that one isn't the ogre and the other the saint. Let kids know that the parent on the scene will do it. None of that "Just wait until your father comes home!" If one parent seems to be more in charge during the week, the other should become the authority figure for the weekend. Be sure to instruct your sitter as to punishments she should carry out, and the infractions that she should report to you.

❑ **848. AT WHAT AGE?** Behavior training starts with babies when you use a pleasant voice and a smiling face for happy times (such as when a baby eats willingly) or a deep and stern voice with a somber face for unhappy times (such as when he throws all his toys out of the playpen). From this point onward, you will be gently correcting and firmly disciplining your youngsters until you are no longer responsible for them.

❑ **849. WHEN PUNISHMENT IS OVER.** When the period of discipline is over, it is over. Sometimes apologies are needed, sometimes not. Teaching children to say, and mean, "I'm sorry" can make others feel better. The parent should give a big hug, forget the incident and not bring it up again at supper, to neighbors, or grandparents. Here are some things you can tell your youngster: "I'm hoping you won't make that mistake again." "I trust you to do the right thing when I'm not watching over you." "I love you too much to let you break the law."

❑ **850.** NO APPEALS. As soon as children are three or four, explain that when a punishment is given, there are to be no appeals to the other parent for leniency. (One family doubles the punishment if kids try this!) Be sure that you have given the youngster every opportunity to talk about what happened before setting the punishment. That way, he will feel that he had a fair hearing. And reassure him that you care so much for him that you can't let him do wrong things.

❑ **851.** ATTENTION GETTING. Preschoolers are often naughty (shouting, kicking, throwing things) in order to gain attention. Firmly set the child down in a safe place on the floor, say nothing, turn away, and walk out of sight. Being deprived of an audience is often sufficient discipline and a child will learn that this behavior was of no benefit.

❑ **852.** BITING. When toddlers bite, some parents try to cure the habit by biting the child in return. This is like teaching a child not to steal by taking him to a store where you steal an item! When a child bites, quickly separate her from the other youngsters. If needed, take appropriate first aid measures for the bitten child. Biting is usually a phase that disappears when kids become more verbal, however, it is distressing and you can help stop it two ways. First, use preventive conversation, spending time with the playmates and giving the child attention, praising her for not biting, and clearly stating what will happen if she bites. Second, use curative measures such as removing the biting child to isolation. Explain simply but very seriously that biting will not be tolerated. Try to find out what triggered the biting and suggest an alternate means of expression. If biting occurs at a party, a park, a friend's home, immediately take the child home, telling her it is because she bit someone. You may have to repeat this process until she understands.

❑ **853.** KEEP IT SIMPLE. For young children who misbe-have, don't go into elaborate explanations. One word— "No!"—can be effective. Occasionally it will be followed by an explanation ("because that's not safe"). Teach kids that "no" means to stop immediately, and the question "why" will be answered after the unacceptable behavior has ceased.

☐ **854.** POWER PLAYS AND TANTRUMS. Stop this bad behavior as soon as a child starts to use it. Don't appear to be upset (although you may well be). Give the child a choice: "Stop screaming and kicking or there will be punishment—you choose. It's up to you." A parent must remain in control when a child is not in control. Discuss the behavior when you are both calm and then decide on a punishment together.

☐ **855.** MEAN WHAT YOU SAY. Ask your youngster if she understands when you say: "If you do that again, you'll get a time-out." Consistency is the basic requisite for good discipline. If you make a threat, you must follow through. Don't say you'll punish when you cannot carry it out. The moment you do, you open the door for kids to behave as they please without paying any heed to your words.

☐ **856.** ONE CHANCE ONLY. Some parents give a second chance before punishing. In a case where a child breaks a known rule, this second chance should not be given. Share with kids your decision to be firm about the rules and that ignoring certain rules, especially those concerned with safety, will cause swift punishment.

☐ **857.** HUMILIATION. The purpose of discipline is to correct, and humiliation should play no part in it. When you humiliate a youngster, the hurt is what is remembered, not the lesson in how to do better. For example, a parent embarrasses a four-year-old who wets his pants by making him spend the rest of the day in the wet pants. Humiliation is a not-so-subtle form of child abuse.

☐ **858.** PARENTAL FRUSTRATION. Sometimes when a child has been naughty, a parent is just so angry that the punishment may be excessive. If in retrospect you feel you have overreacted, sit down quietly with the youngster and apologize. She will be impressed with your honesty! Adjust the punishment if possible. But also explain that a parent wants so much for a child to be good and happy that when a child is naughty, it really hurts the parent. Another time, you might say: "I'm getting angry about this . . ." and that may change the behavior. Don't let kids think parents are always perfect—they'll soon find out otherwise.

❑ **859.** BROKEN CURFEW. One of the most frightening experiences for parents occurs when a youngster doesn't return home on time. Together, establish a curfew and a short grace period. Be very strict the first time the curfew is broken. If the time to return home is 10:45 to 11:00 P.M. be prepared to discipline for even one minute beyond 11:00. If you don't, you'll be taken advantage of on a regular basis. "Campus" a youngster one weekend night for each five minutes late (or portion thereof). Being "campused" means no going out, no phone calls, no TV, no visiting friends. If kids try the old "car ran out of gas" line, investigate the verity of it. Don't accept differences in clocks—tell youngsters that before they leave they should always set their watches in keeping with the family clock.

❑ **860.** NO "GO TO YOUR ROOM!" Many parents think that sending a youngster to his room is proper punishment. It is not. A child's room is his castle—his own precious place—and there should not be bad vibes about it. Besides, there's lots of fun stuff to do there! So, if you must send a child somewhere, send him to your room, or the laundry room, or a corner of the kitchen.

❑ **861.** PUNCH CARD. When taking a youngster out in public, such as to a store, make him a little three-by-five card from a piece of paper. On it draw three smiley faces and three sad faces. Explain that if she's helpful, you'll circle a smiley face. If she is difficult or naughty, you'll circle a sad face. If at the end of the trip there are more circles around the smiley faces, she can choose a treat.

❑ **862.** CHARGE A FEE. If you wish to correct a child who swears, talks in a fresh manner, or whines, here's a good cure. Fill a covered jar with five dollars in quarters. Each time there is an offense, take a quarter out. At the end of the month, the youngster gets any money that is left.

❑ **863.** THE THINKING BENCH. Probably the most common form of punishment for young children, the thinking bench, is also called "time-out" or isolation. The purpose is to stop the wrong activity and give the youngster an opportunity to think about what she did and how else she might have acted. For example, your daughter shoves a friend off a trike and the friend cries. When you've ensured that the friend is all right, take your child to the thinking bench (a real footstool in the laundry room, the second stair tread on the stairway, wherever she can be away from the activity). Put her here and set a timer—the kind that rings a bell. Be explicit about the mistake ("You took the trike, you made your friend cry") and ask her to think about what she did. The timer is set for as many minutes as the child is old, so a three-year-old will sit for three minutes. Early on, explain that if the child leaves the thinking bench, she is put back, and the timer is started again. When the bell rings, return to the child and ask "Since you wanted the trike, what is a better way for you to have gotten to use it?" She may have an answer or you may have to suggest one (asking for the trike, taking turns, offering a trade). Then point out that by being naughty she has missed playtime. Ask if she can now go and play happily and tell her friend she is sorry. Now, this procedure takes your time, but only at first. It will take less time as your child realizes the consequences of wrong behavior and doesn't want to go through this routine over and over again.

❑ **864.** CLEANING UP THE MESS. Sometimes having to clean up a mess—or help to clean it up—is sufficient punishment. (Remember, that playing with numerous toys is not something to be punished, it is creative fun. And, picking up at day's end is not punishment either, but a "given.") However, if a child spills paint, dumps out a drawer, throws all the sand out of the sandbox, or tosses food on the floor, he should clean it up. By the time a child is five, he should clean up most messes entirely by himself with only a few suggestions from the parent. Now the parent may be able to clean it up faster, but that's not the point. Teach the child the consequence of his action and don't deprive him of the lesson gained from the cleanup. Show him how to use rags, a pail of water, a scrub brush—whatever is necessary.

❏ **865.** EVEN STEVEN. Sometimes there is absolutely no way a child can undo what she has done wrong. Perhaps she has cut a hole in her best shirt or wasted thirty minutes of your time by being late when you came to pick her up at the library. The youngster has used up some of your time needlessly—by having to mend the hole or wait in the car. So, she pays you back your time by doing a special task—this is an "Even Steven" punishment. She may fold laundry or dust or weed—any task that can be done alone, in quiet, providing the opportunity to think about the importance of time.

❏ **866.** WRITTEN REPRIMANDS. It can be very impressive for a youngster to see a parent's displeasure in writing. Spoken words are said and gone, but written words are there to read and reread. If the misbehavior is a continual one, consider writing a note and placing it on a youngster's desk: "Dear Mark, I know you love Chipper, but dogs truly need fresh water each day. When you forget, I have to do your job and that makes me sad. Will you try harder? I love you, Mom." A child getting such a note is impressed that you took the time to write—and this often makes it an effective cure.

❏ **867.** WRITTEN COMPLIMENTS. You reinforce good behavior when you are appreciative. Perhaps you will mention the child's good conduct to your spouse or your parents (so the child hears). And, you can write a short note to the child and put it on her pillow: "Dear Diana, You really did a spiffy job on the kitchen counters tonight! It made my after-dinner time much easier and I appreciate that! Every minute counts for a working parent. I love you always, Dad."

❑ **868. LITTLE LECTURES.** In our fast-paced society, we often fail to take the time to fully explain the whys and wherefors. Many youngsters respond favorably to reason and, if you are good with words, you can use this talent to advantage. This is especially effective with kids between six and sixteen who have done something thoughtless or dangerous: playing with matches, running into the street, hurting a pet, mistreating a friend, ignoring chores, or failing to do homework. Make your lecture more than a sentence— repeat your message many different ways, which may seem tedious to the youngster but gets the message across. Following the lecture, ask for input as to how to avoid the same mistake again.

❑ **869. HUGE PUNISHMENTS.** Occasionally a child's disobedience is of such magnitude that you must devise a punishment that will be long remembered. You do this in hope that he will *never* repeat the mistake. Such punishment is reserved for occasions where a child has done something to endanger his own life or the lives of others: drag racing, playing with guns, or using drugs. One parent, whose daughter had violated the family rule about going into the swimming pool fenced area without adult permission (and she even fell into the pool), devised a huge punishment that consisted of being confined to the house after school for the first week. She also had to write a research paper on responsibility and safety, including interviews with neighbors, working on it at least thirty minutes a day. The second week she was enrolled in a CPR class. At the end of the second week she read the research paper out loud to the family and gave a CPR demonstration. While this may seem excessive, one of the younger children said, "Wow, I'll never break that rule 'cause I don't want that punishment to happen to me!" There was never any further breaking of the rule.

DEPRIVATION: A MOST-EFFECTIVE DISCIPLINE

Of all the ways to correct wrong behavior, *deprivation* is one of the best. The word sounds alarming, but it is actually a gentle, persuasive, and thoughtful method. It works with kids as young as three and right on through the teen years.

❑ **870. A FIRST CONVERSATION.** Initiate a dialogue with youngsters concerning society's methods of correcting people: a drunk driver is deprived of his license, a thief is deprived of his freedom. On a smaller scale, if we borrow something and don't return it, we're deprived of borrowing again. Or, if we slurp our juice and wipe our nose on our sleeve, we may be deprived of a party invitation. So, when we lose self-control and behave inappropriately, we lose privileges—we are deprived of them. Make the point clearly: that it is our own choice to act acceptably or unacceptably.

❑ **871. DEPRIVED OF WHAT?** When a child disobeys, she is deprived of something she really likes: a possession or a privilege. So, to use deprivation successfully you have to know what is important to your child. Certainly you know your child well enough to know what is meaningful to her: her bike, use of the telephone, weekend freedom, the car keys, television time, video games, a boom box, the right to spend money, a special toy or collection. Depending on the age of the youngster and the seriousness of the infraction, deprive her of her possession or privilege for a certain length of time—anywhere from a day to an entire month.

❑ **872. ADVANCE NOTICE.** Some deprivations can be known in advance as part of the family rules: If your grade-schooler gets a C minus or less, there will be no weekday TV until the next grading period and an improved grade. If your child disobeys a sitter, he will be put to bed before the sitter comes the next time. If your teen fails to be where she said she'd be, and doesn't phone with the change of place, she's "campused" for a week. If a teen gets a traffic ticket, his car keys and license are taken away. Most kids prefer knowing the rules and penalties in advance.

❑ **873.** BUT IT HURTS! If you have announced the deprivation, don't give in. So it is very important to be sure that you do not make an extremely hurtful deprivation (being forbidden to attend the prom) unless there is a large infraction (driving drunk). You, too, may feel sad when your youngster must miss an important event, but the lesson must be brought home and you can't weaken. So don't say, "If you don't improve your spelling grade you can't be on the soccer team" unless you intend to stick to your decision. And, when you make a concession, make it understood that this is a very special occasion and never likely to happen again.

ELEVEN

CAN CHORES BE FUN?

SECTION 1: WHO DOES WHAT

SECTION 2: GETTING THE JOB DONE WITH FUN

SECTION 3: SKILLS FOR INDEPENDENCE

Many parents think that they're being kind to their children by not having them do any chores. But really, they are raising kids who later in life won't be able to cope with work around the home. Working together provides opportunity for both conversation and horseplay—and it can actually build positive memories. No child is too old, too young, or too busy to contribute to the family.

SECTION 1: WHO DOES WHAT

Although I've written about chores in many of my books, in this chapter I've brought the best ideas together so that you can start early to prepare your child to be a functioning adult by teaching what it takes to maintain a home.

❑ **874.** GET AN ATTITUDE! Talk with the family about what makes a good and fair boss since parents are usually the boss when it comes to assigning chores and judging whether the job is done in a satisfactory way. Be consistent but don't be too strict. Unless the queen is coming for dinner, a child's good effort can be as acceptable as a child's *excellent* effort, which will come by example and practice.

❑ **875.** LET ME SHOW YOU. No matter how simple the task assigned, show a child how to do it. You may have to do this several times, but in the long run it will save *you* time. Be strict about the dangers of working around the house: sharp knives in the dishwasher, a hot dryer, running over the vacuum cord, playing with the lawn mower, and misusing a tool. Don't let poorly done work stop you from giving more instruction and more opportunities to do it successfully.

❑ **876.** REPETITION WINS. When first introducing chores, don't change the chores each week—that can come later. Let a youngster repeat the same tasks for two or three weeks until he can do the job in a satisfactory way. Then talk about how often kids want to change their chores: weekly or monthly.

❑ **877.** PUT IT IN WRITING. You may remember everything there is to do, but kids don't. Each week, make a list for young children and have older ones make their own lists of tasks. Be specific. This might be a gradeschool child's list:

Morning: Feed the dog, make three beds.

Afternoon: Set the table, make a salad.

Evening: Wipe the kitchen counters, tidy the family room.

Weekends: Water the house plants, make Saturday lunch, and participate in a project of building bookshelves.

☐ **878.** NO STEREOTYPES. Don't let home tasks get stuck in cement—Mom the cook, Junior the rubbish, Dad the lawn-mowing, and Sis the laundry folding. Dads can bake and make beds, Junior can do laundry and arrange flowers, Mom can wash the car, and Sis can trim the bushes. Giving kids opportunities to do all the chores will empower them when they're finally on their own.

☐ **879.** HOW MUCH TIME FOR TASKS? While preschoolers can work about fifteen minutes a day, older children should contribute thirty minutes. And, over the weekend, a total of two hours of work can be contributed by each family member (except preschoolers who will work about an hour). You can see that with two children, you'll get nine extra hours each week to spend on something special!

☐ **880.** HOW MANY TASKS? AND IS THERE PAY? Helpful things kids can do fall into three categories: routine daily tasks, assigned weekend tasks, and special tasks that are paid for. The first two categories are "givens"—things kids do because they are part of the family. The special tasks should carry a fee. Sit down with the family and make a list of everything that needs to be done to make the house run smoothly, assigning some as regular chores, others as paid work.

☐ **881.** CHORES FIRST, PLAY SECOND. Most weekday tasks should be done before evening fun and television viewing. And when the weekend work projects are finished, there can be a reward: an excursion, ice-cream sundaes, a video, or a later bedtime. Explain when kids are young that they must plan to get their chores done despite their sports practices, parties, and other activities.

❑ **882.** TODDLER TASKS. As soon as a child can walk and understand a few directions, she's ready for toddler tasks—ones you supervise and really express your appreciation for. These are favorites: delivering things to various rooms of the house ("Please put this shirt on Susie's bed"), picking up leaves in the yard, bringing in the newspaper, helping set the table, and of course, picking up toys.

❑ **883.** PRESCHOOLER ASSIGNMENTS. Learning to follow directions and learning to remember two or three things at a time are valuable lessons. Consider these tasks: helping fold laundry and delivering it, smoothing beds and fluffing pillows, emptying wastebaskets, learning the names of tools and how to fetch and carry them safely, opening blinds and curtains, sweeping the patio, and feeding pets.

❑ **884.** GRADESCHOOLERS' WORK. Bigger, taller kids can empty and load the dishwasher, wipe counter tops, bring in the mail, put up the flag, make flower arrangements, select and play recordings, entertain a baby (while adult is nearby), weed the garden, run sprinklers, rake leaves, groom pets, clean lavatories and bathtubs, bake a cake, water house plants, dust and vacuum, polish silver, sew and mend, shovel snow, and help with grocery shopping.

❑ **885.** JUNIOR HIGH JOBS. Although much less supervision is needed, still try to make some chores a team effort with a parent or sibling. Consider: washing the car, making complete meals, painting fences, planning menus, doing repairs, making flower arrangements, sewing clothes, serving as babysitter while parents nap or bathe, running errands on bicycle, taking trash to the curb for pick-up and bringing containers back later, building a fire in the fireplace, reading reviews and recommending movies, testing younger kids on spelling words, reading stories to younger children, and keeping the family scrapbook or photo album up-to-date.

❑ **886.** HIGH SCHOOL CHORES. By this time, little supervision is needed so be sure some of the chores still involve adult companionship. In addition to the preceding list, consider these: changing the car's oil and oil filter, putting up storm windows or screens, building a backyard fire pit or fence, changing faucet washers and light bulbs, washing windows inside and out, doing the grocery shopping, scrubbing floors, mowing the lawn, babysitting, assisting at parties, defrosting/cleaning/reloading refrigerator or freezer, cleaning out closets and drawers, painting a room, setting up the VCR, helping pay bills, and running errands by car.

❑ **887.** PARENTS GET THE LEFTOVERS. Tasks not assigned belong to parents. Don't be shy about listing these to show how much work you are doing. Talk about these jobs and see if kids want to take some of the load off you. If both parents work, the parent's job list should be equally divided between spouses. If there is an at-home parent, the other parent should still accept responsibility for a fair number of chores.

❑ **888.** FAMILY WORK DAY. Occasionally, on a weekend day or a holiday, make a list of jobs that need doing and an estimate of the time required (no more than ninety minutes). Furnish a bell to be rung as each job is completed. Starting with the youngest child, let each choose which task to accomplish, and then all go to work. When one finishes her job and rings the bell, she looks for another worker and helps him. When they finish and ring the bell, they continue to work with others until all the work is done. Then it's time for fun!

❑ **889.** EFFECTIVE ERRANDS. Rather than allotting many weekend hours to running around town doing errands, include kids in these errands when on your way home from school, from sports practice, or other places. Weekend errands almost disappear when you tie them into other trips. And grocery shopping speeds along with good helpers. Divide your list into sections such as produce, canned goods, breads, or paper supplies, and give each mini-list to a youngster. The job will be done in half the time!

❑ **890.** TOOL TIME. Not every member of the family may find the hardware store fascinating, but expose both boys and girls to the wonders of these chock-full-of-stuff places. As you walk about, name tools and other supplies and explain some uses. Our young grandson's first three word sentence was "Go Home Depot" (the name of a favorite hardware store that his handy father takes him to almost every Saturday). By age five, give youngsters their own toolbox and simple, safe tools of their own.

SECTION 2: GETTING THE JOB DONE WITH FUN

While some youngsters just automatically accomplish their assigned chores, others may need encouragement, especially at the beginning. Here are some ways to get the jobs done without nagging.

❑ **891.** AFTER-SUPPER CHECK. If Fido's bowl is empty and the laundry still stacked and waiting to be delivered to each room, it's best to know about it before bedtime. Not during supper—a pleasant event—but immediately after, ask each family member to check his list and be sure all tasks are completed. Say little to those who scurry off to complete their work, but be full of praise to those who have finished.

❑ **892.** PICTURE CHART. Children who don't yet read can have a picture chart to remind them: a toothbrush picture to remind them to brush teeth, a dog picture means fill Fido's water bowl, a picture of a knife/fork/spoon means set the table, a picture of toys means to pick them up. Explain the pictures so that there is no doubt as to what must be done.

❑ **893.** CHECK IT OFF. Some kids function better by actually checking off the job when it is done. Start with a simple chart with seven boxes for the days of the week. As needed, you can get fancy with stars or stickers or tie the chart into the season or a holiday. Keep the chart somewhere it can easily be seen—on the family bulletin board or refrigerator door. One parent places it right in front of the television screen, indicating that chores come first!

❑ **894.** BE A CHAIRPERSON. Everyone likes to feel "in charge." And you can give kids that feeling of control by putting them in charge of one area in the home and then giving them a title: Chairperson of Pets, Chief Sweeper-upper, Assistant Gourmet Chef, Toy Coordinator, Co-engineer for Maintenance, or Archivist (the one in charge of the family scrapbook and photo album). See who can come up with a catchy title for other chores.

❑ **895.** PICK-UP CHALLENGE. One of the most boring tasks seems to be putting away toys and clothes. For recalcitrant workers, set a timer and issue the challenge: "I bet you can't get everything put away before the bell rings" or "I say this will take you eight minutes—a treat if you can do it in seven."

❑ **896.** CELEBRATION DINNER. On the first weekday of each month, plan a celebration. Be complimentary about all the work the family has accomplished. Ask what new things kids learned while doing chores. If you have been using the star or sticker method to show that a day's work was completed, give a small reward for twenty-five stars (a near-perfect month). And, when there is a perfect month, seat that child at the head of the table and toast him!

❑ **897.** IN THE CRACKS. Teach kids that each task

may require a specified amount of time, but it can take less time if it is done "in the cracks." Some examples: While helping make dinner, set out some of the elements for the next-day's lunch. While walking through the family room, put away one toy. While talking on the phone, brush the dog. While unloading the dishwasher, set the table for the next meal. While picking up your room, select clothes for the next day. While brushing your teeth, memorize a poem taped on the mirror.

SECTION 3:
SKILLS FOR INDEPENDENCE

In order to live useful and satisfying lives, young people need to master the "how to" in many categories. Here are a few you can teach by example or with hands-on experiences so kids will know what to do when on their own.

❑ **898.** FOOD NOT GARBAGE. When kids gain that wonderful teenage freedom, nutritious eating often goes down the tubes in favor of snacking and fast foods. This won't happen as often if you include kids in preparing meals at home. Let them plan menus and teach them how to cook. Interest them in the joys and money-saving merits of baking and preserving. Emphasize the importance of kitchen cleanliness and teach the shelf life of perishable foods. During weekends and vacations, give them titles: Salad Chef, Cookie Creator, Vegetable Goddess, Hamburger Hero, and Potato Potentate.

❑ **899.** HOW TO HOST. Help kids to be comfortable when they're entertaining others. Through your own example when entertaining, or in advance of a youth party, show youngsters just how to greet friends at the door, introduce people, announce the rules of a game, award prizes, encourage guests to enjoy the refreshments, mix friends for dancing, be alert to the use of drugs, provide time for conversation, and end the party on a high note.

❏ **900.** **REPAIRS.** Work together, particularly when repairing broken toys. Teach the names of tools and how to do simple repairs in a safe manner. See if your children can do these things: glue broken china, fix a leaky faucet, repair a garden hose, glue a wobbling chair back, mend a broken door step, oil a squeaking door.

❏ **901.** **SHREWD SHOPPING.** Whether it's clothes, toys, or food, teach youngsters to look for the best values—not just the cheapest price. As an example, buy two brands of canned pear halves that have different prices. Check to see if the cheaper one has just as many halves of the same size as the more expensive can. Is "heavy syrup" versus "packed in its own juice" worth extra money? Does one pair of name brand jeans last longer or look better than one half the price? How long did a faddish purchase stay in style? If you're comparing two sleeping bags, is the one with the movie logo of better quality so that it's worth more? Teach kids to be comparison shoppers and get the best value for their money.

❏ **902.** **PERSONAL CARE.** Most parents make all the arrangements for a child's health, dental, optical care—to the point that many youngsters don't know the contents of their own records or the costs of this care. This information is very important when kids are on their own (and possibly without insurance), so let teens make their own appointments, keep their own records, and ask their own intelligent questions.

❏ **903.** **HOUSECLEANING.** While you may have maid service, this likely won't be the case when kids start out on their own. Be sure kids know there is more to housework than dusting a few table tops and vacuuming the center of the room. Show how to clean bathrooms, baseboards, windows, picture frames, lamps, art objects, refrigerator shelves, ovens, carpets, book shelves, even light bulbs (yes, washing them quarterly when cool will give much more light). And here's an idea for teaching kids how to clean closets and cupboards. Using stick-on notes, put a price on each (twenty-five cents up to two dollars). Let family members sign up on the sticker if they want to do that job within the week. Give good ideas on unloading it, cleaning it, putting down fresh shelf paper, and (unless you choose to do this yourself) returning the contents in an orderly way.

❏ **904.** CLOTHING CARE. As you probably know, you can turn white underwear pale blue by tossing new jeans in the washer with them. Or, you can have green diapers created by a dad who included a small throw rug in with them to save a load. So, to avert disasters, teach laundry skills: sorting, spot-removing, care of wash-and-wear fabrics or wools, and folding. Also teach all children how to sew so that they can create, mend, and properly sew on a button.

❏ **905.** YARD MAINTENANCE. Save money by teaching kids how to mow the lawn and care for the yard (planting, weeding, fertilizing, and composting). Actually, with a power mower safely used, lawn care can be fun. Take kids with you to the garden shop. Teach them the names of some common flowers, shrubs, and trees you have on your property.

❏ **906.** AUTOMOTIVE KNOW-HOW. Teach guys and gals basic car care: how to pump gas, choose the correct gas, read gauges, change oil and oil filter, change a tire, replace car fuses, and wash and vacuum. When you take a car in for service, always take one youngster along. Let him see how problems are described and diagnosed. That way, when a youngster gets her first car, she won't be easily intimidated.

❏ **907.** CLUTTER. Anyone who has visited a youngster's dorm or first apartment realizes that those lessons in housekeeping seem to have been quickly forgotten! Set an example with clutter-free living and help kids to create an environment that is efficient to live in as well as pleasant to look at. Create storage places for items to be recycled and get rid of them monthly. Have a box for out-grown clothing and other items that can be donated to rummage sales or charitable groups. Sort the mail daily and put nonurgent reading and catalogs in a bin for leisure perusal. Provide toy bins with lids so that kids can store similar toys efficiently. Each September, spend time in each child's room—a time to get rid of old clothing, broken toys, and outgrown books, as well as to clear the decks for the new school year. Teach the rule: if it hasn't been used in the last twelve months, give it away so someone else can enjoy it.

TWELVE

CHILD OF THE

TWENTY-FIRST CENTURY

SECTION 1: YOUR EDUCATED CHILD

This book has suggested many things to do with your child. But concerning his education, here are a few things not to do with your child: Don't do his homework. Don't side with her against the teacher until you know all the facts. Don't overload him with extracurricular activities. Don't force her into classes/careers that were your own unfulfilled dreams.

However, it is important for you to understand basic educational concepts. These differentiate between an educated child and one who has merely "sat through" twelve or more years of schooling. Although the best education begins in babyhood, if your youngster is older, you might want to read and put into practice some of these early concepts, just to be sure you haven't missed encouraging any of them.

❑ **908.** **CONCEPTS FOR BABIES AND TODDLERS.** A sense of what is important is taught by our responses to his activities—whether we rant and rave about spilled milk or we eagerly help him pick up toys. That we mean what we say is important for our teens but it is taught earlier in our response when a baby reaches out for something he shouldn't touch. Here we're teaching that no means no, not maybe. Caring for possessions is learned when we encourage a child to care for toys rather than destroy them. Unselfishness is taught in simple play when a baby learns to give a toy to another. Patience is learned when little princes and princesses demand toys or attention right now—and parents don't jump to fill the need, instead teach phrases such as "Not now" or "Later." Satisfaction over an accomplishment is learned when you clap for his success with a toy, or smile when he rocks his doll.

❑ **909.** **CONCEPTS FOR A PRESCHOOLER.** Independence is taught as children learn to be on their own for some activities. Toilet training should be taught but not forced, and a child should learn the descriptive words about it—words you wouldn't mind hearing in public!

Simple table manners should be taught (see chapter 6, section 1) since bad manners can become automatic at a very early age. How to dress oneself using zips/snaps/buttons, tie shoes, and brush hair will require patient parental instruction. Teaching skills such as numbers, colors, left and right, throwing and catching, start in these years. But far more important than teaching a preschooler to actually read is teaching her to love books.

❑ **910.** CONCEPTS FOR YOUNG GRADESCHOOLERS. Before going to kindergarten, it is helpful if a child can print and recognize his own name, know his parent's name/ address/phone number, paint and paste, understand how to take turns, and dress himself for cold weather. Some kindergartens have nap time so youngsters need the home practice of resting (pretending to sleep). Other valued concepts are: speaking loudly enough to be heard, sitting quietly and listening, telling time, caring for possessions, handling lunch money, and knowing how to get to school and return whether it be waiting for a carpool or school bus, or walking.

❑ **911.** THE SUCCESSFUL STUDENT. Some students will succeed no matter what school and home support they receive. However, interested and involved parents are one of the biggest elements of success. Parents should provide a place for study and facilities for research so that a youngster can keep up-to-date on homework. The student needs to know how to organize ideas as well as how to write a coherent paper with proper spelling and grammar (there may not always be a computer to do this). A home computer, used for more than games, will be helpful in using school computers.

❑ **912.** THE MOST VALUABLE EDUCATION. If you can teach a youngster to enjoy reading, you have given him the finest education. If he can read, he can do most anything. Start reading to babies so they become accustomed to paying attention to the words and pictures. Make bedtime reading a must—reading to young children, permitting older ones to stay up fifteen minutes later for reading. Keep books in the car and take them into offices where you may have to wait. Let kids read in the bathtub. Encourage listening to books on tape that can be borrowed from the library.

❑ **913.** GETTING AN ATTITUDE. Educated children need to be able to write persuasively: develop an opinion, back it up with facts and reasons, and consider opposing viewpoints. For practice, have kids write out a request (for a later bedtime or to have her ears pierced). Tell them that their essay request should contain the facts, reasons for change, and consideration of the objections. If the paper is well thoughtout, you may accede to the request!

❑ **914.** SILLY COURSES. An occasional lightweight course may have some merit, but set high standards when helping youngsters choose classes. Ask questions such as: "What will you learn in this class? How can you use this information? How will it fit in with other classes?" If kids want to take a course because it is "fun," explain that it must also be practical or physically or intellectually challenging.

❑ **915.** BE REALISTIC. At the beginning of the school year, help kids to set some desired grade standards (such as two As, two Bs, and one C). After the first semester, challenge a youngster to raise one of the grades. Point out that in the real world, excellence comes by accepting the challenge to be a little better each day.

❑ **916.** TWENTY QUESTIONS. The art of asking questions is important in this information age, so teach kids that just being able to answer questions isn't always as important as knowing what questions to ask. Play games with kids that require questioning: the old familiar Twenty Questions and the currently popular Jeopardy.

❑ **917.** FINDING ANSWERS. Parents and teachers will not always be on hand to answer questions. Teach children the resources of a dictionary and encyclopedia—books you should have at home. As they enter school, make the public library a familiar research location. And then introduce them to the Internet—the way a youngster can access the best minds on any subject.

❑ **918.** **THE DAY CARE OF YOUR DREAMS.** If your baby or toddler must be in day care (as opposed to your care until kindergarten age), choose the best facility with the least number of babies. See that the facility is licensed. Go with your baby and visit and observe the following:

☑ **Staff.** Is there sufficient staff to give personal care? Do they seem calm, interested, and loving? Is staff turnover too frequent to allow for quality care?

☑ **Cribs and diaper-changing area.** Is the bedding clean and the changing surface clean? Does the area have a pleasant odor?

☑ **Kitchen and eating area.** Are the menus posted? Is the food nutritious? Are the high chairs sparkling clean?

☑ **Play area.** Are the playpens clean? Is the floor clean where babies crawl? Are the toys in good condition and stimulating? Are there opportunities for music, book time, outside play?

☑ **Safety.** Is there a full-time staff person with first-aid training? Is there a posted fire/emergency plan? Has there ever been a formal complaint filed against the facility or an employee? (It's your right to ask.) Are you welcome to drop in unannounced?

❑ **919.** **PRESCHOOL IS PLAY SCHOOL.** A day care for a preschooler is quite different from one for babies and toddlers. This is a venue for learning social skills. Avoid the school that is pushing a child out of playtime years and encouraging early learning, which can bring on academic burnout later. Take your preschooler for a visit and be alert to pertinent points in #918, plus these factors:

☑ **Children's ages.** Are there two or more children the same age as yours?

☑ **Curriculum.** Do the activities support eye-hand coordination, motor skills, following directions, learning to dress self and tie shoes, working with others, increasing attention span? Does the school have a teaching philosophy and a general curriculum? Are social skills (bathroom etiquette, table manners, politeness) taught? Are the educational skills taught without pressure to read or use a computer, but rather with an emphasis on learning to think and express ideas clearly?

☑ **Staff.** Are the teachers well-trained including at least one who knows the various stages of child development? Do they teach at a child's eye level, instead of talking and supervising "from above"?

☑ **Equipment.** Is the outside play equipment challenging and in safe condition? Does the inside equipment encourage both active and quiet play? Is there a large library of quality books? (There should be NO television viewing.)

☑ **Quiet Time.** Does the school have a quiet/nap time? Are the mats clean?

☑ **Atmosphere.** Is the atmosphere a happy one?

❑ **920.** **CHECKING OUT A GRADE SCHOOL OR HIGH SCHOOL.** As a taxpayer or tuition payer, you should know what you're getting for your money. Go over the following points with your youngster, then make one or two visits to assess the quality of the school.

☑ **Class size.** No more than twenty-five means better learning opportunities.

☑ **Atmosphere.** Upbeat, casual, happy—as opposed to regimented or rowdy. Be sure to inquire of the administration concerning crime at the school.

☑ **Staff.** Experienced teachers of both sexes who are dedicated to teaching—not merely maintaining order; a strong administration that insists on a teaching plan from each teacher; and a grading system that does not simply pass slower students along before they are ready.

☑ **Curriculum.** Solid education in the basics with special classes for reading encouragement when needed; early teaching of a second language; art, drama, music as part of the regular curriculum; and a minimum offering of lightweight classes like basket weaving or hedgehog raising.

☑ **Equipment.** Computers, an extensive library, musical instruments, scientific supplies.

☑ **Physical education.** A rigorous program with both indoor and outdoor facilities; basic safety instruction on drugs and sex taught at appropriate ages and retaught on a regular basis.

☑ **Extracurricular.** Opportunities beyond school hours like science club, spelling bees, speech tournaments, educational decathlons, statewide essay contests, science fairs, and sports teams with competitive team play only for students maintaining a minimum grade average of C.

☑ **Counseling.** Trained professionals who spot problems early and know how to handle them. Counseling for college and career starting in the tenth grade.

☑ **Safety.** A closed campus (no coming and going during the day). A strict and enforceable policy regarding weapons and drugs.

❑ **921. PROGRESS OR FLUFF?** Don't wait for a report card to know how your child is progressing. And don't rely on a youngster's "Everything is fine" response to your questions. Attend all parent/teacher conferences even if you have to leave work early. If necessary, phone a teacher to get a specific question answered. Go over the following questions with your youngster, add to them, and get the answers at your first conference.

☑ Is my child working up to the proper level?

☑ What are her strengths? Weaknesses?

☑ What does the teacher take into account in grading?

☑ Is the homework completed in a satisfactory manner?

☑ Is the youngster self-disciplined, responsible, cooperative?

☑ How does she take suggestions and criticism?

☑ Are her social skills and self-confidence developing?

☑ What can I do to support a good education?

❑ **922. TESTING TIMES.** Ask your child to tell you when there are going to be statewide standardized tests at school. The day before such events should be special for the student (that way you'll be sure to be informed): no chores, dinner of his choice, a long bath before a sensible bedtime, and his favorite breakfast in the morning. These tests show how effective the school teaching is as well as identifying strengths and weaknesses of the students.

❑ **923.** **"DO YOUR HOMEWORK!"** Your child could probably get a good grade if you did his homework, but that's not the purpose! Homework is the proof of what a child has learned and can put into practice. It is the means of cementing new facts into thought. You can best contribute to good homework by using the PACT System. Let the youngster make the PACT sign that stands for Place, Asking, Checking, Talking. Hang it on the wall near the place he does his homework as a reminder that you have a pact with him to help him be smart, successful, and learn what's necessary for a happy life.

P IS FOR PLACE. Research shows that homework done on a bed or with the TV on isn't as thorough or meaningful as homework done in an educational environment. Enlist your youngster's input for making a pleasant place to do homework. It can be a desk or table with a well-equipped shelf in an area that is free from distractions such as sibling play, the telephone, or a view of the yard.

A IS FOR ASKING. It's a parent's duty to ask that boring question "What is your homework today?" (Even ask high school kids.) And, it's a child's duty to answer. The question shows that you care about his education, it can be a subtle reminder that there is some homework to do, and it keeps you up to speed on his current learning. Other questions are more specific: "How did your report go?" "Did you have the test today?" "Is your math getting any easier?" "What is the plan for the field trip?" "Did the new band music come?" "Have you been given a long-range assignment?" These questions and answers keep you "in the loop" as far as your youngster's education goes.

C IS FOR CHECKING. If you correct math errors in homework, or edit written work, your child will probably repeat the same mistakes. Your job is to make general suggestions ("Problem three is wrong." "The second paragraph could use more exciting adjectives.") For a misspelled word, give a hint how the word begins and let a child look it up in a dictionary. Certainly this takes time, but in the long run it makes for a smarter student. Check on your student during the homework session and offer a snack at half-time.

T IS FOR TALKING. Conversation is a great educator. Choose an academic subject you'd like to share with your child—it can be one on which you're already knowledgeable or one you're eager to learn about. You may also find subjects in the newspaper or magazines that relate to school subjects. Talk about your favorite authors, how you got into business, or plans for the future. Let the talk go both ways—listen to your youngster's plans and dreams, have her describe her soccer skills or computer problems. Show your respect for knowledge: look over completed or graded homework and share her successes with all the family.

❑ **924.** MAJOR PROJECT. When assigned a large project, some kids are overwhelmed and just put it out of thought. Because you ask questions and are aware of the project, you can be helpful in many ways. First, talk about it at dinner—you will be surprised at the good ideas offered by other family members. Mark the calendar for the due date and also mark the date two days before (as the date to show off the project to the family). Let the student list the ideas or elements, and together put the work in a logical order. Then, suggest that she work on it only fifteen minutes each day. She'll soon find it's completed!

❑ **925.** ORDER OF WORK. For the majority of students, it is important to do the most exacting homework first while they're most fresh and eager. But the tendency is to do the easy things first. For most scholars, this is the best order: math, writing, nonfiction reading, science projects, fiction reading. Have the student estimate the time required to complete the homework. Then divide it up into twenty to thirty minute segments with a bend-and-stretch time between each.

❏ **926.** **PAY FOR GRADES?** It's an on-going debate, but nowadays many agree that pay for grades is similar to adult pay for work. The following system works for many families, especially if the pay is sufficient so that a percentage goes into savings. With student input, set up a sliding scale for grades A through C (not C minus). Also set a fee for a grade raised, and a deduction for a grade that falls. Make small bonuses for good character ratings if the report card lists those. Give a small payment for sharing a report card the day it is distributed. Have cash on hand for immediate payment. Do this for each middle-of-term and end-of-term grading period for one year, then discuss the system together to see if it has encouraged better grades.

❏ **927.** **THE CONTRACT.** When a youngster needs academic encouragement, talk about writing a contract together. It might look like this:

THE CONTRACT

Hereby let it be recognized that _____, known hereafter as the Student, and _____, known hereafter as the Parent, have willingly entered into the following contractual agreement. The Student agrees to achieve the following: _____.
In return, the Parent agrees to grant the following: _____. The length of time to complete this contract is from (dates) _____ to _____. The terms of this agreement include no nagging or shouting by the Parent, and no cheating or grumbling by the Student. Signed with love this _____ day of _____, (year) _____.
_____ (Student)
_____ (Parent)

❏ **928.** **TEACHER AT DINNER.** "Oh no!" may be the initial response, but if you start this tradition when children are in grade school, it should go better in the later years. Some teachers detest this idea, others welcome it. If the teacher is married, include the spouse (busy teachers will enjoy not having to cook). Work with your child on planning the food. Allow time to show off his room and time for parent and teacher to talk alone. Don't make it a long event—just a casual time for getting-to-know-you.

❏ **929.** THIS IS MY CHILD. At the start of the school year, write a letter to the teacher describing your young child's interests, her strong and weak points, and including your offer to help. Ask your child what she would like the teacher to know about her. Include your home and business phone numbers.

❏ **930.** IS THIS CHILD GIFTED? Poor grades and apathy can be signs of a child in need of tutoring, but they can also be signs of a bright child not being challenged. While double grade promotions used to be the answer for gifted children, it was found that this often resulted in a child who was socially and physically out-of-step with classmates. In the book *Your Gifted Child* by Joan Smutny, Kathleen Veenker, and Stephen Veenker (New York: Facts on File, 1989), these are the signs of a gifted child:
1. Expresses curiosity about many things with thoughtful questions.
2. Has and uses extensive vocabulary with complex sentences.
3. Solves problems in original and imaginative ways.
4. Has a good memory and can order things in logical sequence.
5. Exhibits unusual talent in art, music, creative drama.
6. Discusses and elaborates on ideas and shows humor.
7. Learns quickly and puts learned concepts in new contexts.
8. Takes initiative, has a sustained attention span, works independently, has persistence in working on challenging tasks.

9. Enjoys reading and can make up stories and tell them.

While the school usually nurtures gifted children, the home environment plays a very important role. Create home opportunities for creativity, effective time management, research, decision making, goal setting, and acceptance of failure and success. Outside the home, provide time for travel, museum visits, and live theater. Hints on raising a gifted child are available free from the Center for Gifted, National-Lewis College, Evanston, IL 60201.

❑ **931.** IS COLLEGE IN THE FUTURE? According to the Bureau of the Census, a college education doubles lifetime earnings and increases quality of life. Starting in tenth grade, work with your youngster and the school counselors to plan a program that will prepare him for several likely colleges. Academic requirements differ from school to school, so it's wise to check entrance requirements a few years in advance. Visits to nearby colleges provide valuable input during the high school years.

❑ **932.** NEW SCHOOL. Take away the fear of the first day at school by making a scouting trip during the summer. Start by going over the route to be walked or driven and determine the travel time needed. (This will help to start the big day on time.) Check out the playground and let kids try the equipment. While you can look in the schoolroom windows, an inside tour may be available. Youngsters are especially interested in a classroom of their grade level, computer lab, art room, locker location, gym, library, principal's and nurse's offices, and cafeteria.

❑ **933.** ADHD? Not all overly active children have Attention Deficit Hyperactivity Disorder. Some kids just have a less-developed attention span and are more mischievous. Pediatricians say it is normal for three-to-five-year-olds to race from one activity to another when they are overly excited, hungry, or tired. Work with your youngster to develop a sustained interest in books, coloring, play with toys, and conversation with you. For a period of about six months, monitor the behavior. If the child is overly active and unsettled all of the time and in every setting, it can be a sign that help is needed.

❑ **934.** CROSS-COUNTRY CHALLENGE. Most kids have a cousin or friend in another part of the country. In the summer, create a cross-country book reading challenge. Let youngsters choose a book that both would enjoy reading that week. At the end of the week, permit a five minute phone call to discuss the finished book—as well as other bits of news.

❑ **935.** COUNTING GAMES. One grandfather, who lives with his son and family, has started a tradition that helps kids learn to count, and then to learn the multiplication table. After the bedtime story, he and the child start counting toward the magic number, which is 100. They alternate calling the next number. As they get older, they count by 2s to 100, or by 3s to 102, and so forth. When they become proficient, they speed up the counting pace.

❑ **936.** FAST MULTIPLYING. Here's a trick that's fun to share with a younger child who is having trouble with the multiplication table for 9. The trick is to add one digit to the left side and subtract one digit on the right side. So, it's 9 plus 1 on the left (19) and subtract 1 on the right (18). From 18 you add 1 on the left (28) and subtract 1 on the right (27). Once you get the hang of it, it's fast fun.

❑ **937.** MATH WIZARD. The game is called Thirteen. On a table, lay out (face up) a pyramid of playing cards. In the top row place just one card, then place two cards overlapping the lower half of the top row. It is important to reveal only the top half, not the full size of the card. Continue making rows of three, four, five, six, and seven cards, each overlapping the bottom half of the row above. Keep the remainder of the deck face down. Now, start the game with the bottom row. If any two cards total thirteen (for example a six and a seven), remove those cards. (Aces are one, picture cards are eleven.) If no two cards total thirteen, turn over one card from the deck. If it, and a card from row seven total thirteen, remove those two cards. Soon, the *full size* of a card or cards in row six will be visible, and those cards can be included in making matches totaling thirteen. Each player has the opportunity to make a match by turning over a card from the deck. If a match is made, he continues. If not, the card goes to the bottom of the deck and the turn goes to the other person playing. Gradually you will work your way both across and up the pyramid. The aim is to collect as many cards making thirteen as possible—and even all of them occasionally. And while having fun, you'll be learning all the combinations that total thirteen.

❑ **938.** DOMINO MATH. Children enjoy playing dominoes—a game that can be adapted for all ages. Little children count the dots on each of the matched pieces. Young gradeschoolers practice addition, announcing the total number on both matched pieces. And, as older gradeschoolers play their piece, they multiply the numbers on the two pieces. Teens can give the square of the dots.

SECTION 2: THE ELECTRONIC FUTURE

❑ **939.** EQUALS. Let learning about the computer be a joint experience. Make a comfortable seat next to your own at the computer keyboard and allow very young children to observe how you work. Show the connection between the keyboard and the screen. When old enough, let the child trade seats with you and operate the keyboard. There are a number of clever symbols on the keyboard [such as the happy face (:>) which is seen when turned on its side, or the sad face (:<)]. Even a young child can enjoy these. Let her key in her name and show how to make her own note paper. When a child has some proficiency, ask the child to teach you what he knows. At the same time, share some tips you have found useful.

❑ **940. CD-ROM.** Just like the CD disks you play on your stereo, your child should have available a CD-ROM drive on the family computer. (The letters stand for compact disk read-only memory.) This is one of the most useful learning devices. The drive shines a low-power laser beam onto the recording surface (the side of the disk without a label) and through binary digits or bits that the computer strings together, it produces pictures, text, and video clips on the monitor. Shop together to pick out exciting age-appropriate titles.

❑ **941. READ UP.** There are many magazines geared to computers, some just for kids. Buy single copies of several and see which are most interesting to your youngster. Subscribe to the best one. Then, let her share new things she's learned by reading it.

❑ **942. SKILLS LEARNED.** A creator of video games shared what he believes are the benefits of these toys: enhanced ability to concentrate, increased manual and mental dexterity, and historical input. The first two benefits are valid. The third is only a possibility if you shop wisely. In helping your youngster choose which games to own, try to select some that really do improve the intellect without emphasis on violence.

❑ **943. FUN, FUN, FUN.** Not every experience in growing up needs to be a deep, educational one. Some things should be just plain enjoyment. However, discuss with your youngster just what is meant by "enjoyment." If his idea of fun is playing video games with shooting, torturing and killing, or ones that delve into the world of demons, you will want to discuss how such activities affect his thinking and point of view. It is your parental right to outlaw activities that harm rather than help your child.

❑ **944.** GAME TIME. Computer games come in all sizes and shapes. Because of mass marketing techniques and attractive pricing, games make welcome gifts (especially from puzzled grandparents). Parents and kids should take the time to inspect the games and read the inviting packaging in order to choose wisely. A good game will hold a child's interest over many play sessions. It needs to be sufficiently challenging, but not too difficult. Games to be avoided are those that stress violence, gore, brutality, trickery, and characters acting in bad faith. It should be possible to win honestly. Many of the top selling games may not be the best for your child. If you and your youngster can see the game demonstrated, you will be better able to judge. And, it goes without saying, just because Susie down the street has a certain game is not a good reason for you to buy it and allow your child to play it.

❑ **945.** LEARN AS YOU PLAY. If a computer game has an educational effect, so much the better. Does it teach skills such as spelling, math, history, and so forth? The best of all worlds is a game that teaches as it amuses and fascinates. When purchasing, encourage your child to select a larger proportion of interesting educational games rather than mostly competitive ones.

❑ **946.** ADDICTION ALERT. The addictive nature of many hand-held, so-called pocket games is well known. These games can be carried everywhere and may divert a child from sports, study, even classroom attention. Before—definitely before—you permit or support the purchase of game video equipment, you need to confer with your child about its use and even put a few important rules in writing. How much game play in a day? (A half-hour could be the max.) When is it played with? (After school, but not after dinner until homework and chores are done.) Who pays for it? (Unless it is a gift occasion, the cost is the youngster's.) Can he be deprived of the use of it? (Yes, for breaking family rules or rules concerning the games.)

❑ **947.** **VIDEO GAME PARLORS.** Every community has one of these noisy places that can gobble up a kid's entire allowance and free time. Many arcade games are addictive and monopolize time without any benefit. Research also shows that most games are inherently frustrating and promote stress and negative behaviors such as aggression, lying, tension, and sullenness. Can this be considered "play"? One psychologist says that the need to score increasingly higher is akin to the chemically dependent person's obsession with "scoring" by using greater amounts of an addictive substance. If video games do not leave your youngster feeling in control, happy, and relaxed, you need to limit their use.

❑ **948.** **WWW.** The Internet or World Wide Web is continually in the news. Some say this will always be an important part of each person's outreach to the larger world, a way to receive and send information, a powerful research tool in every home. If it lives up to the promises, you will want to encourage your child to explore the Web by looking at it with him. Because it can be fascinating and time consuming, this is a good weekend activity. Start for just fifteen minutes to see what is interesting. Make an hour the maximum if it proves to be an enjoyable learning experience for both parent and child.

❑ **949.** **WEB SITES.** Help your youngster connect to these World Wide Web sites with programming for families. (You'll need a modem and access to the Internet.)
- CHILDREN'S LITERATURE WEB GUIDE: read favorite books online. http://www.ucalgary.ca/~dkbrown/index.html
- NASA Spacelink: wonderful for space buffs http://spacelink.msfc.nasa.gov/
- KIDLINK: dialogue with kids from more than seventy countries. http://www.kidlink.org
- DISNEY: rather commercial but has the favorite movies. http://disney.com
- AUNT ANNIE'S CRAFT PAGE: learning, problem solving, creativity. http://www.auntannie.com/

- INTERNET PUBLIC LIBRARY: the homework helper supreme. http://www.ipl.org/
- A GIRL'S WORLD: esteem-building clubhouse for girls ages 7-15. http://www.agirlsworld.com/
- FREE ZONE: the hip place for entertaining activities. http://freezone.com/
- FAMILY PLANET: Top-rated one-stop shopping for family activities. http://family.starwave.com

❑ **950.** **E-MAIL PAL.** Don't permit your youngster to make friends with other folks on the computer unless you have a very good way of checking out the age and background of the person. Rather, encourage an E-mail relationship with a relative or friend. It's so easy to correspond by E-mail and it's always fun to find mail in your own mailbox.

❑ **951.** **SAFETY FIRST.** Teach kids these on-line facts: Not everything you read is true. People on-line may not be who they seem. Never respond to messages or bulletin board items without parental approval. Report messages that are suggestive, obscene, belligerent, or threatening. Never arrange a face-to-face meeting without parental approval. Never give out identifying information such as name, home address, telephone number, school, or credit card or social security numbers.

❑ **952.** **OOPS!** Explain respect for the mechanical workings of the computer. Did you know that the most frequent service call for computers is caused by a soft drink spilled in the keyboard? Show how the keyboard and screen need to be carefully cleaned weekly. This can be a regular chore for kids.

❑ **953.** **BACKING UP.** Early in your teaching sessions, talk about the importance of saving input. Explain how often you need to do so. Then explain how to perform the important function of backing up on a disk. For a responsible youngster, making back-up disks of your work can be a delegated and paid job.

HIGH TECH LIVING

❑ **954.** THE HIGH TECH HOME. Some home repairs involve high technology. Discuss the problem with your youngster, guesstimating what a technician might charge. Then consider learning how to do the repair with kid-help. When the parent goes to a store to get detailed information, take the child along to listen and learn. Then discuss how WE will do it. Allow the child to perform a significant and interesting part of it. If the youngster is a mere tool handler, he will learn nothing and quickly become bored.

❑ **955.** AT THE BEEP . . . The ubiquitous phone answering machine can have a message recorded by your youngster. (This should only be done if the child speaks clearly and can read the manual instructions.) Let her make some calls and listen to other peoples' messages, then write out the brief message, practice it a few times and then record it. When the message needs to be changed, give her the full responsibility.

❑ **956.** GREAT EXPECTATIONS. Expect your child to lead the way in many new technologies. A parent needs the ability to learn from the younger generation. Ask kids what new inventions he can imagine. Suggest he keep a list of these ideas and see if they are marketed. If he has a truly unique idea, you might want to work together to develop, patent, and market it.

❑ **957.** WEATHER TECHNOLOGY. Suggest that a youngster keep a weather record for a whole year. Using a maximum/minimum thermometer, let him take the daily readings, record them, and report to the family at dinner each day. Show him how to make a graph of the high and of the low. If he shows interest, you may want to help him purchase more sophisticated instruments and even turn the research into a science fair project.

❑ **958.** AUTOMOTIVE TECHNOLOGY. Farmers' kids know all about the care and feeding of their horses. Do your children know as much about your car or truck? Bring a child along when you take your vehicle in for repairs. Make sure she can see under the hood as the service writer explains the work needing to be done. Let her master the names of some of the automotive parts, and then, on the way home explain (as best you can) what they do. When she's older, encourage her to take an automotive course at school.

❑ **959.** HI-FI TECHNOLOGY. When assembling a hi-fi system, allow your youngster to tell you what to do and how to do it. If he's wrong, figure out the right way together, letting him take the lead. Work together to place the speakers for the very best balance. Let him adjust the treble, bass, and so forth and tell you why this is important. He may want a well-balanced and well-modulated music system in his own room.

❑ **960.** TIMERS. While not new technology, timers are a big convenience in running a home. But they have to be reset for the twice-a-year time change. Show a child how to do this, then let him do it each six months on his own. Find many uses for timers: turning lights on and off, running sprinklers, controlling night lights, adjusting heating/cooling systems, and so forth.

❑ **961.** HIGH TECH CAMERAS. Photography can be an expensive hobby, especially with some of the fancy new electronic cameras. Before buying a camera for a youngster, let him practice taking pictures with yours. Take several rolls of film and critique each picture for subject, lighting, composition, interest, and so forth. Work together to master the equipment and take good pictures. Only then go shopping for the youngster's own camera.

❑ **962.** **PASSPORT TO THE WORLD.** Short wave radio opens the door to faraway places. Show your youngster how to tune in, and then listen together. See what conversations from other countries you can hear. Find the best times of the day or night to reach the most distant places. Permit radio listening before falling asleep at night.

SECTION 3:
A COMMUNITY WITHOUT VIOLENCE

Fear erodes the quality of family life. Families should not have to be constantly concerned with protecting themselves from violence. This section is shared with the idea of giving youngsters the ability to keep themselves from danger, as well as how to act correctly in threatening situations.

❑ **963.** **EVER ALERT.** When taking a neighborhood walk in the evening, play the AAA Game: Alert/Aware/Attentive. After passing a few houses, ask youngsters if there were houses with the lights on. Midway in the walk, ask how many people you've passed. See if kids can describe them. Walk silently and ask what sounds are heard: talking, barking, screeching wheels, doors slamming. Near the end of a walk, see if kids can describe the makes of cars that have passed you. The three A's are an important part of safety.

❑ **964.** **SAFETY SONG #1.** You don't need a tune for this song, just a good sense of rhythm. Again you'll teach the song to include your own address—don't worry if the middle line doesn't rhyme.

> My address has got a beat:
> 4, 8, 7 on Elm Street.
> Aren't those numbers really neat!

❑ **965.** SAFETY SONG #2. Young children often remember facts easily when they're set to music. A simple tune can help a child learn his telephone number. For example, use the familiar tune of "Twinkle, Twinkle Little Star" but change the words to include your own telephone number. It goes like this:

> Ringo, ringo little phone,
> Here's the number of my home.
> It is 5 and 5 and 5,
> Then just 2, 4, 6, and 8.
> Ringo, ringo little phone,
> That's the number of my home.

❑ **966.** SELF-DEFENSE OF YOUR HOME. Since youngsters may be home alone, you want your home to be safe. Let locking up be an every day procedure so that kids aren't alarmed when you do it. The front door should have a dead bolt and a peep hole. For sliding doors, a bar mounted in the middle is a safety precaution. Train youngsters to never open the door to a stranger, no matter what the outsider says. Trim away tall shrubbery from around the house. Put a large dog bowl on the back doorstep, even if your dog is tiny. If you have a security system, have one that sounds a loud alarm. When you're away, call your family regularly, and when you're vacationing, ask a neighbor or relative to check on your house.

❑ **967.** TELEPHONE SELF-DEFENSE. Instruct children to never reveal to a caller that they are home alone. A good line is "Can I have Dad call you back in a little while?" If you have an answer machine, give the impression that a large dog lives at your house by playing a recording of a barking dog in the background of your message. Hang up immediately on obscene calls or when there is just silence.

❑ **968.** NEIGHBORHOOD SELF-DEFENSE. Neighborhood Watch or other mutual surveillance groups are a good protection. Even if you don't know your neighbors socially, see that they have met your children, and let a trusted neighbor know when your children are home alone. Call a meeting of neighborhood adults for the purpose of listing license numbers of cars that belong to each household. Talk about being alert to strange cars and trucks in the neighborhood, strangers going door-to-door, the importance of keeping garage doors closed and porch lights on, and installing motion detector lights all help cut down on crime.

❑ **969.** AUTOMOBILE SELF-DEFENSE. Teach young drivers to approach their parked car with key in hand and eyes scanning the area. They should always lock the car (and use an antitheft device if the car has one), but they still should look in the back seat before entering the car. Once inside the car, immediately lock the doors. Make it a rule that youngsters never give a ride to a stranger—no matter how cute the person looks. Keep purse or briefcase out of sight so as not to attract smash-and-grab incidents at stoplights or in parking lots. Have a phony set of keys in the front seat tray. If approached, throw those keys out the window and drive away while the criminal is picking them up.

❑ **970.** SELF-DEFENSE WHEN WALKING IN A STRANGE AREA. An assertive walk, a good pace, and head up with eyes scanning will make you a less attractive subject. If children think someone is following them, they should turn and shout "What are you doing?" so as to attract the attention of others. And, youngsters should be taught to walk with others nearby or near shops that are open and offer a safe refuge.

❑ **971.** SELF-DEFENSE IN PUBLIC PLACES. If a youngster feels uncomfortable with someone sitting nearby in a movie, she should get up and tell an usher. If wary of someone in an elevator, press every button (in hopes that others will get on) or press the alarm button. And, when using an ATM at night, select a drive-through one, first locking doors, closing windows that don't need to be open during the transaction, and checking your mirrors.

❑ **972.** SELF-DEFENSE WEAPONS. Consider carrying a pepper spray or personal alarm. At a martial arts store you can buy a slim poking device to hang on your teen's key chain. And a cellular phone is an ideal defense since 911 can be quickly dialed—even at home when the telephone lines have been cut by an intruder.

❑ **973.** NO FEAR. With the media reporting so much violence and because you don't want to raise fearful children, parents have an obligation to balance this negativism with some positive news. Read the first four pages of the daily paper with a youngster—marking pen in hand. Put a green check mark on a positive story, a red check mark on one that reports robbery, murder, chaos, war, and so forth. Talk about the bad things and balance them with items showing how humankind has triumphed.

❑ **974.** GENEROSITY, AN ANSWER. While research shows that there is no overall increase in violence in the United States, it is taking bolder forms (overt racial violence, conflict between off-road vehicles and landowners, violence done in the name of environmentalism). One answer is to teach children to be generous, understanding, and forgiving. Encourage kids to put aside surliness in their conversation, in their driving, and in their activities. Setting a good example within the family will help this moderating attitude carry over into the community.

SECTION 4:
COMMITMENT TO FAMILY

There is no stronger influence for good than a family that practices what it preaches. Each day, encourage your youngsters to be committed to your family values. (See chapter 9 for descriptions of some of these virtues.)

❑ **975.** FAMILY FIRST. Start with toddlers and continue through the years to instill the importance of the family unit. As much as possible, eat meals together, worship together, do work projects together, have a shared activity each day and a larger joint activity each weekend.

❑ **976.** CHANGING YOURSELF. Effective families don't blame each other for problems or take out their frustrations on one another. They find benefits from considering how one can change oneself. For example, if two youngsters are arguing about what music to play, one can defuse the argument by making a personal change: listening to music in another room, putting on headphones, suggesting that one choose the music for an hour, then switch. Teach kids early to ask themselves "What can I do to change the situation?"

❑ **977.** FIRST THINGS FIRST. Much family friction comes from varied priorities—the family going different directions. Have a weekly family planning session and talk over the week's activities, responsibilities, and opportunities. Prioritize, putting "musts" first (homework, chores, lesson practice) then the scheduled events (the dentist, Grandma's birthday, the big concert). Finally, let the less important activities fit in the cracks around the "musts" and scheduled events.

❑ **978.** LISTEN FOR SUBTLE MESSAGES. When talking with a complaining child, you may not hear the real reason at first. For example, if a youngster says that she hates her little brother, accept that statement by repeating it. (If you start right out with a lecture on how to love a little brother, you'll cut the lines of communication.) Hearing you say what she has said gives her a feeling of validity and will start the conversation with both of you going the same direction. As you continue the conversation, you may hear the real reason: she feels he's getting more attention than she gets. Now you are ready to make appropriate remarks—and even actions— to solve the real problem.

❑ **979.** YOUR WAY, MY WAY, OUR WAY. Disagreements don't have to end with winners and losers. Usually there is a solution that is better than those proposed by the two opponents. A very simple example is this: If your daughter wants the family to go to the movies and you want the group to go cycling, cycle to the movies. Try to help youngsters discover the very best solution—not always their own, but something even better.

❑ **980.** RENEWAL. Families should look out for one another in four very important ways that will give them the energy and skills to continue as a successful group. *(1) Love*—loving oneself, family, and others. *(2) Spirituality*—understanding our moral and religious base that defines our responsibilities as members of the world society. *(3) Intellect*—appreciating it in others and nurturing our own ability to think clearly. *(4) Talents*—using our innate talents to the max—so that we can maintain a strong and healthy outlook. These are not one-time skills but ones that require daily renewal.

❑ **981.** BE THERE. Anticipate the times when you will be needed more than usual: the first days of school, during exams, at the final game of a sport season, at and after the school play or recital, and when any educational, social, or health problem arises. While a youngster may not want to have a long discussion about any of these events, your interest and comfort needs expression. Be there when it counts.

❑ **982.** "RESERVED." Starting when youngsters can read. Make a monthly family calendar showing lessons, parties, and other events for each member of the family. Mark one evening each week and one half-day each weekend as "Reserved." Use the evening for games as well as conversation about the family. Use the weekend time for an excursion. Rarely move a reserved time or excuse a family member from it. If you establish reserved time from the early years onward, you shouldn't have any argument about it as kids become teens.

❑ **983.** GIVENS. In every family there are some things that are not to be argued or compromised. They are part of family tradition. If kids complain, tell them that when they are parents they can make their own list of "givens." Here are some worthy items for your list of givens: personal cleanliness, weekly church attendance, no dating before age fifteen, abstinence from premarital sex, no use of alcohol or tobacco, no drug use, no profanity, no shoplifting or stealing, no cheating on tests, no lying about age, and no use of weapons. This may sound like a lot of "NO" items, but if everyone followed the Givens list, the world would be a very fine place!

❑ **984.** SIBLING SNIVELING. Often, especially when close in age, siblings develop a dislike for one another. While you can't force total peace, you can work toward a truce. Despite their feelings, siblings should agree to these five things: aid in case of emergency, no bad-mouthing outside the family, no trying to get the other in trouble, a respect for the other's individuality, and acknowledgment of something good the other does.

❑ **985.** HELP! Some family members behave like the Little Red Hen who has to do everything herself. Develop within the family the commitment to offer assistance (and mean it) when another needs help. Encourage family members to be alert to the needs, moods, problems, and events that touch the lives of others in the family. Then encourage the offering of help even though it may not be accepted. And, be sure to commend the help when given.

❑ **986.** PARENT QUIZ. Honestly answer these questions and then discuss with your youngster any "no" answers.

- ▶ Does my day start on a high note and go up from there?
- ▶ Am I satisfied with my child care arrangements or how my youngster spends after-school time?
- ▶ Is there at least a half hour each day when I am alone with my child?
- ▶ Do I set educational and social goals for my child?
- ▶ Do I set business, social and learning goals for myself?
- ▶ Am I spending time regularly to make our home an enjoyable family center?
- ▶ Am I finding the time to keep my other family relationships vital?
- ▶ Do I arrange after-supper activities so that TV is not the sole highlight of the evening for the family?
- ▶ Is there a pleasant family event each weekend?
- ▶ Do I understand the importance of thinking through my own unpleasant childhood experiences as well as my present-day angers and frustrations?
- ▶ Do I look forward to weekend time with my child, rather than feeling that this time is solely for my own rest and amusement?
- ▶ Do I take my child to a museum, play, or concert almost as often as to the park or a movie?
- ▶ Does my child enjoy the pleasure of book reading at least thirty minutes a day? And do I?
- ▶ As work is done around the home, do I include my child, explain what I'm doing, and let her help?
- ▶ Do I nurture my child, helping him develop morally, spiritually, physically, and mentally?
- ▶ Do I know the name of my child's best friend?
- ▶ Can I name something that really upsets my child and also something that really pleases her?
- ▶ Do I know what my child really likes about me and what he most dislikes about me?
- ▶ Do I know what my child likes to do with her free time and what she would like to do more often with me?

- ▶ Do I know my child's favorite teacher and favorite subject, and his least favorite teacher and least favorite subject?
- ▶ If I could buy my child the gift she most desires, do I know what it would be?
- ▶ Am I aware which of my child's accomplishments gives him the most pleasure?
- ▶ Do I treat my job as parent with the same integrity and organization that I bring to my career or other activities?
- ▶ Am I finding time to grow myself, through reading, classes, activities, or hobbies?
- ▶ Do I tell my child each day that I have confidence in him and in his ability to learn, that he is very special, and that I love him no matter what?
- ▶ Do I usually go to sleep feeling contented with my day?

❑ **987.** **KID QUIZ.** Corral your child for this quick quiz, skipping questions that aren't pertinent. Discuss any "no" answers and see how you can help to change them.

- ▶ Is it fun to live in this home?
- ▶ Do you help with chores around the house?
- ▶ Do you have a place for projects that you don't have to clean up very often?
- ▶ Do you read, or are you read to, each day?
- ▶ Do you know your family rules and what happens if you break them?
- ▶ Do you have a relative (grandparent, uncle, cousin) with whom you feel very close?
- ▶ If the television set disappeared for a week, could you name ten other things you'd like to do?
- ▶ Are you eager to learn new skills and subjects?
- ▶ Do you enjoy family meal times?
- ▶ Do you know your parents' favorite sport, music, food, and book?

▶ Do you know your parents' favorite school subject and least favorite subject?

▶ Can you name something you do that upsets your parent?

▶ Can you name something your parent thinks is special about you?

▶ Do you know what your parent likes to do for fun?

▶ Do you remember what was your parent's most favorite family occasion and why?

▶ Do you know something that your parent would like to do more often with you?

▶ Do you know why your parent works?

▶ Do you show your parents that you love them by your words and your acts?

A FOCUS FOR THE FAMILY

To keep your family strong, take the time to consider together these points that are the basis for living a wonderful life.

THE FAMILY PLATFORM

❑ **988.** LOVE UNCONDITIONALLY. Learn to show love in varied ways. And if that love doesn't seem to be returned, never give up! Each day, see that you say "I love you" or express your affection to each other. Love can solve anything!

❑ **989.** STRENGTHEN FAMILY TIES. Never let a period of "no communication" get a foothold. Both parent and child have an investment of many years in your family, so keep it going by taking an interest in each person—even at times when your interest may be rebuffed. Come to an understanding or compromise when there is a problem. Plan creative get-togethers and reunions.

❑ **990.** RESPECT DIVERSITY. You don't want clones!

Look for and appreciate the precious individuality of each family member. Try to understand another's point of view, especially when it is different from yours. Realize that each member of your family is one very unique part of creation.

☐ **991.** CULTIVATE COMMUNICATION. Think back at how much you loved your little baby and how you spoke words even before the baby comprehended their meaning. Now that little person may be too big to hold, but certainly can comprehend your meaning. Practice speaking with patience and consideration and provide many opportunities for conversation. For faraway family members, communicate on a regular basis by phoning and writing.

☐ **992.** PRACTICE BOTH GIVING AND GETTING. They're both pleasant! Volunteer. Contribute. Serve. Comfort. Take on an activity: visit seniors, advise a youth group, teach Sunday school or sing in the choir, raise funds for a worthy cause, deliver meals to the elderly, coach a team. The list is endless. Choose one that the family can do together. You'll get great satisfaction from this activity.

☐ **993.** DEVELOP A COMMUNITY AND A CIRCLE OF FRIENDS. Enlarge the borders of your family by establishing bonds with others. A work project with other families such as improving the local park, getting road signs posted where children play, or starting a monthly potluck—these generate a feeling of community closeness. You don't have to be blood relatives to be "family." Don't be an island or a cold fish. Enlarge your circle every year no matter what your age. Even if you think you don't need them, they may need you.

☐ **994.** TRY NEW THINGS. Sameness is easy and can mire the family in boredom. Whether it is what you eat, the music you listen to, the kind of books and magazines you read, the sports you engage in, or the daily routine, remember to try your wings on things that are totally different. You may be in for a pleasant surprise. Remember that no one knows everything. Keep a list of places you'd like to visit. Stop by the Chamber of Commerce for ideas, or look in the weekend section of the newspaper.

☐ **995.** **BELIEVE IN YOURSELF.** Act with confidence. Mentally make a list of your many good qualities and don't let anyone belittle you. Speak up for what you know is right. If you make a mistake, learn to laugh at yourself and remember it's not the end of the world. Keep your religious beliefs active and listen for guidance—don't always bull ahead with your own ways.

☐ **996.** **RESPECT THE LAW.** We can't expect to be protected by the law if we cut corners when it suits us. Teach kids to recognize right from wrong and don't support the idea that the end justifies the means. Be law-abiding and just in your thinking as well as in your actions.

☐ **997.** **BE A GOOD NEWS BEARER.** Share positive ideas, not negative gossip. And don't be a complainer, a judge, or a constant arguer. Sure, every life has some lumps but don't let them overshadow the good. Contrary to much of the evening news broadcasts, there truly are good things happening. Search them out, share them with your family, and think of them through the day and as you fall asleep at night.

☐ **998.** **APPRECIATE ONE ANOTHER.** A parent can admit to having had in her youth some wild times, strange songs, and odd clothing habits. Thus, when it comes to safe but unusual teen fads, don't judge but rather keep advice to the minimum. Ask questions. Listen and learn. When you approve of something, give compliments. Each day find something you appreciate in each of your family members.

☐ **999.** **USE YOUR HOME.** Make it the family center, but not the circumference. Plan a party. Invite relatives for a weekend. Make a home craft center. Snuggle up in your warm bed and read magazines. If you get sleepy in front of

TV, turn it off and play a box game with a kid. Share your home with others—don't let it become just a place to sleep, eat, and look at TV. Give it a new look now and then—just rearrange it rather than spend more money.

❏ **1000.** TAKE CONTROL OF YOUR POSSESSIONS. End the clutter. Amassing "things" is selfish. Teach youngsters that things unused deprive others of their use. Give away what you don't need. If you haven't used something in a year or two, pass it on to family, friends, or social services.

1001. HOLDING HANDS

You will hold your child's hand through many of the challenges of growing up. But sometimes you won't be there when a little hand-holding is needed, and that's why you teach your youngster the importance of the family bond, for this means you can always stick together in thought even when you are far apart. Hand-holding takes many forms and continues all through life. When you love your child, hand-holding never ends.

When your child is a tiny baby, you let his whole hand curl around your little finger.

When he is learning to walk, you hold his hand as he takes those first tottering steps.

When he is learning to cross the street, he trustingly takes your hand.

When you gather around the breakfast table, you all hold hands for a quiet moment before parting for the day.

When the family goes for a hike, you hold hands in the steep places.

When he leaves for camp, he gives you a brave handshake in front of the other guys.

When he doesn't feel well, your hands lovingly nurse him back to good health and you sit by his bed, holding his hand.

When he has a tough school assignment or trouble under the hood of his car, you give him a helping hand.

When you fall behind with the chores around the house, he gives you a helping hand.

When he goes on his first date, you press an extra bit of cash into his hand.

When he gets his first after-school job, your hands applaud his achievement.

When he graduates, you give his hand a loving squeeze, and then you give each other a "high five."

When he leaves home, your hands touch briefly in a proud good-bye.

Then come hands across the miles. You mentally hold his

hand through the trials and triumphs of learning to be on his own.

And throughout all time, your hand of love will reach out and support your child—and eventually the next generation of little hands.

So at this moment it is up to you to start your own style of hand-holding. Take the hand of your child and go forward together as a family. You can do it!

Book 2 Index

(Activities indexed by idea number, not page number)